Revenue Statistics in Latin America and the Caribbean 2020

Estadísticas tributarias en América Latina y el Caribe 2020

1990-2018

Please cite this publication as:
OECD et al. (2020), *Revenue Statistics in Latin America and the Caribbean 2020*, OECD Publishing, Paris, *https://doi.org/10.1787/68739b9b-en-es*.

Por favor, cite esta publicación de la siguiente manera:
OCDE et al. (2020), *Estadísticas tributarias en América Latina y el Caribe 2020*, OECD Publishing, Paris, *https://doi.org/10.1787/68739b9b-en-es*.

ISBN 978-92-64-72155-5 (print/impresa)
ISBN 978-92-64-28282-7 (pdf)

Revenue Statistics in Latin America and the Caribbean/*Estadísticas tributarias en América Latina y el Caribe*
ISSN 2410-4728 (print/impresa)
ISSN 2410-4736 (online/en línea)

Photo credits/Imágenes: Cover/Portada © some of the graphic elements in the main cover illustration were adapted from Freepik.com.

Corrigenda to publications may be found on line at: *www.oecd.org/about/publishing/corrigenda.htm*.
Las erratas de las publicaciones se encuentran en línea en: www.oecd.org/about/publishing/corrigenda.htm.

Foreword

Revenue Statistics in Latin America and the Caribbean 2020 *is a joint publication by the Organisation for Economic Co-operation and Development (OECD) Centre for Tax Policy and Administration, the OECD Development Centre, the United Nations Economic Commission for Latin America and the Caribbean (UN-ECLAC), the Inter-American Center of Tax Administrations (CIAT), the Inter-American Development Bank (IDB) and with the support of the European Union Regional Facility for Development in Transition for Latin America and the Caribbean (LAC). It presents detailed, internationally comparable data on tax revenues for 26 Latin American and Caribbean economies, three of which are OECD members. Colombia was not an OECD Member at the time of preparation of this publication. Accordingly, Colombia does not appear in the list of OECD Members and is not included in the zone aggregates. Revenue Statistics in Latin America and the Caribbean's approach is based on the well-established methodology of the OECD Revenue Statistics database, which is an essential reference source for OECD member countries. Comparisons are also made with the average tax indicators for OECD economies.*

The term "taxes" in this publication is confined to compulsory, unrequited payments to general government. As outlined in the Interpretative Guide to Revenue Statistics, taxes are "unrequited" in the sense that benefits provided by government to taxpayers are not normally in proportion to their payments. The OECD methodology classifies a tax according to its base: income, profits and capital gains (classified under heading 1000); payroll (heading 3000); property (heading 4000); goods and services (heading 5000); and other taxes (heading 6000). Compulsory social security contributions paid to general government are treated as taxes and classified under heading 2000. Much greater detail on the tax concept, the classification of taxes and the accrual basis of reporting is set out in the Interpretative Guide in Annex A.

Extending the OECD methodology to Latin American and Caribbean countries enables comparisons of tax systems on a consistent basis both across this region and with OECD countries. In a few cases, this methodology differs from the approach used by ECLAC, CIAT and IDB; these differences are noted in the text and in the tables, either with a footnote or an extra row.

The report provides an overview of the main taxation trends in Latin America and the Caribbean. It examines changes in both the level and the composition of taxation plus the attribution of tax collection by sub-level of government between 1990 and 2018.

Presentación

La publicación Estadísticas tributarias en América Latina y el Caribe 2020 *ha sido elaborada conjuntamente por el Centro de Política y Administración Tributaria de la Organización para la Cooperación y el Desarrollo Económicos (OCDE), el Centro de Desarrollo de la OCDE, la Comisión Económica de las Naciones Unidas para América Latina y el Caribe (NU-CEPAL), el Centro Interamericano de Administraciones Tributarias (CIAT), el Banco Interamericano de Desarrollo (BID) y con el apoyo del Fondo Regional para el Desarrollo en Transición para América Latina y el Caribe (ALC) de la Unión Europea. Esta publicación presenta datos detallados y comparables a nivel internacional sobre los ingresos tributarios de 26 economías latinoamericanas y caribeñas, tres de las cuales son miembros de la OCDE. Colombia no era miembro de la OCDE en el momento de preparar esta publicación. Por consiguiente, Colombia no figura en la lista de miembros de la OCDE y no está incluida en los agregados de la zona. El enfoque de la publicación Estadísticas tributarias en América Latina y el Caribe se basa en la metodología bien establecida de la base de datos* Revenue Statistics *de la OCDE, que se ha convertido en una referencia esencial para los países miembros de la OCDE. Se presentan también comparaciones con los promedios de indicadores tributarios para las economías de la OCDE.*

En la presente publicación, el término "impuestos" se limita exclusivamente a los pagos obligatorios sin contraprestación efectuados al gobierno general. Tal y como lo indica la Guía de Interpretación de Revenue Statistics, los impuestos carecen de contraprestación en el sentido en que, normalmente, las prestaciones proporcionadas por el gobierno a los contribuyentes no guardan relación directa con los pagos realizados por estos. La metodología de la OCDE clasifica un impuesto de acuerdo con su base: renta, utilidades y ganancias del capital (categoría 1000); nómina (categoría 3000); propiedad (categoría 4000); bienes y servicios (categoría 5000); y otros impuestos (categoría 6000). Las contribuciones obligatorias a la seguridad social pagadas al gobierno general se tratan aquí como impuestos y se clasifican en la categoría 2000. Para mayor detalle sobre el concepto de impuesto, su clasificación y su registro según el criterio de devengo, véase la Guía de Interpretación que figura en el Anexo A.

Aplicar la metodología de la OCDE a América Latina y el Caribe posibilita la comparación de sistemas tributarios a partir de una base coherente en la región, entre los países latinoamericanos, y con los países miembros de la OCDE. Sin embargo, en algunas ocasiones, esta metodología difiere de la empleada por la CEPAL, el CIAT y el BID; en esos casos, las diferencias se han indicado en el texto y los cuadros, ya sea con una nota a pie de página, o en una línea adicional.

El informe ofrece un panorama general de las principales tendencias en materia tributaria en América Latina y en el Caribe. Examina los cambios registrados entre 1990 y 2018 en el nivel y la composición de la tributación, así como en la atribución de la recaudación tributaria a los diversos subsectores de gobierno.

Acknowledgements

Revenue Statistics in Latin America and the Caribbean 2020 was jointly produced by the Organisation for Economic Co-operation and Development (OECD) Centre for Tax Policy and Administration, the OECD Development Centre, the United Nations Economic Commission for Latin America and the Caribbean (UN-ECLAC), the Inter-American Center of Tax Administrations (CIAT), the Inter-American Development Bank (IDB) and with the support of the European Union Regional Facility for Development in Transition for Latin America and the Caribbean.

The staff from these organisations with responsibility for producing the publication were: Emmanuelle Modica of the OECD Centre for Tax Policy and Administration, under the supervision of the Director, Pascal Saint-Amans, the Deputy Director, Grace Perez-Navarro, the Head of the Tax Policy and Tax Statistics Division, David Bradbury, and the Head of the Tax Data and Statistical Analysis Unit, Michelle Harding; Jingjing Xia of the OECD Development Centre, under the supervision of the Director, Mario Pezzini, the Deputy Director, Federico Bonaglia, the Head of the Latin America and the Caribbean Unit, Sebastian Nieto Parra, and the Co-ordinator of *Revenue Statistics* for the Development Centre, Alexander Pick; Michael Hanni and Juan Pablo Jiménez of the Economic Development Division of UN-ECLAC, under the supervision of Director Daniel Titelman, and the Chief of the Fiscal Affairs Unit, Noel Pérez Benítez; Julio Alberto López from the CIAT Tax Studies and Research Directorate, under the supervision of Director Santiago Díaz de Sarralde; and Alberto Barreix, Principal Technical Leader in Fiscal Economics at the IDB. Michael Hanni of UN-ECLAC authored the Special feature on fiscal revenues from non-renewable natural resources in Latin America and the Caribbean (Chapter 2). The Special feature on equivalent fiscal pressure in Latin America and the Caribbean (Chapter 3) is based on a paper written by Agnes Rojas and Dalmiro Morán as a joint project between IDB and CIAT, under the supervision of Alberto Barreix and Santiago Díaz de Sarralde. Beatriz García Beltrán, Governance Project Officer at the EUROsociAL+ Programme, provided inputs to Chapter 1.

The authors would like to thank other staff at the OECD Development Centre and the Centre for Tax Policy and Administration for their invaluable support in completing and improving the 2020 edition of this publication. René Orozco and Joe Stead produced the analysis on tax morale included in Chapter 1. Marika Boiron and Delphine Grandrieux from the OECD Development Centre's Communications and Publications team, and statistical editors from the OECD Publications and Communications Directorate, ensured the production of the publication, in both paper and electronic form. Michael Sharratt from the OECD Centre for Tax Policy and Administration provided invaluable assistance with the databases, website and other dissemination tools. Nicolas Miranda and Alexandra Le Cam from the OECD Centre for Tax Policy and Administration provided precious help in checking the translation in Spanish.

Finally, the OECD Centre for Tax Policy and Administration and the Development Centre would like to thank our colleagues working in national entities, with whom we have consulted regularly. In particular, we are grateful to Rosario López Palazzo and Marcelo Adrián Calissano from the Ministry of Finance of Argentina; Diana Marcela Parra Garzón and Andrea Prieto González from Colombia's National Tax and Customs Administration; Jorge Richard Nuñez of Costa Rica´s Ministry of Finance; Fidelia Raulina Pérez Castillo from the Dominican Republic's Finance Ministry; Douglas Pablo Rodríguez, Luis Antonio Campos and Sara Guadalupe García de Reyes from the Ministry of Finance of El Salvador; Cristian Erazo Delgado and David Fernando Pineda Pinto from the Revenue Administration Service, and Neffy Velasquez from the Secretary of Finances in Honduras; Andrea Gregory from Jamaica's Tax Administration and Customs agencies; Emma Isaza from Panama's Finance Ministry; Pedro Galeano and Diego Dominguez from Paraguay's Finance Ministry; and Jorge Rivera Calderón from Peru's Ministry of Economic and Finance.

This document was produced with the financial assistance of the European Commission. The opinions expressed and arguments employed herein do not necessarily reflect the official views of the OECD member countries or the European Union.

In memoriam Luiz Villela

Public finance has lost an outstanding economist who furnished advice of the highest quality in his own country of Brazil, where he held senior positions of responsibility, and throughout Latin America and the Caribbean as a principal fiscal expert of the IDB. His legacy of academic and professional contributions in the fields of taxation and decentralisation will long endure. He will be remembered as a brilliant colleague of impeccable integrity and great humanity.

Agradecimientos

La publicación *Estadísticas tributarias en América Latina y el Caribe 2020* ha sido elaborada conjuntamente por el Centro de Política y Administración Tributaria de la Organización para la Cooperación y el Desarrollo Económicos (OCDE), el Centro de Desarrollo de la OCDE, la Comisión Económica de las Naciones Unidas para América Latina y el Caribe (NU-CEPAL), el Centro Interamericano de Administraciones Tributarias (CIAT), el Banco Interamericano de Desarrollo (BID) y con el apoyo del Fondo Regional para el Desarrollo en Transición para América Latina y el Caribe de la Unión Europea.

Las personas de estas organizaciones responsables de redactar la presente publicación han sido: Emmanuelle Modica del Centro de Política y Administración Tributaria de la OCDE, bajo la supervisión del Director, Pascal Saint-Amans, de la Sub-directora, Grace Perez-Navarro, del Jefe de la División de Políticas y Estadísticas Tributarias, David Bradbury, y de la Jefe de la Unidad de Análisis de Datos Tributarios y Estadísticas, Michelle Harding; Jingjing Xia del Centro de Desarrollo de la OCDE, bajo la supervisión del Director, Mario Pezzini, del Director adjunto, Federico Bonaglia, del Jefe de la Unidad de América Latina y el Caribe, Sebastian Nieto Parra, y del Coordinador de estadísticas tributarias para el Centro de Desarrollo, Alexander Pick; Michael Hanni y Juan Pablo Jiménez de la División de Desarrollo Económico de la CEPAL, bajo la supervisión del Director, Daniel Titelman, y del Jefe de la Unidad de Asuntos Fiscales, Noel Pérez Benítez; Julio Alberto López de la Dirección de Estudios e Investigaciones Tributarias del CIAT, bajo la supervisión del Director, Santiago Díaz de Sarralde; y Alberto Barreix, Líder Técnico Principal en Economía Fiscal del BID. Michael Hanni, de la CEPAL, escribió el capítulo especial sobre ingresos fiscales de recursos naturales no renovables en América Latina y el Caribe (Capítulo 2). El capítulo especial sobre la presión fiscal equivalente en América Latina y el Caribe (Capítulo 3) se basa en un documento originalmente realizado por Agnes Rojas y Dalmiro Morán, supervisado por Alberto Barreix y Santiago Díaz de Sarralde, y publicado en forma conjunta por el Centro Interamericano de Administraciones Tributarias (CIAT) y el Banco Interamericano de Desarrollo (BID). Beatriz García Beltrán, Técnica de Gobernanza Democrática / Programa EUROsociAL+, aportó insumos al capítulo 1.

Los autores desean agradecer a otras personas del Centro de Desarrollo y del Centro de Política y Administración Tributaria de la OCDE por su invaluable contribución a la mejora y finalización de la edición 2020 de esta publicación. René Orozco y Joe Stead realizaron el análisis sobre la moral tributaria en el Capítulo 1. Marika Boiron y Delphine Grandrieux, del equipo de Comunicaciones y Publicaciones del Centro de Desarrollo de la OCDE, y editores estadísticos del equipo de Publicaciones y Comunicaciones de la OCDE, aseguraron la producción de la publicación, tanto física como en formato electrónico. Michael Sharratt, del Centro de Política y Administración Tributaria de la OCDE, brindó una valiosa ayuda con las bases de datos, el sitio web y otras herramientas de difusión. Nicolas Miranda y Alexandra Le Cam, del Centro de Política y Administración Tributaria de la OCDE, proporcionaron una ayuda preciosa para comprobar la traducción al español.

Por último, el Centro de Política y Administración Tributaria y el Centro de Desarrollo de la OCDE quisieran agradecer a nuestros colegas de entidades nacionales, a los que hemos consultado con frecuencia. En particular, damos gracias a Rosario López Palazzo y Marcelo Adrián Calissano, del Ministerio de Hacienda de Argentina; Diana Marcela Parra Garzón y Andrea Prieto González, de la Dirección de Impuestos y Aduanas Nacionales de Colombia; Jorge Richard Nuñez, del Ministerio de Hacienda de Costa Rica; Fidelia Raulina Pérez Castillo, del Ministerio de Hacienda de la República Dominicana; Douglas Pablo Rodríguez, Luis Antonio Campos y Sara Guadalupe García de Reyes, del Ministerio de Hacienda de El Salvador; Cristian Erazo Delgado y David Fernando Pineda Pinto, del Servicio de Administración de Rentas, y Neffy Velasquez, de la Secretaría de Finanzas de Honduras; Andrea Gregory, de la Administración de Impuestos y Aduanas de Jamaica; Emma Isaza, del Ministerio de Hacienda de Panamá; Pedro Galeano y Diego Domínguez, del Ministerio de Hacienda de Paraguay; y Jorge Rivera Calderón, del Ministerio de Economía y Finanzas de Perú.

Este documento fue producido con el apoyo financiero de la Comisión Europea. Las opiniones expresadas y los argumentos aquí empleados no reflejan necesariamente las opiniones oficiales de los países miembros de la OCDE o de la Unión Europea.

In memoriam Luiz Villela

Las finanzas públicas han perdido un gran economista que brindó asesoramiento del más alto nivel en su país, Brasil, donde ocupó cargos de alta responsabilidad, y en América Latina y el Caribe como experto fiscal principal del BID. Sus aportes académicos y profesionales en las áreas de tributación y descentralización perdurarán en el tiempo. Será recordado como un brillante colega de intachable integridad y gran calidad humana.

Table of contents

Índice

LIST OF TABLES/LISTA DE CUADROS

Chapter 1/Capítulo 1
Tax revenue trends, 1990-2018/Tendencias tributarias, 1990-2018

Chapter 2/Capítulo 2
Special feature/Sección especial

Chapter 4/Capítulo 4
Tax levels and tax structures, 1990-2018/ Niveles impositivos y estructuras tributarias, 1990-2018

Chapter 6/Capítulo 6

Tax revenues by sub-sectors of general government/ Ingresos tributarios por sub-sectores de gobierno general

LIST OF FIGURES/LISTA DE GRÁFICOS

Chapter 1/Capítulo 1

Tax revenue trends, 1990-2018/Tendencias tributarias, 1990-2018

Chapter 3/Capítulo 3

Special feature/Sección especial

Executive summary

Revenue Statistics in Latin America and the Caribbean provides internationally comparable data on tax levels and tax structures for 26 Latin American and Caribbean (LAC) countries: Argentina, the Bahamas, Barbados, Belize, Bolivia, Brazil, Chile, Colombia, Costa Rica, Cuba, the Dominican Republic, Ecuador, El Salvador, Guatemala, Guyana, Honduras, Jamaica, Mexico, Nicaragua, Panama, Paraguay, Peru, Saint Lucia, Trinidad and Tobago, Uruguay and Venezuela.

In this publication, "taxes" are defined as compulsory, unrequited payments to general government. Taxes are "unrequited" in the sense that benefits provided by government to taxpayers are not normally in proportion to their payments. Compulsory social security contributions (SSCs) paid to general government are classified as taxes. More information on the tax classification and the basis of reporting is set out in the Interpretative Guide in Annex A.

Tax-to-GDP ratios in the LAC region in 2018

In 2018, the average tax-to-GDP ratio in the LAC region (measured as tax revenues, including SSCs paid to general government, as a proportion of GDP) was 23.1%. The LAC average represents the unweighted average of 25 Latin American and Caribbean countries included in this publication and excludes Venezuela due to data availability issues.

Across the LAC region, tax-to-GDP ratios ranged from 12.1% in Guatemala to 42.3% in Cuba in 2018; all LAC countries other than Cuba recorded a tax-to-GDP ratio below the OECD average of 34.3%. Between 2017 and 2018, the average LAC tax-to-GDP ratio increased by 0.4 percentage points. The increase in the tax-to-GDP ratio in the LAC region reflects in part a slight recovery in the economic environment in the region since 2017 (driven by improvements in domestic demand, increased trade and higher commodity prices) as well as a recovery from the impact of natural disasters in the Caribbean in 2017.

The largest increases in tax-to-GDP ratios between 2017 and 2018 occurred in three Caribbean countries: Trinidad and Tobago (3.3 percentage points), Belize (1.4 percentage points) and Guyana (1.3 percentage points). In Trinidad and Tobago, revenues from taxes on income and profits (especially corporate income tax [CIT]) were the main drivers, underpinned by a strong recovery in the energy sector. Belize and Guyana recorded increases in all main categories of tax revenue in 2018 as a proportion of GDP, due to administrative and policy reforms as well as an improved economic context. Outside these three countries, a further 12 countries reported an increase in their tax-to-GDP ratios, while seven recorded a decrease and three were unchanged from 2017 levels. The largest decreases were seen in Argentina (1.3% of GDP) and Nicaragua (0.8% of GDP), in both cases due to a weaker economic environment.

Evolution of tax-to-GDP ratios in the LAC region since 1990

Between 1990 and 2018, the average tax-to-GDP ratio in LAC countries rose almost continuously, increasing by more than 7 percentage points from 15.9% to 23.1% and converging to the OECD average: the difference against the OECD average tax-to-GDP ratio decreased from 16.0 percentage points in 1990 to 11.2 percentage points in 2018.

The main contributors to the increase in tax revenues in the LAC region were value-added taxes (VAT) and taxes on income and profits. VAT revenue as a percentage of GDP in LAC countries increased by 3.8 percentage points between 1990 and 2018, reaching 6.0% of GDP. Ten LAC countries, notably in the Caribbean, have introduced a VAT since 1990 and most LAC countries have made additional efforts to increase these revenues (for example by increasing VAT rates, expanding the taxable base and strengthening the VAT collection system). Revenues from taxes on income and profits increased by 3.1% of GDP over the same period, mainly driven by the boom in commodity prices after 2003, which drove up CIT revenues from the natural resources sector.

The average tax-to-GDP ratio for the South American sub-region was the same as the LAC average in 2018 at 23.1%. South America has recorded the fastest growth in the tax-to-GDP ratio since 1990 and exceeded the LAC average in 2004. However, it recorded a steady decrease between 2015 and 2017 before recovering in 2018. The averages for the Central America and Mexico sub-region and the Caribbean have increased gradually since 1990, although this trend has diverged since 2016: Central America and Mexico remained relatively flat at 21.0% whereas the Caribbean region has shown strong growth, increasing by 1.5 percentage points over the period to reach 25.7% in 2018.

Tax structures in the LAC region

In 2018, the LAC average tax mix continued to exhibit a relatively high reliance on revenue from taxes on goods and services, which made up about half of total tax revenues, compared with a third in the OECD. VAT and revenues from taxes on income and profits were the biggest sources of revenue on average in the LAC region in 2018, each accounting for 27.8% of total tax revenues.

Within taxes on income and profits, the region is more heavily reliant on revenues from CIT than OECD countries and significantly less reliant on personal income tax (PIT). In 2017, CIT and PIT revenues in the LAC region accounted for 15.3% and 9.7% of total tax revenues respectively, compared with 9.3% and 23.9% in the OECD. Similarly, the average share of SSCs in total tax revenues was 8.7 percentage points lower in the LAC region than in the OECD, on average (17.3% compared to 26.0%).

Environmentally related tax revenues (ERTRs) amounted to 1.1% of GDP on average in 2018 in the 23 LAC countries for which data is available, below the OECD average of 2.3%. Approximately two-thirds of ERTRs in the LAC region are derived from taxes on energy, most commonly excises on diesel and petrol (0.6% of GDP on average). Revenues from motor vehicle and transport service taxes represented most of the remainder. The LAC region has been slow to implement taxes to address environmental issues, although a few LAC countries have introduced significant reforms, including Chile, Mexico and, most recently, Colombia.

Special features

The Report contains two special features. The first identifies trends in fiscal revenues from non-renewable natural resources for selected LAC countries in 2018. Driven by higher international prices, hydrocarbon-related revenues in the LAC region rebounded in 2018 reaching 2.7% of GDP, compared to 2.0% of GDP in both 2016 and 2017. Meanwhile, revenues from mining as a proportion of GDP increased to 0.4% on average in 2018 from 0.3% in 2017, due to a rise in corporate tax receipts following strong profits in 2017. Estimates for 2019 suggest that revenues from non-renewable natural resources declined in the region, driven by a fall in prices. Hydrocarbon-related revenues and mining revenues are estimated to have fallen to 2.5% of GDP and 0.3% of GDP in 2019, respectively.

The second special feature examines Equivalent Fiscal Pressure (EFP) in LAC countries over the period 1990-2018. EFP is the sum of the tax-to-GDP ratio, plus compulsory contributions to private social insurance systems and non-tax revenues from natural resources; it is expressed as a percentage of GDP. In 2018, the average EFP in the LAC region was 25.0% of GDP and had increased by 0.2 percentage points from its level in 2017. Since 1990, the share of compulsory contributions to private social insurance systems as a percentage of GDP has increased by 0.7 percentage points, on average, while revenues from natural resources have been volatile.

Resumen ejecutivo

La publicación *Estadísticas tributarias en América Latina y el Caribe* proporciona datos internacionales comparables sobre los niveles y las estructuras tributarias de 26 países de América Latina y el Caribe: Argentina, Las Bahamas, Barbados, Belice, Bolivia, Brasil, Chile, Colombia, Costa Rica, Cuba, Ecuador, El Salvador, Guatemala, Guyana, Honduras, Jamaica, México, Nicaragua, Panamá, Paraguay, Perú, la República Dominicana, Santa Lucía, Trinidad y Tobago, Uruguay y Venezuela.

En esta publicación, el término "impuestos" se refiere a pagos obligatorios sin contraprestación efectuados a la Administración central. Se dice que los impuestos carecen de contraprestación en el sentido de que los bienes y servicios que las Administraciones brindan a los contribuyentes no suelen tener relación directa con los pagos que estos efectúan. Las cotizaciones a la Seguridad Social obligatorias pagadas a la Administración central se clasifican como impuestos. En la Guía de Interpretación que se incluye en el Anexo A, puede consultarse más información sobre la clasificación de los impuestos y el criterio de registro.

Proporción entre la recaudación tributaria y el PIB en América Latina y el Caribe en 2018

En 2018, la recaudación tributaria en la región de América Latina y el Caribe (en términos de ingresos tributarios como porcentaje del PIB, incluidas las cotizaciones a la Seguridad Social pagadas a la Administración central) se situó en el 23.1%. En la media de América Latina y el Caribe se incluye el promedio no ponderado de los 25 países de América Latina y el Caribe incluidos en esta publicación, sin Venezuela, por problemas de disponibilidad de datos.

En 2018, la recaudación tributaria de los distintos países de la región osciló entre el 12.1% en Guatemala y el 42.3% en Cuba. A excepción de Cuba, todos los países de América Latina y el Caribe registraron una recaudación tributaria inferior al promedio de la OCDE, que se situó en el 34.3%. Entre 2017 y 2018, el promedio de la recaudación tributaria como porcentaje del PIB en América Latina y el Caribe aumentó en 0.4 puntos porcentuales. Este incremento refleja, en parte, la ligera recuperación económica en el entorno económico de la región desde 2017 (impulsada por las mejoras en la demanda interna, un incremento del comercio y el aumento de los precios de los productos básicos), así como la superación de los efectos de los desastres naturales que azotaron el Caribe en 2017.

Los mayores incrementos en la proporción entre la recaudación tributaria y el PIB se registraron entre 2017 y 2018 en tres países caribeños: Trinidad y Tobago (3.3 puntos porcentuales), Belice (1.4 puntos porcentuales) y Guyana (1.3 puntos porcentuales). En Trinidad y Tobago, los ingresos por el impuesto sobre la renta y los beneficios (especialmente el impuesto sobre la renta de sociedades) fueron los principales impulsores, apoyados por una fuerte recuperación del sector energético. En 2018, Belice y Guyana registraron aumentos en todas las categorías principales de ingresos tributarios como proporción del PIB, debido a las reformas administrativas y de políticas públicas, así como a la mejora del contexto económico. Aparte de estos tres países, otros 12 países registraron un aumento de su proporción entre la recaudación tributaria y el PIB, mientras que siete sufrieron una disminución y tres permanecieron estables. La mayor reducción se produjo en Argentina (1.3% del PIB) y Nicaragua (0.8% del PIB), en ambos casos como consecuencia de un entorno económico más débil.

Evolución de la recaudación tributaria como porcentaje del PIB en América Latina y el Caribe desde 1990

Entre 1990 y 2018, el promedio de la proporción entre la recaudación tributaria y el PIB en la región de América Latina y el Caribe aumentó de forma prácticamente constante en más de 7 puntos porcentuales, pasando del 15.9% al 23.1% y acercándose al promedio de la OCDE: la diferencia respecto al promedio de la proporción entre la recaudación tributaria y el PIB de la OCDE se redujo desde los 16.0 puntos porcentuales, en 1990, a los 11.2 puntos porcentuales, en 2018.

Los principales factores del aumento de los ingresos tributarios en la región de América Latina y el Caribe fueron los impuestos sobre el valor añadido (IVA) y los impuestos sobre la renta y los beneficios. La recaudación por IVA como porcentaje del PIB en los países de América Latina y el Caribe aumentó 3.8 puntos porcentuales entre 1990 y 2018, acercándose al 6.0% del PIB. Desde 1990, diez países de América Latina y el Caribe, sobre todo en el Caribe, han adoptado el IVA y la mayoría de los países de América Latina y el Caribe han realizado grandes esfuerzos para aumentar estos ingresos (por ejemplo, incrementando los tipos impositivos del IVA, aumentando la base impositiva y reforzando los sistemas de recaudación del IVA). La recaudación por los impuestos sobre la renta y los beneficios aumentó un 3.1% del PIB durante el mismo periodo, sobre todo impulsada por la expansión que sufrieron los precios de los productos básicos a partir de 2003, que incrementó los ingresos por el impuesto sobre la renta de sociedades del sector de los recursos naturales.

En 2018, el promedio de la subregión de América del Sur fue el mismo que el de América Latina y el Caribe, que se situó en el 23.1%. América del Sur ha registrado el crecimiento más rápido en la proporción entre la recaudación tributaria y el PIB desde 1990 y, en 2004, superó el promedio de América Latina y el Caribe. Sin embargo, sufrió un descenso contante entre 2015 y 2017 antes de recuperarse en 2018. Los promedios de la subregión de Centroamérica y México y del Caribe experimentaron un aumento gradual desde 1990, aunque esta tendencia ha cambiado a partir de 2016: en Centroamérica y México se ha mantenido relativamente estable en el 21.0%, mientras que la región del Caribe ha mostrado un fuerte crecimiento, con un incremento de 1.5 puntos porcentuales durante este periodo hasta alcanzar el 25.7% en 2018.

Estructuras tributarias en la región de América Latina y el Caribe

En 2018, en promedio, la estructura tributaria de los países de América Latina y el Caribe siguió mostrando una dependencia relativamente alta de ingresos procedentes de impuestos sobre bienes y servicios, que suponen aproximadamente la mitad del total de los ingresos tributarios, en comparación con el tercio que estos representan en las economías de la OCDE. En 2018, el IVA y los ingresos procedentes de impuestos sobre la renta y los beneficios fueron las mayores fuentes de ingresos, en promedio, de la región de América Latina y el Caribe, al representar el 27.8% del total de ingresos tributarios.

Dentro de la categoría de impuestos sobre la renta y los beneficios, la región de América Latina y el Caribe está mucho más supeditada a los ingresos procedentes del impuesto sobre la renta de sociedades que los países de la OCDE y depende significativamente menos de los impuestos sobre la renta de personas físicas. En 2017, los ingresos procedentes de los impuestos sobre la renta de sociedades y sobre la renta de personas físicas en la región de América Latina y el Caribe representaron, respectivamente, el 15.3% y el 9.7% del total de los ingresos tributarios, frente al 9.3% y el 23.9% en la OCDE. De igual forma, las cotizaciones a la Seguridad Social como proporción del total de los ingresos tributarios fueron 8.7 puntos porcentuales más bajas en la región de América Latina y el Caribe que el promedio de la OCDE (el 17.3% frente al 26.0%).

En 2018, los ingresos por impuestos relacionados con el medio ambiente equivalieron al 1.1% del PIB, en promedio, en los 23 países de América Latina y el Caribe de los que se dispone de dicha información, por debajo del promedio de la OCDE, que se sitúa en el 2.3%. Aproximadamente dos tercios de los ingresos por impuestos relacionados con el medio ambiente en la región de América Latina y el Caribe proceden de impuestos sobre la energía, por lo general, impuestos sobre el diésel y la gasolina (0.6% del PIB en promedio). La recaudación por impuestos sobre los vehículos motorizados y servicios de transporte representó la mayor parte del resto de este tipo de ingresos. A pesar de la lentitud con que se avanza en la aplicación de los impuestos para abordar las cuestiones ambientales, algunos países de América Latina y el Caribe han introducido reformas fiscales importantes. Es el caso de Chile, México y, más recientemente, Colombia.

Secciones especiales

Este Informe contiene dos secciones especiales. La primera identifica tendencias en los ingresos fiscales procedentes de recursos naturales no renovables para una selección de países de América Latina y el Caribe en 2018. Impulsados por unos precios internacionales más altos, los ingresos derivados de los hidrocarburos en la región de América Latina y el Caribe repuntaron en 2018 hasta alcanzar el 2.7% del PIB, frente al 2.0% del PIB de 2016 y 2017. Los ingresos por minería como porcentaje del PIB aumentaron, en promedio, del 0.3% en 2017 al 0.4% en 2018, debido al incremento de la recaudación del impuesto de sociedades a raíz de las fuertes ganancias obtenidas en 2017. Las estimaciones para 2019 sugieren que los ingresos provenientes de recursos naturales no renovables sufrirán un descenso en la región, como consecuencia de la reducción de los precios de estos recursos. Se estima que los ingresos relacionados con los hidrocarburos y los ingresos de la minería han disminuido al 2.5% y al 0.3% del PIB en 2019, respectivamente.

La segunda sección especial examina la presión fiscal equivalente (PFE) en los países de América Latina y el Caribe para el periodo comprendido entre 1990 y 2018. La presión fiscal equivalente es la suma de la proporción entre la recaudación tributaria y el PIB, las cotizaciones obligatorias a sistemas de seguro social privados y los ingresos no tributarios procedentes de recursos naturales, expresados como porcentaje del PIB. En 2018, el promedio de la PFE en la región de América Latina y el Caribe fue del 25.0% del PIB, 0.2 puntos porcentuales más elevada que en 2017. Desde 1990, las cotizaciones obligatorias a sistemas de seguro social privados como porcentaje del PIB han aumentado en 0.7 puntos porcentuales, en promedio, mientras que los ingresos procedentes de recursos naturales han sido inestables.

Chapter 1

Tax revenue trends, 1990-2018

Capítulo 1

Tendencias tributarias, 1990-2018

Chapter 1

Tax revenue trends, 1990-2018

Financing the development agenda of Latin America and the Caribbean (LAC) and its achievement of the Sustainable Development Goals requires a step change in domestic resource mobilisation (OECD et al., 2019[1]). At the same time as higher levels of revenue generation are required to meet long-term objectives, they are also needed to address urgent demands from citizens across the region to enhance the provision of public goods and mitigate high levels of vulnerability, particularly in the labour market. Fiscal policy also has an important role to play in catalysing inclusive economic growth in the region. These imperatives reflect the multi-dimensional nature of development and underline the need for sustainable, comprehensive policies. This need lies at the heart of the Development in Transition (DiT) agenda as led by the European Commission, with the support of the OECD and its Development Centre, and the Economic Commission for Latin America and the Caribbean (ECLAC).

Improving tax systems across the LAC region is not just a matter of raising higher revenues: the source of these revenues also matters in addressing the region's social and economic goals. The types of taxes used to generate tax revenues (otherwise known as the tax mix or tax structure) have a major bearing on the tax system's redistributive potential and thus its capacity to address income inequality. Taxes can also influence behaviour, for example in incentivising a move away from dependency on fossil fuels in the context of climate change. Taxes can also be raised by different levels of government, with consequent impacts for local service provision and policies to address the challenges of rapid urbanisation.

The Covid-19 pandemic is an unprecedented health crisis which is rapidly spreading around the world. This crisis, together with governments' responses to protect households and businesses, has caused an economic slowdown. One consequence of this slowdown is a probable reduction in public revenues in the region, which is expected to be compounded by the recent decline in commodity prices (particularly in South America, Mexico, and Trinidad and Tobago). The crisis has underlined the need for fiscal systems in LAC to generate higher financing for crucial public services, particularly healthcare, and to expand the fiscal space needed to mitigate possible domestic and external shocks. Looking ahead, it will be necessary to define carefully the role of tax systems in balancing the potentially competing priorities of stimulating inclusive development and repairing governments' fiscal positions.

Revenue Statistics in Latin America and the Caribbean is an integral part of the Regional Facility for Development in Transition for Latin America and the Caribbean. Now in its eighth edition, it provides internationally comparable data on tax revenues in 26 countries in the region both as a basis for in-depth policy analysis and as a common starting point for knowledge sharing and capacity development. This first chapter discusses the evolution of several key tax indicators since 1990, including the tax-to-GDP ratio, the tax mix and the share of tax revenue generation by different levels of government. It also analyses the effectiveness of value-added taxes (VAT, a major source of tax revenues in the region) and revenues from environmental taxes. This chapter highlights recent developments in selected countries' tax systems and complements this analysis with case studies on particular topics. For a detailed country-by-country breakdown of tax revenues, please consult Chapters 5 and 6.

Tax-to-GDP ratios

Tax to-GDP ratios in 2018

The tax-to-GDP ratio measures tax revenues (including social security contributions paid to the general government) as a proportion of gross domestic product (GDP). The LAC average represents the unweighted average of 25 countries included in this publication and excludes Venezuela due to lack of data. Saint Lucia is included in this report for the first time.

The average tax-to-GDP ratio in the LAC region was 23.1% in 2018 (Figure 1.1). Levels varied widely across the region, ranging from 12.1% in Guatemala to 42.3% in Cuba. With the exception of Cuba, all LAC countries recorded a tax-to-GDP ratio below the OECD average[1] of 34.3%.

The highest tax-to-GDP ratios in the LAC region were in Cuba (42.3%), Barbados and Brazil (both 33.1%). The countries with the lowest tax-to-GDP ratios were Guatemala (12.1%), the Dominican Republic (13.2%) and Paraguay (14.0%).

Figure 1.1. **Tax-to-GDP ratios, 2018**

Total tax revenues as percentage of GDP

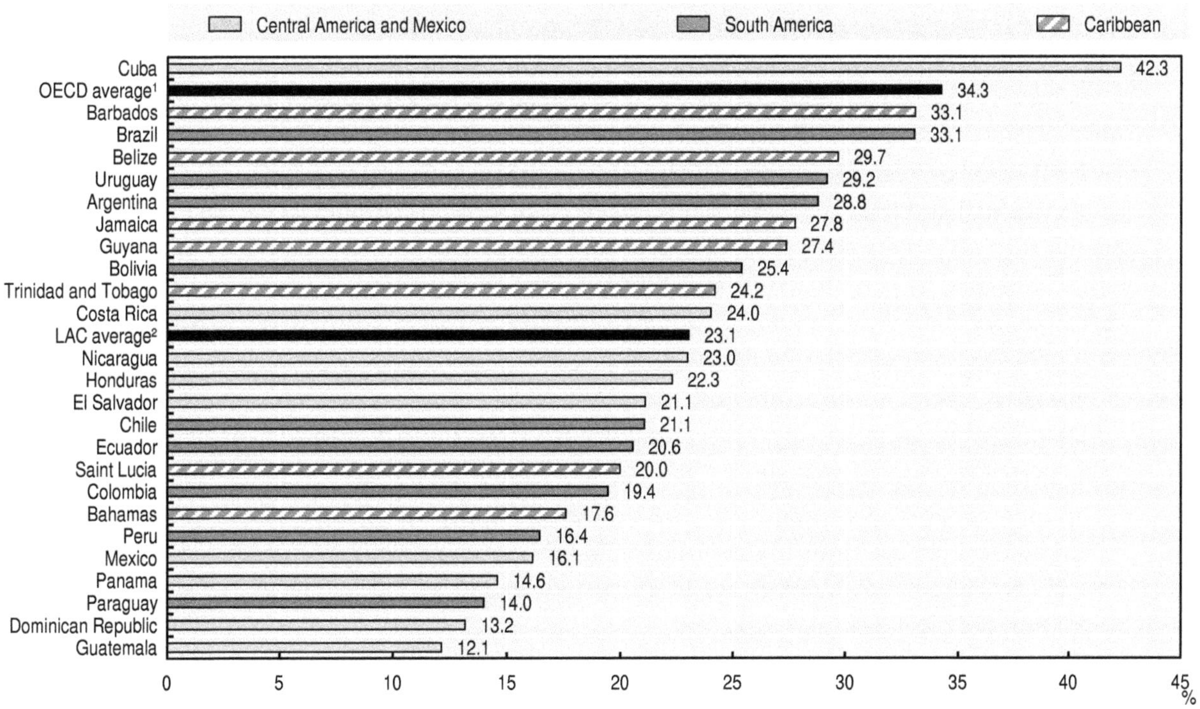

Note: Figures exclude local government revenues for Argentina (but include provincial revenues), the Bahamas, Barbados, the Dominican Republic, Saint Lucia, Trinidad and Tobago and Venezuela as the data are not available.

1. Represents the unweighted average of the 36 OECD member countries. Chile and Mexico are also part of the OECD (36) group. For Mexico, data on state and local government revenues are estimated for 2018.

2. Represents the unweighted average of 25 Latin American and Caribbean countries included in this publication and excludes Venezuela due to data availability issues.

Source: OECD et al. (2020[2]), Table 4.1.

StatLink https://doi.org/10.1787/888934112823

There were important differences in the level of taxation between Central America and Mexico, South America and the Caribbean.[2] Countries in Central America and Mexico typically had lower tax-to-GDP ratios, with an average of 21.0% in 2018, whereas countries in the Caribbean had higher tax-to-GDP ratios and an average of 25.7%. While the tax-to-GDP ratios of South American countries varied widely, they averaged 23.1% in 2018, the same as the LAC average.

In 2018, the average tax-to-GDP ratio for the LAC region as a whole was 0.4 percentage points higher than in 2017, compared to an increase of 0.1 percentage points between 2016 and 2017 (Figure 1.2). This modest increase reflects in part the slow economic recovery in the region since 2017 after a two-year recession. GDP grew by 1.3% (in real terms) in 2017 and by 1.2% in 2018, driven by improvements in domestic demand (ECLAC, 2019[3]) as well as steady increases in commodity prices (OECD/CAF/UN ECLAC, 2018[4]). The rise in the average LAC tax-to-GDP ratio was also partly a result of fiscal consolidation across the region (IDB, 2019[5]).

Changes in tax-to-GDP ratios between 2017 and 2018 varied greatly across the region. The increase in the Caribbean was the largest, at 1.1 percentage points. A recovery from the impact of natural disasters that struck the Caribbean in 2017 contributed to an improved economic context (ECLAC, 2019[3]).

The increase in the average tax-to-GDP ratio in South America between 2017 and 2018 was more modest, at 0.3% of GDP. In contrast, the ratio in Central America and Mexico decreased by 0.1 percentage points. In both regions, economic growth weakened over this period (ECLAC, 2019[3]).

Across the region as a whole, 15 countries reported an increase in their tax-to-GDP ratio in 2018 while seven recorded a decrease and three remained stable. The increases in tax-to-GDP ratios were on average larger than the decreases. The largest increases in tax-to-GDP ratios between 2017 and 2018 occurred in three Caribbean countries: Trinidad and Tobago (3.3 percentage points), Belize (1.4 percentage points) and Guyana (1.3 percentage points).

In Trinidad and Tobago, revenues from taxes on income and profits (especially corporate income tax [CIT]) were the main drivers of revenue growth in 2018 (up by 1.9 percentage points), followed by revenues from VAT (up by 1.4 percentage points).

- The increase in CIT revenues was underpinned by a strong recovery in the energy sector: higher energy prices and increased natural gas production boosted corporate profits (see Chapter 2). Tax revenues from Trinidad and Tobago's oil and gas extraction sector reached 1.8% of GDP, an increase of 0.6 percentage points from the 2017 level. CIT revenues from oil companies represented about a fifth of CIT revenues in 2018.
- The increase in VAT revenues in 2018 followed a sharp fall in 2017 (of 1.3 percentage points). The increase came mainly from outside the energy sector, as Trinidad and Tobago continued efforts to diversify its economic base and reduce dependence on energy revenues (IMF, 2018[6]).

Belize and Guyana recorded increases in all main categories of tax revenue in 2018 as a proportion of GDP, thanks in part to administrative and policy reforms:

- Since 2015, Guyana has made efforts to improve tax administration through the CIAT-SECO Cooperation Program (CIAT, 2017[7]): a large taxpayer unit (LTU) was created; the taxpayer base has grown, thanks to the implementation of risk models; and tax collection processes were strengthened. In 2018, the operations of the LTU and electronic filing were important factors behind an increase in income tax revenues equivalent to 0.5% of GDP (IMF, 2019[8]). In addition, Guyana recorded a 31.6% year-on-year rise in imports in 2018 (Ministry of Finance of Guyana, 2019[9]) mainly related to its oil and gas activities. This underpinned an increase in import duties (equivalent to 0.2% of GDP) and in excises (equivalent to 0.4% of GDP) over the period.

- Revenue from taxes on goods and services in Belize increased by 0.7% of GDP in 2018, driven by an increase in VAT revenues equivalent to 0.5% of GDP. This was the result of a reform to broaden the base of the General Sales Tax (GST) by removing zero-rated items (IMF, 2019[10]). Growth in CIT revenues drove an increase in revenues from taxes on income and profits equivalent to 0.3% of GDP, helped by the economy's continued recovery from a natural disaster in 2016. Growth in 2018 (of 3.0%) was driven mainly by the tourism industry (ECLAC, 2019[11]). In addition, property taxes increased by 0.4% of GDP due to higher revenues from stamp duties.

Figure 1.2. **Changes in tax-to-GDP ratios between 2016-17 and 2017-18**

Percentage points of GDP

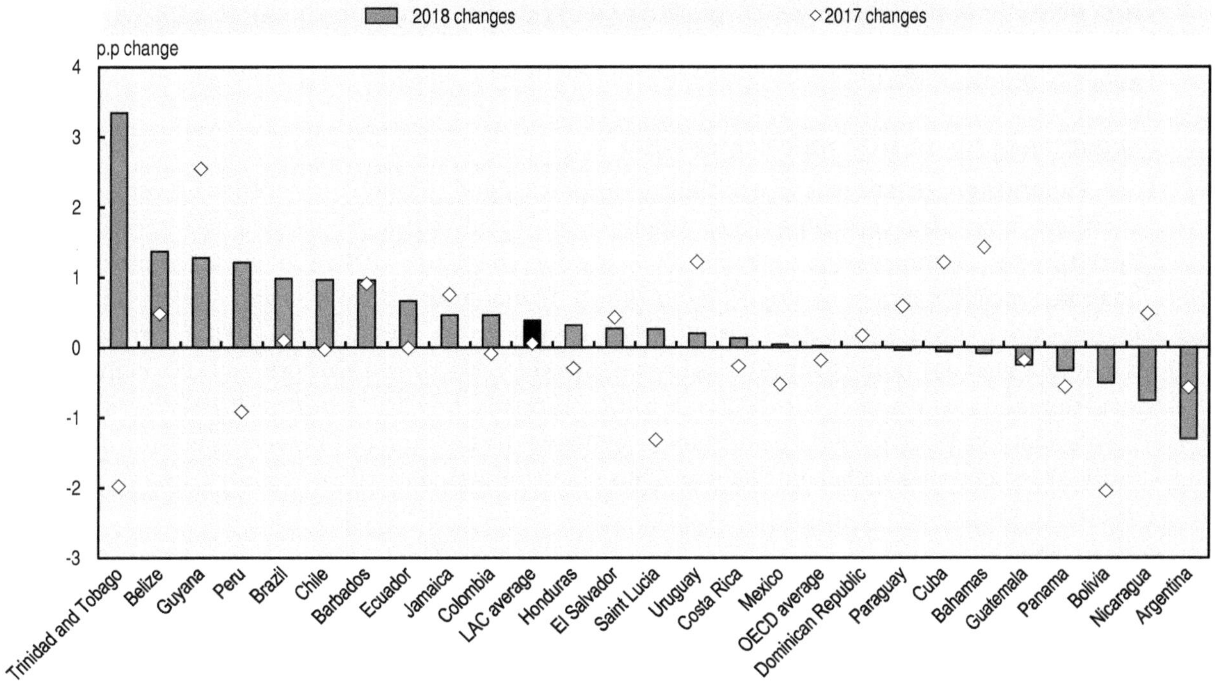

Source: Authors' calculations based on OECD et al. (2020[2]), Table 4.1.

StatLink https://doi.org/10.1787/888934112842

Only Argentina experienced a decrease in tax revenues greater than 1% of GDP between 2017 and 2018 (1.3%). All the main categories of tax revenue recorded a decrease in 2018. Revenues from social security contributions decreased by 0.6 percentage points. Although Argentina implemented significant tax reforms in 2018 (reducing the CIT rate from 35% to 30% and increasing social security contribution rates but narrowing their base), the economic context was the principal driver for the decline in the tax-to-GDP ratio. The economy contracted by 2.5% in real terms in 2018 (ECLAC, 2019[12]; OECD, 2019[13]) Amidst high inflation, Argentina's GDP rose faster in nominal terms than tax revenues (37% versus 31%), leading to a decrease in the tax-to-GDP ratio.

Nicaragua's tax-to-GDP ratio experienced the next-largest decline, equivalent to 0.8% of GDP, over the period, with all other decreases in the region equivalent to less than 0.5% of GDP. Nicaragua's economy also shrank significantly in 2018 (by 3.8% in real terms) amid a political and social crisis that caused significant declines in revenues across all tax categories (ECLAC, 2019[12]). In nominal terms, both taxes and GDP fell, with taxes falling more strongly (4% versus 1%).

As seen in Argentina and Nicaragua, changes in a country's tax-to-GDP ratio are driven by the relative size and direction of change both in nominal tax revenues and nominal GDP. If tax revenues rise more than GDP (or fall less than GDP), the tax-to-GDP ratio will increase. Conversely, if tax revenues rise less than GDP, or fall further, the tax-to-GDP ratio will decline. A higher tax-to-GDP ratio does not necessarily mean that the amount of tax revenues has increased in real or even nominal terms.

Annual GDP growth was positive among all 15 LAC countries whose tax-to-GDP ratio increased between 2017 and 2018, although to a lesser degree than tax revenue growth. All five LAC countries that experienced a decline in their tax-to-GDP ratio in 2018 recorded higher levels of tax revenues in nominal terms than in 2017 but the change in nominal tax revenues was less than the change in nominal GDP. Nicaragua is the only LAC country that experienced negative nominal GDP growth and negative tax revenue growth in 2018, while the Bahamas recorded a decline in GDP and an increase in tax revenues in nominal terms between 2017 and 2018.

Evolution of tax-to-GDP ratios since 2000

Enhancing domestic resource mobilisation, particularly through increased tax revenues, is critical for LAC's sustainable development, as reflected in the DiT agenda (see Box 1.1). With three exceptions (1991, 1996 and 2009), the average tax-to-GDP ratio in LAC countries has risen steadily each year since 1990 (Figure 1.3), increasing by more than 7 percentage points, from 15.9% in 1990 to 23.1% in 2018. This trend contrasts with that in OECD countries, where the average tax-to-GDP ratio has been relatively stable since 1990 (although at a higher level than the LAC average); the OECD tax-to-GDP ratio reached 34.3% in 2018, 2.3 percentage points above its level in 1990. The difference between the LAC and OECD average tax-to-GDP ratios shrank between 1990 and 2008 and has since remained relatively steady (Figure 1.3).

Box 1.1 ***Revenue Statistics in Latin America and the Caribbean* and Development in Transition**

This edition of *Revenue Statistics in Latin America and the Caribbean* is the second to be produced with the support of the European Union (EU) Regional Facility for Development in Transition for Latin America and the Caribbean (LAC). This facility results from a joint work led by the EU, the Organisation for Economic Co-operation and Development (OECD) and its Development Centre, and the Economic Commission for Latin America and the Caribbean (ECLAC).

LAC economies are confronting persistent and new domestic and global vulnerabilities that call for critical transformations to maximise opportunities for development. Four main traps hinder successful transformation and transition to sustainable development. These are the productivity, social vulnerability, institutional and environmental traps, which interact with each other in self-reinforcing dynamics to limit the region's sustainable development opportunities (OECD et al., 2019[1]).

Development in Transition embraces a movement to design better policies, practices and partnerships *both* at home and internationally. Ever-more complex issues require development strategies with more sophisticated policy mixes and greater co-ordination and coherence. Ambitious efforts must be made to overcome the traps and turn vicious circles into virtuous ones. At home, domestic capacities, including tax collection, must be strengthened to better address development challenges. At the international level, international co-operation should act as a facilitator to support countries transitioning towards sustainable development by participating in policy partnerships, as equal partners, and address common concerns, putting LAC national strategies front and centre, strengthen countries' domestic capacities and expand the toolbox of international co-operation modalities and instruments (OECD et al., 2019[1]).

Box 1.1 ***Revenue Statistics in Latin America and the Caribbean* and Development in Transition** *(cont.)*

Fiscal policy is essential to build capacities, address development traps and ensure inclusive and sustainable development in LAC countries. *Revenue Statistics in Latin America and the Caribbean* represents an invaluable resource for governments as they look to strengthen fiscal policy. By providing harmonised and detailed tax data across the region, it allows for in-depth tax-policy analysis, identifying not only how the level of tax revenues varies by country but also which instruments generate these revenues, reflecting the fact that *how* tax revenues are collected can be as important as *how much* is collected. *Revenue Statistics in Latin America and the Caribbean* also represents a common starting point for knowledge-sharing and capacity development between countries, as well as with the broader international community.

Reflecting the critical relationship between effective taxation and effective public spending to promote inclusive and sustainable development, the Development in Transition Facility brings *Revenue Statistics in Latin America and the Caribbean* together with ECLAC's and OECD's work on public expenditure, and social spending in particular. The objective is to provide unprecedented insights and invaluable tools for the development of fiscal policy in the region, thereby unlocking its capacity to fulfil its commitment to Agenda 2030 and implement long-term development strategies.

Figure 1.3. **Tax-to-GDP ratios, LAC and OECD averages, 1990-2018**

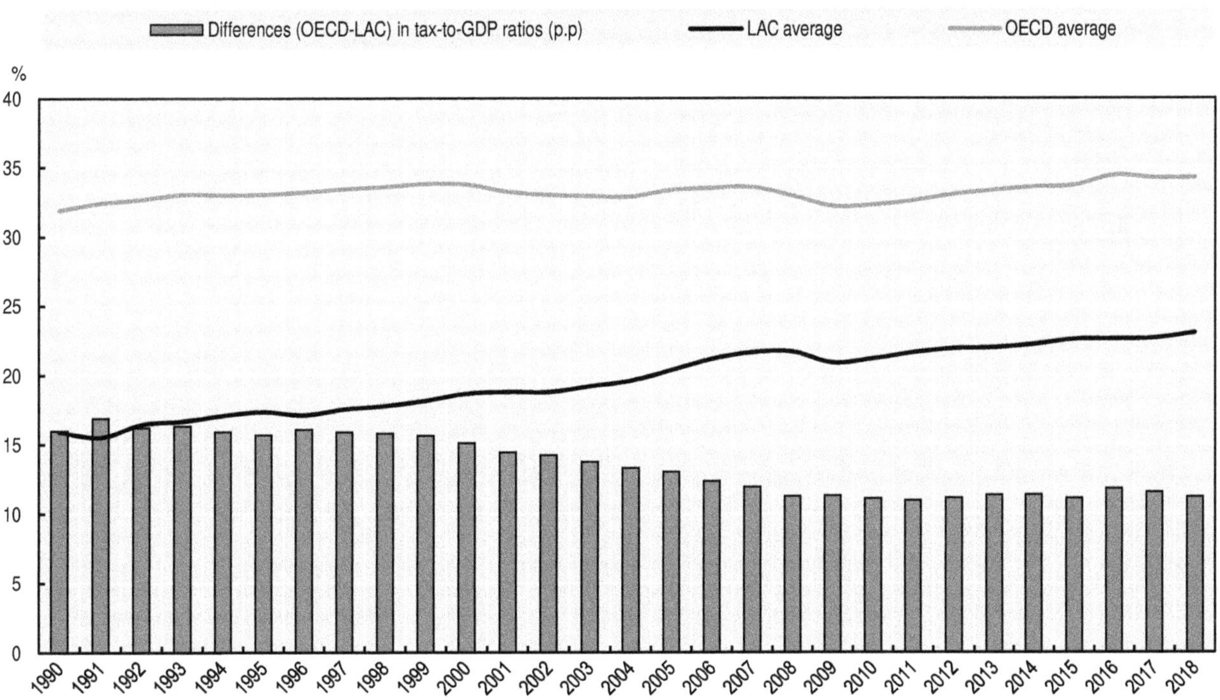

Source: OECD et al. (2020[2]), Table 4.1.

StatLink https://doi.org/10.1787/888934112861

Figure 1.4 shows the evolution of average tax-to-GDP ratios for the three sub-regions of Latin America and the Caribbean since 1990. While all three sub-regions have shown an upward trend in tax levels between 1990 and 2018, their evolution shows notable differences.

- On average, South America recorded the strongest growth over the period and exceeded the LAC average from 2004 until 2018.

- In contrast, the increase in the tax-to-GDP ratios for Central America and Mexico and for the Caribbean has been more gradual. Throughout this period, the tax-to-GDP ratio of Central America and Mexico remained below the average for the LAC region as a whole, whereas the Caribbean's average tax-to-GDP ratio was consistently higher than the LAC average.
- Since 1990, the Caribbean average has been slowly trending towards the LAC average whereas the reverse is observed for Central America and Mexico.
- The evolution of the tax-to-GDP ratios for the three sub-regions has varied in recent years. South America recorded a steady decrease between 2015 and 2017: its tax-to-GDP ratio fell by 0.8 percentage points over the period before recovering in 2018 by 0.3 percentage points (despite the fall in Argentina). The average tax-to-GDP ratio for Central America and Mexico has been steady at 21.0% since 2016, while the Caribbean region has shown steady and strong growth, increasing by 1.5 percentage points between 2016 and 2018.

Figure 1.4. **Average tax-to-GDP ratios, LAC and sub-regions, 1990-2018**

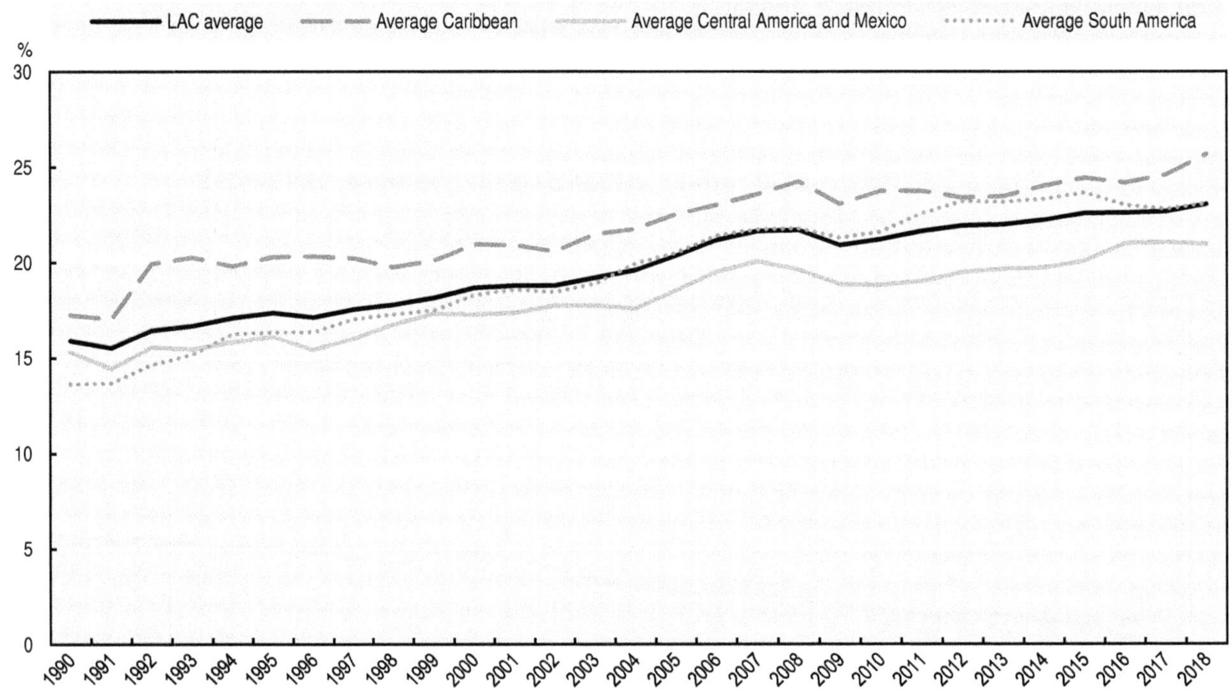

Note: The LAC average represents the unweighted average of 25 LAC countries included in this publication and excludes Venezuela due to data availability issues.

The Caribbean includes seven countries (Bahamas, Barbados, Belize, Guyana, Jamaica, Saint Lucia and Trinidad and Tobago); Central America and Mexico, nine countries (Costa Rica, Cuba, Dominican Republic, El Salvador, Guatemala, Honduras, Mexico, Nicaragua and Panama); and South America, nine countries (Argentina, Bolivia, Brazil, Chile, Colombia, Ecuador, Paraguay, Peru and Uruguay).

Source: Authors' calculations based on OECD et al. (2020[2]), "Revenue Statistics in Latin America: Comparative tables", *OECD Tax Statistics* (database), *http://dx.doi.org/10.1787/data-00641-en*.

StatLink https://doi.org/10.1787/888934112880

Tax-to-GDP ratios in LAC countries increased in the early 1990s after a decade of macroeconomic instability. During the 1980s, many countries ran large fiscal imbalances and some resorted to alternative ways of financing expenditure (borrowing or printing money). This caused rapid inflation across the region, which eroded the real value of countries' tax revenues. Reforms in the 1990s focused on price stability, trade liberalisation and fiscal discipline. Most LAC governments reduced spending and implemented policies aimed at increasing tax revenues; budget management and fiscal balances improved considerably. Policy makers implemented reforms to tax policy and administration to reinforce tax systems against inflationary episodes by shortening collection lags and indexing tax liabilities (ECLAC, 2018[14]).

The introduction of VAT was the most significant tax reform in LAC over the past three decades. In 1980, 12 countries[3] were implementing a VAT system; by the early 1990s, almost all countries were doing so. After this period, reforms have increased the VAT rate, widened the tax base and improved collections. Reforms have also focused on simplifying VAT systems, with most countries reducing the number of items with zero or reduced rates. Several countries have moved towards single-rate VAT schemes (ECLAC, 2018[14]).

LAC countries have undertaken significant efforts to modernise tax administration over the last two decades. New information technology systems have been implemented, the structures of tax administrations were rationalised, tax collection systems became more efficient and staff gained in expertise (IDB, 2013[15]). In addition, some countries simplified their tax systems and broadened their tax bases, reducing the number of exemptions and tax incentives granted to certain activities and sectors principally to incentivise foreign investment. Tax reforms included the introduction or development of simplified regimes for small taxpayers and the taxation of property based on presumed incomes. These measures had a positive effect on revenues in a number of countries thanks to the expansion of taxation to labour and capital income, including dividends (e.g. Colombia, Dominican Republic, Guatemala, El Salvador, Nicaragua, Panama and Peru). Reforms have also included the establishment of minimum taxes, taxes on financial transactions and gradual reductions in the real income level taxed at the top marginal rate (ECLAC, 2013[16]; ECLAC, 2018[14]); Box 1.2 gives examples of ongoing fiscal reforms in three countries.

Box 1.2. **Tax reforms in selected LAC countries**

In 2018, a number of countries undertook major tax policy reforms to simplify tax systems, reduce tax evasion and boost private investment.

Barbados announced a number of measures affecting all main taxes in its 2018 Budget. These included an increase of the CIT rate from 25% to 30%, a new income tax band at 40% for top earners and a new health service contribution on income payable by employers and employees. In addition, Barbados implemented new taxes or increased taxes in the tourist sector and replaced the road tax with a fuel tax (IDB, 2019[5]). In respect to the digital economy, a VAT now applies to all online transactions for the purchase of goods and services by residents of Barbados and a 10% tax applies on transactions for companies such as Airbnb, Homeaway and Expedia (Tax-News.com, 2018[17]; Barbados Revenue Authority, 2018[18]). IDB (2019[5]) explains that these measures are expected to increase revenues by about 3.7% of GDP.

Argentina also embarked on a comprehensive tax reform (Law No. 27430) covering all main tax types, effective from 1 January 2018. Argentina lowered its CIT rate from 35% to 30% and plans to reduce it to 25% from 2020 onwards. In addition, a dividend withholding tax has been implemented and the rate will gradually increase to reach 13% to be applied after 1 January 2020. In respect to PIT, income tax exemptions for interest income and capital gains from different types of investments were eliminated. The different social security rates (which vary depending on the industry) paid by private-sector employers will gradually be unified effective from January 2022. A non-taxable base for SSCs has been implemented since 2018 and its amount will gradually increase until 2022. VAT is applied to digital services provided by residents of Argentina or where the effective use of the services is in Argentina (EY, 2018[19]).

Box 1.2. **Tax reforms in selected LAC countries** *(cont.)*

Colombia approved a comprehensive tax reform in December 2018 that took effect in January 2019. However, a constitutionality review carried out by the Colombian Constitutional Court ruled against the tax reform due to procedural errors during the debate in Congress. This led to a second tax reform (Law No. 2010 of 2019) approved in December 2019 that reproduces almost entirely the comprehensive tax reform of December 2018. Under this reform, CIT rates will decrease from 32% in tax year 2020, to 31% in 2021 and 30% from 2022 onwards. The presumptive income tax rate is reduced from 3.5% to 1.5% in 2019 and 2020, and to 0% from 2021. Reduced CIT rates apply for certain industries (such as hotel services, new projects on theme or ecotourism parks and agrotourism, among others). Income tax exemptions were introduced for income below USD 850 000 from technological and creative industries or agricultural activities. The top PIT rate was increased for all types of income (labour and capital) and a simplified tax regime was implemented for small and medium-sized enterprises to replace the income tax, the general excise tax (when applicable) and industry and commerce tax. Permanent establishments are now taxed on their worldwide attributable income. The tax reform also included measures to address tax evasion, an indirect transfer regime, the creation of a normalisation tax for taxpayers that have omitted assets or included non-existent debts on their income tax returns, a VAT on beer and soda and a new equity tax on Colombian residents' worldwide net worth that will apply for 2019, 2020 and 2021. Innovations such as a VAT refund for the families of low income and one day of the year without VAT are included in the tax reform of 2019. The tax reform is estimated to have yielded additional revenues equivalent to 0.7% of GDP in 2019. (IDB, 2019[5]; EY, 2019[20]).

Between 1990 and 2018, revenues from VAT as a percentage of GDP more than doubled for LAC countries on average, from 2.3% of GDP in 1990 to 6.0% in 2018 (Figure 1.5). Over the same period, revenues from other taxes on goods and services (excises, customs and import duties) in LAC decreased as a percentage of GDP. This decline was associated with trade liberalisation, as a result of which LAC countries changed the way they taxed imported and exported goods as well as specific goods and services. These changes included a reduction of import tariffs, narrowing the base of products and services subject to excises, and the elimination of taxes on exports. One important exception is Argentina, where taxes on exports were re-established in 2002; however, the government abolished export taxes on almost all agricultural products in 2015 (IMF, 2016[21]; World Grain, 2016[22]).

The increase in the average tax-to-GDP ratio in the LAC region since 1990 has largely been driven by increases in revenues from income tax and VAT (Figure 1.5). Four distinct phases in the evolution of tax revenues can be distinguished:

- Between 1990 and 2002, VAT contributed more to the increase in tax revenues than taxes on income and profits (1.8% of GDP versus 1.1%). Over that period, five countries introduced VAT (Barbados, Belize, El Salvador, Jamaica and Paraguay).
- Between 2002 and 2008, the reverse trend is observed: revenue from taxes on income and profits contributed more than VAT revenues to the increase in the average tax-to-GDP ratio (the increases amounted to 1.8% and 1.3% of GDP respectively). The increase in income taxes is partly explained by the commodity price boom after 2003, which drove up CIT revenue from companies in the natural resources sector (ECLAC, 2014[23]; Barreix, Benitez and Pecho, 2017[24]). In several countries, it was also a result of policies that reduced tax incentives in free-trade zones, the introduction of minimum taxes for corporations, reforms in international taxation and agreements between countries to fight tax evasion.

- VAT and revenues from income taxes declined strongly during the global financial crisis. During the subsequent recovery, VAT revenues grew quickly and reached 6% of GDP in 2016, the same level as income tax revenues. During this period, two more Caribbean countries introduced VAT (Saint Lucia in 2012 and Bahamas in 2015). Commodity prices declined steadily and then sharply in 2015.
- From 2016, commodity prices recovered and income tax revenues rebounded. Between 2017 and 2018, revenues from income taxes recorded their highest increase since 2011, at 0.3 percentage points on average. This is largely explained by an increase in CIT revenues (equal to 0.2% of GDP). Factors behind the increase in CIT revenues include strong profits in the mining and oil and gas extraction sectors (see Chapter 2).

Figure 1.5. **Revenue from taxes on income and profits, social security contributions, VAT and other taxes on goods and services, 1990-2018**

Percentage of GDP

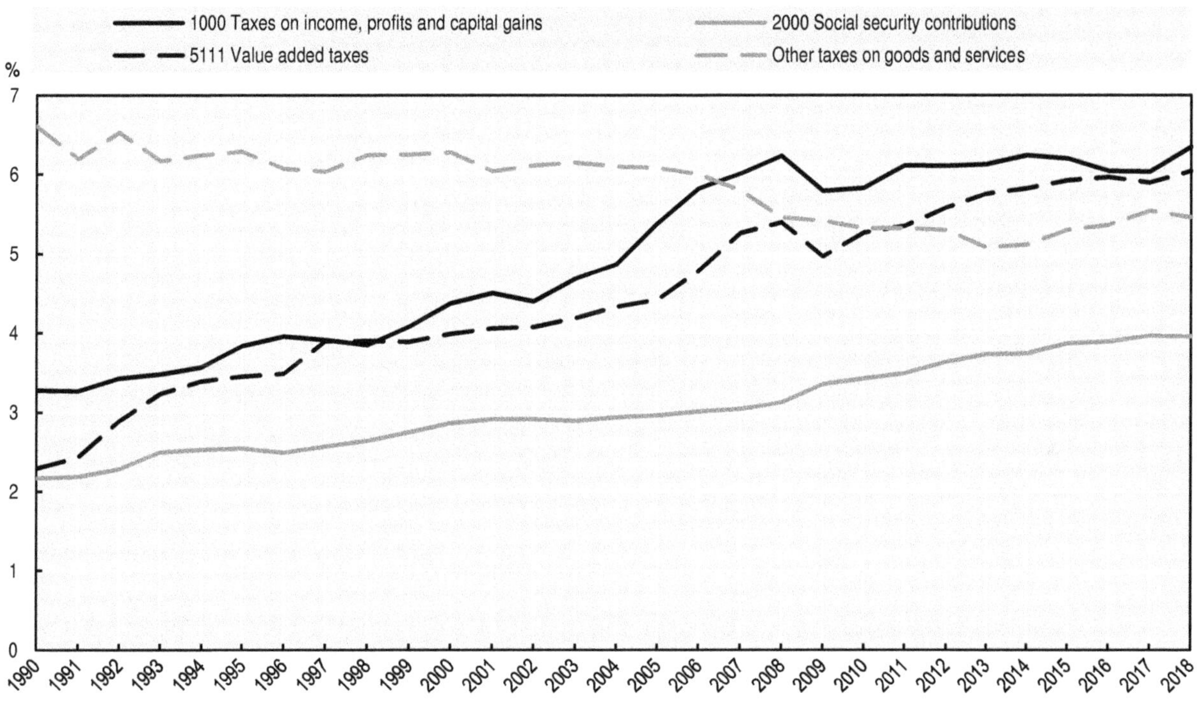

Source: Authors' calculations based on OECD et al. (2020[2]), "Revenue Statistics in Latin America: Comparative tables", *OECD Tax Statistics* (database), *http://dx.doi.org/10.1787/data-00641-en*.

StatLink *https://doi.org/10.1787/888934112899*

Figure 1.6 shows the evolution of CIT and PIT since 2007. In 2018, the LAC averages for CIT and PIT revenues stood at 3.5% and 2.3% of GDP respectively, although Ecuador, Nicaragua and Venezuela are excluded from the calculation due to data issues. Over this period, CIT revenues as a percentage of GDP have been more volatile than revenues from PIT, which have steadily increased. While CIT revenues are principally driven by economic cycles and changes in commodity prices (especially for countries reliant on the exploitation of natural resources), changes to CIT rates are also an important factor. Over this period, the average CIT rate in the LAC region decreased from 27.3% to 25.7% in 2016; it then rose over the next two years, to 26.3% in 2018.[4] Between 2007 and 2018, Argentina, Panama and Uruguay reduced their CIT rate from 30% to 25%. In contrast, some countries increased CIT rates over this period, including Chile (from 17% in 2007 to 25% in 2017) and Mexico (from 28% in 2007 to 30% in 2010) (OECD, 2018[25]).

Figure 1.6. **Revenue from taxes on income and profits, CIT and PIT, 2007-18**

Percentage of GDP

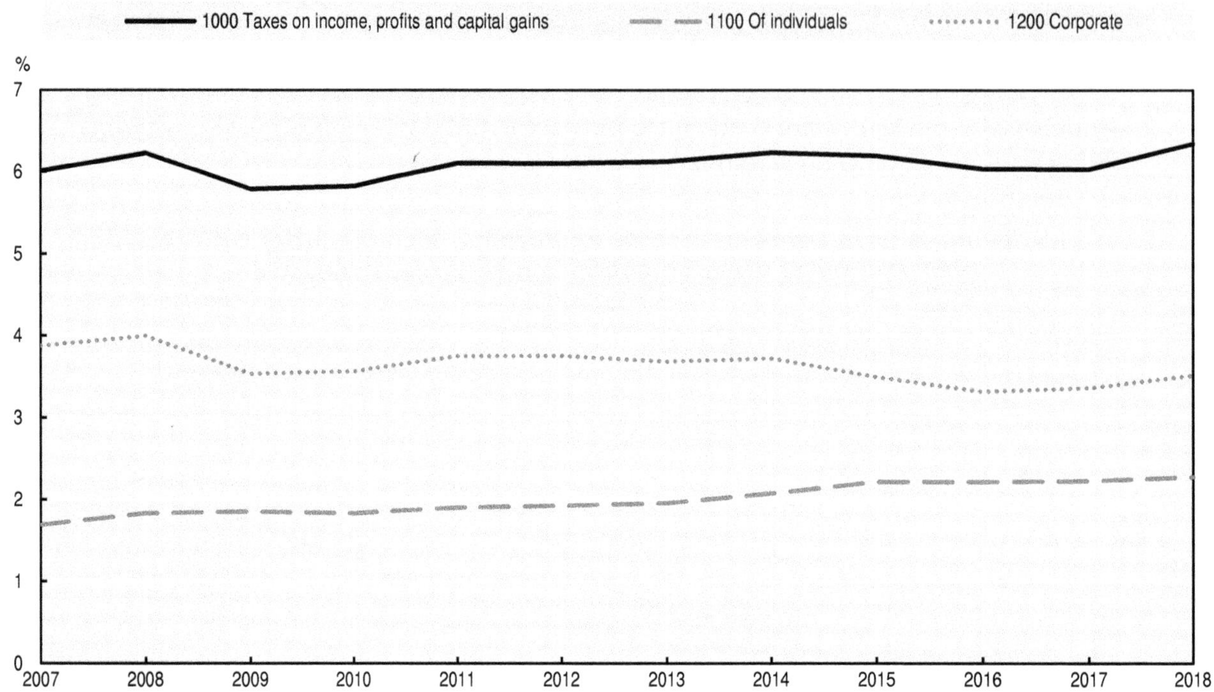

Note: CIT and PIT revenue as a percentage of GDP should be interpreted with caution as Ecuador, Nicaragua and Venezuela are excluded from the calculation. The LAC averages excludes Venezuela due to data availability issues. Ecuador and Nicaragua are excluded from the LAC averages for CIT revenue as a percentage of GDP and PIT revenue as a percentage of GDP as more than a third of their revenue from taxes on income and profits cannot be allocated to CIT revenue (1200) or PIT revenue (1100).

Source: OECD et al. (2020[2]), "Revenue Statistics in Latin America and the Caribbean: Comparative tables", *OECD Tax Statistics* (database), *http://dx.doi.org/10.1787/data-00641-en.*

StatLink *https://doi.org/10.1787/888934112918*

There are notable differences between the three LAC sub-regions when considering the changes in the main tax categories between 1990 and 2018 (Figure 1.7).

- On average, the Caribbean showed the largest increase in VAT revenue as a percentage of GDP (of 6 percentage points). Six of the seven Caribbean countries implemented[5] a VAT system over the period, later than most countries in Central America and Mexico and South America.
- In South America and in Central America and Mexico, the largest increases between 1990 and 2018 were from taxes on income and profits (3.8% of GDP), followed by VAT (3.4% and 2.7% of GDP respectively). Revenues from taxes on income and profits (and indirectly from VAT) were influenced by large increases in mineral and oil prices between 2003 and 2010.

Figure 1.7. **Changes in revenue from taxes on income and profits, social security contributions, VAT and other taxes on goods and services by sub-region, 1990-2018**

Percentage of GDP

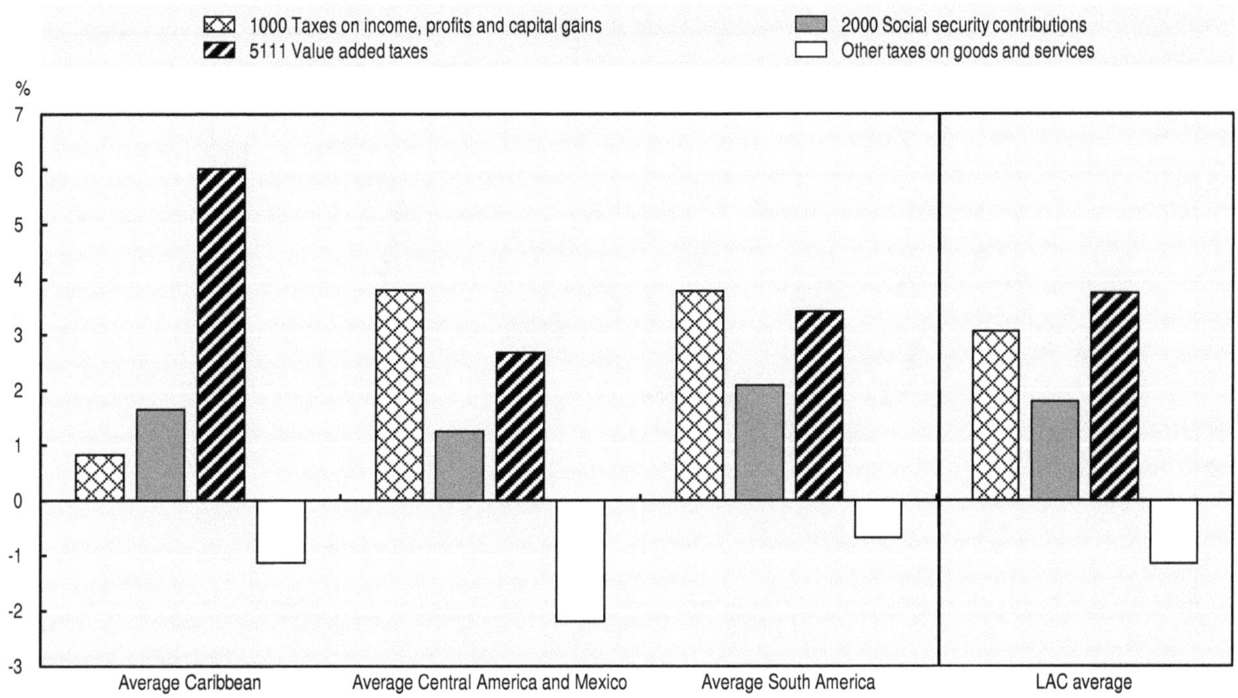

Note: The LAC average represents the unweighted average of 25 LAC countries included in this publication and excludes Venezuela due to data availability issues. The Caribbean includes seven countries (Bahamas, Barbados, Belize, Guyana, Jamaica, Saint Lucia and Trinidad and Tobago); Central America and Mexico, nine countries (Costa Rica, Cuba, Dominican Republic, El Salvador, Guatemala, Honduras, Mexico, Nicaragua and Panama); and South America, nine countries (Argentina, Bolivia, Brazil, Chile, Colombia, Ecuador, Paraguay, Peru and Uruguay).

Source: Authors' calculations based on OECD et al. (2020[2]), "Revenue Statistics in Latin America: Comparative tables", *OECD Tax Statistics* (database), *http://dx.doi.org/10.1787/data-00641-en*.

StatLink *https://doi.org/10.1787/888934112937*

Factors influencing tax-to-GDP ratios

Differences between the LAC and OECD average tax-to-GDP ratios are consistent with the tendency for countries at higher income levels to have higher tax-to-GDP ratios. The data implies a positive correlation between GDP per capita (a measure of the level of income of a country) and tax-to-GDP ratios (Figure 1.8). In general, OECD countries have higher average incomes than LAC countries and collect higher tax revenues as a proportion of GDP. Argentina, Barbados, Brazil and Uruguay show similar tax-to-GDP ratios and levels of income to some OECD countries. Empirical analysis suggests that stronger tax collection, accompanied by better institutions, education and skills, and economic diversification allowed many OECD countries to evade the middle income trap, in contrast to LAC (Melguizo et al., 2017[26]).

Figure 1.8. **GDP per capita in PPP (USD) and tax-to-GDP ratios for countries in the LAC region, the OECD, and a group of African, Asian and Pacific economies, 2017**

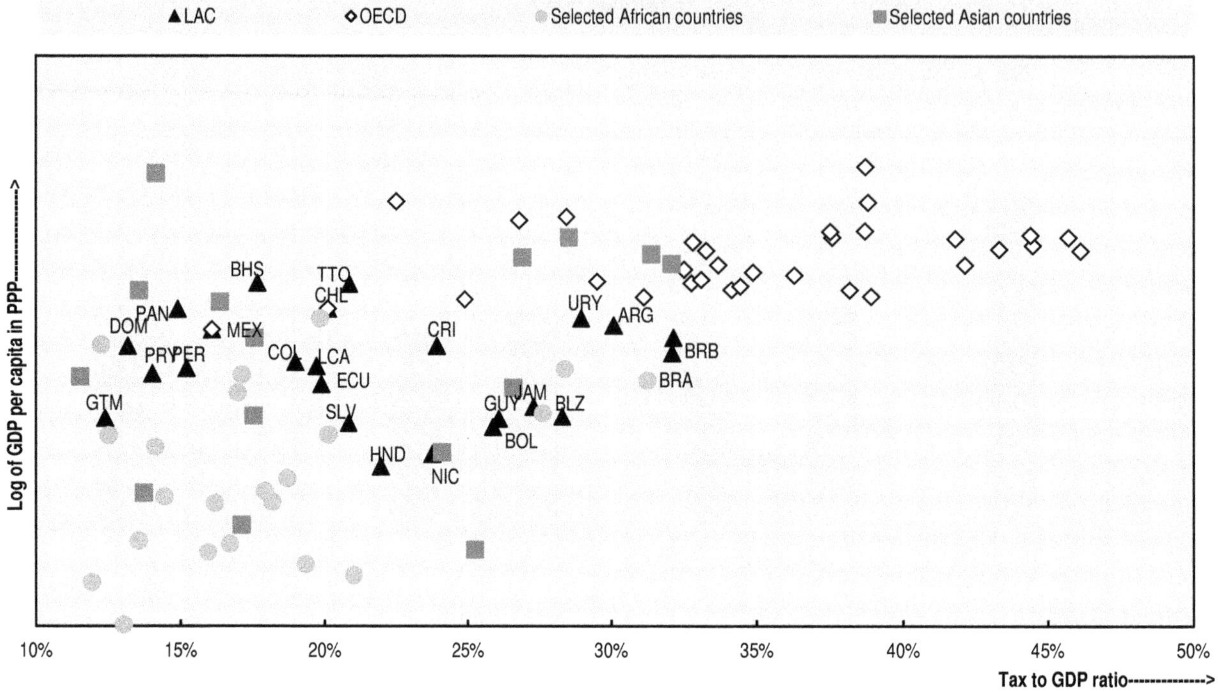

Note: The year of comparison is 2017 as the 2018 data for the tax-to-GDP ratios are not available for the selected African, Asian and Pacific economies. Cuba and Venezuela are not included in this figure due to data availability issues. The purchasing-power-parity (PPP) between two countries is the rate at which the currency of one country needs to be converted into that of a second country to ensure that a given amount of the first country's currency will purchase the same volume of goods and services in the second country as it does in the first. The implied PPP conversion rate is expressed as national currency per current international dollar. An international dollar has the same purchasing power as the U.S. dollar has in the United States. An international dollar is a hypothetical currency that is used as a means of translating and comparing costs from one country to the other using a common reference point, the US dollar (USD).

Source: (IMF, 2019[27]) for figures of GDP per capita. Tax-to-GDP ratios are sourced from the regional *Revenue Statistics* publications (*http://www.oecd.org/tax/tax-policy/global-revenue-statistics-database.htm*).

StatLink https://doi.org/10.1787/888934112956

Tax-to-GDP ratios are influenced by a range of economic and structural factors. GDP per capita, openness to trade, the extent of the informal economy, natural resource endowments and the importance of agriculture in the economy are all factors that can influence tax-to-GDP ratios. Socio-demographic determinants are also important, such as the level of education or the level of female participation in the labour force. The capacity of tax administrations, levels of corruption and tax morale (the willingness of people to pay taxes; see Box 1.3 for further discussion based on (OECD, 2019[28])) are also strongly linked to the level of tax revenues (OECD, 2014[29]). The tax-to-GDP ratio also reflects political choices on the role of the government and its size. Finally, geographic location and historical factors can also influence tax-to-GDP ratios: for example, landlocked countries are less able to impose taxes on goods and services at a port of entry than coastal countries. In addition, international factors, including the tax policies of other countries, can impact tax-to-GDP ratios.

Box 1.3. **Tax morale in Latin America**

Tax morale, the intrinsic motivation to pay taxes, is a key aspect of a tax system and its ability to raise revenues, since most tax systems rely on the voluntary compliance of taxpayers for the bulk of their revenues. A better understanding of what drives differences in tax morale for both individuals and business can help explain variations in tax compliance and holds the potential to inform strategies to increase revenues with (relatively) little enforcement effort. For example, sending messages to Guatemalan taxpayers to nudge their compliance raised tax payment among letter recipients by 5.5 percentage points (Kettle, 2016[30]; The Behavioural Insights Team, 2014[31]).

Tax morale amongst individuals appears to be falling across Latin America, albeit from a high base. The percentage of Latin Americans who would never justify evading paying taxes decreased from 54% in 2011 to 48% in 2015, while the proportion of those who find evading taxes "justifiable" increased from 17% to 27% (Panel A, Figure 1.9). A reduction in tax morale is evident across all economies in the region covered by the Latinobarómetro, although to different degrees (Panel B, Figure 1.9).

Figure 1.9. **Tax morale in Latin America**

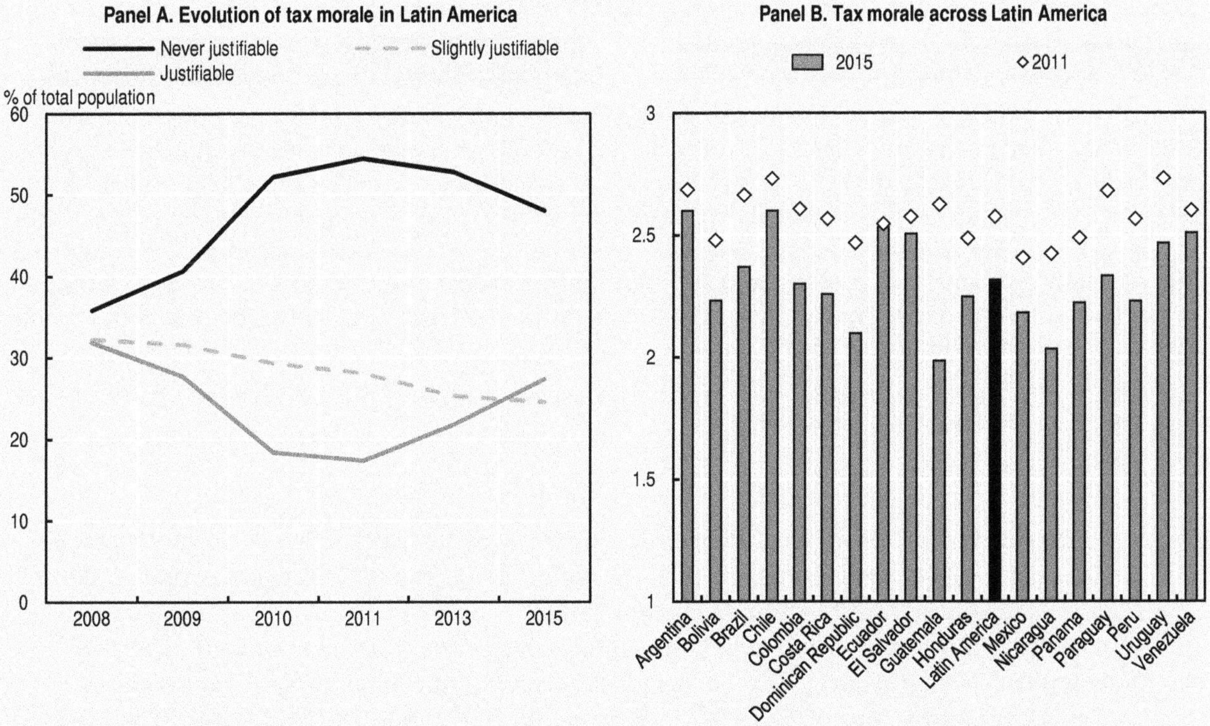

Note: In Panel A, tax morale is measured through the question "Do you justify cheating on taxes if you have the chance?" on a scale of 10 (not at all justifiable) to 1 (totally justifiable). "Never justifiable" is the share of respondents that answered 10; "slightly justifiable" corresponds to the share of respondents who answered between 9 and 6; and "justifiable" is the share of respondents that answered between 1 and 5. In Panel B, tax morale is represented as the average of all available observations for the question "How justifiable do you believe it is to evade paying taxes?" on a scale of 1 (totally justifiable) to 10 (not at all justifiable), and normalised between 1 and 3 for illustration purposes. The black bar is a simple regional average that includes all economies in the Latinobarómetro.

Source: OECD Development Centre/Centre for Tax Policy and Administration calculations based on Latinobarómetro (2016[32])

StatLink https://doi.org/10.1787/888934112975

Institutional and socio-economic factors are strongly linked with individuals' tax morale in Latin America. Recent OECD work (OECD, 2019[28]) uses public opinion surveys (World Values Survey and Latinobarómetro) to better understand the drivers of tax morale. In Latin America, support for democracy, educational attainment and trust in government were all identified as factors influencing tax morale.

Box 1.3. **Tax morale in Latin America** *(cont.)*

The findings highlight the role for taxpayer education in building tax morale. The OECD has surveyed taxpayer education initiatives in 50 countries to be presented in an update in 2020 to the 2015 report *Building Tax Culture, Compliance and Citizenship* (OECD/FIIAPP, 2015$_{[33]}$).

There is limited data to analyse tax morale in businesses. OECD (2019$_{[28]}$) uses data on tax certainty amongst multinational enterprises (MNEs)[6] as a proxy on the basis that MNEs are less likely to engage with the tax system when they perceive it to be less certain. In developing countries, including Latin America, tax certainty appears to have an impact on business behaviour, resulting in modified business structures, increased costs and changes to investment decisions. With some regional variation, both international taxation and the relationship between the authorities and businesses are consistent concerns across developing countries. In Latin America, unpredictable treatment by the tax authorities and considerable bureaucracy were the highest concerns.

Overall, these can be seen as issues of trust, suggesting that trust between taxpayers and authorities is likely to be a key component of tax morale for businesses. To further understand tax morale in business – in Latin America and elsewhere – the OECD is undertaking a survey to assess how tax officials perceive business compliance with voluntary principles on tax, such as the "BIAC Statement of Tax Best Practices for Engaging with Tax Authorities in Developing Countries".

International co-operation can play an important role in improving tax morale by supporting countries to strengthen and simplify tax systems and improve the efficiency and quality of public spending. For example, EUROsociAL+ has programmes in 13 countries with actions related to international taxation (base erosion and profit shifting project), the fight against tax evasion and avoidance, facilitation of tax compliance and territorial taxes and/or fiscal decentralization. One such example is the co-operation between EUROsociAL+ and the Internal Tax Revenue Office of Uruguay (Dirección General Impositiva) regarding the design and implementation of a new model of taxpayer attention and assistance. This initiative has made use of expert advice from the Netherlands Tax and Customs Administration and Spain's State Tax Administration Agency (Agencia Estatal de Administración Tributaria).

Source: OECD (2019$_{[28]}$), *Tax Morale: What Drives People and Businesses to Pay Tax?*, *https://doi.org/10.1787/f3d8ea10-en* and *https://eurosocial.eu/en/democratic-governance-policies/*.

The extent of state participation in financing social security is another important factor underlying the level of tax ratios in the LAC region. From the 1980s onwards, many LAC countries privatised healthcare and pensions to greater or lesser degrees. Chile, El Salvador and Mexico, for example, have shifted their public pension programme to a mostly privately fully funded pension system. In Colombia and Peru, private and public programmes compete and employees opt for one of them (OECD et al., 2015$_{[34]}$; OECD/IDB/The World Bank, 2014$_{[35]}$). On the other hand, Argentina, Brazil and Uruguay follow a model where public and private systems are complementary. In these countries, substantial reforms were undertaken to extend coverage of social security systems to those previously excluded. This has also been instrumental in the increase of tax revenues (ECLAC, 2014$_{[23]}$).

Informality constrains tax collection in LAC countries by significantly reducing the taxable base. More than 50% of workers in Latin America and the Caribbean are informal (OECD/ILO, 2019$_{[36]}$). The high level of informality in the 1990s prompted governments to introduce simplified tax systems for small taxpayers that were to some extent successful in integrating informal workers into the formal sector. These simplified systems varied greatly in success depending on the type of taxpayers covered and the capacity of tax administrations (ECLAC, 2014$_{[23]}$; OECD/IDB/CIAT, 2016$_{[37]}$).

Tax structures

The tax structure (defined as the share of major tax types in total tax revenue) depicts the composition of tax revenues by different tax types. It is an important indicator for understanding the economic and social effects of tax systems in the LAC region.

Evolution of tax structures

Taxes on goods and services provide the largest share of total tax revenues in the LAC region, representing half of total taxation in 2018 on average. Between 1990 and 2018, the average LAC tax mix shifted towards VAT and taxes on income and profits, and away from other taxes on goods and services.

- The share of VAT revenues in total tax revenues reached 27.8% in 2018, corresponding to an increase of 11.6 percentage points since 1990. The revenue share of other taxes on goods and services (including excise, customs and import duties) declined by 19.5 percentage points over the same period (Figure 1.10).
- The share of revenues from taxes on incomes and profits grew by 8.0 percentage points (from 19.7% to 27.8% of total tax revenues) between 1990 and 2018.
- The share of social security contributions in total tax revenues has increased by 4.2 percentage points over the last 28 years, reaching 17.1% in 2018.

Figure 1.10. **Average tax structure in the LAC region, 1990 and 2018**

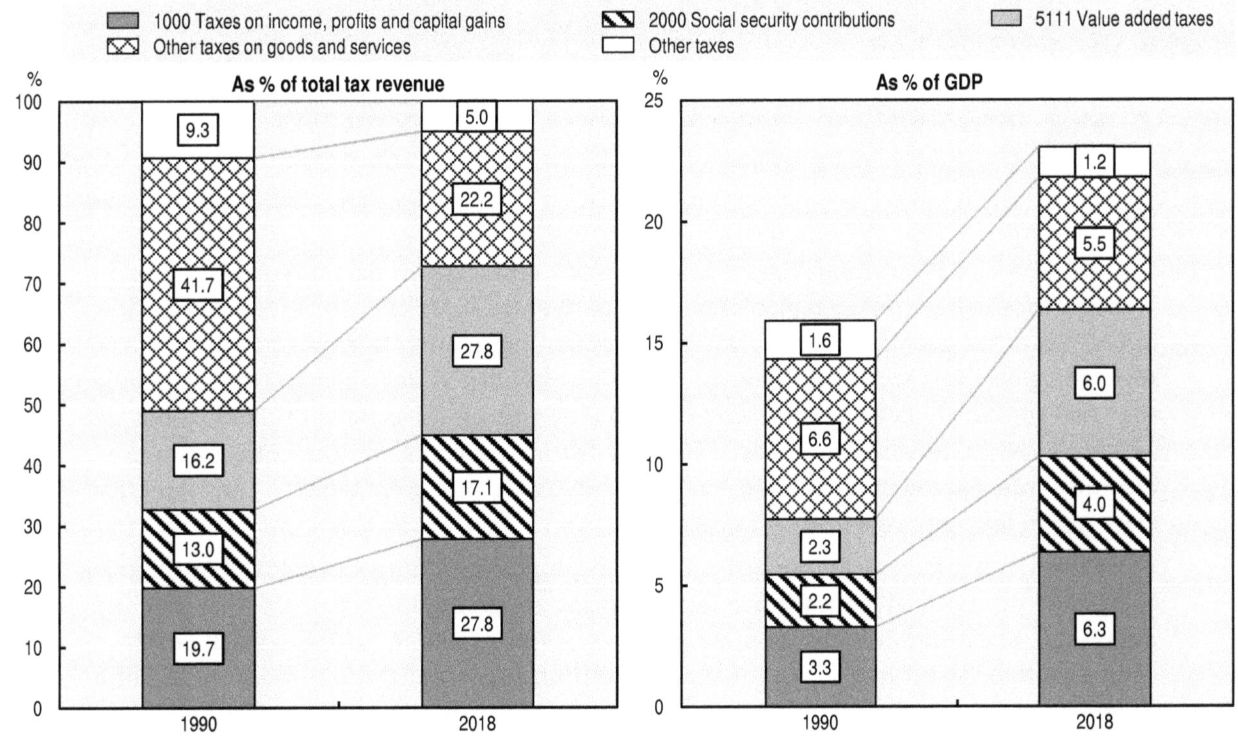

Source: Authors' calculations based on OECD et al. (2020[2]), tables in Chapter 4.

StatLink https://doi.org/10.1787/888934112994

Since 2007, LAC's average tax structure has shifted towards a greater revenue share from PIT and a lower revenue share from CIT, although revenues from CIT remained higher than PIT revenues in 2018 (15.5% of total taxes versus 9.6%) (Figure 1.11).[7]

Figure 1.11. **Average tax structure in the LAC region, 2007 and 2018**

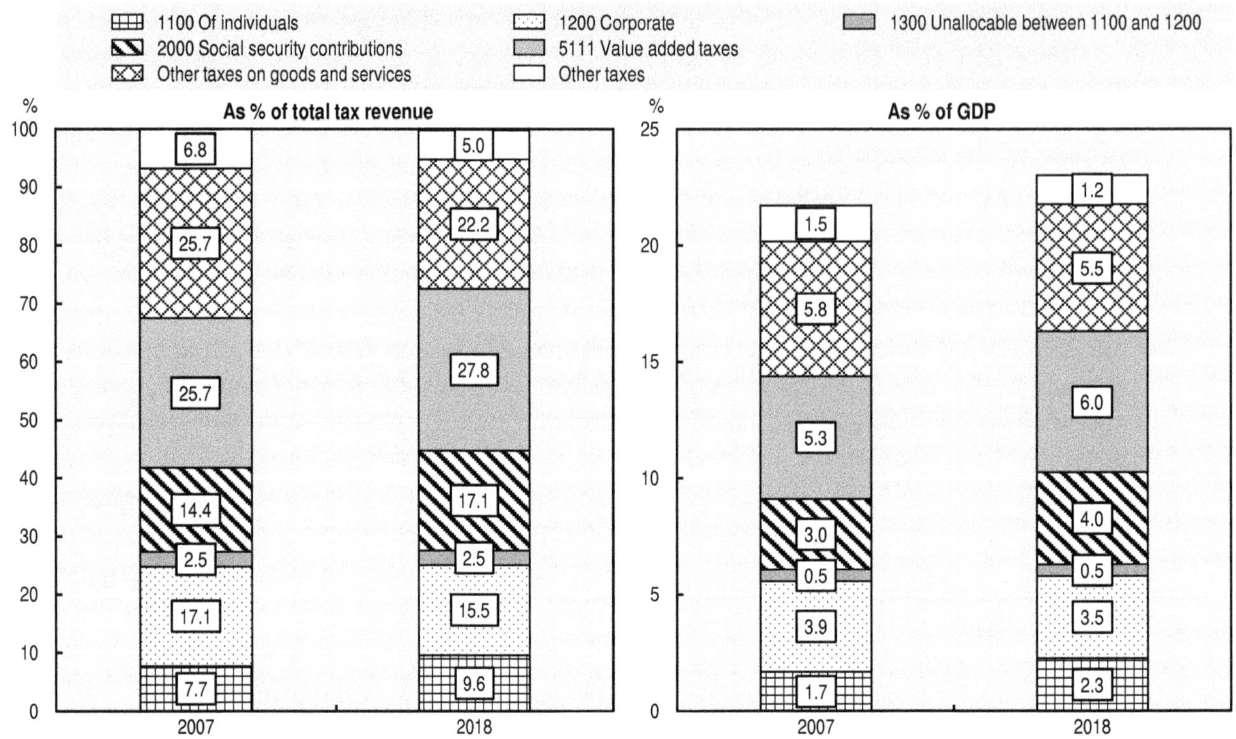

Note: Average CIT revenue and PIT as a percentage of GDP should be interpreted with caution as Ecuador, Nicaragua and Venezuela are excluded from the calculation. The LAC averages exclude Venezuela due to data availability issues. Ecuador and Nicaragua are excluded from the LAC averages for CIT revenue as a percentage of GDP and PIT revenue as a percentage of GDP as more than a third of their revenue from taxes on income and profits cannot be allocated to CIT revenue (1200) or PIT revenue (1100).

Source: Authors' calculations based on OECD et al. (2020$_{[2]}$), "Revenue Statistics in Latin America: Comparative tables", *OECD Tax Statistics* (database), *http://dx.doi.org/10.1787/data-00641-en.*

StatLink *https://doi.org/10.1787/888934113013*

The share of PIT revenues grew between 2007 and 2018, in part due to increases in personal incomes across the region. However, the average share of PIT revenue remains low in LAC countries despite some countries implementing reforms to expand their tax base. After the global financial crisis, several countries established flat rates on capital income that had previously been exempt and implemented progressive rates on labour income (ECLAC, 2014$_{[23]}$). However, there are relatively few taxpayers, given the concentration of income earners at low-income levels: in 2013, only 10% of the population in Latin America were registered taxpayers (IDB, 2013$_{[15]}$).

Several other factors continue to limit PIT revenues, including a small tax base that is comprised primarily of wages (since tax privileges are granted to returns on capital) and high levels of evasion (Barreix, Benitez and Pecho, 2017$_{[24]}$; ECLAC, 2014$_{[23]}$). IDB (2013$_{[15]}$) estimates that "about half of potential revenue from PIT is lost through evasion" in Latin American countries. As a result, LAC's tax system has little impact on inequality and is less effective than that of the OECD countries in the redistribution of income (Hanni, Martner and Podestá, 2017$_{[38]}$). The reduction of the Gini index (an indicator of the level of inequality[8]) after direct taxes and cash and in-kind transfers amounted to 2.2 percentage points in Latin America compared to 16 percentage points in the OECD (OECD et al., 2019$_{[1]}$).

The share of social security contributions in total tax revenues has increased by 4.2 percentage points since 1990, reaching 17.1% in 2018. Two major (and opposing) factors have influenced the trajectory of social security contributions in the region. While rising personal incomes have led to higher collections, this was counter-balanced by the full or partial privatisation of social security that occurred in many countries principally between the mid-1990s and 2010 (OECD et al., 2015[34]).

In 2018, there were notable differences in tax structure across the sub-regions, on average. The Caribbean in particular shows a very different tax structure to other sub-regions.

- In 2018, the largest share of revenue was derived from other taxes on goods and services in the Caribbean, which on average represented 30.3% of total tax revenues. These taxes contributed 17.2% of total tax revenues in South America and 21.1% in Central America and Mexico.
- In contrast, South America had the highest share from VAT revenue in 2018 at 31.0% on average, compared to 27.6% in the Caribbean and 24.8% in Central America and Mexico.
- Social security contributions were lowest in the Caribbean in 2018, at 11.0% of total tax revenues on average, slightly above half of the average for the other sub-regions (18.8% in Central America and Mexico, and 19.6% in South America).
- All three sub-regions generated higher revenues from CIT than from PIT.[9]

Average tax structure in LAC and the OECD

The average tax mix in the LAC region exhibits low revenues from income taxes and social security contributions relative to the OECD average (Figure 1.12). In particular, LAC countries rely heavily on taxes on goods and services on average, which make up more than half of overall tax revenues compared with around one-third in OECD economies on average. However, as a percentage of GDP, revenue from taxes on goods and services in the LAC and OECD regions were similar in 2017, at 11.4% and 10.9% respectively.[10] The level of VAT revenue as a percentage of GDP was also similar, at 5.9% for the LAC average and 6.8% for the OECD.

By contrast, the combined share of taxes on income and profits and social security contributions was much lower in the LAC region than in the OECD (44.6% versus 60.1% in 2017, on average). As a percentage of GDP, these two categories amounted to 10.0% in the LAC region, less than half the average OECD level (20.7%). The tendency towards private provision of social security in many LAC countries explains some of this difference.

On average, CIT generated 15.3% of total tax revenue in the LAC region compared to 9.3% in the OECD area (respectively 3.4% and 3.0% of GDP) (Figure 1.12). The most striking difference between the regions relates to revenues from PIT, which contributed 23.9% of total tax revenues, on average, in the OECD in 2017 and 9.7% of total tax revenues in the LAC region. PIT revenues were equivalent to 2.2% of GDP in the LAC region on average, compared to 8.3% for the OECD.

Figure 1.12. **Tax structure in the LAC and OECD regions, 2017**

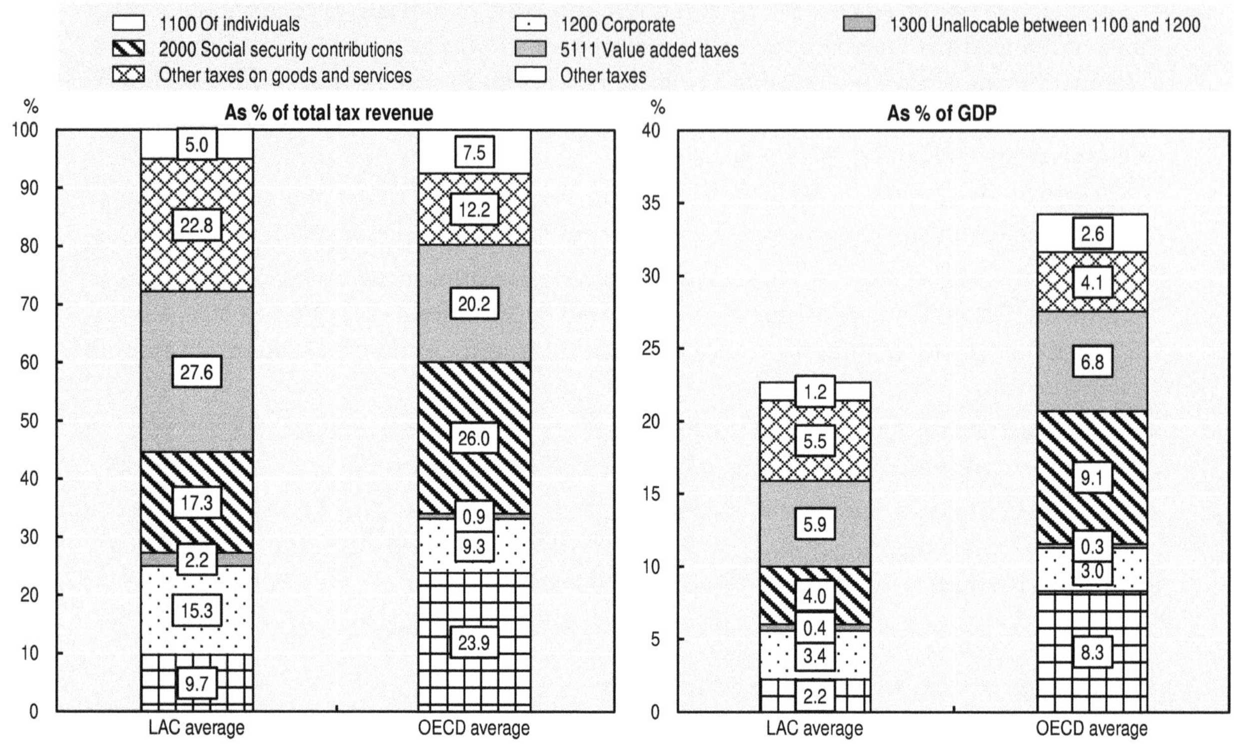

Note: The year of comparison is 2017 as data for the OECD average in 2018 are not available.
The average CIT revenue and PIT as a percentage of GDP for LAC should be interpreted with caution as Ecuador, Nicaragua and Venezuela are excluded from the calculation. The LAC averages exclude Venezuela due to data availability issues. Ecuador and Nicaragua are excluded from the LAC averages for CIT revenue as a percentage of GDP and PIT revenue as a percentage of GDP as more than a third of their revenue from taxes on income and profits cannot be allocated to CIT (1200) or PIT (1100).

Source: Authors' calculations based on OECD et al. (2020[2]), "Revenue Statistics in Latin America: Comparative tables", *OECD Tax Statistics* (database), *http://dx.doi.org/10.1787/data-00641-en*.

StatLink *https://doi.org/10.1787/888934113032*

Taxes on immovable property and payroll (contained within the category "other taxes") are less important sources of revenue for the LAC region on average than in the OECD, although there are challenges with data availability for property taxes.

This edition includes for the first time an indicator of convergence between the tax structures of two countries or of two regions, known as the D-index. Between 2007 and 2017 (the latest year available for the OECD average), the LAC tax structure converged steadily towards the OECD tax structure. The share of revenue from PIT for the LAC average increased towards the OECD average between 2007 and 2017 (from 7.7% of total tax revenues to 9.7% in 2017 compared to 23.9% in the OECD), while the share of revenue from other taxes on goods and services decreased towards the OECD average over the same period (from 25.7% of total tax revenues to 22.8% compared to 12.2% in the OECD). In contrast, the shares for VAT revenues between the LAC region and the OECD have grown more dissimilar over the period. The share for the LAC average increased from 25.7% of total tax revenues in 2007 to 27.6% in 2017, while the OECD average rose more slowly from 19.7% to 20.2% over the same period.

The D-index was first used in *Revenue Statistics 2018* to analyse the convergence of tax structures in OECD countries between 1995 and 2016 (OECD, 2018[39]). Figure 1.13 shows the D-index between the LAC average tax structure with the OECD average. It is calculated as the sum of the absolute differences between the share of each tax category in the LAC average and its share in the OECD average tax mix. A figure of 0 indicates perfect similarity, whereas 200 indicates complete dissimilarity.

Figure 1.13. **Distance between the LAC and OECD average tax structure (D-index), 2007-17**

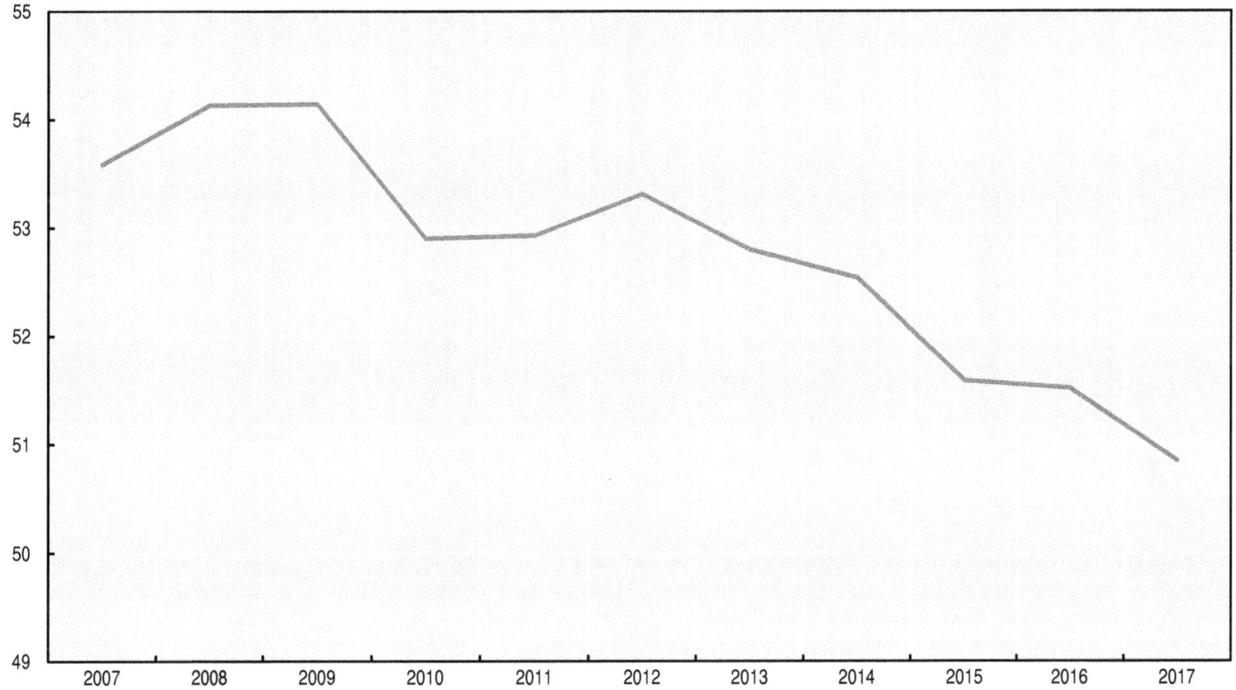

Source: Authors' calculations based on OECD et al. (2020[2]), comparative tables.

StatLink https://doi.org/10.1787/888934113051

Tax structures in LAC countries

Taxes on goods and services are the main source of revenue for all LAC countries except Mexico, Panama and Trinidad and Tobago. For Mexico and Trinidad and Tobago, revenue from taxes on income and profits accounted for the largest share whereas revenue from social security contributions was the most important source of tax revenue for Panama (Figure 1.14).

The contribution of VAT to total tax revenues ranged from 15.6% in Panama to 40.3% in Peru. There is no VAT system in Cuba. The wide variation across countries is partly a result of differences in the design of VAT: rates, tax bases and the number of VAT exemptions differ significantly across the region.

Figure 1.14. **Tax structure in LAC countries, 2018**

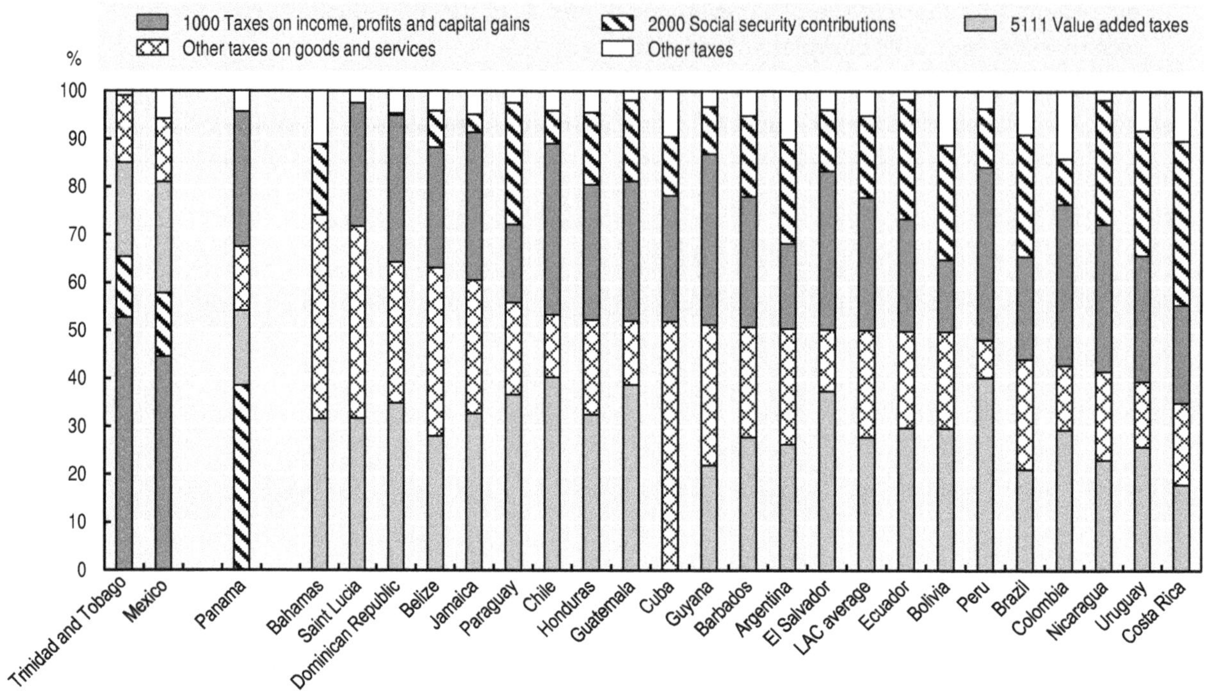

Note: Countries are grouped by the main share of tax revenues between 1000 Taxes on income and profits, 2000 Social security contributions and 5000 Taxes on goods and services. The Bahamas does not have tax income. There is no VAT system in Cuba. Data are not available for social security contributions in Saint Lucia.

Source: Authors' calculations based on OECD et al. (2020[2]), tables in Chapter 4.

StatLink https://doi.org/10.1787/888934113070

In 2018, social security contributions ranged from 0.5% of total tax revenues in Dominican Republic to 38.5% in Panama. The level of these revenues reflects choices on how to finance social security: in countries with public or mixed social security schemes (including Argentina, Brazil, Costa Rica, Panama, Paraguay and Uruguay), social security contributions reach a more significant share (over 20% of total tax revenues).

The D-index was also calculated for each country to analyse the convergence of tax structures in LAC countries with the tax structure of the LAC average. In 2018, the tax structure of Barbados was closest to the LAC average, followed by Honduras. The countries that showed the greatest dissimilarity to the LAC average tax structure were Trinidad and Tobago (due to the high share of income tax), Cuba (due to the absence of VAT and the high share of other taxes on goods and services) and Bahamas (due to the absence of an income tax system).

In 2018, all but six LAC countries had tax structures that were more similar to the LAC average tax structure than in 2000. The four Caribbean countries whose tax structures showed the greatest convergence to the LAC average were also those whose tax structures changed the most: the Bahamas, Belize, Guyana and Saint Lucia. These increases in similarity were explained by the introduction of VAT during the period. Between 2000 and 2018, countries' tax structures have also become more similar across the LAC region as many countries have increased their VAT, PIT and SSC shares while decreasing the share of revenues from other taxes on goods and services.

Figure 1.15. **Distance to LAC average tax structure (D-index) for all LAC countries, 2018**

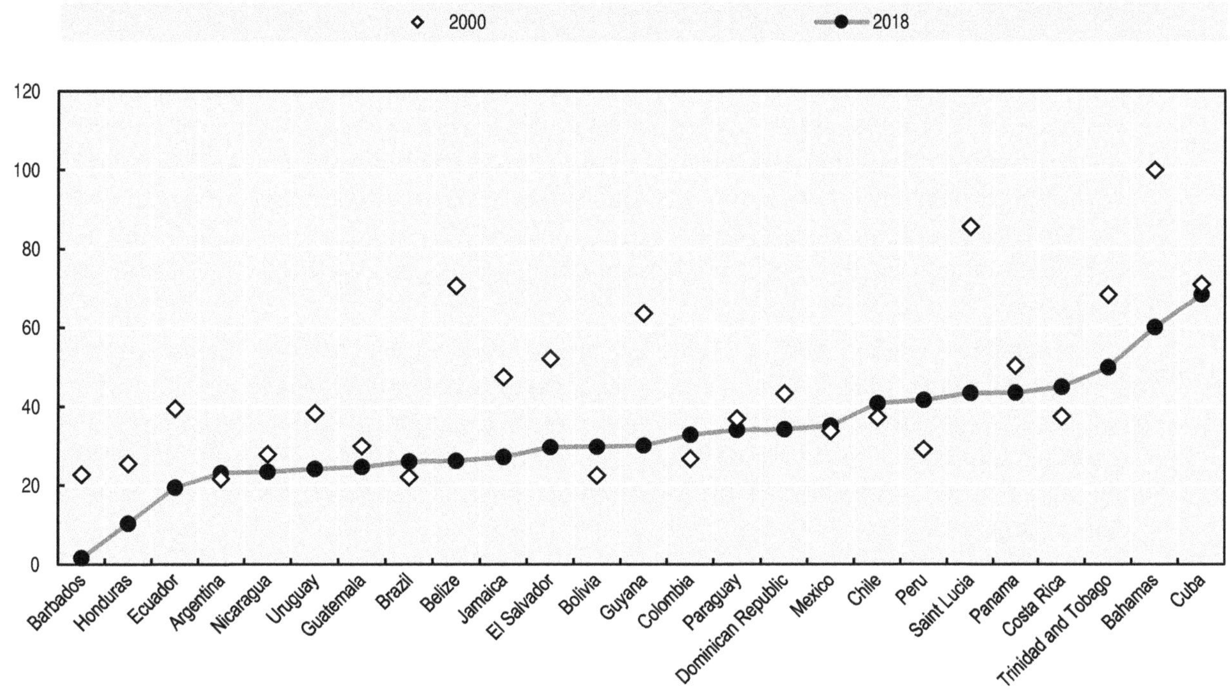

Source: Authors' calculations based on OECD et al. (2020[2]), tables in Chapter 4.

StatLink https://doi.org/10.1787/888934113089

VAT revenue ratio

This section discusses the VAT revenue ratio (VRR) in LAC countries in 2018 (Figure 1.16). The VRR "measures the difference between the VAT revenue actually collected and what would theoretically be raised if VAT was applied at the standard rate to the entire potential tax base in a 'pure' VAT regime and all revenue was collected" (OECD, 2018[40]). The VRR is the ratio of the actual VAT revenues to the product of final consumption (net of VAT revenues) and the standard VAT rate. The calculation is shown below.

$$\frac{\text{VAT revenues}}{\text{(final consumption expenditure-VAT revenues).standard VAT rate}}$$

This indicator provides a sense of VAT revenue loss related to exemptions and reduced rates, fraud, evasion and tax planning as well as weaknesses in tax administrations. However, this indicator needs to be interpreted with reference to the underlying characteristics of the VAT system in each country, as a high VRR could result from cascading effects (for example when exemption occurs early in the supply chain) or from a failure to refund VAT input credits. Other factors may also influence the ratio upwards or downwards, for example when the place of taxation rules for international trade diverge from the destination principle or when the tax on inbound digital supplies is not collected. It is also important to note that the interpretation of the VRR is also more difficult for countries relying significantly on tourism. These countries may record a high VRR due to methodological reasons: purchases by non-residents may not be included in final consumption expenditure (the denominator) whereas the VAT on these purchases is included in the overall VAT revenues (the numerator) (Keen, 2013[41]).

The LAC region's highest VRRs (above 0.80) were recorded in three Caribbean countries (the Bahamas, Belize and Saint Lucia) while the Dominican Republic and Mexico had the lowest VRRs (0.34). The Bahamas, Belize and Saint Lucia have a high share of revenue from tourism compared to the other countries: receipts from international tourism as a percentage of total exports were respectively 68%, 41% and 74% in 2017, compared to an average of 8% in the LAC region as a whole (World Bank, 2020[42]).While this may partly explain the high VRR in these countries, other factors such as reforms introduced by these countries also contributed.

The Bahamas introduced VAT in 2015 following international good practice: a broad-based VAT with a low standard rate, a limited number of exemptions and no reduced rates. In the Bahamas, the standard rate stands at 7.5% (one of the lowest rates in the LAC region, where the average standard VAT rate stands at 14.6%); revenues tripled in 2017 relative to 2015 (in nominal terms), in large part due to the introduction of new systems to collect tax revenues (Schlotterbeck, 2017[43]).

Belize had the second-highest VRR in the selected group of LAC countries in 2018 at 0.89. This strong performance is partly based on measures introduced in FY2018/19 that broadened the GST base by removing zero-rated items and high levels of compliance. The merging of the General Sales Tax and Income Tax departments in August 2019 is likely to further strengthen VAT administration for in Belize (IMF, 2019[10]).

Several factors contribute to the low VRR in Mexico, including the scope of VAT exemptions, the application of a domestic zero rate to numerous goods and services, a reduced VAT rate (11%) in border areas as well as low compliance (OECD, 2018[40]). However, a VAT reform implemented in January 2014 replaced the reduced rate of 11% with the standard rate of 16%. It also removed the zero rate on hotels and related services to foreigners, which are now taxed at the standard rate, and adjusted the regime of inward processing arrangements (*maquiladores*) to reduce the risk of fraud. The VRR in Mexico increased from 0.32 in 2017 to 0.34 in 2018. The VRR may further increase as a result of the broadening of the VAT base which will come into effect in June 2020 to include supplies of digital services from foreign businesses to consumers in Mexico, following the OECD recommendation (KPMG, 2019[44]).

The Dominican Republic has one of the lowest VRRs in the LAC region. VAT collection in the Dominican Republic is also one of the lowest in the LAC region at only 4.6% of GDP compared to the LAC average of 6.0%. A number of tax design and administration factors may contribute to this low VRR (Mele et al., 2017[45]). These include numerous VAT exemptions (for food, health, education, tourism), generous tax exemptions for firms in free economic zones and border regions associated with low compliance (Schlotterbeck, 2017[43]). Mele et al. (2017[45]) estimated that the revenue foregone through the VAT exemptions amounted to 3.3% of GDP on average during the 2008-15 period, a much higher estimate than for peer countries. In addition, the Dominican Republic applied a relatively high VAT rate in 2018 of 18%. Mele et al. (2017[45]) explains that VAT evasion and fraud in the Dominican Republic are among the highest in the region and are the main factors behind the efficiency gap and low VRR.

Figure 1.16. **VAT revenue ratio (VRR) in LAC countries, 2018**

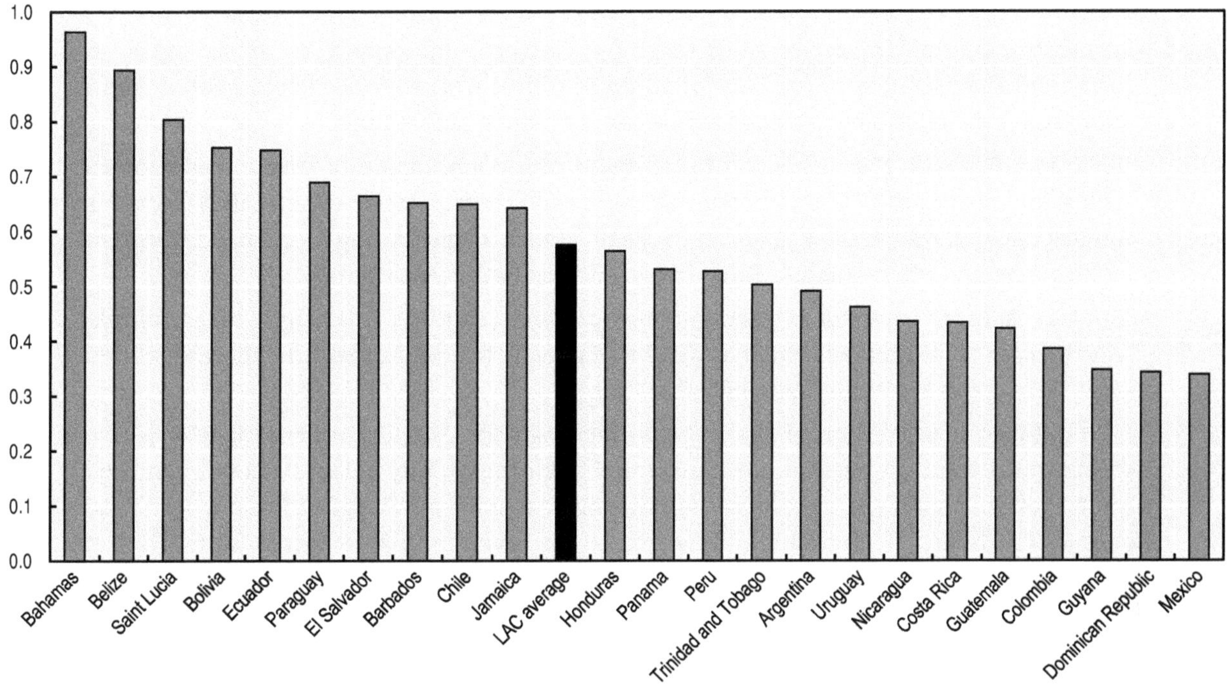

Note: Brazil, Cuba and Venezuela are excluded. Brazil operates a multiple-rate system with tax levied at different rates for each sub-national level. Cuba did not operate a VAT system in 2018. Venezuela tax revenue data are not available for 2018.

Source: VAT rates are sourced from the CIAT, Trading Economics and Deloitte websites, the final expenditure consumption figures from the United Nations Statistics Division website, and VAT revenues from the country tables in OECD et al. (2020[2]), Chapter 5.

StatLink https://doi.org/10.1787/888934113108

Environmental tax revenues

Through the Paris Agreement of 2016, countries have committed to decarbonise their economies by mid-century, implying a shift away from fossil fuels as a source of energy. Environmentally related taxes, and price-based policy instruments more generally, play an increasingly significant role in many countries. By incorporating a price signal into consumer decisions, these taxes give effect to the polluter-pays principle and encourage businesses and households to consider the environmental costs of their behaviour.

An environmentally related tax is a tax whose base is a physical unit (or a proxy of a physical unit) of something that has a proven, specific harmful impact on the environment regardless of whether the tax is intended to change behaviours or is levied for another purpose (OECD, 2005[46]). Revenues from taxes on energy can increase in the medium term if countries increase effective tax rates on the carbon content of fuels (Marten and Van Dender, 2019[47]). A joint ITF and OECD study (OECD/ITF, 2019[48]) shows how revenues from road transport can be stabilised in the long term through a mix of taxing distance driven, vehicles and fuel.

Although environmentally related tax revenues cannot be identified in the standard OECD classification of tax revenues, they can be identified through the detailed list of specific taxes included for most countries within this overarching classification. It is on this basis that they are included in the OECD *Policy Instruments for the Environment (PINE)* database.

Data on environmentally related tax revenue are presented for four mutually exclusive tax-base categories and the total:

- Energy: Energy products (e.g. fossil fuels and electricity) including those used in transportation (e.g. petrol and diesel). This includes all CO_2-related taxes.
- Transport: One-off import or sales taxes on transport equipment, recurrent taxes on ownership, registration or road use of motor vehicles, and other transport-related taxes. Note that this definition excludes excise taxes on automotive fuels.
- Pollution: SOx and NOx emission taxes, taxes on ozone-depleting substances such as chlorofluorocarbons (CFCs), carbon tetrachloride and chlorofluoromethanes (HCFCs), taxes on discharge of wastewater, taxes on packaging (such as plastic bags), on final disposal of solid waste and other waste-related taxes (such as batteries or tyres).
- Resources: Taxes on water extraction, forest products, hunting and fishing taxes, mining royalties, excavation taxes (such as sand and gravel). Note that fees and charges related to water supply are not included (OECD, 2019[49]).

A detailed examination of country-specific taxes for 23 LAC countries in this report demonstrates that, on average, revenue from environmentally related taxes amounted to 1.1%[11] of GDP in 2018, a lower level than the OECD average of 2.3% of GDP (estimated 2018 figure [OECD, 2019[49]]). Environmentally related tax revenue in 2018 varied from 0.02% of GDP in Belize to 2.3% in Honduras (Figure 1.17).

Figure 1.17. **Environmentally related tax revenue in LAC countries by main tax base, 2018**

Percentage of GDP

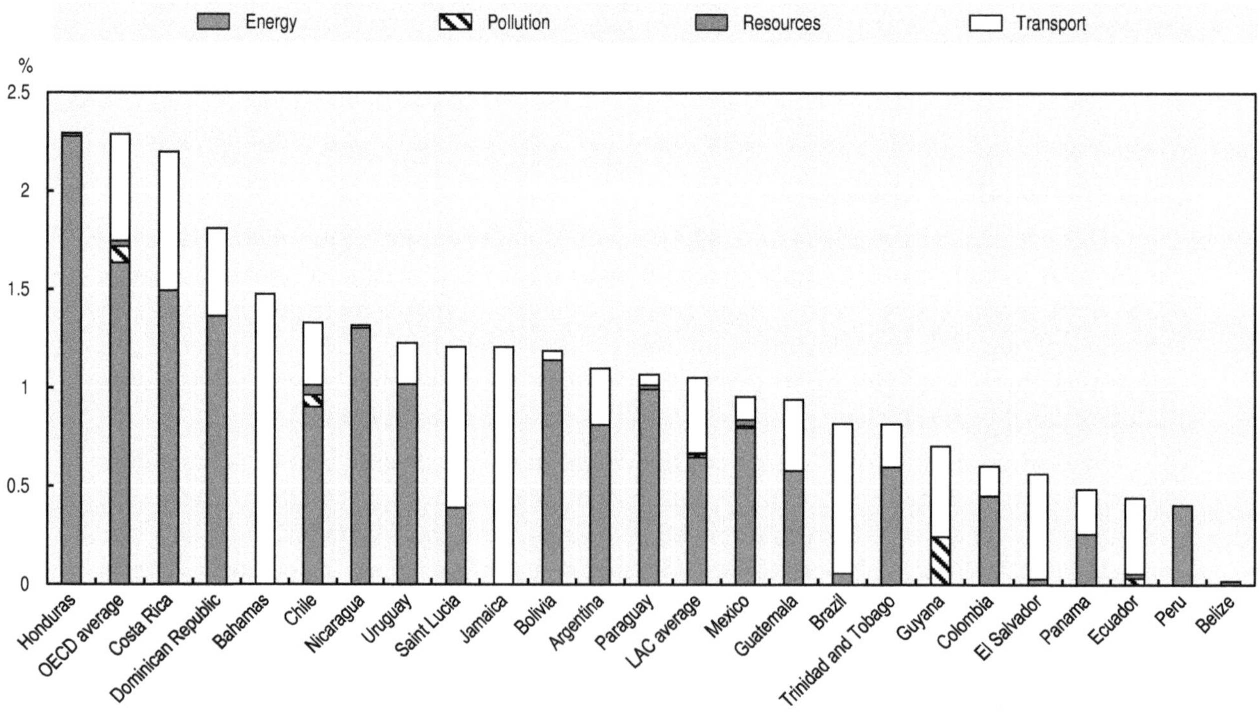

Note: Barbados, Cuba and Venezuela are excluded from the LAC averages. It has not been possible to identify environmentally related tax revenue for Barbados and Cuba. Venezuela is excluded due to data availability issues. The figures for Chile and Mexico use 2017 data based on the *PINE* database that presents more comprehensive data on environmental tax revenues.

Source: *PINE* database for Chile and Mexico, and authors' calculations based on OECD et al. (2020[2]), Chapter 5.

StatLink https://doi.org/10.1787/888934113127

In 2018, revenues from energy taxes (most commonly from diesel and petrol) generated the highest share of total environmentally related tax revenue in the LAC region. Revenues from energy products amounted to 0.6% of GDP on average in 2018, and represented around 60% of environmentally related tax revenue. Revenues from motor vehicle and transport services tax revenue amounted to 0.4 % of GDP and represented most of the remainder (35%) of environmentally related tax revenue. Tax revenues levied on other environmentally related bases were negligible, at 2%, on average. In the OECD, revenues from energy products represent just over 70% of total revenues, whereas taxes on motor vehicles and transport accounted for around one-quarter (OECD, 2019[49]).

Taxes on energy accounted for the largest share of environmentally related tax revenues in all but seven LAC countries. In these seven countries (the Bahamas, Brazil, Ecuador, El Salvador, Guyana, Jamaica and Saint Lucia), revenue from motor vehicles and transport services were the main source (Figure 1.17).

In 2018, taxes on energy were predominantly raised from excises. By contrast, revenues from motor vehicles and transport services taxes were sourced from three different types of taxes: around half came from taxes on use and ownership of vehicles, a quarter came from taxes on specific services (mainly travel or departure tax) and another quarter on excises on vehicles.

While the use of taxation to address environmental issues is well established in many countries, Latin American countries have been slow to implement environmentally related taxes. Although they have introduced fuel taxes (mainly for revenue collection rather than environmental purposes), many LAC countries also provide subsidies for energy products (Lorenzo, 2016[50]) in order to mitigate the impact of high and volatile petroleum prices, control inflation, boost competitiveness and protect the poorest sections of the population. These subsidies largely offset the impact of environmental taxes (Vera, 2019[51]).

Beyond taxes on fuel and the registration or use of vehicles, environmental taxes are still underdeveloped across the LAC region. This can be explained not only by economies' dependency on natural resources, but also by the high proportion of the population with low incomes. Many people live in poverty in LAC countries and there are strong income inequalities. Environmental taxes, and particularly fuel taxes, tend to be regressive as lower income households tend to have higher shares of fuel consumption relative to income than higher income households.

Despite slow progress in the implementation of taxation to address environmental issues, a few LAC countries have introduced significant green tax reforms, including Chile, Mexico and, most recently, Colombia:

- In Chile, a major tax reform including new environmentally related taxes was approved in 2014 (OECD/UN ECLAC, 2016[52]). These included a tax on purchases of motor vehicles, which was introduced in 2015 and raised revenues equivalent to 0.03% of GDP in 2018. Motor vehicle tax rates depend on energy efficiency and emissions. In addition, a tax on polluting fixed sources was implemented in late 2017 and raised revenues worth 0.06% of GDP in 2018. This tax applies on emissions of particulate matter, nitrogen oxides, sulphur dioxide and carbon dioxide produced by establishments whose boilers or turbines have a capacity of 50 thermal megawatts or more.
- Mexico introduced a carbon tax in 2014, applied on the sale and import of fossil fuels according to their carbon content. This increased the proportion of emissions that was taxed, although prices remain relatively low compared to other OECD countries and do

not reflect the full costs associated with the carbon in these fuels (Arlinghaus and van Dender, 2017[53]). However, the carbon tax significantly increased tax revenues between 2014 and 2015, generating revenues equivalent to 1.2% of GDP in 2015 (OECD, 2019[49]). Mexico further increased tax rates on different fossils fuels in 2016.

- In 2016, Colombia introduced a carbon tax and an excise tax on plastic bags. The carbon tax is levied on fossil fuels (specifically gasoline, kerosene, jet fuel, diesel fuel and fuel oil) depending on the amount of carbon. A price of USD 5 is applied for each ton of carbon dioxide produced by fossil fuel combustion. The revenues are allocated to a special fund to address specific environmental issues (coastal erosion, conservation of water sources and ecosystem protection) (Monge, 2018[54]). In 2018, this tax generated revenues worth 0.03% of GDP.

Effective Carbon Rates (OECD, 2018[55]) provides an overview of carbon prices for all energy-related emissions in 42 OECD and G20 countries including Argentina, Brazil, Chile and Mexico. *Taxing Energy Use* (OECD, 2019[56]) contains detailed information on tax rates, energy use and the base they apply to for the same set of countries.

Taxes by level of government

In LAC countries, tax revenues are collected predominantly by central or federal entities; sub-national public spending is financed through transfers from upper to lower levels of government to a greater extent than is the case in OECD countries. Where sub-national data for LAC countries is available, it indicates that tax revenues collected by central government accounted for two-thirds or more of the total collected, whereas the corresponding figure for OECD countries was about 60%. Brazil is a notable exception: central government tax revenue amounted to 43.2% of tax collected in 2017[12] (Table 1.1).

There are two statistical issues to consider when comparing the attribution of revenues for LAC countries with that of OECD members. First, revenues of both groups have been attributed to different levels of government according to guidelines set out in the 2008 System of National Accounts (SNA).[13] The second issue is that some LAC countries lack tax revenue statistics at sub-national level.

For the 19 LAC countries for which sub-national data in 2017 is available, the share of sub-national tax revenues as a proportion of total tax revenue is lower than 8% except in Argentina, Brazil and Colombia. In Brazil, states and municipalities collect about 31% of total tax revenues, indicating a significant degree of decentralisation of tax collection. A large part of the VAT (ICMS – *imposto sobre operações relativas à circulação de mercadorias e prestação de serviços de transporte interestadual e intermunicipal e de comunicação*) is collected at the state level. Sub-national tax revenue in Argentina and Colombia account for more than 15% of total tax revenue. Argentina has a significant collection at state level, which is explained in part by the provincial sales tax (*impuesto sobre los ingresos brutos*). Between 2000 and 2017, the share of revenue raised by sub-national levels of government declined in six countries and rose in 13 countries. The largest decline was in Honduras (3.5% of total tax revenues) and the highest increase was in Paraguay (3.6% of total tax revenues).

These figures reflect the fact that sub-national governments in LAC countries tend to have a relatively narrow range of taxes under their jurisdiction. The taxes most frequently assigned to sub-national entities are property taxes, motor-vehicle licenses, taxes on specific services and municipal fees. The revenue-generation potential of these instruments is relatively limited compared with the tax bases under central jurisdiction, such as VAT and income taxes. In 2017, the entire subnational tax revenue in Belize, Guatemala and Jamaica, and more than 50% of tax revenue collected at the sub-national level in Peru and Uruguay, was sourced from property taxes (Figure 1.18). In Ecuador and Paraguay, about 90% of tax revenues came from evenly distributed property taxes and taxes on goods and services. All other countries rely principally on revenues from taxes on goods and services. Mexico is the only country that also collected revenue from different tax bases. In 2017, 42% of sub-national tax revenue in Mexico came from payroll taxes. In OECD countries, sub-national entities tend to have much broader potential tax bases. A substantial proportion of revenue collection by sub-national governments in OECD countries is through income taxes and profits (representing more than a third of the total collected at sub-national level on average).

Figure 1.18. **Tax mix of sub-national tax revenue, 2017**

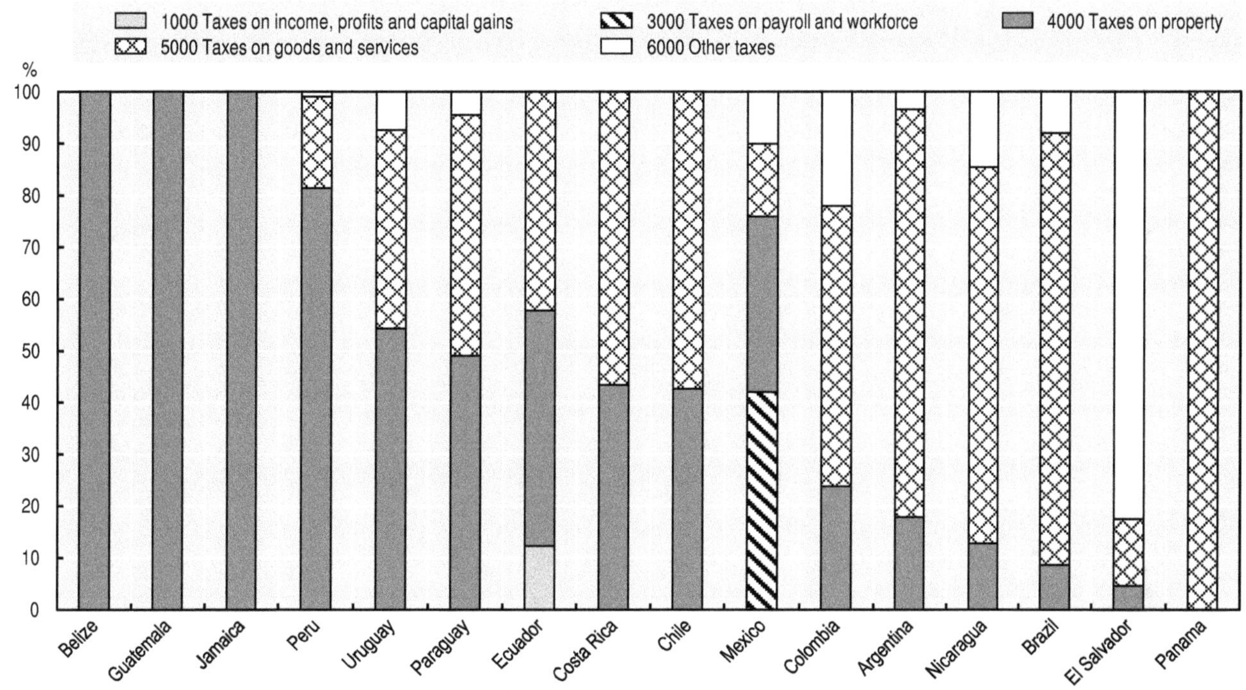

Note: The year of comparison is 2017 as 2018 data for Mexico are not available. The Bahamas, Barbados, Bolivia, Cuba, Dominican Republic, Guyana, Honduras, Saint Lucia, Trinidad and Tobago and Venezuela are excluded as either the sub-national tax revenue data or the breakdown of sub-national tax revenue data by the main type of tax category are not available. The figures exclude local government revenues for Argentina (but include provincial revenues).

Source: Authors' calculations based on OECD et al. (2020[2]), tables in Chapter 6.

StatLink https://doi.org/10.1787/888934113146

Low tax revenues at the sub-national level in LAC countries may also result from a lack of administrative and technical capacity. Property taxes – a common source of sub-national revenue – require sophisticated systems and information and the collection of this revenue is expensive. In addition, appropriate property registers are lacking in many countries; where they exist, they are rarely updated (Canavire-Bacarreza, Martínez-Vázquez and Sepúlveda, 2012[57]). As a result, tax authorities have minimal access to accurate valuations of land and buildings and real estate registries are often reluctant to share this information. Property tax also suffers from a high level of informality: buildings are constructed without permits, properties are not registered and reported prices of some real estate transactions are falsified. As property tax is one of the most controversial taxes with citizens and has high political costs, local politicians are often unwilling to invest the appropriate resources to levy this revenue.

Table 1.1. **Attribution of tax revenue to sub-sectors of general government[1]**

Percentage of total tax revenue

	Central government			State or regional government			Local government			Social Security funds		
	1995	2000	2017	1995	2000	2017	1995	2000	2017	1995	2000	2017
Federal countries												
Argentina	59.0	66.4	59.0	17.5	17.8	18.1	..	..	..	23.4	15.8	22.9
Brazil	44.7	47.8	43.2	26.6	25.1	24.8	3.7	3.4	5.8	25.0	23.7	26.3
Mexico	73.9	78.3	81.1	2.8	2.7	4.1	1.5	1.0	1.6	21.8	18.0	13.3
Venezuela	94.6	94.6	..	..	..	..	..	..	..	5.4	5.4	..
Regional countries												
Colombia[2]	63.2	68.7	74.8	5.5	5.6	5.1	8.6	9.4	12.4	22.7	16.3	7.6
Unitary countries												
Bahamas	89.1	88.1	85.2				..	..	..	10.9	11.9	14.8
Barbados	85.6	84.4	82.5				..	..	..	14.4	15.6	17.5
Belize	93.2	93.5	91.6				0.5	0.7	0.6	6.3	5.8	7.8
Bolivia	94.3	75.7	70.7				5.7	5.5	5.6	0.0	18.8	23.7
Chile	89.9	87.8	86.3				6.5	7.9	7.8	3.6	4.4	5.9
Costa Rica	65.5	63.3	58.5				1.6	1.9	3.0	33.0	34.8	38.5
Cuba[3]	..	..	..				..	..	..	11.3	10.4	12.5
Dominican Republic	99.3	99.0	99.5				..	..	..	0.7	1.0	0.5
Ecuador	70.5	87.7	71.1				4.0	1.6	2.8	25.5	10.7	26.1
El Salvador	80.9	80.5	84.8				..	..	2.0	19.1	19.5	13.2
Guatemala	83.3	83.3	82.2				0.7	0.9	1.0	16.1	15.8	16.7
Guyana	92.6	88.6	89.5				..	..	0.1	7.4	11.4	10.4
Honduras	86.1	85.3	83.2				4.4	5.2	1.8	9.5	9.4	15.0
Jamaica	100.0	99.3	94.6				..	0.7	1.6	0.0	0.0	3.7
Nicaragua	80.4	72.5	69.4				4.6	9.5	6.4	15.0	18.0	24.2
Panama	62.8	59.6	59.9				..	2.2	1.7	37.2	38.2	38.4
Paraguay	100.0	74.4	70.2				..	..	3.6	0.0	25.6	26.2
Peru	88.7	86.5	84.4				..	1.6	2.8	11.3	11.9	12.9
Saint Lucia[4]	100.0	100.0	100.0				..	..	..	..	..	..
Trinidad and Tobago	96.8	93.6	85.2				..	..	..	3.2	6.4	14.8
Uruguay	61.7	63.6	67.9				8.8	8.9	5.5	29.5	27.5	26.5

Notes:

1. The figures exclude local government revenues for Argentina (but include provincial revenues), the Bahamas, Barbados, Cuba, the Dominican Republic, Saint Lucia, Trinidad and Tobago and Venezuela as the data are not available. Local government revenue data are available since 1991 for Nicaragua, since 1994 for Bolivia, since 1995 for Guatemala, since 1998 for Jamaica, since 1999 for Panama, since 2000 for Peru, since 2002 for El Salvador and Guyana, since 2006 for Paraguay and since 1990 for all other countries.
2. Colombia is constitutionally a unitary country with high autonomy of its territorial entities.
3. Data for sub-sectors of general government in Cuba are only available between 2002 and 2012.
4. Social security contributions are not available for Saint Lucia.

Source: OECD et al. ($2020_{[2]}$), Table 4.11.

StatLink https://doi.org/10.1787/888934113507

Notes

1. The figure is provisional and has been calculated by applying the unweighted average percentage change for 2018 in the 34 countries providing data for that year to the overall average tax-to-GDP ratio in 2017.
2. The Caribbean average includes seven countries (Bahamas, Barbados, Belize, Guyana, Jamaica, Saint Lucia and Trinidad and Tobago), Central America and Mexico, nine countries (Costa Rica, Cuba, Dominican Republic, El Salvador, Guatemala, Honduras, Mexico, Nicaragua and Panama), and South America, nine countries (Argentina, Bolivia, Brazil, Chile, Colombia, Ecuador, Paraguay, Peru and Uruguay).
3. This includes Argentina, Brazil, Bolivia, Chile, Colombia, Costa Rica, Ecuador, Honduras, Mexico, Nicaragua, Panama and Peru.
4. These figures include the CIT rates for 22 LAC countries and exclude Cuba, Guyana, Trinidad and Tobago and Venezuela due to data unavailability. The data are principally sourced from KPMG (*https://s3.amazonaws.com/kpmg-global/tax-rates-tool/index_Corporate.html*), CIAT (*https://www.ciat.org/tax-rates-in-latin-america/?lang=en*) and completed for Belize with data found on *https://www.multpl.com/belize-corporate-tax-rate/table/by-year* and other public sources.
5. VAT was introduced in 1991 for Jamaica, 1997 for Barbados, 2006 for Belize (the General Sales Tax), 2007 for Guyana, 2012 for Saint Lucia and 2014 for the Bahamas.
6. The analysis is based on a unique data source, the 2016 OECD business survey that gathered views from senior staff from over 500 companies, almost all MNEs, providing views on tax certainty in 82 developing countries.
7. Around 2.5% of total tax revenue is revenue from taxes on income and profits that cannot be allocated between corporate income tax and personal income tax.
8. The Gini index is a commonly used measurement of inequality. It is a measure of statistical dispersion used to represent the income or wealth distribution of the residents of a country.
9. For the Caribbean, average revenue from taxes on income and profits hides a wide heterogeneity. The Bahamas does not levy income taxes and Trinidad and Tobago raises half of its tax revenue from this source.
10. The year of comparison is 2017 as the 2018 data for the OECD average are not available.
11. Unweighted average of 36 OECD countries.
12. The year of comparison is 2017 as the 2018 data for Mexico are not available.
13. This means that revenues are generally attributed to the level of government that exercises the authority to impose the tax or has the final discretion to set and vary the tax rate. This has implications for situations where one level of government collects tax revenues and transfers them in whole or in part to other levels. Regional examples of this type of mechanism are the Co-participation Law in Argentina, federal participations in Mexico (mandated in the Fiscal Co-ordination Law) and participation funds in Brazil (defined in Article 159 of the Constitution).

References

Arlinghaus, J. and K. van Dender (2017), "The environmental tax and subsidy reform in Mexico", *OECD Taxation Working Papers*, No. 31, OECD Publishing, Paris, *https://dx.doi.org/10.1787/a9204f40-en*. [53]

Barbados Revenue Authority (2018), *Budgetary Proposals 2018: Shared Economy Levy, https://bra.gov.bb/Download.ashx?file=Attachments%2fPolicy+Note+-+Shared+Economy+Levy+2019_02.pdf&id=163&name=Policy+Note+%E2%80%93+Shared+Economy+Levy+.* [18]

Barreix, A., J. Benitez and M. Pecho (2017), "Revisiting personal income tax in Latin America: Evolution and impact", OECD Development Centre Working Papers No. 338, OECD Publishing, Paris, *https://doi.org/10.1787/16d42b4a-en.* [24]

Canavire-Bacarreza, G., J. Martínez-Vázquez and C. Sepúlveda (2012), "Sub-national Revenue Mobilization in Peru", *IDB Working Paper Series No. 299*, Inter-American Development Bank, *https://publications.iadb.org/en/sub-national-revenue-mobilization-peru.* [57]

CIAT (2017), "Tax Administration of Guyana progresses in key areas", Inter-American Center of Tax Administrations, *https://www.ciat.org/as-result-of-the-support-provided-by-the-ciat-seco-cooperation-program-the-tax-administration-of-guyana-progresses-in-key-areas/?lang=en.* [7]

ECLAC (2019), *Argentina - Economic Survey of Latin America and the Caribbean 2019*, Economic Commission for Latin America and the Caribbean, *https://repositorio.cepal.org/bitstream/handle/11362/44675/183/EEI2019_Argentina_en.pdf*. [12]

ECLAC (2019), *Belize- Economic Survey of Latin America and the Caribbean 2019*, Economic Commission for Latin America and the Caribbean, *https://repositorio.cepal.org/bitstream/handle/11362/44675/180/EEI2019_Belize_en.pdf*. [11]

ECLAC (2019), *Preliminary Overview of the Economies of Latin America and the Caribbean 2018*, Economic Commission for Latin America and the Caribbean, *https://repositorio.cepal.org/bitstream/handle/11362/44327/135/S1801218_en.pdf*. [3]

ECLAC (2018), *The Fiscal Panorama of Latin America and the Caribbean*, Economic Commission for Latin America and the Caribbean, *https://www.cepal.org/en/publications/43406-fiscal-panorama-latin-america-and-caribbean-2018-public-policy-challenges*. [14]

ECLAC (2014), *Tax policy in Latin America: Assessment and guidelines for a second generation of reforms*, Economic Commission for Latin America and the Caribbean, *https://repositorio.cepal.org/handle/11362/36806*. [23]

ECLAC (2013), *Fiscal Panorama of Latin America and the Caribbean: Tax reform and renewal of the fiscal covenant*, Economic Commission for Latin America and the Caribbean, *https://www.cepal.org/en/publications/3101-fiscal-panorama-latin-america-and-caribbean-2013-tax-reform-and-renewal-fiscal*. [16]

EY (2019), "Colombia enacts tax reform for 2019", Ernst & Young, *https://taxinsights.ey.com/archive/archive-news/colombia-enacts-tax-reform-for-2019.aspx*. [20]

EY (2018), "Argentine tax reform: A review of key provisions", Ernst & Young, *https://www.ey.com/gl/en/services/tax/international-tax/alert--argentine-tax-reform---a-review-of-key-provisions*. [19]

Hanni, Martner and Podestá (2017), "La incidencia distributiva de la fiscalidad en América Latina", in *Consensos y conflictos en la política tributaria de América Latina*, Economic Commission for Latin America and the Caribbean, *https://repositorio.cepal.org/handle/11362/43863*. [38]

IDB (2019), *Latin American and Caribbean Macroeconomic Report 2019: Building Opportunities for Growth in a Challenging World*, Inter-American Development Bank, *http://dx.doi.org/10.18235/0001633*. [5]

IDB (2013), *More than revenues: Taxation as a development tool*, Inter-American Development Bank, *https://publications.iadb.org/en/publication/more-revenue-taxation-development-tool-executive-summary*. [15]

IMF (2019), "Belize: 2019 Article IV Consultation", Country Report No. 19/364, International Monetary Fund, *https://www.imf.org/en/Publications/CR/Issues/2019/12/09/Belize-2019-Article-IV-Consultation-Press-Release-Staff-Report-and-Statement-by-the-48866*. [10]

IMF (2019), "IMF executive board concludes 2019 Article IV consultation with Guyana", International Monetary Fund, *https://www.imf.org/en/News/Articles/2019/09/16/pr19332-guyana-imf-executive-board-concludes-2019-article-iv-consultation*. [8]

IMF (2019), *World Economic Outlook Database* (October), International Monetary Fund, *https://www.imf.org/external/pubs/ft/weo/2019/02/weodata/index.aspx*. [27]

IMF (2018), "Trinidad and Tobago: 2018 Article IV Consultation", Country Report No. 18/285, International Monetary Fund, *https://www.imf.org/en/Publications/CR/Issues/2018/09/25/Trinidad-and-Tobago-2018-Article-IV-Consultation-Press-Release-and-Staff-Report-46267*. [6]

IMF (2016), "Argentina: 2016 Article IV Consultation", Country Report No. 16/346, International Monetary Fund, *https://www.imf.org/external/pubs/ft/scr/2016/cr16346.pdf*. [21]

Keen, M. (2013), "The anatomy of the VAT", IMF Working Paper No. 13/111, International Monetary Fund, *https://www.imf.org/en/Publications/WP/Issues/2016/12/31/The-Anatomy-of-the-VAT-40543*. [41]

Kettle, S. (2016), "Behavioral Interventions in Tax Compliance: Evidence from Guatemala", Policy Research Working Paper No. WPS7690, World Bank, *http://documents.worldbank.org/curated/en/479561467989537366/pdf/WPS7690.pdf*. [30]

KPMG (2019), "Mexico: Tax reform 2020, VAT on services provided from digital platforms", *https://home.kpmg/us/en/home/insights/2019/11/tnf-mexico-tax-reform-2020-vat-services-digital-platforms.html*. [44]

Latinobarómetro (2016), *Latinobarómetro Database*, *http://www.latinobarometro.org/*. [32]

Lorenzo, F. (2016), "Inventario de instrumentos fiscales verdes en América Latina: Experiencias, efectos y alcances", Project Paper, Economic Commission for Latin America and the Caribbean, *https://repositorio.cepal.org/bitstream/handle/11362/40833/1/S1601174_es.pdf*. [50]

Marten, M. and K. Van Dender (2019), "The use of revenues from carbon pricing", OECD Taxation Working Papers No. 43, OECD Publishing, Paris, *https://doi.org/10.1787/3cb265e4-en.* [47]

Mele, G. et al. (2017), "Gearing up for a more efficient tax system: an assessment of tax efficiency, a cost-benefit analysis of tax expenditures, and an exploration of labor informality and its tax implications", Working Paper No. ACS22697, World Bank, *http://documents.worldbank.org/curated/en/481411518538354879/Gearing-up-for-a-more-efficient-tax-system-an-assessment-of-tax-efficiency-a-cost-benefit-analysis-of-tax-expenditures-and-an-exploration-of-labor-informality-and-its-tax-implications.* [45]

Melguizo, A. et al. (2017), "No sympathy for the devil! Policy priorities to overcome the middle-income trap in Latin America", OECD Development Centre Working Papers No. 340, OECD Publishing, Paris, *http://dx.doi.org/10.1787/26b78724-en.* [26]

Ministry of Finance of Guyana (2019), *Mid-Year Report*, *https://finance.gov.gy/publications/mid-year-report-2019/.* [9]

Monge, C. (2018), "Colombia Puts a Tax on Carbon", *https://www.conservationfinancenetwork.org/2018/11/27/colombia-puts-tax-on-carbon.* [54]

OECD (2019), OECD PINE Database, OECD Publishing, Paris, *http://oe.cd/pine.* [49]

OECD (2019), *Tax Morale: What Drives People and Businesses to Pay Tax?*, OECD Publishing, Paris, *https://doi.org/10.1787/f3d8ea10-en.* [28]

OECD (2019), *Tax Policy Reforms 2019: OECD and Selected Partner Economies*, OECD Publishing, Paris, *https://doi.org/10.1787/da56c295-en.* [13]

OECD (2019), *Taxing Energy Use 2019: Using Taxes for Climate Action*, OECD Publishing, Paris, *https://doi.org/10.1787/058ca239-en.* [56]

OECD (2018), *Consumption Tax Trends 2018: VAT/GST and Excise Rates, Trends and Policy Issues*, OECD publishing, Paris, *https://doi.org/10.1787/ctt-2018-en.* [40]

OECD (2018), *Effective Carbon Rates 2018: Pricing Carbon Emissions Through Taxes and Emissions Trading*, OECD Publishing, Paris, *https://doi.org/10.1787/9789264305304-en.* [55]

OECD (2018), "Statutory Corporate Income Tax Rates", OECD.Stat (database), OECD Publishing, Paris, *https://stats.oecd.org/Index.aspx?DataSetCode=CTS_CIT.* [25]

OECD (2018), *Revenue Statistics 2018*, OECD Publishing, Paris, *https://doi.org/10.1787/rev_stats-2018-en.* [39]

OECD (2014), *Development Co-operation Report 2014: Mobilising Resources for Sustainable Development*, OECD Publishing, Paris, *https://dx.doi.org/10.1787/dcr-2014-en.* [29]

OECD (2005), "Environmental taxes", *Glossary of Statistical Terms*, *https://stats.oecd.org/glossary/detail.asp?ID=6437.* [46]

OECD/CAF/UN ECLAC (2018), *Latin American Economic Outlook 2018: Rethinking Institutions for Development*, OECD Publishing, Paris, *https://dx.doi.org/10.1787/leo-2018-en.* [4]

OECD et al. (2020), *Revenue Statistics in Latin America and the Caribbean 2020*, OECD Publishing, Paris, *https://doi.org/10.1787/35745b02-en.* [2]

OECD et al. (2019), *Latin American Economic Outlook 2019: Development in Transition*, OECD Publishing, Paris, *https://doi.org/10.1787/g2g9ff18-en.* [1]

OECD et al. (2015), *Revenue Statistics in Latin America and the Caribbean 2015*, OECD Publishing, Paris, *https://dx.doi.org/10.1787/rev_lat-2015-en-fr.* [34]

OECD/FIIAPP (2015), *Building Tax Culture, Compliance and Citizenship: A Global Source Book on Taxpayer Education*, OECD Publishing, Paris, *https://doi.org/10.1787/9789264205154-en.* [33]

OECD/IDB/CIAT (2016), *Taxing Wages in Latin America and the Caribbean 2016*, OECD Publishing, Paris, *https://dx.doi.org/10.1787/9789264262607-en.* [37]

OECD/IDB/The World Bank (2014), *Pensions at a Glance: Latin America and the Caribbean*, OECD Publishing, Paris, *https://dx.doi.org/10.1787/pension_glance-2014-en.* [35]

OECD/ILO (2019), Tackling Vulnerability in the Informal Economy, Development Centre Studies, OECD Publishing, Paris, *https://doi.org/10.1787/939b7bcd-en.* [36]

OECD/ITF (2019), *Tax Revenue Implications of Decarbonising Road Transport: Scenarios for Slovenia*, OECD Publishing, Paris, *https://doi.org/10.1787/87b39a2f-en.* [48]

OECD/UN ECLAC (2016), *OECD Environmental Performance Reviews: Chile 2016*, OECD Environmental Performance Reviews, OECD Publishing, Paris, *https://dx.doi.org/10.1787/9789264252615-en.* [52]

Schlotterbeck, S. (2017), "Tax administration reforms in the Caribbean: challenges, achievements, and next steps", IMF Working Paper No. 17/88, International Monetary Fund, *https://www.imf.org/en/Publications/WP/Issues/2017/04/04/Tax-Administration-Reforms-in-the-Caribbean-Challenges-Achievements-and-Next-Steps-44800.* [43]

Tax-News.com (2018), "Tax regime overhaul announced in Barbados", *https://www.tax-news.com/news/Tax_Regime_Overhaul_Announced_In_Barbados____76835.html.* [17]

The Behavioural Insights Team (2014), "Results from BIT tax trial in Guatemala", *https://www.bi.team/blogs/results-from-bit-tax-trial-in-guatemala/.* [31]

Vera, L. (2019), "Impuestos ambientales y equidad: desafíos para América Latina y el Caribe", Friedrich-Ebert-Stiftung (FES), *http://library.fes.de/pdf-files/bueros/kolumbien/15468-20190730.pdf.* [51]

World Bank (2020), "International tourism, receipts (% of total exports)", World Development Indicators (database), *https://data.worldbank.org/indicator/ST.INT.RCPT.XP.ZS.* [42]

World Grain (2016), "Reforms boost Argentine grain industry", *https://www.world-grain.com/articles/6457-reforms-boost-argentine-grain-industry.* [22]

Capítulo 1

Tendencias tributarias, 1990-2018

El financiamiento de la agenda de desarrollo de América Latina y el Caribe y el logro de los Objetivos de Desarrollo Sostenible exigen cambios significativos en la movilización de los recursos nacionales (OCDE et al., 2019[1]). Se requieren más ingresos para cumplir los objetivos a largo plazo, pero también para atender a las necesidades más urgentes de la ciudadanía de la región en cuanto al acceso a los bienes públicos y a la reducción de los altos niveles de vulnerabilidad, en particular en el mercado laboral. Asimismo, la política fiscal tiene un importante papel como catalizador del crecimiento inclusivo en la región. Estos retos reflejan la naturaleza multidimensional del desarrollo y subrayan la necesidad de introducir políticas sostenibles e integrales. Todo ello ocupa un lugar prominente en la agenda de Desarrollo en Transición liderada por la Comisión Europea, con el apoyo de la OCDE y su Centro de Desarrollo, así como de la Comisión Económica para América Latina y el Caribe (CEPAL).

Fortalecer los sistemas tributarios de la región de América Latina y el Caribe, sin embargo, no es solo cuestión de aumentar los ingresos; la procedencia de esos ingresos también es importante para abordar los objetivos socioeconómicos de la región. Los tipos de impuestos utilizados para generar ingresos tributarios (lo que se conoce como estructura tributaria) son fundamentales para el potencial redistributivo del sistema tributario y, por tanto, para su capacidad de hacer frente a las desigualdades de ingreso. Los impuestos también pueden incidir en el comportamiento de las personas; por ejemplo, pueden reducir la dependencia de los combustibles fósiles en el contexto del cambio climático. Asimismo, los impuestos pueden depender de distintas administraciones, con los consiguientes efectos en la prestación de servicios locales y en las políticas para hacer frente a la rápida urbanización.

La pandemia de Covid-19 es una crisis sanitaria sin precedentes que se está propagando rápidamente por todo el mundo. Esta crisis, junto con las respuestas de los gobiernos para proteger a los hogares y las empresas, ha causado una desaceleración económica. Una consecuencia de esta desaceleración es la probable reducción de los ingresos públicos en la región, que se espera se vea agravada por la reciente disminución de los precios de los productos básicos (particularmente en América del Sur, México y Trinidad y Tobago). Esta crisis subraya la necesidad de que los sistemas fiscales en la región generen un mayor financiamiento para servicios públicos cruciales, como es el caso del sector de la salud, y amplíen el espacio fiscal necesario para mitigar los posibles choques internos y externos. Mirando hacia el futuro, será necesario definir cuidadosamente el papel que los sistemas fiscales tienen para determinar las prioridades que estimulen el desarrollo inclusivo y reforzar las posiciones fiscales de los gobiernos.

Este informe *Estadísticas tributarias en América Latina y el Caribe* forma parte de la Facilidad Regional de la UE para el Desarrollo en Transición para América Latina y el Caribe. Actualmente se encuentra en su octava edición y proporciona datos internacionales comparables sobre los ingresos tributarios de 26 países de la región, datos que pueden servir de base para análisis de políticas en profundidad o que pueden ser un punto de partida para intercambiar información y crear capacidad. En este primer capítulo se analiza la evolución de varios indicadores tributarios clave desde 1990; entre ellos, la proporción entre la recaudación tributaria y el PIB, la combinación de impuestos y la generación de ingresos tributarios por parte de los distintos niveles de la Administración. También se analiza la eficacia de los impuestos sobre el valor añadido (el IVA, una de las principales fuentes de ingresos tributarios de la región) y los ingresos procedentes de los impuestos ambientales. En el presente capítulo se destacan asimismo las novedades en los sistemas tributarios de algunos países y se complementa el análisis con estudios de caso sobre determinados temas. Para un desglose de los ingresos tributarios detallado por países, pueden consultar los Capítulos 5 y 6.

La recaudación tributaria como proporción del PIB

La proporción entre la recaudación tributaria y el PIB mide los ingresos tributarios — incluidas las cotizaciones a la Seguridad Social pagadas a la Administración central— como proporción del producto interno bruto (PIB). En el promedio de América Latina y el Caribe se incluye el promedio no ponderado de los 25 países de América Latina y el Caribe incluidos en esta publicación, sin Venezuela, por problemas de disponibilidad de datos. Santa Lucía se ha incluido en el estudio por primera vez.

En 2018, en promedio la recaudación tributaria como proporción del PIB en América Latina y el Caribe se situó en 23.1% (Gráfico 1.1). En la región se registran variaciones considerables: desde el 12.1% de Guatemala hasta el 42.3% de Cuba. A excepción de Cuba, todos los países de América Latina y el Caribe experimentaron una recaudación tributaria como porcentaje del PIB inferior al promedio de la OCDE,[1] que se sitúa en 34.3%.

El porcentaje más alto de este indicador se registró en Cuba (42.3%), y en Barbados y Brasil (33.1% en ambos casos). Los países con la menor recaudación tributaria como porcentaje del PIB fueron Guatemala (12.1%), República Dominicana (13.2%) y Paraguay (14.0%).

Se han detectado diferencias importantes en el nivel de tributación entre Centroamérica y México, América del Sur y el Caribe.[2] Los países de Centroamérica y México presentaron una proporción entre la recaudación tributaria y el PIB más baja, con un promedio de 21.0% en 2018, mientras que en los países del Caribe el porcentaje era más alto, con un promedio de 25.7%. Entre los países de América del Sur se detectan variaciones importantes, pero su promedio fue del 23.1% en 2018, igual que el promedio de América Latina y el Caribe.

Gráfico 1.1. **Recaudación tributaria (% del PIB), 2018**

Total de ingresos tributarios como porcentaje del PIB

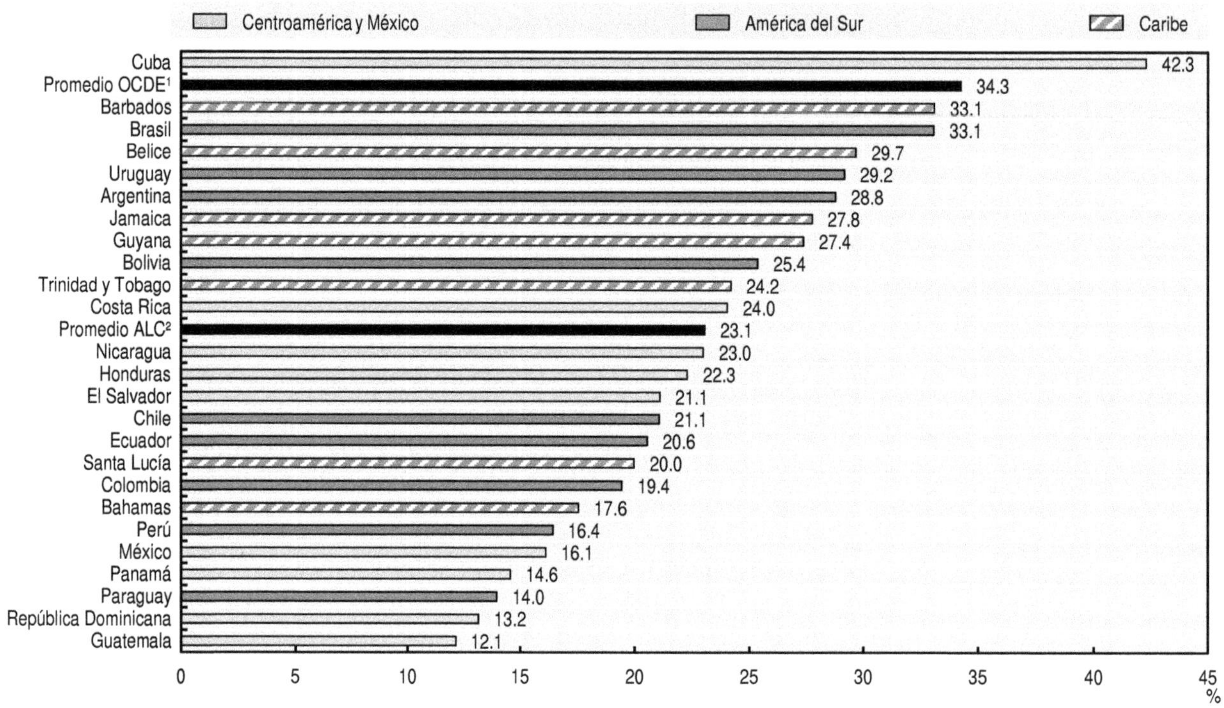

Nota: Las cifras no tienen en cuenta los ingresos de la Administración local de Argentina (sí se incluyen los ingresos de las provincias), las Bahamas, Barbados, la República Dominicana, Santa Lucía, Trinidad y Tobago, y Venezuela, puesto que los datos no se encuentran disponibles.

1. El promedio de la OCDE es el promedio no ponderado de los 36 países miembros de la OCDE. Chile y México también forman parte del grupo de la OCDE (36). Para México, en 2018, se ha hecho una estimación de los datos de ingresos de la Administración central y local.

2. Representa el promedio no ponderado de 25 países de América Latina y el Caribe, sin incluir Venezuela, por problemas de disponibilidad de datos.

Fuente: OCDE et al. (2020[2]), Cuadro 4.1.

StatLink https://doi.org/10.1787/888934113165

En 2018, el promedio de la proporción entre la recaudación tributaria y el PIB en América Latina y el Caribe superó en 0.4 puntos porcentuales la cifra de 2017, lo que contrasta con los 0.1 puntos porcentuales de aumento entre 2016 y 2017 (Gráfico 1.2). Este modesto incremento refleja, en parte, la lenta recuperación económica en la región desde 2017, tras dos años de recesión. El PIB creció un 1.3% (en términos reales) en 2017 y un 1.2% en 2018, impulsado por la recuperación de la demanda interna (CEPAL, 2019[3]), así como por el aumento de los precios de los productos básicos (OCDE/CAF/CEPAL, 2018[4]). El ligero incremento en la recaudación tributaria en América Latina y el Caribe también se debió, en parte, a la consolidación fiscal en toda la región (BID, 2019[5]).

La variación en la proporción entre la recaudación tributaria y el PIB entre 2017 y 2018 no fue homogénea en la región. El incremento en el Caribe fue el más amplio, con 1.1 puntos porcentuales. Superar los efectos de los desastres naturales que azotaron el Caribe en 2017 contribuyó a la mejora del contexto económico (CEPAL, 2019[3]).

Gráfico 1.2. **Variación de la recaudación tributaria entre 2016-2017 y 2017-2018**

Puntos porcentuales del PIB

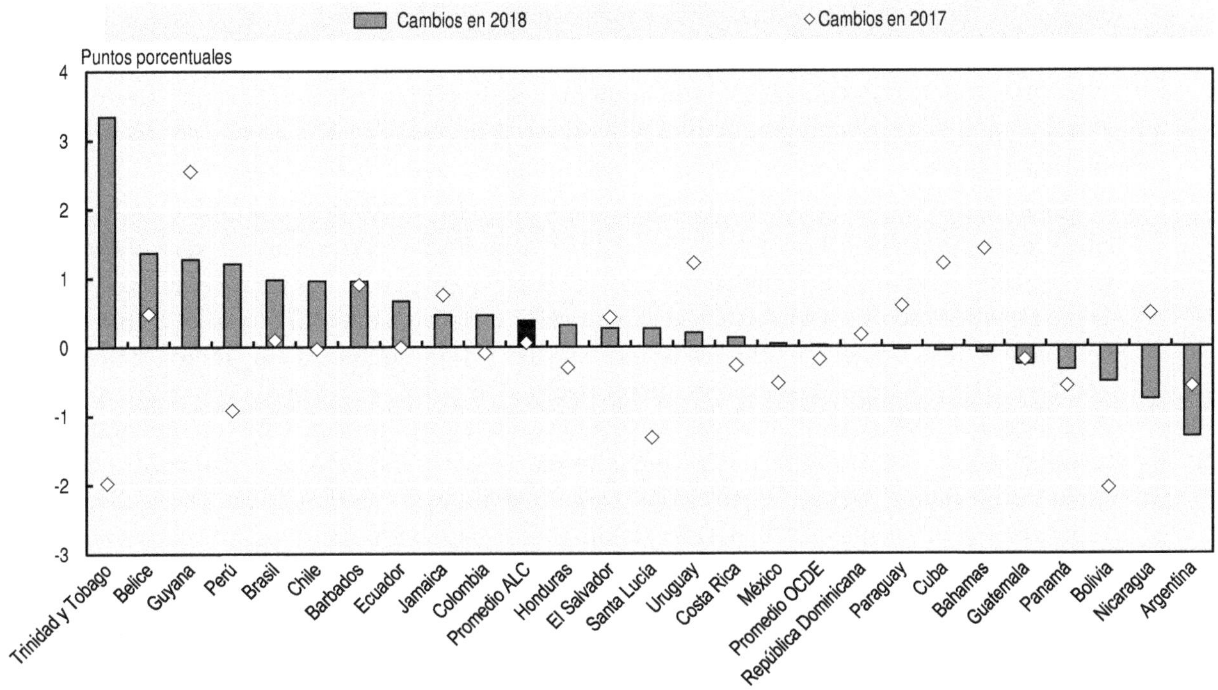

Fuente: Cálculos propios a partir de OCDE et al. (2020[2]), Cuadro 4.1.

StatLink https://doi.org/10.1787/888934113184

El aumento de la recaudación tributaria como proporción del PIB en América del Sur entre 2017 y 2018 fue más modesto (0.3% del PIB). En cambio, Centroamérica y México se redujo en 0.1 puntos porcentuales. En ambas regiones el crecimiento económico se debilitó durante ese período (CEPAL, 2019[3]).

En toda la región, 15 países presentaron un aumento de su proporción entre la recaudación tributaria y el PIB en 2018, mientras que siete registraron una disminución y tres no experimentaron cambios. En general, los incrementos de la proporción entre la recaudación tributaria y el PIB fueron mayores que las disminuciones. Los mayores incrementos entre 2017 y 2018 se registraron en tres países caribeños: Trinidad y Tobago (3.3 puntos porcentuales), Belice (1.4 puntos porcentuales) y Guyana (1.3 puntos porcentuales).

En Trinidad y Tobago, los ingresos de los impuestos sobre la renta y los beneficios (especialmente el impuesto sobre la renta de sociedades) fueron los principales impulsores del repunte en 2018 (1.9 puntos porcentuales), seguidos de los ingresos por el IVA (1.4 puntos porcentuales).

- El aumento de los ingresos por el impuesto sobre la renta de sociedades se debió básicamente a una fuerte recuperación del sector energético: el aumento de los precios de la energía y de la producción de gas natural impulsó los beneficios de las empresas (véase el Capítulo 2). Los ingresos tributarios del sector de extracción de petróleo y gas de Trinidad y Tobago alcanzaron el 1.8% del PIB, lo que supone un aumento de 0.6 puntos porcentuales con respecto al nivel de 2017. Los ingresos del impuesto sobre la renta de sociedades petroleras representaron alrededor de una quinta parte de esta categoría de ingresos en 2018.

- En 2018, los ingresos por IVA repuntaron tras una fuerte caída en 2017 (de 1.3 puntos porcentuales). El aumento se debió sobre todo a sectores ajenos al ámbito energético, puesto que Trinidad y Tobago ha hecho un gran esfuerzo por diversificar su base económica y reducir la dependencia del sector energético (FMI, 2018[6]).

En 2018, Belice y Guyana registraron aumentos en todas las categorías principales de ingresos tributarios como proporción del PIB, debido a ciertas reformas administrativas y de política públicas:

- Desde 2015, Guyana ha apostado por fortalecer su Administración tributaria a través del Programa de Cooperación CIAT-SECO (CIAT, 2017[7]). Se ha creado una unidad consagrada a los grandes contribuyentes; ha aumentado la base de contribuyentes, gracias a la implementación de modelos de riesgo, y se han fortalecido los procesos de recaudación tributaria. En 2018, las operaciones de la Unidad de Grandes Contribuyentes y la presentación electrónica fueron claramente responsables del aumento de ingresos del impuesto sobre la renta equivalente al 0.5% del PIB (FMI, 2019[8]). Además, en 2018 Guyana registró un aumento interanual de las importaciones del 31.6% (Ministerio de Hacienda de Guyana, 2019[9]), principalmente por sus actividades en el sector del petróleo y el gas. A su vez, esto incrementó los derechos de importación (equivalentes al 0.2% del PIB) y los impuestos especiales (gravados principalmente sobre importaciones equivalentes al 0.4% del PIB) durante ese período.
- Los ingresos procedentes del impuesto sobre bienes y servicios en Belice aumentaron un 0.7% como porcentaje del PIB en 2018, impulsado por un aumento de los ingresos por IVA equivalente al 0.5% del PIB. Esto fue el resultado de una reforma para ampliar la base del impuesto sobre las ventas, eliminando los artículos a tipo nulo (0%) (FMI, 2019[10]). El crecimiento de los ingresos por el impuesto sobre la renta de sociedades engrosó las arcas del impuesto sobre la renta y los beneficios en un 0.3% del PIB, con el apoyo de la continua recuperación económica tras el desastre natural de 2016. El crecimiento en 2018 (3.0%) se debe sobre todo al sector turístico (CEPAL, 2019[11]). Además, los impuestos sobre la propiedad aumentaron un 0.4% del PIB por los mayores ingresos en derechos de timbre.

Solo Argentina experimentó una disminución de los ingresos tributarios superior al 1% del PIB entre 2017 y 2018 (1.3%). Todas las categorías principales de ingresos tributarios registraron una disminución en 2018. Los ingresos procedentes de las cotizaciones a la Seguridad Social disminuyeron en 0.6 puntos porcentuales. Si bien Argentina aplicó importantes reformas fiscales en 2018, tales como la reducción de la tasa del impuesto sobre la renta de sociedades del 35% al 30% y aumento de la tasa de cotización a la Seguridad Social (aunque reducción de su base), el contexto económico fue la principal causa para reducir la proporción entre la recaudación tributaria y el PIB. La economía se contrajo un 2.5% en términos reales en 2018 (CEPAL, 2019[12]; OCDE, 2019[13]). En pleno episodio inflacionario, el PIB de Argentina aumentó más rápido en términos nominales que los ingresos tributarios (un 37% frente a un 31%), lo que disminuyó la proporción entre la recaudación tributaria y el PIB.

La siguiente caída más importante de este indicador fue la de Nicaragua, con una reducción equivalente al 0.8% del PIB durante el período. Todas las demás reducciones de la región se sitúan por debajo del 0.5% del PIB. La economía nicaragüense también se contrajo significativamente en 2018 (un 3.8% en términos reales), sumida en una crisis política y social, con una importante reducción de los ingresos en todas las categorías de impuestos (CEPAL, 2019[12]). En términos nominales, tanto los impuestos como el PIB cayeron, aunque la caída de los impuestos fue más pronunciada (un 4% frente a un 1%).

Como se ha visto en Argentina y Nicaragua, la variación en la proporción entre la recaudación tributaria y el PIB de un país se explica tanto por el tamaño relativo del cambio, tanto en los ingresos tributarios nominales como en el PIB nominal. Si los ingresos tributarios aumentan más (o disminuyen menos) que el PIB, la proporción entre la recaudación tributaria y el PIB aumentará. En cambio, si los ingresos tributarios aumentan menos que el PIB (o si caen más), la proporción entre la recaudación tributaria y el PIB se reducirá. Una mayor proporción entre la recaudación tributaria y el PIB, pues, no significa necesariamente que el monto de los ingresos tributarios haya aumentado en términos reales o incluso nominales.

El crecimiento del PIB anual fue positivo en los 15 países de América Latina y el Caribe cuya proporción entre la recaudación tributaria y el PIB aumentó entre 2017 y 2018, aunque en menor grado que el crecimiento de los ingresos tributarios. Los cinco países de América Latina y el Caribe que experimentaron una disminución de la proporción entre la recaudación tributaria y el PIB en 2018 habían aumentado el nivel de ingresos tributarios nominales con respecto a 2017, pero ese aumento había sido inferior a la variación de los niveles del PIB nominal. Nicaragua es el único país de América Latina y el Caribe con crecimiento negativo del PIB nominal y crecimiento negativo de los ingresos tributarios en 2018, mientras que las Bahamas registraron una disminución del PIB y un aumento de los ingresos tributarios en términos nominales entre 2017 y 2018.

Evolución de la proporción entre la recaudación tributaria y el PIB desde el 2000

Aumentar la movilización de recursos nacionales —particularmente a través del aumento de los ingresos tributarios— es fundamental para el desarrollo sostenible de América Latina y el Caribe, un punto que tiene un papel predominante en el enfoque de Desarrollo en Transición (Recuadro 1.1). Con tres excepciones (1991, 1996 y 2009), el promedio de la proporción entre la recaudación tributaria y el PIB en los países de América Latina y el Caribe ha tenido un aumento constante desde 1990 (Gráfico 1.3); el incremento ha sido de más de 7 puntos porcentuales (del 15.9% en 1990 al 23.1% en 2018). Esta tendencia contrasta con la de los países de la OCDE, cuyo promedio de proporción entre la recaudación tributaria y el PIB se ha mantenido relativamente estable desde 1990 (aunque a un nivel más alto que en el caso del promedio de América Latina y el Caribe). La proporción entre la recaudación tributaria y el PIB de la OCDE alcanzó el 34.3% del PIB en 2018, 2.3 puntos porcentuales por encima de los niveles de 1990. La diferencia en el promedio entre América Latina y el Caribe y la OCDE disminuyó entre 1990 y 2008, y a partir de ahí, se ha mantenido relativamente estable (Gráfico 1.3).

Recuadro 1.1. ***Estadísticas tributarias en América Latina y el Caribe y Desarrollo en Transición***

Esta edición del informe *Estadísticas tributarias en América Latina y el Caribe* es la segunda que se elabora con el apoyo de la Facilidad Regional de la Unión Europea (UE) para el Desarrollo en Transición para América Latina y el Caribe. Esta facilidad es el resultado de la labor conjunta liderada por la UE, la Organización para la Cooperación y el Desarrollo Económicos (OCDE) y su Centro de Desarrollo, así como de la Comisión Económica para América Latina y el Caribe (CEPAL).

Las economías de América Latina y el Caribe se enfrentan a nuevas vulnerabilidades nacionales e internacionales, pero también a otras más persistentes, que requieren importantes transformaciones para maximizar las oportunidades de desarrollo. Cuatro trampas principales dificultan su correcta transformación y su transición hacia el desarrollo sostenible: la trampa de la productividad, la trampa de la vulnerabilidad social, la trampa institucional y la trampa ambiental. Estas trampas interactúan entre sí con una dinámica que se retroalimenta para limitar las oportunidades de desarrollo sostenible de la región (OCDE et al., 2019[1]).

El enfoque de Desarrollo en Transición promueve el diseño de mejores políticas, prácticas y asociaciones, tanto a nivel nacional como internacional. Los problemas son cada vez más complejos y requieren estrategias de desarrollo con acciones de políticas más sofisticadas, con mayor coordinación y coherencia. No hay que escatimar esfuerzos para superar las trampas y convertir los círculos viciosos en círculos virtuosos. A nivel nacional, debe fortalecerse la capacidad, incluida la recaudación de impuestos, para abordar mejor los desafíos del desarrollo. A nivel internacional, la cooperación internacional debe actuar como un elemento facilitador para apoyar a los países en su transición hacia el desarrollo sostenible. Se puede recurrir a partenariados en políticas públicas, como socios iguales, para abordar inquietudes compartidas. Las estrategias nacionales de América Latina y el Caribe deben situarse en el centro, para fortalecer la capacidad nacional de los países y ampliar las herramientas de cooperación internacional, en sus distintas modalidades e instrumentos (OCDE et al., 2019[1]).

La política fiscal es fundamental para crear capacidad, abordar las trampas de desarrollo y velar por el desarrollo inclusivo y sostenible de los países de América Latina y el Caribe. Las *Estadísticas tributarias en América Latina y el Caribe* son un recurso extremadamente útil para los gobiernos, pues permiten fortalecer la política fiscal. Al proporcionar datos fiscales armonizados y detallados de toda la región, permiten llevar a cabo un análisis en profundidad de la política tributaria, identificando no solo cómo varía el nivel de ingresos tributarios por país, sino también qué instrumentos generan esos ingresos, teniendo en cuenta que *la forma en que se generan los ingresos fiscales* puede ser tan importante como *la cantidad de ingresos que se generan*. Las *Estadísticas tributarias en América Latina y el Caribe* son por lo tanto un punto de partida compartido para intercambiar información y crear capacidad entre países, incluyendo de una forma amplia la comunidad internacional.

Haciéndose eco de la relación crítica entre tributación eficaz y gasto público eficaz para promover el desarrollo inclusivo y sostenible, la Facilidad para el Desarrollo en Transición aporta las *Estadísticas tributarias en América Latina y el Caribe*, que vienen a unirse a la labor de la CEPAL y de la OCDE en materia de gasto público y, particularmente, de gasto social. El objetivo es brindar una visión sin precedentes, una batería de herramientas de gran valor para el desarrollo de la política fiscal de la región, con vistas a que se puedan cumplir los compromisos de la Agenda 2030 y a que se pongan en práctica estrategias de desarrollo a largo plazo.

Gráfico 1.3. **Recaudación tributaria, América Latina y el Caribe y OCDE, 1990-2018**

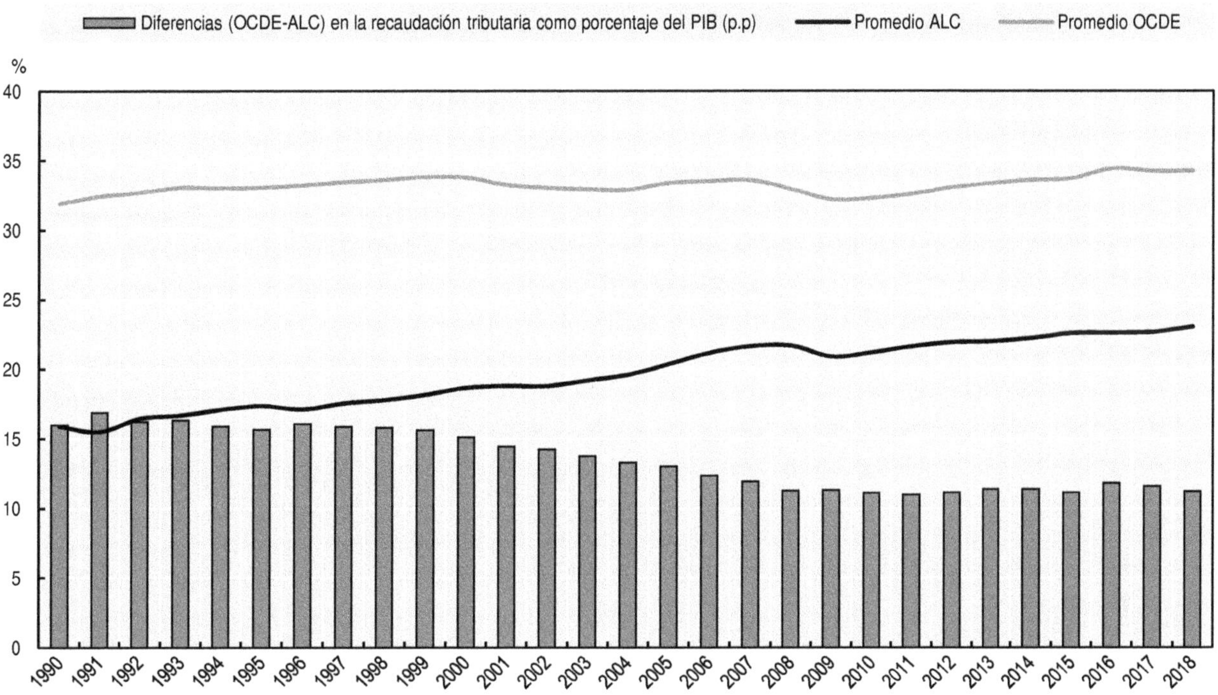

Fuente: OCDE et al. (2020[2]), Cuadro 4.1.

StatLink https://doi.org/10.1787/888934113203

En el Gráfico 1.4 se muestra la evolución del promedio de la proporción entre la recaudación tributaria y el PIB para las tres subregiones de América Latina y el Caribe desde 1990. Mientras que las tres subregiones han mostrado una tendencia al alza en los niveles de impuestos entre 1990 y 2018, su evolución presenta notables diferencias.

- En promedio, América del Sur registró el crecimiento más fuerte en el período y superó el promedio de América Latina y el Caribe de 2004 a 2018.
- En cambio, para Centroamérica y México y para el Caribe, el aumento de la proporción entre la recaudación tributaria y el PIB ha sido más gradual. A lo largo del período, la proporción entre la recaudación tributaria y el PIB de Centroamérica y México se mantuvo por debajo del promedio de la región de América Latina y el Caribe en su conjunto. En cambio, en el Caribe, el promedio de la proporción entre la recaudación tributaria y el PIB ha superado de forma sistemática el de América Latina y el Caribe.
- Desde 1990, el promedio del Caribe se ha ido acercando lentamente al promedio de América Latina y el Caribe, mientras que en Centroamérica y México se observa el movimiento contrario.
- La evolución de la proporción entre la recaudación tributaria y el PIB para las tres subregiones ha variado en los últimos años. América del Sur registró una constante reducción entre 2015 y 2017: su proporción entre la recaudación tributaria y el PIB se redujo en 0.8 puntos porcentuales durante ese período, antes de recuperarse en 2018 en 0.3 puntos porcentuales (a pesar de la caída en Argentina). El promedio de proporción entre la recaudación tributaria y el PIB para Centroamérica y México se ha mantenido estable en 21.0% desde 2016, mientras que la región del Caribe ha mostrado un crecimiento fuerte y constante, con un incremento de 1.5 puntos porcentuales entre 2016 y 2018.

Gráfico 1.4. **Recaudación tributaria, América Latina y el Caribe y subregiones, 1990-2018**

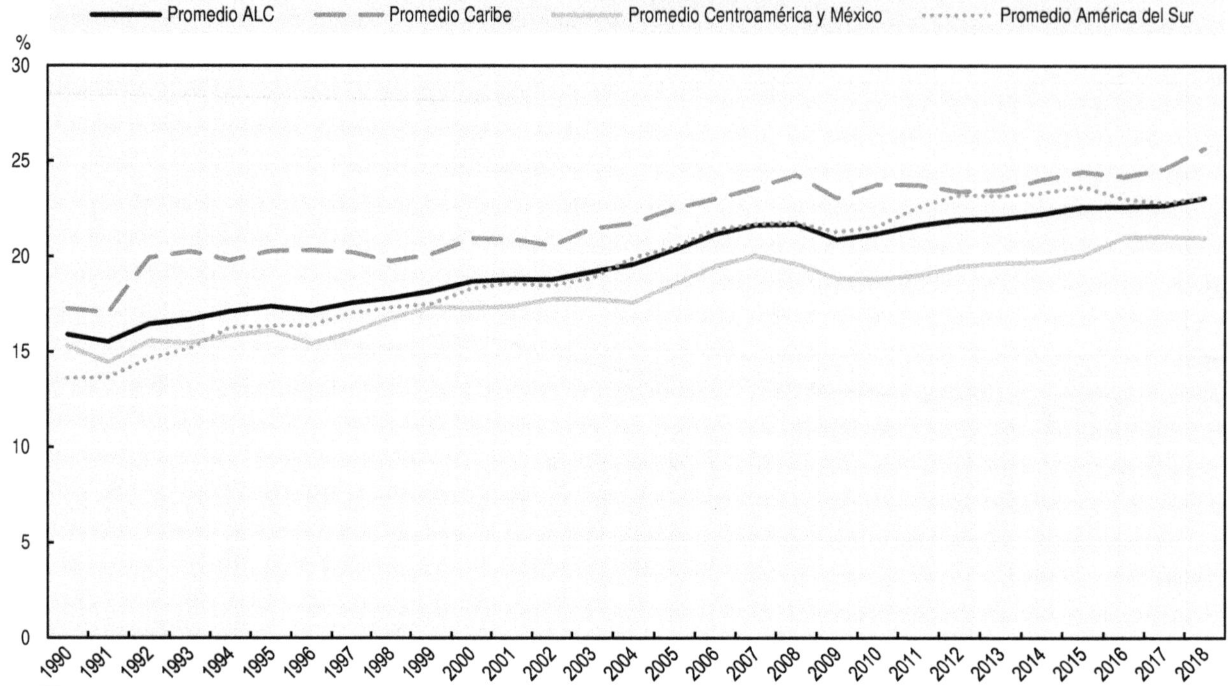

Nota: El promedio de América Latina y el Caribe representa el promedio no ponderado de 25 países de América Latina y el Caribe, sin incluir Venezuela, por problemas de disponibilidad de datos.

El Caribe incluye siete países (Bahamas, Barbados, Belice, Guyana, Jamaica, Santa Lucía, y Trinidad y Tobago); Centroamérica y México, nueve países (Costa Rica, Cuba, El Salvador, Guatemala, Honduras, México, Nicaragua, Panamá y República Dominicana); y América del Sur, nueve países (Argentina, Bolivia, Brasil, Chile, Colombia, Ecuador, Paraguay, Perú y Uruguay).

Fuente: Cálculos propios a partir de OCDE et al. (2020[2]), "Revenue Statistics in Latin America: Comparative tables", *OECD Tax Statistics* (base de datos), *http://dx.doi.org/10.1787/data-00641-en.*

StatLink *https://doi.org/10.1787/888934113222*

La proporción entre la recaudación tributaria y el PIB en los países de América Latina y el Caribe aumentó a principios de los noventa, tras un período de inestabilidad macroeconómica durante el decenio anterior. En los ochenta, numerosos países atravesaron grandes desequilibrios fiscales y algunos recurrieron a métodos alternativos para financiar su gasto (deuda o emisión de moneda). Esto provocó un rápido proceso inflacionario en la región, que erosionó el valor real de sus ingresos fiscales. Las reformas de los años noventa se centraron en la estabilidad de precios, el libre comercio y la disciplina fiscal. La mayoría de gobiernos de América Latina y el Caribe redujeron el gasto público e implementaron políticas para incrementar los ingresos fiscales, lo que mejoró la gestión de los presupuestos y de los saldos fiscales. Las autoridades aplicaron reformas de política fiscal y de administración tributaria para reforzar los sistemas fiscales durante episodios inflacionarios. Esto se logró disminuyendo los tiempos de recaudación e indexando las obligaciones fiscales (CEPAL, 2018[14]).

La introducción del IVA fue la reforma más significativa de los países de América Latina y el Caribe en los últimos tres decenios. En 1980, 12 países[3] estaban implementando el sistema de IVA y, a principios de los años noventa, ya aplicaban IVA prácticamente todos los países. Después de este periodo, las reformas han subido la tasa del IVA, han ampliado la base del impuesto y han reforzado la recaudación. Las reformas también se han centrado en la simplificación de los sistemas de IVA, y la mayoría de los países han reducido el número de artículos con tipo nulo o reducido. Se ha avanzado hacia sistemas de IVA de tasa única en varios países (CEPAL, 2018[14]).

En los últimos dos decenios se han hecho esfuerzos significativos para modernizar la administración de los impuestos. Se han implementado nuevos sistemas informáticos; se ha racionalizado la estructura de las agencias tributarias; los sistemas de recaudación son ahora más eficientes y el personal cuenta ahora con conocimientos especializados (BID, 2013[15]). Además, algunos países han simplificado sus sistemas tributarios y han ampliado la base imponible, reduciendo las exenciones y los incentivos fiscales, que se habían otorgado a ciertas actividades y sectores principalmente para atraer inversión extranjera. Las reformas incluyeron la introducción o el desarrollo de sistemas simplificados para pequeños contribuyentes y la imposición de la propiedad a partir de unos ingresos estimados. Estas medidas han tenido un efecto positivo en los ingresos de varios países gracias a la expansión del impuesto para que abarque todas las rentas del trabajo y del capital, incluidos los dividendos (por ejemplo, Colombia, Guatemala, El Salvador, Nicaragua, Panamá, República Dominicana y Perú). Las reformas también han fijado impuestos mínimos, impuestos sobre las transacciones financieras y reducciones graduales del nivel de renta real gravado al tipo máximo marginal (CEPAL, 2013[16]; CEPAL, 2018[14]). En el Recuadro 1.2 se dan algunos ejemplos de las reformas tributarias actuales en tres países.

Recuadro 1.2. **Reformas tributarias en tres países de América Latina y el Caribe**

En 2018 algunos países emprendieron importantes reformas de política fiscal para simplificar los sistemas tributarios, reducir la evasión fiscal e impulsar la inversión privada.

Barbados anunció una serie de medidas que afectan a los principales impuestos de sus presupuestos de 2018. Entre otras, un aumento de la tasa del impuesto sobre la renta de sociedades (que pasa del 25% al 30%), una nueva banda para el impuesto sobre la renta para las rentas más altas (del 40%), y una nueva contribución a los servicios de salud según la renta, aplicable a empresarios y empleados. Además, Barbados implantó nuevos impuestos o aumentó los existentes en el sector turístico, y sustituyó el impuesto sobre las carreteras por un impuesto sobre el combustible (BID, 2019[5]). Con respecto a la economía digital, ahora se aplica IVA a todas las transacciones de compra de bienes y servicios por Internet de residentes de Barbados, y se aplica un impuesto del 10% a las transacciones de empresas como Airbnb, Homeaway y Expedia (Tax-News.com, 2018[17]; Barbados Revenue Authority, 2018[18]; BID, 2019[5]). BID (2019[5]) apunta que se prevé que estas medidas aumenten los ingresos en torno al 3.7% del PIB.

Argentina también se embarcó en una amplia reforma tributaria (Ley 27430) para modificar las principales tasas y la ley entró en vigor el 1.° de enero de 2018. Se redujo la tasa del impuesto sobre la renta de sociedades (del 35% al 30%) y se prevé que, a partir del 2020, se sitúe en el 25%. Además, se ha aplicado un impuesto de retención de dividendos y la tasa aumentará gradualmente hasta alcanzar el 13% posterior al 1.° de enero de 2020. Con respecto al impuesto sobre la renta de personas físicas, se han eliminado las exenciones para los ingresos por intereses y ganancias de capital de diferentes tipos de inversiones. Los diferentes tipos de cotización a la Seguridad Social (que varían según el sector) de las empresas del sector privado se unificarán gradualmente a partir de enero de 2022. A partir de 2018 se ha establecido una base no imponible para las cotizaciones a la Seguridad Social y su monto aumentará gradualmente hasta 2022. Para servicios digitales prestados por residentes de Argentina o cuando el uso efectivo de los servicios es en Argentina, se aplica IVA (EY, 2018[19]).

Recuadro 1.2. **Reformas tributarias en tres países de América Latina y el Caribe** *(cont.)*

Colombia, por su parte, aprobó una amplia reforma tributaria en diciembre de 2018 que entró en vigor a 1.° de enero de 2019. Sin embargo, la revisión de constitucionalidad llevada a cabo por la Corte Constitucional de Colombia se pronunció en contra de la reforma tributaria debido a errores de procedimiento durante el debate en el Congreso. Esto condujo a una segunda reforma tributaria (Ley N° 2010 de 2019) aprobada en diciembre de 2019 que reproduce casi en su totalidad la reforma tributaria integral de diciembre de 2018. En virtud de esta reforma tributaria, el impuesto sobre la renta de sociedades disminuirá del 33% al 32% para el año fiscal 2020, al 31% para el año fiscal 2021 y al 30% a partir de 2022. La tasa de impuesto sobre la renta presunta se reduce del 3.5% al 1.5% en 2019 y 2020, y al 0% a partir de 2021. Se aplica tasas reducidas para ciertos sectores (como servicios de hotelería y nuevos proyectos de parques temáticos o de ecoturismo, agroturismo, entre otros). Se han introducido exenciones fiscales para las rentas por debajo de USD 850 000 de los sectores tecnológicos y creativos o las actividades agrícolas. Para el impuesto sobre la renta de personas físicas (naturales), la tasa máxima se ha incrementado para todos los tipos de ingresos (trabajo y capital); se ha implementado un régimen fiscal simplificado para pequeñas y medianas empresas en sustitución del impuesto sobre la renta, el impuesto nacional al consumo (si aplica) y el impuesto de industria y comercio. Los establecimientos permanentes están ahora gravados por sus ingresos atribuibles a nivel mundial. En la reforma fiscal también se aborda la evasión fiscal e incluye un régimen de transferencia indirecta, la creación del impuesto de normalización para los contribuyentes que han omitido activos o incluido deudas inexistentes en sus declaraciones de impuestos, se incluye el IVA a cervezas y gaseosas, y se crea un nuevo impuesto al patrimonio neto por los residentes colombianos en todo el mundo, que será aplicable para 2019, 2020 y 2021. Una devolución del IVA para las familias de bajos ingresos y un día del año sin IVA son nuevas modificaciones en la reforma fiscal de 2019. Se estima que la reforma fiscal ha producido ingresos adicionales equivalentes al 0.7% del PIB en 2019. (BID, 2019[5]; EY, 2019[20]).

Entre 1990 y 2018, los ingresos del IVA como proporción del PIB se duplicaron en los países de América Latina y el Caribe, donde se ha pasado del 2.3% del PIB en 1990 al 6.0% del PIB en 2018 (Gráfico 1.5). Durante el mismo período, los ingresos de otros impuestos sobre bienes y servicios (los impuestos específicos y los derechos de aduana y de importación) en América Latina y el Caribe disminuyeron como porcentaje del PIB. Esta caída se asoció a la liberalización del comercio, que implicó que se modificara la imposición de los bienes importados y exportados, así como de los bienes y servicios específicos. Entre estos cambios, se encuentra la reducción de los aranceles a la importación, la reducción de la base de los productos y servicios sujetos a impuestos específicos, y la eliminación de los impuestos sobre las exportaciones. Una importante excepción es Argentina, donde se recuperaron los impuestos sobre las exportaciones en 2002, aunque el Gobierno abolió ese impuesto sobre casi todos los productos agropecuarios en 2015 (FMI, 2016[21]; World Grain, 2016[22]).

El aumento del promedio de la proporción entre la recaudación tributaria y el PIB en la región de América Latina y el Caribe desde 1990 ha estado impulsado, en gran medida, por el incremento de los ingresos procedentes del impuesto sobre la renta y del IVA (Gráfico 1.5). Se pueden distinguir cuatro fases distintas en la evolución de los ingresos tributarios:

- Entre 1990 y 2002, el IVA contribuyó más al aumento de los ingresos tributarios que el impuesto sobre la renta y los beneficios (1.8% del PIB frente al 1.1%). En ese período, cinco países introdujeron el IVA (Barbados, Belice, El Salvador, Jamaica y Paraguay).
- Entre 2002 y 2008, se observa la tendencia inversa: los ingresos procedentes del impuesto sobre la renta y los beneficios contribuyeron más que los ingresos por concepto de IVA al aumento de los ingresos tributarios (incrementos del 1.8% y el 1.3% del PIB,

respectivamente). El aumento de la recaudación a través del impuesto sobre la renta se explica, en parte, por la explosión de los precios de las materias primas a partir de 2003, que hizo subir los ingresos por el impuesto sobre la renta de sociedades del sector de los recursos naturales (CEPAL, 2013[23]; Barreix, Benitez y Pecho, 2017[24]). En varios países también fue el resultado de políticas de reducción de incentivos fiscales en las zonas de libre comercio, de la introducción de impuestos mínimos para las sociedades, de reformas de la fiscalidad internacional y de convenios entre países para combatir la evasión fiscal.

- La recaudación por IVA y por impuestos sobre la renta disminuyó fuertemente durante la crisis financiera mundial del 2008. Durante la recuperación posterior, los ingresos del IVA crecieron rápidamente y alcanzaron el 6% del PIB en 2016, al mismo nivel que los ingresos del impuesto sobre la renta. Durante este período, otros dos países del Caribe empezaron a aplicar el IVA (Santa Lucía, en 2012, y las Bahamas, en 2015). Los precios de los productos básicos fueron disminuyendo de forma constante y, en 2015, experimentaron una caída más pronunciada.
- A partir de 2016, los precios de los productos básicos se recuperaron y los ingresos del impuesto sobre la renta repuntaron. Entre 2017 y 2018, los ingresos por impuestos sobre la renta registraron su mayor aumento desde 2011, con un promedio de 0.3 puntos porcentuales. Esto se debe, en gran medida, al aumento de los ingresos del impuesto sobre la renta de sociedades (0.2% del PIB). Entre los factores que explican el aumento de los ingresos del impuesto sobre la renta de sociedades, figuran los fuertes beneficios registrados por los sectores de la minería y la extracción de petróleo y gas (véase el Capítulo 2 para más detalles).

Gráfico 1.5. **Recaudación a partir del impuesto sobre la renta y los beneficios, contribuciones a la seguridad social, el IVA y otros impuestos sobre bienes y servicios, 1990-2018**

Porcentaje del PIB

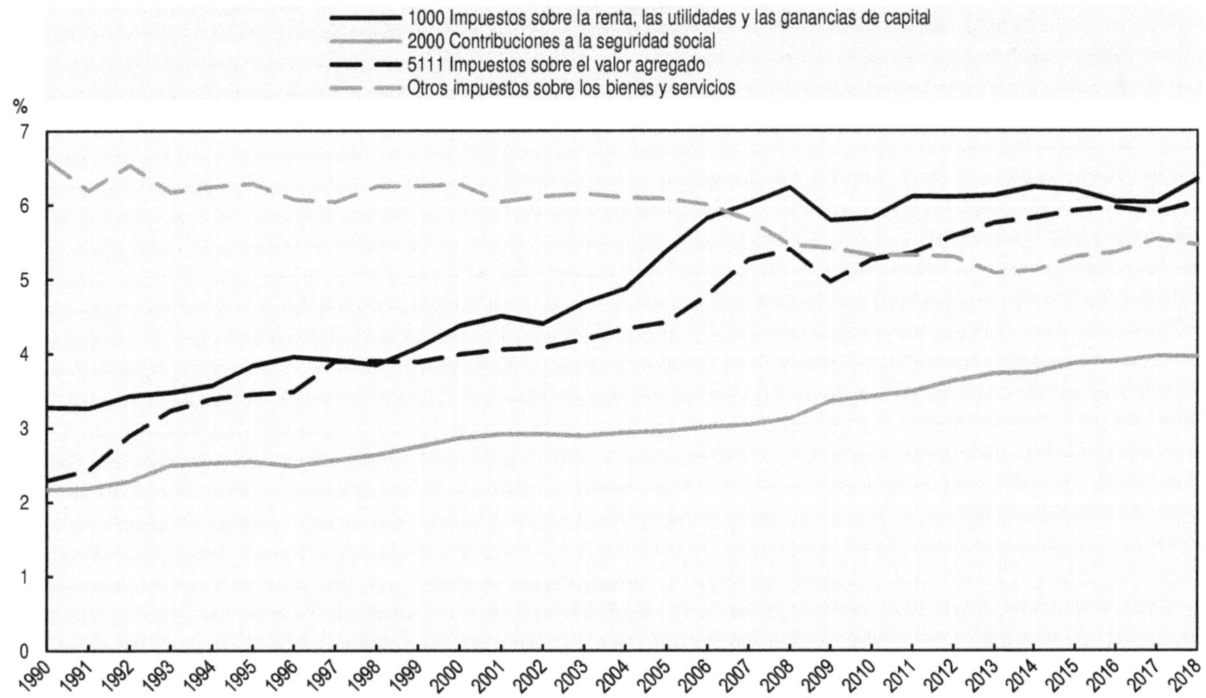

Fuente: Cálculos propios a partir de OCDE et al. (2020[2]), "Revenue Statistics in Latin America: Comparative tables", *OECD Tax Statistics* (base de datos), *http://dx.doi.org/10.1787/data-00641-en*.

StatLink https://doi.org/10.1787/888934113241

El Gráfico 1.6 muestra la evolución del impuesto sobre la renta de sociedades y del impuesto sobre la renta de personas físicas desde 2007. En 2018, los promedios de recaudación de estos impuestos en América Latina y el Caribe se situaron en el 3.5% y el 2.3% del PIB, respectivamente, aunque Ecuador, Nicaragua y Venezuela no se incluyen en el cálculo a falta de datos. Durante este período, los ingresos del impuesto sobre la renta de sociedades como porcentaje del PIB han fluctuado más que los del impuesto sobre la renta de personas físicas, en aumento constante. Si bien los ingresos del impuesto sobre la renta de sociedades reciben sobre todo el impulso de los ciclos económicos y los cambios en los precios de los productos básicos (especialmente para los países que dependen de la explotación de recursos naturales), los cambios en las tasas del impuesto también son importantes. Durante este período, la tata la tasa promedio del impuesto sobre la renta de sociedades en América Latina y el Caribe disminuyó del 27.3% al 25.7% en 2016; en los dos años siguientes aumentó hasta el 26.3% en 2018.[4] Entre 2007 y 2018, Argentina, Panamá y Uruguay redujeron su tasa del impuesto sobre la renta de sociedades del 30% al 25%. En cambio, algunos países aumentaron las tasas de este impuesto en el período, entre ellos Chile (del 17% en 2007 al 25% en 2017) y México (del 28% en 2007 al 30% en 2010) (OCDE, 2018[25]).

Gráfico 1.6. **Recaudación del impuesto sobre la renta y los beneficios, el impuesto sobre la renta de sociedades y el impuesto sobre la renta de personas físicas, 2007-18**

Porcentaje del PIB

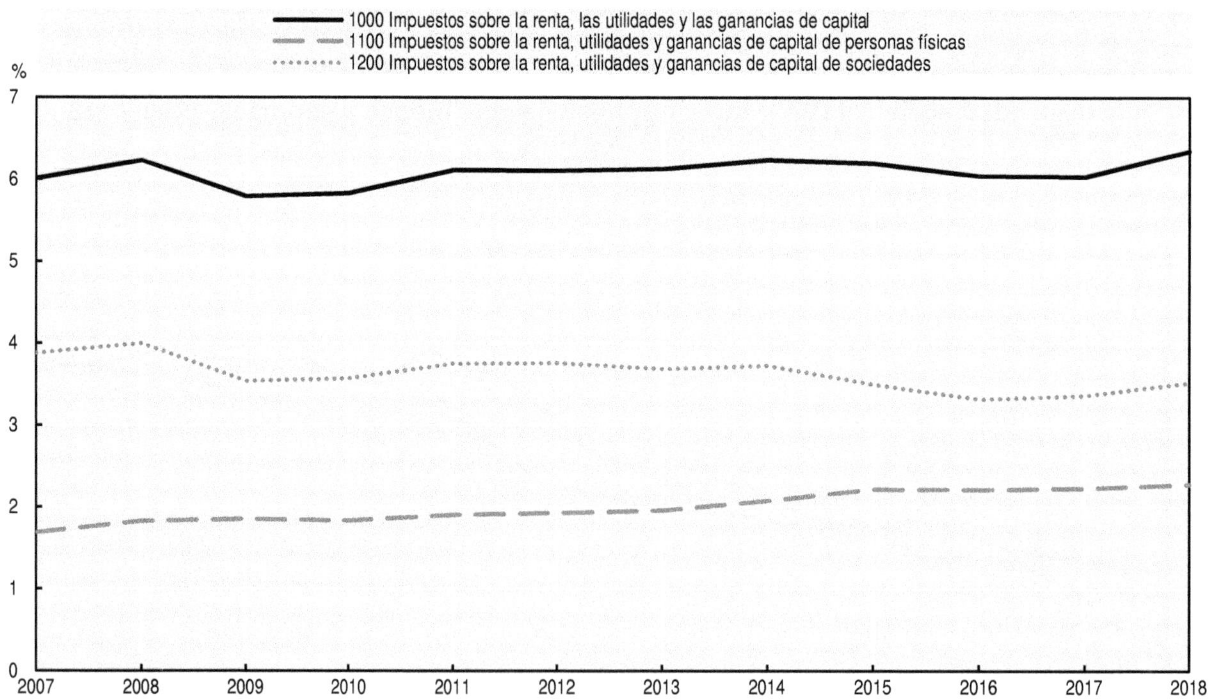

Nota: Los ingresos del impuesto sobre la renta de sociedades y del impuesto sobre la renta de personas físicas como porcentaje del PIB deberían interpretarse con cautela, pues Ecuador, Nicaragua y Venezuela no se incluyen en los cálculos. El promedio de América Latina y el Caribe no incluye Venezuela, por problemas de disponibilidad de datos, y Ecuador y Nicaragua han quedado excluidos porque más de un tercio de su recaudación del impuesto sobre la renta y los beneficios no puede atribuirse a las categorías de renta de sociedades (1200) o renta de personas físicas (1100).

Fuente: OCDE et al. (2020[2]), "Revenue Statistics in Latin America and the Caribbean: Comparative tables", *OECD Tax Statistics* (base de datos), *http://dx.doi.org/10.1787/data-00641-en*.

StatLink *https://doi.org/10.1787/888934113260*

Se constatan diferencias notables entre las tres subregiones de América Latina y el Caribe cuando se analizan las variaciones en las principales categorías de impuestos entre 1990 y 2018 (Gráfico 1.7).

- En promedio, el Caribe es donde más sube la recaudación por IVA como porcentaje del PIB (6.0 puntos porcentuales). Seis de los siete países del Caribe introdujeron[5] el IVA durante el período, más tarde que la mayoría de los países de Centroamérica y México y América del Sur.
- En América del Sur y en Centroamérica y México, los mayores incrementos entre 1990 y 2018 se registraron en el impuesto sobre la renta y los beneficios (3.8% del PIB), seguidos del IVA (3.4% y 2.7% del PIB, respectivamente). La recaudación del impuesto sobre la renta y los beneficios (e indirectamente del IVA) se vio influida por el fuerte aumento de precios de los minerales y el petróleo entre 2003 y 2010.

Gráfico 1.7. **Variación de la recaudación por el impuesto sobre la renta y los beneficios, el IVA, las cotizaciones a la seguridad social y otros impuestos sobre bienes y servicios por subregión, 1990-2018**

Porcentaje del PIB

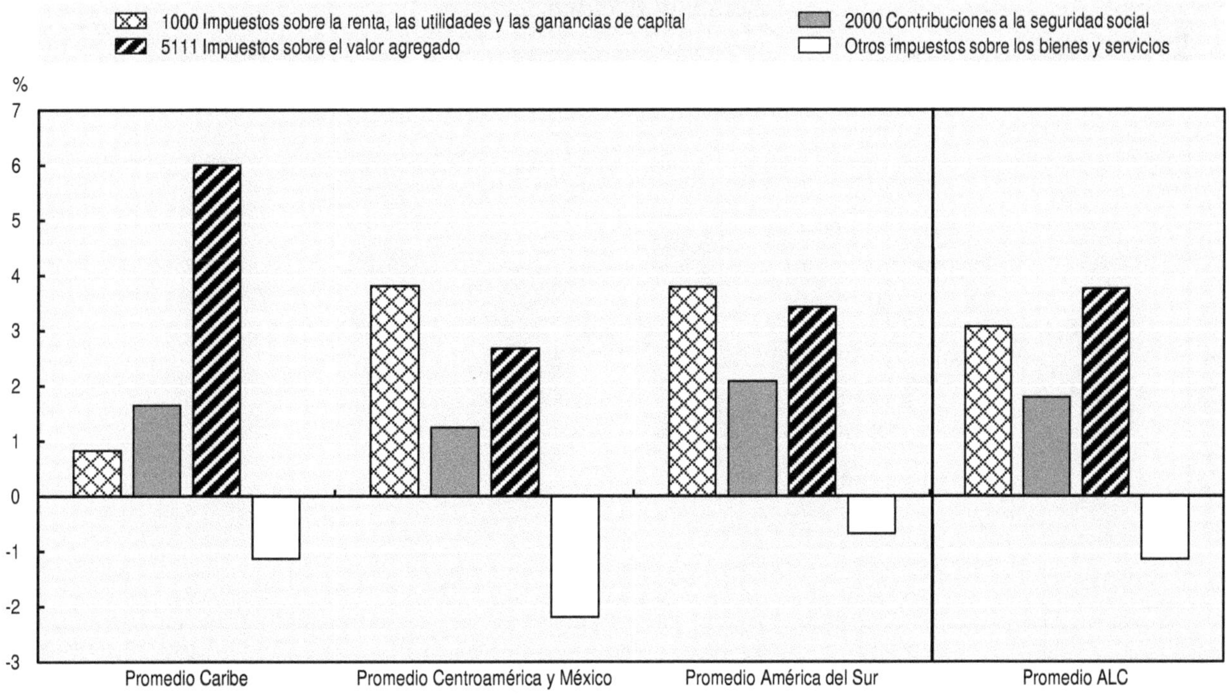

Nota: El promedio América Latina y el Caribe representa el promedio no ponderado de 25 países de América Latina y el Caribe, sin incluir Venezuela, por problemas de disponibilidad de datos. El Caribe incluye siete países (Bahamas, Barbados, Belice, Guyana, Jamaica, Santa Lucía y Trinidad y Tobago); Centroamérica y México, nueve países (Costa Rica, Cuba, El Salvador, Guatemala, Honduras, México, Nicaragua, Panamá y República Dominicana); y América del Sur, nueve países (Argentina, Bolivia, Brasil, Chile, Colombia, Ecuador, Paraguay, Perú y Uruguay).

Fuente: Cálculos propios a partir de OCDE et al. (2020[2]), "Revenue Statistics in Latin America: Comparative tables", *OECD Tax Statistics* (base de datos), *http://dx.doi.org/10.1787/data-00641-en*.

StatLink https://doi.org/10.1787/888934113279

Factores que influyen en la recaudación tributaria como porcentaje del PIB

En lo referente a la proporción entre la recaudación tributaria y el PIB, las diferencias entre los promedios de América Latina y el Caribe y la OCDE son coherentes con la tendencia de que los países con más renta per cápita tienen una proporción más alta. Los datos arrojan una correlación positiva entre el PIB per cápita (indicador del nivel de renta de los países) y la proporción entre la recaudación tributaria y el PIB (Gráfico 1.8). En general, los países de la OCDE tienen ingresos más altos que los países de América Latina y el Caribe, y también tienen una proporción más alta entre la recaudación tributaria y el PIB. Argentina, Barbados, Brasil y Uruguay tienen niveles similares a algunos países de la OCDE en la proporción entre la recaudación tributaria y el PIB. Los análisis empíricos sugieren que la recaudación tributaria más elevada —acompañada de mejores instituciones, mejores índices de educación y competencias, y más diversificación económica— es lo que permite que varios países de la OCDE escapen de la trampa de ingresos medios, lo que contrasta con la región América Latina y el Caribe (Melguizo et al., 2017[26]).

Gráfico 1.8. **PIB per cápita en PPA (USD) y recaudación tributaria como porcentaje del PIB en América Latina y el Caribe, la OCDE y un grupo de países de África, Asia y el Pacífico, 2017**

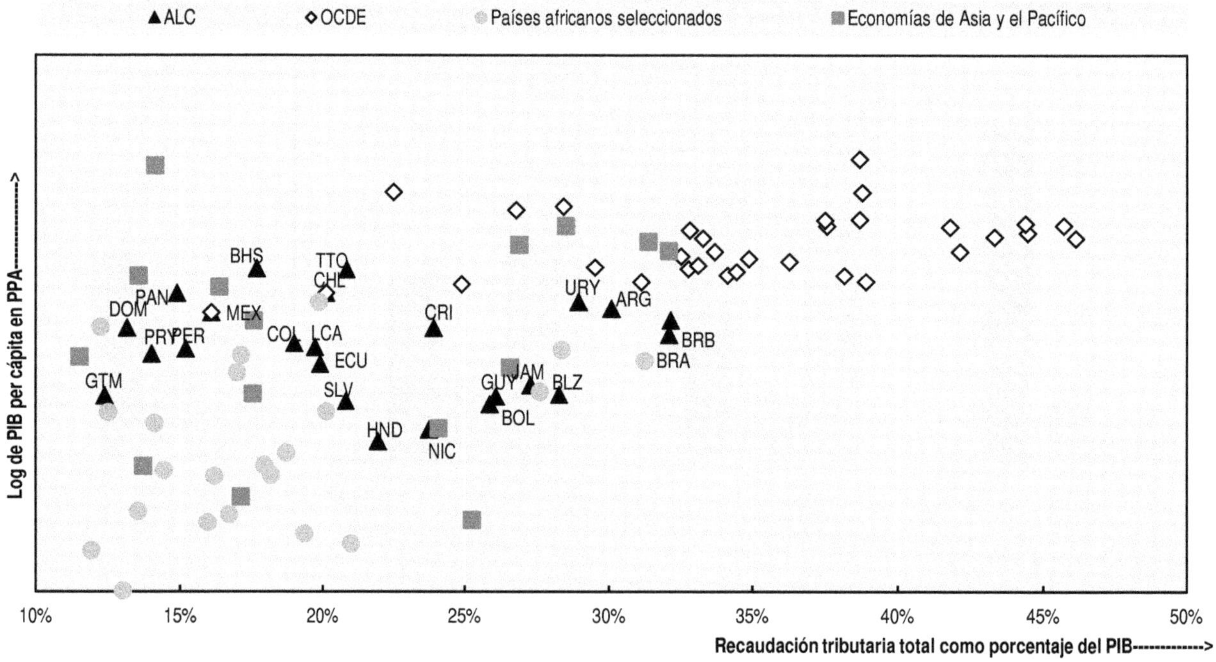

Nota: El año de comparación es 2017, ya que los datos de 2018 para la proporción entre la recaudación tributaria y el PIB no estaban disponibles para los países seleccionados de África, Asia y el Pacífico. Cuba y Venezuela no se incluyen en esta cifra debido a problemas de disponibilidad de datos. La paridad de poder adquisitivo (PPA) entre dos países es el tipo de cambio al que debe convertirse la moneda de un país en la de un segundo país para adquirir el mismo volumen de bienes y servicios en ambos países. El tipo de conversión PPA implícito se expresa como moneda nacional por dólar internacional actual. El dólar internacional tiene el mismo poder adquisitivo que el dólar estadounidense en los Estados Unidos. El dólar internacional es una moneda hipotética que se utiliza como medio para convertir y comparar los costos de un país a otro utilizando un punto de referencia común: el dólar estadounidense (USD).

Fuente: FMI (2019[27]) para las cifras del PIB per cápita. La proporción entre la recaudación tributaria y el PIB se obtiene con datos de las publicaciones regionales de *Revenue Statistics* (*http://www.oecd.org/tax/tax-policy/global-revenue-statistics-database.htm*).

StatLink https://doi.org/10.1787/888934113298

La proporción entre la recaudación tributaria y el PIB se ve influida por una serie de factores económicos y estructurales. El PIB per cápita, la apertura comercial, el tamaño de la economía informal, la dotación de recursos naturales y la importancia del sector agropecuario para la economía son algunos de los factores que influyen la recaudación tributaria. Los determinantes sociodemográficos también son importantes, por ejemplo, el nivel de educación o el grado de participación femenina en la población activa. La capacidad de las agencias tributarias, el nivel de corrupción y la moral tributaria (disposición de la población a pagar impuestos) (véase el Recuadro 1.3 para más detalles basados en [OCDE, 2019$_{[28]}$]) son factores que también van muy ligados al nivel de recaudación tributaria (OCDE, 2014$_{[29]}$). Además, la proporción entre la recaudación tributaria y el PIB refleja las decisiones políticas sobre el papel del gobierno y su tamaño. Para terminar, la ubicación geográfica y los factores históricos también inciden en la proporción entre la recaudación tributaria y el PIB. Por ejemplo, los países sin costa marítima tienen menos posibilidades de gravar bienes y servicios en puertos de entrada. Además, ciertos factores internacionales —entre otros, las políticas tributarias adoptadas por otros países— también pueden afectar a la recaudación tributaria.

El grado de participación del Estado en el financiamiento de la Seguridad Social es otro factor importante para explicar los niveles de recaudación tributaria en América Latina y el Caribe. A partir de los años ochenta, muchos países de América Latina y el Caribe privatizaron la sanidad y las pensiones, en mayor o menor grado. Chile, El Salvador y México son ejemplos de países que han pasado de cobertura pública a un sistema de pensiones administrado sobre todo por el sector privado. En Colombia y Perú, los sistemas públicos y privados compiten, y los empleados deben decidir a cuál se afilian (OCDE et al., 2015$_{[34]}$; OCDE/BID/Banco Mundial, 2015$_{[35]}$). Por otra parte, Argentina, Brasil y Uruguay siguen un modelo en el que los sistemas públicos y privados son complementarios. En estos países se han llevado a cabo reformas para ampliar la cobertura de los sistemas de seguridad social e incluir a los que antes quedaban excluidos. Esto también ha sido un factor importante en el aumento de la recaudación tributaria (CEPAL, 2013$_{[23]}$).

La informalidad erosiona sin duda la recaudación tributaria de los países de América Latina y el Caribe, dado que reduce significativamente la base imponible. Más del 50% de los trabajadores en América Latina y el Caribe son informales (OECD/ILO, 2019). El alto nivel de la economía informal llevó a algunos gobiernos en los años noventa a introducir regímenes fiscales simplificados para los pequeños contribuyentes y, en cierto modo, se logró integrar a trabajadores en el sector estructurado. El éxito de estos sistemas simplificados fue desigual, según el tipo de contribuyente y la capacidad de las agencias tributarias (CEPAL, 2013$_{[23]}$; OCDE/BID/CIAT, 2016$_{[37]}$).

Recuadro 1.3. **La moral tributaria en América Latina**

La moral tributaria, la motivación intrínseca para pagar impuestos, es un aspecto clave del sistema tributario y de su capacidad recaudatoria, ya que la mayoría de los sistemas tributarios se basan en el cumplimiento voluntario de los contribuyentes para el grueso de su recaudación. Entender mejor qué provoca las diferencias en la moral tributaria, tanto en individuos como en empresas, puede contribuir a explicar las variaciones en el cumplimiento de la normativa tributaria y puede fundamentar estrategias para aumentar la recaudación con un esfuerzo (relativamente) bajo para su aplicación. Por ejemplo, el simple hecho de enviar un mensaje a los contribuyentes guatemaltecos para que cumplieran con sus obligaciones fiscales elevó el pago de impuestos entre los destinatarios de las cartas 5.5 puntos porcentuales (Kettle et al., 2016[30]; The Behavioural Insights Team, 2014[31]).

Parece que la moral tributaria de la población se está reduciendo en toda América Latina, aunque es cierto que se parte de una cifra elevada. El porcentaje de latinoamericanos que nunca justificaría la evasión de impuestos disminuyó del 54% en 2011 al 48% en 2015, mientras que la proporción de los que consideran que la evasión de impuestos es "justificable" aumentó del 17% al 27% (Panel A, Gráfico 1.9). La reducción de la moral tributaria se hace evidente en todas las economías de la región cubierta por el Latinobarómetro, aunque en distintos grados (Panel B, Gráfico 1.9).

Gráfico 1.9. **La moral tributaria en América Latina**

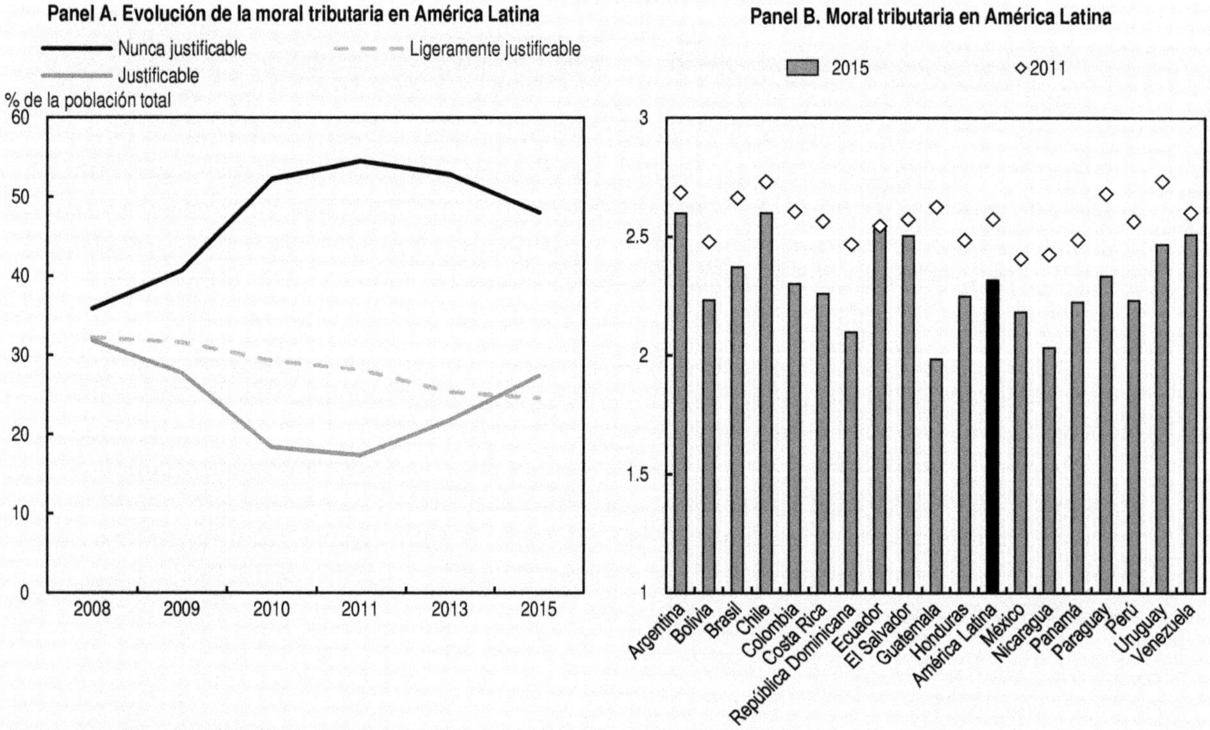

Nota: En el Panel A se calcula la moral tributaria a través de la pregunta "¿Para usted, hacer trampas con los impuestos, si tiene oportunidad, está justificado?". La escala es del 10 (nada justificable) al 1 (totalmente justificable). "Nada justificable" es la parte de los encuestados que respondieron 10; "Más o menos justificable" corresponde a la proporción de encuestados que respondieron entre 9 y 6; y "Justificable" es la parte de los encuestados que respondieron entre 1 y 5. En el Panel B, la moral tributaria se representa como el promedio de todas las observaciones disponibles para la pregunta "¿Hasta qué punto cree usted que es justificable evadir el pago de impuestos?". La escala es 1 (totalmente justificable) a 10 (nada justificable), y se ha normalizado entre 1 y 3 a efectos ilustrativos. La barra negra es el promedio regional simple que incluye todas las economías del Latinobarómetro.

Fuente: Cálculos del Centro de Desarrollo de la OCDE/Centro de Política y Administración Tributaria a partir del Latinobarómetro (2016[32]).

StatLink https://doi.org/10.1787/888934113317

Recuadro 1.3. **La moral tributaria en América Latina** *(cont.)*

Los factores institucionales y socioeconómicos están fuertemente vinculados a la moral tributaria de las personas en América Latina. El reciente trabajo de la OCDE utiliza encuestas de opinión pública (World Values Survey y Latinobarómetro) para comprender mejor lo que fomenta la moral tributaria (OCDE, 2019[28]). En América Latina, el apoyo a la democracia, los logros educativos y la confianza en el gobierno se identificaron como factores que influyen en la moral tributaria.

Los hallazgos destacan el papel del nivel educativo de los contribuyentes en la construcción de la moral tributaria. La OCDE ha estudiado las iniciativas de educación de los contribuyentes en 50 países y en 2020 se presentará una actualización del informe de 2015 *Fomentando la cultura tributaria, el cumplimiento fiscal y la ciudadanía* (OCDE/FIIAPP, 2015[33]).

Con respecto a las empresas, sin embargo, hay pocos datos para analizar su moral tributaria. OCDE (2019[28]) utiliza datos sobre la certidumbre fiscal de las empresas multinacionales[6] como *proxy*, basándose en que es menos probable que las multinacionales se comprometan con el sistema fiscal si no lo consideran seguro. En los países en desarrollo, incluida América Latina, la certidumbre fiscal parece repercutir en el comportamiento empresarial, lo que se traduce en estructuras comerciales modificadas, aumento de los costos y cambios en las decisiones de inversión. Con ciertas variaciones regionales, tanto la fiscalidad internacional como la relación entre las autoridades y las empresas son una constante preocupación para los países en desarrollo. En América Latina, el tratamiento impredecible por parte de las autoridades fiscales y la considerable burocracia es lo que más preocupa.

En general, puede considerarse una cuestión de confianza, por lo que parece probable que la confianza entre contribuyentes y autoridades sea un componente clave de la moral tributaria de las empresas. Para comprender mejor la moral tributaria de las empresas —en América Latina y en otras regiones—, la OCDE está llevando a cabo un estudio para evaluar la forma en que los miembros de la Administración fiscal perciben el cumplimiento por parte de las empresas con respecto a los principios voluntarios en materia fiscal, como el documento "BIAC Statement of Tax Best Practices for Engaging with Tax Authorities in Developing Countries" (Declaración de mejores prácticas fiscales para colaborar con las autoridades fiscales de los países en desarrollo, del Comité Consultivo Empresarial e Industrial de la OCDE [BIAC]).

La cooperación internacional tiene un rol importante para mejorar la moral tributaria al apoyar a los países de América Latina y el Caribe a fortalecer y simplificar los sistemas tributarios y, por otro lado, mejorar la eficiencia y la calidad del gasto público. Por ejemplo, EUROsociAL+ tiene programas en 13 países con acciones relacionadas a la fiscalidad internacional (Erosión de la Base Imponible y Traslado de Beneficios), lucha contra la evasión y elusión fiscal, facilitación del cumplimiento tributario e impuestos territoriales y/o la descentralización fiscal. Uno de estos ejemplos incluye la cooperación con la Dirección General Impositiva (DGI) de Uruguay para el diseño y la implementación de un nuevo modelo de atención y asistencia al contribuyente. Para esta iniciativa se han puesto a disposición de esta administración tributaria las buenas prácticas y la asesoría especializada de las administraciones tributarias de Holanda (The Netherlands Tax and Customs Administration [NTCA]) y de España (Agencia Estatal de Administración Tributaria [AEAT]).

Fuente: OCDE (2019[28]), "Tax Morale: What Drives People and Businesses to Pay Tax?", *https://doi.org/10.1787/f3d8ea10-en* y *https://eurosocial.eu/politicas-de-gobernanza-democratica/*.

Estructuras tributarias

La estructura tributaria (definida como la participación de los principales tipos de impuestos en el total de ingresos tributarios) refleja la recaudación tributaria por tipo de impuesto. Este indicador es importante para comprender los efectos socioeconómicos del sistema tributario en la región de América Latina y el Caribe.

Evolución de las estructuras tributarias

En la región de América Latina y el Caribe, los impuestos sobre bienes y servicios proporcionan la mayor parte del total de ingresos tributarios, lo que en promedio representa la mitad de los impuestos totales en 2018. Entre 1990 y 2018, el promedio de la estructura tributaria de América Latina y el Caribe se desplazó hacia el IVA y el impuesto sobre la renta y los beneficios, y se alejó de otros impuestos sobre bienes y servicios.

- La participación de los ingresos del IVA en el total de ingresos tributarios alcanzó el 27.8% en 2018, lo que corresponde a un aumento de 11.6 puntos porcentuales desde 1990. La proporción de ingresos por impuestos sobre bienes y servicios (incluidos los impuestos específicos, derechos de aduana y de importación) se redujo 19.5 puntos porcentuales durante el mismo periodo (Gráfico 1.10).
- La proporción de ingresos por el impuesto sobre la renta y los beneficios creció en 8.0 puntos porcentuales (de 19.7% a 27.8% del total de ingresos tributarios) entre 1990 y 2018.
- Las cotizaciones a la Seguridad Social, como porcentaje del total de ingresos tributarios, han aumentado 4.2 puntos en los últimos 28 años y en 2018 se situaron en 17.1%.

Gráfico 1.10. **Estructura tributaria promedio en América Latina y el Caribe, 1990 y 2018**

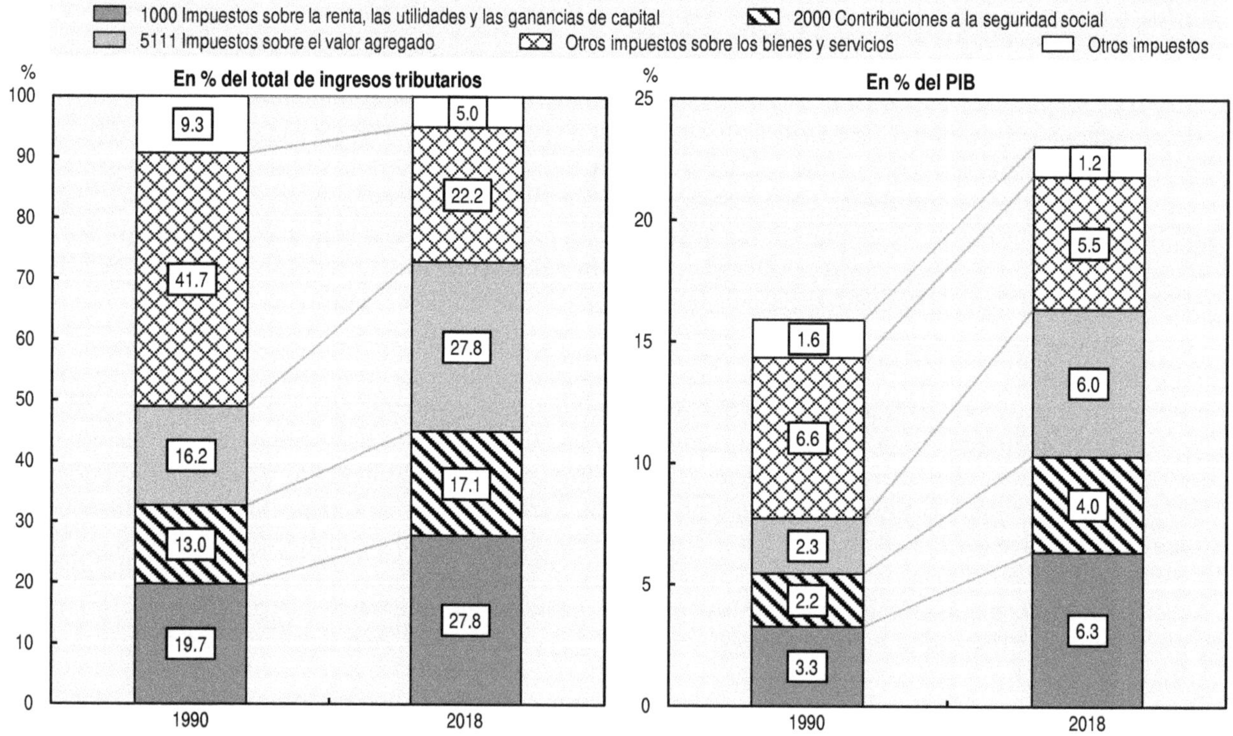

Fuente: Cálculos propios a partir de OCDE et al. (2020[2]), cuadros en el Capítulo 4.

StatLink https://doi.org/10.1787/888934113336

Desde 2007, la estructura tributaria promedio de América Latina y el Caribe se desplazó hacia una mayor proporción de ingresos del impuesto sobre la renta de personas físicas y una menor proporción del impuesto sobre la renta de sociedades, aunque los ingresos del impuesto de sociedades se mantuvieron más altos que el del impuesto sobre la renta de personas físicas en 2018 (el 15.5% del total de impuestos frente al 9.6%) (Gráfico 1.11).[7]

Gráfico 1.11. **Estructura tributaria promedio en América Latina y el Caribe, 2007 y 2018**

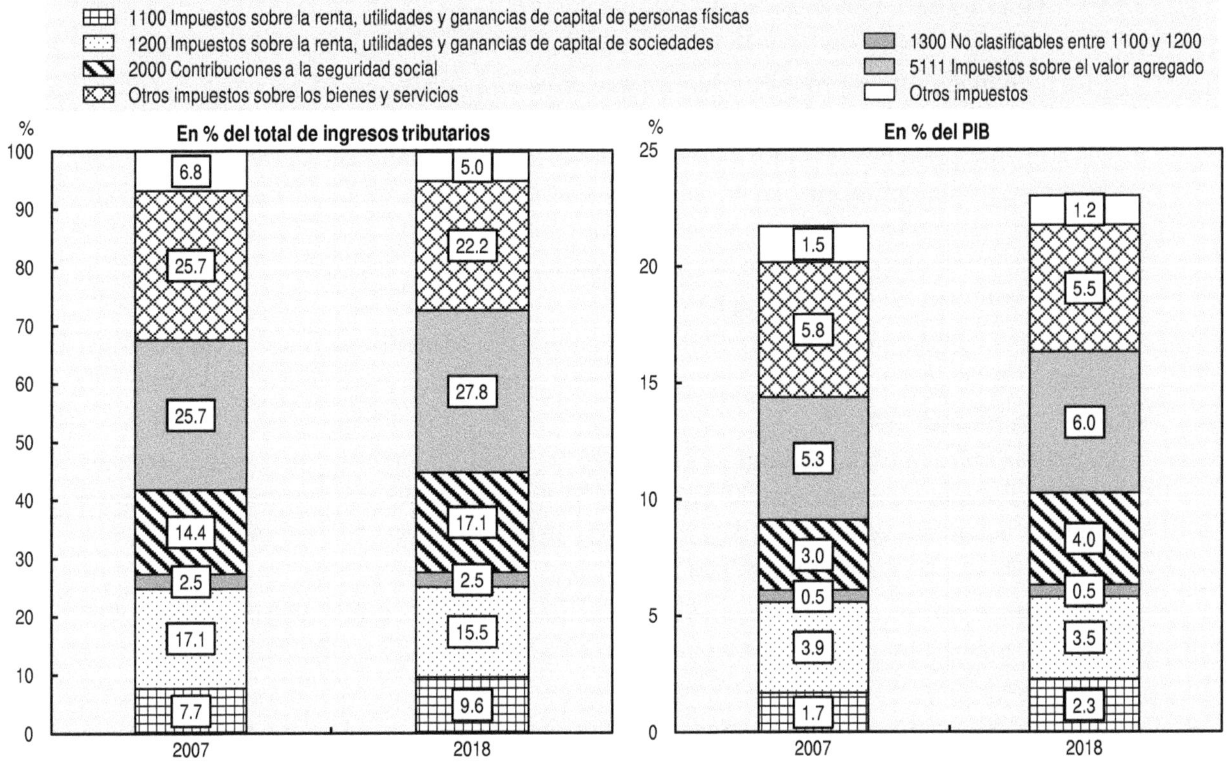

Nota: Los ingresos promedios del impuesto sobre la renta de sociedades y del impuesto sobre la renta de personas físicas como porcentaje del PIB deberían interpretarse con cautela, pues Ecuador, Nicaragua y Venezuela no se incluyen en los cálculos. El promedio de América Latina y el Caribe no incluye Venezuela, por problemas de disponibilidad de datos, y Ecuador y Nicaragua quedan excluidos porque más de un tercio de la recaudación del impuesto sobre la renta y los beneficios no puede atribuirse a las categorías de renta de sociedades (1200) o renta de personas físicas (1100).

Fuente: Cálculos propios a partir de OCDE et al. (2020[2]), "Revenue Statistics in Latin America: Comparative tables", *OECD Tax Statistics* (base de datos), *http://dx.doi.org/10.1787/data-00641-en.*

StatLink *https://doi.org/10.1787/888934113355*

La proporción en los ingresos del impuesto sobre la renta de personas físicas creció entre 2007 y 2018, en parte debido al aumento de los ingresos personales. Sin embargo, el promedio sigue siendo bajo en América Latina y el Caribe, a pesar de las reformas implementadas por algunos países para ampliar su base imponible. Después de la crisis financiera mundial varios países implementaron tipos fijos sobre los rendimientos de capital, que anteriormente eran exentos, e introdujeron tipos progresivos para los ingresos derivados del trabajo (CEPAL, 2013[23]). Sin embargo, son relativamente pocos los contribuyentes con obligaciones tributarias, dada la concentración de personas con bajos ingresos: en 2013 solo el 10% de la población de América Latina constaba como contribuyente tributario registrado (BID, 2013[15]).

Hay otros factores que siguen limitando los ingresos del impuesto sobre la renta de personas físicas; entre otros, la limitada base imponible, comprendida sobre todo de salarios (las rentas del capital cuentan con privilegios), y los altos niveles de evasión (Barreix, Benitez y Pecho, 2017[24]; CEPAL, 2013[23]). BID (2013[15]). Se estima que "alrededor de la mitad del potencial de recaudación del impuesto se pierde a través de la evasión" en los países de América Latina. A consecuencia de ello, el sistema tributario de América Latina y el Caribe tiene un efecto limitado en la desigualdad y es menos eficaz que el de los países de la OCDE para la redistribución de ingresos (Hanni, Martner y Podestá, 2017[38]). La reducción del índice de Gini (indicador del nivel de desigualdad[8]), después de impuestos directos y transferencias en efectivo y en especie, se sitúa en 2.2 puntos porcentuales en América Latina, cuando en la OCDE esa cifra es de 16 puntos porcentuales (OCDE et al., 2019[1]).

La proporción que representan las cotizaciones a la Seguridad Social con respecto al total de ingresos tributarios ha aumentado 4.2 puntos porcentuales desde 1990 y se sitúa en el 17.1% en 2018. Dos factores importantes (y opuestos) han influido en la trayectoria de las cotizaciones a la Seguridad Social en la región. El aumento en la renta per cápita ha llevado a una mayor recaudación tributaria, pero en muchos países esto se ha contrarrestado con la privatización total o parcial de la Seguridad Social, principalmente entre mediados de los noventa y 2010 (OCDE et al., 2015[34]).

En 2018 se produjeron notables diferencias en la estructura tributaria de las subregiones, en promedio. El Caribe, en particular, muestra una estructura tributaria muy diferente a la de las otras subregiones.

- En 2018, la mayor parte de los ingresos se derivó de otros impuestos sobre bienes y servicios en el Caribe, que representan en promedio el 30.3% del total de ingresos tributarios. Estos impuestos contribuyeron con el 17.2% del total de ingresos tributarios en América del Sur y con el 21.1% en Centroamérica y México.
- En contraste, América del Sur registró la mayor proporción de los ingresos por IVA en 2018 con un 31.0% en promedio, en comparación con las otras dos subregiones (27.6% en el Caribe y 24.8% en Centroamérica y México).
- Las contribuciones más bajas a la Seguridad Social se registran en el Caribe en 2018, con un 11.0% del total de ingresos tributarios en promedio, un poco más de la mitad del promedio de las demás subregiones (18.8% en Centroamérica y México, y 19.6% en América del Sur).
- Las tres subregiones generaron más ingresos con el impuesto sobre la renta de sociedades que con el impuesto sobre la renta de personas físicas.[9]

Estructura tributaria promedio en América Latina y el Caribe, y en la OCDE

En promedio, la estructura tributaria de los países de América Latina y el Caribe muestra ingresos relativamente bajos procedentes de los impuestos sobre la renta y las cotizaciones a la Seguridad Social en relación con el promedio de la OCDE (Gráfico 1.12). En particular, los países de América Latina y el Caribe, en promedio, dependen mucho de los impuestos sobre bienes y servicios, que constituyen más de la mitad del total de ingresos tributarios; esto contrasta con el promedio de las economías de la OCDE, para las que estos impuestos representan en torno a un tercio. Sin embargo, como porcentaje del PIB, en 2017, los ingresos por impuestos sobre bienes y servicios en América Latina y el Caribe y en la OCDE se mantuvieron en niveles similares, con un 11.4% y un 10.9%, respectivamente.[10] El nivel de ingresos por IVA como porcentaje del PIB también fue similar, con un 5.9% para el promedio de América Latina y el Caribe y un 6.8% para la OCDE.

En cambio, si sumamos el impuesto sobre la renta y los beneficios y las cotizaciones a la Seguridad Social, la cifra de América Latina y el Caribe es mucho menor que la de la OCDE (44.6% frente a 60.1% en 2017, en promedio). Como porcentaje del PIB, estas dos categorías representaron el 10.0% en la región de América Latina y el Caribe, menos de la mitad del nivel promedio de la OCDE (20.7%). La tendencia a la contratación privada en lo relativo a la seguridad social en muchos países de América Latina y el Caribe explica algunas de las diferencias en esta categoría.

En promedio, el impuesto sobre la renta de sociedades generó el 15.3% del total de ingresos tributarios en la región de América Latina y el Caribe, en comparación con el 9.3% en la OCDE (respectivamente, 3.4% y 3.0% como porcentaje del PIB) (Gráfico 1.12). La diferencia más notable entre las regiones se ve en los ingresos del impuesto sobre la renta de personas físicas, que contribuyó con un promedio del 23.9% del total de ingresos tributarios en la OCDE en 2017 y el 9.7% en América Latina y el Caribe. Los ingresos del impuesto sobre la renta de personas físicas equivalían en promedio al 2.2% del PIB en América Latina y el Caribe, y al 8.3% en la OCDE.

Gráfico 1.12. **Estructura tributaria en América Latina y el Caribe, y la OCDE, 2017**

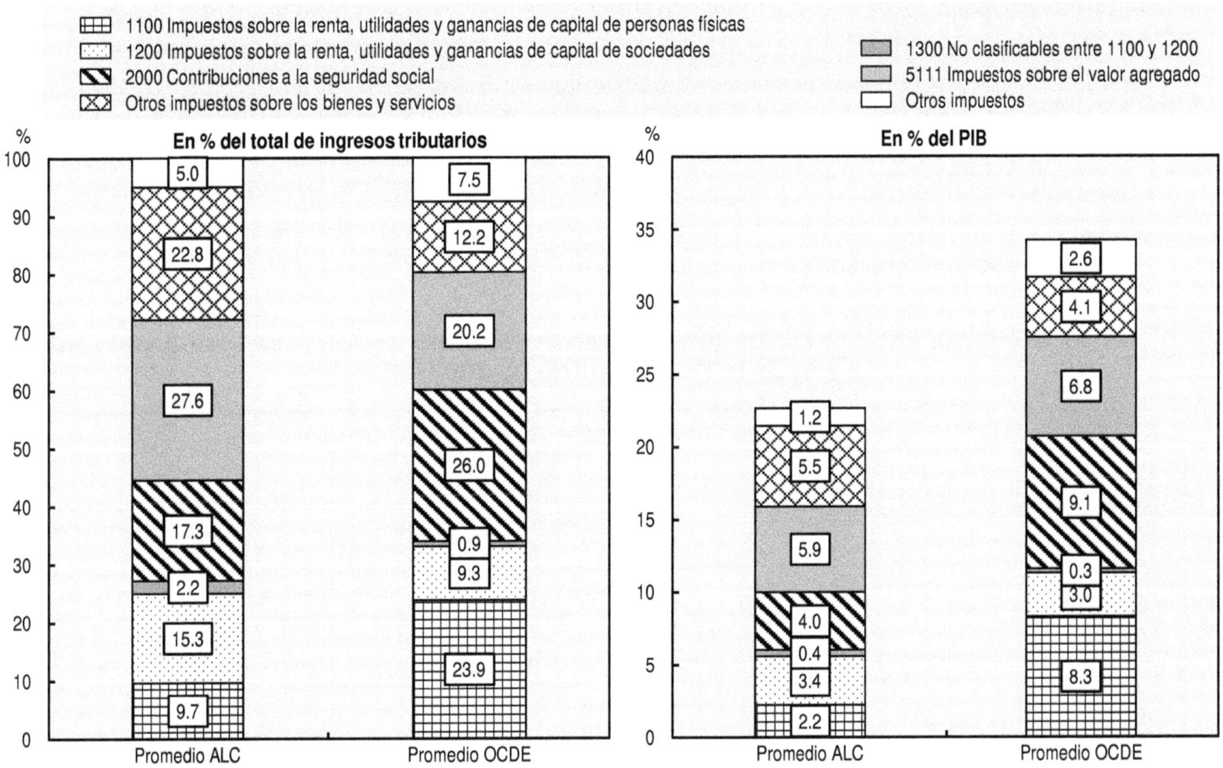

Nota: El año de comparación es 2017, ya que los datos de 2018 para el promedio de la OCDE no están disponibles. Los ingresos promedio del impuesto sobre la renta de sociedades y del impuesto sobre la renta de personas físicas como porcentaje del PIB para América Latina y el Caribe deben interpretarse con cautela, pues Ecuador, Nicaragua y Venezuela no se incluyen en los cálculos. El promedio de América Latina y el Caribe no incluye a Venezuela, debido a problemas de disponibilidad de datos, y Ecuador y Nicaragua quedan excluidos porque más de un tercio de la recaudación de impuesto sobre la renta y los beneficios no puede atribuirse a las categorías de impuesto sobre la renta de sociedades (1200) o impuesto sobre la renta de personas físicas (1100).

Fuente: Cálculos propios a partir de OCDE et al. (2020[2]), "Revenue Statistics in Latin America: Comparative tables", *OECD Tax Statistics* (base de datos), *http://dx.doi.org/10.1787/data-00641-en*.

StatLink https://doi.org/10.1787/888934113374

Los impuestos sobre bienes inmuebles y sobre las nóminas (agrupados en la categoría "otros impuestos") son, en promedio, fuentes de ingresos menos importantes en América Latina y el Caribe con respecto a la OCDE, aunque hay que tener en cuenta ciertas dificultades en la disponibilidad de datos para la categoría de impuestos sobre los bienes inmuebles.

Esta edición incluye por primera vez un indicador de convergencia entre las estructuras tributarias de dos países o de dos regiones: el índice-D. Entre 2007 y 2017 (último año disponible para el promedio de la OCDE), la estructura tributaria de América Latina y el Caribe ha ido avanzando de forma constante hacia la convergencia con la estructura tributaria de la

OCDE. Entre 2007 y 2017, la proporción de ingresos procedentes del impuesto sobre la renta de personas físicas para el promedio de América Latina y el Caribe ha ido aumentando con respecto al promedio de la OCDE (del 7.7% de total de ingresos tributarios al 9.7% en 2017, frente al 23.9% de la OCDE); con respecto a la proporción de los ingresos procedentes de otros impuestos sobre bienes y servicios, ha disminuido, acercándose al promedio de la OCDE durante el mismo período (del 25.7% del total de ingresos tributarios al 22.8%, en comparación con el 12.2% en la OCDE). Por el contrario, la proporción de los ingresos por concepto de IVA entre la región de América Latina y el Caribe y la OCDE ha ampliado sus diferencias durante el período. La proporción del promedio de América Latina y el Caribe aumentó del 25.7% del total de ingresos tributarios en 2007 al 27.6% en 2017, mientras que el promedio de la OCDE aumentó más lentamente: del 19.7% al 20.2% en el mismo período.

El índice-D se utilizó por primera vez en el informe *Estadísticas tributarias de 2018* para analizar la convergencia de las estructuras tributarias de los países de la OCDE entre 1995 y 2016 (OCDE, 2018[39]). El Gráfico 1.13 muestra el índice-D entre la estructura tributaria promedio de América Latina y el Caribe y el promedio de la OCDE. Se calcula como la suma de las diferencias absolutas entre la proporción de cada categoría tributaria en el promedio de América Latina y el Caribe y su proporción en el promedio de la OCDE. Una cifra de 0 indica paridad perfecta, en tanto que una cifra de 200 indica una disparidad absoluta.

Gráfico 1.13. **Distancia entre la estructura tributaria promedio de América Latina y el Caribe, y la de la OCDE (índice-D), 2007-17**

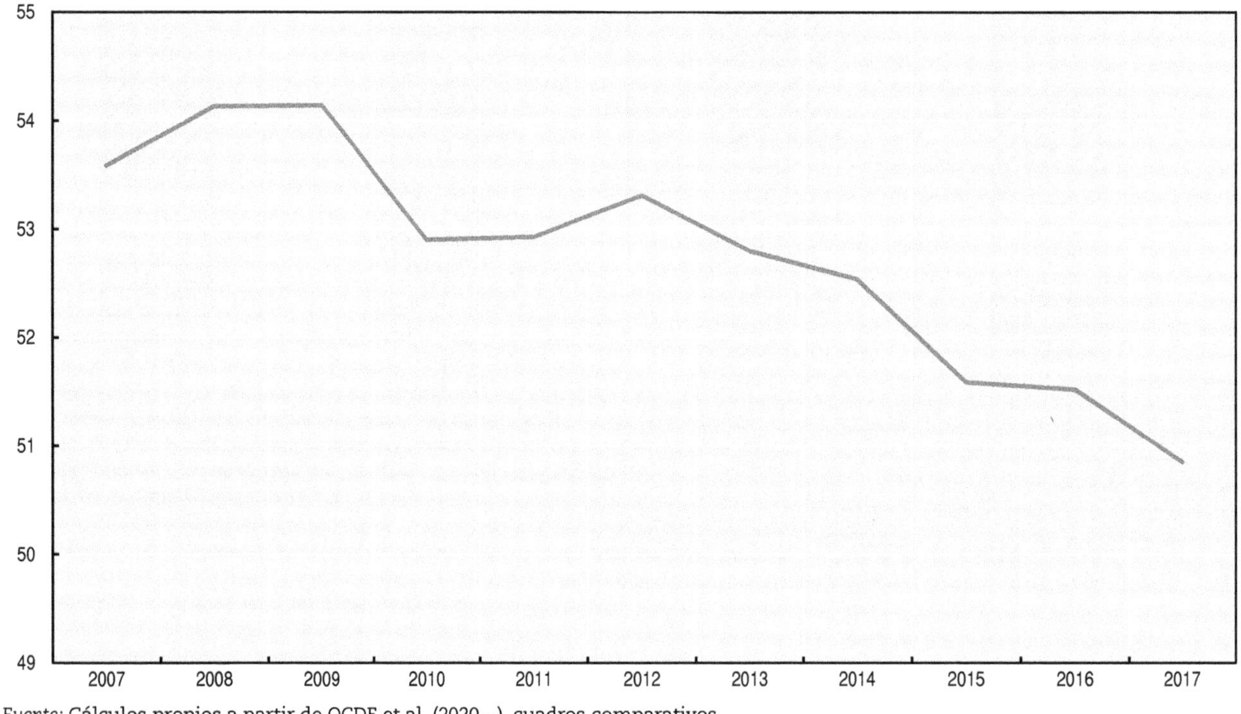

Fuente: Cálculos propios a partir de OCDE et al. (2020[2]), cuadros comparativos.

StatLink https://doi.org/10.1787/888934113393

Estructuras tributarias en países de América Latina y el Caribe

Los impuestos sobre bienes y servicios son la principal fuente de ingresos para todos los países de América Latina y el Caribe, salvo para México, Panamá, y Trinidad y Tobago. Para México y Trinidad y Tobago, los ingresos por el impuesto sobre la renta y los beneficios representaron la mayor proporción, mientras que, en Panamá, las cotizaciones a la Seguridad Social fueron la fuente más importante de ingresos tributarios (Gráfico 1.14).

La contribución del IVA al total de ingresos tributarios osciló entre el 15.6% en Panamá y el 40.3% en Perú. En Cuba no se aplica el IVA. La amplia variación entre países es, en parte, el resultado de las diferencias en el diseño del IVA, ya que las tasas, las bases impositivas y el número de exenciones del IVA difieren significativamente en la región.

Gráfico 1.14. **Estructura tributaria en países de América Latina y el Caribe, 2018**

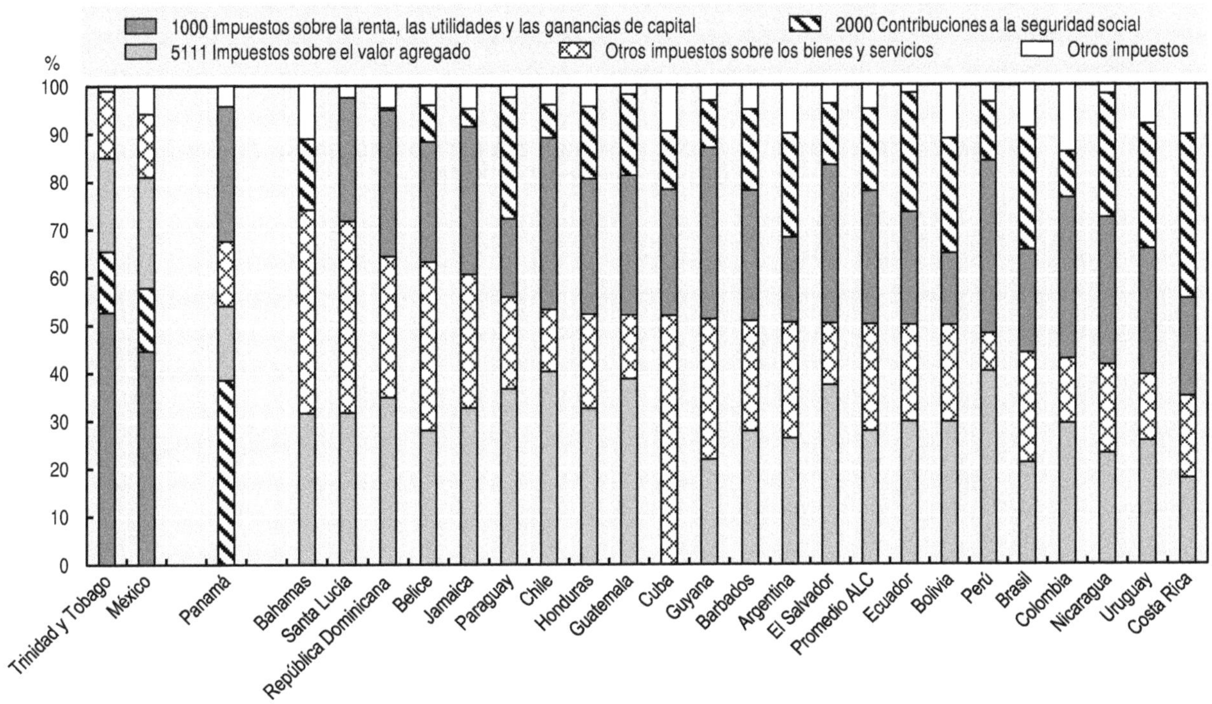

Nota: Los países se agrupan por la parte principal de los ingresos tributarios entre 1000 - Impuesto sobre la renta y los beneficios, 2000 - Cotizaciones a la Seguridad Social y 5000 - Impuestos sobre bienes y servicios. Las Bahamas no tienen impuesto sobre la renta; en Cuba no se aplica el IVA, y no se dispone de datos sobre las cotizaciones a la Seguridad Social en Santa Lucía.

Fuente: Cálculos propios a partir de OCDE et al. (2020[2]), cuadros en el Capítulo 4.

StatLink *https://doi.org/10.1787/888934113412*

En 2018, las cotizaciones a la Seguridad Social variaron ampliamente con respecto al total de ingresos tributarios: del 0.5% en la República Dominicana al 38.5% en Panamá. El nivel de estos ingresos refleja las opciones sobre cómo financiar la Seguridad Social: en los países con sistemas de Seguridad Social públicos o mixtos (incluidos Argentina, Brasil, Costa Rica, Panamá, Paraguay y Uruguay), las cotizaciones alcanzan una participación más significativa (más del 20% del total de ingresos tributarios).

Se calculó el índice-D para cada país para analizar la convergencia de la estructura tributaria de los países de América Latina y el Caribe, y la OCDE. En 2018, la estructura tributaria de Barbados era la más cercana al promedio de América Latina y el Caribe, seguida de Honduras. Los países que mostraron mayores diferencias con la estructura tributaria promedio de América Latina y el Caribe fueron Trinidad y Tobago (debido a la elevada proporción del impuesto sobre la renta), Cuba (debido a la ausencia de IVA y a la elevada proporción de otros impuestos sobre bienes y servicios) y las Bahamas (debido a la ausencia de impuesto sobre la renta).

En 2018, todos los países de América Latina y el Caribe, excepto seis, tenían estructuras tributarias más similares a la estructura promedio de América Latina y el Caribe que en el año 2000. Los cuatro países del Caribe cuyas estructuras tributarias mostraron la mayor convergencia con el promedio de América Latina y el Caribe fueron también los que más cambiaron sus estructuras tributarias: las Bahamas, Belice, Guyana y Santa Lucía. Estos aumentos en la similitud se explican por la introducción del IVA durante el período. Entre 2000 y 2018, la estructura tributaria de los países también se ha vuelto más homogénea en toda la región de América Latina y el Caribe, ya que muchos países han aumentado su contribución por IVA, por el impuesto sobre la renta de personas físicas y por las cotizaciones a la Seguridad Social, al tiempo que han disminuido la contribución de los ingresos procedentes de otros impuestos sobre bienes y servicios.

Gráfico 1.15. **Distancia con respecto a la estructura tributaria promedio de América Latina y el Caribe (índice-D), 2018**

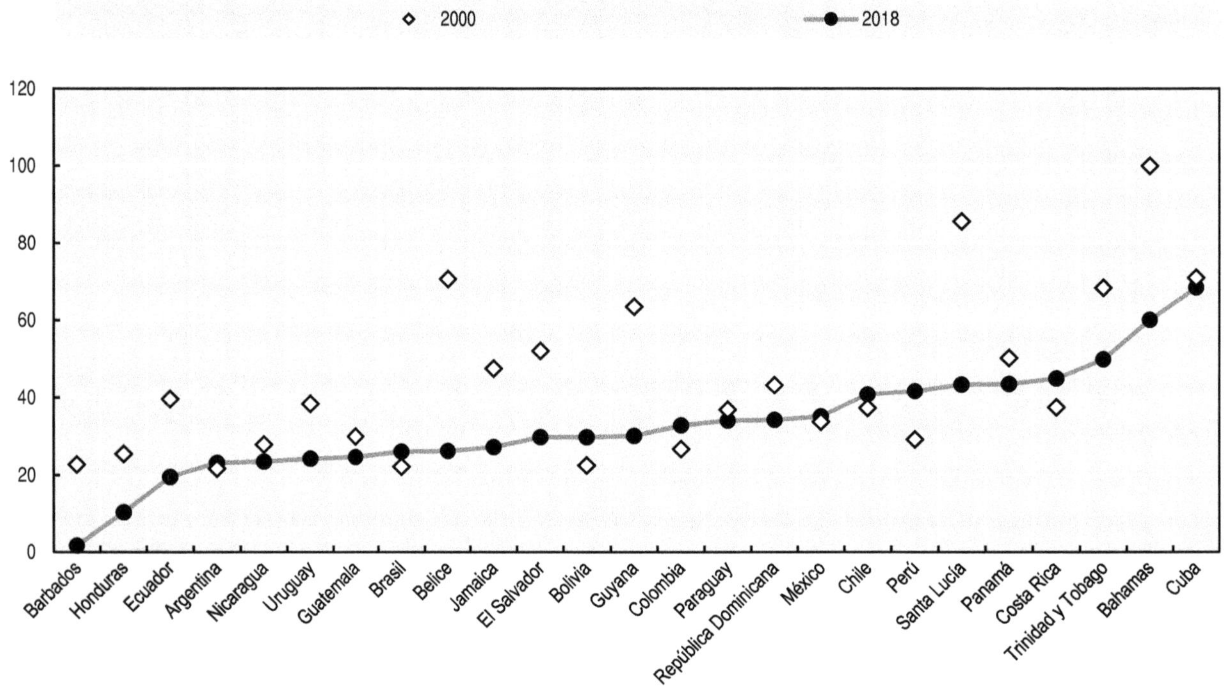

Fuente: Cálculos propios a partir de OCDE et al. (2020[2]), cuadros en el Capítulo 4.

StatLink https://doi.org/10.1787/888934113431

Ratio de recaudación de IVA

Esta sección analiza el ratio de recaudación de IVA en América Latina y el Caribe en 2018 (Gráfico 1.16). Esta relación mide la diferencia entre la recaudación observada del IVA y la recaudación teórica o potencial del IVA si este fuese aplicado a un tipo único a toda la base impositiva en un régimen de IVA "puro" (OCDE, 2018[40]). Este ratio es la relación entre los ingresos reales del IVA con respecto al producto del consumo final (neto de los ingresos del IVA) y el tipo estándar del IVA. La fórmula se muestra a continuación:

$$\frac{\text{Recaudación de IVA}}{\text{(Gasto de consumo final-Recaudación de IVA).Tipo general de IVA}}$$

Este indicador da una idea de los ingresos por IVA que se pierden a causa de las exenciones y los tipos reducidos, el fraude, la evasión y la planificación fiscal, así como por las deficiencias de las agencias tributarias. Sin embargo, este indicador debe interpretarse teniendo en cuenta las características subyacentes del sistema del IVA de cada país, ya que un ratio de recaudación de IVA elevada podría ser el resultado de efectos en cascada (por ejemplo, cuando la exención se produce en las primeras etapas de la cadena de suministro) o porque no se ha conseguido recuperar un crédito por IVA soportado. Otros factores también pueden influir en la proporción hacia arriba o hacia abajo: por ejemplo, cuando las normas sobre el lugar de imposición para el comercio internacional difieren del principio de destino o cuando no se recauda el impuesto sobre los suministros digitales entrantes. También es importante señalar que la interpretación del ratio es más difícil para los países que dependen significativamente del turismo. Esos países pueden tener un ratio elevada por razones metodológicas: las compras de los no residentes no pueden incluirse en el gasto de consumo final (el denominador) mientras que el IVA de esas compras sí se incluye en los ingresos globales del IVA (el numerador) (Keen, 2013[41]).

Los mayores ratios de recaudación de IVA de la región de América Latina y el Caribe (más de 0.80) se registraron en tres países del Caribe (las Bahamas, Belice y Santa Lucía), mientras que México y la República Dominicana presentan los ratios más bajas (0.34). En las Bahamas, Belice y Santa Lucía se observa una alta proporción de ingresos procedentes del turismo en comparación con los demás países: los ingresos del turismo internacional como porcentaje del total de las exportaciones fueron, respectivamente, el 68%, el 41% y el 74% en 2017, lo que contrasta con el promedio del 8% de América Latina y el Caribe en su conjunto (Banco Mundial, 2020[42]). Si bien esto puede explicar el elevado ratio de recaudación de IVA en esos países, también hay otros factores que han contribuido a ese elevado ratio, a saber, ciertas reformas introducidas.

Las Bahamas introdujeron el IVA en 2015, en aplicación de las buenas prácticas internacionales: un IVA de base amplia con un tipo bajo, un número limitado de exenciones y sin tipo reducido. En las Bahamas, el tipo general es del 7.5% (uno de los más bajos de América Latina y el Caribe, con un tipo general promedio del 14.6%); los ingresos se triplicaron en 2017 con respecto a 2015 (en términos nominales), en gran parte debido a los nuevos sistemas para recaudar los impuestos (Schlotterbeck, 2017[43]).

Belice obtuvo segundo ratio de recaudación de IVA más alto en el grupo seleccionado de países de América Latina y el Caribe en 2018, con un 0.89. Este buen resultado se debe, en parte, a las medidas introducidas en el ejercicio fiscal 2018/19 —unas medidas que ampliaron la base del impuesto sobre las ventas, al eliminar los artículos a tipo nulo (0%)— y también se debe a los altos niveles de cumplimiento. La fusión de los departamentos del Impuesto sobre las Ventas y el Impuesto sobre la Renta, en agosto de 2019, es probable que fortalezca aún más la gestión del IVA en Belice (FMI, 2019[10]).

En cuanto a México, son varios los elementos que pueden explicar el bajo ratio de recaudación de IVA registrado; entre otros, el alcance de las exenciones del IVA, la aplicación de un tipo nulo a numerosos bienes y servicios nacionales, un tipo reducido del 11% en zonas fronterizas y el bajo nivel de cumplimiento (OCDE, 2018[40]). Ahora bien, en enero de 2014 se implementó una reforma al IVA que aumentó el tipo reducido (11%) de las zonas fronterizas al 16%, el tipo general. La reforma también eliminó el tipo nulo para hoteles y servicios provistos a extranjeros, que ahora se gravan al tipo general, y se ajustó el régimen de las maquiladoras para reducir el riesgo de fraude. El ratio de recaudación de IVA en México se incrementó de 0.32 en 2017 a 0.34 en 2018. El ratio de recaudación de IVA puede aumentar aún más como resultado de la ampliación de la base del IVA que entrará en vigor en junio de 2020 para incluir los suministros de servicios digitales de empresas extranjeras a consumidores en México, siguiendo la recomendación de la OCDE (KPMG, 2019[44]).

La República Dominicana presenta unos de los ratios de recaudación de IVA más bajos de América Latina y el Caribe. Sus cifras de recaudación de IVA son también de las más bajas de la región de América Latina y el Caribe, con solo un 4.6% del PIB, frente al 6.0% de promedio de América Latina y el Caribe. Varios factores de diseño y administración de impuestos pueden contribuir a la recaudación de IVA (Mele et al., 2017[45]). Entre ellos se incluyen numerosas exenciones de IVA (para alimentos, salud, educación, turismo), generosas exenciones fiscales para empresas en zonas económicas libres y regiones fronterizas asociadas con un bajo cumplimiento (Schlotterbeck, 2017[43]). Mele et al. (2017[45]) estimó que los ingresos que se perdían por las exenciones del IVA ascendían al 3.3% del PIB en promedio durante el período 2008-15, una estimación mucho más alta que la de países similares. Además, la República Dominicana aplicaba un tipo de IVA relativamente alto en el 2018, un 18%, frente al 14.6% en promedio de los 24 países de América Latina y el Caribe. Mele et al. (2017[45]) explica que la evasión y el fraude del IVA en la República Dominicana se encuentran entre los más altos de la región, y esos son los principales factores que explican la brecha de eficiencia y el bajo ratio de recaudación de IVA.

Gráfico 1.16. **Ratio de recaudación de IVA en los países de América Latina y el Caribe, 2018**

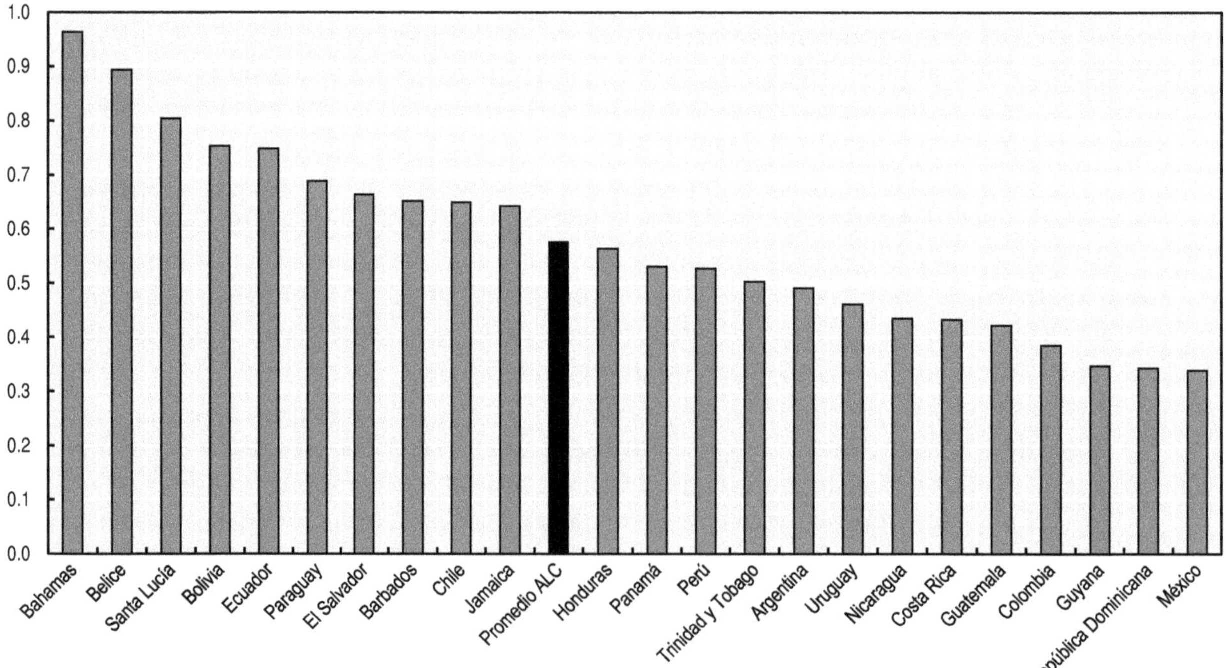

Nota: Brasil, Cuba y Venezuela no se incluyen. Brasil opera un sistema de tipos múltiples con impuestos a tipos diferentes para cada nivel subnacional; Cuba no aplicaba IVA en 2018, y no se dispone de datos sobre los ingresos tributarios de Venezuela para 2018.

Fuente: Los tipos de IVA provienen de los sitios web del Centro Interamericano de Administraciones Tributarias (CIAT), Trading Economics y Deloitte; las cifras de consumo de gastos finales, del sitio web de la División de Estadística de las Naciones Unidas, y los ingresos por IVA, de las cuadros de países del OCDE et al. (2020[2]), Capítulo 5.

StatLink https://doi.org/10.1787/888934113450

Ingresos por impuestos ambientales

A raíz del Acuerdo de París de 2016, los países se comprometieron a reducir las emisiones de carbono de sus economías para mediados de siglo, lo que implica que es preciso sustituir los combustibles fósiles como fuente de energía. Los impuestos relacionados con el medio ambiente, y los instrumentos de política basados en el precio, de forma más general, han ido ganando protagonismo en muchos países. Al incorporar una señal de precio en las decisiones de los consumidores, estos impuestos implementan el principio de que "quien contamina, paga", y llevan a empresas y hogares a plantearse el costo social de sus acciones.

Un impuesto relacionado con el medio ambiente es un impuesto cuya base es una unidad física (o un *proxy* de una unidad física) de algo que tiene un impacto pernicioso específico y comprobado en el medio ambiente, con independencia de si el impuesto está destinado a cambiar los comportamientos o si se impone por otro motivo (OCDE, 2005[46]). Los ingresos de los impuestos sobre la energía pueden aumentar a mediano plazo, si los países aumentan los tipos impositivos efectivos sobre el contenido de carbono de los combustibles (Marten y Van Dender, 2019[47]). Un estudio conjunto de la Federación Internacional de Trabajadores del Transporte (FIT) y la OCDE (OCDE/ITF, 2019[48]) muestra cómo los ingresos del transporte por carretera pueden estabilizarse a largo plazo mediante una combinación de impuestos sobre la distancia recorrida, sobre los vehículos y sobre el combustible.

Si bien los ingresos tributarios relacionados con el medio ambiente no pueden identificarse en la clasificación general de impuestos de la OCDE, sí se detallan en la lista de impuestos específicos incluidos para la mayoría de los países, dentro de la clasificación general. De este modo, se incluyen en la base de datos de *Instrumentos de políticas para el medio ambiente* (*Policy Instruments for the Environment*, PINE) de la OCDE.

Los datos sobre los ingresos tributarios relacionados con el medio ambiente se desgranan en cuatro categorías excluyentes de base imponible y en total:

- Energía: Productos energéticos (como los combustibles fósiles y la electricidad), incluidos los combustibles para el transporte (como la gasolina y el diésel). Todos los impuestos relacionados con el CO_2 se clasifican aquí.
- Transporte: Impuestos a las importaciones o ventas sobre equipos de transporte, impuestos recurrentes a la propiedad, registro o uso de vehículos motorizados en carretera y otros impuestos relacionados con el transporte. (Obsérvese que esta definición excluye los impuestos especiales sobre los combustibles de automoción.)
- Contaminación: impuestos a la emisión de dióxido de azufre (SOx) y óxido de nitrógeno (NOx); impuestos a sustancias que destruyen el ozono, como los clorofluorocarbonos (CFC), tetracloruro de carbono y clorofluorometanos (HCFC); impuestos sobre vertidos de aguas residuales; impuestos sobre los embalajes, como las bolsas de plástico, sobre la eliminación final de residuos sólidos, y otros impuestos relacionados con residuos, como baterías o neumáticos.
- Recursos: Impuestos sobre la extracción de agua, productos forestales, impuestos de caza y pesca, cánones de minería, impuestos de excavación (como arena y grava). Obsérvese que no se incluyen las tasas y cargos relacionados con el suministro de agua (OCDE, 2019[49]).

Un análisis detallado de los impuestos específicos por país para 23 países de América Latina y el Caribe demuestra que, en promedio, los ingresos por impuestos relacionados con el medio ambiente se situaban en el 1.1%[11] del PIB en 2018, un nivel más bajo que el promedio de la OCDE, que es del 2.3% del PIB (cifra estimada para 2018) (OCDE, 2019[49]). Los ingresos tributarios relacionados con el medio ambiente en 2018 variaron del 0.02% del PIB en Belice al 2.3% en Honduras (Gráfico 1.17).

Gráfico 1.17. **Ingresos tributarios relacionados con el medio ambiente por base imponible principal, 2018**

Porcentaje del PIB

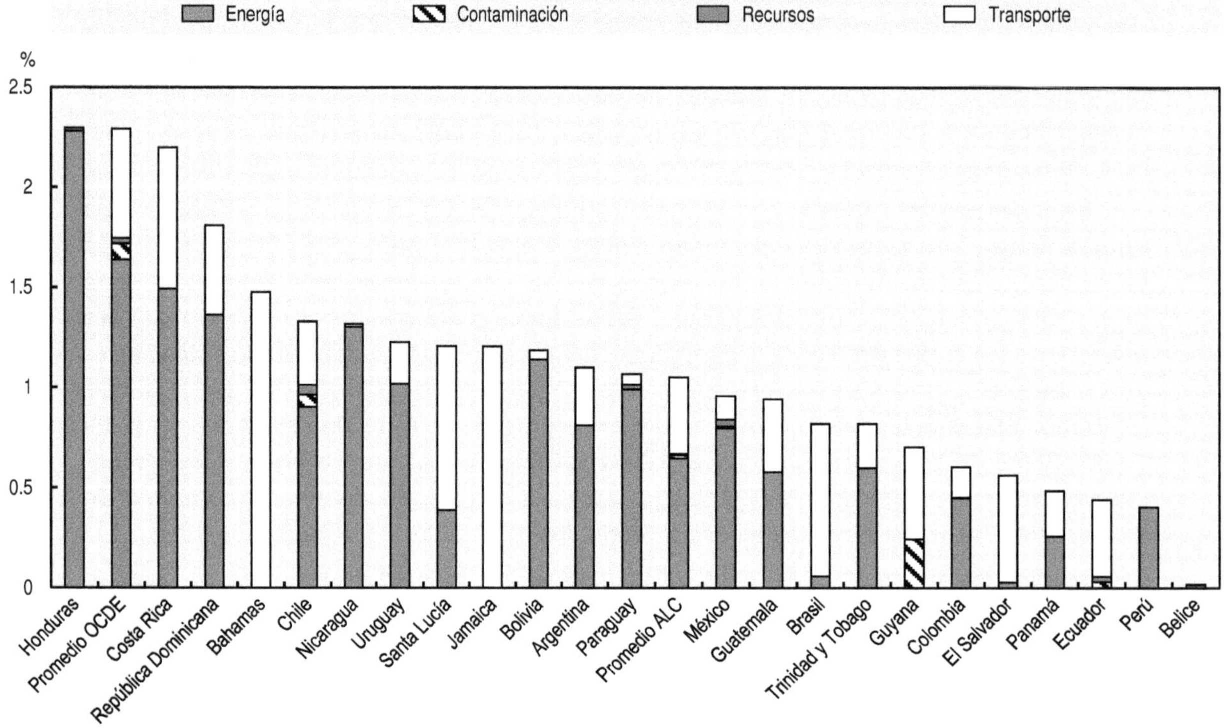

Nota: Barbados, Cuba y Venezuela están excluidos de los promedios de América Latina y el Caribe. No ha sido posible identificar los ingresos relacionados con el impuesto al medio ambiente para Barbados y Cuba, y Venezuela no se incluye por problemas de disponibilidad de datos. Las cifras correspondientes a Chile y México utilizan datos de 2017 basados en la base de datos *PINE*, que presenta datos más completos sobre los ingresos en concepto de impuestos ambientales.

Fuente: Base de datos *PINE* para Chile y México, y cálculos propios a partir de OCDE et al. (2020[2]), Capítulo 5.

StatLink *https://doi.org/10.1787/888934113469*

En 2018, los ingresos provenientes de la imposición energética (más comúnmente, sobre el diésel y la gasolina) representaron la mayor proporción de ingresos tributarios relacionados con el medio ambiente en la región de América Latina y el Caribe. Los ingresos procedentes de productos relacionados con la energía ascendieron al 0.6% del PIB en promedio en 2018, y representaron en torno al 60% de los ingresos tributarios relacionados con el medio ambiente. La recaudación por impuestos sobre los vehículos motorizados y servicios de transporte asciende al 0.4% del PIB y representa la mayor parte del resto (35%) de los ingresos tributarios relacionados con el medio ambiente. Los ingresos tributarios recaudados en otras bases relacionadas con el medio ambiente fueron poco significativos (un 2% en promedio). En la OCDE, los ingresos por productos energéticos representan un poco más del 70% de los ingresos totales, mientras que los impuestos sobre los vehículos motorizados y el transporte representaron alrededor de un cuarto de los ingresos totales (OCDE, 2019[49]).

Los impuestos sobre la energía representaron la mayor parte de los ingresos tributarios relacionados con el medio ambiente en todos los países de América Latina y el Caribe, excepto en siete. En esos siete países (Bahamas, Brasil, Ecuador, El Salvador, Guyana, Jamaica y Santa Lucía) los ingresos por vehículos motorizados y servicios de transporte fueron la fuente principal (Gráfico 1.17).

En 2018, los impuestos sobre la energía se recaudaron sobre todo mediante impuestos especiales. En cambio, los ingresos en concepto de impuestos sobre vehículos motorizados y servicios de transporte se obtuvieron de tres tipos diferentes de impuestos: en torno a la mitad procedía de los impuestos sobre el uso y la propiedad de los vehículos; una cuarta parte, de los impuestos sobre servicios específicos (principalmente el impuesto de viaje o de salida), y otra cuarta parte, de los impuestos especiales sobre los vehículos.

Si bien el uso de los impuestos para abordar las cuestiones ambientales está bien asentado en muchos países, los países de América Latina han sido lentos al aplicar impuestos relacionados con el medio ambiente. Si bien han introducido impuestos sobre los combustibles (principalmente con fines recaudatorios, no con fines ambientales), muchos países de América Latina y el Caribe también otorgan subsidios a los productos energéticos para mitigar el impacto de los altos y volátiles precios del petróleo, controlar la inflación, fomentar la competitividad y proteger a los sectores más pobres de la población (Lorenzo, 2016[50]). Estos subsidios contrarrestan, en gran medida, el efecto de los impuestos ambientales (Vera, 2019[51]).

Más allá de los impuestos sobre el combustible y la matriculación o el uso de vehículos, los impuestos ambientales todavía están poco desarrollados en la región de América Latina y el Caribe. Esto puede explicarse no solo por la dependencia de las economías de los recursos naturales, sino también por la elevada proporción de la población con ingresos bajos. En los países de América Latina y el Caribe, son muchas las personas que viven en la pobreza, y la desigualdad de ingresos es elevada. Los impuestos ambientales y, en particular, los impuestos sobre los combustibles tienden a ser regresivos: los hogares con menos ingresos suelen tener una mayor proporción de consumo de combustible en relación con sus ingresos que los hogares con más ingresos.

A pesar de la lentitud con que se avanza en la aplicación de los impuestos para abordar las cuestiones ambientales, algunos países de América Latina y el Caribe han introducido reformas fiscales importantes. Es el caso de Chile, México y, más recientemente, Colombia:

- En Chile se aprobó una importante reforma tributaria que incluye nuevos impuestos relacionados con el medio ambiente en 2014 (OCDE/CEPAL, 2016[52]). Estos incluyen un impuesto sobre las compras de vehículos motorizados, que se introdujo en 2015 y generó ingresos equivalentes al 0.03% del PIB en 2018. Las tasas impositivas de vehículos motorizados dependen de la eficiencia energética y las emisiones. Además, a finales de 2017, se introdujo un impuesto sobre las fuentes fijas contaminantes que recaudó ingresos por valor del 0.06% del PIB en 2018. Este impuesto se aplica a las emisiones de partículas, óxidos de nitrógeno, dióxido de azufre y dióxido de carbono producidos por establecimientos cuyas calderas o turbinas tienen una capacidad de 50 megavatios térmicos o más.
- México introdujo un impuesto sobre el carbono en 2014, aplicado a la venta e importación de combustibles fósiles, de acuerdo con su contenido de carbono. Esto ha aumentado la proporción de emisiones gravadas, aunque los precios siguen siendo relativamente bajos en comparación con otros países de la OCDE y no reflejan los costos totales asociados con el carbono en estos combustibles (Arlinghaus y van Dender, 2017[53]). Con todo, el impuesto al carbono aumentó significativamente los ingresos tributarios entre 2014 y 2015, y generó ingresos equivalentes al 1.2% del PIB en 2015 (OCDE, 2019[49]). México incrementó aún más los tipos impositivos sobre diferentes combustibles fósiles en 2016.

- En 2016, Colombia introdujo un impuesto al carbono y un impuesto al consumo para las bolsas de plástico. El impuesto al carbono se aplica a los combustibles fósiles (específicamente, gasolina, queroseno, combustible para aviones, combustible diésel y fuelóleo) dependiendo de la cantidad de carbono. Se aplica un precio de USD 5 por cada tonelada de dióxido de carbono producida por la combustión de combustibles fósiles. Los ingresos se asignan a un fondo especial para abordar asuntos ambientales específicos (erosión costera, conservación de las fuentes de agua y protección del ecosistema) (Monge, $2018_{[54]}$). En 2018, este impuesto generó ingresos por valor del 0.03% del PIB.

El documento *Effective Carbon Rates* (OCDE, $2018_{[55]}$) ofrece una descripción general de los precios del carbono en todas las emisiones relacionadas con la energía en 42 países de la OCDE y el G-20 (entre otros, Argentina, Brasil, Chile y México). Para el mismo conjunto de países, el documento *Taxing Energy Use* (OCDE, $2019_{[56]}$) ofrece información detallada sobre los tipos de los impuestos, el uso de la energía y la base a la que se aplican.

Impuestos por nivel de gobierno

En países de América Latina y el Caribe, los impuestos se recaudan sobre todo a través de la Administración central o las agencias federales; los gobiernos subnacionales dependen más de un sistema de transferencias de niveles superiores a niveles inferiores de gobierno para su financiamiento que en el caso de los países de la OCDE. Para los países en los cuales se dispone de datos de recaudación subnacional en América Latina y el Caribe, los ingresos tributarios de la Administración central constituyen dos tercios o más de toda la recaudación. El monto correspondiente en países de la OCDE es del 60%. Brasil es una notable excepción: la Administración central recaudó un 43.2% de todos los ingresos en 2017[12] (Cuadro 1.1).

Existen dos elementos estadísticos que deben tenerse en cuenta al comparar la atribución de la recaudación para los países de América Latina y el Caribe y la de países miembros de la OCDE. Primero, los ingresos tributarios de ambos grupos se han atribuido a diferentes niveles de gobierno de acuerdo con las guías del Sistema de Cuentas Nacionales (SCN) de 2008.[13] Segundo, los promedios en América Latina y el Caribe pueden verse afectados por la falta de datos a nivel subnacional en algunos países.

Para los 19 países de América Latina y el Caribe para los que se dispone de datos en 2017, el porcentaje total de ingresos tributarios recaudados por los gobiernos subnacionales es inferior al 8%, salvo en el caso de Argentina, Brasil y Colombia. En Brasil, los estados y los municipios recaudan alrededor del 31% del total de ingresos tributarios, lo que indica un alto grado de descentralización tributaria. Una gran parte del IVA (*imposto sobre operações relativas à circulação de mercadorias e prestação de serviços de transporte interestadual e intermunicipal e de comunicação*, ICMS) se recauda a través de los estados. La recaudación subnacional en Argentina y Colombia representa más del 15% del total de ingresos tributarios. Argentina presenta una sustancial recaudación a nivel provincial, que se explica en gran parte por su impuesto sobre los ingresos brutos. Entre 2000 y 2017, la proporción de ingresos tributarios recaudada a nivel subnacional disminuyó en seis países y aumentó en 13. La mayor caída se registró en Honduras (3.5% del total de ingresos tributarios) y el mayor incremento se observó en Paraguay (3.6% del total de ingresos tributarios).

Estas cifras reflejan que, en los países de América Latina y el Caribe, los gobiernos subnacionales no suelen tener muchos impuestos bajo su titularidad. Los impuestos que con mayor frecuencia se asignan a los gobiernos subnacionales son los impuestos sobre la propiedad, los impuestos sobre vehículos motorizados, los impuestos sobre servicios específicos y las tasas municipales. El potencial de generación de ingresos de estos impuestos es mucho más limitado que el de los impuestos bajo la titularidad del gobierno central, tales como el IVA o el impuesto sobre la renta. En 2017, toda la recaudación subnacional de Belice, Guatemala y Jamaica, y más del 50% de la recaudación subnacional de Perú y Uruguay provenía de los impuestos sobre la propiedad (Gráfico 1.18). En Ecuador y Paraguay, alrededor del 90% de los ingresos tributarios procedía de los impuestos sobre la propiedad y los impuestos sobre bienes y servicios, distribuidos casi por igual. Todos los demás países dependen básicamente de la recaudación de impuestos sobre bienes y servicios. México es el único país que utiliza bases tributarias diferentes a las descritas anteriormente. En 2017, el 42% de la recaudación subnacional de México procedía de los impuestos retenidos en la nómina. En los países miembros de la OCDE, las entidades subnacionales suelen tener impuestos con bases mucho más amplias. Una proporción significativa de la recaudación de los gobiernos subnacionales en los países de la OCDE proviene de los impuestos sobre la renta y los beneficios (más de un tercio de la recaudación promedio total a nivel subnacional).

Gráfico 1.18. **Estructura tributaria de los ingresos tributarios subnacionales, 2017**

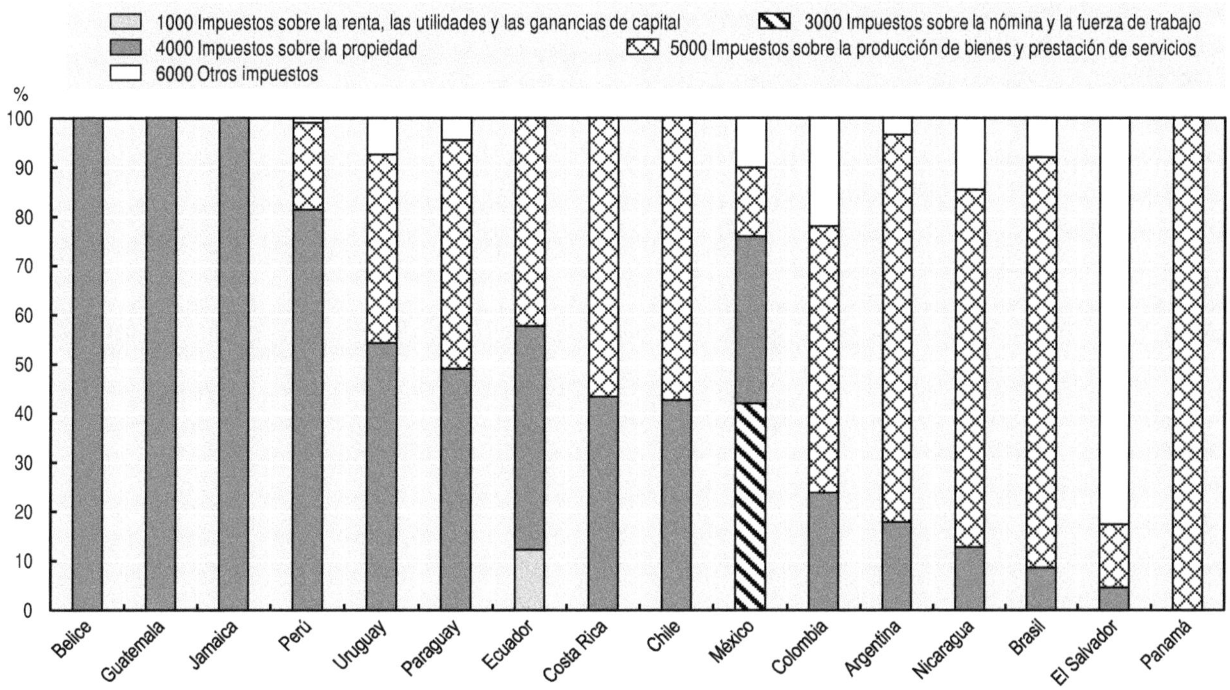

Nota: El año de comparación es 2017, ya que los datos de 2018 para México no están disponibles. No se incluyen las Bahamas, Barbados, Bolivia, Cuba, Guyana, Honduras, la República Dominicana, Santa Lucía, Trinidad y Tobago y Venezuela, ya que no se dispone de datos sobre los ingresos tributarios subnacionales ni del desglose de los datos sobre los ingresos tributarios subnacionales por tipo principal de categoría tributaria. Las cifras tampoco incluyen los ingresos de la Administración local de Argentina (aunque sí se incluyen los ingresos de las provincias).

Fuente: Cálculos propios a partir de OCDE et al. (2020[2]), cuadros en el Capítulo 6.

StatLink https://doi.org/10.1787/888934113488

Los bajos niveles de recaudación subnacional en América Latina y el Caribe también pueden deberse a una capacidad administrativa y técnica inadecuada. Los impuestos sobre la propiedad, fuente habitual de ingresos subnacionales, requieren sofisticados sistemas y datos, por lo que su recaudación es costosa. Además, numerosos países carecen de registros de la propiedad apropiados y, de haberlos, raramente se actualizan (Canavire-Bacarreza, Martínez-Vázquez y Sepúlveda, 2012[57]). A consecuencia de ello, las autoridades tributarias no tienen un acceso adecuado a tasaciones precisas de terrenos y edificios, y las agencias inmobiliarias se muestran reticentes a compartir esa información. Los impuestos sobre la propiedad también se ven afectados por la alta presencia de la economía informal: los edificios muchas veces se construyen sin los debidos permisos; muchas propiedades no se inscriben en el registro y los precios de venta de algunos bienes inmuebles se falsifican. El impuesto sobre la propiedad es uno de los impuestos más controvertidos a ojos de la ciudadanía y conlleva altos costos políticos, por lo que las administraciones locales rara vez están dispuestas a invertir los recursos necesarios para recaudar este impuesto.

Cuadro 1.1. **Atribución de los ingresos tributarios a los subsectores de la Administración central[1]**

Porcentaje del total de ingresos tributarios

	Gobierno central			Gobierno estatal o regional			Gobierno local			Fondos de seguridad social		
	1995	2000	2017	1995	2000	2017	1995	2000	2017	1995	2000	2017
Países federales												
Argentina	59.0	66.4	59.0	17.5	17.8	18.1	..	..	..	23.4	15.8	22.9
Brasil	44.7	47.8	43.2	26.6	25.1	24.8	3.7	3.4	5.8	25.0	23.7	26.3
México	73.9	78.3	81.1	2.8	2.7	4.1	1.5	1.0	1.6	21.8	18.0	13.3
Venezuela	94.6	94.6	..	..	..	..	..	..	..	5.4	5.4	..
País régional												
Colombia[2]	63.2	68.7	74.8	5.5	5.6	5.1	8.6	9.4	12.4	22.7	16.3	7.6
Países unitarios												
Bahamas	89.1	88.1	85.2				..	..	..	10.9	11.9	14.8
Barbados	85.6	84.4	82.5				..	..	..	14.4	15.6	17.5
Belice	93.2	93.5	91.6				0.5	0.7	0.6	6.3	5.8	7.8
Bolivia	94.3	75.7	70.7				5.7	5.5	5.6	0.0	18.8	23.7
Chile	89.9	87.8	86.3				6.5	7.9	7.8	3.6	4.4	5.9
Costa Rica	65.5	63.3	58.5				1.6	1.9	3.0	33.0	34.8	38.5
Cuba[3]	..	..	..				..	..	..	11.3	10.4	12.5
República Dominicana	99.3	99.0	99.5				..	..	..	0.7	1.0	0.5
Ecuador	70.5	87.7	71.1				4.0	1.6	2.8	25.5	10.7	26.1
El Salvador	80.9	80.5	84.8				..	..	2.0	19.1	19.5	13.2
Guatemala	83.3	83.3	82.2				0.7	0.9	1.0	16.1	15.8	16.7
Guyana	92.6	88.6	89.5				..	..	0.1	7.4	11.4	10.4
Honduras	86.1	85.3	83.2				4.4	5.2	1.8	9.5	9.4	15.0
Jamaica	100.0	99.3	94.6				..	0.7	1.6	0.0	0.0	3.7
Nicaragua	80.4	72.5	69.4				4.6	9.5	6.4	15.0	18.0	24.2
Panamá	62.8	59.6	59.9				..	2.2	1.7	37.2	38.2	38.4
Paraguay	100.0	74.4	70.2				..	..	3.6	0.0	25.6	26.2
Perú	88.7	86.5	84.4				..	1.6	2.8	11.3	11.9	12.9
Santa Lucía[4]	100.0	100.0	100.0				..	..	..	..	..	..
Trinidad y Tobago	96.8	93.6	85.2				..	..	..	3.2	6.4	14.8
Uruguay	61.7	63.6	67.9				8.8	8.9	5.5	29.5	27.5	26.5

Notas:

1. Las cifras no tienen en cuenta los ingresos de la Administración local de Argentina (aunque sí se incluyen los ingresos de las provincias), las Bahamas, Barbados, Cuba, la República Dominicana, Santa Lucía, Trinidad y Tobago, y Venezuela, puesto que los datos no se encuentran disponibles. Se dispone de datos sobre los ingresos de la Administración local desde 1991 para Nicaragua, desde 1994 para Bolivia, desde 1995 para Guatemala, desde 1998 para Jamaica, desde 1999 para Panamá, desde 2000 para Perú, desde 2002 para El Salvador y Guyana, desde 2006 para Paraguay, y desde 1990 para los demás países.
2. Colombia constitucionalmente es un país unitario con una alta autonomía de sus territorios.
3. Los datos correspondientes a los subsectores de la Administración central de Cuba solo están disponibles entre 2002 y 2012.
4. No se dispone de datos sobre las cotizaciones a la Seguridad Social en Santa Lucía.

Fuente: OCDE et al. (2020), Cuadro 4.11.

StatLink https://doi.org/10.1787/888934113526

Notas

1. Esta cifra es provisional y, para calcularla, se ha aplicado el porcentaje de cambio promedio no ponderado para 2018 de los 34 países que proporcionaron datos para ese año al promedio de la proporción entre la recaudación tributaria y el PIB general de 2017.
2. El promedio del Caribe incluye siete países (Bahamas, Barbados, Belice, Guyana, Jamaica, Santa Lucía, y Trinidad y Tobago), Centroamérica y México, nueve países (Costa Rica, Cuba, El Salvador, Guatemala, Honduras, México, Nicaragua, Panamá y República Dominicana), y América del Sur, nueve países (Argentina, Bolivia, Brasil, Chile, Colombia, Ecuador, Paraguay, Perú y Uruguay).
3. Esto incluye a Argentina, Brasil, Bolivia, Chile, Colombia, Costa Rica, Ecuador, Honduras, México, Nicaragua, Panamá y Perú.
4. Estas cifras incluyen las tasas de impuesto sobre la renta de empresas de 22 países de América Latina y el Caribe y excluyen a Cuba, Guyana, Trinidad y Tobago y Venezuela debido a la indisponibilidad de datos. Los datos proceden principalmente de KPMG (*https://s3.amazonaws.com/kpmg-global/tax-rates-tool/index_Corporate.html*), el CIAT (*https://www.ciat.org/tax-rates-in-latin-america/?lang=en*) y se completan para Belice con los datos que se encuentran en *https://www.multpl.com/belize-corporate-tax-rate/table/by-year* y otras fuentes públicas.
5. El IVA se introdujo en Jamaica en 1991; en 1997, en Barbados; en 2006, en Belice (impuesto general a las ventas); en 2007, en Guyana, en 2012, en Santa Lucía y en 2014, en las Bahamas.
6. El análisis se basa en una única fuente de datos —la encuesta a empresas de la OCDE de 2016—, que recogió las opiniones de altos cargos de más de 500 empresas, casi todas multinacionales, sobre la certidumbre fiscal de 82 países en desarrollo.
7. En torno al 2.5% del total de ingresos tributarios son ingresos del impuesto sobre la renta y los beneficios que no se pueden asignar entre el impuesto a las sociedades y a las personas físicas.
8. El índice de Gini es un indicador que se usa para medir la desigualdad. Mide la dispersión estadística utilizada para representar la distribución de los ingresos o la riqueza de los residentes de un país.
9. Para el Caribe, el promedio de los ingresos derivados del impuesto sobre la renta y los beneficios oculta una gran heterogeneidad. Las Bahamas no tienen impuesto sobre la renta, y Trinidad y Tobago recauda la mitad de sus ingresos tributarios por esa vía.
10. El año de comparación es 2017, ya que los datos de 2018 para el promedio de la OCDE no están disponibles.
11. Promedio no ponderado de los 36 países de la OCDE.
12. El año de comparación es 2017, ya que los datos de 2018 para México no están disponibles.
13. Esto implica que los ingresos suelen atribuirse a la Administración que tiene la titularidad del impuesto o que puede imponer o modificar el tipo impositivo. Esto tiene implicaciones en situaciones en que un nivel del gobierno recauda el impuesto y transfiere lo recaudado parcial o totalmente a otros niveles de gobierno. Algunos ejemplos de este tipo de mecanismo son la legislación de coparticipación en Argentina y las participaciones federales en México (regida por la Ley de Coordinación Fiscal), y los Fondos de Participación de Brasil (definidos en el artículo 159 de la Constitución).

Referencias

Arlinghaus, J. y K. van Dender (2017), "The environmental tax and subsidy reform in Mexico", *OECD Taxation Working Papers No. 31*, OECD Publishing, Paris, *https://dx.doi.org/10.1787/a9204f40-en*. [53]

Banco Mundial (2020), "International tourism, receipts (% of total exports)", *World Development Indicators (base de datos)*, *https://data.worldbank.org/indicator/ST.INT.RCPT.XP.ZS*. [42]

Barbados Revenue Authority (2018), "Budgetary Proposals 2018: Shared Economy Levy", *https://bra.gov.bb/Download.ashx?file=Attachments%2fPolicy+Note+-+Shared+Economy+Levy+2019_02.pdf&id=163&name=Policy+Note+%E2%80%93+Shared+Economy+Levy+*. [18]

Barreix, A., J. Benitez y M. Pecho (2017), "Revisiting personal income tax in Latin America: Evolution and impact", *OECD Development Centre Working Papers No. 338*, OECD Publishing, Paris, *https://doi.org/10.1787/16d42b4a-en*. [24]

BID (2019), *Informe Macroeconómico de América Latina y el Caribe 2019: Construir oportunidades para crecer en un mundo desafiante*, Banco Interamericano de Desarrollo, *http://dx.doi.org/10.18235/0001633*. [5]

BID (2013), *More than Revenue: Taxation as a Development Tool*, Banco Interamericano de Desarrollo, *https://publications.iadb.org/en/publication/more-revenue-taxation-development-tool-executive-summary*. [15]

Canavire-Bacarreza, G., J. Martínez-Vázquez y C. Sepúlveda (2012), "Sub-national revenue mobilization in Peru", *IDB Working Paper Series No. 299*, Banco Interamericano de Desarrollo, *https://publications.iadb.org/en/sub-national-revenue-mobilization-peru*. [57]

CEPAL (2019), *Balance Preliminar de las Economías de América Latina y el Caribe 2018*, Comisión Económica para América Latina y el Caribe, *https://doi.org/10.18356/7867aa0a-es*. [3]

CEPAL (2019), *Estudio Económico de América Latina y el Caribe 2019: Argentina*, Comisión Económica para América Latina y el Caribe, *https://repositorio.cepal.org/bitstream/handle/11362/44674/218/EEE2019_Argentina_es.pdf*. [12]

CEPAL (2019), *Estudio Económico de América Latina y el Caribe 2019: Belice*, Comisión Económica para América Latina y el Caribe, *https://repositorio.cepal.org/bitstream/handle/11362/44674/234/EEE2019_Belice_es.pdf*. [11]

CEPAL (2018), *Panorama Fiscal de América Latina y el Caribe 2018*, Comisión Económica para América Latina y el Caribe, *https://www.cepal.org/es/publicaciones/43405-panorama-fiscal-america-latina-caribe-2018-desafios-politicas-publicas-marco-la*. [14]

CEPAL (2013), *Panorama fiscal de América Latina y el Caribe 2013*, Comisión Económica para América Latina y el Caribe, *https://www.cepal.org/es/publicaciones/3097-panorama-fiscal-america-latina-caribe-2013-reformas-tributarias-renovacion-pacto*. [16]

CEPAL (2013), *Política tributaria en América Latina: Agenda para una segunda generación de reformas*, Comisión Económica para América Latina y el Caribe, *https://repositorio.cepal.org//handle/11362/5368*. [23]

CIAT (2017), *La Administración Tributaria de Guyana avanza en áreas clave*, Centro Interamericano de Administraciones Tributarias, *https://www.ciat.org/como-resultado-del-apoyo-brindado-por-el-programa-de-cooperacion-ciat-seco-la-administracion-tributaria-de-guyana-avanza-en-areas-clave/*. [7]

EY (2019), *Colombia enacts tax reform for 2019*, Ernst & Young, *https://taxinsights.ey.com/archive/archive-news/colombia-enacts-tax-reform-for-2019.aspx*. [20]

EY (2018), *Argentine tax reform: A review of key provisions*, Ernst & Young, *https://www.ey.com/gl/en/services/tax/international-tax/alert--argentine-tax-reform---a-review-of-key-provisions*. [19]

FMI (2019), "Belize: 2019 Article IV Consultation", *Country Report No. 19/364*, Fondo Monetario Internacional, *https://www.imf.org/en/Publications/CR/Issues/2019/12/09/Belize-2019-Article-IV-Consultation-Press-Release-Staff-Report-and-Statement-by-the-48866*. [10]

FMI (2019), *IMF executive board concludes 2019 Article IV consultation with Guyana*, Fondo Monetario Internacional, *https://www.imf.org/en/News/Articles/2019/09/16/pr19332-guyana-imf-executive-board-concludes-2019-article-iv-consultation*. [8]

FMI (2019), *World Economic Outlook Database (October)*, Fondo Monetario Internacional, *https://www.imf.org/external/pubs/ft/weo/2019/02/weodata/index.aspx*. [27]

FMI (2018), "Trinidad and Tobago: 2018 Article IV Consultation", *Country Report No. 18/285*, Fondo Monetario Internacional, *https://www.imf.org/en/Publications/CR/Issues/2018/09/25/Trinidad-and-Tobago-2018-Article-IV-Consultation-Press-Release-and-Staff-Report-46267*. [6]

FMI (2016), "Argentina: 2016 Article IV Consultation", *Country Report No. 16/346*, Fondo Monetario Internacional, *https://www.imf.org/external/pubs/ft/scr/2016/cr16346.pdf*. [21]

Hanni, M., R. Martner y A. Podestá (2017), "La incidencia distributiva de la fiscalidad en América Latina", *Consensos y conflictos en la política tributaria de América Latina*, Comisión Económica para América Latina y el Caribe, *https://repositorio.cepal.org/handle/11362/43863*. [38]

Keen, M. (2013), "The anatomy of the VAT", *IMF Working Paper No. 13/111*, Fondo Monetario Internacional, *https://www.imf.org/en/Publications/WP/Issues/2016/12/31/The-Anatomy-of-the-VAT-40543*. [41]

Kettle, S. et al. (2016), "Behavioral Interventions in Tax Compliance: Evidence from Guatemala", *Policy Research Working Paper No. WPS7690*, Banco Mundial, *http://documents.worldbank.org/curated/en/479561467989537366/Behavioral-interventions-in-tax-compliance-evidence-from-Guatemala*. [30]

KPMG (2019), "Mexico: Tax reform 2020, VAT on services provided from digital platforms", *https://home.kpmg/us/en/home/insights/2019/11/tnf-mexico-tax-reform-2020-vat-services-digital-platforms.html*. [44]

Latinobarómetro (2016), *Latinobarómetro Database*, *http://www.latinobarometro.org/*. [32]

Lorenzo, F. (2016), "Inventario de instrumentos fiscales verdes en América Latina: Experiencias, efectos y alcances", *Documento de Proyecto*, Comisión Económica para América Latina y el Caribe, *https://repositorio.cepal.org/bitstream/handle/11362/40833/1/S1601174_es.pdf.* [50]

Marten, M. y K. Van Dender (2019), "The use of revenues from carbon pricing", *OECD Taxation Working Papers No. 43*, OECD Publishing, Paris, *https://doi.org/10.1787/3cb265e4-en.* [47]

Medina, Jonelis y Cangul (2017), "The Informal Economy in Sub-Saharan Africa Size and Determinants", *IMF Working Paper No. 17/156*, Fondo Monetario Internacional, *https://www.imf.org/en/Publications/WP/Issues/2017/07/10/The-Informal-Economy-in-Sub-Saharan-Africa-Size-and-Determinants-45017.* [36]

Mele, G. et al. (2017), "Hacia un sistema tributario más eficiente : evaluación de la eficiencia fiscal, análisis de costos y beneficios de los gastos tributarios y estudio sobre el empleo informal y sus repercusiones en el sistema tributario", *Documento de trabajo No. ACS22697*, Banco Mundial, *http://documentos.bancomundial.org/curated/es/481411518538354879/Gearing-up-for-a-more-efficient-tax-system-an-assessment-of-tax-efficiency-a-cost-benefit-analysis-of-tax-expenditures-and-an-exploration-of-labor-informality-and-its-tax-implications.* [45]

Melguizo, A. et al. (2017), "No sympathy for the devil! Policy priorities to overcome the middle-income trap in Latin America", *OECD Development Centre Working Papers No. 340*, OECD Publishing, Paris, *http://dx.doi.org/10.1787/26b78724-en.* [26]

Ministerio de Hacienda de Guyana (2019), *Mid-Year Report*, *https://finance.gov.gy/publications/mid-year-report-2019/.* [9]

Monge, C. (2018), "Colombia puts a tax on carbon", *https://www.conservationfinancenetwork.org/2018/11/27/colombia-puts-tax-on-carbon.* [54]

OCDE (2019), *OECD PINE Database*, OECD Publishing, Paris, *http://oe.cd/pine.* [49]

OCDE (2019), *Tax Morale: What Drives People and Businesses to Pay Tax?*, OECD Publishing, Paris, *https://doi.org/10.1787/f3d8ea10-en.* [28]

OCDE (2019), *Tax Policy Reforms 2019: OECD and Selected Partner Economies*, OECD Publishing, Paris, *https://doi.org/10.1787/da56c295-en.* [13]

OCDE (2019), *Taxing Energy Use 2019: Using Taxes for Climate Action*, OECD Publishing, Paris, *https://doi.org/10.1787/058ca239-en.* [56]

OCDE (2018), *"Statutory Corporate Income Tax Rates", OECD.Stat (base de datos)*, OECD Publishing, Paris, *https://stats.oecd.org/Index.aspx?DataSetCode=CTS_CIT.* [25]

OCDE (2018), *Consumption Tax Trends 2018: VAT/GST and Excise Rates, Trends and Policy Issues*, OECD Publishing, Paris, *https://doi.org/10.1787/ctt-2018-en.* [40]

OCDE (2018), *Effective Carbon Rates 2018: Pricing Carbon Emissions Through Taxes and Emissions Trading*, OECD Publishing, Paris, *https://doi.org/10.1787/9789264305304-en.* [55]

OCDE (2018), *Revenue Statistics 2018*, OECD Publishing, Paris, *https://doi.org/10.1787/rev_stats-2018-en.* [39]

OCDE (2014), *Development Co-operation Report 2014: Mobilising Resources for Sustainable Development*, OECD Publishing, Paris, *https://dx.doi.org/10.1787/dcr-2014-en.* [29]

OCDE (2005), "Environmental taxes", *Glossary of Statistical Terms*, *https://stats.oecd.org/glossary/detail.asp?ID=6437.* [46]

OCDE/BID/Banco Mundial (2015), *Un Panorama de las Pensiones en America Latina y el Caribe*, OECD Publishing, Paris, *https://doi.org/10.1787/9789264233195-es.* [35]

OCDE/BID/CIAT (2016), *Taxing Wages in Latin America and the Caribbean 2016*, OECD Publishing, Paris, *https://dx.doi.org/10.1787/9789264262607-en.* [37]

OCDE/CAF/CEPAL (2018), *Perspectivas económicas de América Latina 2018: Repensando las instituciones para el desarrollo*, OECD Publishing, Paris, *https://doi.org/10.1787/leo-2018-es.* [4]

OCDE/CEPAL (2016), *OECD Environmental Performance Reviews: Chile 2016*, OECD Environmental Performance Reviews, OECD Publishing, Paris, *https://dx.doi.org/10.1787/9789264252615-en.* [52]

OCDE et al. (2020), *Estadísticas tributarias en América Latina y el Caribe 2020*, OECD Publishing, Paris, *https://doi.org/10.1787/35745b02-en.* [2]

OCDE et al. (2019), *Perspectivas económicas de América Latina 2019: Desarrollo en transición*, OECD Publishing, Paris, *https://doi.org/10.1787/g2g9ff1a-es.* [1]

OCDE et al. (2015), *Estadísticas tributarias en América Latina y el Caribe 2015*, OECD Publishing, Paris, *https://dx.doi.org/10.1787/rev_lat-2015-en-fr*. [34]

OCDE/FIIAPP (2015), *Fomentando la cultura tributaria, el cumplimiento fiscal y la ciudadanía: Guía sobre educación tributaria en el mundo*, OECD Publishing, Paris, *https://doi.org/10.1787/9789264222786-es*. [33]

OECD/ILO (2019), Tackling Vulnerability in the Informal Economy, Development Centre Studies, OECD Publishing, Paris, *https://doi.org/10.1787/939b7bcd-en*. [58]

OCDE/ITF (2019), *Tax Revenue Implications of Decarbonising Road Transport: Scenarios for Slovenia*, OECD Publishing, Paris, *https://doi.org/10.1787/87b39a2f-en*. [48]

Schlotterbeck, S. (2017), "Tax administration reforms in the Caribbean: challenges, achievements, and next steps", *IMF Working Paper No. 17/88*, Fondo Monetario Internacional, *https://www.imf.org/en/Publications/WP/Issues/2017/04/04/Tax-Administration-Reforms-in-the-Caribbean-Challenges-Achievements-and-Next-Steps-44800*. [43]

Tax-News.com (2018), "Tax regime overhaul announced in Barbados", *https://www.tax-news.com/news/Tax_Regime_Overhaul_Announced_In_Barbados____76835.html*. [17]

The Behavioural Insights Team (2014), "Results from BIT tax trial in Guatemala", *https://www.bi.team/blogs/results-from-bit-tax-trial-in-guatemala/*. [31]

Vera, L. (2019), "Impuestos ambientales y equidad: desafíos para América Latina y el Caribe", Friedrich-Ebert-Stiftung (FES), *http://library.fes.de/pdf-files/bueros/kolumbien/15468-20190730.pdf*. [51]

World Grain (2016), "Reforms boost Argentine grain industry", *https://www.world-grain.com/articles/6457-reforms-boost-argentine-grain-industry*. [22]

Chapter 2

SPECIAL FEATURE

Fiscal revenues from non-renewable natural resources in Latin America and the Caribbean

Capítulo 2

SECCIÓN ESPECIAL

Ingresos fiscales provenientes de recursos naturales no renovables en América Latina y el Caribe

Chapter 2

SPECIAL FEATURE

Fiscal revenues from non-renewable natural resources in Latin America and the Caribbean

Hydrocarbon-related revenues rebounded in 2018 amid market volatility

In 2018, the global oil market experienced significant volatility as a result of a confluence of macroeconomic, political and production factors. In the first part of the year, the principal quoted spot prices in the market – Western Texas Intermediate (WTI), Brent and Dubai – rose as a result of a greater than agreed cut in production among OPEC members, particularly in Venezuela, and stronger global macroeconomic fundamentals. This dynamic was reinforced in May as the United States announced its unilateral withdrawal from Joint Cooperative Plan of Action – the so-called Iran nuclear deal – and the possibility of new sanctions against Iran, which would begin to impact global production later in the year.

In response to this potential disruption, OPEC and the Russian Federation agreed to increase their output to offset this decline. Nonetheless, the market remained tight as traditional importers of Iranian crude oil reduced their purchases in light of the looming sanctions. In the fourth quarter of the year, spot prices dropped sharply when the United States awarded sanction waivers to a group of countries, most notably China and India, and a surge in production in the Russian Federation and Saudi Arabia pushed the market into oversupply. Nevertheless, taken as an annual average, the average spot price of oil rose significantly, to USD 68 per barrel from USD 53 per barrel in 2017, a 29% increase (Figure 2.1).

Figure 2.1. **Crude oil spot price, January 2016 to December 2018**

USD per barrel

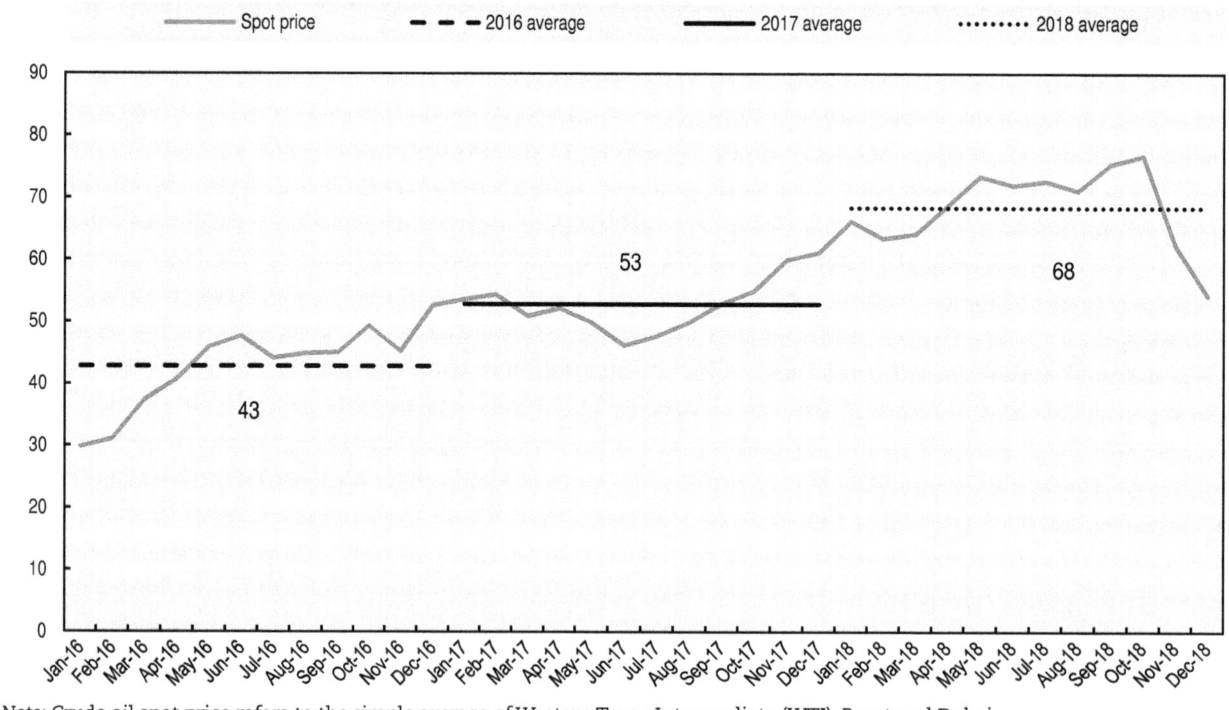

Note: Crude oil spot price refers to the simple average of Western Texas Intermediate (WTI), Brent and Dubai.

Source: Economic Commission for Latin America and the Caribbean (ECLAC), based on World Bank (2020[1]).

StatLink https://doi.org/10.1787/888934113545

Despite heightened volatility in global oil markets, fiscal revenues from oil and gas exploration and production – up-stream activities – strengthened considerably in LAC during 2018.[1] Overall revenues from exploration and production of hydrocarbons reached an average of 2.7% of GDP, compared with 2.0% in 2017 (Figure 2.2 and Table 2.1). Non-tax revenues, receipts of property rents such as royalties and other participations in the commercial value of production, accounted for much of this increase, rising to 2.3% of GDP from 1.7% of GDP in 2017. The increase in spot prices did not translate directly into higher non-tax revenues as production in the region trended lower over the year: crude oil and condensates were down 8.2% over the 2017 levels, or 2.2% excluding Venezuela, and natural gas fell 2.1% (BP, 2019[2]).

Figure 2.2. **Fiscal revenues from oil and gas extraction in nine LAC countries, by instrument, 2010-18**

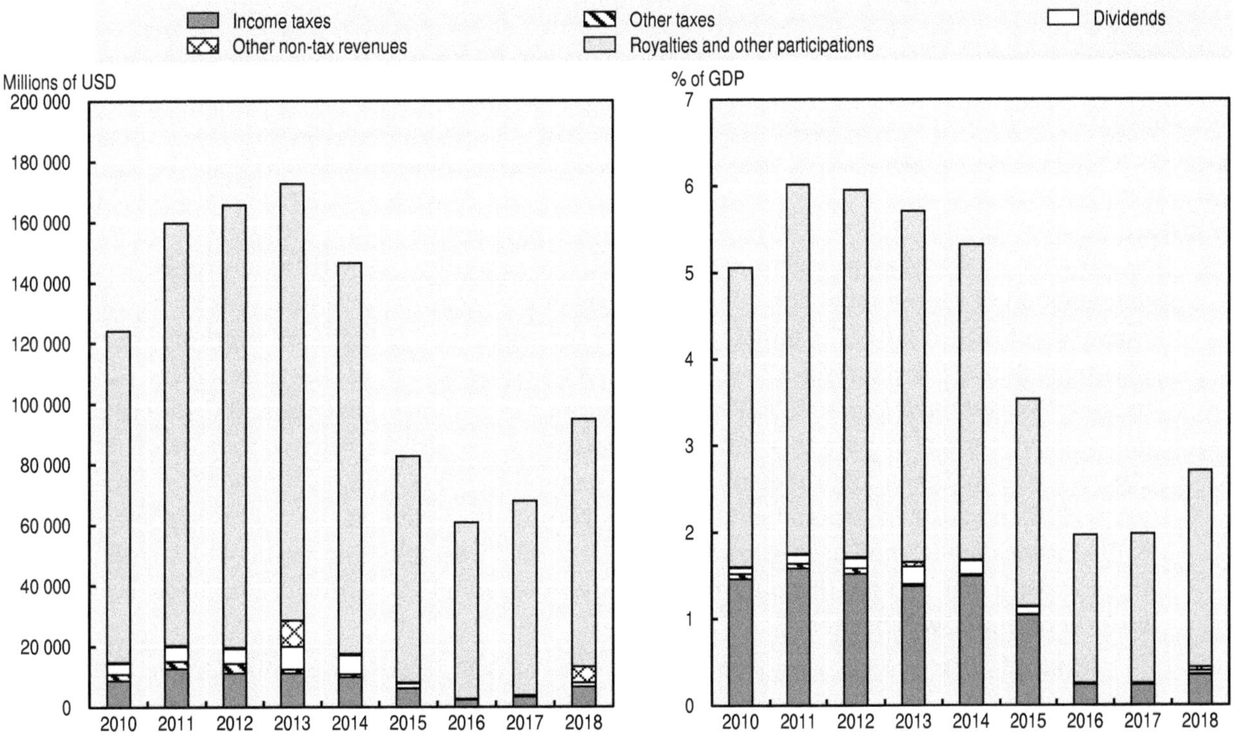

Note: Country sample includes Argentina, Bolivia (Plurinational State of), Brazil, Colombia, Ecuador, Guatemala, Mexico, Peru, and Trinidad and Tobago. Percentage of GDP data is the simple average of all countries in the sample.

Source: Economic Commission for Latin America and the Caribbean (ECLAC), based on data from CEPALSTAT (ECLAC, 2020[3]).

StatLink https://doi.org/10.1787/888934113564

Tax revenues from the sector also rose during the year, reaching an average of 0.4% of GDP compared to 0.2% of GDP in 2017, as corporate income tax (CIT) receipts jumped on the back of higher profitability among oil producers in the region (Table 2.1). Colombia and Trinidad and Tobago registered significant increases in tax revenues over the year, a factor of importance in the latter country where CIT is the predominate mechanism for capturing rents generated by the sector. Despite this up-tick in tax revenues, as Figure 2.2 shows, they play a relatively small role in overall hydrocarbon revenues.

Table 2.1. **Fiscal revenues from oil and gas extraction in nine LAC countries, by instrument, 2017-18**

Percentage of GDP

Country	Total		Tax revenues		Non-tax revenues		Total revenues 2018	
	2017	2018	2017	2018	2017	2018	Millions of US dollars	Year-on-year variation (%)
Argentina	0.4	0.5	0.1	0.1	0.3	0.4	2 680	-4
Bolivia (Plur. State of)	4.0	4.6	0.3	0.3	3.8	4.3	1 845	23
Brazil	0.4	1.2	0.03	0.1	0.4	1.1	22 271	149
Colombia	1.1	1.8	0.4	0.7	0.7	1.1	6 112	83
Ecuador	5.6	8.0	0.0	0.0	5.6	8.0	8 621	48
Guatemala	0.05	0.07	0.01	0.01	0.03	0.05	53	53
Mexico	3.8	4.2	-0.01	0.02	3.8	4.2	51 124	16
PEMEX	1.8	1.9	...	...	1.8	1.9	22 688	10
Federal government	2.0	2.3	-0.01	0.02	2.0	2.3	28 435	22
Peru	0.5	0.6	0.1	0.2	0.4	0.5	1 402	33
Trinidad and Tobago	2.0	3.4	1.2	1.8	0.8	1.6	772	76
Simple average / total in million USD	2.0	2.7	0.2	0.4	1.7	2.3	94 880	40

Note: Figures may not sum to total due to rounding. In Mexico, hydrocarbon-related tax revenues registered a net refund in 2017 as some companies operating in the sector made use of loss carry-forward provisions in their annual tax declarations.

Source: Economic Commission for Latin America and the Caribbean (ECLAC), based on data from *CEPALSTAT* (ECLAC, 2020[3]).

StatLink https://doi.org/10.1787/888934113773

Higher oil and gas production during 2018 in **Argentina**, as well as a pronounced depreciation of the national currency, helped push hydrocarbon revenues to 0.5% of GDP from 0.4% of GDP in 2017. The principal driver of this increase was higher receipts of royalty payments during the year, which brought non-tax revenues to 0.4% of GDP from 0.3% of GDP in 2017. Tax revenues, however, fell in absolute (both in national currency and USD terms) and relative terms. In part this reflected changes to the CIT framework as part of the 2017 tax reform, including a reduction in the general CIT rate from 35% to 30% for fiscal years 2018 and 2019. In September 2018, the government reinstated the tax on exports of hydrocarbons (which had been allowed to expire in 2017), establishing a rate of 12% with a threshold of 3 or 4 ARS per US dollar, depending on the product. The impact of this measure on 2018 revenues was limited.

In **Bolivia**, natural gas revenues reached 4.6% of GDP in 2018, up from 4.0% of GDP in 2017, on the back of an up-tick in non-tax revenues from instruments related to the commercial value of production, such as the Direct Tax on Hydrocarbons (*Impuesto Directo a los Hidrocarburos*) and royalties. Nevertheless, the increase in prices did not pass directly to the evolution of revenues as natural gas production fell in volume terms during the year (-6.5%) as a result of weaker demand from Argentina – where natural gas production increased – and Brazil – due to high hydroelectric production and weaker industrial output (Ministerio de Economia y Finanzas Publicas, 2019[4]).

Oil and natural gas revenues in **Brazil** jumped in 2018 despite a decline in hydrocarbons production, reaching 1.2% of GDP in comparison with 0.4% of GDP in 2017.[2] A nearly five-fold increase in CIT receipts pushed tax revenues from the sector to 0.1% of GDP, up from 0.03% in 2017, their highest level since 2009. Nonetheless, the rise in overall revenues was principally due to a jump in non-tax revenues, which reached 1.1% of GDP compared to 0.4% of GDP in 2017, in part due to a 14% depreciation of the Brazilian real during the year. Revenues from the government's special participation in production more than doubled[3] (to 0.43% of GDP from 0.17% of GDP in 2017) as Petrobras ramped up production in fields that were subjected to higher tax rates (Petrobras, 2019[5]). Non-tax revenues were also buoyed by receipts from signature bonuses at the completion of the 15th bidding round for oil and gas exploration and production concessions (equivalent to 0.3% of GDP).

In **Colombia**, hydrocarbon revenues rose to 1.8% of GDP compared with 1.1% of GDP in 2017, largely because of robust financial results at Ecopetrol, the state-owned producer, brought about by higher oil and gas production and prices. Operating income at the company nearly doubled in 2017 and rose a further 40% in 2018 (Ecopetrol, 2019[6]). This dynamic drove tax revenues up to 0.7% of GDP in 2018 from 0.4% in 2017, buoyed by the settlement of CIT liabilities for calendar year 2017 and strong estimated tax prepayments for calendar year 2018. In a similar vein, the rebound in profitability had a knock-on effect on non-tax revenues, with dividend payments by Ecopetrol to the central government rising to 0.3% of GDP compared to 0.1% of GDP in 2017.

Oil revenues in **Ecuador** rose sharply, reaching 8.0% of GDP in 2018 up from 5.6% of GDP in 2017, despite a decline in hydrocarbon production. A decline in export volumes was largely compensated by the increase in prices. However, the leap in oil revenues was largely due to increased internal sales by state-owned oil producers, in line with higher import volumes of hydrocarbon derivatives. In **Guatemala**, hydrocarbon revenues increased to 0.07% of GDP from 0.05% of GDP in 2017, as higher prices lifted revenues from the government's participation in the value of production.

In **Mexico**, the increase in international spot prices was offset by a continued decline in crude oil production (-7.8% in 2018), which weighed heavily on hydrocarbon revenues in 2018 (SHCP, 2019[7]). Overall, hydrocarbon revenues rose to 4.2% of GDP, up from 3.8% of GDP in 2017, due largely to an increase in non-tax revenues accrued by the federal government as a result of higher prices. The revenues of Pemex – which is consolidated in the federal public sector – were subdued, increasing by 0.1% of GDP between 2017 and 2018. In contrast, an up-tick in oil production in **Peru** compensated for a decline in the production of natural gas and liquefied natural gas (LNG), which in turn allowed hydrocarbon revenues to rise to 0.6% of GDP from 0.5% of GDP in 2017. Non-tax revenues, particularly royalties, were also bolstered by the value of LNG exports that were directed to the more lucrative markets of Europe and Asia (Perúpetro, 2019[8]).

Revenues from hydrocarbons in **Trinidad and Tobago** rebounded sharply in 2018, rising to 3.4% of GDP from 2.0% of GDP in 2017. Unlike most hydrocarbon-producing countries in the region, where a state-owned champion accounts for a large share of overall production and revenues, the principal actors in Trinidad and Tobago are large multinational enterprises.[4] CIT therefore plays a crucial role in capturing rents from the exploitation of the country's hydrocarbon assets. Higher profitability in 2017 and 2018 brought about by higher crude oil prices bolstered tax revenues from the sector, which reached 1.8% of GDP compared with 1.2% of GDP in 2017. The adoption of a 12.5% royalty rate on the extraction of natural gas resulted in a doubling of non-tax revenues from the sector (1.6% of GDP compared with 0.8% of GDP in 2017) (Ministry of Finance of Trinidad and Tobago, 2018[9]).

Fiscal revenues from mining maintained an upward trend in 2018

Spot prices in international markets for a wide range of industrial minerals and metals remained strong in the first half of 2018, maintaining or even building on gains observed in the second half of 2017 (Figure 2.3). However, growing concerns about economic activity in China and increasing trade tensions between China and the United States provoked a contraction in international prices during the second half of 2018. Between the second and third quarter of the year, spot prices fell sharply for copper (-11%), lead (-12%) and zinc (19%). Precious metals – which are in some cases blended into ore concentrates exported from the region, principally in the case of copper concentrates – also registered a significant downward correction in prices over the same period that affected gold (-7%), platinum (9%) and silver (-9%).

Figure 2.3. **Spot prices and Chinese import volumes of selected industrial metals and minerals, Q1 2017-Q4 2018**

Index, Q1 2017 = 100

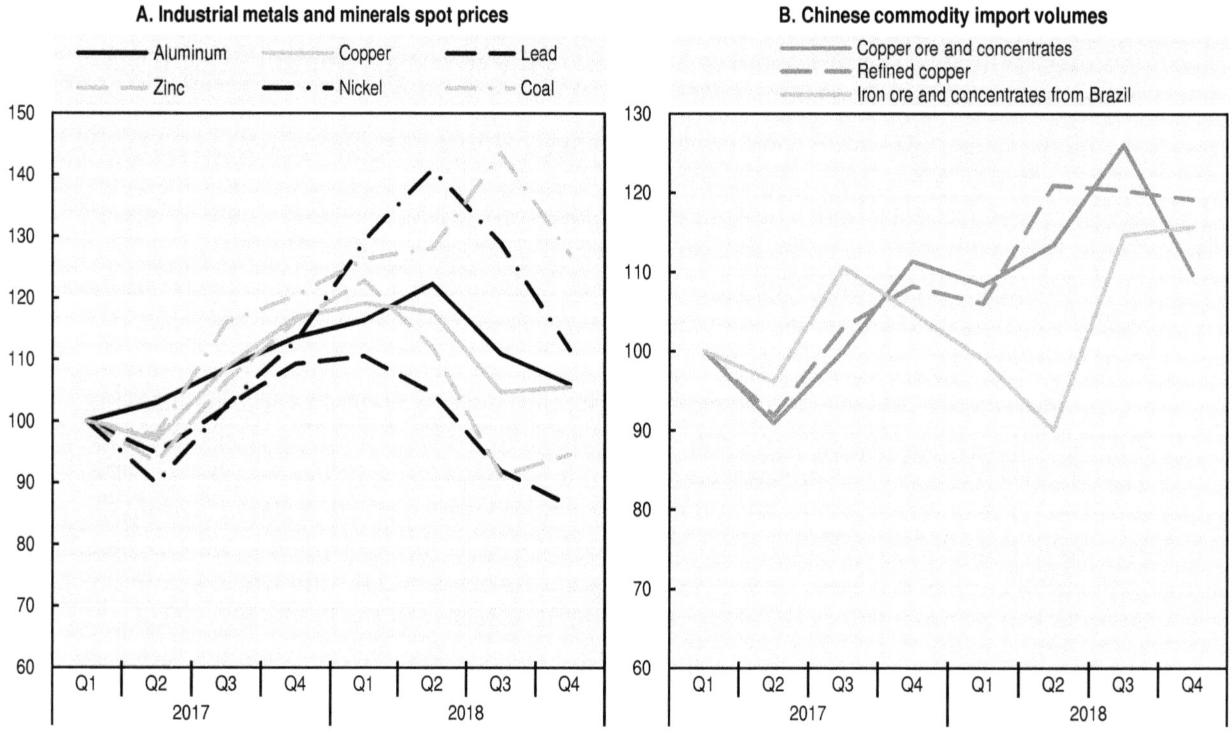

Source: Economic Commission for Latin America and the Caribbean (ECLAC), based on World Bank (2020[1]).

StatLink https://doi.org/10.1787/888934113583

The shift in prices caused by changing market sentiment did not necessarily reflect underlying fundamentals. Chinese import demand remained strong throughout the year, bolstered in part by the tightening of environmental regulations and measures to restrict the import of scrap metal [(World Bank, 2019[10]); (World Bank, 2019[11])]. Rising steel production in China – up 6.6% in 2018 compared with 2017, to a record high of 928.3 million tonnes – sustained demand for coal, iron ore and nickel (World Steel Association, 2019[12]). As a result, continued demand from China put a floor under the price correction observed in the second half of the year. Despite these price dynamics, annual average prices of some of the region's principal exported non-renewable natural resources did rise, including coal (21.0%), copper (5.8%) and nickel (26.0%).

Mining revenues in LAC rose in 2018, reaching 0.39% of GDP in 2018 compared with 0.33% of GDP in 2017. This increase was principally due to a surge in tax revenues – consisting of receipts from CIT and other tax instruments whose base is income – which reached 0.23% of GDP in comparison with 0.18% of GDP in 2017, or an increase of 41% in USD terms (Figure 2.4 and Table 2.2).[5] The rise in CIT revenues, driven by the liquidation of 2017 tax liabilities and payment of estimated taxes for 2018, was in large part due to a rebound in prices – both in 2017 and 2018 – and the concomitant impact on operating income of firms operating in the sector.

Figure 2.4. **Fiscal revenues from mining in 11 LAC countries, by instrument, 2010-18**

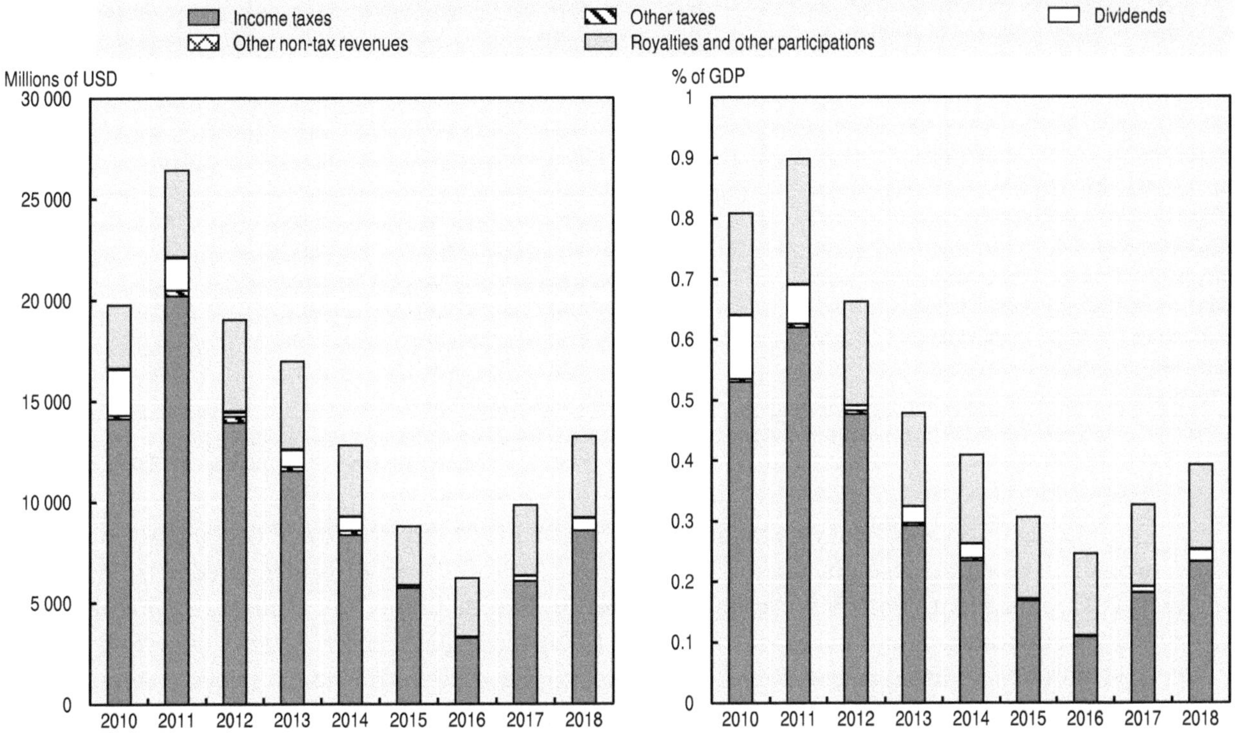

Note: Country sample includes Argentina, Bolivia (Plurinational State of), Brazil, Chile, Colombia, Dominican Republic, Ecuador, Guatemala, Jamaica, Mexico and Peru. Percentage of GDP data is the simple average of all countries in the sample.

Source: Economic Commission for Latin America and the Caribbean (ECLAC), based on CEPALSTAT (ECLAC, 2020[3])

StatLink https://doi.org/10.1787/888934113602

Non-tax revenues, in contrast, registered a more muted increase, rising to 0.16% of GDP on average in 2018 as compared to 0.14% of GDP in 2017, or a 24% up-tick in USD terms (Table 2.2). This increase was due in part to a significant dividend payment by the Chilean state-owned mining firm CODELCO to the Chilean government. Revenues from royalties and other participations tied to the commercial value of production – calculated on the prevailing spot price at the time of production – were less dynamic compared to 2017, due largely to a correction in international prices during the second half of the year (rising 15% in USD terms).

At the country level, fiscal revenues from mining in **Argentina** held steady at 0.04% of GDP during 2018, although they were heavily influenced by domestic and external factors (Table 2.2). Mine production fell sharply during the year, most notably for copper (-48% in volume), gold (-34%) and silver (-17%). Nevertheless, despite the decline in production, mining revenues expressed in terms of Argentinian pesos (ARS) continued to rise – roughly in line with the increase in nominal GDP – as the currency depreciated sharply in 2018 (70%, annual average).

Table 2.2. **Fiscal revenues from mining in 11 LAC countries, by instrument, 2017-18**

Percentage of GDP

Country	Total		Tax revenues		Non-tax revenues		Total revenues 2018	
	2017	2018	2017	2018	2017	2018	Millions of US dollars	Year-on-year variation (%)
Argentina	0.04	0.04	0.03	0.03	0.01	0.01	187	-22
Bolivia (Plur. State of)	0.76	0.85	0.27	0.37	0.49	0.48	342	20
Brazil	0.07	0.10	0.04	0.05	0.03	0.05	1 925	34
Chile	0.94	1.40	0.46	0.82	0.48	0.58	4 188	60
CODELCO	0.49	0.60	0.01	0.02	0.48	0.58	1 798	32
Private sector	0.45	0.80	0.45	0.80	0.00	0.00	2 390	90
Colombia	0.40	0.45	0.19	0.20	0.21	0.25	1 489	18
Dominican Republic	0.41	0.21	0.35	0.15	0.06	0.05	176	-46
Ecuador	0.06	0.07	0.02	0.02	0.05	0.05	77	15
Guatemala	0.06	0.03	0.03	0.01	0.03	0.02	21	-50
Jamaica	0.03	0.04	0.00	0.00	0.03	0.04	5	26
Mexico	0.19	0.23	0.16	0.20	0.03	0.03	2 787	25
Peru	0.62	0.90	0.46	0.72	0.16	0.19	2 039	53
Simple average / total in million USD	0.33	0.39	0.18	0.23	0.14	0.16	13 235	35

Source: Economic Commission for Latin America and the Caribbean (ECLAC), based on CEPALSTAT (ECLAC, 2020[3]).

StatLink https://doi.org/10.1787/888934113792

Mining revenues in **Bolivia** reached 0.85% of GDP in 2018 from 0.76% of GDP in 2017, as a result of rising tax receipts. Tax revenues rose to 0.37% of GDP in 2018, compared to 0.27% in 2017, equivalent to a 20% increase in USD terms. Profitability of the mining sector rose in 2017 supported by an increase in zinc prices (38%) and higher export volumes of metallic gold (43%). In addition to boosting CIT receipts, higher profits also led to higher receipts deriving from the additional corporate tax rate applied to the sector of 12.5%. Non-tax revenues in 2018 fell marginally, reaching 0.48% of GDP compared to 0.49% of GDP in 2017, reflecting the downward trend of minerals and metals prices during the year.

In **Brazil**, mining revenues rose to 0.10% of GDP in 2018 from 0.07% of GDP in 2017, supported by higher iron ore prices during the year. While tax revenues held steady relative to GDP (0.04% of GDP), they increased 35% in USD terms. Non-tax revenues were particularly dynamic in 2018, despite the decline in the annual average prices, reaching 0.05% of GDP in comparison to 0.03% of GDP in 2017 (a 34% increase in USD terms). Higher production volumes of ferrous minerals bolstered this result, with Vale S.A. reporting a 6% increase for iron ore fines and 9% for pellets (Vale S.A., 2019[13]). The increase in non-tax revenues was also due to changes in the calculation of royalty payments. The tax base of the royalty (*Compensação Financeira pela Exploração de Recursos Minerais*) was changed from net sales excluding taxes and other qualifying expenses to gross sales excluding only taxes. Additionally, the reform brought changes in the rate of the levy, most notably for iron ore, which increased to 3.5%.

Mining revenues in **Chile** rose sharply in 2018, due largely to increased tax payments by the country's private producers. Overall revenues stood at 1.4% of GDP in 2018 compared to 0.94% of GDP in 2017 (a 60% increase in USD terms). Tax revenues, corporate tax receipts and payments of the special tax on mining, were up sharply due to higher receipts from tax filings for fiscal year 2017 and estimated tax prepayments in 2018, which in turn were boosted by an increase in the corporate tax rate (from 25.5% to 27%).[6] Non-tax revenues, essentially transfers of profits from the State-owned producer CODELCO to the central government and payments by CODELCO on its exports of copper, also trended higher, rising from 0.48% of GDP in 2017 to 0.58% of GDP.

Rising international prices for coal (21%) buoyed mining revenues in **Colombia**, which rose to 0.45% of GDP from 0.40% of GDP in 2017 (an 18% increase in USD terms). Non-tax revenues, especially royalties from the production value of coal, rose from 0.21% of GDP in 2017 to 0.25% of GDP (24% in USD terms). Tax revenues from the sector rose marginally, passing from 0.19% of GDP in 2017 to 0.20% of GDP. Lower gold production at the Pueblo Viejo mine (-11%), a joint venture of Barrick Gold (Canada) and Newmont Goldcorp (United States), negatively impacted mining revenues in the **Dominican Republic**, which fell to 0.21% of GDP from 0.41% of GDP in 2017. The bulk of this decline was due to a contraction in tax revenues – falling to 0.15% of GDP from 0.35% of GDP in 2017 – reflecting in part the impact of a 25% contraction in income in 2017 from the Pueblo Viejo mine (Barrick Gold Corporation, 2019[14]).

Mining revenues in **Ecuador** edged up marginally in 2018, increasing to 0.07% of GDP compared to 0.06% of GDP in 2017. Large-scale mining projects are under development in the country and fiscal revenues are projected to increase in the coming years. Non-tax revenues are currently the most notable component of overall mining revenues, largely consisting of royalty prepayments by companies in the pre-production stage of operations. For example, Lundin Gold Inc. (Canada) entered into an agreement with the government of Ecuador in 2016, which included – among other fiscal measures – a schedule of prepayments of USD 25 million in 2016 and USD 20 million in 2017 and 2018 (Lundin Gold, 2017[15]).

Revenues from mining in **Guatemala** declined to 0.03% of GDP in 2018 from 0.06% of GDP in 2017. Tax and non-tax revenues were down, largely due to a decline in production of metals – mainly iron oxide and nickel – in 2017 and 2018. In July 2017, the Supreme Court of Guatemala suspended the licenses of two of the largest mines in the country. This decision was reaffirmed by the country's Constitutional Court in September 2018, which ordered that the Ministry of Mines and Energy conduct an ILO 169 consultation with local communities within the framework of the Indigenous and Tribal Peoples Convention (1989).

In **Jamaica**, mining revenues remained subdued, reaching 0.04% of GDP in 2018. This marks a stark contrast from a high of 0.8% of GDP in 2016. Tax revenues from mining – CIT receipts from the bauxite and alumina sector – remained nil, continuing a trend that began in FY 2012/13. Non-tax revenues did trend higher, rising from 0.03% of GDP in 2017 to 0.04% of GDP in 2018, equivalent to a 26% up-tick in USD terms. Bauxite royalties from a levy of USD 0.50 per dry metric tonne of ore shipped rose as export volumes increased 26.5% in 2018. The bauxite levy – with a base statutory rate of USD 5 per dry metric tonne – showed little dynamism as payments of the levy have been provisionally waived for some firms. The government has also entered into bespoke profit-sharing agreements with some firms operating in the country, which establish a take of 17.33% of earnings before interest, taxes and depreciation, or the payment of the bauxite levy at a rate of USD 1.50 per dry metric tonne shipped, whichever is greater.

A combination of an up-tick in copper production (2% in volume), stronger international copper prices in 2017 and 2018 and depreciation of the national currency bolstered fiscal revenues from mining in **Mexico**, which rose to 0.23% of GDP from 0.19% of GDP in 2017. Tax revenues strengthened – reaching 0.20% of GDP compared to 0.16% of GDP in 2017 – in response to higher year-end tax settlements on higher profits in 2017. Non-tax revenues rose in absolute terms (11% in USD) but remained at 0.03% of GDP.

In **Peru**, mining revenues rose sharply as CIT receipts from the sector surged. Overall, revenues rose to 0.9% of GDP from 0.62% of GDP in 2017, equivalent to a 53% increase in USD terms. Tax revenues were buoyant – rising to 0.72% of GDP from 0.46% of GDP in 2017 – thanks to settlement payments for 2017 taxes and strong estimated tax pre-payments in the first half of 2018. A decline in copper production and a relatively smaller increase in annual average prices resulted in a more muted increase in non-tax revenues from mining, which rose to 0.19% of GDP from 0.16% of GDP in 2017.

Estimates point to declining revenues from non-renewable natural resources in 2019

Global macroeconomic conditions in 2019 were not favourable for the region's producers of non-renewable natural resources. Global economic growth slowed sharply, from 3.1% in 2018 to 2.5% in 2019, its lowest level since the financial crisis of 2008-09 (ECLAC, 2019[16]). Global trade volumes also faltered during the year, registering an outright contraction in the first three quarters of the year after having posted modest growth of 3.4% in 2018. At the same time, prices of several important non-renewable natural resources for the region slid in 2019, including coal (-27%), crude oil (-10%) and copper (-8%) (Figure 2.5). A rise in iron ore prices during the year did not correspond to strengthened market fundamentals, but rather reflected the impact of the tragic tailings dam failure at the Córrego do Feijão iron ore mine owned by Vale S.A. in Minas Gerais, Brazil, that resulted in the death of 272 individuals.

Figure 2.5. **Observed prices of selected commodities, 2014-19**

Index, 2014 = 100

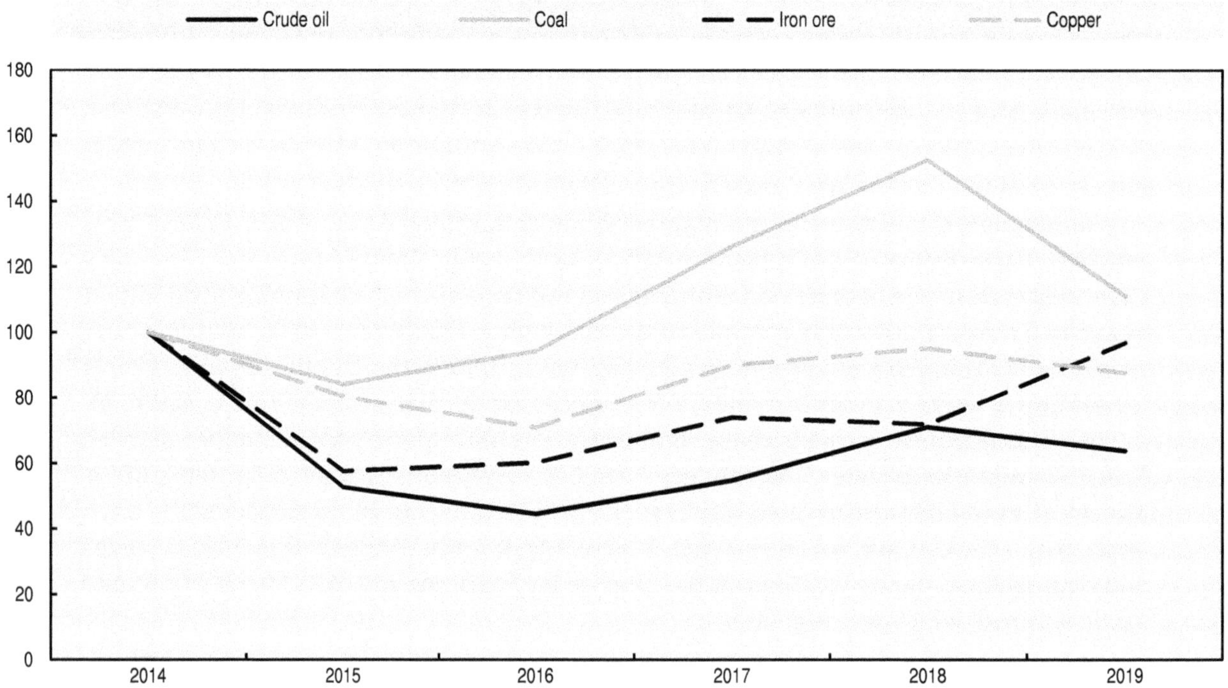

Source: Economic Commission for Latin America and the Caribbean (ECLAC), based on World Bank (2020[1]).

StatLink https://doi.org/10.1787/888934113621

Revenues from non-renewable natural resources are estimated to have fallen in LAC in 2019 (Figure 2.6). Oil and gas revenues, which had rebounded, are estimated to have averaged 2.5% of GDP, down from 2.7% of GDP in 2018. Reductions are expected in many of the countries of the sample, particularly those that rely principally on non-tax revenues that move in time with the evolution of prices (royalties and other participations shares in the commercial value of production). In contrast, oil revenues may have increased in Colombia and Trinidad and Tobago as CIT payments on 2018 profits offset the decline in non-tax revenues.

Figure 2.6. **Observed and estimated fiscal revenues from hydrocarbons and mining in selected LAC countries, 2010-19**

Percentage of GDP

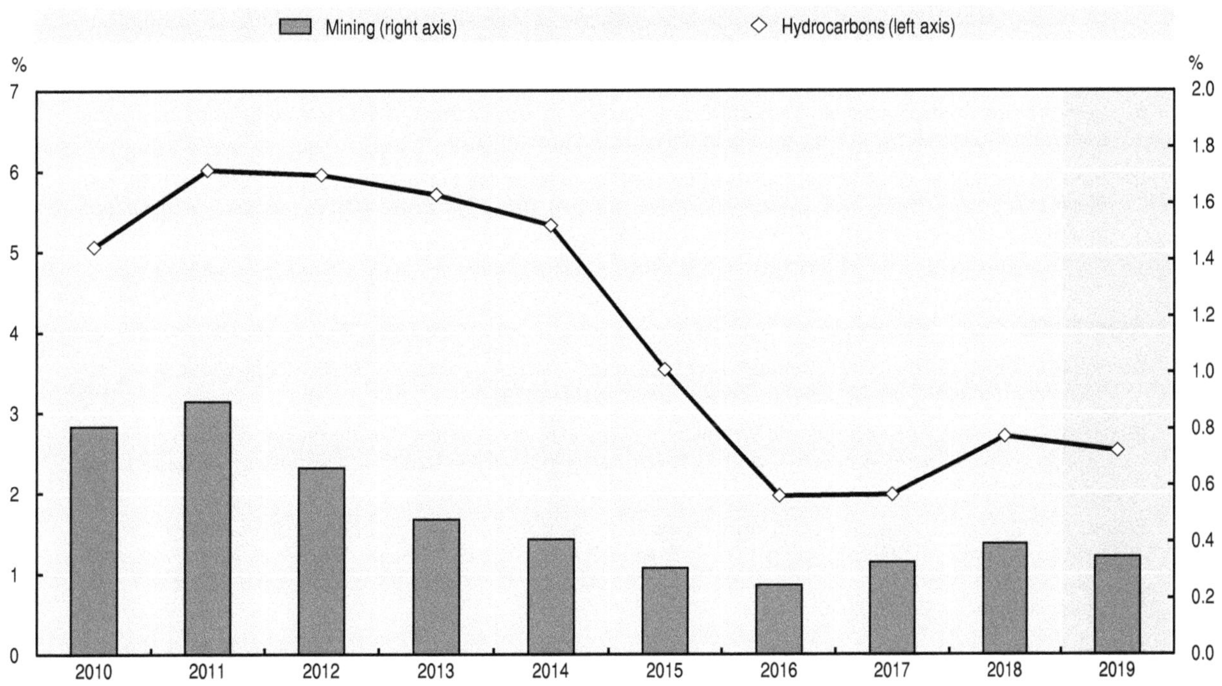

Note: Mining country sample includes: Argentina, Bolivia (Plurinational State of), Brazil, Chile, Colombia, Dominican Republic, Ecuador, Guatemala, Jamaica, Mexico and Peru. Hydrocarbons country sample includes: Argentina, Bolivia (Plurinational State of), Brazil, Colombia, Ecuador, Guatemala, Mexico, Peru, and Trinidad and Tobago. Values for 2019 are based on official government estimates from 2020 budget documents or from preliminary annual figures. When figures for 2019 were not available, they were estimated using monthly data (typically for the first nine months of the year). When monthly data was not available, revenues were estimated by applying the year-on-year change in the price for the most representative product – or basket of products in the case of mining – for the country expressed in national currency terms to 2018 revenues.

Source: Economic Commission for Latin America and the Caribbean (ECLAC), based on *CEPALSTAT* (ECLAC, 2020[3]).

StatLink https://doi.org/10.1787/888934113640

Mining revenues are also estimated to have declined on average, falling to 0.3% of GDP in 2019 from 0.4% in 2018. However, this reduction is not likely to have been uniform across countries as in the case of producers of hydrocarbons. The trajectory of revenues reflects in large part the evolution of prices and production relevant to each countries' basket of exports. Nevertheless, lower prices are likely to have dragged on tax and non-tax revenues during the year.

Notes

1. Guatemala is included for the first time in this analysis.
2. In December 2017, the federal government of Brazil enacted a new taxation model for the sector – which came into effect in January 2018 – that established a new special regime for exploration, development and production of oil, gas and other liquid hydrocarbons. The new model introduced modifications to the customs oil and gas customs regime, allowing for – among other changes – the exemption from federal taxes on the importation of goods for permanent use in the country. The new framework also definitively established the deduction of exploration and production costs from the tax base of the CIT and the social contribution on net profit tax (CSLL). Subsequently, some Brazilian states agreed to grant tax incentives related to the VAT (ICMS) on transactions covered by the new regime (Petrobras, 2019[5]).
3. A levy of 10% to 40% on sales value of production, adjusted by qualifying deductions, with the rate set depending on the level of production or profitability of a concession.
4. In November 2018, the state-owned oil company, Petroleum Company of Trinidad and Tobago Limited (Petrotrin), was liquidated. The activities of the former company were divided among four new State-owned enterprises, one of which – Heritage Petroleum Company Limited – will continue to operate in the area of oil exploration, development, production and marketing.
5. Regional averages in this year's edition are marginally lower than in previous editions due to the inclusion of Ecuador and Guatemala in the sample of countries.
6. Income tax filings for 2017 were also influenced by an increase of the CIT rate from 24% to 25.5% (for filers of the semi-integrated system). In a similar way, pre-payments of 2018 taxes were impacted by a further increase in the CIT rate from 25.5% to 27%.

References

Barrick Gold Corporation (2019), *Annual Report 2018*, *https://barrick.q4cdn.com/788666289/files/annual-report/Barrick-Annual-Report-2018.pdf* (accessed on 2 March 2020). [14]

BP (2019), *BP Statistical Review of World Energy*, *https://www.bp.com/content/dam/bp/business-sites/en/global/corporate/pdfs/energy-economics/statistical-review/bp-stats-review-2019-full-report.pdf* (accessed on 2 March 2020). [2]

ECLAC (2020), "Fiscal revenues from non-renewable natural resources", *CEPALSTAT (database)*, United Nations Economic Commission for Latin America and the Caribbean, *https://cepalstat-prod.cepal.org/cepalstat/tabulador/ConsultaIntegrada.asp?IdAplicacion=6&idTema=939&idIndicador=3354&idioma=e* (accessed on 3 March 2020). [3]

ECLAC (2019), *Preliminary Overview of the Economies of Latin America and the Caribbean 2019*, United Nations Economic Commission for Latin America and the Caribbean, *https://repositorio.cepal.org/handle/11362/45001* (accessed on 2 March 2020). [16]

Ecopetrol (2019), *Integrated Sustainable Management Report 2018*, *https://www.ecopetrol.com.co/documentos/Ecopetrol-Integrated-Sustainability-Report-2018.pdf* (accessed on 2 March 2020). [6]

Lundin Gold (2017), *Annual Report 2016*, *https://www.lundingold.com/site/assets/files/1707/2016_annual_report_new.pdf* (accessed on 2 March 2020). [15]

Ministerio de Economia y Finanzas Publicas (2019), *Memoria de la Economía Boliviana 2018*, *https://www.economiayfinanzas.gob.bo/memoria-de-la-economia-boliviana-2018.html* (accessed on 3 March 2020). [4]

Ministry of Finance of Trinidad and Tobago (2018), *Review of the Economy 2018*, *https://www.finance.gov.tt/wp-content/uploads/2018/10/Review-Of-The-Economy-2018.pdf* (accessed on 2 March 2020). [9]

Perúpetro (2019), *Memoria anual 2018*, *https://www.perupetro.com.pe/wps/wcm/connect/corporativo/469bffbe-b3f2-42b0-baff-fbf7ff4df270/MEMORIA+PERUPETRO+2018a.pdf?MOD=AJPERES&MemoriaAnual2018* (accessed on 2 March 2020). [8]

Petrobras (2019), "Form 20-F filing to the United States Securities and Exchange Commission", Petróleo Brasileiro S.A., *https://www.investidorpetrobras.com.br/enu/892/Form-20F-2018-Ingles_2.pdf* (accessed on 2 March 2020). [5]

SHCP (2019), *Informes sobre la Situación Económica, las Finanzas Públicas y la Deuda Pública*, Secretaría de Hacienda y Crédito Público, Gobierno de México, *https://www.finanzaspublicas.hacienda.gob.mx/work/models/Finanzas_Publicas/docs/congreso/infotrim/2018/ivt/01inf/itindc_201804.pdf* (accessed on 2 March 2020). [7]

Vale S.A. (2019), "Form 20-F filing to the United States Securities and Exchange Commission", *http://www.vale.com/EN/investors/information-market/annual-reports/20f/20FDocs/Vale_20-F%20FY2018%20-%20final_i.pdf* (accessed on 2 March 2020). [13]

World Bank (2020), "World Bank commodities price data (the pink sheet)", *http://pubdocs.worldbank.org/en/596831580311438199/CMO-Pink-Sheet-February-2020.pdf* (accessed on 3 March 2020). [1]

World Bank (2019), *Commodity Markets Outlook, April 2019*, *http://documents.worldbank.org/curated/en/992831556034429620/Commodity-Markets-Outlook-April-2019* (accessed on 2 March 2020). [11]

World Bank (2019), *Commodity Markets Outlook, October 2018*, *http://pubdocs.worldbank.org/en/236551540394193458/CMO-October-2018-Full-Report.pdf* (accessed on 2 March 2020). [10]

World Steel Association (2019), "Global crude steel output increases by 4.6% in 2018", *https://www.worldsteel.org/media-centre/press-releases/2019/Global-crude-steel-output-increases-by-4.6--in-2018.html* (accessed on 2 March 2020). [12]

Capítulo 2

SECCIÓN ESPECIAL

Ingresos fiscales provenientes de recursos naturales no renovables en América Latina y el Caribe

Los ingresos relacionados con la exploración y producción de los hidrocarburos se recuperaron en 2018 a pesar de la volatilidad en el mercado mundial de petróleo

En 2018, el mercado mundial del petróleo experimentó alta volatilidad como resultado de una confluencia de factores macroeconómicos, políticos y de producción. En la primera parte del año, los principales precios spot en el mercado (Western Texas Intermediate [WTI], Brent y Dubai) aumentaron como resultado de un corte de producción mayor al acordado entre los miembros de la OPEP, particularmente en Venezuela, y sólidos fundamentos macroeconómicos mundiales. Esta dinámica se reforzó en mayo cuando Estados Unidos anunció su retirada unilateral del Plan de Acción Cooperativa Conjunta, el llamado acuerdo nuclear de Irán, y la posibilidad de nuevas sanciones contra el mismo país que comenzarían a afectar la producción mundial más adelante en el año.

En respuesta a esta potencial interrupción, la OPEP y la Federación Rusa acordaron aumentar su producción para compensar esta disminución. No obstante, el mercado se mantuvo apretado ya que los importadores tradicionales de petróleo crudo iraní redujeron sus compras a la luz de las inminentes sanciones. En el cuarto trimestre del año, los precios al contado cayeron bruscamente cuando Estados Unidos otorgó exenciones de sanciones a un grupo de países, principalmente China e India, y un aumento en la producción en Federación Rusa y Arabia Saudita empujó al mercado a un exceso de oferta. Sin embargo, tomado como un promedio anual, el precio del petróleo aumentó significativamente, llegando a USD 68 por barril en comparación con los USD 53 por barril en 2017, lo que equivale a un aumento del 29% (Gráfico 2.1).

Gráfico 2.1. **Precio spot del petróleo crudo, enero de 2016 a diciembre de 2018**

USD por barril

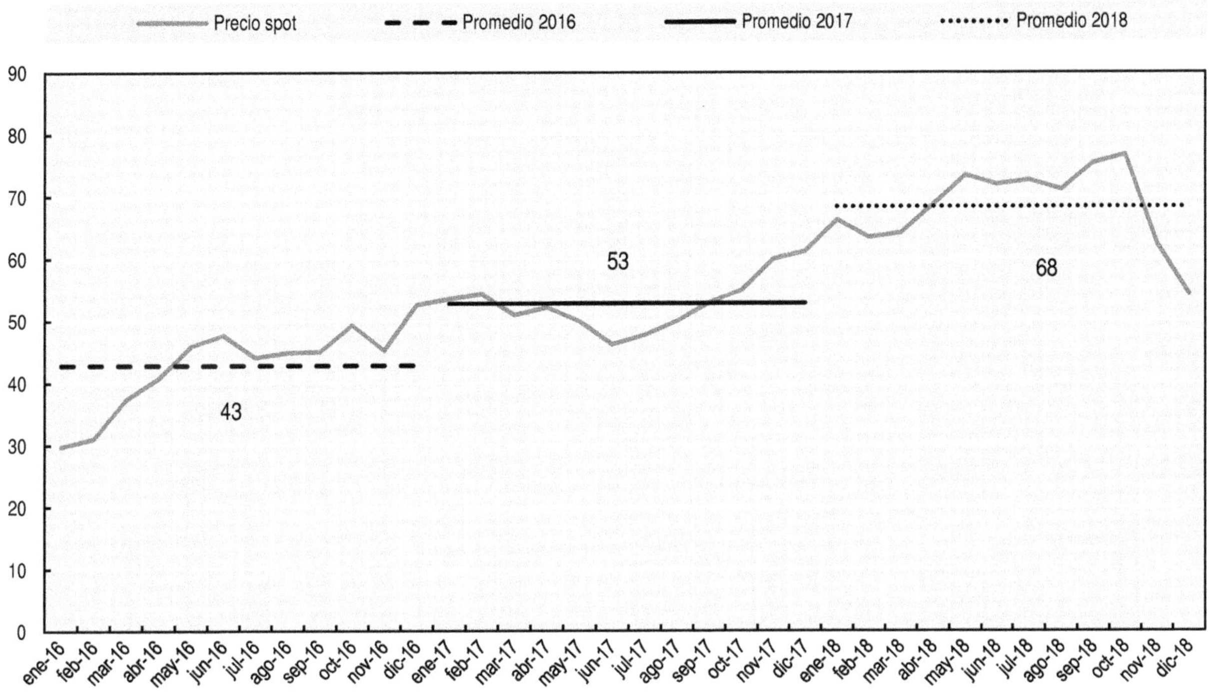

Nota: El precio spot del petróleo crudo se refiere al promedio simple de Western Texas Intermediate (WTI), Brent y Dubai.

Fuente: Comisión Económica para América Latina y el Caribe (CEPAL), sobre la base de Banco Mundial (2020[1]).

StatLink https://doi.org/10.1787/888934113659

A pesar de la mayor volatilidad en los mercados mundiales de petróleo, los ingresos fiscales de la exploración y producción de petróleo y gas —actividades de "*up-stream*"— se fortalecieron en ALC durante 2018.[1] Los ingresos totales provenientes de la exploración y producción de hidrocarburos alcanzaron un promedio del 2.7% del PIB, en comparación con un 2.0% en 2017 (Gráfico 2.2 y Cuadro 2.1). Los ingresos no tributarios —mayormente ingresos por rentas de la propiedad, como regalías y otras participaciones en el valor comercial de la producción— representaron gran parte de este aumento, incrementando del 1.7% del PIB en 2017 al 2.3% en 2018. Vale mencionar que el alza en los precios spot no se tradujo directamente en mayores ingresos no tributarios, ya que la producción en la región mostró una tendencia a la baja durante el año: el petróleo crudo y los condensados cayeron un 8.2% respecto de los niveles de 2017, o un 2.2% excluyendo a Venezuela, y el gas natural cayó 2.1% (BP, 2019[2]).

Gráfico 2.2. **Ingresos fiscales provenientes de exploración y producción de hidrocarburos en nueve países de ALC, por instrumento, 2010-18**

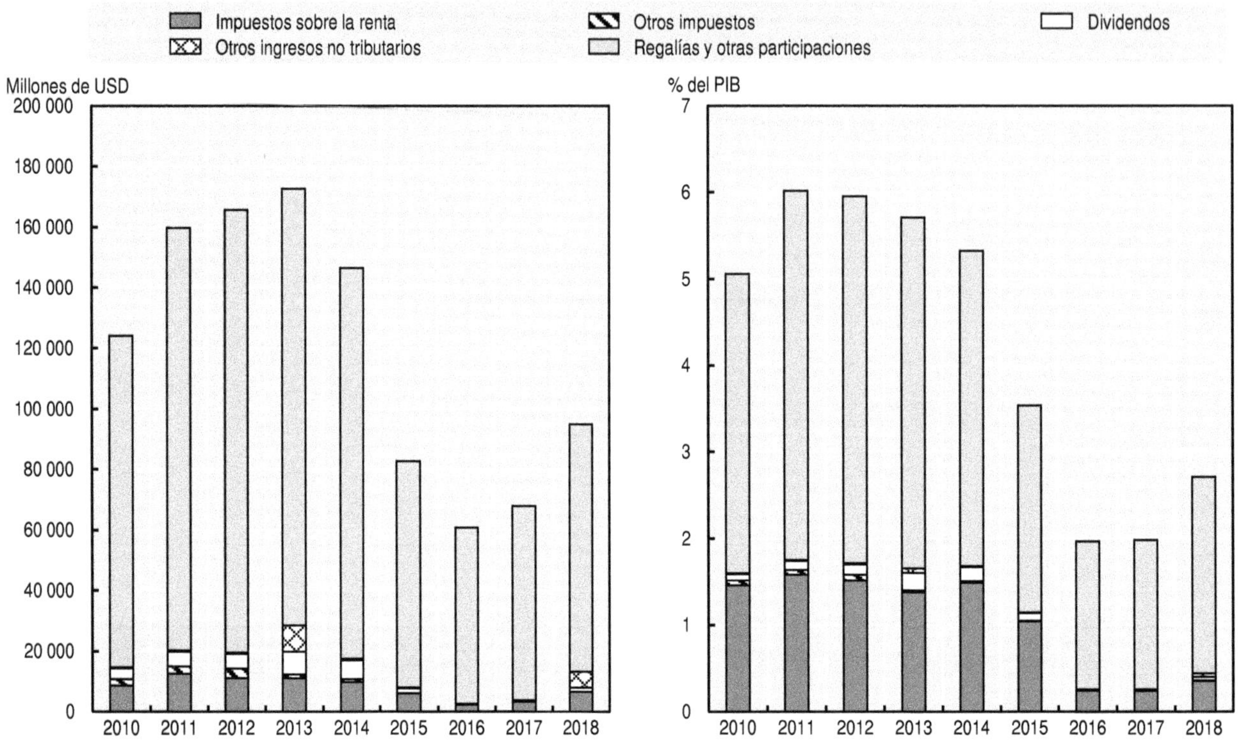

Nota: La muestra de países para la exploración y producción de hidrocarburos incluye: Argentina, Bolivia (Estado Plurinacional de), Brasil, Colombia, Ecuador, Guatemala, México, Perú y Trinidad y Tobago.
El porcentaje del PIB es el promedio simple de todos los países de la muestra.
Fuente: Comisión Económica para América Latina y el Caribe (CEPAL), sobre la base de cifras de *CEPALSTAT* (CEPAL, 2020[3]).
StatLink *https://doi.org/10.1787/888934113678*

Los ingresos tributarios del sector también aumentaron durante el año, alcanzando un promedio del 0.4% del PIB en comparación con el 0.2% del PIB en 2017, ya que los ingresos del impuesto sobre la renta corporativa (ISR) aumentaron en línea con la mayor rentabilidad entre los productores de petróleo en la región (Cuadro 2.1). Colombia y Trinidad y Tobago registraron aumentos significativos en sus ingresos tributarios durante el año, un factor de importancia en este último país, donde el ISR es el mecanismo predominante para capturar las rentas generadas por el sector. A pesar del incremento en los ingresos tributarios, a nivel regional juegan un papel relativamente pequeño en los ingresos fiscales provenientes de la exploración y producción de hidrocarburos (Gráfico 2.2).

Cuadro 2.1. **Ingresos fiscales provenientes de exploración y producción de hidrocarburos en nueve países de ALC, por instrumento, 2017-18**

Porcentaje del PIB

País	Total		Ingresos tributarios		Ingresos no tributarios		Ingresos totales 2018	
	2017	2018	2017	2018	2017	2018	Millones de USD	Variación interanual (%)
Argentina	0.4	0.5	0.1	0.1	0.3	0.4	2 680	-4
Bolivia (Est. Plur. de)	4.0	4.6	0.3	0.3	3.8	4.3	1 845	23
Brasil	0.4	1.2	0.03	0.1	0.4	1.1	22 271	149
Colombia	1.1	1.8	0.4	0.7	0.7	1.1	6 112	83
Ecuador	5.6	8.0	0.0	0.0	5.6	8.0	8 621	48
Guatemala	0.05	0.07	0.01	0.01	0.03	0.05	53	53
México	3.8	4.2	-0.01	0.02	3.8	4.2	51 124	16
PEMEX	1.8	1.9	...	...	1.8	1.9	22 688	10
Gobierno federal	2.0	2.3	-0.01	0.02	2.0	2.3	28 435	22
Perú	0.5	0.6	0.1	0.2	0.4	0.5	1 402	33
Trinidad y Tobago	2.0	3.4	1.2	1.8	0.8	1.6	772	76
Promedio simple / total en milliones de USD	2.0	2.7	0.2	0.4	1.7	2.3	94 880	40

Nota: Las cifras pueden no sumar debido al redondeo. En 2017, los ingresos tributarios relacionados con la exploración y producción de los hidrocarburos en México registraron un reembolso neto, ya que algunas empresas que operan en el sector hicieron uso de las disposiciones de transferencia de pérdidas en sus declaraciones juradas.

Fuente: Comisión Económica para América Latina y el Caribe (CEPAL), sobre la base de cifras de CEPALSTAT (CEPAL, 2020[3]).

StatLink https://doi.org/10.1787/888934113811

Una mayor producción de petróleo y gas durante 2018 en **Argentina**, así como una pronunciada depreciación de la moneda nacional, conllevaron un incremento en los ingresos de hidrocarburos, los cuales alcanzaron un 0.5% del PIB en comparación con un 0.4% del PIB en 2017. El principal impulsor de este aumento fueron los mayores ingresos por concepto de regalías durante el año, que llevó los ingresos no tributarios al 0.4% del PIB en comparación con el 0.3% del PIB en 2017. Sin embargo, los ingresos tributarios cayeron en términos absolutos (tanto en moneda nacional como en dólares estadounidenses) y en términos relativos. En parte, esto reflejó cambios en el marco de ISR como parte de la reforma fiscal de 2017, incluida una reducción en la tasa general de ISR del 35% al 30% para los años fiscales 2018 y 2019. En septiembre de 2018, el gobierno restableció el impuesto a las exportaciones de hidrocarburos (que había caducado en 2017), estableciendo una tasa del 12% con un umbral de 3 o 4 ARS por dólar estadounidense, según el producto. El impacto de esta medida en los ingresos de 2018 fue limitado.

En **Bolivia**, los ingresos fiscales relacionados con el gas natural alcanzaron el 4.6% del PIB en 2018 en comparación con el 4.0% del PIB en 2017. Esto se debe a un aumento en los ingresos no tributarios de instrumentos relacionados con el valor comercial de la producción, como el impuesto directo sobre hidrocarburos y regalías. Sin embargo, el aumento de los precios no se reflejó en la evolución de los ingresos, ya que la producción de gas natural en volumen disminuyó durante el año (-6.5%) como resultado de una menor demanda por parte de Argentina, donde aumentó la producción de gas natural, y Brasil, debido a alta producción hidroeléctrica y producción industrial más débil (Ministerio de Economia y Finanzas Publicas, 2019[4]).

Los ingresos fiscales por petróleo y gas natural en **Brasil** aumentaron en 2018 a pesar de una disminución en la producción de hidrocarburos, alcanzando el 1.2% del PIB en comparación con el 0.4% del PIB en 2017.[2] Un aumento de casi cinco veces en los ingresos de ISR impulsó los ingresos tributarios del sector a 0.1% del PIB, por encima del 0.03% en 2017, su nivel más alto desde 2009. Sin embargo, el aumento de los ingresos totales se debió principalmente a un salto en los ingresos no tributarios, que alcanzaron un 1.1% del PIB en comparación con un 0.4% del PIB en 2017, en parte debido a una depreciación del 14% del real brasileño durante el año. Los ingresos de la participación especial del gobierno en la producción[3] aumentaron más del doble (a 0.43% del PIB por encima del 0.17% del PIB en 2017) a medida que Petrobras aumentó la producción en campos que estaban sujetos a tasas impositivas más altas (Petrobras, 2019[5]). Los ingresos no tributarios también se vieron impulsados por ingresos derivados de los bonos de firma al finalizar la 15ª ronda de licitación para concesiones de exploración y producción de petróleo y gas (equivalente al 0.3% del PIB).

En **Colombia**, los ingresos por hidrocarburos casi se duplicaron en 2018, alcanzando el 1.8% del PIB en comparación con el 1.1% del PIB en 2017, en gran parte debido a los sólidos resultados financieros de Ecopetrol, el productor estatal, provocado por una mayor producción y mejores precios de petróleo y gas. Las utilidades operacionales de la compañía casi se duplicaron en 2017 y aumentaron un 40% más en 2018 (Ecopetrol, 2019[6]). Los ingresos tributarios aumentaron hasta un 0.7% del PIB en 2018, en comparación con un 0.4% en 2017, impulsado por la liquidación de pasivos ISR para el año calendario 2017 y fuertes prepagos de impuestos estimados para el año calendario 2018. En una línea similar, la recuperación de la rentabilidad tuvo un efecto adicional en los ingresos no tributarios: el pago de dividendos por parte de Ecopetrol al gobierno central aumentó al 0.3% del PIB en comparación con un 0.1% del PIB en 2017.

Los ingresos petroleros en **Ecuador** aumentaron significativamente, alcanzando un 8.0% del PIB en 2018 frente a un 5.6% del PIB en 2017, a pesar de una disminución en la producción de hidrocarburos. La disminución en el volumen exportado fue compensada en gran medida por el incremento en el precio del petróleo. Sin embargo, el salto en los ingresos del petróleo se debió en parte al aumento de las ventas internas de los productores estatales, en línea con los mayores volúmenes de importación de derivados de hidrocarburos. En **Guatemala**, los ingresos por hidrocarburos aumentaron al 0.07% del PIB del 0.05% del PIB en 2017, a medida que los precios más altos elevaron los ingresos de la participación del gobierno en el valor de la producción.

En **México**, el aumento en los precios spot internacionales fue contrarrestado por una disminución en la producción de petróleo crudo (-7.8% en 2018), que afectó la evolución de los ingresos de hidrocarburos en 2018 (SHCP, 2019[7]). A nivel general, estos ingresos aumentaron al 4.2% del PIB, frente al 3.8% del PIB en 2017, debido a un aumento en los ingresos no tributarios percibidos por el gobierno federal como resultado de los precios más altos. El crecimiento de los ingresos propios de Pemex, que se consolida en el sector público federal, fue moderado, incrementando en 0.1% del PIB entre 2017 y 2018. En contraste, un aumento en la producción de petróleo en **Perú** compensó una disminución en la producción de gas natural y gas natural licuado (GNL). Esta dinámica permitió un aumento en los ingresos de hidrocarburos hasta el 0.6% del PIB frente al 0.5% del PIB en 2017. Los ingresos no tributarios, particularmente de regalías, se vieron reforzados por los mayores ingresos asociados con las exportaciones de GNL dirigidas a los mercados más lucrativos de Europa y Asia (Perúpetro, 2019[8]).

Los ingresos por hidrocarburos en **Trinidad y Tobago** se recuperaron en 2018, aumentando a 3.4% del PIB desde 2.0% del PIB en 2017. A diferencia de la mayoría de los países productores de hidrocarburos en la región, donde un productor estatal representa una gran parte de la producción total e ingresos, en Trinidad y Tobago los principales actores son las grandes empresas multinacionales.[4] El ISR, por lo tanto, juega un papel crucial en la captura de rentas de la explotación de los activos de hidrocarburos del país. La mayor rentabilidad en 2017 y 2018 provocada por los precios más altos del petróleo crudo impulsó los ingresos tributarios del sector, que alcanzaron el 1.8% del PIB en comparación con el 1.2% del PIB en 2017. La adopción de una tasa unificada de regalía del 12.5% para la extracción de gas natural resultó en una duplicación de los ingresos no tributarios del sector (1.6% del PIB comparado con 0.8% del PIB en 2017) (Ministerio de Hacienda Trinidad y Tobago, 2018[9]).

Los ingresos fiscales provenientes de la minería mantuvieron su tendencia al alza en 2018

Los precios spot en los mercados internacionales para una amplia gama de minerales y metales industriales se mantuvieron fuertes en la primera mitad de 2018, manteniendo o incluso aprovechando las ganancias observadas en la segunda mitad de 2017 (Gráfico 2.3). Sin embargo, las crecientes preocupaciones sobre la actividad económica en China y las tensiones comerciales entre China y los Estados Unidos provocaron una contracción en los precios internacionales durante la segunda mitad de 2018. Entre el segundo y el tercer trimestre del año, los precios spot cayeron para el cobre (-11%), plomo (-12%) y zinc (-19%). Los metales preciosos, que en algunos casos se mezclan con concentrados de mineral exportados desde la región, principalmente en el caso de los concentrados de cobre, también registraron una corrección a la baja en los precios durante el mismo período que afectó al oro (-7%), platino (-9%) y plata (-9%).

Gráfico 2.3. **Metales y minerales industriales seleccionados: variación interanual en los precios spot y los volúmenes de importación chinos, T1 2017-T4 2018**

Índice, T1 2017 = 100

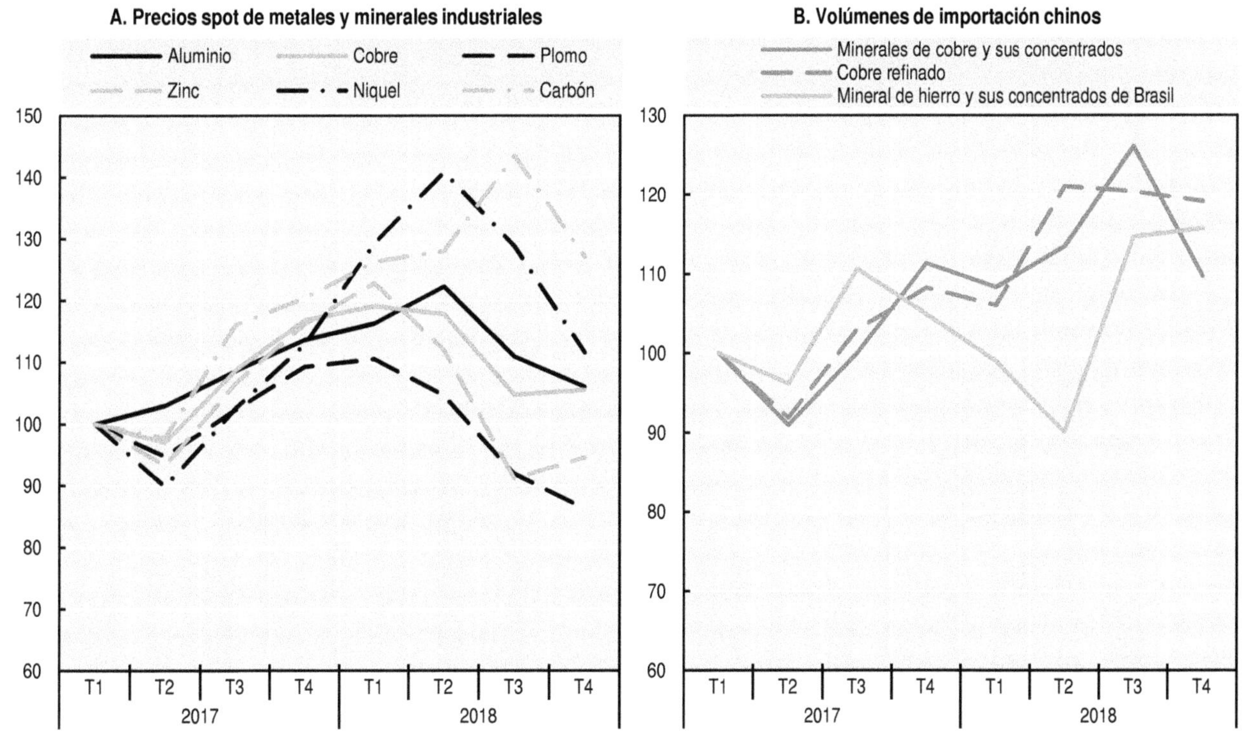

Fuente: Comisión Económica para América Latina y el Caribe (CEPAL), sobre la base de Banco Mundial (2020[1]).

StatLink https://doi.org/10.1787/888934113697

El ajuste en los precios causado por el cambio en el sentimiento del mercado no reflejó necesariamente los fundamentos subyacentes. La demanda de importación china se mantuvo fuerte durante todo el año, reforzada en parte por un endurecimiento de las regulaciones ambientales y nuevas medidas para restringir la importación de chatarra (Banco Mundial, 2019[10]; Banco Mundial, 2019[11]). La producción de acero en China alcanzó un récord histórico de 928.3 millones de toneladas —un aumento de 6.6% en 2018 sobre el 2017— lo cual sostuvo la demanda para carbón, mineral de hierro y níquel (Asociación Mundial del Acero, 2019[12]). En este contexto, la continua demanda de China estableció un piso bajo para la corrección de precios observada en la segunda mitad del año. A pesar de la tendencia a la baja en los precios para la mayoría de los metales y minerales, el promedio anual de algunos de los principales recursos naturales no renovables exportados de la región aumentó, incluido el carbón (21.0%), el cobre (5.8%) y el níquel (26.0%).

Los ingresos fiscales mineros en ALC aumentaron en 2018, alcanzando el 0.39% del PIB en 2018 en comparación con el 0.33% del PIB en 2017. Este resultado se debió principalmente a un aumento de los ingresos tributarios - principalmente ingresos por concepto del ISR y otros instrumentos tributarios cuya base son las utilidades - que alcanzaron el 0.23% del PIB en comparación con el 0.18% del PIB en 2017, o un aumento del 41% en términos de USD (Gráfico 2.4 y Cuadro 2.2).[5] El incremento en los ingresos tributarios relacionados con el ISR, impulsado principalmente por la liquidación de pasivos tributarios del año anterior y pagos de impuestos estimados, se debió en gran parte al repunte en los precios y al impacto concomitante en los ingresos operacionales de las empresas que operan en el sector.

Gráfico 2.4. **Ingresos fiscales provenientes de minería en 11 países de ALC, por instrumento, 2010-18**

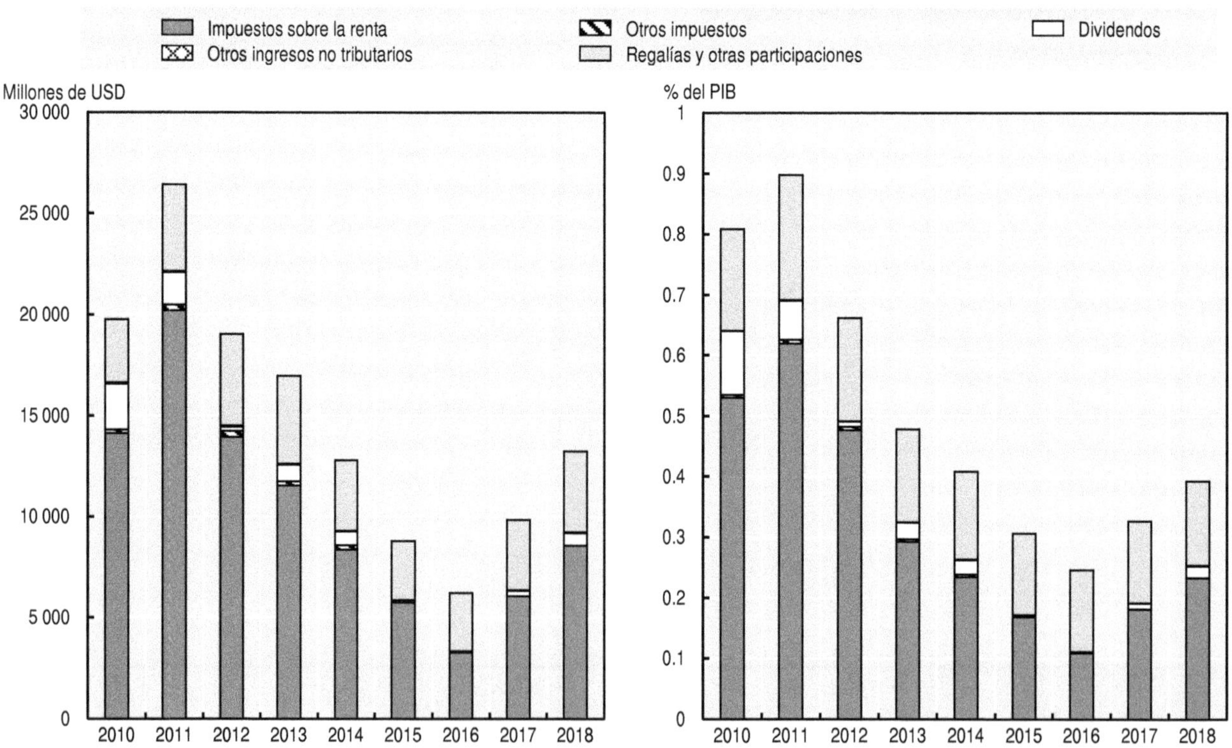

Nota: La muestra de países para la minería incluye: Argentina, Bolivia (Estado Plurinacional de), Brasil, Chile, Colombia, Ecuador, Guatemala, Jamaica, México, Perú y República Dominicana. El porcentaje del PIB es el promedio simple de todos los países de la muestra.

Fuente: Comisión Económica para América Latina y el Caribe (CEPAL), sobre la base de cifras de CEPALSTAT (CEPAL, 2020[3]).

StatLink https://doi.org/10.1787/888934113716

Los ingresos no tributarios, por el contrario, registraron un aumento más moderado, llegando al 0.16% del PIB en promedio en 2018 en comparación con el 0.14% del PIB en 2017, o un aumento del 24% en términos de USD (Cuadro 2.2). Este aumento se debió en parte a un importante pago de dividendos por parte de la firma minera estatal chilena CODELCO al gobierno chileno. Los ingresos por regalías y otras participaciones vinculadas al valor comercial de la producción, calculados sobre el precio spot vigente en el momento de la producción, fueron menos dinámicos en comparación con 2017, debido a la corrección en los precios internacionales durante la segunda mitad del año (un aumento de 15% en términos de USD).

A nivel de país, los ingresos fiscales de la minería en **Argentina** se mantuvieron estables en 0.04% del PIB durante 2018, aunque estuvieron fuertemente influenciados por factores internos y externos (Cuadro 2.2). La producción minera cayó significativamente durante el año, especialmente en los casos de cobre (-48% en volumen), oro (-34%) y plata (-17%). Sin embargo, a pesar de la disminución en la producción, los ingresos mineros expresados en términos de pesos argentinos (ARS) continuaron aumentando, aproximadamente en línea con el aumento del PIB nominal, ya que la moneda se depreció fuertemente en 2018 (70%, promedio anual).

Cuadro 2.2. **Ingresos fiscales provenientes de minería en 11 países de ALC, por instrumento, 2017-18**

Porcentaje del PIB

País	Total		Ingresos tributarios		Ingresos no tributarios		Ingresos totales 2018	
	2017	2018	2017	2018	2017	2018	Millones de USD	Variación interanual (%)
Argentina	0.04	0.04	0.03	0.03	0.01	0.01	187	-22
Bolivia (Est. Plur. de)	0.76	0.85	0.27	0.37	0.49	0.48	342	20
Brasil	0.07	0.10	0.04	0.05	0.03	0.05	1 925	34
Chile	0.94	1.40	0.46	0.82	0.48	0.58	4 188	60
CODELCO	0.49	0.60	0.01	0.02	0.48	0.58	1 798	32
Sector privado	0.45	0.80	0.45	0.80	0.00	0.00	2 390	90
Colombia	0.40	0.45	0.19	0.20	0.21	0.25	1 489	18
Ecuador	0.06	0.07	0.02	0.02	0.05	0.05	77	15
Guatemala	0.06	0.03	0.03	0.01	0.03	0.02	21	-50
Jamaica	0.03	0.04	0.00	0.00	0.03	0.04	5	26
México	0.19	0.23	0.16	0.20	0.03	0.03	2 787	25
Perú	0.62	0.90	0.46	0.72	0.16	0.19	2 039	53
Rep. Dominicana	0.41	0.21	0.35	0.15	0.06	0.05	176	-46
Promedio simple / total en milliones de USD	0.33	0.39	0.18	0.23	0.14	0.16	13 235	35

Fuente: Comisión Económica para América Latina y el Caribe (CEPAL), sobre la base de cifras de CEPALSTAT (CEPAL, 2020[3]).

StatLink https://doi.org/10.1787/888934113830

Los ingresos fiscales mineros en **Bolivia** alcanzaron el 0.85% del PIB en 2018 desde el 0.76% del PIB en 2017, como resultado del aumento de los ingresos tributarios. Los ingresos tributarios alcanzaron un 0.37% del PIB en 2018, en comparación con un 0.27% en 2017, lo que equivale a un incremento del 20% en términos de USD. La rentabilidad del sector minero aumentó en 2017 respaldada por un alza en el precio del zinc (38%) y mayores volúmenes de exportación de oro metálico (43%). Además de aumentar los ingresos por concepto del ISR, mayores ganancias también condujeron a mayores ingresos derivados de la tasa adicional del impuesto sobre la renta corporativa aplicada al sector del 12.5%. Los ingresos no tributarios en 2018 cayeron marginalmente, alcanzando el 0.48% del PIB en comparación con el 0.49% del PIB en 2017, lo que reflejó la tendencia a la baja de los precios de los minerales y metales durante el año.

En **Brasil**, los ingresos mineros aumentaron al 0.10% del PIB en 2018 desde el 0.07% del PIB en 2017, respaldados por los mayores precios del mineral de hierro durante el año. Si bien los ingresos tributarios se mantuvieron estables en relación con el PIB (0.04% del PIB), aumentaron 35% en términos de USD. Los ingresos no tributarios fueron particularmente dinámicos en 2018, a pesar de la disminución en los precios promedio anuales, alcanzando el 0.05% del PIB en comparación con el 0.03% del PIB en 2017 (un aumento del 34% en términos de USD). Los mayores volúmenes de producción de minerales ferrosos reforzaron este resultado, con Vale S.A. reportando un aumento del 6% para los finos de mineral de hierro y del 9% para los gránulos (Vale S.A., 2019[13]). El aumento en los ingresos no tributarios también se debió a ajustes en el cálculo de los pagos de regalías. La base imponible de la regalía (*Compensação Financeira pela Exploração de Recursos Minerais*) cambió de ventas netas sin impuestos y otros gastos calificados a ventas brutas excluyendo solo impuestos. Además, esta reforma trajo cambios en la tasa del gravamen, especialmente para el mineral de hierro, que aumentó al 3.5%.

Los ingresos mineros en **Chile** aumentaron fuertemente en 2018, debido en gran parte al aumento de los pagos de impuestos de los productores privados del país. Los ingresos totales se situaron en el 1.4% del PIB en 2018 en comparación con el 0.94% del PIB en 2017 (un aumento del 60% en términos de USD). Los ingresos tributarios, los ingresos por el ISR y los pagos del impuesto especial a la minería incrementaron considerablemente debido a mayores pagos por la liquidación de pasivos tributarios para el año fiscal 2017 y los pagos anticipados de impuestos estimados en 2018, que a su vez se vieron impulsados por un aumento en la tasa de impuestos corporativos (del 25.5% al 27%).[6] Los ingresos no tributarios, esencialmente transferencias de ganancias del productor estatal CODELCO al gobierno central y los pagos de CODELCO por sus exportaciones de cobre, también mostraron una tendencia al alza, al pasar del 0.48% del PIB en 2017 al 0.58% del PIB.

El aumento de los precios internacionales del carbón (21%) impulsó los ingresos mineros en **Colombia**, que alcanzaron el 0.45% del PIB desde frente 0.40% del PIB en 2017 (un aumento del 18% en términos de USD). Los ingresos no tributarios, especialmente las regalías del valor de producción del carbón aumentaron del 0.21% del PIB en 2017 al 0.25% del PIB (24% en términos de USD). Los ingresos tributarios del sector fueron menos dinámicos, pasando del 0.19% del PIB en 2017 al 0.20% del PIB. La menor producción de oro en la mina Pueblo Viejo (-11%), una empresa conjunta de Barrick Gold (Canadá) y Newmont Goldcorp (Estados Unidos), impactó negativamente los ingresos mineros en la **República Dominicana**, que cayeron al 0.21% del PIB desde el 0.41% del PIB en 2017. La mayor parte de esta disminución se debió a una contracción en los ingresos tributarios, que cayeron al 0.15% del PIB desde el 0.35% del PIB en 2017, lo que refleja en parte el impacto de una contracción del 25% en las utilidades en 2017 del Pueblo Mina Viejo (Barrick Gold Corporation, 2019[14]).

Los ingresos mineros en **Ecuador** aumentaron marginalmente en 2018, aumentando a 0.07% del PIB en comparación con 0.06% del PIB en 2017. Se están desarrollando proyectos mineros a gran escala en el país y se proyecta que los ingresos fiscales aumenten en los próximos años. Los ingresos no tributarios son actualmente el componente más notable de los ingresos mineros, y consisten principalmente en pagos anticipados de regalías por parte de las empresas en la etapa de preproducción de las operaciones. Por ejemplo, Lundin Gold Inc. (Canadá) firmó un acuerdo con el gobierno de Ecuador en 2016, que incluía, entre otras medidas fiscales, un calendario de pagos anticipados de regalías de USD 25 millones en 2016 y USD 20 millones en 2017 y 2018 (Lundin Gold, 2017[15]).

Los ingresos de la minería en **Guatemala** disminuyeron al 0.03% del PIB en 2018 del 0.06% del PIB en 2017. Los ingresos tributarios y no tributarios disminuyeron, en gran parte debido a una disminución en la producción de metales, principalmente óxido de hierro y níquel, en 2017 y 2018. En julio de 2017, la Corte Suprema de Guatemala suspendió las licencias de dos de las minas más grandes del país. Esta decisión fue reafirmada por el Tribunal Constitucional del país en septiembre de 2018, que ordenó que el Ministerio de Minas y Energía llevara a cabo una consulta de la OIT 169 con las comunidades locales en el marco del Convenio sobre pueblos indígenas y tribales (1989).

En **Jamaica**, los ingresos mineros se mantuvieron bajos, alcanzando el 0.04% del PIB en 2018. Esto marca un contraste con un máximo reciente del 0.8% del PIB en 2016. Los ingresos tributarios de la minería —provenientes del pago del ISR por parte del sector de bauxita y alúmina— permanecieron nulos, continuando una tendencia que comenzó en el año fiscal 2012/13. Los ingresos no tributarios mostraron una tendencia al alza, al pasar del 0.03% del PIB en 2017 al 0.04% del PIB en 2018, lo que equivale a un aumento del 26% en términos de USD. Las regalías de bauxita, un gravamen de USD 0.50 por tonelada métrica seca de mineral enviado, aumentaron a medida que los volúmenes de exportación aumentaron un 26.5% en 2018. El gravamen de bauxita, con una tasa legal base de USD 5 por tonelada métrica seca, mostró poco dinamismo. El gobierno ha firmado acuerdos a medida con algunas empresas que operan en el país, que establecen una participación del 17.33% de las ganancias antes de intereses, impuestos y depreciación, o el pago de la tasa de bauxita a una tasa de USD 1.50 por seco tonelada métrica enviada, lo que sea mayor.

Una combinación de un repunte en la producción de cobre (2% en volumen), precios internacionales del cobre más fuertes en 2017 y 2018 y la depreciación de la moneda nacional impulsaron los ingresos fiscales de la minería en **México**, que aumentaron a 0.23% del PIB desde 0.19% de PIB en 2017. Los ingresos tributarios se fortalecieron, alcanzando el 0.20% del PIB en comparación con el 0.16% del PIB en 2017, en respuesta a las mayores liquidaciones de los pasivos tributarios del ISR asociados con mayores las ganancias realizadas en 2017. Los ingresos no tributarios aumentaron en términos absolutos (11% en USD) pero se mantuvo en 0.03% del PIB.

En **Perú**, los ingresos mineros aumentaron considerablemente apoyado por mayores ingresos vinculados con el ISR. Los ingresos totales alcanzaron el 0.9% del PIB desde frente al 0.62% del PIB en 2017, lo que equivale a un aumento del 53% en términos de USD. Los ingresos tributarios fueron boyantes: incrementaron al 0.72% del PIB desde el 0.46% del PIB en 2017, gracias a los pagos de liquidación del ISR para el año fiscal 2017 y a los pagos anticipados de impuestos estimados en el primer semestre de 2018. Una disminución en la producción de cobre y un aumento relativamente menor en los precios promedio anuales resultó en un aumento más moderado en los ingresos no tributarios de la minería, que llegaron al 0.19% del PIB desde el 0.16% del PIB en 2017.

Se prevé una caída en los ingresos fiscales provenientes de los recursos naturales no renovables en 2019

Las condiciones macroeconómicas mundiales en 2019 no fueron favorables para los productores de recursos naturales no renovables de la región. El crecimiento económico mundial se desaceleró bruscamente, del 3.1% en 2018 al 2.5% en 2019, su nivel más bajo desde la crisis económica y financiera de 2008-09 (CEPAL, 2019[16]). Los volúmenes del comercio mundial también se tambalearon durante el año, experimentando una contracción en los primeros tres trimestres del año después de registrar un modesto crecimiento del 3.4% en 2018. Al mismo tiempo, los precios de varios recursos naturales no renovables importantes para la región cayeron en 2019, incluido carbón (-27%), petróleo crudo (-10%) y cobre (-8%) (Gráfico 2.5). Un aumento en los precios del mineral de hierro durante el año no correspondió a los fundamentos del mercado fortalecidos, sino que reflejó el impacto de la trágica falla de la presa de relaves en la mina de mineral de hierro Córrego do Feijão, propiedad de Vale S.A. en Minas Gerais, Brasil, que resultó en la muerte de 272 individuos.

Gráfico 2.5. **Productos seleccionados: precios observados, 2014-19**

Índice, 2014 = 100

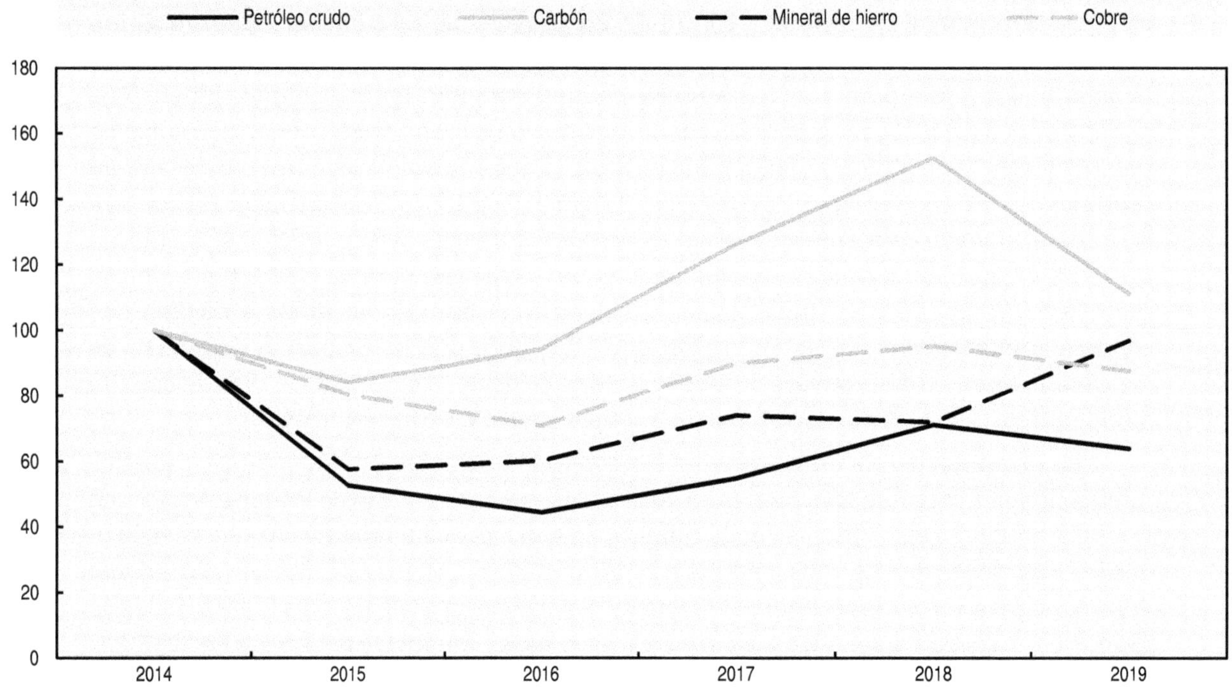

Fuente: Comisión Económica para América Latina y el Caribe (CEPAL), sobre la base de Banco Mundial (2020[1])

StatLink https://doi.org/10.1787/888934113735

Se estima que los ingresos fiscales provenientes de recursos naturales no renovables cayeron en ALC en 2019 (Gráfico 2.6). Se prevé que los ingresos relacionados con la exploración y producción de hidrocarburos alcanzarían el 2.5% del PIB, por debajo del 2.7% del PIB en 2018. Se esperan reducciones en muchos de los países de la muestra, particularmente aquellos que dependen principalmente de ingresos no tributarios que se mueven al ritmo de la evolución de los precios (regalías y otras participaciones en el valor comercial de la producción). En contraste, los ingresos petroleros pueden haber aumentado en Colombia y Trinidad y Tobago, ya que los pagos del ISR sobre las ganancias de 2018 compensarían la disminución de los ingresos no tributarios.

Gráfico 2.6. **América Latina y el Caribe: ingresos fiscales observados y estimados provenientes de la exploración y producción de hidrocarburos y de minería, 2010-19**

Porcentaje del PIB

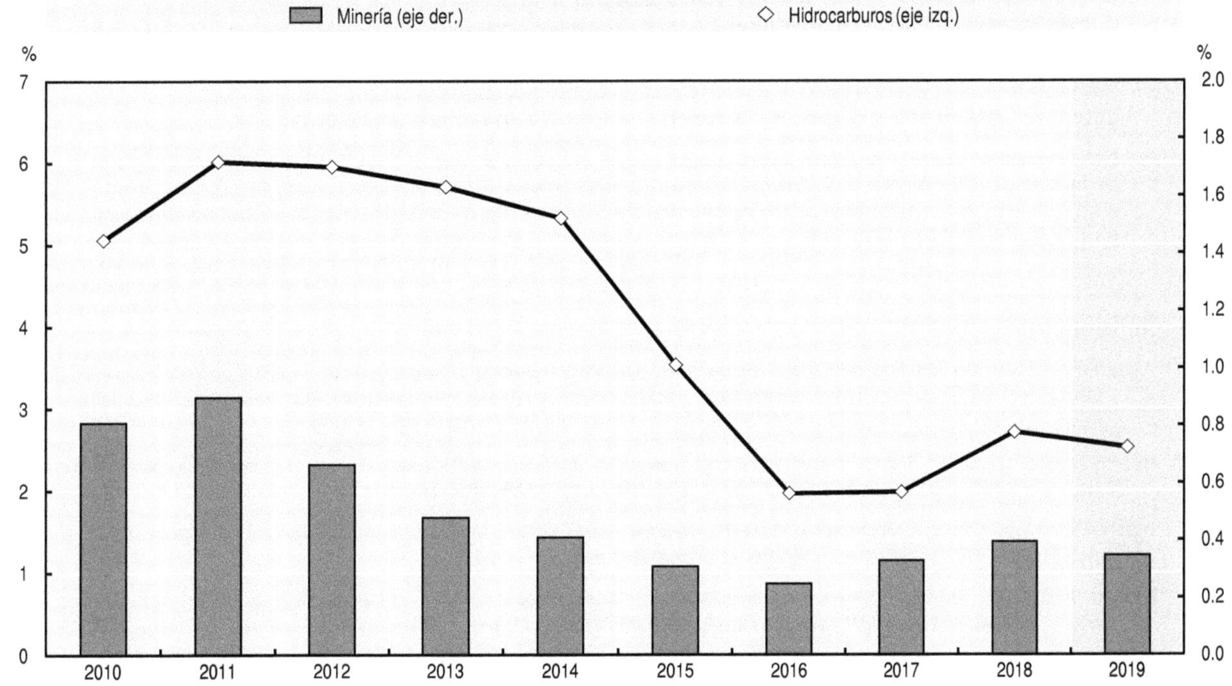

Nota: La muestra de países para la minería incluye: Argentina, Bolivia (Estado Plurinacional de), Brasil, Chile, Colombia, Ecuador, Guatemala, Jamaica, México, Perú y República Dominicana. La muestra de países para la exploración y producción de hidrocarburos incluye: Argentina, Bolivia (Estado Plurinacional de), Brasil, Colombia, Ecuador, Guatemala, México, Perú y Trinidad y Tobago. Los valores para 2019 se basan en estimaciones oficiales del gobierno a partir de los documentos presupuestarios de 2020 o de cifras anuales preliminares. Cuando las cifras para 2019 no estaban disponibles, se estimaron utilizando datos mensuales (generalmente durante los primeros 9 meses del año). Cuando no se disponía de datos mensuales, los ingresos se estimaron aplicando el cambio interanual en el precio del producto más representativo (o cesta de productos en el caso de la minería) para el país, expresado en términos de moneda nacional, a los ingresos observados de 2018.

Fuente: Comisión Económica para América Latina y el Caribe (CEPAL), sobre la base de las cifras de CEPALSTAT (CEPAL, 2020[3]).

StatLink https://doi.org/10.1787/888934113754

También se proyecta que los ingresos mineros disminuyeron en promedio, cayendo a 0.3% del PIB en 2019 desde 0.4% en 2018. Sin embargo, es probable que esta reducción no haya sido uniforme en todos los países, como en el caso de los productores de hidrocarburos. La trayectoria de los ingresos mineros refleja en gran medida la evolución de los precios y la producción relevantes para la canasta de exportaciones de cada país. Sin embargo, es probable que los precios más bajos hayan arrastrado los ingresos tributarios y no tributarios durante el año.

Notas

1. Guatemala se incluye en el análisis por primera vez.
2. En diciembre de 2017, el gobierno federal de Brasil promulgó un nuevo modelo de impuestos para el sector, que entró en vigor en enero de 2018, que estableció un nuevo régimen especial para la exploración, el desarrollo y la producción de petróleo, gas y otros hidrocarburos líquidos. El nuevo modelo introdujo modificaciones al régimen aduanero de petróleo y gas, permitiendo, entre otros cambios, la exención de impuestos federales sobre la importación de bienes para uso permanente en el país. El nuevo marco también estableció definitivamente la deducción de los costos de exploración y producción de la base impositiva del ISR y la contribución social al impuesto a las ganancias netas (CSLL). Posteriormente, algunos estados brasileños acordaron otorgar incentivos fiscales relacionados con el IVA (ICMS) en las transacciones cubiertas por el nuevo régimen (Petrobras, 2019[5]).

3. Un gravamen del 10% al 40% sobre el valor de venta de la producción, ajustado mediante deducciones calificadas, con la tasa establecida según el nivel de producción o la rentabilidad de una concesión.
4. En noviembre de 2018, la compañía petrolera estatal, Petroleum Company of Trinidad and Tobago Limited (Petrotrin), fue liquidada. Las actividades de la antigua empresa se dividieron entre cuatro nuevas empresas estatales, una de las cuales, Heritage Petroleum Company Limited, continuará operando en el área de exploración, desarrollo, producción y comercialización de petróleo.
5. Los promedios regionales en la edición de este año son marginalmente más bajos que en ediciones anteriores debido a la inclusión de Ecuador y Guatemala en la muestra de países.
6. Las declaraciones de impuestos sobre la renta para 2017 también se vieron influidas por un aumento de la tasa de ISR del 24% al 25.5% (para los contribuyentes del sistema semi-integrado). De manera similar, los pagos anticipados de los impuestos de 2018 se vieron afectados por un aumento adicional en la tasa ISR del 25.5% al 27%.

Referencias

Asociación Mundial del Acero (2019), "Global crude steel output increases by 4.6% in 2018", *https://www.worldsteel.org/media-centre/press-releases/2019/Global-crude-steel-output-increases-by-4.6--in-2018.html.* [12]

Banco Mundial (2020), "World Bank commodities price data (the pink sheet)", *http://pubdocs.worldbank.org/en/596831580311438199/CMO-Pink-Sheet-February-2020.pdf.* [1]

Banco Mundial (2019), *Commodity Markets Outlook, April 2019*, *http://documents.worldbank.org/curated/en/992831556034429620/Commodity-Markets-Outlook-April-2019.* [11]

Banco Mundial (2019), *Commodity Markets Outlook, October 2018*, *http://pubdocs.worldbank.org/en/236551540394193458/CMO-October-2018-Full-Report.pdf.* [10]

Barrick Gold Corporation (2019), *Annual Report 2018*, *https://barrick.q4cdn.com/788666289/files/annual-report/Barrick-Annual-Report-2018.pdf.* [14]

BP (2019), *BP Statistical Review of World Energy*, *https://www.bp.com/content/dam/bp/business-sites/en/global/corporate/pdfs/energy-economics/statistical-review/bp-stats-review-2019-full-report.pdf.* [2]

CEPAL (2020), "Ingresos públicos provenientes de recursos naturales no renovables", CEPALSTAT *(base de datos)*, Comisión Economica para America Latina y el Caribe, *https://cepalstat-prod.cepal.org/cepalstat/tabulador/ConsultaIntegrada.asp?IdAplicacion=6&idTema=939&idIndicador=3354&idioma=e.* [3]

CEPAL (2019), *Balanço Preliminar das Economias da América Latina e do Caribe 2019*, Comisión Economica para America Latina y el Caribe, *https://repositorio.cepal.org/handle/11362/45085.* [16]

CEPAL (2019), CEPALSTAT, Economic Comision for Latin American and the Caribbean, *https://estadisticas.cepal.org/cepalstat/Portada.html?idioma=english* (accessed on 3 October 2019). [17]

Ecopetrol (2019), *Integrated Sustainable Management Report 2018*, *https://www.ecopetrol.com.co/documentos/Ecopetrol-Integrated-Sustainability-Report-2018.pdf.* [6]

Lundin Gold (2017), *Annual Report 2016*, *https://www.lundingold.com/site/assets/files/1707/2016_annual_report_new.pdf.* [15]

Ministerio de Economia y Finanzas Publicas (2019), *Memoria de la Economía Boliviana 2018*, *https://www.economiayfinanzas.gob.bo/memoria-de-la-economia-boliviana-2018.html.* [4]

Ministerio de Hacienda Trinidad y Tobago (2018), *Review of the Economy 2018*, *https://www.finance.gov.tt/wp-content/uploads/2018/10/Review-Of-The-Economy-2018.pdf.* [9]

Perúpetro (2019), *Memoria anual 2018*, *https://www.perupetro.com.pe/wps/wcm/connect/corporativo/469bffbe-b3f2-42b0-baff-fbf7ff4df270/MEMORIA+PERUPETRO+2018a.pdf?MOD=AJPERES&Memoria Anual2018.* [8]

Petrobras (2019), "Form 20-F filing to the United States Securities and Exchange Commission", Petróleo Brasileiro S.A., *https://www.investidorpetrobras.com.br/enu/892/Form-20F-2018-Ingles_2.pdf.* [5]

SHCP (2019), *Informes sobre la Situación Económica, las Finanzas Públicas y la Deuda Pública*, Secretaría de Hacienda y Crédito Público, Gobierno de México, *https://www.finanzaspublicas.hacienda.gob.mx/work/models/Finanzas_Publicas/docs/congreso/infotrim/2018/ivt/01inf/itindc_201804.pdf.* [7]

Vale S.A. (2019), "Form 20-F filing to the United States Securities and Exchange Commission", *http://www.vale.com/EN/investors/information-market/annual-reports/20f/20FDocs/Vale_20-F%20FY2018%20-%20final_i.pdf.* [13]

Chapter 3

SPECIAL FEATURE

Equivalent fiscal pressure in Latin America and the Caribbean: Enlarging the map of the region's fiscal revenues

Capítulo 3

SECCIÓN ESPECIAL

La presión fiscal equivalente en América Latina y el Caribe: Ampliando el mapa de los ingresos fiscales de la región

Chapter 3

SPECIAL FEATURE

Equivalent fiscal pressure in Latin America and the Caribbean: Enlarging the map of the region's fiscal revenues

Introduction

Over recent decades, it has been possible to identify common features and trends of fiscal revenues among the different countries of Latin America and the Caribbean (LAC). Yet, in many respects, the region is highly diverse, which has limited the comparability of conventional standards and of the economic variables generally used for such purposes. In this regard, Equivalent Fiscal Pressure (EFP), a different methodology for calculating fiscal pressure in LAC, seeks to measure the resources raised by the countries of the region more broadly. By including structural elements of public financing in the LAC countries, this methodological approach also makes it possible to standardise fiscal pressure and make it more comparable between countries and regions.

Equivalent Fiscal Pressure and its implications

A country's tax revenue as a share of GDP is a variable defined as the amount of monetary resources that a given country captures by applying a set of taxes and similar instruments that, in general, comprise the essential basis of State financing. In conventional terms, this indicator is usually expressed in relation to a country's gross domestic product (GDP), so as to ensure a comparable unit of measure.

Because of an array of factors, however, the importance of tax systems can be underestimated when alternative sources of public revenues or different configurations of basic State functions exist in different countries. Hence, for example, the widespread availability of renewable or non-renewable natural resources allows some countries in the region to supplement public financing by implementing tax regimes that enable State appropriation of part of the revenues derived from activities linked to those resources. The best-known case relates to the economic exploitation of hydrocarbon and mineral deposits that have great commercial value world-wide. Similarly, extensive public social security systems in certain countries require an abundant supply of tax resources to ensure that such systems function properly and are financially sustainable. This is in contrast, however, to other countries that have opted to introduce no less extensive private systems based on individual capitalisation in the areas of health and social security. These systems may replace, complement or compete with the alternative public system.

This special feature proposes the concept of Equivalent Fiscal Pressure (EFP), which takes account of two other sources of revenue in addition to tax revenues (including public social security contributions, SSCs), and that amount to a tax effort demanded of taxpayers when payment of them is compulsory: contributions to private systems (pensions and healthcare) and non-tax fiscal revenues derived from the exploitation of natural resources (Barreix et al., 2013[1]).

EFP may be defined as follows:

$$EFP = TR + SSCpub + SSCpriv + NRnoT$$

Where:

- TR: general government tax revenues

- SSCpub: social security contributions (public systems)
- SSCpriv: social insurance contributions (private systems).
- NRnoT: non-tax revenues derived from the exploitation of natural resources.

It should be noted that while consideration of these diverse components helps nourish and enrich analysis of fiscal conditions in LAC countries, it does not invalidate or contradict conventional measures that quantify the level of public financing in each country. Indeed, albeit with different names and criteria, they are all considered in the methodologies that are most widespread internationally (Box 3.1). Rather, the aim is to expand the possibilities for regional and international comparison and to provide new elements that are, at least for the specific context in LAC, crucial to achieving a broad and comprehensive perspective of these issues.

Box 3.1. **Methodological issues in classifying tax revenues**

The definition of Equivalent Fiscal Pressure (EFP) includes elements of public financing that, in several LAC countries, acquire a great deal of importance both in terms of resources from compulsory contributions to private social protection schemes (pensions and health insurance) and non-tax fiscal revenue from the exploitation of natural resources (mainly hydrocarbons and minerals). This allows regional and international comparisons to be made from a perspective other than the conventional one, but several matters have to be made clear. In fact, the two items mentioned are not usually part of the total tax burden in the methodologies of other recognised information sources, and may lead to different conclusions in particular cases.

On the one hand, compulsory (obligatory) contributions made to private social insurance systems by employers or employees, and related to the jobs of those employees, are considered "non-tax compulsory payments" (NTCPs) in the OECD's methodological criteria. With a similar reasoning to that underlying their inclusion in EFP, NTCPs are part of an employer's total labour costs, and of employees' total remuneration, influencing their individual decisions in a similar way to what happens with labour taxes. Given that, the OECD has included indicators of compulsory payments in order to make inter-country comparisons more uniform and consistent (OECD, 2019[2]). In fact, a total of 22 OECD countries have this type of instrument, among which Chile, Iceland, Israel, the Netherlands, Poland, Switzerland and the United States are notable for their relative importance in those countries and for their scale within average labour costs.

On the other hand, the availability of renewable and non-renewable natural resources has led the producing countries to design a variety of special tax regimes to ensure adequate appropriation of the revenues generated by their economic exploitation. These strategies include not only a range of tax instruments (corporate income tax and *ad hoc* taxes) and non-tax instruments (mainly royalties and usage rights), but also different forms of State participation in the production, administration and marketing of raw materials and services, including the operation of public enterprises in these activities. In general, the tax resources associated with them are usually included in the overall figures for revenues from the taxes levied, except in specific cases. In order to make a more uniform comparison, however, and though they are not part of the total tax burden, it would be helpful to consider the non-tax resources also associated with the extractive sectors, which are substantially important in several OECD countries such as Australia, Canada, Mexico, Norway, Poland, the United Kingdom (Scotland) and the United States.

Source: Based on (OECD, 2019[2]).

As Figure 3.1 shows, the traditional methodology indicates that tax take as a share of GDP in LAC, which comprises tax revenues (including public SSCs), stood at 23.1% of GDP in 2018. Using the EFP methodology, the new resources add 1.9% of GDP to tax revenue in 2018, bringing the total to 25% of GDP. During mineral price booms, resources from exploitation of the countries' natural wealth alone has managed to contribute 2% of GDP (2013).[1]

As regards the structural composition of EFP, tax revenues (including social security contributions) have remained relatively stable since 1990. In 2018, they accounted for 92.3% of government revenues as per EFP's definition; considering only tax resources – excluding public SSCs – they fluctuated around 75% throughout this period. The share of private SSCs has increased since its implementation in several countries of the region in the 1990s, and today accounts for 3.8% of LAC's EFP. For their part, the share of non-tax revenues from natural resources has been volatile within the structure of EFP, in line with the variable behaviour of this kind of revenue.

Figure 3.1. **Equivalent Fiscal Pressure in Latin America and the Caribbean, 1990-2018**

Percentage of GDP

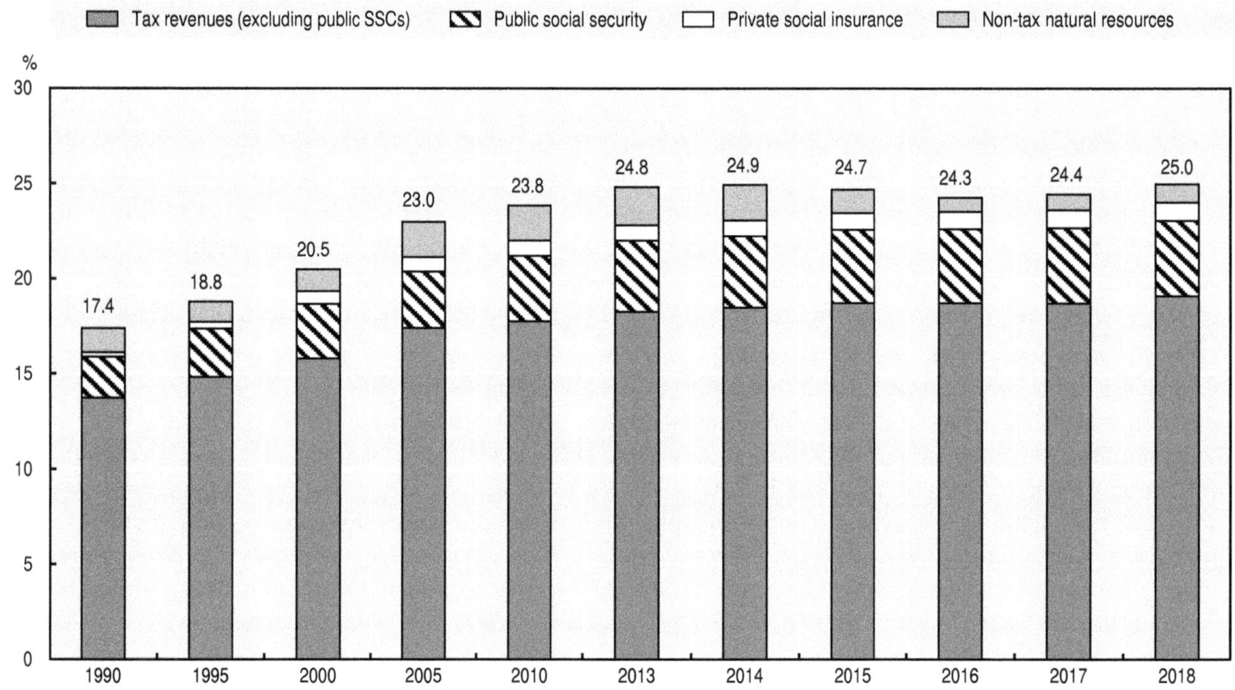

Note: Data refers to the simple average of the 25 Latin American and Caribbean countries included in this publication, and excludes Venezuela due to data availability issues.

Source: Prepared by the authors based on data in (IDB-CIAT, 2020[3]) and (OECD et al., 2020[2]).

StatLink https://doi.org/10.1787/888934113849

A comparison of overall tax revenue to GDP between LAC and the OECD[2] in 2017 shows that, as a simple average, tax revenues (including public SSCs) amounted to 22.7% of GDP in LAC and 35.2% of GDP in the OECD (34 countries, excluding Chile and Mexico to avoid duplication). When these figures are weighted by the current GDP of each country, they stood at 25.1% of GDP for LAC and 31.8% for the OECD (Figure 3.2). Nonetheless, when the new resources (private SSCs and natural resources) are taken into account, the simple average of EFP in LAC reaches 24.4% and the weighted average is 27.6%. In other words, the gap between LAC and the OECD narrows significantly, from 12.5 points (35.2% – 22.7%) to 4.6 points (32.1% – 27.6%) when the new resources are considered in the average, weighted by the size of the respective economies.

Something that should be made clear in the comparisons included in this special feature is that, in some OECD member countries, "additional" resources from components of EFP are also important, such as compulsory payments to private social insurance systems or non-tax revenues related to the exploitation of strategic natural resources.[3] Indeed, although compulsory contributions to certain healthcare systems are not usually counted in the fiscal pressure of OECD countries (for example, those linked to the Patient Protection and Affordable Care Act in the United States), they would in fact fit in and should be part of their respective EFPs. Similarly, resources collected by means of the State's ability to obtain revenues from the public domain, such as natural resources, would be part of EFP – an example in the OECD being Norway's non-tax revenues from the exploitation of its oil reserves (Box 3.1).

Figure 3.2. **Comparison of Tax Revenues (TR) and Equivalent Fiscal Pressure (EFP) in LAC and OECD-34, 2017**

Percentage of GDP

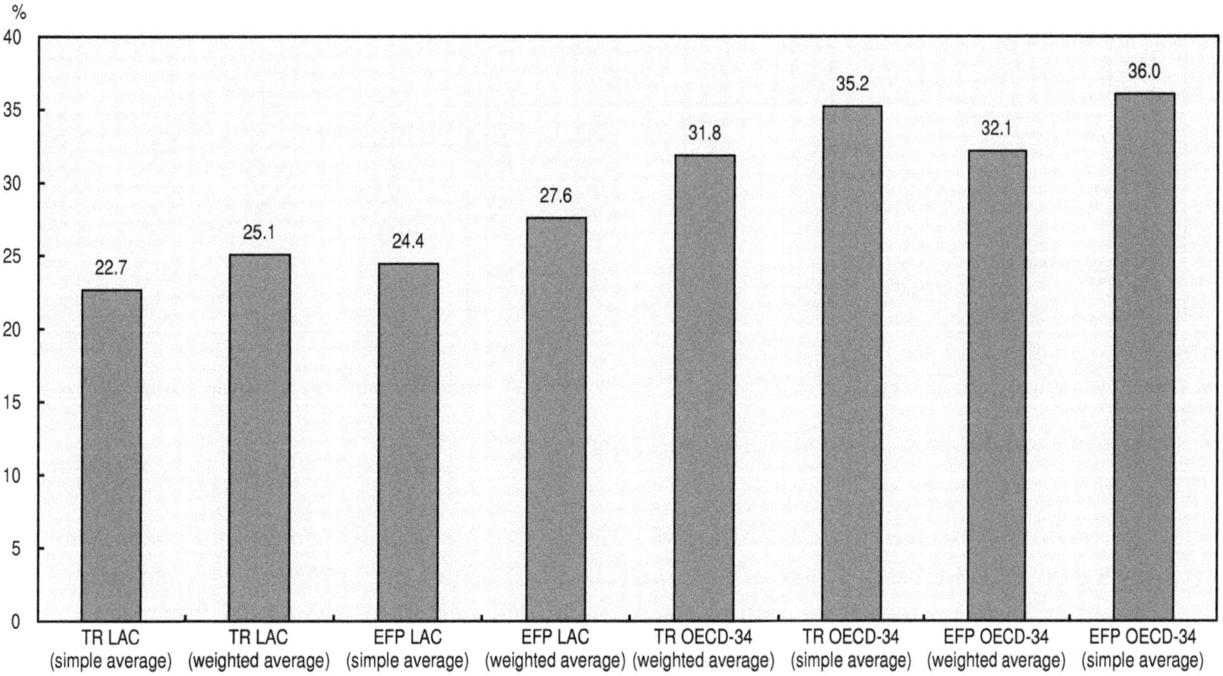

Note: The OECD-34 averages exclude Chile and Mexico to avoid duplication in the comparison with LAC's EFP.

Source: Prepared by the authors based on data in (IDB-CIAT, 2020[4]) and (OECD et al., 2020[2]).

StatLink https://doi.org/10.1787/888934113868

Evolution of EFP in LAC: Achievements and obstacles with wide regional diversity

Regional evolution, 1990-2018

In 2018, the region achieved its highest level of EFP since 1990.[4] This growth in revenues was sustained by an increase in the region's fiscal pillars.[5] These pillars, which determine regional fiscal sustainability, are: value added tax (VAT),[6] income tax,[7] compulsory public SSCs and compulsory private SSCs. Although non-tax revenues from the exploitation of natural resources are an important income source for the region, they are not regarded as pillars because of their volatility. Figure 3.3 shows the evolution of the region's EFP from 1990 to 2018, disaggregated by fiscal pillars, non-tax natural resources, and other taxes.

Figure 3.3. **Fiscal pillars and other components of EFP in Latin America and the Caribbean, 1990-2018**

Percentage of GDP

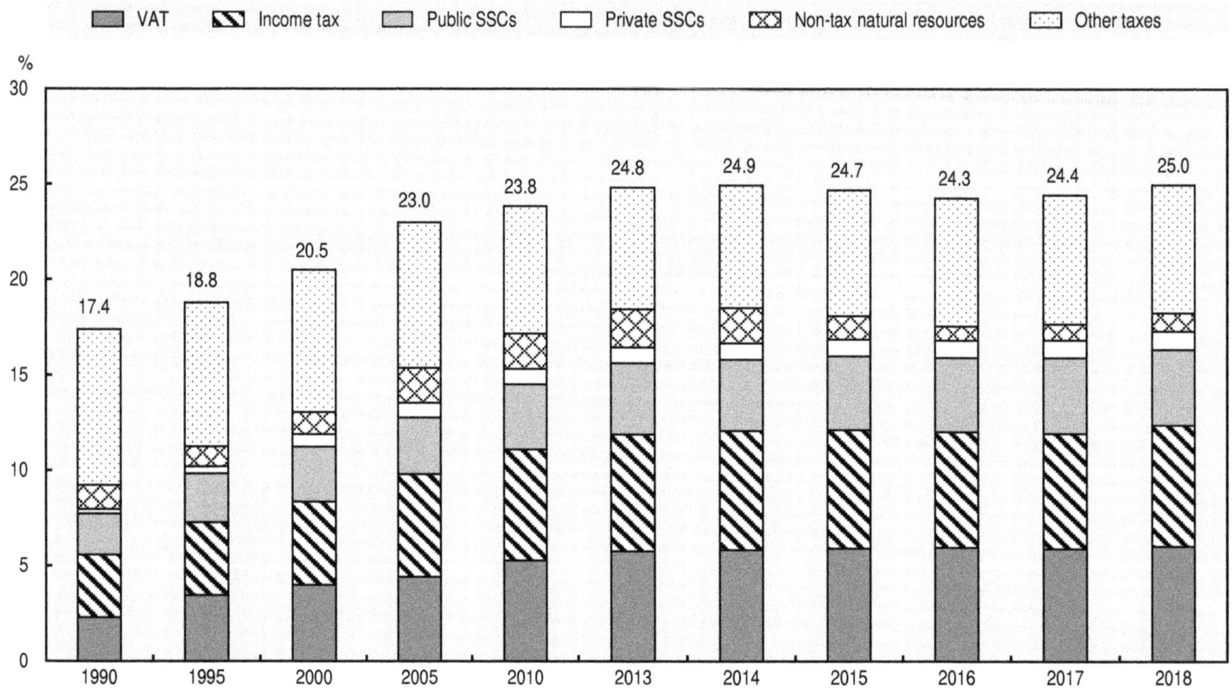

Note: Data refers to the simple average of the 25 countries included in this publication and excludes Venezuela due to data availability issues.

Source: Prepared by the authors based on data in (IDB-CIAT, 2020[4]) and (OECD et al., 2020[2]).

StatLink https://doi.org/10.1787/888934113887

Between 1990 and 2018, VAT, income tax, public SSCs and private SSCs grew, respectively, by 3.8% of GDP, 3.1% of GDP, 1.8% of GDP, and 0.7% of GDP. These performances were partially offset by lower revenue from natural resources, bringing about an overall EFP increase of 7.6% of GDP.

In the past five-year period (2013-18), EFP in the region grew by just 0.2% of GDP. Income tax and public SSCs grew by only 0.2% of GDP, while revenues from natural resources declined by 1% of GDP. This slowing of EFP growth was brought about mainly by changes in the international context, the overall downturn in economic growth rates and the fall in minerals prices, which significantly affected the region's fiscal accounts. This latter circumstance reflects the region's high degree of fiscal sensitivity to changes in commodities prices.

The structure of EFP in LAC also includes a heading referred to as "Others". This includes the categories of taxes on property and financial transactions, payroll, other taxes on goods and services (including excise taxes, levies on international trade and general consumption taxes, as in Argentina, Brazil, Colombia and Cuba), simplified tax regimes for SMEs, and most subnational taxes, among others. In 1990, this group of taxes, whose composition varies from one country to another, accounted for 47% of EFP and up to 2018, it was gradually replaced by the fiscal pillars; it now accounts for a much smaller but still significant share of total EFP (27%).

Level and structure of EFP by country

The LAC region is characterised by wide diversity in its level of fiscal revenues. At the individual country level, the ranges between maximum and minimum levels of EFP among countries are very significant (Figure 3.4). Cuba has the highest tax burden in the region (42.3% of GDP in 2018), and Guatemala has the lowest (12.1%). As mentioned earlier, the regional average is 25% and it is notable that, for countries whose EFP is around or below the regional average, the tax burden falls substantially when we discount the additional resources included in EFP. This is the case, for example, in Bolivia, Chile, and Trinidad and Tobago.

Figure 3.4. **Equivalent Fiscal Pressure and Tax Revenue in Latin America and the Caribbean, 2018**

Percentage of GDP

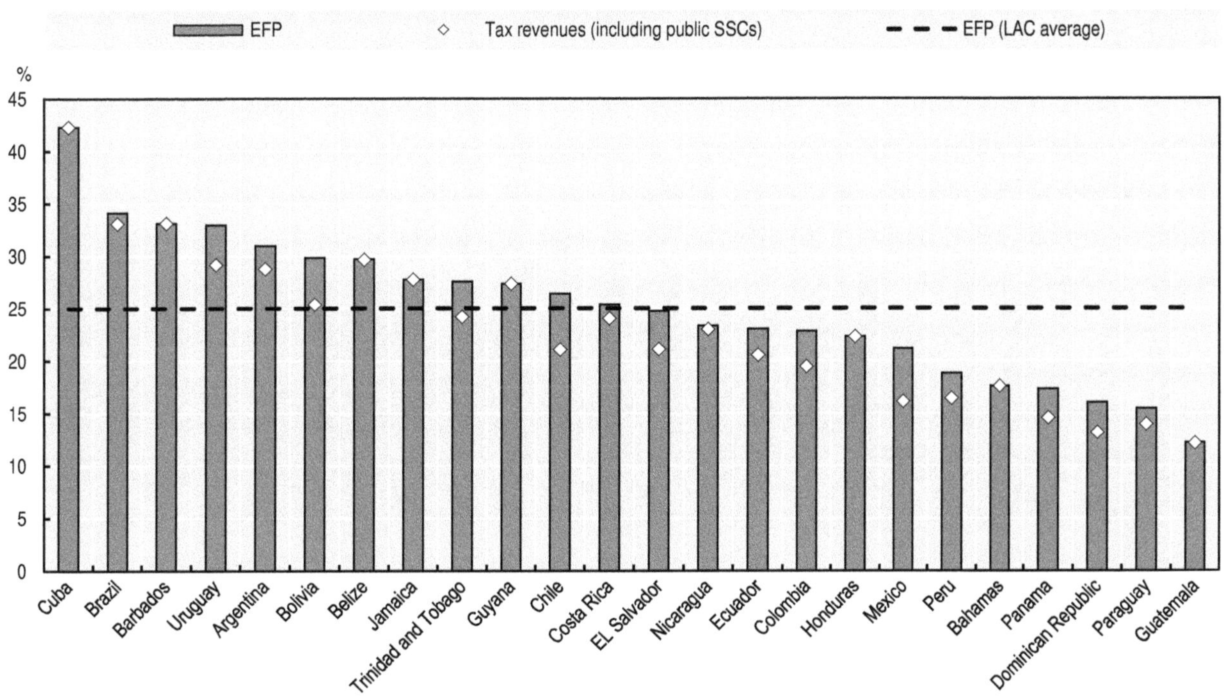

Note: The LAC average is a simple average of countries included in this publication and excludes Venezuela due to data availability issues. The LAC average includes Saint Lucia's tax revenues but excludes the country's social security contributions, contributions to private insurance plans and non-tax revenues from non-renewable resources because of a lack of data.

Source: Prepared by the authors based on data in (IDB-CIAT, 2020[4]) and (OECD et al., 2020[2]).

StatLink *https://doi.org/10.1787/888934113906*

Analysis of the ranking of the countries according to their EFP levels shows some important changes that have been apparent over recent years. Taking as a reference the most recent update to the EFP database (Barreix et al., 2017[3]), the countries that fell the most on the regional EFP ranking are Bolivia, Trinidad and Tobago, Argentina and Paraguay. By contrast, it is worth noting the progress made by Uruguay in consolidating its position as one of the countries with the highest tax burden in the region as a result of a substantial increase in income tax revenue, especially personal income tax. The regional average rose, moreover, because of the inclusion of countries such as Cuba, Guyana and Jamaica in the EFP database.

Regarding the tax structure, Figure 3.5 shows the composition of EFP by country. The highest revenue figures for the "VAT" fiscal pillar relate to Barbados (9.2% of GDP) and Jamaica (9.1% of GDP).[8] As regards income tax, Trinidad and Tobago has the highest level in the region at 12.8% of GDP, followed by Cuba (11.1% of GDP) and Guyana (9.8% of GDP). In 2018, public SSCs reached 8.4% of GDP in Brazil and 8.2% in Costa Rica. In private systems, Chile leads the region in revenue with 4.7% of GDP; also important are Uruguay (3.8%), El Salvador (3.5%) and the Dominican Republic (2.8%).

Figure 3.5. **Fiscal pillars and other components of EFP by country, 2018**

Percentage of GDP

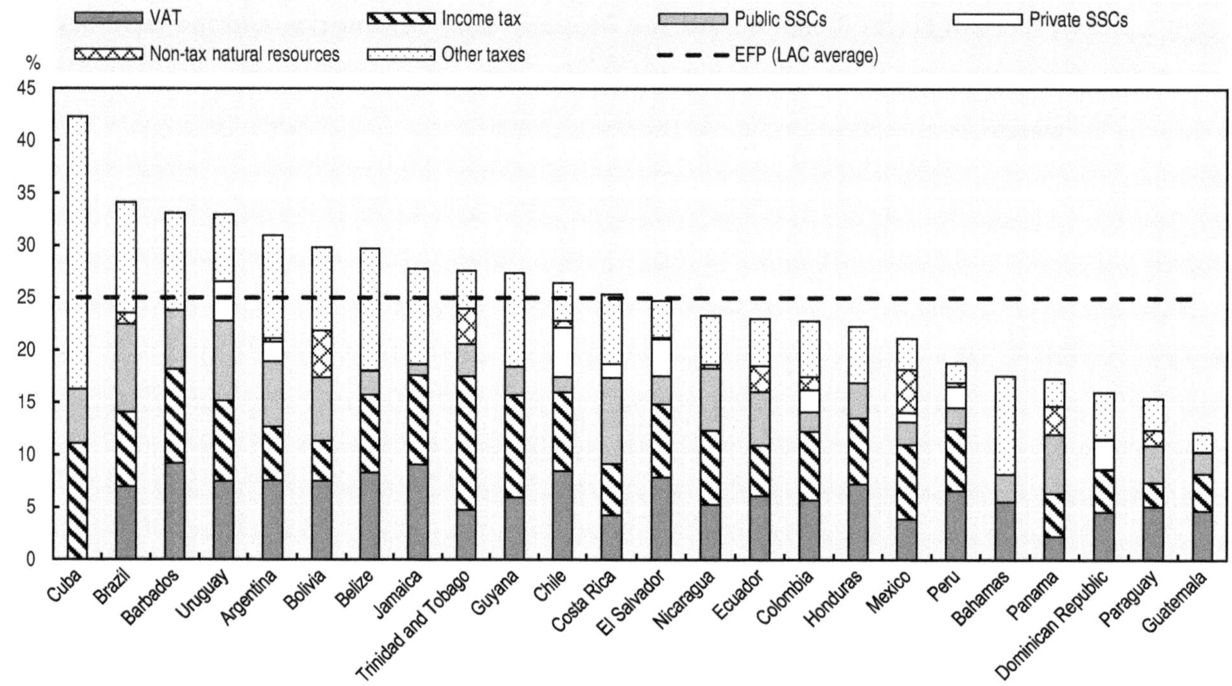

Note: The LAC average is the simple average of the 25 countries included in this publication and excludes Venezuela due to data availability issues. The LAC average includes Saint Lucia's tax revenues but excludes the country's social security contributions, contributions to private insurance plans, and non-tax revenues from non-renewable resources because of a lack of data.

Source: Prepared by the authors based on data in (IDB-CIAT, 2020[3]) and (OECD et al., 2020[2]).

StatLink https://doi.org/10.1787/888934113925

As regards non-tax revenues from natural resources, the countries that generated the most in 2018 were Bolivia (4.5% of GDP), Mexico (4.2% of GDP), and Trinidad and Tobago (3.4% of GDP). As mentioned earlier, there is a striking contrast between revenues in Bolivia and Trinidad and Tobago in the final year of analysis, and levels during the boom years of mineral and hydrocarbon prices (in 2012, both countries raised about 11% of GDP in this category).

Comparison with the OECD

Since 1990, greater fiscal effort, tax reforms and favourable external circumstances have allowed LAC countries to converge towards levels of tax revenue as a share of GDP prevailing in countries with greater tax development, such as those in the OECD. The differences with the OECD narrowed most particularly in the first decade of this century, coinciding with the boom in mineral prices. LAC's EFP stood at 51.3% of EFP in the OECD countries in 1990 (34 countries, excluding Chile and Mexico), at 57.4% in 2000, and at 67.8% in 2017 (Figure 3.6).

Since 2010, the differences in EFP between LAC and the OECD have been relatively stable, coinciding with an adverse international environment, a fall in demand for LAC's natural resources, and the consequent decline in the prices of the main hydrocarbons and minerals exported from the region, which has lessened their influence on regional convergence.

Figure 3.6. **Comparison (ratio) of LAC's EFP with the OECD, with and without natural resources, 1990-2017**

Percentage of OECD-34 average

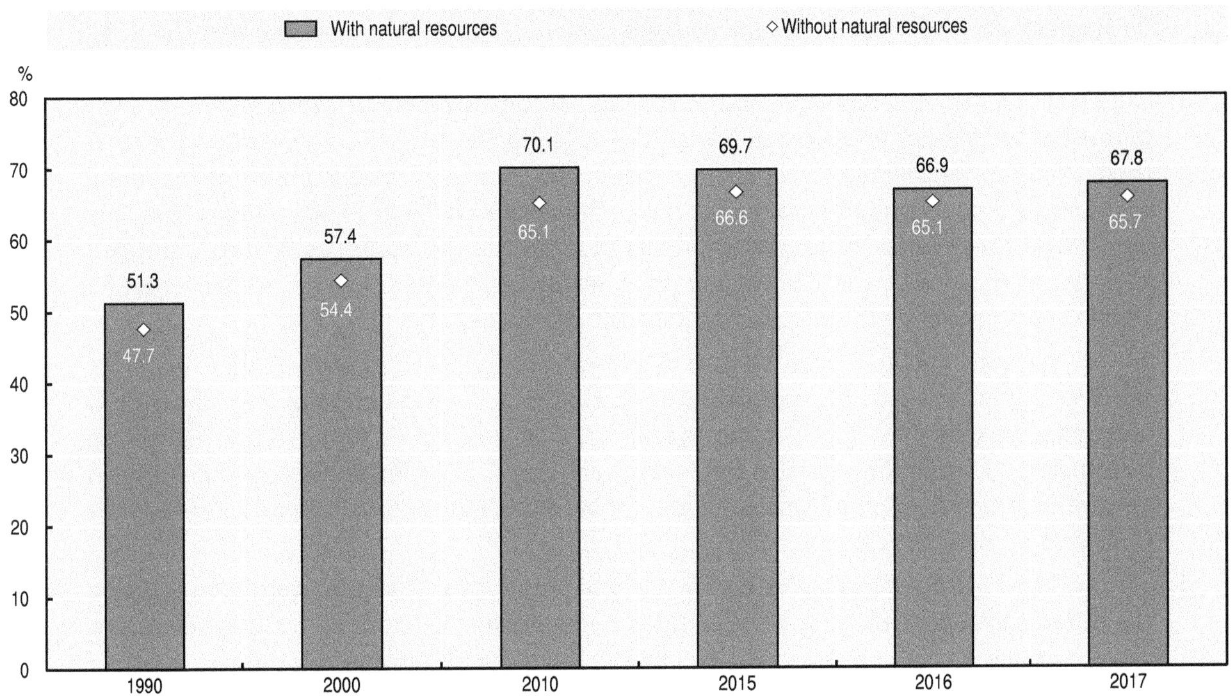

Note: Data refer to the simple averages of 25 Latin American and Caribbean countries and 34 OECD countries. The OECD-34 average does not include Chile and Mexico to avoid duplication in the comparison with LAC's EFP.

Source: Prepared by the authors based on data in (IDB-CIAT, 2020[3]) and (OECD et al., 2020[2]).

StatLink https://doi.org/10.1787/888934113944

As regards the EFP comparison with the OECD by type of tax, LAC and the OECD have moved closest together in VAT. In this field, LAC-wide, revenues are practically at the same level as the OECD; for the Caribbean and Southern Cone countries such as Argentina, Brazil, Chile and Uruguay, revenue even surpasses the level in several developed countries.

By contrast, in the area of social security contributions as a share of GDP, the gaps between LAC and the OECD are very clear. Considering only public SSCs, the LAC average is equivalent to just 41.5% of the average figure for the OECD, aside from the significant amounts raised in countries such as Argentina, Bolivia, Brazil, Costa Rica and Uruguay, at a level similar to or even higher than levels in several OECD countries. The situation is not substantially better if we add contributions to private systems, since revenues are only 47.3% of the OECD average.

The performance of income tax has not been favourable and, despite some progress and reforms over the past decade,[9] revenue amounts to only slightly more than half (51%) of that in the OECD. The lower level of income tax convergence stems from LAC's low yield in revenue from personal income tax. LAC countries collect a fairly similar amount of corporate income tax to that of the OECD (2.9% of GDP for the OECD-34 in 2017, and 3.4% of

GDP for LAC). The big difference is in revenue from personal income tax: in the OECD, this stood at an average of 8.6% of GDP in 2017, while in LAC it was at just 2.2%. In LAC, personal income tax is paid by individuals in the formal sector who receive high salaries and are in the upper income deciles. It is estimated that 90% of LAC's population is exempt from this tax (Barreix, Benítez and Pecho, $2017_{[4]}$). Because of these factors, the income tax structure is skewed towards legal entities in most LAC countries.

Finally, the wide diversity apparent throughout the region has always made it difficult to engage in wide-ranging analyses and to group countries according to certain basic criteria. A frequent alternative is to classify the countries according to their geographic location, as in other sections of this study. For example, they can be grouped into categories such as "South America," "Central America" and "the Caribbean", despite the sharp differences within each of these sub-regions. Another option would be to group the countries according to the level (current, recent or average for a given period) of the countries' total tax burden, including social security contributions and the tax resources of subnational levels of government. This would lead, for example, to countries such as Argentina, Brazil and Uruguay being grouped together as those with the highest tax revenues in Latin America, together with several Caribbean countries such as Barbados, Belize and Jamaica.

In this case, and as a possible way of grouping countries, it is interesting to consider the differences between LAC and the OECD in relation to the development level and overall taxpaying capacity of each country in the region. This would yield four regional subgroups comprising: *i)* Central America plus the Dominican Republic; *ii)* the Caribbean; *iii)* the Andean Community countries plus Venezuela; and *iv)* the Mercosur member countries, as well as Chile and Mexico (Barreix et al., $2017_{[3]}$).

As Figure 3.7 shows, taking both total GDP and per capita GDP at purchasing power parity, the difference between LAC and the OECD is much greater, because of: *i)* the difference in greater proportion of product in various taxes; and *ii)* the difference in purchasing power represented by the size of each economy.[10] Similarly, it can be seen that income tax plays a much more important role in the OECD countries, (the difference being concentrated in the tax paid by individuals). Moreover, there is a certain parity with respect to total SSCs (taking public and private systems together) and VAT is more important for LAC as a source of public resources.

Figure 3.7. Comparative per capita fiscal pressure in current US dollars (PPP) by region, 2017

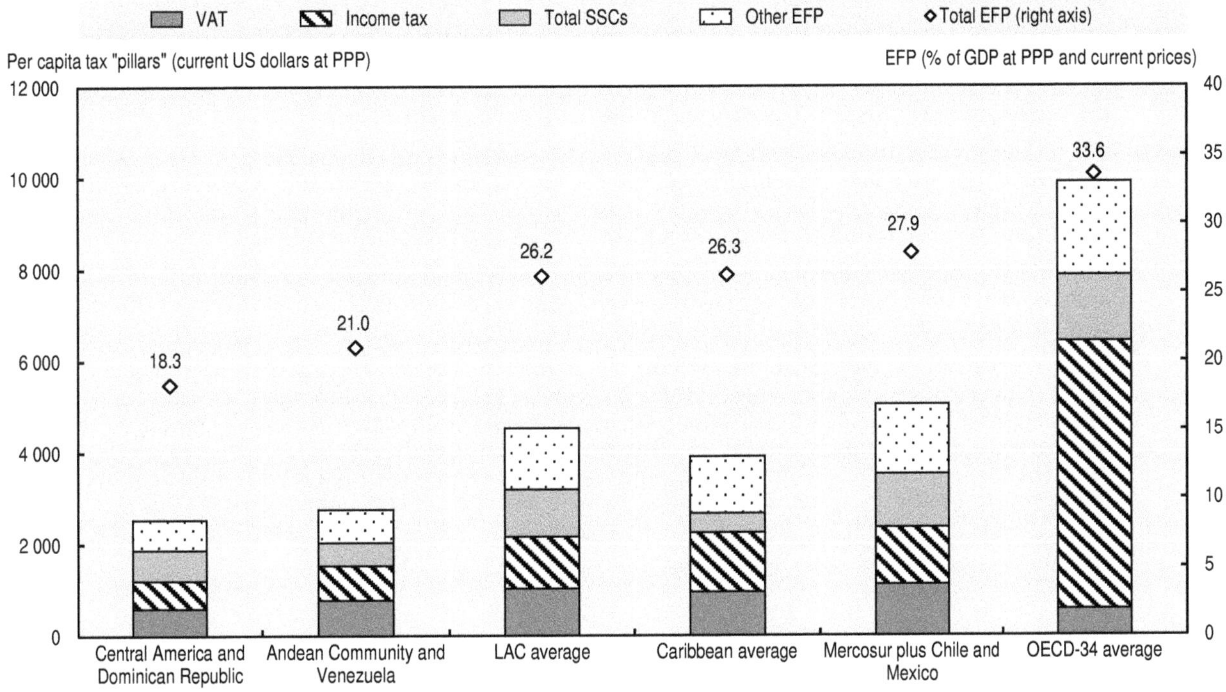

Note: Data refer to averages weighted by GDP. The OECD-34 average does not include Chile and Mexico to avoid duplication in the comparison with LAC's EFP. The "Total SSCs" component includes public and private systems, while "Other EFP" includes the other tax revenues, as well as non-tax revenues from strategic natural resource sectors.

Source: Prepared by the authors based on data in (IDB-CIAT, 2020[5]), (OECD et al., 2020[2]) and (IMF, 2019[7]) for each country's per capita GDP at PPP and GDP at PPP.

StatLink https://doi.org/10.1787/888934113963

In short, the true amount of resources available to the tax authorities is much higher in the developed world than in the LAC countries, especially when tax burdens are considered in relation to the size of the economy and the per capita level of taxation. These comparisons have implications when sources of public financing are linked to the level of total public spending in each region and country, and they call for a careful assessment of potential tax and fiscal reform options that seek to expand the mobilisation of domestic resources in the region.

Notes

1. Throughout this special feature, statistical data from the IDB-CIAT *Equivalent Fiscal Pressure Database* (IDB-CIAT, 2020[5]) are used. Regional averages do not include Venezuela because of a lack of information.
2. Throughout this special feature, the OECD-34 average is used. This does not include Chile or Mexico in order to avoid duplication in the comparison with LAC's EFP.
3. Informal calculations using data provided by the OECD show the simple average EFP for the OECD-34 to be 36% of GDP in 2017 (32.1% on average, weighted by the size of each economy). This suggests, in general, a lower relative weight of private social insurance and non-tax natural resources (with some exceptions) for developed countries overall than prevails in LAC.
4. This year is taken as a reference for comparison since it marks the beginning of the period analysed in the tax statistics presented throughout this document using a standardised methodology (OECD, 2019[6]). Estimates for previous periods, however, confirm that the current ratio of average tax revenue to GDP is the highest in the region's history (see [CIAT, 2017[7]]).

5. A fiscal pillar is a tax that has a broad base and can generate significant and stable revenues over time (Barreix and Roca, 2007[8]).
6. Although VAT is the main tax levied on consumption, some countries in the region have broad-based general taxes on goods and services that have characteristics similar to those of VAT. Examples include: the tax on gross income (provincial) in Argentina; COFINS and PIS/PASEP (federal) and ISS (municipal) in Brazil; and the Industry and Trade Tax (municipal) in Colombia.
7. The "income tax" pillar refers to net tax collection linked to income tax, including all other taxes on income that are under the authority of central or subnational governments, whether they are levied on a particular sector, have alternative basis for calculation, are temporary and extraordinary, and/or are levied on specific types of income not covered by traditional income tax.
8. It should be noted that if revenues from other general taxes on goods and services comparable to VAT are considered, revenue is also very significant in Argentina and Brazil (11.4% and 12.4% of GDP in 2018, respectively).
9. In 2006, Uruguay was the pioneer in adopting a system of dual income taxation, through which it began to tax labour income separately, with a progressive scale of rates, and capital income with a relatively low proportional rate. This same path has been followed by countries such as Peru in 2009 and several Central American countries between 2009 and 2011, in a practical effort to include different forms of capital income in the income tax base. More recently, Argentina and Mexico have joined this trend of dual systems for personal income tax with similar characteristics.
10. Both total EFP and the main per capita taxes are averages weighted by each country's total GDP in US dollars at purchasing power parity (PPP).

References

Barreix, A., J. Benítez and M. Pecho (2017), "Revisiting personal income tax in Latin America: Evolution and impact", *OECD Development Centre Working Papers*, No. 338, OECD Publishing, Paris, *https://dx.doi.org/10.1787/16d42b4a-en.* [6]

Barreix, A. and J. Roca (2007), "Strengthening a fiscal pillar: The Uruguayan dual income tax", *CEPAL Review* 92, Vol. August, pp. 121-140, *https://repositorio.cepal.org/bitstream/handle/11362/11216/92121140I_en.pdf?sequence=1&isAllowed=y.* [10]

Barreix, A. et al. (2017), "Updating of Equivalent Fiscal Pressure in Latin America and the Caribbean", *Discussion Paper*, No. 548, IDB, *https://publications.iadb.org/publications/english/document/Updating-of-Equivalent-Fiscal-Pressure-in-Latin-America-and-the-Caribbean.pdf.* [5]

Barreix, A. et al. (2013), *Putting Pressure: Estimating the real fiscal burden in Latin America and the Caribbean. Concept, development and international comparisons*, IDB, CIAT, IEF, *https://www.ciat.org/Biblioteca/DocumentosdeTrabajo/2013/2013_Putting_pressure_barreix_bes_velayos_pecho_benitez.pdf.* [1]

IDB-CIAT (2020), *IDB-CIAT Revenue Collection database*, *https://www.ciat.org/idb-ciat-revenue-collection-database/?lang=en.* [3]

IMF (2019), *World Economic Outlook Database April 2019*, International Monetary Fund, *https://www.imf.org/external/pubs/ft/weo/2019/01/weodata/index.aspx* (accessed on 16 September 2019). [7]

Inter American Center of Tax Administrations (ed.) (2017), *CIAT: Fifty years in Latin American taxation*, *https://www.ciat.org/Biblioteca/Publicaciones_CIAT/Libro_50_anos/2017_LB_50_ing.pdf* (accessed on 2 March 2020). [9]

OECD (2019), *Global Revenue Statistics Database*, OECD, *https://stats.oecd.org/Index.aspx?DataSetCode=RS_GBL* (accessed on 16 September 2019). [11]

OECD (2019), *OECD.Stat*, OECD, Paris, *https://stats-2.oecd.org/index.aspx?DatasetCode=DACSECTOR.* [8]

OECD (2019), *Taxing Wages 2017-2018 Associated Paper: Non-tax compulsory payments*, OECD Publishing, Paris, *https://www.oecd.org/tax/tax-policy/non-tax-compulsory-payments.pdf.* [2]

OECD et al. (2020), *Revenue Statistics in Latin America and the Caribbean 2020*, OECD Publishing, Paris, *https://doi.org/10.1787/35745b02-en..* [4]

Capítulo 3

SECCIÓN ESPECIAL

La presión fiscal equivalente en América Latina y el Caribe: Ampliando el mapa de los ingresos fiscales de la región

Introducción

Si bien a lo largo de las últimas décadas ha sido posible identificar rasgos y tendencias comunes entre los distintos países que la componen, debe reconocerse que América Latina y el Caribe (ALC) es una región muy heterogénea en numerosas dimensiones. Esta cualidad ha atentado, históricamente, contra la comparabilidad de los casos observados a través de los estándares convencionales y de las variables económicas generalmente utilizadas a tales efectos. En ese sentido, la Presión Fiscal Equivalente (PFE) es una metodología diferente de cálculo de la presión fiscal en ALC que busca medir, de una manera más amplia, los recursos recaudados por los países de la región. Este enfoque metodológico, al incorporar elementos estructurales del financiamiento público de los países de ALC, también permite estandarizar y hacer más comparable la presión fiscal entre países y regiones.

El concepto de "Presión Fiscal Equivalente" y sus implicancias

La recaudación tributaria sobre PIB de un país es aquella variable definida por el monto de recursos monetarios que un determinado país logra captar a partir de la aplicación de un conjunto de diferentes impuestos y otros instrumentos similares los cuales, en general, constituyen la base fundamental de financiamiento del Estado. De manera convencional, este indicador suele estar expresado con relación al producto interior bruto (PIB) de cada país para asegurar una unidad de medida comparable.

Sin embargo, por una serie de distintos factores, la importancia de los sistemas tributarios puede verse relativizada cuando existen otras fuentes alternativas de recursos públicos o distintas configuraciones de las funciones básicas del Estado en los distintos países. Así, por ejemplo, la disponibilidad amplia de recursos naturales —sean éstos de naturaleza renovable o no renovable— permite a algunos países de la región complementar el financiamiento público a partir de la instrumentación de regímenes fiscales para la apropiación estatal de una parte de las rentas generadas en las actividades vinculadas a los mismos (el caso más conocido es el vinculado a la explotación económica de los yacimientos de hidrocarburos y minerales). En una línea similar, la existencia de amplios sistemas públicos de seguridad social en determinados países requiere del abastecimiento de un caudaloso flujo de recursos tributarios que asegure su adecuado funcionamiento y sostenibilidad financiera. Esto contrasta con otros países que han optado por introducir sistemas privados —no menos amplios— de capitalización individual, tanto en el área de salud como de previsión social, que reemplazan, complementan o compiten con la alternativa de un esquema público.

En relación con lo anterior, en esta sección especial se plantea el concepto de "Presión Fiscal Equivalente" (PFE), el cual incorpora dos fuentes adicionales de ingresos a los ingresos tributarios (incluyendo contribuciones a la seguridad social pública), que representan un esfuerzo fiscal exigido a los contribuyentes cuando son de carácter obligatorio: las contribuciones a los sistemas privados de pensiones y atención de la salud, y los ingresos fiscales no tributarios provenientes de la explotación de recursos naturales (Barreix et al., 2013[1]).

La PFE queda definida de la siguiente manera:

$$PFE = IT + CSSpub + CSSpriv + RNnoT$$

Donde:

- IT: Ingresos tributarios del gobierno general
- CSSpub: Contribuciones a la Seguridad Social (esquemas públicos)
- CSSpriv: Contribuciones a los sistemas de seguro social (esquemas privados)
- RNnoT: Ingresos no tributarios provenientes de la explotación de recursos naturales.

Cabe aclarar que la consideración de todos estos componentes de heterogeneidad contribuye a nutrir y profundizar los análisis de la situación fiscal de los países de ALC, pero no invalida o contradice las mediciones convencionales que cuantifican el nivel de financiamiento público en cada uno de los mismos. De hecho, aunque con distintas denominaciones y criterios, todos ellos están contemplados en las metodologías más difundidas a nivel internacional (Recuadro 3.1). En cambio, se pretende expandir las posibilidades de comparación regional e internacional y proveer nuevos elementos que resultan, al menos para el contexto específico de la región, indispensables para lograr una perspectiva amplia y completa de estas cuestiones.

Recuadro 3.1. **Cuestiones metodológicas para la clasificación de los ingresos fiscales**

La definición de la Presión Fiscal Equivalente (PFE) incorpora elementos del financiamiento público que, en varios países de ALC, adquieren una relevancia significativa tanto en lo que se refiere a los recursos por contribuciones sociales obligatorias a regímenes privados de protección social (pensiones y seguros de salud) como a los ingresos fiscales no tributarios provenientes de la explotación de recursos naturales estratégicos (principalmente hidrocarburos y minerales). Esto permite efectuar comparaciones regionales e internacionales desde una perspectiva diferente a la convencional, pero requiere una serie de aclaraciones. De hecho, los dos ítems mencionados no suelen formar parte de la carga tributaria total en las metodologías de otras reconocidas fuentes de información y pueden conducir a conclusiones diferentes en casos particulares.

Por un lado, las contribuciones compulsivas (obligatorias) que se realizan a esquemas privados de seguro social, por parte de empleadores o empleados y en relación con la actividad laboral de estos últimos, son considerados "pagos compulsivos no tributarios" (PCNT) en los criterios metodológicos de la OCDE. Con lógica similar a la que da sustento a su inclusión dentro de la PFE, los PCNT forman parte de los costos laborales totales que enfrenta el empleador, así como de la retribución total del empleado influyendo sobre sus decisiones individuales de manera similar a la que opera con los impuestos al trabajo. Debido a esto, la OCDE ha incorporado indicadores de pagos obligatorios para realizar comparaciones entre países de una manera más homogénea y consistente (OCDE, 2019[2]). De hecho, un total de 22 países de la OCDE poseen este tipo de instrumentos, entre los que se destacan Chile, Estados Unidos, Islandia, Israel, los Países Bajos, Polonia y Suiza, por su importancia relativa y por su magnitud dentro de los costos promedios laborales.

Por otro lado, la disponibilidad de recursos naturales renovables y no renovables ha llevado a los países productores a diseñar una variedad de regímenes fiscales especiales para asegurar la adecuada apropiación de las rentas generadas por su explotación económica. Estas estrategias incluyen no sólo un abanico de instrumentos tributarios (impuesto sobre la renta [ISR] corporativo e impuestos *ad hoc*) y no tributarios (principalmente regalías y derechos de utilización), sino también distintas formas de participación del Estado en la producción, la administración y la comercialización de materias primas y servicios hasta la operación de empresas públicas en estas actividades. En general, los recursos tributarios asociados a las mismas suelen estar incorporados en las cifras globales de recaudación de los impuestos aplicados salvo casos específicos. Sin embargo, para lograr una comparación más homogénea y, aunque no forman parte de la carga tributaria total, resultaría conveniente considerar los recursos no tributarios también asociados a los sectores extractivos, los cuales muestran relevancia significativa en varios países de la OCDE como Australia, Canadá, Estados Unidos, México, Noruega, Polonia y Reino Unido (Escocia).

Fuente: Elaboración propia sobre la base de (OCDE, 2019[2]).

Como puede observarse en el Gráfico 3.1, con la metodología tradicional la recaudación tributaria como porcentaje del PIB de ALC, que son los ingresos tributarios (incluyendo a las contribuciones a la seguridad social pública), alcanzó el 23.1% del PIB en 2018. Considerando la metodología de la PFE, los nuevos recursos aportan 1.9% del PIB a la recaudación tributaria sobre PIB en 2018, alcanzando el 25% del PIB. En períodos de bonanza de los precios de los minerales, solo los recursos provenientes de la explotación de la riqueza natural de los países han llegado a contribuir con 2% del PIB (año 2013).[1]

En cuanto a la composición estructural de la PFE, los ingresos tributarios (incluyendo impuestos y contribuciones a la seguridad social pública) se han mantenido relativamente estables desde 1990 y en 2018 concentraron el 92.3% de los ingresos del gobierno como se definen en la PFE. Si tomamos los impuestos solamente, sin las contribuciones a la seguridad social pública, éstos oscilan en torno al 75% a lo largo de todo el período analizado. La participación de CSS privadas ha crecido en importancia desde su implementación en varios países de la región durante la década de 1990 y hoy representa el 3.8% de la PFE de la región. Por su parte, los ingresos no tributarios por recursos naturales se han caracterizado por una participación volátil dentro de la estructura de la PFE, en concordancia con el comportamiento variable de este tipo de ingresos.

Gráfico 3.1. **Presión Fiscal Equivalente – América Latina y El Caribe, 1990-2018**

Porcentaje del PIB

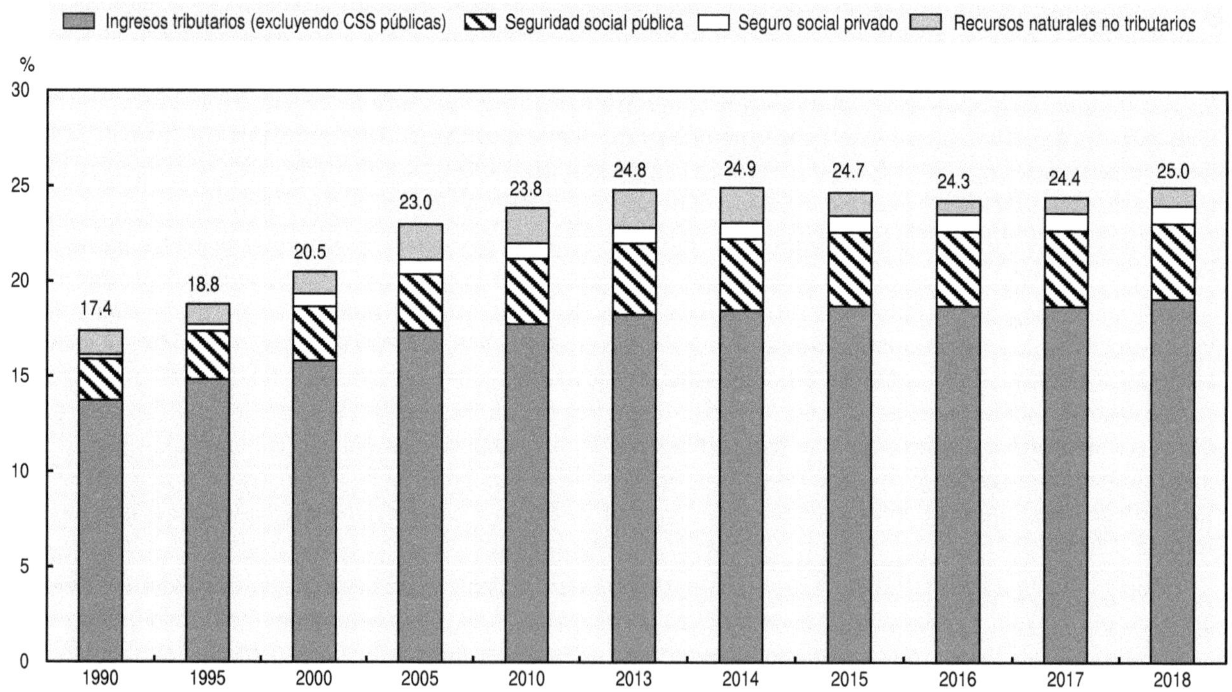

Nota: Los datos se refieren al promedio simple de los 25 países de América Latina y el Caribe incluidos en esta publicación, y no incluyen a Venezuela por falta de información.

Fuente: Elaboración propia sobre la base de cifras contenidas en (BID-CIAT, 2020[3]) y (OCDE et al., 2020[2]).

StatLink https://doi.org/10.1787/888934113982

Realizando un ejercicio de comparación de la recaudación tributaria sobre PIB de ALC y OCDE[2] para el año 2017 se tiene que, en promedio simple, los ingresos tributarios (incluyendo CSS públicas) de ALC alcanzan el 22.7% del PIB y para OCDE el 35.2% del PIB (34 países, excluyendo a Chile y México para evitar duplicaciones). Cuando se ponderan esas mismas cifras por el PIB corriente de cada país, éstas alcanzan el 25.1% del PIB para ALC y 31.8% para la OCDE (Gráfico 3.2). Sin embargo, cuando se consideran los nuevos recursos (CSS privadas y recursos naturales), la PFE de ALC en promedio simple llega a 24.4% y en promedio ponderado a 27.6%. Es decir, las brechas entre ALC y OCDE se reducen notablemente, de 12.5 puntos (35.2% - 22.7%) a 4.6 puntos (32.1% - 27.6%), cuando se consideran los nuevos recursos en promedio ponderado por el tamaño de las respectivas economías.

Una aclaración que merece ser considerada en las comparaciones incluidas en esta sección especial es que en algunos de los países miembros de la OCDE también adquieren relevancia los recursos "adicionales" por componentes de la PFE como los pagos obligatorios a sistemas privados de seguridad social o los ingresos no tributarios asociados a la explotación de recursos naturales estratégicos.[3] En efecto, aunque las contribuciones obligatorias a ciertos regímenes de salud no suelen ser contabilizadas en la presión fiscal de los países de la OCDE en general (por ejemplo, las vinculadas a la Ley para la Protección de los Pacientes y para el Cuidado Asequible en el caso de los Estados Unidos), sí encajarían y debieran formar parte de su respectiva PFE. Igualmente, formarían parte de la PFE los recursos recaudados por la capacidad del Estado de obtener rentas derivadas del dominio público, como los recursos naturales, siendo un ejemplo a nivel de la OCDE los ingresos no tributarios de Noruega provenientes de la explotación de sus reservas de petróleo (Recuadro 3.1).

Gráfico 3.2. **Comparativo de Ingresos Tributarios (IT) y Presión Fiscal Equivalente (PFE) entre ALC y OCDE-34, 2017**

Porcentaje del PIB

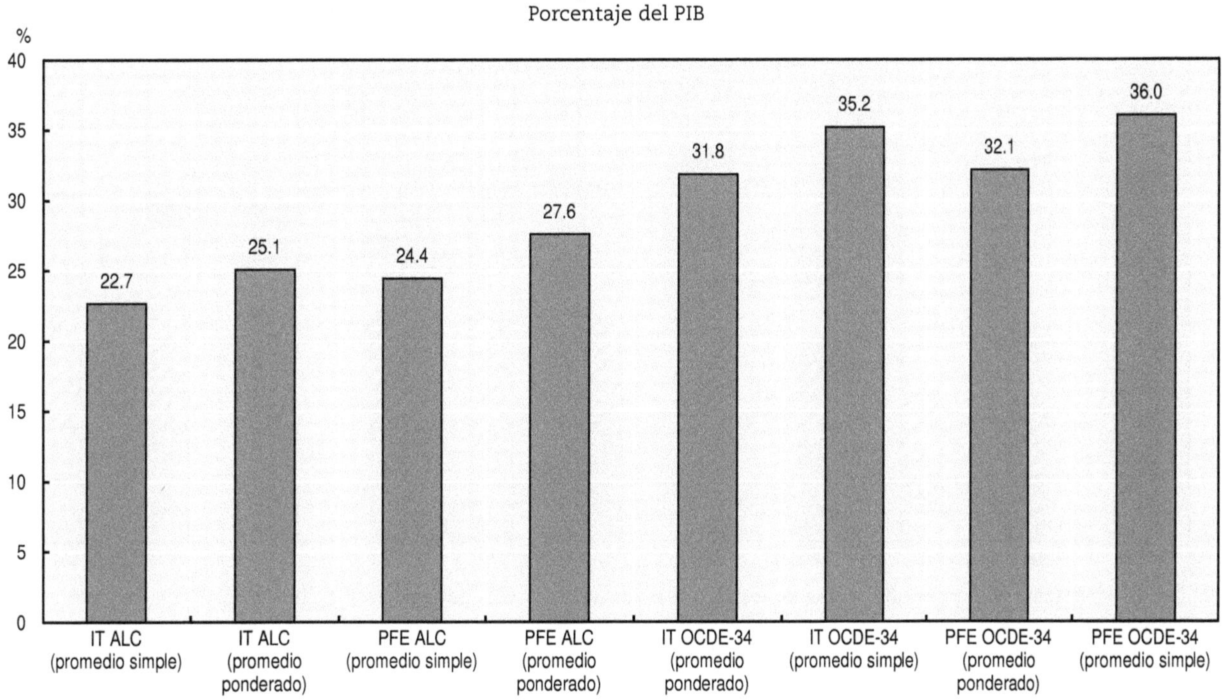

Nota: El promedio OCDE-34 no incluye a Chile ni México para evitar duplicaciones en la comparación con la PFE de ALC.

Fuente: Elaboración propia sobre la base de cifras contenidas en (BID-CIAT, 2020[3]) y (OCDE et al., 2020[2]).

StatLink https://doi.org/10.1787/888934114001

Evolución de la PFE en los países de ALC: Logros y obstáculos con gran heterogeneidad regional

Evolución regional, 1990-2018

Como fue señalado, en 2018 la región alcanzó el nivel máximo de PFE desde 1990.[4] Esta mayor recaudación fue sostenida por el incremento en los pilares fiscales de la región.[5] Estos pilares determinan la sostenibilidad fiscal regional y son: el Impuesto al Valor Agregado (IVA),[6] el Impuesto sobre la Renta (ISR)[7] y las contribuciones a la Seguridad Social pública (CSS públicas) y contribuciones obligatorias a los sistemas de seguro social privado (CSS privadas). Si bien los ingresos no tributarios por la explotación de recursos naturales representan una fuente de recursos importante para la región, no son considerados pilares por su alta variabilidad. El Gráfico 3.3 muestra la evolución de la PFE de la región desde 1990 hasta 2018, desagregada por pilares fiscales, recursos naturales no tributarios y otros impuestos.

Gráfico 3.3. **Pilares fiscales y otros componentes de la PFE – América Latina y el Caribe, 1990-2018**

Porcentaje del PIB

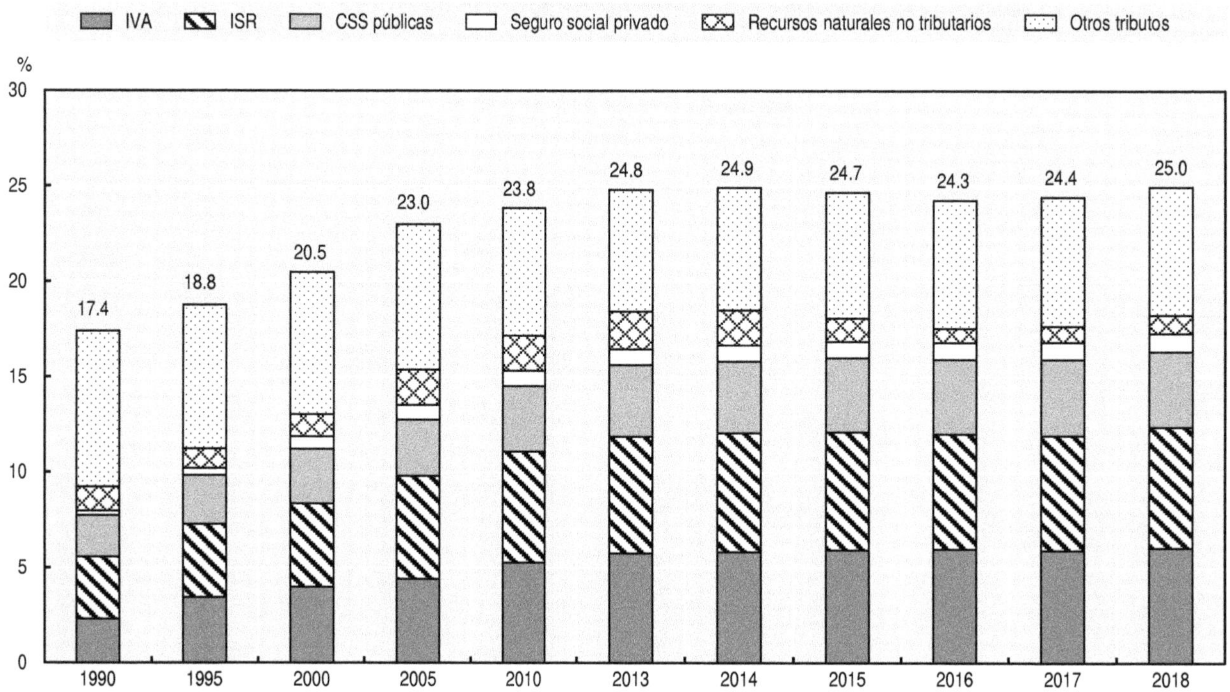

Nota: Los datos se refieren al promedio simple de los 25 países incluidos en esta publicación y no incluyen a Venezuela por falta de información.

Fuente: Elaboración propia sobre la base de cifras contenidas en (BID-CIAT, 2020[3]) y (OCDE et al., 2020[2]).

StatLink https://doi.org/10.1787/888934114020

Desde 1990 hasta 2018, el IVA, el ISR, las CSS públicas y las CSS privadas crecieron 3.8% del PIB, 3.1% del PIB, 1.8% del PIB y 0.7% del PIB, respectivamente. Estos desempeños fueron parcialmente menguados por la menor recaudación por concepto de recursos naturales y determinaron un aumento global de la PFE de 7.6% del PIB.

En el último quinquenio (2013-18), el crecimiento de la presión fiscal equivalente en la región fue de solo 0.2% del PIB. El ISR y las CSS públicas crecieron tan solo 0.2% del PIB, mientras que los ingresos por recursos naturales disminuyeron 1% del PIB. Esta desaceleración en la PFE fue ocasionada principalmente por los cambios en el contexto internacional, la desaceleración general en las tasas de crecimiento económico y la caída en los precios de los minerales, que afectaron significativamente las cuentas fiscales de la región. Esta última circunstancia refleja la alta sensibilidad fiscal de la región a cambios en los precios de los *commodities*.

La estructura de la PFE de ALC además cuenta en sus componentes con un rubro denominado "Otros tributos". Este rubro contiene las categorías de impuestos a la propiedad y a las transacciones financieras, nómina salarial, otros impuestos sobre bienes y servicios (incluyendo impuestos especiales, al comercio internacional y tributos generales sobre el consumo como en los casos de Argentina, Brasil, Colombia o Cuba), regímenes simplificados y la mayoría de los tributos subnacionales, entre otros. En 1990 este grupo de impuestos, cuya composición interna varía de un país a otro, representaba el 47% de la PFE y hasta 2018 fue desplazado gradualmente por los pilares fiscales, participando actualmente de un porcentaje mucho menor aunque aún significativo de la PFE total (27%).

Nivel y estructura de la PFE por países

La región de ALC se caracteriza por una elevada heterogeneidad en términos de su nivel de ingresos fiscales. A nivel individual de países, los rangos entre niveles máximos y mínimos de la PFE entre países son muy significativos (Gráfico 3.4). Cuba presenta la mayor carga fiscal de la región (42.3% del PIB) y Guatemala la menor (12.1%). Como fue señalado, el promedio regional es de 25% y es de destacar que, para los países cuya PFE se encuentra alrededor o por debajo de la media regional, la carga tributaria disminuye sustancialmente cuando se descuentan los recursos adicionales que incorpora la PFE, como por ejemplo en Bolivia, Chile, y Trinidad y Tobago.

Gráfico 3.4. **Presión Fiscal Equivalente y recaudación tributaria – América Latina y el Caribe, 2018**

Porcentaje del PIB

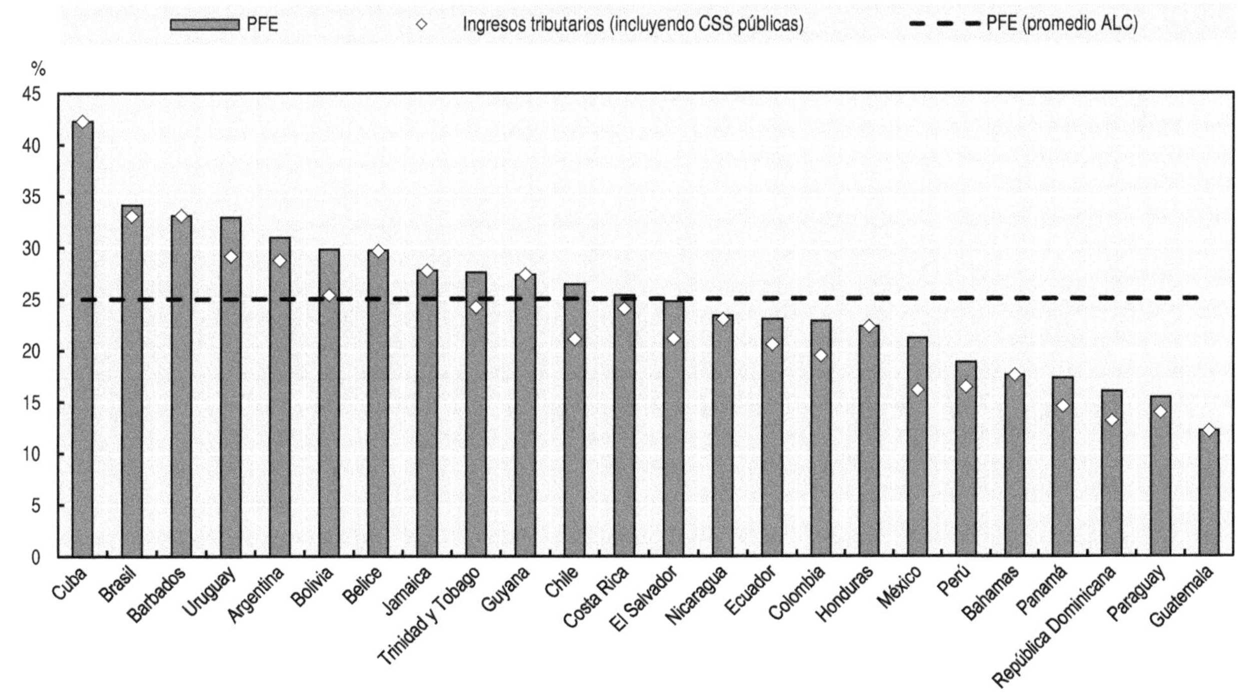

Nota: El promedio ALC es el promedio simple de los 25 países incluidos en esta publicación y no incluye a Venezuela por falta de información. El promedio incluye los ingresos tributarios de Santa Lucía, pero excluye las contribuciones a la seguridad social, las contribuciones a los planes de seguros privados y los ingresos no tributarios procedentes de recursos no renovables para dicho país debido a la falta de datos.

Fuente: Elaboración propia sobre la base de cifras contenidas en (BID-CIAT, 2020[3]) y (OCDE et al., 2020[2]).

StatLink https://doi.org/10.1787/888934114039

Analizando el ordenamiento de los países de acuerdo con el nivel de la PFE, deben señalarse algunos cambios importantes observados en los años más recientes. Tomando como referencia la última actualización de esta base de datos que llegaba al año 2015 (Barreix et al., 2017[5]), los países que más retrocedieron en el ranking regional de la variable PFE son Bolivia, Trinidad y Tobago, Argentina y Paraguay. Al contrario, destacan los avances del Uruguay consolidándose como uno de los países de mayor recaudación tributaria de la región, como resultado de un aumento sustancial de la recaudación del ISR, especialmente del gravamen aportado por personas físicas. Adicionalmente, el promedio regional se ha visto incrementado por la incorporación de países tales como Cuba, Guyana y Jamaica dentro de la base de datos de la PFE.

En cuanto a la estructura tributaria, en el Gráfico 3.5 se detalla la composición de la PFE por país. Las mayores cifras de recaudación del pilar fiscal "IVA" se localizan en Barbados (9.2% del PIB) y Jamaica (9.1% del PIB).[8] En cuanto al "ISR", Trinidad y Tobago recauda 12.8% del PIB, el nivel más elevado de la región, seguido de Cuba (11.1% del PIB) y Guyana (9.8% del PIB). En 2018, las CSS públicas en Brasil alcanzaron el 8.4% del PIB y en Costa Rica el 8.2%. En regímenes privados, Chile lidera la recaudación regional con 4.7% del PIB, siendo importantes en Uruguay (3.8%), El Salvador (3.5%) y la República Dominicana (2.8%).

Gráfico 3.5. **Pilares fiscales y otros componentes de la PFE por países, 2018**

Porcentaje del PIB

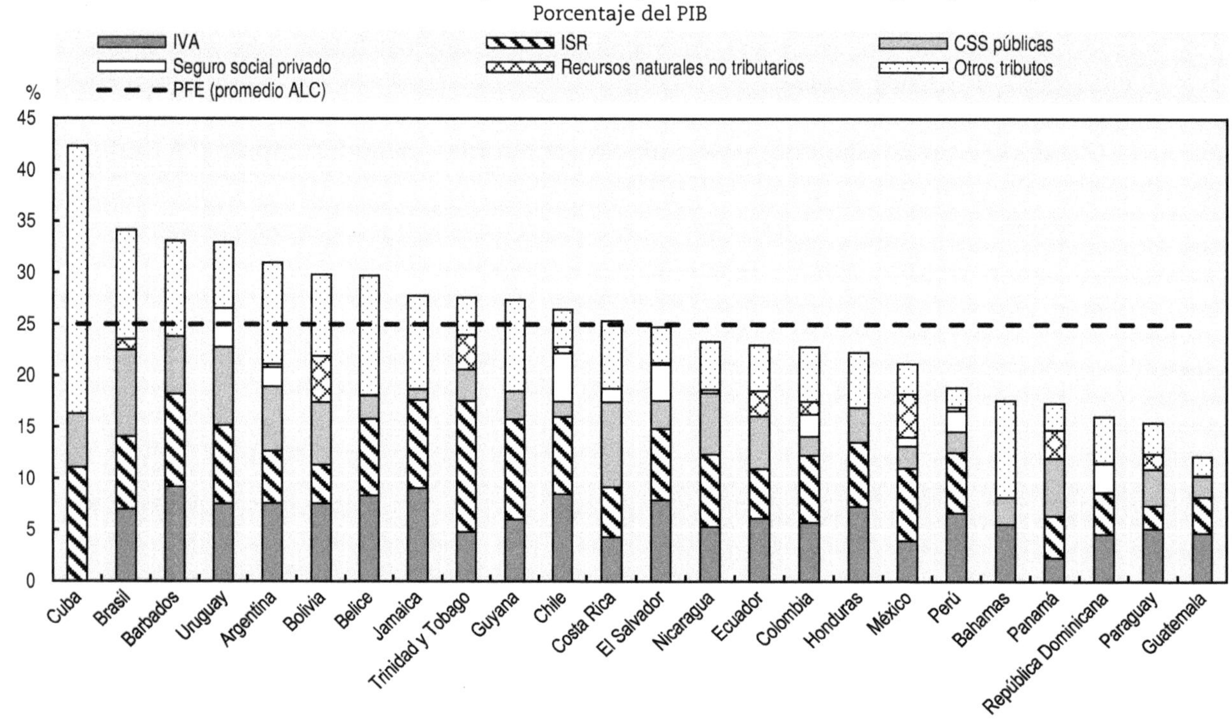

Nota: El promedio ALC es el promedio simple de los 25 países incluidos en esta publicación y no incluye a Venezuela por falta de información. El promedio de ALC incluye los ingresos tributarios de Santa Lucía, pero excluye las contribuciones a la seguridad social, las contribuciones a los planes de seguros privados y los ingresos no tributarios procedentes de recursos no renovables para dicho país debido a la falta de datos.

Fuente: Elaboración propia sobre la base de cifras contenidas en (BID-CIAT, 2020[3]) y (OCDE et al., 2020[2]).

StatLink https://doi.org/10.1787/888934114058

En cuanto a los ingresos no tributarios por recursos naturales, individualmente los que más recaudaron en 2018 fueron Bolivia (4.5% del PIB), México (4.2% del PIB) y Trinidad y Tobago (3.4% del PIB). Como fue mencionado en párrafos anteriores, es llamativo el contraste de lo recaudado por Bolivia y Trinidad y Tobago en el último año analizado, en comparación con lo recaudado en los años del auge de los precios de los minerales e hidrocarburos (ambos países llegaron a recaudar en 2012 alrededor de 11% del PIB en esta categoría).

Comparación con la OCDE

Desde 1990, el mayor esfuerzo fiscal, las reformas tributarias emprendidas y contextos favorables externos les han permitido a los países de ALC acercarse a la recaudación tributaria como porcentaje del PIB de países con mayor desarrollo tributario como los de la OCDE. Las diferencias con el promedio de OCDE-34 se redujeron particularmente durante los años de la década del 2000, coincidiendo con el boom de los precios de los minerales. Así, en 1990 la PFE de ALC representaba el 51.3% de la PFE de la OCDE (34 países, excluyendo a Chile y México), en el año 2000 el 57.4% y en 2017 el 67.8% (Gráfico 3.6). Desde 2010, las diferencias en la PFE entre ALC y la OCDE se han mantenido relativamente estables, lo que coincide con un entorno internacional adverso, la reducción en la demanda por los recursos naturales de ALC y la consiguiente caída en los precios de los hidrocarburos y principales minerales exportados desde la región, lo que ha reducido su influencia en la convergencia regional.

Gráfico 3.6. **Comparativo (ratio) con OCDE de la PFE de ALC, con y sin recursos naturales, 1990-2017**

Porcentaje de la recaudación promedio de OCDE-34

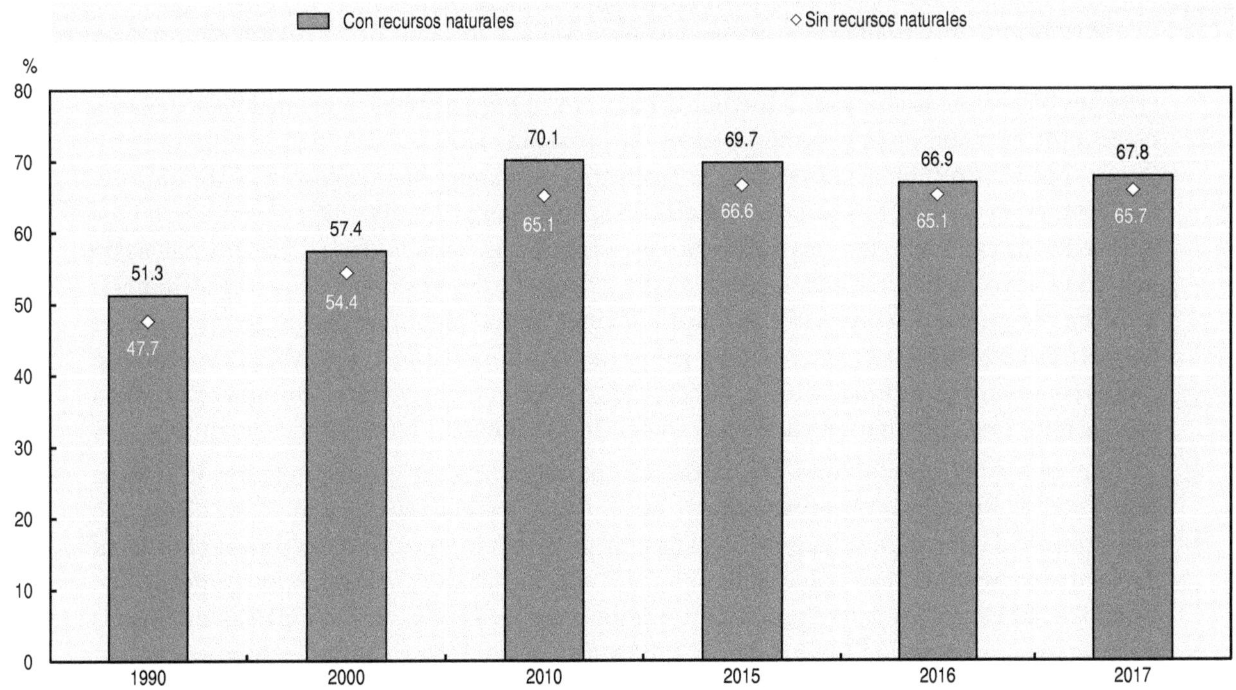

Nota: Los datos se refieren a los promedios simples de 25 países de América Latina y el Caribe y 34 países de la OCDE. El promedio OCDE-34 no incluye a Chile ni México para evitar duplicaciones en la comparación con la PFE de ALC.

Fuente: Elaboración propia sobre la base de cifras contenidas en (BID-CIAT, 2020[3]) y (OCDE et al., 2020[2]).

StatLink https://doi.org/10.1787/888934114077

En cuanto a la comparación entre la PFE con la OCDE por tipo de impuesto, el mayor acercamiento se ha producido en IVA, donde a nivel regional se recauda prácticamente al mismo nivel de la OCDE e incluso para el Caribe y los países del Cono Sur como Argentina, Brasil, Chile o Uruguay, la recaudación sobrepasa a la de varios países desarrollados.

En contribuciones a la seguridad social sobre PIB, en cambio, las brechas entre ALC y la OCDE resultan muy evidentes. Considerando solamente las CSS públicas, el promedio de ALC representa sólo el 41.5% del valor medio para la OCDE, más allá de los significativos montos recaudados por países tales como Argentina, Bolivia, Brasil, Costa Rica y Uruguay, a un nivel similar o incluso superior de varios países de la OCDE. Cuando se suman las contribuciones de los regímenes privados, la situación no mejora de manera sustancial, pues en ALC solo se llega a recaudar el 47.3% de lo que hace OCDE en promedio.

En el ISR el desempeño no ha sido favorable y, a pesar de ciertos avances y reformas observados a lo largo de la última década,[9] se recauda apenas más de la mitad de lo que promedia la OCDE (51%). Este resultado se explica, fundamentalmente, por el bajo rendimiento obtenido por la región en la recaudación del ISR de personas físicas. En el ISR aportado por las sociedades, los países de ALC recaudan un porcentaje relativamente similar al de OCDE (en 2017, OCDE-34 recaudó 2.9% del PIB y ALC 3.4%). La gran diferencia está en los ingresos del ISR de personas naturales, que para OCDE alcanzan un promedio de 8.6% del PIB y para ALC tan sólo el 2.2% en ese mismo año. En ALC, el ISR de personas naturales es pagado por individuos en el sector formal y con altos salarios, ubicados en los deciles de mayores ingresos, y se estima que casi el 90% de la población de ALC está exenta del pago de este impuesto (Barreix, Alberto; Benitez, Juan Carlos y Pecho, Miguel, 2017[6]). Estos factores hacen que la estructura del ISR se vea sesgada hacia las personas jurídicas en la gran mayoría de los países de ALC.

Por último, la elevada heterogeneidad observada a lo largo de la región siempre ha dificultado los análisis globales y los agrupamientos de países de acuerdo a determinados criterios básicos. Una alternativa frecuente consiste en efectuar clasificaciones de los países de acuerdo a su ubicación geográfica – como se presenta en otras secciones de este trabajo – lo que, por ejemplo, en este caso podría realizarse con categorías tales como "América del Sur", "América Central" y "Caribe", más allá de saberse las profundas diferencias existentes al interior de cada una de estas sub-regiones. Otra opción sería la de agrupar los países de acuerdo al nivel (actual, reciente o promedio de un período determinado) de la carga tributaria total de los países, incluyendo las contribuciones de la seguridad social y los recursos tributarios de niveles subnacionales de gobierno. Esto conduciría a agrupar, por ejemplo, a países como Argentina, Brasil y Uruguay como los de mayor recaudación tributaria en América Latina, a los que se sumarían varios países del Caribe como Barbados, Belice y Jamaica.

En este caso, y como otra forma de agrupamiento de los países, resulta de interés ponderar las diferencias observadas entre ALC y OCDE en relación con el nivel de desarrollo y la capacidad contributiva general de cada país de la región. Esto resultaría en la obtención de cuatro subgrupos regionales dados por: *i)* Centroamérica más República Dominicana; *ii)* Caribe; *iii)* los países de la Comunidad Andina más Venezuela; y *iv)* los países miembros del Mercosur, además de Chile y México (Barreix et al., 2017[5]). Como se puede observar en el Gráfico 3.7, tomando tanto el PIB total como el PIB per cápita en paridad del nivel adquisitivo la diferencia entre ALC y la OCDE es mucho mayor ya sea por: *i)* la diferencia en mayor proporción de producto en varios impuestos; así como por *ii)* la diferencia de poder adquisitivo representada por la magnitud de cada economía.[10] Del mismo modo, se puede apreciar que la imposición sobre la renta tiene un rol mucho más importante en los países de la OCDE (diferencia que se concentra en el impuesto aportado por las personas físicas). Además, se percibe cierta paridad respecto de las CSS totales (considerando regímenes públicos y privados en conjunto) y se comprueba para la región una relevancia superior del IVA como fuente generadora de recursos públicos.

Gráfico 3.7. **Presión fiscal per cápita comparada en dólares estadounidenses corrientes (PPA) por regiones, 2017**

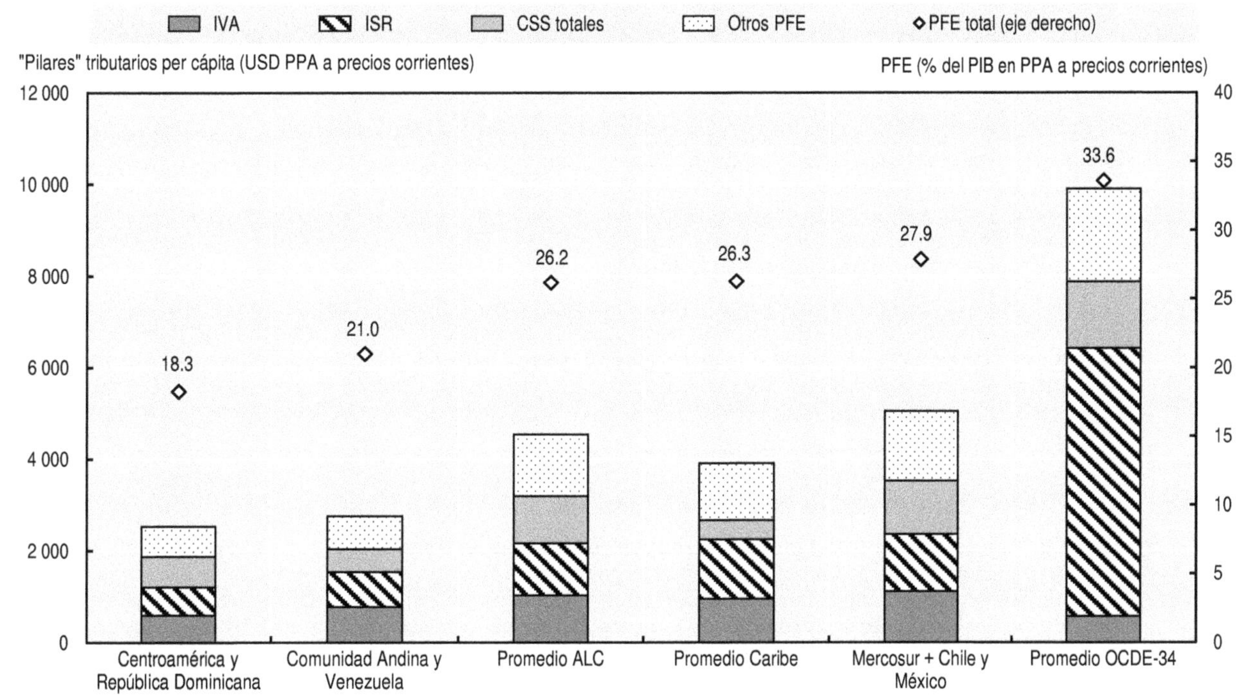

Nota: Los datos se refieren a los promedios ponderados por el PIB. El promedio OCDE-34 no incluye a Chile ni México para evitar duplicaciones en la comparación con la PFE de ALC. El componente "CSS Totales" abarca sistemas públicos y privados, mientras que "Otros PFE" comprende el resto de los ingresos tributarios más aquellos no tributarios provenientes de sectores de recursos naturales estratégicos.

Fuente: Elaboración propia sobre la base de cifras contenidas en (BID-CIAT, 2020[3]), (OCDE et al., 2020[2]), y (FMI, 2019[7]) para el PIB per cápita en PPA y el PIB en PPA de cada país.

StatLink *https://doi.org/10.1787/888934114096*

En definitiva, la cantidad real de recursos disponibles para el fisco es muy superior en el mundo desarrollado que la observada en los países de ALC, especialmente cuando se consideran las cargas tributarias en relación con el tamaño de la economía y el nivel de imposición a nivel per cápita. Este tipo de comparaciones tiene implicancias al momento de vincular estas fuentes de financiamiento público con el nivel de gasto público total de cada región y cada país, y obliga a evaluar con cautela las potenciales opciones de reforma tributaria y fiscal que buscan ampliar la movilización de recursos domésticos en los países de la región.

Notas

1. A lo largo de esta sección especial se utilizan datos estadísticos provenientes de la base de datos de *Presión Fiscal Equivalente BID-CIAT* (BID-CIAT, 2020[3]). Los promedios regionales no incluyen a Venezuela por falta de información.
2. A lo largo de esta sección especial se considera el promedio OCDE-34, el cual no incluye a Chile ni a México para evitar duplicaciones en la comparación con la PFE de ALC.
3. Si bien constituyen cálculos preliminares, a partir de estadísticas provistas por OCDE, se ha calculado el valor promedio (simple) de la PFE para la OCDE-34 en 36% del PIB para el año 2017 (32.1% en promedio ponderado por el tamaño de cada economía). Esto sugiere, en general, un menor peso relativo de los ítems de seguro social privado y recursos naturales no tributarios —salvo algunas excepciones— para el conjunto de países desarrollados respecto del observado en América Latina y el Caribe.

4. Se toma este año como referencia de la comparación por corresponder con el año de inicio del período analizado en las estadísticas tributarias presentadas a lo largo de este documento bajo una metodología estandarizada (OCDE, 2019[11]). No obstante, existen estimaciones para períodos anteriores que confirman que los valores actuales de promedio de la recaudación tributaria sobre PIB son los más elevados en la historia de la región. Para mayor información, véase (CIAT, 2017[9]).
5. Un pilar fiscal es aquel tributo que tiene una base amplia y es capaz de generar recaudaciones significativas y estables a lo largo del tiempo (Barreix y Roca, 2007[6]).
6. Si bien el IVA es el principal tributo aplicado sobre el consumo, en algunos países de la región existen impuestos generales sobre bienes y servicios de base amplia y con características asimilables a las del IVA. Como ejemplos pueden mencionarse, entre otros: el impuesto sobre ingresos brutos (provincial) en Argentina; el COFINS y PIS/PASEP (federal) y el ISS (municipal) en Brasil; y el Impuesto de Industria y Comercio (municipal) en Colombia.
7. El pilar fiscal "ISR" se refiere a la recaudación tributaria neta vinculada al Impuesto sobre la Renta, incluyendo también al resto de gravámenes sobre los ingresos que sean potestad del gobierno central o subnacional, ya sea que recaigan sobre un sector particular, tengan otra base de cálculo alternativa, sean de carácter temporal y extraordinario y/o graven tipos de ingresos específicos no alcanzados por el ISR tradicional.
8. Cabe remarcar que, si se consideran los ingresos por otros tributos generales sobre bienes y servicios asimilables al IVA, la recaudación también resulta muy significativa en los casos de Argentina y Brasil (11.4% y 12.4% del PIB en 2018, respectivamente).
9. En 2006, Uruguay fue el país pionero en adoptar un sistema de imposición dual, a través del cual comenzó a gravar en forma separada las rentas del trabajo, con una escala progresiva de alícuotas, y las rentas de capital con una tasa proporcional relativamente baja. Ese mismo camino ha sido seguido por países como el Perú en 2009 y varios países de Centroamérica entre 2009 y 2011, en un intento práctico por incorporar distintas rentas de capital dentro de la base gravable del ISR. En años más recientes, Argentina y México también se sumaron a esta tendencia de reformas con impuestos duales con similares características.
10. Tanto los valores de la PFE total como de los principales impuestos per cápita son promedios ponderados por el PIB total de cada país en dólares estadounidenses a paridad de poder adquisitivo (PPA).

Referencias

Barreix, A., J. Benitez y M. Pecho (2017), "Revisando el impuesto a la renta personal en América Latina: Evolución e impacto", Banco Interamericano de Desarrollo, *https://publications.iadb.org/es/revisando-el-impuesto-la-renta-personal-en-america-latina-evolucion-e-impacto.* [6]

Barreix, A. y J. Roca (2007), "Reforzando un pilar fiscal: El impuesto a la renta dual a la uruguaya", *Revista de la CEPAL* 92, pp. 123-142, *https://repositorio.cepal.org/handle/11362/11195.* [9]

Barreix, A. et al. (2017), "Actualización de la presión fiscal equivalente en América Latina y el Caribe", Banco Interamericano de Desarrollo, *http://dx.doi.org/10.18235/0000879.* [5]

Barreix, A. et al. (2013), "Metiendo Presión: Estimando la verdadera carga fiscal de América Latina y el Caribe", BID, CIAT, IEF, *https://www.ciat.org/Biblioteca/Estudios/2013_Metiendo_Presion_ief_ciat_bid_es.pdf* [1]

BID-CIAT (2020), *Base de datos de recaudación BID-CIAT*, *https://www.ciat.org/base-de-datos-de-recaudacion-bid-ciat/.* [3]

CIAT (2017), *Cincuenta años en el quehacer tributario de América Latina*, Centro Interamericano de Administraciones Tributarias, *https://www.ciat.org/Biblioteca/Publicaciones_CIAT/Libro_50_anos/2017_LB_50_es.pdf.* [10]

FMI (2019), *World Economic Outlook Database April 2019*, Fondo Monetario Internacional, *https://www.imf.org/external/pubs/ft/weo/2019/01/weodata/index.aspx.* [7]

OCDE (2019), *OECD.Stat*, OCDE, Paris, *https://stats-2.oecd.org/index.aspx?DatasetCode=DACSECTOR.* [11]

OCDE (2019), *Taxing Wages 2017-2018 Associated Paper: Non-tax compulsory payments*, OECD Publishing, Paris, *https://www.oecd.org/tax/tax-policy/non-tax-compulsory-payments.pdf.* [2]

OCDE (2019), *Global Revenue Statistics Database*, OECD Publishing, *https://stats.oecd.org/Index.aspx?DataSetCode=RS_GBL* [8]

OCDE et al. (2020), *Estadísticas tributarias en América Latina y el Caribe 2020*, OECD Publishing, Paris, *https://doi.org/10.1787/35745b02-en.* [4]

Chapter 4

Tax levels and tax structures, 1990-2018

Capítulo 4

Niveles impositivos y estructuras tributarias, 1990-2018

Chapter 4 / Capítulo 4

4.1. Comparative tables, 1990-2018

In all of the following tables a (..) indicates not available. The main series in this volume cover the years 1990 to 2018.

Figures referring to 1991-99, 2001-06 and 2008-09 in Tables 4.1 to 4.2 and Tables 4.15 to 4.17, figures relating to 1991-99, 2001-09 and 2011-16 in Tables 4.5 to 4.10 and figures relating to 1990-94, 1996-99 and 2001-16 in Tables 4.11 to 4.13 have been omitted because of lack of space. Complete series are, however, available on line at www.latameconomy.org and in the database OECD (2020), "Revenue Statistics in Latin America: Comparative tables", *OECD Tax Statistics*, http://dx.doi.org/10.1787/data-00641-en.

4.2. Cuadros comparativos, 1990-2018

En todos los cuadros siguientes, (..) indica dato indisponible. Las principales series de datos de esta sección cubren el periodo que va de 1990 a 2018.

Las cifras relativas a 1991-99, 2001-06 y a 2008-09 en Cuadros 4.1 hasta 4.2 y Cuadros 4.15 hasta 4.17 y las cifras relativas a 1991-99, 2001-09 y 2011-16 en Cuadros 4.5 hasta 4.10 y las cifras relativas a 1990-94, 1996-99 y 2001-16 en Cuadros 4.11 hasta 4.13 a se han omitido por falta de espacio. Sin embargo, las series completas están disponibles en línea en www.latameconomy.org y en la base de datos OCDE (2020), "Revenue Statistics in Latin America: Comparative tables", *OECD Tax Statistics, http://dx.doi.org/10.1787/data-00641-en.*

Table 4.1. **Total tax revenue as % of GDP, 1990-2018**
Cuadro 4.1. **Total de ingresos tributarios en % del PIB, 1990-2018**

	1990	2000	2007	2010	2013	2014	2015	2016	2017	2018
Argentina	13.7	19.8	26.4	29.1	31.2	31.1	31.5	30.7	30.1	28.8
Bahamas[1]	9.7	12.2	13.1	12.7	13.6	13.9	15.5	16.3	17.7	17.6
Barbados[1]	25.3	30.9	30.0	30.0	29.4	28.9	29.6	31.2	32.1	33.1
Belize / Belice	21.6	19.1	25.3	26.5	25.5	27.4	26.9	27.8	28.3	29.7
Bolivia[1]	6.5	20.2	22.2	22.9	26.7	27.9	29.5	27.9	25.9	25.4
Brazil / Brasil	27.8	29.4	34.7	32.3	32.3	31.6	31.9	32.0	32.1	33.1
Chile	16.9	18.8	22.7	19.6	19.9	19.6	20.4	20.1	20.1	21.1
Colombia	9.2	14.8	19.3	18.1	20.0	19.6	19.9	19.1	19.0	19.4
Costa Rica	22.5	21.2	23.3	22.4	23.5	23.3	23.6	24.2	23.9	24.0
Cuba	31.9	37.2	44.0	37.2	36.5	37.1	38.1	41.1	42.4	42.3
Dominican Republic / República Dominicana	8.3	12.3	14.9	12.3	13.6	13.4	12.9	13.0	13.2	13.2
Ecuador[1]	7.1	11.6	15.1	16.0	19.5	19.2	21.3	19.9	19.9	20.6
El Salvador	11.3	14.2	18.6	18.6	19.9	19.7	19.7	20.4	20.8	21.1
Guatemala	8.2	12.2	13.8	12.2	12.9	12.9	12.3	12.6	12.4	12.1
Guyana	20.6	20.8	24.4	24.2	22.9	23.8	24.2	23.5	26.1	27.4
Honduras	12.4	17.2	19.6	18.1	19.0	20.2	20.8	22.3	22.0	22.3
Jamaica	20.3	22.2	24.8	24.9	24.9	24.8	25.8	26.5	27.3	27.8
Mexico / México[2]	12.1	11.5	12.0	12.8	13.3	13.7	15.9	16.6	16.1	16.1
Nicaragua	..	14.3	18.8	19.3	21.2	21.8	22.3	23.3	23.8	23.0
Panama / Panamá[1]	15.6	15.5	15.5	16.4	16.8	15.5	15.0	15.5	14.9	14.6
Paraguay[1]	9.6	11.6	10.8	12.1	12.6	14.3	13.7	13.4	14.0	14.0
Peru / Perú	12.0	15.2	18.5	17.8	18.9	19.2	17.4	16.1	15.2	16.4
Saint Lucia / Santa Lucía[3]	..	19.4	19.6	19.3	20.1	20.4	20.7	21.0	19.7	20.0
Trinidad and Tobago / Trinidad y Tobago	23.3	21.9	27.8	28.7	27.8	29.0	28.4	22.8	20.9	24.2
Uruguay	20.0	23.2	25.7	26.3	27.5	27.4	27.3	27.8	29.0	29.2
Venezuela[4]	18.1	13.6	17.0	11.8	14.4	..	..	..	..	..
Unweighted average / Promedio no ponderado										
LAC / ALC[5]	**15.9**	**18.7**	**21.6**	**21.2**	**22.0**	**22.2**	**22.6**	**22.6**	**22.7**	**23.1**
OECD / OCDE[6]	**31.9**	**33.8**	**33.6**	**32.3**	**33.4**	**33.6**	**33.7**	**34.4**	**34.2**	**34.3**

Note: The figures exclude local government revenues for Argentina (but include provincial revenues), the Bahamas, Barbados, Cuba (except for 2002-2012), the Dominican Republic, Saint Lucia, Trinidad and Tobago and Venezuela as the data are not available. Local government revenue data are available since 1991 for Nicaragua, since 1994 for Bolivia, since 1995 for Guatemala, since 1998 for Jamaica, since 1999 for Panama, since 2000 for Peru, since 2002 for El Salvador and Guyana, since 2006 for Paraguay and since 1990 for all other countries.

1. The data include the following estimations: Bahamas (social security contributions from 2017), Barbados (social security contributions are government projections for 2015-2018), Bolivia (local tax revenues and healthcare social security contributions for 2018), Ecuador (local tax revenues for 2018), Panama (Local tax revenues for 2018), Paraguay (Local tax revenues for 2018). See the corresponding country tables for more information.
2. Data on state and local government revenues are estimated for 2018.
3. Social security contributions are not available.
4. Some tax revenue data are not available between 2014 and 2017 and therefore total figures have not been included. Data for 2018 are not available.
5. Represents the group of 25 Latin American and Caribbean countries included in this publication and excludes Venezuela due to data availability issues. Chile and Mexico are also part of the OECD (36) group.
6. Calculated by applying the unweighted average percentage change for 2018 in the 34 countries providing data for that year to the overall average tax to GDP ratio in 2017.

Nota : Las cifras excluyen los ingresos subnacionales para Argentina (pero se incluyen los ingresos de las provincias), Las Bahamas, Barbados, Cuba (excepto 2002-2012), República Dominicana, Santa Lucía, Trinidad y Tobago y Venezuela, dado que los datos no están disponibles. Los datos de ingresos subnacionales están disponibles desde 1991 para Nicaragua, desde 1994 para Bolivia, desde 1995 para Guatemala, desde 1998 para Jamaica, desde 1999 para Panamá, desde 2000 para Perú, desde 2002 para El Salvador y Guyana, desde 2006 para Paraguay y desde 1990 para todos los demás países.

1. Los datos incluyen las siguientes estimaciones: Bahamas (contribuciones a la seguridad social de 2017), Barbados (las contribuciones a la seguridad social son proyecciones gubernamentales para 2015-2018), Bolivia (ingresos fiscales locales y contribuciones a la seguridad social en salud para 2018), Ecuador (ingresos fiscales locales para 2018), Panamá (ingresos fiscales locales para 2018), Paraguay (ingresos fiscales locales para 2018). Consulte las tablas de países correspondientes para obtener más información.
2. Los datos estimados incluyen ingresos esperados a nivel estatal y local para el 2018.
3. Las cotizaciones a la seguridad social no están disponibles.
4. Algunos datos de ingresos fiscales no están disponibles entre 2014 y 2017 y, por lo tanto, no se han incluido las cifras totales. Los datos para 2018 no están disponibles.
5. Representa al grupo de 25 países de América Latina y el Caribe incluidos en esta publicación y excluye a Venezuela debido a problemas de disponibilidad de datos. Chile y México también forman parte del grupo OCDE (36).
6. Calculado mediante la aplicación del cambio porcentual promedio no ponderado para 2018 en los 34 países que proporcionan datos para ese año al promedio del recaudación tributario sobre PIB en 2017

StatLink https://doi.org/10.1787/888934114115

Table 4.2. **Total tax revenue in millions of USD at market exchange rates, 1990-2018**
Cuadro 4.2. **Total de ingresos tributarios en millones de US dólares a tipos de cambio de mercado, 1990-2018**

	1990	2000	2007	2010	2013	2014	2015	2016	2017	2018
Argentina	20 952	61 084	75 919	123 456	190 650	175 337	202 079	170 714	193 434	149 521
Bahamas[1]	505	965	1 360	1 277	1 445	1 490	1 761	1 934	2 157	2 151
Barbados[1]	513	946	1 412	1 368	1 379	1 357	1 406	1 521	1 609	1 692
Belize / Belice	89	159	326	370	411	464	473	503	527	571
Bolivia[1]	317	1 696	2 940	4 527	8 255	9 258	9 805	9 547	9 777	10 296
Brazil / Brasil	132 859	192 434	485 484	712 552	799 373	777 092	573 936	574 881	662 142	623 665
Chile	5 829	14 645	39 427	42 814	55 286	51 101	49 734	50 416	55 852	62 839
Colombia	5 136	14 655	39 800	51 846	76 503	74 534	58 377	53 940	59 207	64 370
Costa Rica	1 286	3 177	6 246	8 416	11 844	11 901	13 102	13 983	14 024	14 535
Cuba	6 870	11 367	25 787	23 949	28 173	29 940	33 182	37 597	41 021	42 307
Dominican Republic / República Dominicana	664	2 986	6 586	6 633	8 512	9 039	9 208	9 848	10 542	11 274
Ecuador[1]	1 078	2 125	7 698	11 133	18 581	19 577	21 146	19 883	20 745	22 277
El Salvador	543	1 669	3 172	3 426	4 385	4 451	4 628	4 929	5 193	5 498
Guatemala	573	2 097	4 693	5 051	6 957	7 565	7 849	8 633	9 367	9 523
Guyana	104	234	425	549	685	733	774	825	927	1 067
Honduras	515	1 219	2 405	2 841	3 520	3 988	4 369	4 839	5 078	5 308
Jamaica	1 027	1 998	3 192	3 286	3 543	3 433	3 647	3 744	4 026	4 338
Mexico / México	36 267	81 139	126 471	135 822	169 551	180 123	186 360	179 131	186 359	..
Nicaragua	..	733	1 399	1 693	2 332	2 586	2 846	3 092	3 288	3 016
Panama / Panamá[1]	895	1 942	3 298	4 815	7 650	7 740	8 090	8 958	9 272	9 489
Paraguay[1]	471	1 029	1 921	3 302	4 843	5 777	4 967	4 843	5 469	5 645
Peru / Perú	3 389	7 672	18 915	26 458	38 110	38 771	33 310	31 388	32 619	37 037
Saint Lucia / Santa Lucía[2]	..	160	254	273	303	323	346	362	365	386
Trinidad and Tobago / Trinidad y Tobago	1 158	1 746	5 893	6 261	7 480	7 948	7 339	5 188	4 617	5 449
Uruguay	2 051	5 307	6 026	10 614	15 845	15 703	14 555	14 623	17 247	17 402
Venezuela[3]	8 737	16 027	37 634	34 780	33 810	..	..	..	..	..

Note: The figures exclude local government revenues for Argentina (but include provincial revenues), the Bahamas, Barbados, Cuba (except for 2002-2012), the Dominican Republic, Saint Lucia, Trinidad and Tobago and Venezuela as the data are not available. Local government revenue data are available since 1991 for Nicaragua, since 1994 for Bolivia, since 1995 for Guatemala, since 1998 for Jamaica, since 1999 for Panama, since 2000 for Peru, since 2002 for El Salvador and Guyana, since 2006 for Paraguay and since 1990 for all other countries.

1. The data include the following estimations: Bahamas (social security contributions from 2017), Barbados (social security contributions are government projections for 2015-2018), Bolivia (local tax revenues and healthcare social security contributions for 2018), Ecuador (local tax revenues for 2018), Panama (Local tax revenues for 2018), Paraguay (Local tax revenues for 2018). See the corresponding country tables for more information.
2. Social security contributions are not available.
3. Some tax revenue data are not available between 2014 and 2017 and therefore total figures have not been included. Data for 2018 are not available.

Nota : Las cifras excluyen los ingresos subnacionales para Argentina (pero se incluyen los ingresos de las provincias), Las Bahamas, Barbados, Cuba (excepto 2002-2012), República Dominicana, Santa Lucía, Trinidad y Tobago y Venezuela, dado que los datos no están disponibles. Los datos de ingresos subnacionales están disponibles desde 1991 para Nicaragua, desde 1994 para Bolivia, desde 1995 para Guatemala, desde 1998 para Jamaica, desde 1999 para Panamá, desde 2000 para Perú, desde 2002 para El Salvador y Guyana, desde 2006 para Paraguay y desde 1990 para todos los demás países.

1. Los datos incluyen las siguientes estimaciones: Bahamas (contribuciones a la seguridad social de 2017), Barbados (las contribuciones a la seguridad social son proyecciones gubernamentales para 2015-2018), Bolivia (ingresos fiscales locales y contribuciones a la seguridad social en salud para 2018), Ecuador (ingresos fiscales locales para 2018), Panamá (ingresos fiscales locales para 2018), Paraguay (ingresos fiscales locales para 2018). Consulte las tablas de países correspondientes para obtener más información.
2. Las cotizaciones a la seguridad social no están disponibles.
3. Algunos datos de ingresos fiscales no están disponibles entre 2014 y 2017 y, por lo tanto, no se han incluido las cifras totales. Los datos para 2018 no están disponibles

StatLink https://doi.org/10.1787/888934114134

Table 4.3. **Tax revenue of main headings as % of GDP, 2018**
Cuadro 4.3. **Ingresos tributarios en las principales partidas en % del PIB, 2018**

	1000 Income & profits / Ingresos y utilidades	2000 Social security / Seguridad social	3000 Payroll / Nómina	4000 Property / Propiedad	5000 Goods and services / Bienes y servicios	6000 Others / Otros
Argentina	5.1	6.3	0.0	2.7	14.5	0.2
Bahamas[1]	0.0	2.6	0.0	1.9	13.0	0.0
Barbados[1]	9.0	5.6	0.0	1.7	16.8	0.0
Belize / Belice	7.5	2.3	0.0	1.2	18.7	0.0
Bolivia[1]	3.8	6.1	0.0	0.2	12.7	2.6
Brazil / Brasil	7.1	8.4	0.6	1.5	14.6	0.9
Chile	7.5	1.5	0.0	1.1	11.2	-0.2
Colombia	6.5	1.9	0.4	1.6	8.3	0.8
Costa Rica	4.9	8.2	1.4	0.4	8.4	0.6
Cuba	11.1	5.2	1.3	0.0	22.0	2.8
Dominican Republic / República Dominicana	4.0	0.1	0.0	0.6	8.5	0.0
Ecuador[1]	4.8	5.1	0.0	0.3	10.3	0.0
El Salvador	7.0	2.7	0.0	0.5	10.6	0.4
Guatemala	3.5	2.1	0.0	0.2	6.3	0.0
Guyana	9.8	2.7	0.0	0.5	14.0	0.3
Honduras	6.3	3.4	0.0	0.6	11.6	0.4
Jamaica	8.5	1.0	0.0	1.2	16.8	0.1
Mexico / México[2]	7.1	2.2	0.4	0.3	5.8	0.2
Nicaragua	7.1	5.9	0.0	0.2	9.5	0.2
Panama / Panamá[1]	4.1	5.6	0.2	0.4	4.2	0.1
Paraguay[1]	2.3	3.5	0.0	0.3	7.8	0.1
Peru / Perú	5.9	2.0	0.0	0.4	7.9	0.2
Saint Lucia / Santa Lucía	5.1	..	0.0	0.5	14.3	0.0
Trinidad and Tobago / Trinidad y Tobago	12.8	3.1	0.0	0.2	8.1	0.0
Uruguay	7.7	7.6	0.0	2.2	11.5	0.2
Venezuela[3]	..	..	0.0	1.2	7.4	0.1
Unweighted average / Promedio no ponderado						
LAC / ALC[4]	**6.3**	**4.0**	**0.2**	**0.8**	**11.5**	**0.4**
OECD / OCDE[5]	**11.6**	**9.1**	**0.4**	**1.9**	**10.9**	**0.1**

Note: The figures exclude local government revenues for Argentina (but include provincial revenues), the Bahamas, Barbados, Cuba (except for 2002-2012), the Dominican Republic, Saint Lucia, Trinidad and Tobago and Venezuela as the data are not available. Local government revenue data are available since 1991 for Nicaragua, since 1994 for Bolivia, since 1995 for Guatemala, since 1998 for Jamaica, since 1999 for Panama, since 2000 for Peru, since 2002 for El Salvador and Guyana, since 2006 for Paraguay and since 1990 for all other countries.

1. The data include the following estimations: Bahamas (social security contributions from 2017), Barbados (social security contributions are government projections for 2015-2018), Bolivia (local tax revenues and healthcare social security contributions for 2018), Ecuador (local tax revenues for 2018), Panama (Local tax revenues for 2018), Paraguay (Local tax revenues for 2018). See the corresponding country tables for more information.
2. Data for 2017 are used for 3000 and 4000 (local and state government data). Other data have been updated to 2018. Federal government data are used for 1000, 5000 and 6000.
3. Data for 2017 as the data for 2018 are not available. The data for headings 1000 taxes on income and profits and 2000 social security contributions are not available in 2017.
4. Represents the group of 25 Latin American and Caribbean countries included in this publication and excludes Venezuela due to data availability issues. Chile and Mexico are also part of the OECD (36) group. The figure for revenues from social security contributions needs to be considered with caution as these revenues are not available for Saint Lucia.
5. Represents the unweighted average for OECD member countries. Data for 2017 are used as data for 2018 was not available at the time of publication.

Nota : Las cifras excluyen los ingresos subnacionales para Argentina (pero se incluyen los ingresos de las provincias), Las Bahamas, Barbados, Cuba (excepto 2002-2012), República Dominicana, Santa Lucía, Trinidad y Tobago y Venezuela, dado que los datos no están disponibles. Los datos de ingresos subnacionales están disponibles desde 1991 para Nicaragua, desde 1994 para Bolivia, desde 1995 para Guatemala, desde 1998 para Jamaica, desde 1999 para Panamá, desde 2000 para Perú, desde 2002 para El Salvador y Guyana, desde 2006 para Paraguay y desde 1990 para todos los demás países.

1. Los datos incluyen las siguientes estimaciones: Bahamas (contribuciones a la seguridad social de 2017), Barbados (las contribuciones a la seguridad social son proyecciones gubernamentales para 2015-2018), Bolivia (ingresos fiscales locales y contribuciones a la seguridad social en salud para 2018), Ecuador (ingresos fiscales locales para 2018), Panamá (ingresos fiscales locales para 2018), Paraguay (ingresos fiscales locales para 2018). Consulte las tablas de países correspondientes para obtener más información.
2. Los datos de 2017 se utilizan para 3000 y 4000 (datos del gobierno local y estatal). Los otros datos se han actualizado para 2018. Los datos del gobierno federal se utilizan para 1000, 5000 y 6000
3. Los datos son para 2017 ya que los datos para 2018 no están disponibles. Los datos para las categorías de 1000 impuestos sobre la renta y las ganancias y 2000 contribuciones a la seguridad social no están disponibles en 2017.
4. Representa al grupo de 25 países de América Latina y el Caribe incluidos en esta publicación y excluye a Venezuela debido a problemas de disponibilidad de datos. Chile y México también forman parte del grupo OCDE (36). La cifra de los ingresos de las contribuciones a la seguridad social debe considerarse con cautela ya que estos ingresos no están disponibles para Santa Lucía.
5. Representa el promedio no ponderado de los países miembros de la OCDE. Los datos de 2017 se utilizan porque los datos de 2018 no estaban disponibles en el momento de la publicación.

StatLink https://doi.org/10.1787/888934114153

Table 4.4. **Tax revenue of main headings as % of total tax revenue, 2018**
Cuadro 4.4. **Ingresos tributarios en las principales partidas en % del total de ingresos tributarios, 2018**

	1000 Income & profits / Ingresos y utilidades	2000 Socialsecurity / Seguridad social	3000 Payroll / Nómina	4000 Property / Propiedad	5000 Goods and services / Bienes y servicios	6000 Others / Otros
Argentina	17.8	21.7	0.0	9.3	50.4	0.8
Bahamas[1]	0.0	14.9	0.0	11.0	74.1	0.0
Barbados[1]	27.2	16.9	0.0	5.1	50.8	0.0
Belize / Belice	25.2	7.6	0.0	4.1	63.1	0.0
Bolivia[1]	15.0	24.0	0.0	0.8	49.9	10.4
Brazil / Brasil	21.5	25.4	1.8	4.5	44.1	2.6
Chile	35.8	6.9	0.0	5.1	53.3	-1.1
Colombia	33.7	9.6	1.8	8.0	42.8	4.2
Costa Rica	20.4	34.3	6.0	1.8	35.0	2.6
Cuba	26.2	12.3	3.0	0.0	51.9	6.5
Dominican Republic / República Dominicana	30.6	0.5	0.0	4.6	64.4	0.0
Ecuador[1]	23.5	24.9	0.0	1.6	49.9	0.1
El Salvador	33.1	12.8	0.0	2.2	50.2	1.7
Guatemala	29.2	16.9	0.0	1.9	52.0	0.0
Guyana	35.7	9.9	0.0	2.0	51.2	1.2
Honduras	28.2	15.1	0.0	2.5	52.2	1.9
Jamaica	30.8	3.7	0.0	4.4	60.6	0.4
Mexico / México[2]	44.6	13.3	2.4	1.9	36.4	1.5
Nicaragua	30.7	25.9	0.0	1.0	41.5	0.8
Panama / Panamá[1]	28.2	38.5	1.4	2.6	29.0	0.4
Paraguay[1]	16.3	25.4	0.0	1.8	55.9	0.7
Peru / Perú	36.1	12.2	0.0	2.2	48.1	1.4
Saint Lucia / Santa Lucía[3]	25.8	..	0.0	2.5	71.8	0.0
Trinidad and Tobago / Trinidad y Tobago	52.7	12.7	0.0	1.0	33.6	0.0
Uruguay	26.3	26.1	0.0	7.6	39.4	0.6
Venezuela[4]	..	..	..	..	..	..
Unweighted average / Promedio no ponderado						
LAC / ALC[5]	**27.8**	**17.1**	**0.7**	**3.6**	**50.1**	**1.5**
OECD / OCDE[6]	**34.0**	**26.0**	**1.1**	**5.8**	**32.4**	**0.4**

Note: The figures exclude local government revenues for Argentina (but include provincial revenues), the Bahamas, Barbados, Cuba (except for 2002-2012), the Dominican Republic, Saint Lucia, Trinidad and Tobago and Venezuela as the data are not available. Local government revenue data are available since 1991 for Nicaragua, since 1994 for Bolivia, since 1995 for Guatemala, since 1998 for Jamaica, since 1999 for Panama, since 2000 for Peru, since 2002 for El Salvador and Guyana, since 2006 for Paraguay and since 1990 for all other countries.

1. The data include the following estimations: Bahamas (social security contributions from 2017), Barbados (social security contributions are government projections for 2015-2018), Bolivia (local tax revenues and healthcare social security contributions for 2018), Ecuador (local tax revenues for 2018), Panama (Local tax revenues for 2018), Paraguay (Local tax revenues for 2018). See the corresponding country tables for more information.
2. Data for 2017 are used as the state and local government revenue data (3000 and 4000) for 2018 are not available.
3. The figures need to be considered with caution as revenues from social security contributions are not available
4. The tax structure is not available for 2014-2018 due to lack of data in some main revenues categories in those years.
5. Represents the group of 25 Latin American and Caribbean countries included in this publication and excludes Venezuela due to data availability issues. Chile and Mexico are also part of the OECD (36) group.
6. Represents the unweighted average for OECD member countries. Data for 2017 are used as data for 2018 was not available at the time of publication.

Nota : Las cifras excluyen los ingresos subnacionales para Argentina (pero se incluyen los ingresos de las provincias), Las Bahamas, Barbados, Cuba (excepto 2002-2012), República Dominicana, Santa Lucía, Trinidad y Tobago y Venezuela, dado que los datos no están disponibles. Los datos de ingresos subnacionales están disponibles desde 1991 para Nicaragua, desde 1994 para Bolivia, desde 1995 para Guatemala, desde 1998 para Jamaica, desde 1999 para Panamá, desde 2000 para Perú, desde 2002 para El Salvador y Guyana, desde 2006 para Paraguay y desde 1990 para todos los demás países.

1. Los datos incluyen las siguientes estimaciones: Bahamas (contribuciones a la seguridad social de 2017), Barbados (las contribuciones a la seguridad social son proyecciones gubernamentales para 2015-2018), Bolivia (ingresos fiscales locales y contribuciones a la seguridad social en salud para 2018), Ecuador (ingresos fiscales locales para 2018), Panamá (ingresos fiscales locales para 2018), Paraguay (ingresos fiscales locales para 2018). Consulte las tablas de países correspondientes para obtener más información.
2. Los datos de 2017 se utilizan ya que los datos de ingresos del gobierno estatal y local (3000 y 4000) para 2018 no están disponibles.
3. Las cifras deben considerarse con cautela (precaucion) ya que los ingresos de las contribuciones a la seguridad social no están disponibles.
4. La estructura fiscal no está disponible para 2014-2018 debido a la falta de datos en algunas categorías principales de ingresos en esos años.
5. Representa al grupo de 25 países de América Latina y el Caribe incluidos en esta publicación y excluye a Venezuela debido a problemas de disponibilidad de datos. Chile y México también forman parte del grupo OCDE (36).
6. Representa el promedio no ponderado de los países miembros de la OCDE. Los datos de 2017 se utilizan porque los datos de 2018 no estaban disponibles en el momento de la publicación.

StatLink https://doi.org/10.1787/888934114172

Table 4.5. **Taxes on income and profits (1000) as % of GDP and as % of total tax revenue**
Cuadro 4.5. **Impuestos sobre la renta y las utilidades (1000) en % del PIB y del total de ingresos tributarios**

	% of GDP / % del PIB					% of total tax revenue / % del total de ingresos tributarios				
	1990	2000	2010	2017	2018	1990	2000	2010	2017	2018
Argentina	0.7	3.7	4.7	5.3	5.1	5.3	18.5	16.2	17.5	17.8
Bahamas	0.0	0.0	0.0	0.0	0.0	0.0	0.0	0.0	0.0	0.0
Barbados	6.1	9.8	8.4	7.8	9.0	24.3	31.7	28.0	24.3	27.2
Belize / Belice	4.5	4.6	8.9	7.2	7.5	20.9	23.9	33.6	25.5	25.2
Bolivia	0.4	2.3	4.6	3.9	3.8	6.7	11.5	20.0	15.1	15.0
Brazil / Brasil	5.1	5.7	6.7	7.0	7.1	18.3	19.5	20.6	21.7	21.5
Chile	3.9	4.4	7.5	6.9	7.5	23.2	23.3	38.1	34.5	35.8
Colombia	2.8	3.4	4.8	6.3	6.5	29.9	23.2	26.6	33.0	33.7
Costa Rica	2.3	2.8	3.8	4.7	4.9	10.0	13.2	17.1	19.8	20.4
Cuba	0.1	6.0	5.6	10.3	11.1	0.2	16.1	15.0	24.2	26.2
Dominican Republic / República Dominicana	2.2	2.7	2.7	4.1	4.0	26.0	22.3	22.0	31.0	30.6
Ecuador	0.9	1.5	3.4	4.0	4.8	12.9	12.6	21.2	19.9	23.5
El Salvador	2.0	3.6	5.4	7.0	7.0	17.6	25.7	29.1	33.4	33.1
Guatemala	1.6	2.3	3.0	3.7	3.5	19.7	18.7	24.4	30.1	29.2
Guyana	6.9	7.9	8.5	9.3	9.8	33.5	37.8	35.4	35.6	35.7
Honduras	2.5	2.7	4.4	6.1	6.3	20.3	15.9	24.5	27.7	28.2
Jamaica	10.3	9.9	10.3	8.2	8.5	50.9	44.8	41.3	30.1	30.8
Mexico / México[1]	4.1	4.1	5.1	7.2	7.1	34.0	36.0	39.8	44.6	44.6
Nicaragua	..	1.8	4.5	6.9	7.1	..	12.3	23.1	28.9	30.7
Panama / Panamá	3.8	3.9	4.5	3.9	4.1	24.2	25.0	27.4	26.4	28.2
Paraguay	1.2	1.5	1.6	2.3	2.3	12.7	13.1	13.4	16.6	16.3
Peru / Perú	0.7	2.9	6.5	5.7	5.9	5.8	19.0	36.5	37.5	36.1
Saint Lucia / Santa Lucía[2]	..	6.2	5.9	5.1	5.1	..	31.8	30.5	25.7	25.8
Trinidad and Tobago / Trinidad y Tobago	12.3	12.4	19.6	10.8	12.8	52.7	56.8	68.5	51.8	52.7
Uruguay	0.9	3.2	5.3	7.3	7.7	4.7	13.6	20.0	25.3	26.3
Venezuela[3]	15.1	5.9	3.6	..	..	83.7	43.2	30.7	..	..
Unweighted average / Promedio no ponderado										
LAC / ALC[4]	**3.3**	**4.4**	**5.8**	**6.0**	**6.3**	**19.7**	**22.7**	**26.9**	**27.2**	**27.8**
OECD / OCDE[5]	**12.1**	**11.9**	**10.6**	**11.6**	..	**37.5**	**34.8**	**32.8**	**34.0**	..

Note: The figures exclude local government revenues for Argentina (but include provincial revenues), the Bahamas, Barbados, Cuba (except for 2002-2012), the Dominican Republic, Saint Lucia, Trinidad and Tobago and Venezuela as the data are not available. Local government revenue data are available since 1991 for Nicaragua, since 1994 for Bolivia, since 1995 for Guatemala, since 1998 for Jamaica, since 1999 for Panama, since 2000 for Peru, since 2002 for El Salvador and Guyana, since 2006 for Paraguay and since 1990 for all other countries.

1. For the figures as % of total tax revenue data for 2017 are used as the state and local government revenue data for 2018 are not available.
2. The figures as a percentage of total tax revenue need to be considered with caution as revenues from social security contributions are not available
3. Some tax revenue data between 2014 and 2017 and all data for 2018 are not available. In those years data as % of total tax revenue cannot be calculated.
4. Represents the group of 25 Latin American and Caribbean countries included in this publication and excludes Venezuela due to data availability issues. Chile and Mexico are also part of the OECD (36) group.
5. Represents the unweighted average for OECD member countries.

Nota : Las cifras excluyen los ingresos subnacionales para Argentina (pero se incluyen los ingresos de las provincias), Las Bahamas, Barbados, Cuba (excepto 2002-2012), República Dominicana, Santa Lucía, Trinidad y Tobago y Venezuela, dado que los datos no están disponibles. Los datos de ingresos subnacionales están disponibles desde 1991 para Nicaragua, desde 1994 para Bolivia, desde 1995 para Guatemala, desde 1998 para Jamaica, desde 1999 para Panamá, desde 2000 para Perú, desde 2002 para El Salvador y Guyana, desde 2006 para Paraguay y desde 1990 para todos los demás países.

1. Para los ingresos como un porcentaje de los ingresos fiscales totales, se utilizan los datos de 2017 porque los datos de ingresos de los gobiernos estatales y locales no están disponibles para 2018.
2. Las cifras de ingresos como un porcentaje de los ingresos fiscales totales deben considerarse con cautela ya que los ingresos de las contribuciones a la seguridad social no están disponibles.
3. Algunos datos de ingresos fiscales entre 2014 y 2017 y todos los datos de 2018 no están disponibles. Para esos años, no se pueden calcular los ingresos como un porcentaje de los ingresos fiscales totales.
4. Representa al grupo de 25 países de América Latina y el Caribe incluidos en esta publicación y excluye a Venezuela debido a problemas de disponibilidad de datos. Chile y México también forman parte del grupo OCDE (36).
5. Representa el promedio no ponderado para los países miembros de la OCDE.

StatLink https://doi.org/10.1787/888934114191

Table 4.6. **Social security contributions (2000) as % of GDP and as % of total tax revenue**
Cuadro 4.6. **Contribuciones a la seguridad social (2000) en % del PIB y del total de ingresos tributarios**

	% of GDP / % del PIB					% of total tax revenue / % del total de ingresos tributarios				
	1990	2000	2010	2017	2018	1990	2000	2010	2017	2018
Argentina	3.5	3.1	6.2	6.9	6.3	25.3	15.8	21.2	22.9	21.7
Bahamas[1]	1.3	1.5	1.7	2.6	2.6	13.2	11.9	13.1	14.8	14.9
Barbados[1]	3.3	4.8	6.2	5.6	5.6	13.1	15.6	20.6	17.5	16.9
Belize / Belice	1.2	1.1	2.2	2.2	2.3	5.7	5.8	8.2	7.8	7.6
Bolivia[1]	0.0	3.8	3.8	6.1	6.1	0.0	18.8	16.7	23.7	24.0
Brazil / Brasil	6.8	7.0	8.1	8.4	8.4	24.3	23.7	25.2	26.3	25.4
Chile	1.5	1.4	1.3	1.5	1.5	9.0	7.3	6.8	7.3	6.9
Colombia	0.7	2.4	2.1	1.5	1.9	7.9	16.3	11.7	7.6	9.6
Costa Rica	6.5	6.4	7.4	8.0	8.2	28.9	30.4	33.1	33.5	34.3
Cuba	3.5	3.9	4.6	5.3	5.2	11.0	10.4	12.4	12.5	12.3
Dominican Republic / República Dominicana	0.1	0.1	0.1	0.1	0.1	0.8	1.0	0.8	0.5	0.5
Ecuador	1.6	1.2	3.7	5.2	5.1	22.5	10.7	22.8	26.1	24.9
El Salvador	2.2	2.8	2.5	2.7	2.7	19.2	19.5	13.7	13.2	12.8
Guatemala	1.4	1.9	1.9	2.1	2.1	17.0	15.8	15.5	16.7	16.9
Guyana	0.8	2.4	2.2	2.7	2.7	3.7	11.4	9.0	10.4	9.9
Honduras	1.0	1.6	2.9	3.3	3.4	8.5	9.4	16.0	15.0	15.1
Jamaica	0.0	0.0	0.7	1.0	1.0	0.0	0.0	2.9	3.7	3.7
Mexico / México[2]	2.0	2.1	2.1	2.1	2.2	16.8	18.0	16.2	13.3	13.3
Nicaragua	..	2.6	4.3	5.7	5.9	..	18.0	22.4	24.2	25.9
Panama / Panamá	4.7	5.9	5.6	5.7	5.6	30.3	38.2	34.0	38.4	38.5
Paraguay	0.0	3.0	2.8	3.7	3.5	0.0	25.6	22.7	26.2	25.4
Peru / Perú	0.9	1.8	1.9	2.0	2.0	7.8	11.9	10.6	12.9	12.2
Saint Lucia / Santa Lucía[3]	..	..	..	..	..	..	..	..	..	..
Trinidad and Tobago / Trinidad y Tobago	0.9	1.4	1.9	3.1	3.1	3.7	6.4	6.7	14.8	12.7
Uruguay[4]	6.0	6.4	6.2	7.7	7.6	29.9	27.5	23.4	26.5	26.1
Venezuela[5]	0.9	0.7	1.0	..	..	4.9	5.4	8.1	..	..
Unweighted average / Promedio no ponderado										
LAC / ALC[6]	**2.2**	**2.9**	**3.4**	**4.0**	**4.0**	**13.0**	**15.4**	**16.1**	**17.3**	**17.1**
OECD / OCDE[7]	**7.3**	**8.6**	**8.8**	**9.1**	..	**22.0**	**25.0**	**26.8**	**26.0**	..

Note: The figures exclude local government revenues for Argentina (but include provincial revenues), the Bahamas, Barbados, Cuba (except for 2002-2012), the Dominican Republic, Saint Lucia, Trinidad and Tobago and Venezuela as the data are not available. Local government revenue data are available since 1991 for Nicaragua, since 1994 for Bolivia, since 1995 for Guatemala, since 1998 for Jamaica, since 1999 for Panama, since 2000 for Peru, since 2002 for El Salvador and Guyana, since 2006 for Paraguay and since 1990 for all other countries.

1. The social security contributions data are estimated in the following countries: Bahamas (from 2017 onward), Barbados (from 2015 onward), and Bolivia (heathcare contributions only, for 2018).
2. For the figures as % of total tax revenue data for 2017 are used as the state and local government revenue data for 2018 are not available.
3. Social security contributions are not available.
4. Figures for 1990-98 are estimated by the Direction General of Taxes as the methodology they use to calculate social security contributions was not employed until 1999.
5. Some tax revenue data between 2014 and 2017 and all data for 2018 are not available. In those years data as % of total tax revenue cannot be calculated.
6. Represents the group of 25 Latin American and Caribbean countries included in this publication and excludes Venezuela due to data availability issues. Chile and Mexico are also part of the OECD (36) group.
7. Represents the unweighted average for OECD member countries.

Nota : Las cifras excluyen los ingresos subnacionales para Argentina (pero se incluyen los ingresos de las provincias), Las Bahamas, Barbados, Cuba (excepto 2002-2012), República Dominicana, Santa Lucía, Trinidad y Tobago y Venezuela, dado que los datos no están disponibles. Los datos de ingresos subnacionales están disponibles desde 1991 para Nicaragua, desde 1994 para Bolivia, desde 1995 para Guatemala, desde 1998 para Jamaica, desde 1999 para Panamá, desde 2000 para Perú, desde 2002 para El Salvador y Guyana, desde 2006 para Paraguay y desde 1990 para todos los demás países.

1. Las contribuciones a la seguridad social se estiman en los siguientes países: Bahamas (desde 2017), Barbados (desde 2015) y Bolivia (contribuciones al seguro médico para 2018).
2. Para los ingresos como un porcentaje de los ingresos fiscales totales, se utilizan los datos de 2017 porque los datos de ingresos de los gobiernos estatales y locales no están disponibles para 2018.
3. Las cotizaciones a la seguridad social no están disponibles.
4. Las cifras de 1990-98 son estimaciones por la Dirección General de Impuestos dado que el empleo de la metodología actual utilizada para calcular las contribuciones a la seguridad social tuvo lugar en 1999.
5. Algunos datos de ingresos fiscales entre 2014 y 2017 y todos los datos de 2018 no están disponibles. Para esos años, no se pueden calcular los ingresos como un porcentaje de los ingresos fiscales totales.
6. Representa al grupo de 25 países de América Latina y el Caribe incluidos en esta publicación y excluye a Venezuela debido a problemas de disponibilidad de datos. Chile y México también forman parte del grupo OCDE (36).
7. Representa el promedio no ponderado para los países miembros de la OCDE.

StatLink https://doi.org/10.1787/888934114210

Table 4.7. **Taxes on payroll (3000) as % of GDP and as % of total tax revenue**
Cuadro 4.7. **Impuestos sobre la nómina (3000) en % del PIB y del total ingresos tributarios**

	% of GDP / % del PIB					% of total tax revenue / % del total de ingresos tributarios				
	1990	2000	2010	2017	2018	1990	2000	2010	2017	2018
Argentina	0.0	0.0	0.0	0.0	0.0	0.0	0.0	0.0	0.0	0.0
Bahamas	0.0	0.0	0.0	0.0	0.0	0.0	0.0	0.0	0.0	0.0
Barbados	0.0	0.0	0.0	0.0	0.0	0.0	0.0	0.0	0.0	0.0
Belize / Belice	0.0	0.0	0.0	0.0	0.0	0.0	0.0	0.0	0.0	0.0
Bolivia	0.0	0.0	0.0	0.0	0.0	0.0	0.0	0.0	0.0	0.0
Brazil / Brasil	0.4	0.5	0.5	0.6	0.6	1.6	1.5	1.7	1.9	1.8
Chile	0.0	0.0	0.0	0.0	0.0	0.0	0.0	0.0	0.0	0.0
Colombia	0.0	0.6	0.7	0.3	0.4	0.0	4.2	4.1	1.8	1.8
Costa Rica	1.4	1.3	1.3	1.4	1.4	6.4	6.3	5.9	6.0	6.0
Cuba	0.0	3.2	6.9	1.4	1.3	0.0	8.5	18.4	3.4	3.0
Dominican Republic / República Dominicana	0.0	0.0	0.0	0.0	0.0	0.0	0.0	0.0	0.0	0.0
Ecuador	0.0	0.0	0.0	0.0	0.0	0.0	0.0	0.0	0.0	0.0
El Salvador	0.0	0.0	0.0	0.0	0.0	0.0	0.0	0.0	0.0	0.0
Guatemala	0.0	0.0	0.0	0.0	0.0	0.0	0.0	0.0	0.0	0.0
Guyana	0.0	0.0	0.0	0.0	0.0	0.0	0.0	0.0	0.0	0.0
Honduras	0.0	0.0	0.0	0.0	0.0	0.0	0.0	0.0	0.0	0.0
Jamaica	0.0	0.0	0.0	0.0	0.0	0.0	0.0	0.0	0.0	0.0
Mexico / México[1]	0.2	0.2	0.3	0.4	0.4	1.8	1.5	2.2	2.4	2.4
Nicaragua	..	0.0	0.0	0.0	0.0	..	0.0	0.0	0.0	0.0
Panama / Panamá	0.0	0.3	0.2	0.2	0.2	0.0	1.9	1.2	1.4	1.4
Paraguay	0.0	0.0	0.0	0.0	0.0	0.0	0.0	0.0	0.0	0.0
Peru / Perú	0.0	0.7	0.0	0.0	0.0	0.0	4.4	0.0	0.0	0.0
Saint Lucia / Santa Lucía	..	0.0	0.0	0.0	0.0	..	0.0	0.0	0.0	0.0
Trinidad and Tobago / Trinidad y Tobago	0.0	0.0	0.0	0.0	0.0	0.0	0.0	0.0	0.0	0.0
Uruguay	0.0	0.0	0.0	0.0	0.0	0.0	0.0	0.0	0.0	0.0
Venezuela[2]	0.0	0.0	0.0	0.0	..	0.0	0.0	0.0	..	..
Unweighted average / Promedio no ponderado										
LAC / ALC[3]	**0.1**	**0.3**	**0.4**	**0.2**	**0.2**	**0.4**	**1.1**	**1.3**	**0.7**	**0.7**
OECD / OCDE[4]	**0.3**	**0.4**	**0.3**	**0.4**	..	**1.0**	**0.9**	**1.0**	**1.1**	..

Note: The figures exclude local government revenues for Argentina (but include provincial revenues), the Bahamas, Barbados, Cuba (except for 2002-2012), the Dominican Republic, Saint Lucia, Trinidad and Tobago and Venezuela as the data are not available. Local government revenue data are available since 1991 for Nicaragua, since 1994 for Bolivia, since 1995 for Guatemala, since 1998 for Jamaica, since 1999 for Panama, since 2000 for Peru, since 2002 for El Salvador and Guyana, since 2006 for Paraguay and since 1990 for all other countries.

1. Data for 2017 are used as the state and local government revenue data (3000 and 4000) for 2018 are not available.
2. Some tax revenue data between 2014 and 2017 and all data for 2018 are not available. In those years data as % of total tax revenue cannot be calculated.
3. Represents the group of 25 Latin American and Caribbean countries included in this publication and excludes Venezuela due to data availability issues. Chile and Mexico are also part of the OECD (36) group.
4. Represents the unweighted average for OECD member countries.

Nota : Las cifras excluyen los ingresos subnacionales para Argentina (pero se incluyen los ingresos de las provincias), Las Bahamas, Barbados, Cuba (excepto 2002-2012), República Dominicana, Santa Lucía, Trinidad y Tobago y Venezuela, dado que los datos no están disponibles. Los datos de ingresos subnacionales están disponibles desde 1991 para Nicaragua, desde 1994 para Bolivia, desde 1995 para Guatemala, desde 1998 para Jamaica, desde 1999 para Panamá, desde 2000 para Perú, desde 2002 para El Salvador y Guyana, desde 2006 para Paraguay y desde 1990 para todos los demás países.

1. Los datos de 2017 se utilizan ya que los datos de ingresos del gobierno estatal y local (3000 y 4000) para 2018 no están disponibles.
2. Algunos datos de ingresos fiscales entre 2014 y 2017 y todos los datos de 2018 no están disponibles. Para esos años, no se pueden calcular los ingresos como un porcentaje de los ingresos fiscales totales.
3. Representa al grupo de 25 países de América Latina y el Caribe incluidos en esta publicación y excluye a Venezuela debido a problemas de disponibilidad de datos. Chile y México también forman parte del grupo OCDE (36).
4. Representa el promedio no ponderado para los países miembros de la OCDE.

StatLink https://doi.org/10.1787/888934114229

Table 4.8. **Taxes on property (4000) as % of GDP and as % of total tax revenue**
Cuadro 4.8. **Impuestos sobre la propiedad (4000) en % del PIB y del total de ingresos tributarios**

	% of GDP / % del PIB					% of total tax revenue / % del total de ingresos tributarios				
	1990	2000	2010	2017	2018	1990	2000	2010	2017	2018
Argentina	1.6	1.3	2.6	2.9	2.7	11.4	6.3	9.0	9.5	9.3
Bahamas	1.1	2.6	2.7	1.9	1.9	11.2	21.6	21.1	10.8	11.0
Barbados	3.6	1.8	1.4	1.5	1.7	14.4	5.7	4.8	4.6	5.1
Belize / Belice	4.2	0.8	0.8	0.9	1.2	19.2	4.2	3.1	3.1	4.1
Bolivia	0.0	0.0	0.3	0.2	0.2	0.1	0.0	1.2	0.7	0.8
Brazil / Brasil	1.6	2.0	1.4	1.4	1.5	5.9	6.7	4.2	4.3	4.5
Chile	1.0	1.3	0.8	1.1	1.1	6.2	7.0	4.1	5.4	5.1
Colombia	0.2	1.0	1.6	2.0	1.6	2.2	6.6	8.7	10.3	8.0
Costa Rica	0.3	0.2	0.3	0.4	0.4	1.3	0.9	1.5	1.8	1.8
Cuba	0.0	0.0	0.0	0.0	0.0	0.0	0.0	0.0	0.0	0.0
Dominican Republic / República Dominicana	0.1	0.2	0.7	0.6	0.6	1.2	1.4	5.5	4.6	4.6
Ecuador	0.1	0.1	0.2	0.3	0.3	1.5	0.8	1.4	1.7	1.6
El Salvador	0.5	0.1	0.1	0.5	0.5	4.8	0.7	0.6	2.2	2.2
Guatemala	0.5	0.3	0.4	0.2	0.2	5.8	2.1	3.0	1.8	1.9
Guyana	0.2	0.3	0.3	0.5	0.5	1.0	1.6	1.4	1.9	2.0
Honduras	0.1	0.3	0.3	0.6	0.6	0.7	1.5	1.8	2.6	2.5
Jamaica	2.5	1.1	0.9	1.2	1.2	12.5	4.9	3.5	4.6	4.4
Mexico / México[1]	0.2	0.2	0.3	0.3	0.3	1.9	1.8	2.3	1.9	1.9
Nicaragua	..	0.0	0.2	0.2	0.2	..	0.1	1.2	0.9	1.0
Panama / Panamá	0.6	0.3	0.5	0.4	0.4	3.6	2.2	2.9	2.7	2.6
Paraguay	0.3	0.2	0.2	0.2	0.3	3.0	2.0	1.7	1.8	1.8
Peru / Perú	1.6	0.2	0.5	0.4	0.4	13.6	1.2	3.0	2.4	2.2
Saint Lucia / Santa Lucía[2]	..	0.5	0.5	0.5	0.5	..	2.5	2.6	2.6	2.5
Trinidad and Tobago / Trinidad y Tobago	0.4	0.3	0.1	0.2	0.2	1.8	1.6	0.5	1.0	1.0
Uruguay	1.8	2.0	2.3	2.3	2.2	8.9	8.6	8.9	7.8	7.6
Venezuela[3]	0.1	0.5	0.0	1.2	..	0.3	3.7	0.2	..	..
Unweighted average / Promedio no ponderado										
LAC / ALC[4]	**1.0**	**0.7**	**0.8**	**0.8**	**0.8**	**5.7**	**3.7**	**3.9**	**3.6**	**3.6**
OECD / OCDE[5]	**1.8**	**1.8**	**1.7**	**1.9**	..	**5.8**	**5.4**	**5.4**	**5.8**	..

Note: The figures exclude local government revenues for Argentina (but include provincial revenues), the Bahamas, Barbados, Cuba (except for 2002-2012), the Dominican Republic, Saint Lucia, Trinidad and Tobago and Venezuela as the data are not available. Local government revenue data are available since 1991 for Nicaragua, since 1994 for Bolivia, since 1995 for Guatemala, since 1998 for Jamaica, since 1999 for Panama, since 2000 for Peru, since 2002 for El Salvador and Guyana, since 2006 for Paraguay and since 1990 for all other countries.

1. Data for 2017 are used as the state and local government revenue data (3000 and 4000) for 2018 are not available.
2. The figures as a percentage of total tax revenue need to be considered with caution as revenues from social security contributions are not available
3. Some tax revenue data between 2014 and 2017 and all data for 2018 are not available. In those years data as % of total tax revenue cannot be calculated.
4. Represents the group of 25 Latin American and Caribbean countries included in this publication and excludes Venezuela due to data availability issues. Chile and Mexico are also part of the OECD (36) group.
5. Represents the unweighted average for OECD member countries.

Nota : Las cifras excluyen los ingresos subnacionales para Argentina (pero se incluyen los ingresos de las provincias), Las Bahamas, Barbados, Cuba (excepto 2002-2012), República Dominicana, Santa Lucía, Trinidad y Tobago y Venezuela, dado que los datos no están disponibles. Los datos de ingresos subnacionales están disponibles desde 1991 para Nicaragua, desde 1994 para Bolivia, desde 1995 para Guatemala, desde 1998 para Jamaica, desde 1999 para Panamá, desde 2000 para Perú, desde 2002 para El Salvador y Guyana, desde 2006 para Paraguay y desde 1990 para todos los demás países.

1. Los datos de 2017 se utilizan ya que los datos de ingresos del gobierno estatal y local (3000 y 4000) para 2018 no están disponibles.
2. Las cifras deben considerarse con cautela (precaucion) ya que los ingresos de las contribuciones a la seguridad social no están disponibles.
3. Algunos datos de ingresos fiscales entre 2014 y 2017 y todos los datos de 2018 no están disponibles. Para esos años, no se pueden calcular los ingresos como un porcentaje de los ingresos fiscales totales.
4. Representa al grupo de 25 países de América Latina y el Caribe incluidos en esta publicación y excluye a Venezuela debido a problemas de disponibilidad de datos. Chile y México también forman parte del grupo OCDE (36).
5. Representa el promedio no ponderado para los países miembros de la OCDE.

StatLink https://doi.org/10.1787/888934114248

Table 4.9. **Taxes on goods and services (5000) as % of GDP and as % of total tax revenue**
Cuadro 4.9. **Impuestos sobre bienes y servicios (5000) en % del PIB y del total de ingresos tributarios**

	% of GDP / % del PIB					% of total tax revenue / % del total de ingresos tributarios				
	1990	2000	2010	2017	2018	1990	2000	2010	2017	2018
Argentina	7.5	11.2	15.2	14.4	14.5	55.2	56.5	52.4	47.8	50.4
Bahamas	7.4	7.9	7.8	13.1	13.0	76.4	64.3	61.1	74.4	74.1
Barbados	12.2	14.5	14.0	17.2	16.8	48.2	47.0	46.6	53.6	50.8
Belize / Belice	11.7	12.7	14.6	18.0	18.7	54.1	66.1	55.2	63.6	63.1
Bolivia	5.9	12.9	12.9	13.1	12.7	90.3	63.8	56.4	50.7	49.9
Brazil / Brasil	13.5	14.1	14.8	13.9	14.6	48.7	48.1	46.0	43.2	44.1
Chile	10.6	12.0	10.0	11.0	11.2	62.9	63.8	51.2	54.8	53.3
Colombia	4.9	6.9	8.2	8.2	8.3	53.8	46.3	45.1	43.1	42.8
Costa Rica	10.2	9.9	9.0	8.7	8.4	45.5	46.7	40.3	36.4	35.0
Cuba	27.7	22.0	19.1	22.8	22.0	86.9	59.2	51.3	53.8	51.9
Dominican Republic / República Dominicana	5.8	9.1	8.8	8.4	8.5	69.5	74.2	71.8	63.9	64.4
Ecuador	4.5	8.8	8.7	10.4	10.3	63.0	75.7	54.5	52.2	49.9
El Salvador	5.4	7.7	10.2	10.3	10.6	47.7	54.1	54.8	49.6	50.2
Guatemala	4.7	7.7	7.0	6.4	6.3	57.5	63.4	57.1	51.4	52.0
Guyana	8.7	10.1	12.8	13.3	14.0	42.0	48.6	53.0	50.9	51.2
Honduras	8.2	11.7	9.7	11.6	11.6	66.2	68.0	53.5	52.9	52.2
Jamaica	7.4	11.1	13.0	16.7	16.8	36.4	50.1	52.1	61.2	60.6
Mexico / México[1]	5.3	4.8	4.9	5.9	5.8	44.0	41.7	38.0	36.4	36.4
Nicaragua	..	8.6	10.1	10.7	9.5	..	60.0	52.4	45.1	41.5
Panama / Panamá	6.1	4.9	5.5	4.6	4.2	39.0	31.3	33.7	30.7	29.0
Paraguay	7.3	6.7	7.3	7.7	7.8	75.7	58.0	60.6	54.8	55.9
Peru / Perú	8.5	9.2	8.6	7.2	7.9	71.4	60.8	48.6	47.1	48.1
Saint Lucia / Santa Lucía[2]	..	12.7	12.9	14.1	14.3	..	65.7	66.9	71.8	71.8
Trinidad and Tobago / Trinidad y Tobago	9.7	7.7	7.0	6.8	8.1	41.7	35.2	24.3	32.4	33.6
Uruguay	11.3	11.6	12.4	11.5	11.5	56.6	50.1	47.1	39.8	39.4
Venezuela[3]	2.0	6.5	7.2	7.4	..	11.1	47.7	61.1	..	..
Unweighted average / Promedio no ponderado										
LAC / ALC[4]	**8.9**	**10.3**	**10.6**	**11.4**	**11.5**	**58.0**	**56.0**	**51.0**	**50.5**	**50.1**
OECD / OCDE[5]	**10.0**	**10.9**	**10.6**	**10.9**	..	**32.5**	**33.0**	**33.2**	**32.4**	..

Note: The figures exclude local government revenues for Argentina (but include provincial revenues), the Bahamas, Barbados, Cuba (except for 2002-2012), the Dominican Republic, Saint Lucia, Trinidad and Tobago and Venezuela as the data are not available. Local government revenue data are available since 1991 for Nicaragua, since 1994 for Bolivia, since 1995 for Guatemala, since 1998 for Jamaica, since 1999 for Panama, since 2000 for Peru, since 2002 for El Salvador and Guyana, since 2006 for Paraguay and since 1990 for all other countries.

1. In 2018, federal government data are used for the figure as % of GDP. For the figure as % of total tax revenue, data for 2017 are used as the state and local government revenue data for 2018 are not available.
2. The figures as a percentage of total tax revenue need to be considered with caution as revenues from social security contributions are not available
3. Some tax revenue data between 2014 and 2017 and all data for 2018 are not available. In those years data as % of total tax revenue cannot be calculated.
4. Represents the group of 25 Latin American and Caribbean countries included in this publication and excludes Venezuela due to data availability issues. Chile and Mexico are also part of the OECD (36) group.
5. Represents the unweighted average for OECD member countries.

Nota : Las cifras excluyen los ingresos subnacionales para Argentina (pero se incluyen los ingresos de las provincias), Las Bahamas, Barbados, Cuba (excepto 2002-2012), República Dominicana, Santa Lucía, Trinidad y Tobago y Venezuela, dado que los datos no están disponibles. Los datos de ingresos subnacionales están disponibles desde 1991 para Nicaragua, desde 1994 para Bolivia, desde 1995 para Guatemala, desde 1998 para Jamaica, desde 1999 para Panamá, desde 2000 para Perú, desde 2002 para El Salvador y Guyana, desde 2006 para Paraguay y desde 1990 para todos los demás países.

1. Para 2018, los datos del gobierno federal se utilizan para la cifra como porcentaje del PIB. Para la cifra como porcentaje de los ingresos fiscales totales, los datos de 2017 se utilizan ya que los datos de ingresos del gobierno estatal y local para 2018 no están disponibles.
2. Las cifras deben considerarse con cautela (precaucion) ya que los ingresos de las contribuciones a la seguridad social no están disponibles.
3. Algunos datos de ingresos fiscales entre 2014 y 2017 y todos los datos de 2018 no están disponibles. Para esos años, no se pueden calcular los ingresos como un porcentaje de los ingresos fiscales totales.
4. Representa al grupo de 25 países de América Latina y el Caribe incluidos en esta publicación y excluye a Venezuela debido a problemas de disponibilidad de datos. Chile y México también forman parte del grupo OCDE (36).
5. Representa el promedio no ponderado para los países miembros de la OCDE.

StatLink https://doi.org/10.1787/888934114267

Table 4.10. **Value added taxes (5111) as % of GDP and as % of total tax revenue**
Cuadro 4.10. **Impuesto al valor agregado (5111) en % del PIB y del total de ingresos tributarios**

	% of GDP / % del PIB					% of total tax revenue / % del total de ingresos tributarios				
	1990	2000	2010	2017	2018	1990	2000	2010	2017	2018
Argentina	2.1	6.2	7.0	7.2	7.6	15.6	31.1	24.1	23.9	26.3
Bahamas	0.0	0.0	0.0	5.2	5.6	0.0	0.0	0.0	29.6	31.6
Barbados	0.0	8.0	8.4	8.9	9.2	0.0	26.0	28.1	27.6	27.8
Belize / Belice	..	0.0	7.1	7.9	8.3	..	0.0	26.9	27.7	28.0
Bolivia	2.8	5.7	7.4	7.8	7.5	43.0	28.1	32.5	30.1	29.7
Brazil / Brasil	8.0	6.9	6.9	6.7	7.0	28.7	23.4	21.4	20.9	21.1
Chile	6.3	7.9	7.5	8.4	8.5	37.4	41.8	38.5	41.6	40.2
Colombia	2.1	4.1	5.3	5.5	5.7	22.6	27.6	29.3	29.0	29.4
Costa Rica	4.1	4.8	4.7	4.4	4.3	18.1	22.8	21.0	18.4	17.8
Cuba	0.0	0.0	0.0	0.0	0.0	0.0	0.0	0.0	0.0	0.0
Dominican Republic / República Dominicana	1.3	2.5	4.1	4.5	4.6	15.1	20.5	33.3	33.9	34.9
Ecuador	2.0	5.0	5.4	6.4	6.1	28.0	43.5	33.8	32.0	29.8
El Salvador	0.0	6.1	7.8	7.6	7.9	0.0	42.8	41.8	36.7	37.4
Guatemala	2.4	4.7	5.1	4.7	4.7	29.7	38.5	41.7	38.0	38.7
Guyana	0.0	0.0	5.8	5.8	6.0	0.0	0.0	24.2	22.2	21.9
Honduras	2.0	4.8	5.4	7.2	7.3	16.2	28.1	29.7	32.9	32.5
Jamaica	0.8	5.7	7.1	8.9	9.1	3.8	25.5	28.7	32.5	32.7
Mexico / México[1]	3.2	2.8	3.8	3.7	3.9	26.1	24.7	29.4	23.1	23.1
Nicaragua	..	4.5	5.5	6.1	5.3	..	31.5	28.6	25.9	23.0
Panama / Panamá	1.4	0.6	2.6	2.5	2.3	9.0	3.6	15.9	16.5	15.6
Paraguay	0.0	3.7	4.6	5.1	5.1	0.0	32.1	38.3	36.5	36.6
Peru / Perú	2.1	5.5	6.9	5.9	6.6	17.1	36.0	38.9	38.6	40.3
Saint Lucia / Santa Lucía	..	0.0	0.0	6.2	6.3	..	0.0	0.0	31.3	31.7
Trinidad and Tobago / Trinidad y Tobago	4.4	3.8	4.4	3.4	4.8	18.8	17.3	15.2	16.2	19.7
Uruguay	5.5	6.5	8.7	7.6	7.5	27.5	28.0	32.8	26.2	25.7
Venezuela[2]	..	4.1	5.5	5.6	..	..	30.2	46.7	..	..
Unweighted average / Promedio no ponderado										
LAC / ALC[3]	**2.3**	**4.0**	**5.3**	**5.9**	**6.0**	**16.2**	**22.9**	**26.2**	**27.6**	**27.8**
OECD / OCDE[4]	**5.2**	**6.4**	**6.5**	**6.8**	..	**16.7**	**19.3**	**20.3**	**20.2**	..

Note: The figures exclude local government revenues for Argentina (but include provincial revenues), the Bahamas, Barbados, Cuba (except for 2002-2012), the Dominican Republic, Saint Lucia, Trinidad and Tobago and Venezuela as the data are not available. Local government revenue data are available since 1991 for Nicaragua, since 1994 for Bolivia, since 1995 for Guatemala, since 1998 for Jamaica, since 1999 for Panama, since 2000 for Peru, since 2002 for El Salvador and Guyana, since 2006 for Paraguay and since 1990 for all other countries.

1. For the figures as % of total tax revenue data for 2017 are used as the state and local government revenue data for 2018 are not available.
2. Some tax revenue data between 2014 and 2017 and all data for 2018 are not available. In those years data as % of total tax revenue cannot be calculated.
3. Represents the group of 25 Latin American and Caribbean countries included in this publication and excludes Venezuela due to data availability issues. Chile and Mexico are also part of the OECD (36) group.
4. Represents the unweighted average for OECD member countries.

Nota : Las cifras excluyen los ingresos subnacionales para Argentina (pero se incluyen los ingresos de las provincias), Las Bahamas, Barbados, Cuba (excepto 2002-2012), República Dominicana, Santa Lucía, Trinidad y Tobago y Venezuela, dado que los datos no están disponibles. Los datos de ingresos subnacionales están disponibles desde 1991 para Nicaragua, desde 1994 para Bolivia, desde 1995 para Guatemala, desde 1998 para Jamaica, desde 1999 para Panamá, desde 2000 para Perú, desde 2002 para El Salvador y Guyana, desde 2006 para Paraguay y desde 1990 para todos los demás países.

1. Para los ingresos como un porcentaje de los ingresos fiscales totales, se utilizan los datos de 2017 porque los datos de ingresos de los gobiernos estatales y locales no están disponibles para 2018.
2. Algunos datos de ingresos fiscales entre 2014 y 2017 y todos los datos de 2018 no están disponibles. Para esos años, no se pueden calcular los ingresos como un porcentaje de los ingresos fiscales totales.
3. Representa al grupo de 25 países de América Latina y el Caribe incluidos en esta publicación y excluye a Venezuela debido a problemas de disponibilidad de datos. Chile y México también forman parte del grupo OCDE (36).
4. Representa el promedio no ponderado para los países miembros de la OCDE.

StatLink https://doi.org/10.1787/888934114286

Table 4.11. **Tax revenues of sub-sectors of general government as % of total tax revenue**
Cuadro 4.11. **Ingresos tributarios por subsector del gobierno general, en % del total de ingresos tributarios**

	Central government / Gobierno central			State or Regional government / Gobierno estatal o regional			Local government / Gobierno local			Social Security Funds / Fondos de seguridad social		
	1995	2000	2017	1995	2000	2017	1995	2000	2017	1995	2000	2017
Federal countries / Países federales												
Argentina	59.0	66.4	59.0	17.5	17.8	18.1	..	..	..	23.4	15.8	22.9
Brazil / Brasil	44.7	47.8	43.2	26.6	25.1	24.8	3.7	3.4	5.8	25.0	23.7	26.3
Mexico / México	73.9	78.3	81.1	2.8	2.7	4.1	1.5	1.0	1.6	21.8	18.0	13.3
Venezuela[1]	94.6	94.6	..	..	..	..	..	..	..	5.4	5.4	..
Regional country / País régional												
Colombia	63.2	68.7	74.8	5.5	5.6	5.1	8.6	9.4	12.4	22.7	16.3	7.6
Unitary countries / Países unitarios												
Bahamas[2]	89.1	88.1	85.2	..	..	..	..	..	..	10.9	11.9	14.8
Barbados[2]	85.6	84.4	82.5	..	..	..	..	..	..	14.4	15.6	17.5
Belize / Belice	93.2	93.5	91.6	..	..	..	0.5	0.7	0.6	6.3	5.8	7.8
Bolivia[2]	94.3	75.7	70.7	..	..	..	5.7	5.5	5.6	..	18.8	23.7
Chile	89.9	87.8	86.3	..	..	..	6.5	7.9	7.8	3.6	4.4	5.9
Costa Rica	65.5	63.3	58.5	..	..	..	1.6	1.9	3.0	33.0	34.8	38.5
Cuba	..	..	..	..	..	..	..	..	..	11.3	10.4	12.5
Dominican Republic / República Dominicana	99.3	99.0	99.5	..	..	..	..	..	..	0.7	1.0	0.5
Ecuador	70.5	87.7	71.1	..	..	..	4.0	1.6	2.8	25.5	10.7	26.1
El Salvador	80.9	80.5	84.8	..	..	..	..	..	2.0	19.1	19.5	13.2
Guatemala	83.3	83.3	82.2	..	..	..	0.7	0.9	1.0	16.1	15.8	16.7
Guyana	92.6	88.6	89.5	..	..	..	..	..	0.1	7.4	11.4	10.4
Honduras	86.1	85.3	83.2	..	..	..	4.4	5.2	1.8	9.5	9.4	15.0
Jamaica	100.0	99.3	94.6	..	..	..	..	0.7	1.6	..	..	3.7
Nicaragua	80.4	72.5	69.4	..	..	..	4.6	9.5	6.4	15.0	18.0	24.2
Panama / Panamá	62.8	59.6	59.9	..	..	..	..	2.2	1.7	37.2	38.2	38.4
Paraguay	100.0	74.4	70.2	..	..	..	..	..	3.6	..	25.6	26.2
Peru / Perú	88.7	86.5	84.4	..	..	..	..	1.6	2.8	11.3	11.9	12.9
Saint Lucia / Santa Lucía[3]	100.0	100.0	100.0	..	..	..	..	..	..	..	..	..
Trinidad and Tobago / Trinidad y Tobago	96.8	93.6	85.2	..	..	..	..	..	..	3.2	6.4	14.8
Uruguay	61.7	63.6	67.9	..	..	..	8.8	8.9	5.5	29.5	27.5	26.5

Note: The figures exclude local government revenues for Argentina (but include provincial revenues), the Bahamas, Barbados, Cuba (except for 2002-2012), the Dominican Republic, Saint Lucia, Trinidad and Tobago and Venezuela as the data are not available. Local government revenue data are available since 1991 for Nicaragua, since 1994 for Bolivia, since 1995 for Guatemala, since 1998 for Jamaica, since 1999 for Panama, since 2000 for Peru, since 2002 for El Salvador and Guyana, since 2006 for Paraguay and since 1990 for all other countries.

1. Some tax revenue data are not available between 2014 and 2017 and the breakdown by sub-sectors of general government is not available for those years
2. The social security contributions data are estimated in the following countries: Bahamas (from 2017 onward), Barbados (from 2015 onward), and Bolivia (heathcare contributions only, for 2018).
3. The figures as a percentage of total tax revenue need to be considered with caution as revenues from social security contributions are not available

Nota : Las cifras excluyen los ingresos subnacionales para Argentina (pero se incluyen los ingresos de las provincias), Las Bahamas, Barbados, Cuba (excepto 2002-2012), República Dominicana, Santa Lucía, Trinidad y Tobago y Venezuela, dado que los datos no están disponibles. Los datos de ingresos subnacionales están disponibles desde 1991 para Nicaragua, desde 1994 para Bolivia, desde 1995 para Guatemala, desde 1998 para Jamaica, desde 1999 para Panamá, desde 2000 para Perú, desde 2002 para El Salvador y Guyana, desde 2006 para Paraguay y desde 1990 para todos los demás países.

1. Algunos ingresos fiscales no están disponibles entre 2014 y 2017 y la desagregación por subsectores del gobierno general no está disponible para esos años.
2. Las contribuciones a la seguridad social se estiman en los siguientes países: Bahamas (desde 2017), Barbados (desde 2015) y Bolivia (contribuciones al seguro médico para 2018).
3. Las cifras deben considerarse con cautela (precaucion) ya que los ingresos de las contribuciones a la seguridad social no están disponibles.

StatLink https://doi.org/10.1787/888934114305

Table 4.12. **Main central government taxes as % of total tax revenues of central government, 2016**

Cuadro 4.12. **Impuestos principales del gobierno central en % del total de ingresos tributarios del gobierno central, 2016**

	1000 Income & profits / Ingresos y utilidades	2000 Social security / Seguridad social[1]	3000 Payroll / Nómina	4000 Property / Propiedad	5000 Goods and services / Bienes y servicios	6000 Others / Otros
Federal countries / Países federales						
Argentina	29.6	0.0	0.0	10.6	56.8	3.0
Brazil / Brasil	50.2	0.0	4.3	3.9	41.0	0.5
Mexico / México	55.0	0.0	0.0	0.0	43.9	1.1
Venezuela	..	..	..	..	..	..
Regional country / País régional						
Colombia	44.1	0.0	2.4	8.1	45.0	0.4
Unitary countries / Países unitarios						
Bahamas	0.0	0.0	0.0	12.7	87.3	0.0
Barbados	29.5	0.0	0.0	5.6	65.0	0.0
Belize / Belice	27.8	0.0	0.0	2.7	69.5	0.0
Bolivia	21.4	0.0	0.0	1.0	71.7	5.8
Chile	40.0	1.6	0.0	2.4	58.3	-2.3
Costa Rica	33.8	1.5	0.0	0.9	59.4	4.3
Cuba	..	..	..	..	..	..
Dominican Republic / República Dominicana	31.1	0.0	0.0	4.6	64.3	0.0
Ecuador	27.5	0.0	0.0	0.6	71.8	0.1
El Salvador	39.3	0.0	0.0	2.4	58.2	0.0
Guatemala	36.6	0.0	0.0	1.0	62.5	0.0
Guyana	39.7	0.0	0.0	2.1	56.9	1.3
Honduras	33.3	0.0	0.0	3.1	63.6	0.0
Jamaica	31.8	0.0	0.0	3.1	64.7	0.4
Nicaragua	41.6	0.0	0.0	0.1	58.3	0.0
Panama / Panamá	44.1	0.0	2.3	4.5	48.5	0.6
Paraguay	23.6	0.0	0.0	0.0	75.7	0.8
Peru / Perú	44.4	0.0	0.0	0.2	55.2	0.2
Saint Lucia / Santa Lucía	25.7	0.0	0.0	2.6	71.8	0.0
Trinidad and Tobago / Trinidad y Tobago	60.8	0.0	0.0	1.2	38.0	0.0
Uruguay	37.3	0.0	0.0	7.0	55.4	0.3

Note: Excluding social security contributions collected by social security funds.

1. These comprise social security contributions collected by central government.

Nota : Se excluyen las contribuciones a la seguridad social que recaudados por los fondos de la seguridad social.

1. Estos comprenden contribuciones a la seguridad social recaudados por el gobierno central.

StatLink https://doi.org/10.1787/888934114324

Table 4.13. **Main state government taxes as % of total tax revenues of state government, 2016**
Cuadro 4.13. **Impuestos principales del gobierno estatal en % del total de ingresos tributarios del gobierno estatal, 2016**

	1000 Income & profits / Ingresos y utilidades	2000 Social security / Seguridad social	3000 Payroll / Nómina	4000 Property / Propiedad	5000 Goods and services / Bienes y servicios	6000 Others / Otros
Federal countries / Países federales						
Argentina	0.0	0.0	0.0	17.9	78.8	3.4
Brazil / Brasil	0.0	0.0	0.0	1.4	92.1	6.6
Mexico / México	0.0	0.0	58.3	18.1	18.6	5.0
Venezuela	..	..	..	..	..	..
Regional country / País régional						
Colombia	0.0	0.0	0.0	0.0	72.9	27.1
Unitary countries / Países unitarios						
Bahamas	..	..	..	..	..	..
Barbados	..	..	..	..	..	..
Belize / Belice	..	..	..	..	..	..
Bolivia	..	..	..	..	..	..
Chile	..	..	..	..	..	..
Costa Rica	..	..	..	..	..	..
Cuba	..	..	..	..	..	..
Dominican Republic / República Dominicana	..	..	..	..	..	..
Ecuador	..	..	..	..	..	..
El Salvador	..	..	..	..	..	..
Guatemala	..	..	..	..	..	..
Guyana	..	..	..	..	..	..
Honduras	..	..	..	..	..	..
Jamaica	..	..	..	..	..	..
Nicaragua	..	..	..	..	..	..
Panama / Panamá	..	..	..	..	..	..
Paraguay	..	..	..	..	..	..
Peru / Perú	..	..	..	..	..	..
Saint Lucia / Santa Lucía	..	..	..	..	..	..
Trinidad and Tobago / Trinidad y Tobago	..	..	..	..	..	..
Uruguay	..	..	..	..	..	..

StatLink https://doi.org/10.1787/888934114343

Table 4.14. **Main local government taxes as % of total tax revenues of local government, 2016**
Cuadro 4.14. **Impuestos principales del gobierno local en % del total de ingresos tributarios del gobierno local, 2016**

	1000 Income & profits / Ingresos y utilidades	2000 Social security / Seguridad social	3000 Payroll / Nómina	4000 Property / Propiedad	5000 Goods and services / Bienes y servicios	6000 Others / Otros
Federal countries / Países federales						
Argentina	..	..	..	..	..	..
Brazil / Brasil	0.0	0.0	0.0	39.7	46.2	14.1
Mexico / México	0.0	0.0	0.0	74.6	2.5	22.9
Venezuela	..	..	..	..	..	..
Regional country / País régional						
Colombia	0.0	0.0	0.0	33.6	46.4	19.9
Unitary countries / Países unitarios						
Bahamas	..	..	..	..	..	..
Barbados	..	..	..	..	..	..
Belize / Belice	0.0	0.0	0.0	100.0	0.0	0.0
Bolivia	0.0	0.0	0.0	0.0	0.0	100.0
Chile	0.0	0.0	0.0	42.6	57.4	0.0
Costa Rica	0.0	0.0	0.0	43.4	56.6	0.1
Cuba	..	..	..	..	..	..
Dominican Republic / República Dominicana	..	..	..	..	..	..
Ecuador	12.3	0.0	0.0	45.5	42.2	0.0
El Salvador	0.0	0.0	0.0	4.6	12.8	82.6
Guatemala	0.0	0.0	0.0	100.0	0.0	0.0
Guyana	0.0	0.0	0.0	0.0	0.0	100.0
Honduras	0.0	0.0	0.0	0.0	0.0	100.0
Jamaica	0.0	0.0	0.0	100.0	0.0	0.0
Nicaragua	0.0	0.0	0.0	12.8	72.7	14.5
Panama / Panamá	0.0	0.0	0.0	0.0	100.0	0.0
Paraguay	0.0	0.0	0.0	49.0	46.5	4.4
Peru / Perú	0.0	0.0	0.0	81.5	17.6	0.9
Saint Lucia / Santa Lucía	..	..	..	..	..	..
Trinidad and Tobago / Trinidad y Tobago	..	..	..	..	..	..
Uruguay	0.0	0.0	0.0	54.3	38.3	7.4

StatLink https://doi.org/10.1787/888934114362

Table 4.15. **Gross domestic product for tax reporting years at market prices, in millions of national currency**

Cuadro 4.15. **Producto interno bruto para los años fiscales a precios de mercado, en millones de moneda local**

		1990	2000	2007	2010	2013	2014	2015	2016	2017	2018
Argentina	ARS	74 710	308 491	896 980	1 661 721	3 348 308	4 579 086	5 954 511	8 228 160	10 644 779	14 605 790
Bahamas	BSD	5 218	7 880	10 393	10 039	10 642	10 738	11 333	11 902	12 203	12 229
Barbados	BBD	4 059	6 116	9 403	9 124	9 364	9 402	9 488	9 734	10 011	10 225
Belize / Belice	BZD	824	1 664	2 581	2 793	3 217	3 386	3 525	3 613	3 725	3 850
Bolivia	BOB	15 443	51 928	103 009	137 876	211 856	228 004	228 031	234 533	259 185	278 388
Brazil / Brasil	BRL	12	1 199 092	2 720 263	3 885 847	5 331 619	5 778 953	5 995 787	6 269 328	6 583 319	6 889 176
Chile	CLP	10 522 684	42 005 194	90 702 903	111 508 611	137 876 216	148 599 454	159 553 348	169 469 507	180 211 290	191 248 711
Colombia	COP	28 065 889	206 560 673	427 518 882	543 187 690	713 626 705	762 903 000	804 692 000	863 782 000	920 194 000	978 478 000
Costa Rica	CRC	523 319	4 607 291	13 816 351	19 596 937	24 860 944	27 226 883	29 281 373	31 136 211	33 014 819	34 693 418
Cuba	CUP	19 645	30 565	58 604	64 328	77 148	80 656	87 133	91 370	96 851	100 023
Dominican Republic / República Dominicana	DOP	77 344	393 303	1 458 417	1 983 202	2 619 770	2 925 665	3 205 655	3 487 293	3 802 656	4 235 847
Ecuador	USD	15 232	18 319	51 008	69 555	95 130	101 726	99 290	99 938	104 296	108 398
El Salvador	USD	4 818	11 785	17 012	18 448	21 991	22 593	23 438	24 154	24 928	26 057
Guatemala	GTQ	31 176	133 428	261 760	333 093	423 098	454 053	488 128	521 837	555 649	589 960
Guyana	GYD	25 432	205 128	352 120	462 910	613 653	635 377	660 227	723 581	734 150	805 664
Honduras	HNL	17 141	106 654	233 567	299 286	376 539	414 634	460 405	495 922	542 570	572 945
Jamaica	JMD	38 145	395 009	885 632	1 152 781	1 431 934	1 541 746	1 659 532	1 760 824	1 894 686	2 025 075
Mexico / México	MXN	843 623	6 693 683	11 504 076	13 366 377	16 277 187	17 473 842	18 551 459	20 116 689	21 921 242	23 543 546
Nicaragua	NIO	519	64 812	136 950	187 053	271 530	308 403	347 707	380 261	416 013	413 911
Panama / Panamá	PAB	5 723	12 502	21 296	29 440	45 600	49 921	54 092	57 908	62 219	65 128
Paraguay	PYG	6 031 160	30 874 088	89 866 049	128 989 495	166 714 587	179 721 609	188 230 723	204 447 278	219 188 417	231 489 278
Peru / Perú	PEN	5 322	175 862	319 693	420 738	546 124	574 302	609 365	656 182	698 420	740 562
Saint Lucia / Santa Lucía	XCD	1 420	2 228	3 499	3 807	4 072	4 283	4 521	4 645	4 997	5 216
Trinidad and Tobago / Trinidad y Tobago	TTD	21 105	50 098	133 468	138 557	172 417	175 747	164 185	148 823	149 392	152 095
Uruguay	UYU	12 010	276 152	549 470	808 079	1 178 332	1 330 508	1 455 848	1 589 195	1 707 109	1 831 132
Venezuela	VES	0	1	5	10	22	30	80	281	2 009	2 038 603

Source: OECD National Accounts data for Chile and Mexico, the World Economic Outlook (IMF) for Barbados, Belize, and Trinidad & Tobago, and official National Accounts data for Bolivia, Brazil, Ecuador, El Salvador, Guatemala, Nicaragua, Paraguay, Peru and Uruguay. For Argentina, Bahamas, Colombia, Costa Rica, Dominican Republic, Guyana, Honduras, Jamaica, Panama, Saint Lucia, and Venezuela, official national sources were used where available, together with data from the IMF. For Cuba, figures between 1996 and 2018 come from Oficina Nacional de Estadística e Información (ONEI), while data before 1996 come from ECLAC/CEPAL. For Bahamas, Barbados, Belize, Saint Lucia and Trinidad and Tobago, GDP figures are reported on a fiscal year basis. For Jamaica, GDP reported for 1990-2003 are reported on a fiscal year basis, while for other years, they are reported on a calendar year basis.

Fuente : Datos de las Cuentas Nacionales de la OCDE para Chile y México, Perspectivas de la economía mundial (FMI) para Barbados, Belice y Trinidad y Tobago, y datos de cuentas nacionales para Bolivia, Brasil, Ecuador, El Salvador, Guatemala, Nicaragua, Paraguay, Perú y Uruguay. Para Argentina, Bahamas, Colombia, Costa Rica, República Dominicana, Guyana, Honduras, Jamaica, Panamá, Santa Lucía y Venezuela, se utilizan fuentes nacionales oficiales donde los datos están disponibles, junto con los datos del FMI. Para Cuba, las cifras entre 1996 y 2018 provienen de la Oficina Nacional de Estadística e Información, mientras que los datos anteriores a 1996 provienen de la CEPAL. Para Bahamas, Barbados, Belice, Santa Lucía y Trinidad y Tobago, las cifras del PIB se informan sobre la base del año fiscal. Para Jamaica, el PIB reportado para 1990-2003 se presenta sobre una base de año fiscal, mientras que para otros años, se presenta sobre un base de año calendario.

StatLink https://doi.org/10.1787/888934114381

Table 4.16. **Gross domestic product for tax reporting years at market prices, in USD**
Cuadro 4.16. **Producto interno bruto para los años fiscales a precios de mercado, en US dólares**

	1990	2000	2007	2010	2013	2014	2015	2016	2017	2018
Argentina	153 205	308 491	287 921	424 729	611 471	563 614	642 464	556 774	642 928	519 487
Bahamas	5 218	7 880	10 393	10 039	10 642	10 738	11 333	11 902	12 203	12 229
Barbados	2 030	3 058	4 702	4 562	4 682	4 701	4 744	4 867	5 006	5 113
Belize / Belice	412	832	1 291	1 397	1 609	1 693	1 763	1 807	1 863	1 925
Bolivia	4 868	8 385	13 216	19 786	30 883	33 237	33 241	34 189	37 782	40 581
Brazil / Brasil	477 882	655 454	1 397 115	2 208 704	2 471 718	2 456 055	1 800 045	1 796 622	2 062 842	1 885 469
Chile	34 512	77 847	173 606	218 538	278 384	260 542	243 919	250 340	277 746	298 231
Colombia	55 879	98 931	205 755	286 039	381 844	381 240	293 493	282 720	311 796	330 974
Costa Rica	5 716	14 965	26 856	37 634	50 326	51 181	55 410	57 828	58 654	60 464
Cuba	21 541	30 565	58 604	64 328	77 148	80 656	87 133	91 370	96 851	100 023
Dominican Republic / República Dominicana	7 995	24 306	44 067	53 921	62 758	67 264	71 254	75 777	80 082	85 630
Ecuador	15 232	18 319	51 008	69 555	95 130	101 726	99 290	99 938	104 296	108 398
El Salvador	4 818	11 785	17 012	18 448	21 991	22 593	23 438	24 154	24 928	26 057
Guatemala	6 950	17 187	34 113	41 338	53 851	58 722	63 767	68 663	75 620	78 461
Guyana	504	1 124	1 741	2 273	2 988	3 078	3 197	3 504	3 555	3 899
Honduras	4 169	7 104	12 275	15 730	18 499	19 757	20 980	21 718	23 101	23 803
Jamaica	5 058	8 997	12 881	13 193	14 211	13 864	14 153	14 107	14 753	15 633
Mexico / México	299 944	707 910	1 052 697	1 057 801	1 274 444	1 314 569	1 170 567	1 077 830	1 158 229	1 223 401
Nicaragua	519	5 109	7 423	8 759	10 983	11 880	12 757	13 286	13 844	13 118
Panama / Panamá	5 723	12 502	21 296	29 440	45 600	49 921	54 092	57 908	62 219	65 128
Paraguay	4 904	8 856	17 856	27 239	38 585	40 277	36 164	36 054	39 009	40 385
Peru / Perú	28 326	50 414	102 187	148 931	202 091	202 308	191 316	194 391	214 182	225 292
Saint Lucia / Santa Lucía	526	825	1 296	1 410	1 508	1 586	1 675	1 720	1 851	1 932
Trinidad and Tobago / Trinidad y Tobago	4 966	7 986	21 199	21 841	26 897	27 438	25 878	22 719	22 134	22 512
Uruguay	10 270	22 832	23 461	40 285	57 531	57 236	53 275	52 687	59 530	59 651
Venezuela	48 391	117 676	221 953	294 507	234 401	212 347	323 595	279 249	143 841	98 437

Source: The figures are derived by dividing the GDP data in Table 4.15 by the exchange rate in Table 4.17.
Fuente : Las cifras se obtienende la división de los datos del PIB en el Cuadro 4.15 por el tipo de cambio en el Cuadro 4.17.

StatLink https://doi.org/10.1787/888934114400

Table 4.17. **Exchange rates used, national currency per US dollar at market exchange rates**
Cuadro 4.17. **Tasas de cambio utilizadas, moneda local por US dólares a precios de mercado**

		1990	2000	2007	2010	2013	2014	2015	2016	2017	2018
Argentina	ARS	0.488	1.000	3.115	3.912	5.476	8.125	9.268	14.778	16.557	28.116
Bahamas	BSD	1.000	1.000	1.000	1.000	1.000	1.000	1.000	1.000	1.000	1.000
Barbados	BBD	2.000	2.000	2.000	2.000	2.000	2.000	2.000	2.000	2.000	2.000
Belize / Belice	BZD	2.000	2.000	2.000	2.000	2.000	2.000	2.000	2.000	2.000	2.000
Bolivia	BOB	3.172	6.193	7.794	6.968	6.860	6.860	6.860	6.860	6.860	6.860
Brazil / Brasil	BRL	0.000	1.829	1.947	1.759	2.157	2.353	3.331	3.490	3.191	3.654
Chile	CLP	304.903	539.588	522.464	510.249	495.273	570.348	654.124	676.958	648.834	641.277
Colombia	COP	502.262	2 087.927	2 077.806	1 899.000	1 868.894	2 001.107	2 741.776	3 055.256	2 951.269	2 956.359
Costa Rica	CRC	91.553	307.871	514.460	520.724	493.998	531.972	528.449	538.428	562.874	573.786
Cuba	CUP	0.912	1.000	1.000	1.000	1.000	1.000	1.000	1.000	1.000	1.000
Dominican Republic / República Dominicana	DOP	9.674	16.181	33.095	36.780	41.744	43.495	44.989	46.020	47.485	49.467
Ecuador	USD	1.000	1.000	1.000	1.000	1.000	1.000	1.000	1.000	1.000	1.000
El Salvador	USD	1.000	1.000	1.000	1.000	1.000	1.000	1.000	1.000	1.000	1.000
Guatemala	GTQ	4.486	7.763	7.673	8.058	7.857	7.732	7.655	7.600	7.348	7.519
Guyana	GYD	50.460	182.498	202.270	203.662	205.372	206.425	206.515	206.501	206.491	206.633
Honduras	HNL	4.112	15.013	19.028	19.026	20.355	20.987	21.945	22.835	23.487	24.070
Jamaica	JMD	7.541	43.907	68.755	87.378	100.762	111.205	117.256	124.822	128.430	129.541
Mexico / México	MXN	2.813	9.456	10.928	12.636	12.772	13.292	15.848	18.664	18.927	19.244
Nicaragua	NIO	1.000	12.686	18.449	21.356	24.723	25.960	27.256	28.621	30.050	31.553
Panama / Panamá	PAB	1.000	1.000	1.000	1.000	1.000	1.000	1.000	1.000	1.000	1.000
Paraguay	PYG	1 229.845	3 486.234	5 032.821	4 735.471	4 320.710	4 462.140	5 204.920	5 670.585	5 618.919	5 732.061
Peru / Perú	PEN	0.188	3.488	3.129	2.825	2.702	2.839	3.185	3.376	3.261	3.287
Saint Lucia / Santa Lucía	XCD	2.700	2.700	2.700	2.700	2.700	2.700	2.700	2.700	2.700	2.700
Trinidad and Tobago / Trinidad y Tobago	TTD	4.250	6.273	6.296	6.344	6.410	6.405	6.344	6.551	6.749	6.756
Uruguay	UYU	1.169	12.095	23.421	20.059	20.482	23.246	27.327	30.163	28.676	30.697
Venezuela	VES	0.000	0.000	0.000	0.000	0.000	0.000	0.000	0.001	0.014	20.710

Note: Annual average market exchange rates.
Source: World Economic Outlook (IMF), October 2019.
Nota : Se utilizan tasas de cambio de mercado promedios anuales.
Fuente : Perspectivas de la economía mundial (FMI), octubre de 2019.

StatLink https://doi.org/10.1787/888934114419

Chapter 5

Country tables, 1990-2018 – Tax revenues

Capítulo 5

Cuadros país, 1990-2018 – Ingresos tributarios

Table 5.1. **Argentina**

Details of tax revenue / Ingresos tributarios detallados

Million ARS

	1990	2000	2007	2010	2013	2014	2015	2016	2017	2018
Total tax revenue	**10 217**	**61 084**	**236 516**	**483 014**	**1 043 967**	**1 424 523**	**1 872 915**	**2 522 854**	**3 202 629**	**4 203 894**
1000 Taxes on income, profits and capital gains	**542**	**11 303**	**44 226**	**78 427**	**185 688**	**269 809**	**384 536**	**436 927**	**559 755**	**746 994**
1100 Of individuals	141	3 937	12 777	23 980	79 803	125 503	188 218	174 483	236 284	296 224
1110 On income and profits	130	3 854	12 715	23 858	79 449	125 067	187 663	173 721	234 117	293 344
1120 On capital gains	11	82	62	122	354	436	555	762	2 167	2 880
1200 Corporate	357	6 575	29 145	50 664	99 346	132 178	185 725	236 286	297 111	401 683
1210 On profits	357	6 575	29 145	50 664	99 346	132 178	185 725	236 286	297 111	401 683
Corporate income taxes	198	5 956	27 837	49 012	97 614	129 881	183 207	233 028	294 546	399 623
Tax on assets	160	19	9	4	3	6	4	12	5	5
Tax on assumed minimum income	0	600	1 299	1 648	1 728	2 291	2 513	3 246	2 560	2 055
1220 On capital gains	..	..	..	..	..	..	..	..	..	..
1300 Unallocable between 1100 and 1200	43	792	2 304	3 783	6 539	12 128	10 593	26 159	26 360	49 086
Non resident taxpayers	11	792	2 304	3 783	6 539	12 128	10 593	26 159	26 360	49 086
Other	33	0	0	0	0	0	0	0	0	0
2000 Social security contributions	**2 583**	**9 670**	**36 612**	**102 460**	**236 072**	**307 656**	**415 410**	**556 067**	**733 527**	**913 427**
2100 Employees	..	2 486	7 052	37 990	91 779	121 276	163 590	219 446	288 985	361 756
2110 On a payroll basis	..	2 486	7 052	37 990	91 779	121 276	163 590	219 446	288 985	361 756
2120 On an income tax basis	..	0	0	0	0	0	0	0	0	0
2200 Employers	..	6 069	23 939	54 713	132 999	174 965	235 610	314 628	413 212	514 144
2210 On a payroll basis	..	6 069	23 939	54 713	132 999	174 965	235 610	314 628	413 212	514 144
2220 On an income tax basis	..	0	0	0	0	0	0	0	0	0
2300 Self-employed or non-employed	98	1 115	5 620	9 757	11 293	11 416	16 210	21 994	31 330	37 527
2310 On a payroll basis	98	1 115	5 620	9 757	11 293	11 416	16 210	21 994	31 330	37 527
2320 On an income tax basis	0	0	0	0	0	0	0	0	0	0
2400 Unallocable between 2100, 2200 and 2300	2 485	0	0	0	0	0	0	0	0	0
2410 On a payroll basis	2 485	..	..	..	..	..	..	..	..	..
2420 On an income tax basis	0	..	..	..	..	..	..	..	..	..
3000 Taxes on payroll and workforce	**0**	**0**	**0**	**0**	**0**	**0**	**0**	**0**	**0**	**0**
4000 Taxes on property	**1 164**	**3 867**	**23 978**	**43 538**	**96 679**	**129 065**	**166 182**	**224 193**	**303 382**	**389 073**
4100 Recurrent taxes on immovable property	419	1 809	3 025	5 035	14 097	17 547	21 738	32 770	44 236	58 672
4110 Households	0	0	0	0	0	0	0	0	0	0
4120 Others	419	1 809	3 025	5 035	14 097	17 547	21 738	32 770	44 236	58 672
4200 Recurrent taxes on net wealth	246	1 084	2 557	5 248	10 471	14 575	18 538	19 976	22 786	15 296
4210 Individual	3	1 024	2 492	5 147	10 296	14 356	18 210	19 541	22 165	14 517
Personal assets	0	1 024	2 492	5 147	10 296	14 356	18 210	19 541	22 165	14 517
Recurrent taxes on net wealth	3	0	0	0	0	0	0	0	0	0
4220 Corporate	242	60	65	101	175	220	327	435	621	778
4300 Estate, inheritance and gift taxes	0	0	0	0	0	0	0	0	0	0
4310 Estate and inheritance taxes	..	..	..	..	..	..	..	..	..	..
4320 Gift taxes	..	..	..	..	..	..	..	..	..	..
4400 Taxes on financial and capital transactions	459	904	18 390	33 252	72 111	96 943	125 906	171 447	236 360	315 105
Immovable property transfers	0	54	382	539	734	912	1 256	2 052	4 091	5 935
Movable property transfers	44	0	0	0	0	0	0	0	0	0
Bank accounts' credits and debits	205	0	15 065	26 885	56 515	76 740	97 480	131 669	172 838	234 300
Stamp taxes	211	850	2 942	5 829	14 862	19 291	27 170	37 726	59 431	74 870
4500 Non-recurrent taxes	40	70	6	3	0	0	0	0	0	0
4510 On net wealth	0	0	0	0	..	..	..	..	..	..
4520 Other non-recurrent taxes	40	70	6	3	..	..	..	..	..	..
4600 Other recurrent taxes on property	0	0	0	0	0	0	0	0	0	0
5000 Taxes on goods and services	**5 636**	**34 539**	**128 329**	**253 092**	**517 591**	**704 677**	**889 323**	**1 176 337**	**1 529 578**	**2 120 200**
5100 Taxes on production, sale, transfer, etc	5 462	34 288	128 321	252 550	513 926	703 883	881 120	1 167 379	1 520 300	2 113 011
5110 General taxes	2 384	25 123	86 803	167 534	381 630	515 090	671 297	901 584	1 188 317	1 671 320
5111 Value added taxes	1 594	19 009	62 669	116 386	249 006	331 203	433 076	583 217	765 336	1 104 580
5112 Sales tax	0	0	0	0	0	0	0	0	0	0
5113 Other	791	6 114	24 134	51 148	132 624	183 887	238 221	318 367	422 981	566 740
5120 Taxes on specific goods and services	3 077	9 166	41 517	85 016	132 296	188 793	209 822	265 795	331 983	441 691
5121 Excises	1 866	5 850	13 164	26 208	49 680	69 977	92 349	129 790	182 818	205 182
Alcoholic beverages	25	36	95	238	525	673	985	1 163	1 591	2 147
Non alcoholic beverages	25	90	312	501	1 195	1 586	2 168	2 477	3 136	3 627
Beers	0	50	149	212	650	879	1 384	1 171	2 811	4 729
Tobacco products	425	1 875	3 881	6 884	12 343	17 432	26 152	42 183	60 249	67 264
Liquid fuel and gas	1 073	3 478	7 466	15 269	31 010	44 490	56 478	75 664	102 846	116 409
Electricity	72	205	538	591	547	607	590	637	1 768	2 358
Motor vehicles	59	20	0	27	185	121	88	265	476	337
Other	189	96	724	2 485	3 225	4 189	4 503	6 229	9 942	8 311
5122 Profits of fiscal monopolies	0	0	0	0	0	0	0	0	0	0

Table 5.1. **Argentina** *(cont.)*

Details of tax revenue / Ingresos tributarios detallados

Million ARS

	1990	2000	2007	2010	2013	2014	2015	2016	2017	2018
5123 Customs and import duties	219	1 976	7 015	11 428	23 551	30 058	35 512	56 365	70 635	107 178
Import duties	166	1 938	6 859	11 183	23 134	29 482	34 822	55 305	69 259	104 991
Import fees	53	38	156	246	416	576	691	1 060	1 376	2 187
5124 Taxes on exports	724	32	20 450	45 547	55 465	84 088	75 939	71 509	66 121	114 160
5125 Taxes on investment goods	0	0	0	0	0	0	0	0	0	0
5126 Taxes on specific services	163	1 233	674	1 429	2 677	3 533	4 420	5 782	7 792	9 293
Insurance services	42	194	11	21	46	65	88	118	167	198
Financial services	32	855	1	0	0	0	0	0	0	0
Telephone services	82	33	417	936	1 605	1 983	2 301	2 911	4 061	4 626
Other specific services	7	151	246	472	1 026	1 486	2 031	2 753	3 564	4 469
5127 Other taxes on internat. trade and transactions	98	74	214	404	924	1 136	1 601	2 349	4 616	5 876
5128 Other taxes	8	0	0	0	0	0	0	0	0	0
5130 Unallocable between 5110 and 5120	0	0	0	0	0	0	0	0	0	0
5200 Taxes on use of goods and perform activities	177	833	1 921	3 598	9 059	12 010	17 035	23 941	34 232	41 789
5210 Recurrent taxes	177	833	1 921	3 598	9 059	12 010	17 035	23 941	34 232	41 789
5211 Paid by households: motor vehicles	177	833	1 921	3 598	9 059	12 010	17 035	23 941	34 232	41 789
5212 Paid by others: motor vehicles	0	0	0	0	0	0	0	0	0	0
5213 Paid in respect of other goods	0	0	0	0	0	0	0	0	0	0
5220 Non-recurrent taxes	0	0	0	0	0	0	0	0	0	0
5300 Unallocable between 5100 and 5200	-3	-583	-1 912	-3 056	-5 394	-11 215	-8 831	-14 983	-24 953	-34 600
6000 Other taxes	**292**	**1 704**	**3 371**	**5 497**	**7 937**	**13 316**	**17 463**	**129 330**	**76 386**	**34 201**
6100 Paid solely by business	0	354	1 063	2 093	4 423	4 259	5 624	6 873	10 544	16 052
Simplified system for small taxpayers	..	354	1 063	2 093	4 423	4 259	5 624	6 873	10 544	16 052
6200 Other	292	1 351	2 308	3 404	3 514	9 056	11 839	122 457	65 842	18 148
Tax debt payments	135	24	38	293	-1 313	1 340	1 306	110 721	46 131	-8 646
Special payments	79	6	0	0	0	0	0	0	0	0
Other national level	0	12	0	0	0	0	0	0	0	0
Other provincial level	78	1 309	2 269	3 110	4 827	7 716	10 533	11 736	19 711	26 795

Note: Year ending 31st December.
The data are on a cash basis.
The figures exclude local government tax revenues as the data are not available (but include provincial revenues).
Heading 5212: In ECLAC data, property tax on motor vehicles is classified in category 4000.
Heading 5300: The figures are negative as they represent general reimbursements of exports and specific taxes on goods and services.
Heading 6200: The tax debt payments from 2016 include revenue following the implementation of a new voluntary disclosure regime in July 2016 (Law 27260).

Source: Subsecretaría de Ingresos Públicos, Dirección Nacional de Investigaciones y Análisis Fiscal, Ministerio de Hacienda (Undersecretary of Public Revenue, National Direction of Research and Fiscal Analysis, Ministry of Finance)

StatLink https://doi.org/10.1787/888934114438

Table 5.2. **Bahamas**

Details of tax revenue / Ingresos tributarios detallados

Million BSD

	1990	2000	2007	2010	2013	2014	2015	2016	2017	2018
Total tax revenue	**505**	**965**	**1 360**	**1 277**	**1 445**	**1 490**	**1 761**	**1 934**	**2 157**	**2 151**
1000 Taxes on income, profits and capital gains	**0**	**0**	**0**	**0**	**0**	**0**	**0**	**0**	**0**	**0**
1100 Of individuals	0	0	0	0	0	0	0	0	0	0
1110 On income and profits	..	..	..	..	..	..	..	..	..	..
1120 On capital gains	..	..	..	..	..	..	..	..	..	..
1200 Corporate	0	0	0	0	0	0	0	0	0	0
1210 On profits	..	..	..	..	..	..	..	..	..	..
1220 On capital gains	..	..	..	..	..	..	..	..	..	..
1300 Unallocable between 1100 and 1200	0	0	0	0	0	0	0	0	0	0
2000 Social security contributions	**66**	**115**	**155**	**167**	**229**	**245**	**260**	**258**	**320**	**320**
2100 Employees	..	..	..	60	87	91	98	101	..	..
2110 On a payroll basis	..	..	..	..	..	..	..	..	..	..
2120 On an income tax basis	..	..	..	..	..	..	..	..	..	..
2200 Employers	..	..	..	104	137	149	157	152	..	..
2210 On a payroll basis	..	..	..	..	..	..	..	..	..	..
2220 On an income tax basis	..	..	..	..	..	..	..	..	..	..
2300 Self-employed or non-employed	..	..	..	3	6	6	6	6	..	..
2310 On a payroll basis	..	..	..	..	..	..	..	..	..	..
2320 On an income tax basis	..	..	..	..	..	..	..	..	..	..
2400 Unallocable between 2100, 2200 and 2300	66	115	155	0	-1	-1	-1	-1	320	320
2410 On a payroll basis	..	..	..	..	..	..	..	..	..	..
2420 On an income tax basis	..	..	..	..	..	..	..	..	..	..
3000 Taxes on payroll and workforce	**0**	**0**	**0**	**0**	**0**	**0**	**0**	**0**	**0**	**0**
4000 Taxes on property	**56**	**208**	**450**	**269**	**293**	**268**	**298**	**204**	**233**	**237**
4100 Recurrent taxes on immovable property	19	32	79	92	115	104	107	104	121	124
4110 Households	0	0	0	0	0	0	0	0	0	0
4120 Others	19	32	79	92	115	104	107	104	121	124
4200 Recurrent taxes on net wealth	0	0	0	0	0	0	0	0	0	0
4210 Individual	..	..	..	..	..	..	..	..	..	..
4220 Corporate	..	..	..	..	..	..	..	..	..	..
4300 Estate, inheritance and gift taxes	0	0	0	0	0	0	0	0	0	0
4310 Estate and inheritance taxes	..	..	..	..	..	..	..	..	..	..
4320 Gift taxes	..	..	..	..	..	..	..	..	..	..
4400 Taxes on financial and capital transactions	37	176	371	177	178	164	191	100	112	114
Stamp Tax from Imports	0	102	143	15	18	0	0	0	0	0
Stamp Tax from Exports	0	0	0	0	0	0	0	0	0	0
All Other Stamp Tax	37	74	228	162	160	164	191	100	112	114
4500 Non-recurrent taxes	0	0	0	0	0	0	0	0	0	0
4510 On net wealth	..	..	..	..	..	..	..	..	..	..
4520 Other non-recurrent taxes	..	..	..	..	..	..	..	..	..	..
4600 Other recurrent taxes on property	0	0	0	0	0	0	0	0	0	0
5000 Taxes on goods and services	**386**	**620**	**737**	**780**	**937**	**986**	**1 203**	**1 472**	**1 604**	**1 593**
5100 Taxes on production, sale, transfer, etc	354	552	638	657	788	772	993	1 296	1 384	1 405
5110 General taxes	0	0	0	0	0	0	219	628	638	680
5111 Value added taxes	0	0	0	0	0	0	219	628	638	680
5112 Sales tax	..	..	..	..	..	..	0	0	0	0
5113 Other	..	..	..	..	..	..	0	0	0	0
5120 Taxes on specific goods and services	354	552	638	657	788	772	775	668	746	725
5121 Excises	0	0	0	188	246	249	262	230	287	255
5122 Profits of fiscal monopolies	0	0	0	0	0	0	0	0	0	0
5123 Customs and import duties	289	435	507	348	332	336	307	264	287	271
5124 Taxes on exports	6	13	14	14	14	10	9	12	8	17
5125 Taxes on investment goods	0	0	0	0	0	0	0	0	0	0
5126 Taxes on specific services	59	104	117	106	196	178	197	162	163	180
Departure tax	27	64	77	70	144	125	147	135	135	143
Gaming tax	27	20	14	10	10	8	25	26	27	37
Hotel occupancy tax	5	20	26	25	42	45	25	1	1	0
5127 Other taxes on internat. trade and transactions	0	0	0	0	0	0	0	0	0	0
5128 Other taxes	0	0	0	0	0	0	0	0	0	0
5130 Unallocable between 5110 and 5120	0	0	0	0	0	0	0	0	0	0
5200 Taxes on use of goods and perform activities	32	69	99	123	149	214	209	177	220	189
5210 Recurrent taxes	32	69	99	123	149	214	209	177	220	189
Motor vehicle tax	10	14	20	21	28	29	29	30	31	37
5211 Paid by households: motor vehicles	..	..	..	..	..	..	..	..	..	..
5212 Paid by others: motor vehicles	..	..	..	..	..	..	..	..	..	..

Table 5.2. **Bahamas** *(cont.)*

Details of tax revenue / Ingresos tributarios detallados

Million BSD

	1990	2000	2007	2010	2013	2014	2015	2016	2017	2018
5213 Paid in respect of other goods	22	55	78	102	121	185	180	146	189	151
Company fees and registration	0	5	5	5	5	5	5	6	6	7
International business companies	0	17	20	19	17	17	16	15	15	14
Others	22	33	54	78	99	163	159	125	167	130
5220 Non-recurrent taxes	0	0	0	0	0	0	0	0	0	0
5300 Unallocable between 5100 and 5200	0	0	0	0	0	0	0	0	0	0
6000 Other taxes	**-4**	**21**	**17**	**60**	**-15**	**-8**	**0**	**0**	**0**	**0**
6100 Paid solely by business	0	0	0	0	0	0	0	0	0	0
6200 Other	-4	21	17	60	-15	-8	0	0	0	0
Incentive acts and other refunds	-8	14	-5	11	-15	-8	0	0	0	0
Other taxes	4	7	22	49	0	0	0	0	0	0

Note: Fiscal year ending on 30th June. For example, the data for 2018 represent July 2017 to June 2018.
The data for 2018 are preliminary and taken from the Central Bank of The Bahamas.
The figures exclude local government tax revenues as the data are not available.
Heading 2000: The data are estimated for 2017 and 2018.
Heading 2400: This heading includes refunds of social security contributions as reported by the National Insurance Board (NIB).
Heading 4400: All stamp taxes have been recorded under heading 4400 in this edition. They were previously recorded under heading 5120 and 6200.
Heading 5111: A value added tax was enforced on 1st January 2015.

Source: The Central Bank of The Bahamas; National Insurance Board of The Bahamas.

StatLink https://doi.org/10.1787/888934114457

Table 5.3. **Barbados**

Details of tax revenue / Ingresos tributarios detallados

Million BBD

	1990	2000	2007	2010	2013	2014	2015	2016	2017	2018
Total tax revenue	**1 026**	**1 892**	**2 824**	**2 736**	**2 757**	**2 715**	**2 813**	**3 041**	**3 218**	**3 385**
1000 Taxes on income, profits and capital gains	**250**	**599**	**947**	**766**	**657**	**678**	**714**	**802**	**783**	**921**
1100 Of individuals	140	293	335	395	379	441	433	492	463	482
1110 On income and profits	140	293	335	395	379	441	433	492	463	482
Personal income tax	140	293	335	395	365	413	397	488	463	482
Consolidation tax	0	0	0	0	14	28	36	3	0	0
1120 On capital gains	..	..	..	..	..	..	..	..	..	..
1200 Corporate	95	269	521	294	175	156	215	248	275	355
1210 On profits	95	269	521	294	175	156	215	248	275	355
1220 On capital gains	..	..	..	..	..	..	..	..	..	..
1300 Unallocable between 1100 and 1200	15	37	91	76	104	81	66	63	45	83
2000 Social security contributions	**134**	**295**	**487**	**565**	**598**	**532**	**546**	**547**	**562**	**572**
2100 Employees	..	..	..	..	..	..	..	..	..	..
2110 On a payroll basis	..	..	..	..	..	..	..	..	..	..
2120 On an income tax basis	..	..	..	..	..	..	..	..	..	..
2200 Employers	..	..	..	..	..	..	..	..	..	..
2210 On a payroll basis	..	..	..	..	..	..	..	..	..	..
2220 On an income tax basis	..	..	..	..	..	..	..	..	..	..
2300 Self-employed or non-employed	..	..	..	..	..	..	..	..	..	..
2310 On a payroll basis	..	..	..	..	..	..	..	..	..	..
2320 On an income tax basis	..	..	..	..	..	..	..	..	..	..
2400 Unallocable between 2100, 2200 and 2300	134	295	487	565	598	532	546	547	562	572
2410 On a payroll basis	..	..	..	..	..	..	..	..	..	..
2420 On an income tax basis	..	..	..	..	..	..	..	..	..	..
3000 Taxes on payroll and workforce	**0**	**0**	**0**	**0**	**0**	**0**	**0**	**0**	**0**	**0**
4000 Taxes on property	**147**	**108**	**125**	**130**	**168**	**207**	**143**	**145**	**148**	**172**
4100 Recurrent taxes on immovable property	46	95	103	118	156	196	133	135	138	161
Property tax	46	95	103	118	156	164	133	135	138	161
Municipal solid waste tax	0	0	0	0	0	32	0	0	0	0
4110 Households	..	..	..	..	..	..	..	..	..	..
4120 Others	..	..	..	..	..	..	..	..	..	..
4200 Recurrent taxes on net wealth	0	0	0	0	0	0	0	0	0	0
4210 Individual	..	..	..	..	..	..	..	..	..	..
4220 Corporate	..	..	..	..	..	..	..	..	..	..
4300 Estate, inheritance and gift taxes	0	0	0	0	0	0	0	0	0	0
4310 Estate and inheritance taxes	..	..	..	..	..	..	..	..	..	..
4320 Gift taxes	..	..	..	..	..	..	..	..	..	..
4400 Taxes on financial and capital transactions	101	13	22	12	12	11	10	9	11	11
Stamp duties	101	13	22	12	12	11	10	9	11	11
4500 Non-recurrent taxes	0	0	0	0	0	0	0	0	0	0
4510 On net wealth	..	..	..	..	..	..	..	..	..	..
4520 Other non-recurrent taxes	..	..	..	..	..	..	..	..	..	..
4600 Other recurrent taxes on property	0	0	0	0	0	0	0	0	0	0
5000 Taxes on goods and services	**495**	**889**	**1 265**	**1 276**	**1 334**	**1 298**	**1 410**	**1 547**	**1 726**	**1 719**
5100 Taxes on production, sale, transfer, etc	424	788	1 151	1 105	1 218	1 193	1 291	1 423	1 610	1 520
5110 General taxes	197	492	790	768	909	806	861	920	1 039	990
5111 Value added taxes	0	492	790	768	909	806	861	890	887	941
5112 Sales tax	197	0	0	0	0	0	0	29	152	49
Social responsibility levy	0	0	..	..	..	..	..	29	152	49
Consumption tax	197	0	..	..	..	..	..	0	0	0
5113 Other	0	0	0	0	0	0	0	0	0	0
5120 Taxes on specific goods and services	227	296	362	337	309	386	430	503	570	530
5121 Excises	91	175	164	146	115	136	169	226	303	271
Excises	0	160	164	146	115	136	169	226	303	271
Levies	91	15	0	0	0	0	0	0	0	0
5122 Profits of fiscal monopolies	0	0	0	0	0	0	0	0	0	0
5123 Customs and import duties	118	121	197	191	194	224	232	245	219	214
5124 Taxes on exports	0	0	0	0	0	0	0	0	0	0
5125 Taxes on investment goods	0	0	0	0	0	0	0	0	0	0
5126 Taxes on specific services	17	1	0	0	0	27	29	33	49	45
Hotel and restaurant tax	17	1	..	..	..	0	0	0	0	0
Banks and other asset tax	0	0	..	..	..	27	29	33	49	45
5127 Other taxes on internat. trade and transactions	0	0	0	0	0	0	0	0	0	0
5128 Other taxes	0	0	0	0	0	0	0	0	0	0
5130 Unallocable between 5110 and 5120	0	0	0	0	0	0	0	0	0	0
5200 Taxes on use of goods and perform activities	71	101	114	171	117	105	119	124	116	199
5210 Recurrent taxes	71	101	114	171	117	105	119	124	116	199
5211 Paid by households: motor vehicles	0	0	0	0	0	0	0	0	0	0

Table 5.3. **Barbados** *(cont.)*

Details of tax revenue / Ingresos tributarios detallados

Million BBD

	1990	2000	2007	2010	2013	2014	2015	2016	2017	2018
5212 Paid by others: motor vehicles	0	0	0	0	0	0	0	0	0	0
5213 Paid in respect of other goods	71	101	114	171	117	105	119	124	116	199
5220 Non-recurrent taxes	0	0	0	0	0	0	0	0	0	0
5300 Unallocable between 5100 and 5200	0	0	0	0	0	0	0	0	0	0
6000 Other taxes	**0**	**0**	**0**	**0**	**0**	**0**	**0**	**0**	**0**	**0**
6100 Paid solely by business	..	..	..	..	..	..	..	..	..	..
6200 Other	..	..	..	..	..	..	..	..	..	..

Note: Year ending 31st March. For example, the data for 2018 represent April 2018 to March 2019.

The data are on a cash basis.

The figures exclude local government tax revenues as the data are not available.

Tax revenues are revised with latest data from the Central Bank of Barbados and tax structure has been modified accordingly in this edition.

Heading 1300: This heading includes withholding taxes levied on both individuals and corporate entities.

Heading 2000: Social security contributions refer to contribution income of National Insurance Scheme obtained from Actuarial Reviews of the National Insurance, Unemployment and Severance Funds. Data for 2015-18 are intermediate projections in the 15th Actuarial Review.

Heading 5213: This heading includes miscellaneous indirect taxes levied on a recurrent basis such as revenues from various licenses.

Source: The Central Bank of Barbados; National Insurance Board of Barbados.

StatLink https://doi.org/10.1787/888934114476

Table 5.4. **Belize / Belice**

Details of tax revenue / Ingresos tributarios detallados

Million BZD

	1990	2000	2007	2010	2013	2014	2015	2016	2017	2018
Total tax revenue	**178**	**318**	**652**	**740**	**822**	**927**	**947**	**1 005**	**1 054**	**1 142**
1000 Taxes on income, profits and capital gains	**37**	**76**	**180**	**248**	**245**	**272**	**254**	**261**	**269**	**287**
1100 Of individuals	21	19	45	52	64	74	82	88	93	98
1110 On income and profits	21	19	45	52	64	74	82	88	93	98
Income tax (PAYE)	20	19	45	52	64	74	82	88	93	98
Income tax on individuals	1	0	0	0	0	0	0	0	0	0
1120 On capital gains	..	..	..	..	..	..	..	..	..	..
1200 Corporate	12	51	127	189	172	183	159	162	166	178
Income tax (companies)	12	1	11	51	18	16	1	0	0	2
Income tax (business tax)	0	51	115	138	150	167	158	162	166	176
Income tax (supplemental petroleum tax)	0	0	0	0	4	0	0	0	0	0
1210 On profits	..	..	..	..	..	..	..	..	..	..
1220 On capital gains	..	..	..	..	..	..	..	..	..	..
1300 Unallocable between 1100 and 1200	4	6	9	7	10	15	13	11	10	11
Income tax (arrears)	4	3	5	1	2	2	2	2	2	2
Income tax (withholding)	0	3	4	6	8	13	11	9	8	9
2000 Social security contributions	**10**	**18**	**53**	**60**	**67**	**72**	**77**	**80**	**83**	**87**
2100 Employees	..	..	..	..	..	..	..	..	..	..
2110 On a payroll basis	..	..	..	..	..	..	..	..	..	..
2120 On an income tax basis	..	..	..	..	..	..	..	..	..	..
2200 Employers	..	..	..	..	..	..	..	..	..	..
2210 On a payroll basis	..	..	..	..	..	..	..	..	..	..
2220 On an income tax basis	..	..	..	..	..	..	..	..	..	..
2300 Self-employed or non-employed	..	..	..	..	..	..	..	..	..	..
2310 On a payroll basis	..	..	..	..	..	..	..	..	..	..
2320 On an income tax basis	..	..	..	..	..	..	..	..	..	..
2400 Unallocable between 2100, 2200 and 2300	10	18	53	60	67	72	77	80	83	87
2410 On a payroll basis	..	..	..	..	..	..	..	..	..	..
2420 On an income tax basis	..	..	..	..	..	..	..	..	..	..
3000 Taxes on payroll and workforce	**0**	**0**	**0**	**0**	**0**	**0**	**0**	**0**	**0**	**0**
4000 Taxes on property	**34**	**13**	**31**	**23**	**31**	**35**	**35**	**31**	**32**	**47**
4100 Recurrent taxes on immovable property	1	2	7	7	6	6	5	7	6	6
4110 Households	1	2	7	7	6	6	5	7	6	6
4120 Others	0	0	0	0	0	0	0	0	0	0
4200 Recurrent taxes on net wealth	0	0	0	0	0	0	0	0	0	0
4210 Individual	..	..	..	..	..	..	..	..	..	..
4220 Corporate	..	..	..	..	..	..	..	..	..	..
4300 Estate, inheritance and gift taxes	0	0	0	0	0	0	0	0	0	0
4310 Estate and inheritance taxes	..	0	0	0	0	0	0	0	0	0
4320 Gift taxes	..	0	0	0	0	0	0	0	0	0
4400 Taxes on financial and capital transactions	33	11	24	16	25	29	29	25	26	40
Stamp duties on customs	28	0	0	0	0	0	0	0	0	0
Stamp duties (other departments)	5	11	24	16	25	29	29	25	26	40
4500 Non-recurrent taxes	0	0	0	0	0	0	0	0	0	0
4510 On net wealth	..	..	..	..	..	..	..	..	..	..
4520 Other non-recurrent taxes	..	..	..	..	..	..	..	..	..	..
4600 Other recurrent taxes on property	0	0	0	0	0	0	0	0	0	0
5000 Taxes on goods and services	**97**	**211**	**389**	**409**	**478**	**548**	**580**	**633**	**670**	**721**
5100 Taxes on production, sale, transfer, etc.	94	207	380	400	469	540	571	630	662	708
5110 General taxes	0	82	175	199	237	270	275	292	292	320
5111 Value added taxes	..	0	174	199	237	270	275	292	292	320
5112 Sales tax	..	82	0	0	0	0	0	0	0	0
5113 Other	..	0	0	0	0	0	0	0	0	0
5120 Taxes on specific goods and services	94	125	205	200	232	269	296	338	369	388
5121 Excises	35	47	72	31	35	38	39	159	187	190
Revenue replacement duty	18	39	49	7	13	15	15	1	1	1
Excise duties	17	8	22	22	21	22	23	157	186	189
Excise on locally refined petroleum products	0	0	0	0	0	0	1	0	1	0
Excise on locally extracted crude oil	0	0	0	1	2	1	0	1	0	1
5122 Profits of fiscal monopolies	0	0	0	0	0	0	0	0	0	0
5123 Customs and import duties	50	64	113	144	165	196	221	154	139	143
Import duties	50	64	92	123	140	167	190	123	98	101
Environmental tax	0	0	21	21	25	29	31	31	40	42
Imports into EPZs	0	0	0	0	0	0	0	0	0	0
5124 Taxes on exports	0	0	0	0	0	0	0	0	0	0
5125 Taxes on investment goods	0	0	0	0	0	0	0	0	0	0
5126 Taxes on specific services	0	0	0	0	0	0	0	0	0	0

Table 5.4. **Belize / Belice** *(cont.)*

Details of tax revenue / Ingresos tributarios detallados

Million BZD

	1990	2000	2007	2010	2013	2014	2015	2016	2017	2018
5127 Other taxes on internat. trade and transactions	8	14	21	25	32	35	35	24	43	55
Goods in transit - administration charge	3	1	1	1	1	1	1	1	1	1
Goods in transit - social fee	0	5	6	8	11	12	11	10	17	23
Taxes on foreign currency transactions	6	8	14	16	20	22	23	13	25	31
5128 Other taxes	0	0	0	0	0	0	0	0	0	0
5130 Unallocable between 5110 and 5120	0	0	0	0	0	0	0	0	0	0
5200 Taxes on use of goods and perform activities	3	4	8	9	9	9	9	3	9	13
5210 Recurrent taxes	3	4	8	9	9	9	9	3	9	13
5211 Paid by households: motor vehicles	2	3	6	3	4	4	4	0	5	0
5212 Paid by others: motor vehicles	0	0	0	0	0	0	0	0	0	0
5213 Paid in respect of other goods	1	1	3	6	6	5	5	3	4	13
5220 Non-recurrent taxes	0	0	0	0	0	0	0	0	0	0
5300 Unallocable between 5100 and 5200	0	0	0	0	0	0	0	0	0	0
6000 Other taxes	**0**	**0**	**0**	**0**	**0**	**0**	**0**	**0**	**0**	**0**
6100 Paid solely by business	..	..	..	..	..	..	..	..	..	..
6200 Other	..	..	..	..	..	..	..	..	..	..

Note: Year ending 31st March. For example, the data for 2018 represent April 2018 to March 2019.

The data are on a cash basis.

The data for 2018 represent the revised estimates for the 2018/19 fiscal year reported in the Approved Estimates of Revenue and Expenditure for Fiscal Year 2019/2020.

Heading 4400: Stamp duties on customs has been recorded under heading 4400 in this edition. It was previously recorded under heading 5123.

Heading 5213: Revenues from Oil mining & prospecting licenses and Mining fee have been removed from heading 5213 in this edition.

Source: Ministry of Finance of Belize; Social Security Board Belize.

StatLink https://doi.org/10.1787/888934114495

Table 5.5. **Bolivia**

Details of tax revenue / Ingresos tributarios detallados

Million BOB

	1990	2000	2007	2010	2013	2014	2015	2016	2017	2018
Total tax revenue	**1 005**	**10 504**	**22 912**	**31 549**	**56 629**	**63 508**	**67 264**	**65 492**	**67 072**	**70 634**
1000 Taxes on income, profits and capital gains	**68**	**1 209**	**3 433**	**6 294**	**11 644**	**12 723**	**12 809**	**10 876**	**10 152**	**10 591**
1100 Of individuals	68	214	217	263	364	439	508	496	502	525
1110 On income and profits	68	214	217	263	364	439	508	496	502	525
Value added supplementary scheme	62	161	195	237	333	401	461	442	441	475
Fiscal notes on value added supplementary scheme	6	53	23	26	31	38	47	55	61	50
1120 On capital gains	..	..	..	..	..	..	..	..	..	..
1200 Corporate	0	995	3 215	6 031	11 280	12 284	12 302	10 379	9 650	10 066
1210 On profits	..	995	3 215	6 031	11 280	12 284	12 302	10 379	9 650	10 066
Corporate tax	..	804	2 922	5 089	7 914	9 062	10 260	8 638	8 655	9 165
Fiscal notes on corporate tax	..	192	293	942	3 366	3 222	2 041	1 742	995	901
1220 On capital gains	..	..	..	..	..	..	..	..	..	..
1300 Unallocable between 1100 and 1200	0	0	0	0	0	0	0	0	0	0
2000 Social security contributions	**0**	**1 977**	**3 598**	**5 265**	**10 334**	**12 513**	**14 235**	**14 828**	**15 915**	**16 930**
2100 Employees	..	..	..	..	..	..	..	..	..	..
2110 On a payroll basis	..	..	..	..	..	..	..	..	..	..
2120 On an income tax basis	..	..	..	..	..	..	..	..	..	..
2200 Employers	..	..	..	..	..	..	..	..	..	..
2210 On a payroll basis	..	..	..	..	..	..	..	..	..	..
2220 On an income tax basis	..	..	..	..	..	..	..	..	..	..
2300 Self-employed or non-employed	..	..	..	..	..	..	..	..	..	..
2310 On a payroll basis	..	..	..	..	..	..	..	..	..	..
2320 On an income tax basis	..	..	..	..	..	..	..	..	..	..
2400 Unallocable between 2100, 2200 and 2300	..	1 977	3 598	5 265	10 334	12 513	14 235	14 828	15 915	16 930
2410 On a payroll basis	..	1 977	3 598	5 265	10 334	12 513	14 235	14 828	15 915	16 930
2420 On an income tax basis	..	0	0	0	0	0	0	0	0	0
3000 Taxes on payroll and workforce	**0**	**0**	**0**	**0**	**0**	**0**	**0**	**0**	**0**	**0**
4000 Taxes on property	**1**	**3**	**334**	**367**	**412**	**433**	**424**	**455**	**492**	**543**
4100 Recurrent taxes on immovable property	0	0	0	0	0	0	0	0	0	0
4110 Households	..	..	..	..	..	..	..	..	..	..
4120 Others	..	..	..	..	..	..	..	..	..	..
4200 Recurrent taxes on net wealth	0	0	0	0	0	0	0	0	0	0
4210 Individual	..	..	..	..	..	..	..	..	..	..
4220 Corporate	..	..	..	..	..	..	..	..	..	..
4300 Estate, inheritance and gift taxes	1	3	11	20	28	32	36	15	1	0
4310 Estate and inheritance taxes	1	3	11	20	28	32	36	15	1	0
4320 Gift taxes	0	0	0	0	0	0	0	0	0	0
4400 Taxes on financial and capital transactions	0	0	324	347	384	401	388	439	491	543
4500 Non-recurrent taxes	0	0	0	0	0	0	0	0	0	0
4510 On net wealth	..	..	..	..	..	..	..	..	..	..
4520 Other non-recurrent taxes	..	..	..	..	..	..	..	..	..	..
4600 Other recurrent taxes on property	0	0	0	0	0	0	0	0	0	0
5000 Taxes on goods and services	**907**	**6 697**	**14 261**	**17 791**	**30 994**	**33 910**	**34 759**	**33 441**	**34 022**	**35 215**
5100 Taxes on production, sale, transfer, etc.	907	6 697	14 261	17 791	30 994	33 910	34 759	33 441	34 022	35 215
5110 General taxes	584	3 955	9 568	12 541	22 736	24 714	25 247	24 327	24 591	25 615
5111 Value added taxes	432	2 949	7 487	10 259	19 033	20 580	20 756	19 902	20 199	20 977
VAT (internal market)	178	1 204	3 001	4 100	7 805	9 273	9 914	10 318	9 910	10 155
VAT (imports)	178	1 445	3 734	5 193	8 709	9 389	9 738	8 458	9 154	9 387
VAT fiscal notes (internal market)	56	223	654	581	783	760	666	622	439	411
VAT fiscal notes (imports)	20	76	99	385	1 736	1 158	438	504	696	1 024
5112 Sales tax	0	0	0	0	0	0	0	0	0	0
5113 Other	151	1 007	2 081	2 282	3 703	4 134	4 491	4 425	4 392	4 638
Transactions tax	136	943	1 905	2 174	3 587	4 081	4 463	4 386	4 323	4 547
Fiscal note on transactions tax	15	64	176	107	116	53	28	39	69	92
5120 Taxes on specific goods and services	324	2 742	4 693	5 250	8 258	9 196	9 511	9 114	9 430	9 600
5121 Excises	118	2 087	3 546	3 658	5 012	5 663	5 853	6 040	6 032	6 191
Excises (internal market)	61	244	598	933	1 468	1 365	1 486	1 687	1 450	1 649
Excises (Imports)	22	298	485	379	719	1 051	1 109	917	953	1 091
Special tax on hydrocarbons and derivatives	0	1 387	2 073	1 070	1 681	1 998	2 581	2 695	3 105	3 076
Fiscal notes on excises	35	118	119	155	47	328	262	103	442	272
Fiscal notes on special tax on hydrocarb. and deriv.	0	40	271	1 121	1 098	921	415	638	82	103
5122 Profits of fiscal monopolies	0	0	0	0	0	0	0	0	0	0
5123 Customs and import duties	204	640	1 114	1 545	2 849	3 102	3 254	2 893	3 198	3 185
Customs and import duties	163	616	1 079	1 504	2 663	2 879	3 057	2 786	3 043	2 937
Fiscal notes on customs and import duties	41	24	34	41	186	223	197	107	155	248
5124 Taxes on exports	0	0	0	0	0	0	0	0	0	0
5125 Taxes on investment goods	0	0	0	0	0	0	0	0	0	0

Table 5.5. **Bolivia** *(cont.)*

Details of tax revenue / Ingresos tributarios detallados

Million BOB

	1990	2000	2007	2010	2013	2014	2015	2016	2017	2018
5126 Taxes on specific services	2	15	33	47	91	120	127	175	200	224
Air departure tax	2	15	33	47	71	90	102	116	122	128
Tax on gambling	0	0	0	0	20	30	25	59	78	96
5127 Other taxes on internat. trade and transactions	0	0	0	0	306	311	277	6	0	0
5128 Other taxes	0	0	0	0	0	0	0	0	0	0
5130 Unallocable between 5110 and 5120	0	0	0	0	0	0	0	0	0	0
5200 Taxes on use of goods and perform activities	0	0	0	0	0	0	0	0	0	0
5210 Recurrent taxes	..	..	..	..	..	..	..	..	..	..
5211 Paid by households: motor vehicles	..	..	..	..	..	..	..	..	..	..
5212 Paid by others: motor vehicles	..	..	..	..	..	..	..	..	..	..
5213 Paid in respect of other goods	..	..	..	..	..	..	..	..	..	..
5220 Non-recurrent taxes	..	..	..	..	..	..	..	..	..	..
5300 Unallocable between 5100 and 5200	0	0	0	0	0	0	0	0	0	0
6000 Other taxes	**30**	**617**	**1 286**	**1 832**	**3 245**	**3 929**	**5 037**	**5 893**	**6 491**	**7 355**
6100 Paid solely by business	4	6	8	12	17	20	25	35	30	33
Simplified tax regime	3	6	8	12	17	20	25	35	30	33
Integrated tax system	1	0	0	0	0	0	0	0	0	0
6200 Other	25	611	1 278	1 819	3 228	3 908	5 012	5 858	6 461	7 322
Municipal taxes	0	575	961	1 381	1 955	2 145	2 585	3 073	3 737	4 496
Other taxes	20	35	279	422	1 241	1 716	2 378	2 696	2 685	2 784
Fiscal notes on other taxes	3	0	31	3	9	25	23	63	8	9
Unified agricultural regime	2	1	7	14	23	23	26	27	31	32

Note: Year ending 31st December.

The data are on a cash basis.

Tax revenues are revised with latest data from the Ministerio de Economía y Finanzas Públicas de Bolivia and Unidad de Análisis de Políticas Sociales y Económicas in this edition. Tax structure has been modified accordingly. Local tax revenues for 2018 are estimated.

Heading 1210: Corporate tax under heading 1210 includes revenues from IUE (corporate tax), IUE-RE (corporate tax remittances) and IUM (mining profits) in this edition.

Heading 2000: The figures in this edition include social security contributions to Bolivia's pension system and healthcare related funds. For healthcare related funds, the contributions for 2018 are estimated.

Heading 5113: This heading includes both IT (transactions tax) and its fiscal notes in this edition.

Heading 5127: This heading includes IVME (tax on the sales of foreign currency).

Heading 6200: The municipal taxes are estimated in 2018. Other taxes include revenues from conceptos varios (miscellaneous concepts), programa transitorio (transitional programme) and otros ingresos en efectivo (other cash revenue). Fiscal notes on other taxes include fiscal notes on conceptos varios.

Source: Ministerio de Economía y Finanzas Públicas de Bolivia (Ministry of Economy and Public Finance of Bolivia); Unidad de Análisis de Políticas Sociales y Económicas (Social and Economic Policy Analysis Unit).

StatLink https://doi.org/10.1787/888934114514

Table 5.6. **Brazil / Brasil**

Details of tax revenue / Ingresos tributarios detallados

Million BRL

	1990	2000	2007	2010	2013	2014	2015	2016	2017	2018
Total tax revenue	**3**	**352 041**	**945 265**	**1 253 617**	**1 724 287**	**1 828 452**	**1 911 727**	**2 006 054**	**2 113 150**	**2 278 765**
1000 Taxes on income, profits and capital gains	**1**	**68 667**	**193 022**	**258 738**	**360 561**	**381 844**	**400 993**	**453 127**	**458 312**	**489 863**
1100 Of individuals	0	3 406	60 332	87 828	126 018	140 420	148 739	161 833	177 377	193 089
1110 On income and profits	0	3 406	60 332	87 828	126 018	140 420	148 739	161 833	177 377	193 089
Withholding income tax (IRRF)	0	0	47 626	71 579	101 830	114 638	121 540	133 549	146 872	160 576
Other personal income taxes	0	3 406	12 706	16 248	24 188	25 782	27 199	28 285	30 504	32 513
1120 On capital gains	..	..	..	..	..	..	..	..	..	..
1200 Corporate	0	25 430	99 062	128 255	171 003	171 352	164 057	197 941	184 501	194 814
1210 On profits	0	25 430	99 062	128 255	171 003	171 352	164 057	197 941	184 501	194 814
Corporate income tax	0	16 680	65 767	82 474	109 316	109 020	104 910	131 181	113 815	119 063
Social contribution on net profits (CSLL)	0	8 750	33 295	45 780	61 687	62 332	59 147	66 760	70 686	75 751
1220 On capital gains	..	..	..	..	..	..	..	..	..	..
1300 Unallocable between 1100 and 1200	0	39 831	33 629	42 656	63 540	70 072	88 196	93 353	96 434	101 961
Withholding tax on non-resident income (remittances abroad)	..	..	7 862	11 537	18 582	19 703	24 669	24 892	27 270	35 337
Withholding tax on capital income	..	..	21 367	24 887	37 121	41 288	53 692	59 404	59 470	53 585
Withholding tax on other income	..	..	4 400	6 232	7 837	9 082	9 836	9 057	9 694	13 039
2000 Social security contributions	**1**	**83 469**	**213 918**	**315 789**	**443 927**	**481 296**	**501 944**	**526 445**	**555 054**	**579 228**
2100 Employees	..	..	..	..	..	..	..	..	..	..
2110 On a payroll basis	..	..	..	..	..	..	..	..	..	..
2120 On an income tax basis	..	..	..	..	..	..	..	..	..	..
2200 Employers	0	18 709	43 602	64 271	98 045	108 782	118 323	124 713	128 743	124 428
2210 On a payroll basis	0	18 709	43 602	64 271	98 045	108 782	118 323	124 713	128 743	124 428
2220 On an income tax basis	0	0	0	0	0	0	0	0	0	0
2300 Self-employed or non-employed	..	..	..	..	..	..	..	..	..	..
2310 On a payroll basis	..	..	..	..	..	..	..	..	..	..
2320 On an income tax basis	..	..	..	..	..	..	..	..	..	..
2400 Unallocable between 2100, 2200 and 2300	1	64 760	170 317	251 519	345 882	372 514	383 622	401 732	426 311	454 800
2410 On a payroll basis	1	64 760	170 317	251 519	345 882	372 514	383 622	401 732	426 311	454 800
2420 On an income tax basis	0	0	0	0	0	0	0	0	0	0
3000 Taxes on payroll and workforce	**0**	**5 437**	**13 680**	**20 974**	**31 912**	**35 295**	**37 192**	**37 901**	**39 085**	**41 800**
Payroll-based contribution to education	0	2 791	7 089	11 049	16 561	18 411	19 039	19 473	20 010	21 979
"S" System contributions	0	2 646	6 592	9 925	15 351	16 884	18 153	18 428	19 075	19 820
4000 Taxes on property	**0**	**23 524**	**61 867**	**52 841**	**68 068**	**72 635**	**83 672**	**85 931**	**91 664**	**103 608**
4100 Recurrent taxes on immovable property	0	4 753	13 140	17 929	24 760	27 673	32 626	35 459	39 700	47 388
Tax on rural land property (ITR)	0	234	317	485	764	900	1 105	1 126	1 273	1 419
Tax on urban land property (IPTU)	0	4 519	12 822	17 444	23 996	26 773	31 521	34 333	38 427	45 970
4110 Households	..	..	..	..	..	..	..	..	..	..
4120 Others	..	..	..	..	..	..	..	..	..	..
4200 Recurrent taxes on net wealth	0	0	0	0	0	0	0	0	0	0
4210 Individual	..	..	..	..	..	..	..	..	..	..
4220 Corporate	..	..	..	..	..	..	..	..	..	..
4300 Estate, inheritance and gift taxes	0	329	1 207	2 518	4 142	4 698	6 461	7 345	7 242	8 162
4310 Estate and inheritance taxes	..	..	..	..	..	..	..	..	..	..
4320 Gift taxes	..	..	..	..	..	..	..	..	..	..
4400 Taxes on financial and capital transactions	0	18 442	47 520	32 393	39 166	40 263	44 586	43 126	44 722	48 057
Tax on financial operations (IOF)	0	3 096	7 818	26 571	29 417	29 756	34 681	33 645	34 660	36 615
Tax on real estate property transfers (ITBI)	0	950	3 383	5 840	9 749	10 507	9 904	9 482	10 062	11 442
Other	0	14 396	36 320	-18	0	0	0	0	0	0
4500 Non-recurrent taxes	0	0	0	0	0	0	0	0	0	0
4510 On net wealth	..	..	..	..	..	..	..	..	..	..
4520 Other non-recurrent taxes	..	..	..	..	..	..	..	..	..	..
4600 Other recurrent taxes on property	0	0	0	0	0	0	0	0	0	0
5000 Taxes on goods and services	**2**	**169 181**	**404 839**	**576 335**	**778 666**	**812 437**	**840 087**	**849 682**	**912 634**	**1 004 186**
5100 Taxes on production, sale, transfer, etc	2	163 887	388 317	552 138	745 446	776 015	799 627	806 346	868 824	960 379
5110 General taxes	1	136 743	334 672	482 405	659 215	684 312	703 349	721 364	777 737	854 677
5111 Value added taxes	1	82 279	187 190	268 117	363 190	384 287	396 428	413 175	441 039	480 524
Tax on the circulation of goods and services (ICMS)	1	82 279	187 190	268 117	363 190	384 287	396 428	413 175	441 039	480 524
5112 Sales tax	0	0	0	0	0	0	0	0	0	0
5113 Other	0	54 464	147 482	214 288	296 025	300 025	306 921	308 189	336 698	374 153
Contribution to COFINS	0	38 707	100 946	140 939	197 545	194 696	199 876	201 517	221 670	244 287
Contribution to PIS	0	8 339	21 813	30 714	41 745	41 950	42 632	42 808	47 051	51 678
Contribution to PASEP	0	1 312	4 049	9 880	8 775	9 491	9 958	10 026	11 574	12 272
Tax on general services (ISS)	0	6 106	20 673	32 756	47 960	53 888	54 455	53 838	56 403	65 916
5120 Taxes on specific goods and services	0	27 144	53 645	69 732	86 231	91 703	96 278	84 982	91 086	105 703

Table 5.6. **Brazil / Brasil** (*cont.*)

Details of tax revenue / Ingresos tributarios detallados

Million BRL

	1990	2000	2007	2010	2013	2014	2015	2016	2017	2018
5121 Excises	0	18 699	39 241	45 053	43 657	49 227	51 320	47 853	52 863	57 949
Vehicles	..	..	5 229	5 787	3 799	4 940	4 367	3 299	4 467	5 713
Beverages	..	..	2 589	2 431	3 455	3 401	2 599	2 684	2 944	2 768
Tobacco	..	..	2 800	3 704	5 117	5 688	5 692	5 718	5 210	5 208
Fuels	..	..	7 943	7 759	734	26	3 271	6 001	5 821	3 963
Other excises	..	..	20 681	25 372	30 552	35 172	35 391	30 150	34 421	40 297
5122 Profits of fiscal monopolies	0	0	0	0	0	0	0	0	0	0
5123 Customs and import duties	0	8 445	12 157	21 072	36 829	36 612	38 870	31 308	32 284	40 575
5124 Taxes on exports	0	0	61	47	144	162	99	139	66	129
5125 Taxes on investment goods	0	0	0	0	0	0	0	0	0	0
5126 Taxes on specific services	0	0	1 381	2 349	3 367	3 204	3 005	2 741	2 862	2 988
Merchant marine renewal tax (AFRMM)	..	..	1 381	2 349	3 367	3 204	3 005	2 741	2 862	2 988
5127 Other taxes on internat. trade and transactions	0	0	805	1 212	2 233	2 499	2 983	2 940	3 011	4 062
CIDE on remittances abroad	..	..	805	1 212	2 233	2 499	2 983	2 940	3 011	4 062
5128 Other taxes	0	0	0	0	0	0	0	0	0	0
5130 Unallocable between 5110 and 5120	0	0	0	0	0	0	0	0	0	0
5200 Taxes on use of goods and perform activities	0	5 294	16 523	24 197	33 220	36 422	40 460	43 336	43 810	43 807
5210 Recurrent taxes	0	5 294	16 523	24 197	33 220	36 422	40 460	43 336	43 810	43 807
5211 Paid by households: motor vehicles	0	5 294	16 523	24 197	33 220	36 422	40 460	43 336	43 810	43 807
Motor vehicle property tax (IPVA)	0	5 294	14 627	21 367	29 232	32 453	36 219	39 093	40 509	41 495
Contributions to DPVAT	0	0	1 896	2 830	3 988	3 969	4 242	4 243	3 302	2 312
5212 Paid by others: motor vehicles	0	0	0	0	0	0	0	0	0	0
5213 Paid in respect of other goods	0	0	0	0	0	0	0	0	0	0
5220 Non-recurrent taxes	0	0	0	0	0	0	0	0	0	0
5300 Unallocable between 5100 and 5200	0	0	0	0	0	0	0	0	0	0
6000 Other taxes	**0**	**1 763**	**57 938**	**28 941**	**41 154**	**44 945**	**47 839**	**52 968**	**56 401**	**60 080**
6100 Paid solely by business	0	0	307	0	0	0	0	0	0	0
Revenue service development fund (FUNDAF)	..	..	307	..	..	..	..	..	..	..
6200 Other	0	1 763	57 631	28 941	41 154	44 945	47 839	52 968	56 401	60 080

Note: Year ending 31st December.

The data are on a cash basis.

Heading 2000: Contributions to costs of military pensions are classified under heading 2000 in this edition. They were previously under heading 3000.

Heading 3000: Contributions to labour union are removed in this edition as they are voluntary contributions. They were previously under heading 3000.

Heading 4100: Tax on rural land property and tax on urban land property are classified under heading 4100 in this edition as they are levied on both individuals and corporations. They were previously under heading 4120.

Heading 4300: Tax on inheritance and donations is classified under heading 4300 in this edition. It was previously under heading 4310.

Heading 5113: Contributions to COFINS, PIS and PASEP are classified under heading 5113 in this edition as they are levied on gross revenues and income of corporations. Contributions to COFINS and PIS were previously under heading 5112. Contributions to PASEP were previously under heading 3000. Contributions to PASEP are included in contributions to PIS before 2000 as they cannot be distinguished.

Heading 5121: Tax on industrialised products (IPI) is classified under heading 5121 in this edition as it is a tax on specific goods. It has been renamed "other excises" and its values correspond to the remaining IPI in addition to IPI on vehicles, beverages and tobacco. It was previously under heading 5111.

Heading 5124: Tax on exports is classified under heading 5124 in this edition. It was previously under heading 5123. Tax on exports before 2002 is included in tax on imports as they cannot be distinguished.

Heading 5126: The figure for 2018 is estimated.

Heading 5127: CIDE on remittances abroad is classified under heading 5127 in this edition. It was previously under heading 5128.

Heading 5210: Administrative fees for state governments are removed in this edition. They were previously under heading 5210.

Heading 5211: Motor vehicle property tax (IPVA) is classified under heading 5211 in this edition. It was previously under heading 4600. Contributions to DPVAT are added under heading 5211 in this edition.

Heading 6100: Contributions to FUNDAF after 2008 are included in heading 6200.

Heading 6200: Administrative fees for federal government are removed in this edition. They were previously under heading 6200. The figure for 2018 is estimated.

Source: Ministério da Fazenda (Ministry of Finance); Secretaria do Tesouro Nacional (National Treasury Secretariat).

StatLink https://doi.org/10.1787/888934114533

Table 5.7. **Chile**

Details of tax revenue / Ingresos tributarios detallados

Million CLP

	1990	2000	2007	2010	2013	2014	2015	2016	2017	2018
Total tax revenue	**1 777 218**	**7 901 998**	**20 598 963**	**21 845 693**	**27 381 686**	**29 145 219**	**32 532 354**	**34 129 307**	**36 238 557**	**40 297 426**
1000 Taxes on income, profits and capital gains	**412 974**	**1 841 630**	**9 412 056**	**8 329 060**	**9 520 709**	**9 628 037**	**11 840 521**	**11 444 570**	**12 516 154**	**14 418 859**
1100 Of individuals	99 154	604 100	989 348	1 492 837	1 964 172	2 114 296	3 199 876	2 990 653	3 500 023	2 701 416
Second category tax	65 552	490 980	993 129	1 449 099	1 981 699	2 140 345	2 350 120	2 458 249	2 585 694	2 848 205
Global complementary tax	33 603	113 120	-3 781	43 738	-17 527	-26 050	-36 757	-213 365	50 495	-146 789
Others	0	0	0	0	0	0	886 513	745 769	863 834	0
1110 On income and profits	..	..	..	..	..	..	..	..	..	..
1120 On capital gains	..	..	..	..	..	..	..	..	..	..
1200 Corporate	219 586	882 896	6 054 487	4 448 745	6 041 089	6 196 077	6 839 133	7 146 657	7 658 420	8 920 497
First category tax	200 891	815 747	5 084 996	3 913 870	5 473 355	5 182 214	6 183 830	6 689 101	7 049 471	7 836 379
Surtax on state owned enterprises	16 074	47 634	113 334	194 203	124 220	100 851	132 352	88 362	193 058	184 442
Mining tax	0	0	835 452	298 558	324 577	801 647	323 507	105 653	101 970	184 382
Other	2 621	19 516	20 705	42 114	118 937	111 365	199 444	263 541	313 921	715 293
1210 On profits	..	..	..	..	..	..	..	..	..	..
1220 On capital gains	..	..	..	..	..	..	..	..	..	..
1300 Unallocable between 1100 and 1200	94 233	354 634	2 368 221	2 387 478	1 515 449	1 317 664	1 801 512	1 307 260	1 357 711	2 796 947
Additional tax	59 082	350 301	1 462 715	1 414 057	1 337 721	1 454 847	1 429 758	1 331 564	1 453 577	2 127 948
Other	35 151	4 332	905 507	973 421	177 727	-137 183	371 755	-24 304	-95 865	668 998
2000 Social security contributions	**159 559**	**576 758**	**1 148 647**	**1 493 987**	**1 968 973**	**2 110 087**	**2 252 489**	**2 441 419**	**2 627 558**	**2 786 173**
2100 Employees	154 021	553 937	1 098 620	1 433 159	1 906 340	2 044 356	2 188 575	2 373 777	2 553 916	2 703 261
2110 On a payroll basis	154 021	553 937	1 098 620	1 433 159	1 906 340	2 044 356	2 188 575	2 373 777	2 553 916	2 703 261
2120 On an income tax basis	0	0	0	0	0	0	0	0	0	..
2200 Employers	5 538	22 821	50 027	60 828	62 633	65 731	63 914	67 642	73 643	82 912
2210 On a payroll basis	5 538	22 821	50 027	60 828	62 633	65 731	63 914	67 642	73 643	82 912
2220 On an income tax basis	0	0	0	0	0	0	0	0	0	..
2300 Self-employed or non-employed	0	0	0	0	0	0	0	0	0	0
2310 On a payroll basis	..	..	..	..	..	..	..	..	..	..
2320 On an income tax basis	..	..	..	..	..	..	..	..	..	..
2400 Unallocable between 2100, 2200 and 2300	0	0	0	0	0	0	0	0	0	0
2410 On a payroll basis	..	..	..	..	..	..	..	..	..	..
2420 On an income tax basis	..	..	..	..	..	..	..	..	..	..
3000 Taxes on payroll and workforce	**0**	**0**	**0**	**0**	**0**	**0**	**0**	**0**	**0**	**0**
4000 Taxes on property	**109 319**	**554 037**	**1 013 571**	**898 607**	**1 133 765**	**1 228 961**	**1 421 274**	**1 731 723**	**1 950 217**	**2 071 113**
4100 Recurrent taxes on immovable property	59 968	302 244	496 311	662 368	840 842	924 062	1 056 920	1 171 399	1 229 195	1 357 743
4110 Households	..	..	..	..	..	..	..	..	..	..
4120 Others	..	..	..	..	..	..	..	..	..	..
4200 Recurrent taxes on net wealth	0	0	0	0	0	0	0	0	0	0
4210 Individual	..	..	..	..	..	..	..	..	..	..
4220 Corporate	..	..	..	..	..	..	..	..	..	..
4300 Estate, inheritance and gift taxes	3 444	10 906	28 501	39 338	45 550	31 340	92 236	100 490	202 376	125 649
4310 Estate and inheritance taxes	..	..	..	..	..	..	..	..	..	..
4320 Gift taxes	..	..	..	..	..	..	..	..	..	..
4400 Taxes on financial and capital transactions	45 907	240 886	488 759	196 901	247 373	273 559	272 118	459 834	518 645	587 721
4500 Non-recurrent taxes	0	0	0	0	0	0	0	0	0	0
4510 On net wealth	..	..	..	..	..	..	..	..	..	..
4520 Other non-recurrent taxes	..	..	..	..	..	..	..	..	..	..
4600 Other recurrent taxes on property	0	0	0	0	0	0	0	0	0	..
5000 Taxes on goods and services	**1 118 722**	**5 041 769**	**9 023 666**	**11 185 156**	**14 779 915**	**16 127 855**	**17 597 378**	**18 629 617**	**19 858 881**	**21 468 973**
5100 Taxes on production, sale, transfer, etc	1 074 009	4 789 827	8 578 636	10 532 904	13 869 529	15 131 675	16 515 485	17 449 222	18 597 180	19 951 557
5110 General taxes	664 421	3 306 350	6 781 501	8 399 926	11 170 794	12 133 710	13 273 958	14 073 050	15 069 540	16 211 646
5111 Value added taxes	664 421	3 306 350	6 781 501	8 399 926	11 170 794	12 133 710	13 273 958	14 073 050	15 069 540	16 211 646
5112 Sales tax	0	0	0	0	0	0	0	0	0	..
5113 Other	0	0	0	0	0	0	0	0	0	..
5120 Taxes on specific goods and services	409 588	1 483 477	1 797 135	2 132 978	2 698 735	2 997 965	3 241 527	3 376 172	3 527 640	3 739 911
5121 Excises	166 050	816 160	1 299 844	1 561 205	1 987 475	2 224 223	2 412 773	2 568 863	2 682 659	2 796 033
Cigarettes and tobacco	60 604	283 275	455 595	647 637	815 991	856 595	981 422	1 009 034	978 696	981 456
Gasoline and diesel	105 445	532 885	844 249	913 568	1 171 483	1 361 724	1 388 218	1 502 039	1 629 561	1 727 392
Oil stabilisation fund	0	0	0	0	0	0	0	0	0	0
Fisheries Law Extraction Rights	0	0	0	0	0	5 890	8 558	9 998	11 749	19 623
Additional tax on new motor vehicles	0	0	0	0	0	14	34 575	47 792	62 654	67 561
5122 Profits of fiscal monopolies	0	0	0	0	0	0	0	0	0	0
5123 Customs and import duties	222 486	548 571	300 416	267 331	303 393	337 839	343 491	308 871	321 156	347 555
5124 Taxes on exports	0	0	0	0	0	0	0	0	0	0
5125 Taxes on investment goods	0	0	0	0	0	0	0	0	0	0
5126 Taxes on specific services	21 052	118 746	196 875	304 442	407 867	435 903	485 263	498 438	523 824	596 323
5127 Other taxes on internat. trade and transactions	0	0	0	0	0	0	0	0	0	0
5128 Other taxes	0	0	0	0	0	0	0	0	0	0
5130 Unallocable between 5110 and 5120	0	0	0	0	0	0	0	0	0	0

Table 5.7. **Chile** *(cont.)*

Details of tax revenue / Ingresos tributarios detallados

Million CLP

	1990	2000	2007	2010	2013	2014	2015	2016	2017	2018
5200 Taxes on use of goods and perform activities	44 714	251 942	445 030	652 252	910 386	996 180	1 081 893	1 180 395	1 261 702	1 517 416
5210 Recurrent taxes	44 714	251 942	445 030	652 252	910 386	996 180	1 081 893	1 180 395	1 261 702	1 402 064
Motor vehicles	24 469	93 880	155 158	218 219	330 754	365 316	397 608	434 137	482 009	539 639
5211 Paid by households: motor vehicles	0	0	0	0	0	0	0	0	0	..
5212 Paid by others: motor vehicles	0	0	0	0	0	0	0	0	0	..
5213 Paid in respect of other goods	20 245	158 062	289 872	434 033	579 632	630 864	684 285	746 258	779 693	862 425
Municipal permits	18 401	136 138	263 996	396 944	527 955	578 671	630 943	692 974	725 954	806 975
Mining patents	3 374	34 730	25 184	36 213	50 094	50 448	51 767	51 641	52 254	53 854
Other	-1 530	-12 806	692	876	1 583	1 745	1 575	1 643	1 485	1 596
5220 Non-recurrent taxes	0	0	0	0	0	0	0	0	0	115 352
Tax on polluting fixed sources	0	0	0	0	0	0	0	0	0	115 352
5300 Unallocable between 5100 and 5200	0	0	0	0	0	0	0	0	0	0
6000 Other taxes	**-23 356**	**-112 195**	**1 023**	**-61 117**	**-21 676**	**50 279**	**-579 308**	**-118 021**	**-714 253**	**-447 692**
6100 Paid solely by business	0	0	0	0	0	0	0	0	0	..
6200 Other	-23 356	-112 195	1 023	-61 117	-21 676	50 279	-579 308	-118 021	-714 253	-447 692

Note: Year ending 31st December.

The data are on a cash basis.

Heading 5121: In ECLAC data, figures from the Oil Prices Stabilisation Fund (FEPP) are considered as non-tax revenues.

Source: Servicio de Impuestos Internos (Chile's Tax Service).

StatLink https://doi.org/10.1787/888934114552

Table 5.8. **Colombia**

Details of tax revenue / Ingresos tributarios detallados

Million COP

	1990	2000	2007	2010	2013	2014	2015	2016	2017	2018
Total tax revenue	**2 579 426**	**30 598 630**	**82 697 457**	**98 455 335**	**142 976 023**	**149 150 432**	**160 056 025**	**164 800 001**	**174 735 823**	**190 299 911**
1000 Taxes on income, profits and capital gains	**771 694**	**7 103 525**	**24 010 404**	**26 218 852**	**47 743 096**	**50 083 349**	**52 656 876**	**54 326 726**	**57 615 236**	**64 043 928**
1100 Of individuals	47 210	1 499 345	4 751 580	5 192 384	7 787 050	8 344 422	9 736 861	9 833 084	10 367 606	12 215 963
1110 On income and profits	47 210	1 499 345	4 751 580	5 192 384	7 787 050	8 344 422	9 736 861	9 833 084	10 367 606	12 215 963
1120 On capital gains	..	..	..	..	..	..	..	..	..	..
1200 Corporate	359 758	5 119 828	18 427 899	20 405 209	38 788 077	40 435 726	41 070 208	42 351 554	44 970 528	48 529 320
1210 On profits	359 758	5 119 828	18 427 899	20 405 209	38 788 077	40 435 726	41 070 208	42 351 554	44 970 528	48 529 320
Income tax	359 758	5 119 828	18 427 899	20 405 209	35 848 498	27 974 251	27 144 039	28 240 820	40 124 337	48 396 597
Pro Equity Income Tax - CREE	0	0	0	0	2 939 579	12 461 475	13 926 169	14 110 734	4 846 190	132 723
1220 On capital gains	..	..	..	..	..	..	..	..	..	..
1300 Unallocable between 1100 and 1200	364 726	484 352	830 925	621 258	1 167 968	1 303 200	1 849 807	2 142 087	2 277 102	3 298 645
Income tax	364 726	484 352	830 925	621 258	1 167 968	1 303 200	1 849 807	2 142 087	2 277 102	3 298 645
Pro Equity Income Tax - CREE	0	0	0	0	0	0	0	0	0	0
2000 Social security contributions	**203 596**	**4 989 000**	**9 694 000**	**11 478 085**	**16 644 445**	**13 715 710**	**13 585 138**	**15 443 016**	**13 351 711**	**18 192 049**
2100 Employees	..	..	..	..	..	..	..	..	..	..
2110 On a payroll basis	..	..	..	..	..	..	..	..	..	..
2120 On an income tax basis	..	..	..	..	..	..	..	..	..	..
2200 Employers	..	..	..	..	..	..	..	..	..	..
2210 On a payroll basis	..	..	..	..	..	..	..	..	..	..
2220 On an income tax basis	..	..	..	..	..	..	..	..	..	..
2300 Self-employed or non-employed	..	..	..	..	..	..	..	..	..	..
2310 On a payroll basis	..	..	..	..	..	..	..	..	..	..
2320 On an income tax basis	..	..	..	..	..	..	..	..	..	..
2400 Unallocable between 2100, 2200 and 2300	203 596	4 989 000	9 694 000	11 478 085	16 644 445	13 715 710	13 585 138	15 443 016	13 351 711	18 192 049
2410 On a payroll basis	203 596	4 989 000	9 694 000	11 478 085	16 644 445	13 715 710	13 585 138	15 443 016	13 351 711	18 192 049
2420 On an income tax basis	0	0	0	0	0	0	0	0	0	0
3000 Taxes on payroll and workforce	**0**	**1 286 803**	**2 798 906**	**4 022 503**	**3 527 459**	**2 627 958**	**2 797 308**	**2 998 237**	**3 200 238**	**3 461 352**
4000 Taxes on property	**56 160**	**2 027 654**	**6 459 259**	**8 535 238**	**14 907 909**	**15 984 365**	**18 156 105**	**18 090 331**	**17 950 494**	**15 265 472**
4100 Recurrent taxes on immovable property	56 160	991 070	2 298 829	3 338 935	4 735 321	5 424 320	6 061 965	6 571 134	7 310 244	7 981 989
4110 Households	0	0	0	0	0	0	0	0	0	0
4120 Others	56 160	991 070	2 298 829	3 338 935	4 735 321	5 424 320	6 061 965	6 571 134	7 310 244	7 981 989
4200 Recurrent taxes on net wealth	0	0	1 170 908	1 970 530	4 274 832	4 118 075	5 352 940	4 440 142	3 868 595	467 925
4210 Individual	..	..	1 170 908	1 970 530	4 274 832	4 118 075	5 352 940	4 440 142	3 868 595	467 925
4220 Corporate	..	..	0	0	0	0	0	0	0	0
4300 Estate, inheritance and gift taxes	0	0	0	0	0	0	0	0	0	0
4310 Estate and inheritance taxes	..	..	..	..	..	..	..	..	..	..
4320 Gift taxes	..	..	..	..	..	..	..	..	..	..
4400 Taxes on financial and capital transactions	0	1 036 584	2 989 522	3 225 773	5 897 755	6 441 969	6 741 200	7 079 055	6 771 655	6 815 558
4500 Non-recurrent taxes	0	0	0	0	0	0	0	0	0	0
4510 On net wealth	..	..	..	..	..	..	..	..	..	..
4520 Other non-recurrent taxes	..	..	..	..	..	..	..	..	..	..
4600 Other recurrent taxes on property	0	0	0	0	0	0	0	0	0	0
5000 Taxes on goods and services	**1 388 653**	**14 180 450**	**36 766 741**	**44 411 642**	**55 285 569**	**60 969 982**	**65 610 838**	**66 962 420**	**75 381 123**	**81 408 789**
5100 Taxes on production, sale, transfer, etc	1 388 653	14 048 655	36 447 297	44 038 074	54 326 006	59 908 784	64 582 352	65 786 951	74 003 567	79 935 336
5110 General taxes	672 368	9 585 866	26 910 512	33 333 802	40 479 366	45 197 474	48 579 171	49 355 123	58 565 799	64 316 019
5111 Value added taxes	583 078	8 445 776	23 377 821	28 811 682	34 642 822	38 749 869	41 553 967	41 878 886	50 619 849	55 879 110
5112 Sales tax	89 290	1 140 090	3 532 691	4 522 121	5 836 544	6 447 605	7 025 204	7 476 238	7 945 950	8 436 909
Industry and commerce tax (State)	89 290	1 140 090	3 532 691	4 522 121	5 836 544	6 447 605	7 025 204	7 476 238	7 945 950	8 436 909
5113 Other	0	0	0	0	0	0	0	0	0	0
5120 Taxes on specific goods and services	716 285	4 462 789	9 536 785	10 704 271	13 846 640	14 711 310	16 003 181	16 431 827	15 437 768	15 619 317
5121 Excises	404 699	2 718 692	5 276 999	6 052 273	9 949 457	10 724 586	11 412 250	12 318 641	11 616 844	12 061 132
Oil	141 270	833 004	1 211 511	1 418 766	2 883 410	2 980 883	3 297 392	3 335 157	1 352 793	1 517 546
Tobacco (State)	52 898	213 412	330 016	390 472	496 513	481 589	524 357	595 476	887 534	1 145 879
Beer (State)	85 722	471 135	1 203 838	1 432 453	2 031 349	2 108 721	2 305 895	2 549 949	2 572 771	2 637 674
Liquors (State)	124 808	520 394	834 390	929 328	1 292 743	1 345 827	1 253 466	1 574 864	1 907 802	1 800 605
Restaurant, vehicles sale and mobile telephony	0	0	0	0	1 181 998	1 648 467	1 684 179	1 700 069	1 948 718	2 047 419
Carbon	0	0	0	0	0	0	0	0	474 596	288 373
Plastic bags	0	0	0	0	0	0	0	0	6 546	28 099
Medicinal cannabis	0	0	0	0	0	0	0	0	10	3
Diesel surcharge	0	85 716	388 091	500 405	572 022	579 952	598 993	590 233	546 243	579 613
Petrol surcharge	0	595 031	1 309 154	1 380 848	1 491 423	1 579 147	1 747 969	1 972 893	1 919 830	2 015 922
5122 Profits of fiscal monopolies	0	0	0	0	0	0	0	0	0	0
5123 Customs and import duties	311 586	1 744 097	4 259 786	4 651 999	3 897 184	3 986 724	4 590 931	4 113 187	3 820 924	3 558 185
Custom duties	180 989	1 744 097	4 259 786	4 651 999	3 897 184	3 986 724	4 590 931	4 113 187	3 820 924	3 558 185
Imports surcharge	130 597	0	0	0	0	0	0	0	0	0
5124 Taxes on exports	0	0	0	0	0	0	0	0	0	0
5125 Taxes on investment goods	0	0	0	0	0	0	0	0	0	0
5126 Taxes on specific services	0	0	0	0	0	0	0	0	0	0

Table 5.8. **Colombia** *(cont.)*

Details of tax revenue / Ingresos tributarios detallados

Million COP

	1990	2000	2007	2010	2013	2014	2015	2016	2017	2018
5127 Other taxes on internat. trade and transactions	0	0	0	0	0	0	0	0	0	0
5128 Other taxes	0	0	0	0	0	0	0	0	0	0
5130 Unallocable between 5110 and 5120	0	0	0	0	0	0	0	0	0	0
5200 Taxes on use of goods and perform activities	0	131 795	319 444	373 568	959 563	1 061 198	1 028 485	1 175 469	1 377 556	1 473 453
5210 Recurrent taxes	..	131 795	319 444	373 568	959 563	1 061 198	1 028 485	1 175 469	1 377 556	1 473 453
5211 Paid by households: motor vehicles	..	131 795	319 444	373 568	959 563	1 061 198	1 028 485	1 175 469	1 377 556	1 473 453
Tax on motor vehicle ownership	..	131 795	319 444	373 568	959 563	1 061 198	1 028 485	1 175 469	1 377 556	1 473 453
5212 Paid by others: motor vehicles	..	0	0	0	0	0	0	0	0	0
5213 Paid in respect of other goods	..	0	0	0	0	0	0	0	0	0
5220 Non-recurrent taxes	..	0	0	0	0	0	0	0	0	0
5300 Unallocable between 5100 and 5200	0	0	0	0	0	0	0	0	0	0
6000 Other taxes	**159 323**	**1 011 197**	**2 968 147**	**3 789 014**	**4 867 545**	**5 769 069**	**7 249 761**	**6 979 271**	**7 237 021**	**7 928 320**
6100 Paid solely by business	0	0	0	0	0	0	0	0	0	0
6200 Other	159 323	1 011 197	2 968 147	3 789 014	4 867 545	5 769 069	7 249 761	6 979 271	7 237 021	7 928 320
Stamp tax	0	401 497	759 787	357 160	58 378	72 425	105 729	97 492	75 493	79 868
Other	78 306	79 287	86 297	126 602	200 465	260 721	318 271	357 863	403 473	461 160
Other (sub-national)	81 017	530 413	2 122 062	3 305 252	4 608 702	5 435 923	6 825 762	6 523 916	6 758 055	7 387 293

Note: "Year ending 31st December.

The data are on a cash basis.

Includes the reported consolidated revenues of the territorial entities (departments and municipalities).

Headings 1100 and 1200: The data are estimated.

Heading 2000: Before 2013, social security contributions did not include all the contributions entering FOSYGA (Solidarity and Guarantee Fund). Only the portion of the contributions used to finance the subsidised regime (up to 1.5 pp of the 12.5% of the monthly wage paid by employers and employees as an obligatory health contribution) was included. The part of the contributions entering FOSYGA to finance the contributory regime was classified in the social security sector as "other incomes". From 2013 onwards, all of the health contributions entering FOSYGA are classified as social security contributions. The portion of the contributions not entering FOSYGA that is both collected and spent by the health insurers – EPS - is not part of the fiscal accounts.

Heading 5121: The data includes the Petrol surcharge (previously classified under heading 6200 (Other taxes)) and the Diesel Surcharge (previously not recorded in the total tax revenues).The Diesel surcharge revenues feed into an extra-budgetary fund and are considered as tax revenues according to the OECD classification, described in the Interpretative Guide in Annex A. Colombia does not include revenues from the diesel surcharge in their total tax revenues as these revenues do not feed into budget revenues.

Heading 5211: The data includes the tax on motor vehicle ownership (previously classified under heading 6200 (Other taxes))."

Source: Dirección de Impuestos y Aduanas Nacionales de Colombia, Ministerio de Hacienda y Crédito Público y Banco Central de Colombia. (National Tax and Customs Administration, Ministry of Finance and Public Credit and Central Bank of Colombia).

StatLink https://doi.org/10.1787/888934114571

Table 5.9. **Costa Rica**

Details of tax revenue / Ingresos tributarios detallados

Million CRC

	1990	2000	2007	2010	2013	2014	2015	2016	2017	2018
Total tax revenue	**117 711**	**978 114**	**3 213 401**	**4 382 367**	**5 851 096**	**6 330 931**	**6 923 575**	**7 528 752**	**7 893 642**	**8 339 991**
1000 Taxes on income, profits and capital gains	**11 820**	**128 805**	**531 552**	**748 093**	**1 014 440**	**1 091 470**	**1 247 308**	**1 416 218**	**1 562 063**	**1 699 258**
1100 Of individuals	..	..	123 194	202 849	316 894	349 139	386 241	414 247	446 519	483 645
1110 On income and profits	..	..	123 194	202 849	316 894	349 139	386 241	414 247	446 519	483 645
1120 On capital gains	..	..	..	..	..	..	..	..	..	..
1200 Corporate	..	..	348 826	450 312	545 183	574 137	659 951	742 011	843 879	915 284
1210 On profits	..	..	348 826	450 312	545 183	574 137	659 951	742 011	843 879	915 284
1220 On capital gains	..	..	..	..	..	..	..	..	..	..
1300 Unallocable between 1100 and 1200	11 820	128 805	59 531	94 932	152 363	168 194	201 116	259 961	271 664	300 330
2000 Social security contributions	**33 990**	**297 069**	**885 053**	**1 450 531**	**1 928 082**	**2 114 124**	**2 305 133**	**2 539 755**	**2 640 785**	**2 859 467**
2100 Employees	..	..	..	..	..	..	..	..	..	..
2110 On a payroll basis	..	..	..	..	..	..	..	..	..	..
2120 On an income tax basis	..	..	..	..	..	..	..	..	..	..
2200 Employers	3 447	37 313	107 398	207 206	272 706	294 486	318 652	331 124	361 161	368 865
Government contributions	3 447	37 313	107 398	207 206	272 706	294 486	318 652	331 124	361 161	368 865
2210 On a payroll basis	..	..	..	..	..	..	..	..	..	..
2220 On an income tax basis	..	..	..	..	..	..	..	..	..	..
2300 Self-employed or non-employed	..	..	..	..	..	..	..	..	..	..
2310 On a payroll basis	..	..	..	..	..	..	..	..	..	..
2320 On an income tax basis	..	..	..	..	..	..	..	..	..	..
2400 Unallocable between 2100, 2200 and 2300	30 543	259 756	777 654	1 243 325	1 655 376	1 819 638	1 986 481	2 208 631	2 279 624	2 490 602
Contributions by employees and non-government employers	30 543	249 182	727 844	1 139 265	1 511 383	1 648 831	1 785 522	1 985 151	2 042 620	2 242 663
Contributions for the special regimes	0	10 574	49 811	104 060	143 993	170 806	200 959	223 480	237 004	247 939
2410 On a payroll basis	..	..	..	..	..	..	..	..	..	..
2420 On an income tax basis	..	..	..	..	..	..	..	..	..	..
3000 Taxes on payroll and workforce	**7 575**	**61 796**	**170 996**	**260 664**	**352 755**	**388 869**	**423 616**	**453 369**	**471 206**	**498 577**
Contributions by non-government employers	7 484	59 129	165 677	248 259	337 696	372 869	406 296	435 328	453 128	478 523
Contributions by government employers	91	2 666	5 320	12 405	15 059	16 000	17 321	18 041	18 078	20 054
4000 Taxes on property	**1 566**	**8 396**	**42 658**	**63 706**	**99 030**	**114 313**	**123 261**	**134 332**	**145 955**	**149 310**
4100 Recurrent taxes on immovable property	1 200	5 390	23 293	48 963	70 785	81 613	90 003	97 869	107 156	113 586
Land tax	0	0	0	0	0	0	0	0	0	0
Additional land tax	0	0	0	0	0	0	0	0	0	0
Tax on sumptuary constructions	0	0	0	0	0	0	0	0	0	0
Immovable property tax	0	0	0	3 527	3 998	4 013	4 076	4 098	4 255	4 468
Municipal immovable property tax	1 200	5 390	23 293	45 436	66 787	77 600	85 927	93 771	102 901	109 119
4110 Households	..	..	..	..	..	..	..	..	..	..
4120 Others	..	..	..	..	..	..	..	..	..	..
4200 Recurrent taxes on net wealth	0	0	0	0	0	0	0	0	0	0
4210 Individual	..	..	..	..	..	..	..	..	..	..
4220 Corporate	..	..	..	..	..	..	..	..	..	..
4300 Estate, inheritance and gift taxes	0	0	0	0	0	0	0	0	0	0
4310 Estate and inheritance taxes	..	..	..	..	..	..	..	..	..	..
4320 Gift taxes	..	..	..	..	..	..	..	..	..	..
4400 Taxes on financial and capital transactions	366	3 007	19 366	14 743	28 246	32 700	33 258	36 462	38 799	35 724
4500 Non-recurrent taxes	0	0	0	0	0	0	0	0	0	0
4510 On net wealth	..	..	..	..	..	..	..	..	..	..
4520 Other non-recurrent taxes	..	..	..	..	..	..	..	..	..	..
4600 Other recurrent taxes on property	0	0	0	0	0	0	0	0	0	0
5000 Taxes on goods and services	**53 509**	**456 851**	**1 505 510**	**1 766 914**	**2 302 986**	**2 468 087**	**2 661 902**	**2 794 229**	**2 875 333**	**2 918 471**
5100 Taxes on production, sale, transfer, etc	49 867	425 713	1 406 100	1 600 302	2 092 588	2 222 962	2 388 900	2 508 186	2 575 411	2 608 864
5110 General taxes	21 326	222 775	797 850	920 298	1 212 471	1 306 110	1 368 601	1 420 938	1 466 986	1 513 677
5111 Value added taxes	21 326	222 775	797 850	920 298	1 176 745	1 266 798	1 336 075	1 414 358	1 453 348	1 487 620
5112 Sales tax	0	0	0	0	0	0	0	0	0	0
5113 Other	0	0	0	0	35 726	39 313	32 526	6 580	13 638	26 057
5120 Taxes on specific goods and services	28 541	202 939	608 250	680 004	880 117	916 851	1 020 299	1 087 248	1 108 425	1 095 187
5121 Excises	11 096	157 204	447 168	523 617	689 528	706 016	798 412	846 864	870 225	858 424
Fuels and energy	0	0	250 577	320 638	404 210	404 901	457 827	472 644	510 260	517 666
Alcohol beverages	0	8 229	23 802	28 035	35 254	36 293	43 095	43 400	43 176	45 610
Non alcoholic beverages	0	0	18 263	26 566	32 519	34 874	36 353	39 764	39 781	40 182
Soaps	0	0	883	1 317	1 989	1 493	2 562	2 912	2 332	2 712
Cement	0	0	0	227	291	340	304	267	311	289
Tobacco	0	0	0	0	38 860	32 277	33 681	32 560	30 590	30 766
Abolished specific taxes on production and consumption	0	0	0	0	0	0	0	0	0	0
Other specific taxes on consumption	11 096	148 975	153 643	146 834	176 405	195 838	224 590	255 317	243 775	221 200
5122 Profits of fiscal monopolies	0	0	0	0	0	0	0	0	0	0

Table 5.9. **Costa Rica** *(cont.)*

Details of tax revenue / Ingresos tributarios detallados

Million CRC

	1990	2000	2007	2010	2013	2014	2015	2016	2017	2018
5123 Customs and import duties	15 052	40 485	134 576	126 134	154 576	169 120	174 568	185 544	179 188	175 368
Import duties	13 977	32 336	107 565	103 851	130 634	142 226	148 666	158 559	152 756	149 017
Custom duties	1 075	8 149	27 011	22 284	23 942	26 894	25 902	26 986	26 432	26 351
5124 Taxes on exports	2 113	2 238	2 432	3 973	4 877	4 853	4 468	5 073	5 638	5 468
Export duties	2 113	2 088	2 260	3 816	4 104	3 067	2 701	3 250	3 673	3 594
Export duties Law 133	0	0	0	0	0	0	0	0	0	0
Export duties Law 5519	0	0	0	0	0	0	0	0	0	0
Tax on banana exports	0	150	172	157	168	176	156	184	199	193
Export duties on ground transportation	0	0	0	0	605	1 610	1 611	1 638	1 766	1 682
5125 Taxes on investment goods	0	0	0	0	0	0	0	0	0	0
5126 Taxes on specific services	280	2 929	23 242	24 767	28 571	34 081	38 687	44 934	48 290	50 554
Casinos and gambling	0	225	442	445	1 019	940	1 455	1 609	891	1 060
Port cargo movements	0	6	0	0	0	0	0	0	0	0
Overseas departure tax	0	0	22 799	24 322	27 552	33 141	37 232	43 325	47 399	49 494
10% on public shows	0	0	0	0	0	0	0	0	0	0
Pro-national airport's stamp tax	0	0	0	0	0	0	0	0	0	0
Stamp tax on the use of borders and ports	280	2 697	0	0	0	0	0	0	0	0
5127 Other taxes on internat. trade and transactions	0	83	832	1 513	2 565	2 782	3 093	3 512	3 695	3 785
5128 Other taxes	0	0	0	0	0	0	1 071	1 320	1 389	1 589
5130 Unallocable between 5110 and 5120	0	0	0	0	0	0	0	0	0	0
5200 Taxes on use of goods and perform activities	3 642	31 138	99 410	166 612	210 398	245 125	273 003	286 044	299 922	309 607
5210 Recurrent taxes	3 642	31 138	99 410	166 612	210 398	245 125	273 003	286 044	299 922	309 607
5211 Paid by households: motor vehicles	0	0	0	0	0	0	0	0	0	0
5212 Paid by others: motor vehicles	1 425	15 374	52 511	94 102	113 727	130 000	145 894	156 517	164 034	171 523
Property tax on vehicles, aircraft and boats	1 425	15 374	52 511	94 102	113 727	130 000	145 894	156 517	164 034	171 523
5213 Paid in respect of other goods	2 217	15 763	46 899	72 510	96 671	115 125	127 109	129 527	135 888	138 084
Local taxes	1 262	11 898	43 874	68 808	91 163	110 120	122 248	124 862	130 639	132 514
Hunting and fishing licences	0	0	0	0	0	0	0	0	0	0
Spirits licence	0	0	0	0	0	0	0	0	0	0
Revenue stamps	955	3 866	3 025	3 702	5 508	5 005	4 861	4 664	5 249	5 571
Sport stamp tax	0	0	0	0	0	0	0	0	0	0
5220 Non-recurrent taxes	0	0	0	0	0	0	0	0	0	0
5300 Unallocable between 5100 and 5200	0	0	0	0	0	0	0	0	0	0
6000 Other taxes	**9 251**	**25 198**	**77 632**	**92 460**	**153 803**	**154 069**	**162 355**	**190 850**	**198 300**	**214 908**
6100 Paid solely by business	0	0	0	0	0	0	0	0	0	0
6200 Other	9 251	25 198	77 632	92 460	153 803	154 069	162 355	190 850	198 300	214 908
Transfers of vehicles, aircraft and boats	497	2 530	9 937	12 311	17 177	19 099	20 999	23 022	21 872	22 265
Tax revenue from decentralised units	2 764	15 048	22 257	29 969	45 700	46 591	49 334	67 584	68 127	63 329
Other taxes	5 990	7 620	45 438	50 180	90 926	88 379	92 022	100 243	108 302	129 314

Note: Year ending 31st December.

The data are on a cash basis.

The local government tax revenues data have been expanded and start in 1990 in this edition.

Heading 2000: In ECLAC data, social security contributions also include INA (National Institute of Apprenticeship), IMAS (Joint Social Aid Institute), and FODESAF (Social Development and Family Allowances Fund).

Heading 3000: In Costa Rica and for ECLAC, social security contributions from decentralised institutions are classified under heading 2000.

Heading 5212: In ECLAC data, tax on ownership of vehicles, aircraft and boats is classified in category 4000.

Heading 5213: This includes local tax revenue previously classified under heading 5126 up to 2011 and under heading 5130 from 2012.

Heading 6200: The figures have been revised and include the tax revenue of decentralised bodies (other than social security contributions) that was not accounted for in previous editions. The tax revenue of decentralised bodies is classified under central government for this publication. In Costa Rica this revenue is classified under a separate unit (decentralised) considered to be separate from the central government.

In ECLAC data, the tax on the transfer of used vehicles Law No. 7088 of 30/11/87 is classified as a property tax.

Source: Secretaría Técnica de la Autoridad Presupuestaria, Ministerio de Finanzas y Contraloría General de la República (Technical Secretary of the Budgeting Authority, Ministry of Finance and National General Comptroller).

StatLink https://doi.org/10.1787/888934114590

Table 5.10. **Cuba**

Details of tax revenue / Ingresos tributarios detallados

Million CUP

	1990	2000	2007	2010	2013	2014	2015	2016	2017	2018
Total tax revenue	**6 265**	**11 367**	**25 787**	**23 949**	**28 173**	**29 940**	**33 182**	**37 597**	**41 021**	**42 307**
1000 Taxes on income, profits and capital gains	**14**	**1 826**	**3 403**	**3 603**	**5 292**	**5 995**	**6 676**	**8 018**	**9 931**	**11 094**
1100 Of individuals	14	291	404	554	1 055	1 308	1 848	2 343	3 279	4 002
1110 On income and profits	..	..	..	..	..	..	..	..	..	..
1120 On capital gains	..	..	..	..	..	..	..	..	..	..
1200 Corporate	0	1 535	2 999	3 049	4 237	4 687	4 828	5 675	6 651	7 092
1210 On profits	..	..	..	..	..	..	..	..	..	..
1220 On capital gains	..	..	..	..	..	..	..	..	..	..
1300 Unallocable between 1100 and 1200	0	0	0	0	0	0	0	0	0	0
2000 Social security contributions	**691**	**1 181**	**2 412**	**2 974**	**3 123**	**3 622**	**4 322**	**4 710**	**5 108**	**5 206**
2100 Employees	..	..	..	..	..	..	..	..	..	..
2110 On a payroll basis	..	..	..	..	..	..	..	..	..	..
2120 On an income tax basis	..	..	..	..	..	..	..	..	..	..
2200 Employers	..	..	..	..	..	..	..	..	..	..
2210 On a payroll basis	..	..	..	..	..	..	..	..	..	..
2220 On an income tax basis	..	..	..	..	..	..	..	..	..	..
2300 Self-employed or non-employed	..	..	..	..	..	..	..	..	..	..
2310 On a payroll basis	..	..	..	..	..	..	..	..	..	..
2320 On an income tax basis	..	..	..	..	..	..	..	..	..	..
2400 Unallocable between 2100, 2200 and 2300	691	1 181	2 412	2 974	3 123	3 622	4 322	4 710	5 108	5 206
2410 On a payroll basis	691	1 181	2 412	2 974	3 123	3 622	4 322	4 710	5 108	5 206
2420 On an income tax basis	0	0	0	0	0	0	0	0	0	0
3000 Taxes on payroll and workforce	**0**	**970**	**3 417**	**4 414**	**3 424**	**2 939**	**2 753**	**2 411**	**1 385**	**1 273**
4000 Taxes on property	**0**	**0**	**0**	**0**	**0**	**0**	**0**	**0**	**0**	**0**
4100 Recurrent taxes on immovable property	..	..	..	..	..	..	..	..	..	..
4110 Households	..	..	..	..	..	..	..	..	..	..
4120 Others	..	..	..	..	..	..	..	..	..	..
4200 Recurrent taxes on net wealth	..	..	..	..	..	..	..	..	..	..
4210 Individual	..	..	..	..	..	..	..	..	..	..
4220 Corporate	..	..	..	..	..	..	..	..	..	..
4300 Estate, inheritance and gift taxes	..	..	..	..	..	..	..	..	..	..
4310 Estate and inheritance taxes	..	..	..	..	..	..	..	..	..	..
4320 Gift taxes	..	..	..	..	..	..	..	..	..	..
4400 Taxes on financial and capital transactions	..	..	..	..	..	..	..	..	..	..
4500 Non-recurrent taxes	..	..	..	..	..	..	..	..	..	..
4510 On net wealth	..	..	..	..	..	..	..	..	..	..
4520 Other non-recurrent taxes	..	..	..	..	..	..	..	..	..	..
4600 Other recurrent taxes on property	..	..	..	..	..	..	..	..	..	..
5000 Taxes on goods and services	**5 443**	**6 732**	**15 875**	**12 283**	**15 588**	**15 912**	**17 742**	**20 309**	**22 055**	**21 969**
5100 Taxes on production, sale, transfer, etc	5 443	6 732	15 875	12 283	15 588	15 912	17 742	20 309	22 055	21 969
5110 General taxes	5 017	6 131	14 464	10 525	14 057	14 171	15 611	17 690	17 961	17 623
5111 Value added taxes	0	0	0	0	0	0	0	0	0	0
5112 Sales tax	5 017	6 131	14 464	10 525	14 057	14 171	15 611	17 690	17 961	17 623
5113 Other	0	0	0	0	0	0	0	0	0	0
5120 Taxes on specific goods and services	426	602	1 412	1 758	1 531	1 740	2 131	2 618	4 094	4 346
5121 Excises	..	..	..	..	..	..	..	..	..	..
5122 Profits of fiscal monopolies	..	..	..	..	..	..	..	..	..	..
5123 Customs and import duties	..	..	..	..	..	..	..	..	..	..
5124 Taxes on exports	..	..	..	..	..	..	..	..	..	..
5125 Taxes on investment goods	..	..	..	..	..	..	..	..	..	..
5126 Taxes on specific services	..	..	..	..	..	..	..	..	..	..
5127 Other taxes on internat. trade and transactions	..	..	..	..	..	..	..	..	..	..
5128 Other taxes	..	..	..	..	..	..	..	..	..	..
5130 Unallocable between 5110 and 5120	0	0	0	0	0	0	0	0	0	0
5200 Taxes on use of goods and perform activities	0	0	0	0	0	0	0	0	0	0
5210 Recurrent taxes	..	..	..	..	..	..	..	..	..	..
5211 Paid by households: motor vehicles	..	..	..	..	..	..	..	..	..	..
5212 Paid by others: motor vehicles	..	..	..	..	..	..	..	..	..	..
5213 Paid in respect of other goods	..	..	..	..	..	..	..	..	..	..
5220 Non-recurrent taxes	..	..	..	..	..	..	..	..	..	..
5300 Unallocable between 5100 and 5200	0	0	0	0	0	0	0	0	0	0
6000 Other taxes	**117**	**657**	**681**	**675**	**747**	**1 472**	**1 690**	**2 149**	**2 543**	**2 766**
6100 Paid solely by business	..	..	..	..	..	..	..	..	..	..
6200 Other	..	..	..	..	..	..	..	..	..	..

Note: Year ending 31st December.

The data are on a cash basis.

The figures for the sub-category under the heading 5120 are not available.

National tax revenues are no longer presented as central government tax revenues in this edition as central and local government data are added between 2002 and 2012.

There are minor discrepancies between national tax revenue data and the sum of central tax revenues and local tax revenues mainly due to different rounding methods.

Heading 5112: Taxes on circulation and sales (Impuesto de circulación y sobre Ventas) are larger for national data than the combined central and local data by approximately CUP 538.8 million in 2012.

Source: Ministerio de Finanzas y Precios de la República de Cuba (Ministry of Finance and Prices of the Republic of Cuba); Oficina Nacional de Estadísticas de Cuba (National Statistics Office of Cuba).

StatLink https://doi.org/10.1787/888934114609

Table 5.11. **Dominican Republic / República Dominicana**

Details of tax revenue / Ingresos tributarios detallados

Million DOP

	1990	2000	2007	2010	2013	2014	2015	2016	2017	2018
Total tax revenue	**6 424**	**48 310**	**217 960**	**243 942**	**355 314**	**393 157**	**414 245**	**453 191**	**500 583**	**557 681**
1000 Taxes on income, profits and capital gains	**1 670**	**10 782**	**55 232**	**53 643**	**108 853**	**125 098**	**119 819**	**135 700**	**155 024**	**170 561**
1100 Of individuals	..	4 088	14 665	17 088	27 147	31 525	35 549	40 193	43 553	51 425
1110 On income and profits	..	4 070	14 577	16 901	26 723	31 119	35 187	39 775	43 097	51 031
1120 On capital gains	..	18	87	187	424	406	361	418	456	394
1200 Corporate	..	4 679	29 203	21 475	58 923	72 865	61 695	69 362	83 047	88 079
1210 On profits	..	4 605	29 063	21 325	58 597	72 628	61 455	69 079	82 785	87 822
1220 On capital gains	..	74	140	151	326	238	240	283	262	257
Casinos	..	59	140	151	187	173	184	228	237	228
Racetracks	..	15	0	0	0	0	0	0	0	0
Phone gaming	..	0	0	0	139	64	56	55	25	30
1300 Unallocable between 1100 and 1200	1 670	2 015	11 365	15 080	22 782	20 708	22 576	26 144	28 425	31 057
2000 Social security contributions	**53**	**490**	**860**	**1 845**	**1 552**	**1 515**	**1 483**	**1 550**	**2 635**	**2 514**
2100 Employees	..	..	775	1 720	1 408	1 355	1 321	1 392	1 535	..
2110 On a payroll basis	..	..	..	..	..	..	..	..	..	..
2120 On an income tax basis	..	..	..	..	..	..	..	..	..	..
2200 Employers	..	..	85	125	144	160	163	158	1 099	..
2210 On a payroll basis	..	..	..	..	..	..	..	..	..	..
2220 On an income tax basis	..	..	..	..	..	..	..	..	..	..
2300 Self-employed or non-employed	..	..	0	0	0	0	0	0	0	..
2310 On a payroll basis	..	..	..	..	..	..	..	..	..	..
2320 On an income tax basis	..	..	..	..	..	..	..	..	..	..
2400 Unallocable between 2100, 2200 and 2300	53	490	0	0	0	0	0	0	0	2 514
2410 On a payroll basis	53	490	..	..	..	..	..	..	..	2 514
2420 On an income tax basis	0	0	..	..	..	..	..	..	..	0
3000 Taxes on payroll and workforce	**0**	**0**	**0**	**0**	**0**	**0**	**0**	**0**	**0**	**0**
4000 Taxes on property	**74**	**689**	**9 996**	**13 315**	**22 928**	**18 183**	**19 044**	**20 717**	**22 942**	**25 716**
4100 Recurrent taxes on immovable property	9	115	594	555	1 518	1 579	1 755	1 871	2 166	2 527
4110 Households	9	115	594	555	1 518	1 579	1 755	1 871	2 166	2 527
4120 Others	0	0	0	0	0	0	0	0	0	0
4200 Recurrent taxes on net wealth	0	0	1 281	2 449	8 666	3 458	3 445	3 544	4 113	4 609
Tax on assets	..	..	1 281	2 449	3 337	3 454	3 445	3 544	4 113	4 609
4210 Individual	..	..	..	..	..	..	..	..	..	..
4220 Corporate	..	..	..	..	5 329	4	..	..	..	..
4300 Estate, inheritance and gift taxes	11	96	143	231	315	325	418	388	455	526
4310 Estate and inheritance taxes	..	..	..	..	..	..	..	..	..	..
4320 Gift taxes	..	..	..	..	..	..	..	..	..	..
4400 Taxes on financial and capital transactions	40	377	7 375	8 658	11 209	11 394	12 067	13 265	13 995	15 675
Tax on checks	0	0	3 833	4 262	5 168	5 620	5 951	6 591	7 117	8 139
Real estate operations	22	217	3 291	3 864	5 236	4 876	5 169	5 668	5 802	6 320
Tax on the transfer of immovable property	18	160	252	533	805	898	947	1 005	1 076	1 215
4500 Non-recurrent taxes	3	32	270	488	412	677	591	681	711	553
4510 On net wealth	3	32	270	488	412	677	591	681	711	553
4520 Other non-recurrent taxes	0	0	0	0	0	0	0	0	0	0
4600 Other recurrent taxes on property	11	70	333	934	810	751	769	969	1 503	1 827
5000 Taxes on goods and services	**4 467**	**35 853**	**150 325**	**175 139**	**221 981**	**248 361**	**273 898**	**295 223**	**319 980**	**358 888**
5100 Taxes on production, sale, transfer, etc	4 398	35 135	143 884	168 641	214 540	239 526	263 435	282 288	306 680	344 706
5110 General taxes	970	9 912	66 613	81 226	112 731	130 447	147 039	159 212	169 629	194 725
5111 Value added taxes	970	9 912	66 613	81 226	112 731	130 447	147 039	159 212	169 629	194 725
5112 Sales tax	0	0	0	0	0	0	0	0	0	0
5113 Other	0	0	0	0	0	0	0	0	0	0
5120 Taxes on specific goods and services	3 429	25 224	77 271	87 415	101 809	109 080	116 396	123 076	137 051	149 981
5121 Excises	495	6 614	47 888	56 024	68 434	72 399	74 586	78 105	89 681	97 278
Alcoholic beverages	251	2 451	13 101	15 054	17 969	19 779	22 371	23 617	25 694	28 882
Tobacco products	102	469	3 284	4 529	4 356	4 382	4 532	4 117	5 120	4 355
Petroleum products	89	3 143	29 985	34 598	42 222	44 335	43 315	45 698	53 075	57 053
Other excises	52	551	1 518	1 843	3 887	3 904	4 367	4 674	5 792	6 988
5122 Profits of fiscal monopolies	0	0	0	0	0	0	0	0	0	0
5123 Customs and import duties	1 548	13 459	19 337	19 455	19 043	21 315	25 212	27 286	28 703	32 096
Import duties	615	13 456	19 336	19 455	18 916	21 238	24 378	26 397	27 276	30 931
Others	933	3	1	0	126	76	834	889	1 426	1 165
5124 Taxes on exports	6	4	83	146	34	12	8	0	0	0
5125 Taxes on investment goods	0	0	0	0	0	0	0	0	0	0

Table 5.11. **Dominican Republic / República Dominicana** *(cont.)*

Details of tax revenue / Ingresos tributarios detallados

Million DOP

	1990	2000	2007	2010	2013	2014	2015	2016	2017	2018
5126 Taxes on specific services	344	1 590	9 211	11 411	13 863	14 956	16 245	17 361	18 287	20 173
Telecommunications	85	0	3 867	4 886	5 897	6 129	6 375	6 607	6 781	7 146
Insurance premiums	33	584	2 211	3 088	3 674	3 965	4 301	4 828	5 236	5 976
Departure tax	204	809	3 131	3 428	4 283	4 839	5 535	5 892	6 252	6 933
Hotels	22	191	0	0	0	0	0	0	0	0
Others	0	7	2	9	9	24	35	34	18	119
5127 Other taxes on internat. trade and transactions	1 037	3 556	753	379	436	397	346	323	380	435
Exchange commission	857	3 412	233	70	0	0	0	0	0	0
Consular fees	77	32	342	132	143	142	137	149	153	153
Others	103	112	178	176	293	256	209	174	227	281
5128 Other taxes	0	0	0	0	0	0	0	0	0	0
5130 Unallocable between 5110 and 5120	0	0	0	0	0	0	0	0	0	0
5200 Taxes on use of goods and perform activities	69	718	6 441	6 498	7 442	8 835	10 463	12 935	13 300	14 182
5210 Recurrent taxes	69	718	2 301	2 265	2 569	2 736	2 958	3 365	3 553	3 804
5211 Paid by households: motor vehicles	45	268	1 391	1 277	1 073	1 289	1 558	1 932	2 081	2 310
5212 Paid by others: motor vehicles	0	0	0	0	0	0	0	0	0	0
5213 Paid in respect of other goods	24	450	910	988	1 496	1 447	1 400	1 433	1 472	1 494
Licences to carry firearms	17	237	316	296	240	200	171	190	176	192
Licences to operate gambling houses	0	114	217	211	1 229	1 221	1 208	1 210	1 250	1 262
Licences to operate slot machines	4	60	371	458	0	0	0	0	0	0
Others	4	39	7	24	28	26	21	34	46	41
5220 Non-recurrent taxes	0	0	4 140	4 234	4 872	6 099	7 505	9 570	9 747	10 378
Vehicle property registration	..	..	4 140	4 234	4 595	5 683	6 990	8 903	9 072	9 667
Ecological taxes	..	..	0	0	277	416	515	667	675	711
5300 Unallocable between 5100 and 5200	0	0	0	0	0	0	0	0	0	0
6000 Other taxes	**159**	**495**	**1 546**	**0**	**0**	**1**	**1**	**1**	**1**	**1**
6100 Paid solely by business	0	0	0	..	0	0	0	0	0	0
6200 Other	159	495	1 546	..	0	1	1	1	1	1

Note: Year ending 31st December.

The data are on a cash basis.

The figures exclude local government tax revenues as the data are not available.

Heading 2000: The data exclude social security contributions to general government managed by the private sector. An additional breakdown is available since 2015 to discern between social security contributions paid by employees and those paid by employers.

Source: Ministerio de Hacienda (Ministry of Finance).

StatLink https://doi.org/10.1787/888934114628

Table 5.12. **Ecuador**

Details of tax revenue / Ingresos tributarios detallados

Million USD

	1990	2000	2007	2010	2013	2014	2015	2016	2017	2018
Total tax revenue	**1 078**	**2 125**	**7 698**	**11 133**	**18 581**	**19 577**	**21 146**	**19 883**	**20 745**	**22 277**
1000 Taxes on income, profits and capital gains	**139**	**268**	**1 743**	**2 363**	**3 882**	**4 219**	**4 780**	**4 386**	**4 134**	**5 236**
1100 Of individuals	..	10	39	80	162	177	192	224	180	193
1110 On income and profits	..	10	39	80	161	177	192	224	180	193
Personal income tax	..	10	39	80	161	177	192	164	176	193
Solidarity contribution on remuneration	..	0	0	0	0	0	0	60	5	0
1120 On capital gains	..	..	..	0	0	0	0	0	0	..
1200 Corporate	..	53	424	485	1 023	1 121	1 575	1 377	1 074	1 894
1210 On profits	..	53	424	485	1 023	1 121	1 575	1 377	1 074	1 894
Corporate income tax	..	53	424	474	946	1 045	1 507	943	991	1 808
Income tax on oil companies and others	..	0	0	11	76	77	68	79	63	81
Solidarity contribution on profits	..	0	0	0	0	0	0	355	19	4
1220 On capital gains	..	..	..	..	..	..	..	..	..	..
1300 Unallocable between 1100 and 1200	139	206	1 279	1 798	2 698	2 920	3 013	2 784	2 880	3 149
Withholding tax	0	190	1 047	1 560	2 398	2 584	2 702	2 411	2 578	2 858
Income tax advances	0	14	227	298	342	381	335	335	343	353
Income tax refunds	0	0	0	-75	-86	-113	-99	-32	-112	-132
Other income taxes (local)	1	2	5	15	44	69	75	71	71	71
2000 Social security contributions	**243**	**228**	**1 792**	**2 541**	**4 547**	**4 718**	**5 057**	**4 741**	**5 415**	**5 553**
2100 Employees	..	..	..	..	..	..	..	..	..	..
2110 On a payroll basis	..	..	..	..	..	..	..	..	..	..
2120 On an income tax basis	..	..	..	..	..	..	..	..	..	..
2200 Employers	..	..	..	..	..	..	..	..	..	..
2210 On a payroll basis	..	..	..	..	..	..	..	..	..	..
2220 On an income tax basis	..	..	..	..	..	..	..	..	..	..
2300 Self-employed or non-employed	..	..	..	..	..	..	..	..	..	..
2310 On a payroll basis	..	..	..	..	..	..	..	..	..	..
2320 On an income tax basis	..	..	..	..	..	..	..	..	..	..
2400 Unallocable between 2100, 2200 and 2300	243	228	1 792	2 541	4 547	4 718	5 057	4 741	5 415	5 553
2410 On a payroll basis	..	..	..	..	..	..	..	..	..	..
2420 On an income tax basis	..	..	..	..	..	..	..	..	..	..
3000 Taxes on payroll and workforce	**0**	**0**	**0**	**0**	**0**	**0**	**0**	**0**	**0**	**0**
4000 Taxes on property	**16**	**17**	**91**	**159**	**252**	**261**	**303**	**639**	**347**	**354**
4100 Recurrent taxes on immovable property	13	8	48	68	119	124	134	142	162	174
Rural land tax	0	0	0	3	6	10	9	8	7	2
4110 Households	0	0	0	0	0	0	0	0	0	0
4120 Others	13	8	48	66	113	113	125	134	155	172
Tax on urban properties	12	7	40	55	96	96	106	113	129	..
Tax on rural properties	1	1	8	10	17	17	19	21	26	..
4200 Recurrent taxes on net wealth	0	0	0	35	48	44	49	47	35	30
4210 Individual	..	..	..	0	0	0	0	0	0	0
4220 Corporate	..	..	..	35	48	44	49	47	35	30
Tax on foreign assets	..	..	..	35	48	44	49	47	35	30
4300 Estate, inheritance and gift taxes	0	0	3	5	9	11	29	15	26	27
4310 Estate and inheritance taxes	..	..	3	5	9	11	29	15	26	27
4320 Gift taxes	..	..	0	0	0	0	0	0	0	0
4400 Taxes on financial and capital transactions	0	0	0	0	0	0	0	0	0	1
4500 Non-recurrent taxes	0	0	0	0	0	0	0	343	19	7
4510 On net wealth	..	..	..	..	..	..	..	343	19	7
Solidarity contribution on equity	..	..	..	..	..	..	..	202	16	6
Solidarity contribution on foreign assets	..	..	..	..	..	..	..	141	3	1
4520 Other non-recurrent taxes	..	..	..	..	..	..	..	0	0	0
4600 Other recurrent taxes on property	3	9	40	50	76	83	91	92	106	115
5000 Taxes on goods and services	**679**	**1 609**	**4 072**	**6 066**	**9 913**	**10 378**	**10 996**	**10 098**	**10 830**	**11 111**
5100 Taxes on production, sale, transfer, etc	671	1 580	3 958	5 863	9 468	9 905	10 503	9 639	10 371	10 608
5110 General taxes	306	928	2 819	3 801	6 123	6 454	6 431	6 116	6 718	6 706
5111 Value added taxes	302	923	2 787	3 759	6 056	6 376	6 352	6 042	6 643	6 633
VAT (internal operations)	..	557	1 518	2 506	4 096	4 513	4 778	4 375	4 672	4 789
VAT (imports)	..	381	1 486	1 668	2 090	2 035	1 722	1 329	1 646	1 947
2% contribution on VAT	..	0	0	0	0	0	0	402	412	4
VAT refunds	..	-14	-218	-416	-130	-172	-148	-65	-87	-107
Other VATs (local)	..	0	0	0	0	0	0	0	0	0
5112 Sales tax	0	0	0	0	0	0	0	0	0	0
5113 Other	4	5	32	41	67	78	79	74	75	74
5120 Taxes on specific goods and services	365	652	1 139	2 062	3 346	3 451	4 072	3 524	3 653	3 902

Table 5.12. **Ecuador** *(cont.)*

Details of tax revenue / Ingresos tributarios detallados

Million USD

	1990	2000	2007	2010	2013	2014	2015	2016	2017	2018
5121 Excises	90	89	269	508	729	783	806	769	919	955
Beer	..	29	81	119	170	166	188	194	237	239
Cigarettes	..	30	74	117	176	178	195	158	126	112
Fizzy drinks	..	9	16	40	57	53	59	109	103	94
Vehicles	..	6	11	55	84	106	98	50	67	63
Alcohol and alcoholic products	..	4	11	23	43	45	44	35	38	43
Non-returnable plastic bottles	..	0	0	0	16	22	22	28	31	35
Telephone	..	0	0	0	0	0	0	24	37	32
Water heaters	..	0	0	0	0	0	3	14	32	26
Perfumes	..	0	0	17	8	19	44	23	24	25
Non-alcoholic drinks	..	0	0	0	0	0	0	8	11	11
Other excises (internal operations)	..	0	0	0	0	5	13	2	4	5
Excises on imports	..	10	76	138	175	188	142	124	209	271
5122 Profits of fiscal monopolies	0	0	0	0	0	0	0	0	0	0
5123 Customs and import duties	227	217	679	1 153	1 352	1 357	2 026	1 633	1 468	1 561
5124 Taxes on exports	0	0	0	0	0	0	0	0	0	0
5125 Taxes on investment goods	0	0	0	0	0	0	0	0	0	0
5126 Taxes on specific services	26	343	192	30	40	52	146	157	169	180
Contribution to comprehensive cancer care	0	0	0	0	0	0	81	90	97	104
Prepaid television services	0	0	0	14	31	40	54	56	60	64
Club membership fees	0	0	0	0	1	0	1	1	1	1
Casino services	0	0	0	8	0	0	0	0	0	0
Telecommunications	0	0	188	0	0	3	0	0	0	0
Capital circulation tax	0	322	0	0	0	0	0	0	0	0
Departure tax	7	16	0	0	0	0	0	0	0	0
Tax on credit operations	18	2	0	1	0	0	0	0	0	0
Other service taxes (local)	1	2	4	7	9	8	10	9	10	0
5127 Other taxes on internat. trade and transactions	22	4	0	371	1 225	1 260	1 094	965	1 098	1 206
Foreign Currency Exit Tax (ISD)	0	0	..	371	1 225	1 260	1 094	965	1 098	1 206
Tax on purchase of foreign currency	22	4	..	0	0	0	0	0	0	0
5128 Other taxes	0	0	0	0	0	0	0	0	0	0
5130 Unallocable between 5110 and 5120	0	0	0	0	0	0	0	0	0	0
5200 Taxes on use of goods and perform activities	8	29	114	203	445	472	493	459	460	503
5210 Recurrent taxes	5	28	114	203	431	460	473	441	441	482
5211 Paid by households: motor vehicles	5	23	85	168	346	363	358	328	323	355
Motor vehicle tax	5	23	85	168	231	248	245	216	212	236
Environmental tax on vehicle pollution	0	0	0	0	115	115	113	112	111	119
5212 Paid by others: motor vehicles	0	0	0	0	0	0	0	0	0	0
5213 Paid in respect of other goods	1	5	29	35	85	97	115	113	118	126
5220 Non-recurrent taxes	2	1	0	0	14	12	20	18	18	22
5300 Unallocable between 5100 and 5200	0	0	0	0	0	0	0	0	0	0
6000 Other taxes	**2**	**2**	**1**	**4**	**-13**	**1**	**10**	**18**	**19**	**23**
6100 Paid solely by business	0	0	0	0	0	0	0	0	0	0
6200 Other	2	2	1	4	-13	1	10	18	19	23
Simplified taxation system of Ecuador (RISE)	0	0	0	6	15	20	20	19	22	23
Other tax refunds	0	0	0	-2	-28	-18	-10	-1	-3	-2
Other taxes (local)	2	2	1	1	0	0	0	0	0	2

Note: Year ending 31st December.

The data are on a cash basis unless noted otherwise.

Additional country specific taxes have been added and tax structure has been adjusted accordingly in this edition based on information from Internal Revenue Service (SRI) of Ecuador. Local government tax data in 2018 are estimated.

Heading 2000: The data are collected from non-financial public sector operations published by the Central Bank of Ecuador and are on accrual basis.

Heading 4500: Solidarity contribution on equity is recorded under heading 4500 in this edition. It was previously under heading 4200.

Heading 5123: The data are collected from general budget of the consolidated state government published by the Central Bank of Ecuador and are on accrual basis.

Heading 5126: Tax on credit operations under heading 5126 is collected from general budget of the consolidated state government published by the Central Bank of Ecuador and are on accrual basis.

Heading 5127: Tax on purchase of foreign currency under heading 5127 is collected from general budget of the consolidated state government published by the Central Bank of Ecuador and are on accrual basis.

Heading 5211: Motor vehicle tax is recorded under heading 5211 in this edition. It was previously under heading 5212.

Heading 6200: Credit notes are removed in this edition as they are non-tax revenues.

Source: Servicio de Rentas Internas (Internal Revenue Service); Banco Central del Ecuador (Central Bank of Ecuador).

StatLink https://doi.org/10.1787/888934114647

Table 5.13. **El Salvador**

Details of tax revenue / Ingresos tributarios detallados

Million USD

	1990	2000	2007	2010	2013	2014	2015	2016	2017	2018
Total tax revenue	**543**	**1 669**	**3 172**	**3 426**	**4 385**	**4 451**	**4 628**	**4 929**	**5 193**	**5 498**
1000 Taxes on income, profits and capital gains	**95**	**429**	**933**	**996**	**1 479**	**1 521**	**1 545**	**1 659**	**1 733**	**1 819**
1100 Of individuals	..	..	395	590	694	686	774	732	759	795
1110 On income and profits	..	..	395	590	694	686	774	732	759	795
1120 On capital gains	..	..	..	..	..	..	..	..	..	..
1200 Corporate	..	..	573	420	666	693	622	763	804	845
1210 On profits	..	..	573	420	666	693	622	763	804	845
1220 On capital gains	..	..	..	..	..	..	..	..	..	..
1300 Unallocable between 1100 and 1200	95	429	-35	-14	119	142	148	164	170	180
Withholding income tax	..	..	0	41	146	170	178	195	209	220
Income tax refunds	..	..	-35	-55	-27	-28	-30	-31	-39	-40
2000 Social security contributions	**104**	**325**	**390**	**470**	**547**	**570**	**607**	**655**	**683**	**704**
2100 Employees	..	75	88	99	114	119	130	143	151	156
2110 On a payroll basis	..	75	88	99	114	119	130	143	151	156
2120 On an income tax basis	..	0	0	0	0	0	0	0	0	0
2200 Employers	..	176	214	238	276	288	314	347	368	380
2210 On a payroll basis	..	176	214	238	276	288	314	347	368	380
2220 On an income tax basis	..	0	0	0	0	0	0	0	0	0
2300 Self-employed or non-employed	..	13	29	33	40	42	45	48	52	54
2310 On a payroll basis	..	13	29	33	40	42	45	48	52	54
2320 On an income tax basis	..	0	0	0	0	0	0	0	0	0
2400 Unallocable between 2100, 2200 and 2300	104	62	59	100	117	120	119	116	112	114
2410 On a payroll basis	104	62	59	100	117	120	119	116	112	114
2420 On an income tax basis	0	0	0	0	0	0	0	0	0	0
3000 Taxes on payroll and workforce	**0**	**0**	**0**	**0**	**0**	**0**	**0**	**0**	**0**	**0**
4000 Taxes on property	**26**	**12**	**24**	**19**	**26**	**51**	**112**	**112**	**112**	**119**
4100 Recurrent taxes on immovable property	0	0	3	3	5	5	5	5	5	6
4110 Households	..	..	..	..	..	..	..	..	..	..
4120 Others	..	..	..	..	..	..	..	..	..	..
4200 Recurrent taxes on net wealth	16	0	0	0	0	0	0	0	0	0
4210 Individual	..	..	..	..	..	..	..	..	..	..
4220 Corporate	..	..	..	..	..	..	..	..	..	..
4300 Estate, inheritance and gift taxes	0	0	0	0	0	0	0	0	0	0
4310 Estate and inheritance taxes	..	..	..	..	..	..	..	..	..	..
4320 Gift taxes	..	..	..	..	..	..	..	..	..	..
4400 Taxes on financial and capital transactions	10	12	21	16	21	46	107	107	107	113
Property transfers	10	12	21	16	21	24	20	23	23	24
Checks and electronic transfers of funds	0	0	0	0	0	15	55	54	53	56
Withholding for liquidity control	0	0	0	0	0	7	31	31	32	34
4500 Non-recurrent taxes	0	0	0	0	0	0	0	0	0	0
4510 On net wealth	..	..	..	..	..	..	..	..	..	..
4520 Other non-recurrent taxes	..	..	..	..	..	..	..	..	..	..
4600 Other recurrent taxes on property	0	0	0	0	0	0	0	0	0	0
5000 Taxes on goods and services	**259**	**903**	**1 775**	**1 878**	**2 250**	**2 217**	**2 278**	**2 413**	**2 578**	**2 763**
5100 Taxes on production, sale, transfer, etc	259	903	1 770	1 863	2 227	2 193	2 254	2 386	2 550	2 732
5110 General taxes	133	714	1 389	1 433	1 731	1 720	1 764	1 813	1 903	2 054
5111 Value added taxes	0	714	1 389	1 433	1 731	1 720	1 764	1 813	1 903	2 054
5112 Sales tax	0	0	0	0	0	0	0	0	0	0
5113 Other	133	0	0	0	0	0	0	0	0	0
5120 Taxes on specific goods and services	127	189	381	431	496	473	490	573	647	678
5121 Excises	65	49	169	224	254	261	285	355	423	437
Alcoholic beverages	..	..	15	22	22	22	22	23	24	24
Cigarettes	..	..	27	38	31	34	29	28	27	24
Soft drinks	..	..	25	31	42	43	48	49	49	49
Beer	..	..	30	29	49	49	55	61	65	73
Weapons, ammunition and explosives	..	..	1	1	1	1	1	1	1	1
Ad-valorem on fuels	..	..	0	0	0	0	7	9	8	7
Special contribution- Sugar	..	..	1	1	1	1	1	1	1	1
Special contribution- Public transportation	..	..	0	35	36	37	40	43	45	47
Special contribution- FOVIAL	..	..	70	69	72	74	80	86	89	93
Special contribution- Public security	..	..	0	0	0	0	2	56	116	118
5122 Profits of fiscal monopolies	0	0	0	0	0	0	0	0	0	0
5123 Customs and import duties	61	141	204	151	199	181	194	206	211	227
5124 Taxes on exports	0	0	0	0	0	0	0	0	0	0
5125 Taxes on investment goods	0	0	0	0	0	0	0	0	0	0
5126 Taxes on specific services	0	0	8	56	43	31	11	12	13	14
5127 Other taxes on internat. trade and transactions	0	0	0	0	0	0	0	0	0	0
5128 Other taxes	0	0	0	0	0	0	0	0	0	0

Table 5.13. **El Salvador** *(cont.)*

Details of tax revenue / Ingresos tributarios detallados

Million USD

	1990	2000	2007	2010	2013	2014	2015	2016	2017	2018
5130 Unallocable between 5110 and 5120	0	0	0	0	0	0	0	0	0	0
5200 Taxes on use of goods and perform activities	0	0	5	15	23	24	24	26	27	30
5210 Recurrent taxes	..	..	5	7	12	13	12	12	14	15
5211 Paid by households: motor vehicles	..	..	0	0	0	0	0	0	0	0
5212 Paid by others: motor vehicles	..	..	0	0	0	0	0	0	0	0
5213 Paid in respect of other goods	..	..	5	7	12	13	12	12	14	15
5220 Non-recurrent taxes	..	..	0	7	11	11	12	14	14	15
5300 Unallocable between 5100 and 5200	0	0	0	0	0	0	0	0	0	0
6000 Other taxes	**58**	**0**	**49**	**63**	**84**	**91**	**86**	**91**	**88**	**93**
6100 Paid solely by business	0	0	0	0	0	0	0	0	0	0
6200 Other	58	0	49	63	84	91	86	91	88	93

Note: Year ending 31st December.
The data are on a cash basis.
Additional municipal tax data have been included in this edition and will impact heading 4100, heading 5200 and heading 6200.
Heading 1000: Disaggregated individual and corporate income taxes are not available before 2002. Their figures in 2018 are estimated based on aggregate income tax data.
Heading 2000: The figures include social security contributions paid to the Salvadoran Institute of Social Security (ISSS), National Public Employees Pension Institute (INPEP), Social Security Institute of the Armed Forces (IPSFA) and Salvadoran Institute of Teacher Welfare (ISBM). The figures exclude payments to privately managed pension funds (AFPs) and may include small amount of voluntary contributions which are undistinguishable from the public social security contribution data.

Source: Dirección General de Tesorería en Ministerio de Hacienda (General Treasury Directorate in Ministry of Finance); Dirección General de Contabilidad Gubernamental en Ministerio de Hacienda (General Directorate of Government Accounting in Ministry of Finance); Instituto Salvadoreño del Seguro Social (Salvadoran Social Security Institute); Centro Interamericano de Administraciones Tributarias (Inter-American Center of Tax Administrations).

StatLink https://doi.org/10.1787/888934114666

Table 5.14. **Guatemala**

Details of tax revenue / Ingresos tributarios detallados

Million GTQ

	1990	2000	2007	2010	2013	2014	2015	2016	2017	2018
Total tax revenue	**2 569**	**16 278**	**36 008**	**40 703**	**54 663**	**58 497**	**60 081**	**65 609**	**68 829**	**71 602**
1000 Taxes on income, profits and capital gains	**507**	**3 041**	**8 342**	**9 933**	**16 041**	**17 752**	**17 534**	**20 572**	**20 693**	**20 893**
1100 Of individuals	25	137	877	1 225	1 246	1 784	1 826	2 082	2 468	2 603
1110 On income and profits	25	137	877	1 225	1 246	1 784	1 826	2 082	2 468	2 603
1120 On capital gains	..	..	..	..	..	..	..	..	..	..
1200 Corporate	482	2 902	5 417	6 134	11 532	12 426	11 801	14 418	13 846	13 633
1210 On profits	482	2 902	5 417	6 134	11 532	12 426	11 801	14 418	13 846	13 633
Corporate income tax	482	1 610	5 408	6 132	11 529	12 423	11 801	14 417	13 839	13 633
Commercial and agricultural enterprises	0	1 291	9	2	3	3	0	1	6	0
1220 On capital gains	..	..	..	..	..	..	..	..	..	..
1300 Unallocable between 1100 and 1200	0	2	2 048	2 574	3 263	3 543	3 907	4 072	4 380	4 656
Extraordinary and temporary solidarity tax in support of peace agreements	..	0	2 047	44	21	9	1	1	28	10
Solidarity tax	..	0	0	2 530	3 243	3 533	3 906	4 070	4 352	4 646
Extraordinary and temporary solidarity tax	..	2	1	0	0	0	0	0	0	0
2000 Social security contributions	**436**	**2 569**	**5 069**	**6 312**	**8 485**	**9 263**	**9 778**	**10 974**	**11 523**	**12 102**
2100 Employees	..	..	..	..	..	..	..	..	..	..
2110 On a payroll basis	..	..	..	..	..	..	..	..	..	..
2120 On an income tax basis	..	..	..	..	..	..	..	..	..	..
2200 Employers	..	..	..	..	..	..	..	..	..	..
2210 On a payroll basis	..	..	..	..	..	..	..	..	..	..
2220 On an income tax basis	..	..	..	..	..	..	..	..	..	..
2300 Self-employed or non-employed	..	..	..	..	..	..	..	..	..	..
2310 On a payroll basis	..	..	..	..	..	..	..	..	..	..
2320 On an income tax basis	..	..	..	..	..	..	..	..	..	..
2400 Unallocable between 2100, 2200 and 2300	436	2 569	5 069	6 312	8 485	9 263	9 778	10 974	11 523	12 102
2410 On a payroll basis	436	2 569	5 069	6 312	8 485	9 263	9 778	10 974	11 523	12 102
2420 On an income tax basis	0	0	0	0	0	0	0	0	0	0
3000 Taxes on payroll and workforce	**0**	**0**	**0**	**0**	**0**	**0**	**0**	**0**	**0**	**0**
4000 Taxes on property	**149**	**347**	**832**	**1 202**	**1 063**	**1 035**	**1 050**	**957**	**1 247**	**1 354**
4100 Recurrent taxes on immovable property	0	153	426	621	623	661	693	565	710	865
4110 Households	..	0	0	0	0	0	0	0	0	0
4120 Others	..	153	426	621	623	661	693	565	710	865
Property tax	..	6	1	1	1	1	1	1	1	2
Property tax (municipal)	..	147	426	620	621	660	692	564	709	863
4200 Recurrent taxes on net wealth	0	0	0	0	0	0	0	0	0	0
4210 Individual	..	..	..	..	..	..	..	..	..	..
4220 Corporate	..	..	..	..	..	..	..	..	..	..
4300 Estate, inheritance and gift taxes	0	0	0	0	0	0	0	0	0	0
4310 Estate and inheritance taxes	..	..	..	..	..	..	..	..	..	..
4320 Gift taxes	..	..	..	..	..	..	..	..	..	..
4400 Taxes on financial and capital transactions	149	194	406	581	440	373	357	393	537	489
Stamp duty	104	182	392	572	430	359	336	370	508	463
Tax on property transfer	45	12	14	10	10	14	20	23	29	26
4500 Non-recurrent taxes	0	0	0	0	0	0	0	0	0	0
4510 On net wealth	..	..	..	..	..	..	..	..	..	..
4520 Other non-recurrent taxes	..	..	..	..	..	..	..	..	..	..
4600 Other recurrent taxes on property	0	0	0	0	0	0	0	0	0	0
5000 Taxes on goods and services	**1 477**	**10 317**	**21 764**	**23 255**	**29 073**	**30 447**	**31 719**	**33 105**	**35 365**	**37 253**
5100 Taxes on production, sale, transfer, etc	1 449	10 131	21 411	22 750	27 543	29 128	30 088	31 356	33 586	35 420
5110 General taxes	762	6 259	15 382	16 980	21 874	23 153	23 271	24 215	26 187	27 733
5111 Value added taxes	762	6 259	15 382	16 980	21 874	23 153	23 271	24 215	26 187	27 733
VAT domestic	361	2 903	6 647	7 995	10 405	11 325	12 023	13 308	14 380	14 573
VAT imports	401	4 189	10 532	11 127	13 619	14 094	13 630	13 361	14 148	15 560
Tax credit refunds	0	-834	-1 797	-2 142	-2 150	-2 267	-2 381	-2 455	-2 342	-2 401
5112 Sales tax	0	0	0	0	0	0	0	0	0	0
5113 Other	0	0	0	0	0	0	0	0	0	0
5120 Taxes on specific goods and services	687	3 872	6 029	5 770	5 669	5 975	6 816	7 140	7 400	7 687
5121 Excises	181	1 797	2 946	3 101	3 372	3 579	4 289	4 422	4 518	4 668
Tobacco and derivatives	76	205	355	347	385	404	369	365	348	337
Beer	0	97	144	159	217	243	293	306	314	322
Alcoholic beverages	0	77	87	97	90	86	88	90	96	103
Soft drinks	0	15	195	220	282	300	328	348	348	365
Other beverages	0	12	1	2	1	0	0	1	0	0
Cement	0	0	117	99	100	100	312	117	114	123
Oil and derivatives	105	1 389	2 047	2 179	2 297	2 445	2 899	3 195	3 296	3 417
5122 Profits of fiscal monopolies	0	0	0	0	0	0	0	0	0	0
5123 Customs and import duties	506	1 806	2 654	2 368	1 965	2 044	2 157	2 323	2 455	2 576

Table 5.14. **Guatemala** *(cont.)*

Details of tax revenue / Ingresos tributarios detallados

Million GTQ

	1990	2000	2007	2010	2013	2014	2015	2016	2017	2018
5124 Taxes on exports	0	0	0	0	0	0	0	0	0	0
5125 Taxes on investment goods	0	0	0	0	0	0	0	0	0	0
5126 Taxes on specific services	0	269	429	301	332	352	370	396	427	443
Departure tax	..	135	229	224	240	252	263	280	300	312
INGUATE	..	40	78	73	89	96	104	110	120	125
Transportation and communications	..	94	122	3	3	4	4	5	7	6
5127 Other taxes on internat. trade and transactions	0	0	0	0	0	0	0	0	0	0
5128 Other taxes	0	0	0	0	0	0	0	0	0	0
5130 Unallocable between 5110 and 5120	0	0	0	0	0	0	0	0	0	0
5200 Taxes on use of goods and perform activities	28	186	353	505	1 530	1 320	1 631	1 750	1 779	1 834
5210 Recurrent taxes	28	186	353	505	1 530	1 320	1 631	1 750	1 779	1 834
5211 Paid by households: motor vehicles	0	0	0	0	694	747	914	967	953	953
5212 Paid by others: motor vehicles	28	186	353	505	836	572	717	782	826	881
5213 Paid in respect of other goods	0	0	0	0	0	0	0	0	0	0
5220 Non-recurrent taxes	0	0	0	0	0	0	0	0	0	0
5300 Unallocable between 5100 and 5200	0	0	0	0	0	0	0	0	0	0
6000 Other taxes	**0**	**4**	**1**	**1**	**1**	**0**	**0**	**0**	**0**	**0**
6100 Paid solely by business	..	0	0	0	0	0	0	0	0	0
6200 Other	..	4	1	1	1	0	0	0	0	0

Note: Year ending 31st December.

The data are on a cash basis.

Local government tax revenues include revenues from the municipal property tax (IUSI).

Heading 1000: Taxes on income from financial products are removed in this edition as they have been included in personal and corporate income taxes.

Heading 2000: Figures include contributions to the Guatemalan Social Security Institute (IGSS) and payments by public employees to the government's pension fund.

Heading 4400: Stamp duty has been placed under heading 4400 in this edition. It was previously under heading 6200. Before 2000, tax on property transfer under heading 4400 also includes other central government property tax under heading 4120 as they cannot be distinguished.

Heading 5121: Other beverages contain all alcoholic and non-alcoholic beverages before 2000.

Source: Superintendencia de Administración Tributaria (Superintendency of Tax Administration); Ministerio de Finanzas Públicas (Ministry of Public Finance).

StatLink https://doi.org/10.1787/888934114685

Table 5.15. **Guyana**

Details of tax revenue / Ingresos tributarios detallados

Million GYD

	1990	2000	2007	2010	2013	2014	2015	2016	2017	2018
Total tax revenue	**5 232**	**42 750**	**85 991**	**111 906**	**140 678**	**151 382**	**159 895**	**170 305**	**191 513**	**220 457**
1000 Taxes on income, profits and capital gains	**1 752**	**16 179**	**29 520**	**39 561**	**46 587**	**51 611**	**55 011**	**61 127**	**68 088**	**78 713**
1100 Of individuals	333	7 734	12 832	17 816	18 506	21 389	23 300	26 773	26 564	31 377
1110 On income and profits	333	7 734	12 832	17 816	18 506	21 389	23 300	26 773	26 564	31 377
Personal	306	7 157	12 832	15 419	15 199	17 900	19 894	22 727	21 669	25 808
Self-employed	27	577	0	2 397	3 307	3 490	3 407	4 045	4 895	5 570
1120 On capital gains	0	0	0	0	0	0	0	0	0	0
1200 Corporate	1 375	8 266	16 460	21 427	27 622	29 794	31 200	33 852	41 183	46 857
1210 On profits	0	0	0	0	0	0	0	0	0	0
1220 On capital gains	0	0	0	0	0	0	0	0	0	0
1300 Unallocable between 1100 and 1200	43	179	229	317	459	428	511	502	341	478
2000 Social security contributions	**191**	**4 868**	**8 061**	**10 047**	**13 195**	**14 985**	**16 644**	**18 211**	**19 911**	**21 766**
2100 Employees	0	0	0	0	0	0	0	0	0	0
2110 On a payroll basis	0	0	0	0	0	0	0	0	0	0
2120 On an income tax basis	0	0	0	0	0	0	0	0	0	0
2200 Employers	0	0	0	0	0	0	0	0	0	0
2210 On a payroll basis	0	0	0	0	0	0	0	0	0	0
2220 On an income tax basis	0	0	0	0	0	0	0	0	0	0
2300 Self-employed or non-employed	0	0	0	0	0	0	0	0	0	0
2310 On a payroll basis	0	0	0	0	0	0	0	0	0	0
2320 On an income tax basis	0	0	0	0	0	0	0	0	0	0
2400 Unallocable between 2100, 2200 and 2300	191	4 868	8 061	10 047	13 195	14 985	16 644	18 211	19 911	21 766
2410 On a payroll basis	0	0	0	0	0	0	0	0	0	0
2420 On an income tax basis	0	0	0	0	0	0	0	0	0	0
3000 Taxes on payroll and workforce	**0**	**0**	**0**	**0**	**0**	**0**	**0**	**0**	**0**	**0**
4000 Taxes on property	**53**	**701**	**962**	**1 593**	**2 608**	**2 423**	**3 237**	**3 209**	**3 618**	**4 421**
4100 Recurrent taxes on immovable property	40	681	943	1 562	2 572	2 381	3 201	3 172	3 579	4 377
4110 Households	0	0	0	0	0	0	0	0	0	0
4120 Others	40	681	943	1 562	2 572	2 381	3 201	3 172	3 579	4 377
4200 Recurrent taxes on net wealth	0	0	0	0	0	0	0	0	0	0
4210 Individual	0	0	0	0	0	0	0	0	0	0
4220 Corporate	0	0	0	0	0	0	0	0	0	0
4300 Estate, inheritance and gift taxes	13	20	19	31	37	42	37	37	39	44
4310 Estate and inheritance taxes	13	20	19	31	37	42	37	37	39	44
4320 Gift taxes	0	0	0	0	0	0	0	0	0	0
4400 Taxes on financial and capital transactions	0	0	0	0	0	0	0	0	0	0
4500 Non-recurrent taxes	0	0	0	0	0	0	0	0	0	0
4510 On net wealth	0	0	0	0	0	0	0	0	0	0
4520 Other non-recurrent taxes	0	0	0	0	0	0	0	0	0	0
4600 Other recurrent taxes on property	0	0	0	0	0	0	0	0	0	0
5000 Taxes on goods and services	**2 200**	**20 798**	**46 544**	**59 360**	**76 691**	**81 104**	**83 924**	**86 445**	**97 502**	**112 891**
5100 Taxes on production, sale, transfer, etc	2 162	20 530	45 937	58 846	76 072	80 431	83 227	85 499	96 386	111 796
5110 General taxes	1 399	14 861	22 755	27 044	34 317	37 307	35 374	37 468	42 728	48 181
5111 Value added taxes	0	0	21 329	27 044	34 317	37 307	35 374	36 268	42 423	48 181
Imports	0	0	0	14 877	20 036	20 370	19 366	18 477	23 261	0
Domestic supply	0	0	0	12 168	14 281	16 937	16 008	17 791	19 162	0
5112 Sales tax	0	0	0	0	0	0	0	0	0	0
5113 Other	1 399	14 861	1 426	0	0	0	0	1 200	305	0
5120 Taxes on specific goods and services	763	5 669	23 182	31 802	41 755	43 124	47 853	48 031	53 659	63 615
5121 Excises	32	609	16 057	22 070	28 343	29 267	33 827	31 083	35 162	41 659
Imports	0	0	0	18 935	24 147	25 044	29 953	27 043	29 111	0
Domestic supply	0	0	0	2 358	3 124	3 190	3 377	4 040	4 348	0
Purchase tax - motor cars	32	475	159	0	0	0	0	0	0	0
Environmental tax	0	134	514	777	1 072	1 033	496	0	1 703	1 979
5122 Profits of fiscal monopolies	0	0	0	0	0	0	0	0	0	0
5123 Customs and import duties	544	3 943	6 005	8 302	11 866	12 167	12 357	14 887	16 273	19 321
5124 Taxes on exports	94	7	9	7	14	14	12	13	23	33
5125 Taxes on investment goods	0	0	0	0	0	0	0	0	0	0
5126 Taxes on specific services	92	1 110	1 112	1 423	1 532	1 676	1 658	2 048	2 201	2 603
Entertainment tax	12	27	1	0	0	0	0	0	0	0
Travel tax	80	1 084	1 112	1 423	1 532	1 676	1 658	2 048	2 201	2 603
5127 Other taxes on internat. trade and transactions	0	0	0	0	0	0	0	0	0	0
5128 Other taxes	0	0	0	0	0	0	0	0	0	0
5130 Unallocable between 5110 and 5120	0	0	0	0	0	0	0	0	0	0
5200 Taxes on use of goods and perform activities	38	268	607	514	620	673	697	945	1 116	1 095
5210 Recurrent taxes	38	268	607	514	620	673	697	945	1 116	1 095
5211 Paid by households: motor vehicles	27	239	306	475	587	637	653	868	1 039	1 095
5212 Paid by others: motor vehicles	0	0	0	0	0	0	0	0	0	0

Table 5.15. **Guyana** *(cont.)*

Details of tax revenue / Ingresos tributarios detallados

Million GYD

	1990	2000	2007	2010	2013	2014	2015	2016	2017	2018
5213 Paid in respect of other goods	12	29	301	39	33	35	44	78	77	0
Other licences	12	29	301	39	33	35	44	78	77	0
5220 Non-recurrent taxes	0	0	0	0	0	0	0	0	0	0
5300 Unallocable between 5100 and 5200	0	0	0	0	0	0	0	0	0	0
6000 Other taxes	**1 037**	**204**	**904**	**1 346**	**1 596**	**1 259**	**1 079**	**1 313**	**2 394**	**2 666**
6100 Paid solely by business	0	0	0	0	0	0	0	0	0	0
6200 Other	1 037	204	904	1 346	1 596	1 259	1 079	1 313	2 394	2 666

Note: Year ending 31st December.

The data are on a cash basis.

Central government tax revenues of the latest year come from Bank of Guyana which has the most updated data. Data for earlier years come from Ministry of Finance which has the most disaggregated data. Local government data come from Bank of Guyana for all years.

Heading 1000: Income taxes for self-employed persons and corporations are estimated in 2018.

Heading 2000: The figures include contributions to National Insurance Scheme.

Source: Ministry of Finance; Bank of Guyana; National Insurance Scheme.

StatLink https://doi.org/10.1787/888934114704

Table 5.16. **Honduras**

Details of tax revenue / Ingresos tributarios detallados

Million HNL

	1990	2000	2007	2010	2013	2014	2015	2016	2017	2018
Total tax revenue	**2 118**	**18 299**	**45 763**	**54 060**	**71 653**	**83 702**	**95 882**	**110 485**	**119 266**	**127 756**
1000 Taxes on income, profits and capital gains	**431**	**2 907**	**11 833**	**13 232**	**19 366**	**21 347**	**25 003**	**29 584**	**33 055**	**36 071**
1100 Of individuals	157	992	3 919	4 528	6 478	7 312	8 147	9 566	10 533	11 368
1110 On income and profits	157	992	3 919	4 528	6 478	7 312	8 147	9 566	10 533	11 368
1120 On capital gains	..	..	..	..	..	..	..	..	..	..
1200 Corporate	274	1 916	7 915	8 705	12 888	14 034	16 856	20 018	22 522	24 702
1210 On profits	274	1 916	7 915	8 705	12 888	14 034	16 856	20 018	22 522	24 702
Corporate income tax	274	1 916	6 877	7 400	11 523	12 756	15 206	18 020	20 668	22 082
Income tax surcharge	0	0	1 038	1 305	1 352	1 265	1 637	1 985	1 841	2 601
Special contribution of the cooperative sector	0	0	0	0	13	13	13	13	14	19
1220 On capital gains	..	..	..	..	..	..	..	..	..	..
1300 Unallocable between 1100 and 1200	0	0	0	0	0	0	0	0	0	0
2000 Social security contributions	**179**	**1 727**	**6 037**	**8 671**	**12 529**	**12 467**	**13 524**	**14 402**	**17 911**	**19 302**
2100 Employees	..	..	..	..	..	..	..	..	..	..
2110 On a payroll basis	..	..	..	..	..	..	..	..	..	..
2120 On an income tax basis	..	..	..	..	..	..	..	..	..	..
2200 Employers	..	..	..	..	..	..	..	..	..	..
2210 On a payroll basis	..	..	..	..	..	..	..	..	..	..
2220 On an income tax basis	..	..	..	..	..	..	..	..	..	..
2300 Self-employed or non-employed	..	..	..	..	..	..	..	..	..	..
2310 On a payroll basis	..	..	..	..	..	..	..	..	..	..
2320 On an income tax basis	..	..	..	..	..	..	..	..	..	..
2400 Unallocable between 2100, 2200 and 2300	179	1 727	6 037	8 671	12 529	12 467	13 524	14 402	17 911	19 302
2410 On a payroll basis	179	1 727	6 037	8 671	12 529	12 467	13 524	14 402	17 911	19 302
2420 On an income tax basis	0	0	0	0	0	0	0	0	0	0
3000 Taxes on payroll and workforce	**0**	**0**	**0**	**0**	**0**	**0**	**0**	**0**	**0**	**0**
4000 Taxes on property	**16**	**266**	**439**	**994**	**1 446**	**2 300**	**2 635**	**2 726**	**3 046**	**3 243**
4100 Recurrent taxes on immovable property	16	189	291	254	298	275	298	330	344	435
4110 Households	..	..	..	..	..	..	..	..	..	..
4120 Others	..	..	..	..	..	..	..	..	..	..
4200 Recurrent taxes on net wealth	0	78	148	359	245	389	334	294	349	278
4210 Individual	..	..	..	..	..	..	..	..	..	..
4220 Corporate	..	..	..	..	..	..	..	..	..	..
4300 Estate, inheritance and gift taxes	0	0	0	0	0	0	0	0	0	0
4310 Estate and inheritance taxes	..	..	..	..	..	..	..	..	..	..
4320 Gift taxes	..	..	..	..	..	..	..	..	..	..
4400 Taxes on financial and capital transactions	0	0	0	0	903	1 636	2 003	2 102	2 353	2 531
4500 Non-recurrent taxes	0	0	0	380	0	0	0	0	0	0
4510 On net wealth	..	..	0	0	..	..	..	..	..	..
4520 Other non-recurrent taxes	..	..	0	380	..	..	..	..	..	..
4600 Other recurrent taxes on property	0	0	0	0	0	0	0	0	0	0
5000 Taxes on goods and services	**1 401**	**12 436**	**25 985**	**28 937**	**35 908**	**44 945**	**52 217**	**58 638**	**63 111**	**66 735**
5100 Taxes on production, sale, transfer, etc	1 401	12 436	25 985	28 937	35 908	44 945	52 217	58 638	63 111	66 735
5110 General taxes	344	5 146	14 170	16 050	20 637	27 734	32 273	36 521	39 228	41 562
5111 Value added taxes	344	5 146	14 170	16 050	20 637	27 734	32 273	36 521	39 228	41 562
5112 Sales tax	0	0	0	0	0	0	0	0	0	0
5113 Other	0	0	0	0	0	0	0	0	0	0
5120 Taxes on specific goods and services	1 057	7 290	11 815	12 887	15 270	17 211	19 944	22 117	23 883	25 173
5121 Excises	256	4 592	7 606	8 458	10 119	11 588	13 349	14 953	16 405	17 011
Beer	70	376	358	376	503	525	668	824	974	1 150
Soft drinks	25	240	419	514	725	754	838	890	938	979
Liquors	32	48	80	121	165	188	194	190	192	227
Petroleum products	43	347	0	0	0	0	0	0	0	0
Cigarettes	57	369	582	607	495	610	598	564	563	565
Fuel tax	0	2 954	5 578	6 288	7 613	8 874	10 317	11 594	12 773	13 061
Other	28	258	589	551	618	638	735	890	965	1 028
5122 Profits of fiscal monopolies	0	0	0	0	0	0	0	0	0	0
5123 Customs and import duties	498	2 083	2 869	2 505	2 651	2 974	3 541	3 998	4 244	4 485
Petroleum	0	297	0	0	0	0	0	0	0	0
Other	498	1 786	2 869	2 505	2 651	2 974	3 541	3 998	4 244	4 485
5124 Taxes on exports	217	6	0	0	101	107	84	72	79	90
Bananas	39	5	..	..	0	0	0	0	0	0
Coffee	1	0	..	..	0	0	0	0	0	0
Temporary export tax	163	0	..	..	0	0	0	0	0	0
Special contribution of the mining sector	0	0	..	..	101	107	84	72	79	90
Other	15	1	..	..	0	0	0	0	0	0
5125 Taxes on investment goods	0	0	0	0	0	0	0	0	0	0

Table 5.16. **Honduras** *(cont.)*

Details of tax revenue / Ingresos tributarios detallados

Million HNL

	1990	2000	2007	2010	2013	2014	2015	2016	2017	2018
5126 Taxes on specific services	0	0	0	0	87	90	91	86	84	80
Special contribution of mobile services	..	..	..	..	66	67	67	60	55	49
Special contribution of the food and services sector	..	..	..	..	18	20	21	23	25	26
Special contribution of casino games and slot machines	..	..	..	..	3	3	3	3	4	4
5127 Other taxes on internat. trade and transactions	0	0	0	0	0	0	0	0	0	0
5128 Other taxes	87	610	1 340	1 924	2 312	2 451	2 880	3 007	3 070	3 508
5130 Unallocable between 5110 and 5120	0	0	0	0	0	0	0	0	0	0
5200 Taxes on use of goods and perform activities	0	0	0	0	0	0	0	0	0	0
5210 Recurrent taxes	..	..	..	..	..	..	..	..	..	..
5211 Paid by households: motor vehicles	..	..	..	..	..	..	..	..	..	..
5212 Paid by others: motor vehicles	..	..	..	..	..	..	..	..	..	..
5213 Paid in respect of other goods	..	..	..	..	..	..	..	..	..	..
5220 Non-recurrent taxes	..	..	..	..	..	..	..	..	..	..
5300 Unallocable between 5100 and 5200	0	0	0	0	0	0	0	0	0	0
6000 Other taxes	**91**	**962**	**1 469**	**2 225**	**2 404**	**2 644**	**2 503**	**5 136**	**2 142**	**2 404**
6100 Paid solely by business	0	0	0	0	0	0	0	0	0	0
6200 Other	91	962	1 469	2 225	2 404	2 644	2 503	5 136	2 142	2 404

Note: Year ending 31st December.

The data are on a cash basis.

Heading 4100: Tax on real estate is classified under heading 4100 in this edition. It was previously under heading 4600.

Heading 4200: Tax on net assets is classified under heading 4200 in this edition. It was previously under heading 4600.

Source: Servicio de Administración de Rentas (Revenue Administration Service); Secretaría de Finanzas (Ministry of Finance).

StatLink https://doi.org/10.1787/888934114723

Table 5.17. **Jamaica**

Details of tax revenue / Ingresos tributarios detallados

Million JMD

	1990	2000	2007	2010	2013	2014	2015	2016	2017	2018
Total tax revenue	**7 748**	**87 713**	**219 435**	**287 139**	**357 046**	**381 799**	**427 640**	**467 350**	**517 091**	**562 009**
1000 Taxes on income, profits and capital gains	**3 944**	**39 277**	**97 924**	**118 708**	**129 951**	**134 698**	**149 990**	**158 409**	**155 790**	**173 122**
1100 Of individuals	1 687	17 441	48 220	54 798	66 283	70 868	74 538	72 175	60 306	62 644
1110 On income and profits	1 687	17 441	48 220	54 798	66 283	70 868	74 538	72 175	60 306	62 644
PAYE	1 489	16 515	45 533	50 828	62 172	66 645	70 075	67 591	54 879	57 472
Other individuals	198	926	2 687	3 969	4 111	4 223	4 463	4 584	5 427	5 173
1120 On capital gains	..	..	..	..	..	..	..	..	..	..
1200 Corporate	1 280	7 627	19 758	33 091	34 539	32 606	40 198	47 530	61 401	62 504
1210 On profits	1 280	7 627	19 758	33 091	34 539	32 606	40 198	47 530	61 401	62 504
Bauxite/alumina	134	430	1 626	866	0	0	0	0	0	0
Other companies	1 146	7 197	18 132	32 224	34 539	31 991	39 668	46 823	60 431	61 427
Minimum business tax	0	0	0	0	0	615	529	707	970	1 077
1220 On capital gains	..	..	..	..	..	..	..	..	..	..
1300 Unallocable between 1100 and 1200	977	14 209	29 946	30 820	29 130	31 224	35 255	38 704	34 083	47 974
Tax on dividends	68	854	1 928	1 059	1 695	1 904	979	1 408	1 801	1 987
Tax on interests	605	9 535	18 120	16 970	10 185	10 103	13 519	14 451	6 417	17 446
Education tax	305	3 821	9 898	12 792	17 249	19 217	20 757	22 845	25 865	28 541
2000 Social security contributions	**0**	**0**	**6 349**	**8 199**	**13 875**	**15 865**	**16 449**	**17 978**	**19 249**	**21 033**
2100 Employees	..	..	..	..	..	..	..	..	..	..
2110 On a payroll basis	..	..	..	..	..	..	..	..	..	..
2120 On an income tax basis	..	..	..	..	..	..	..	..	..	..
2200 Employers	..	..	..	..	..	..	..	..	..	..
2210 On a payroll basis	..	..	..	..	..	..	..	..	..	..
2220 On an income tax basis	..	..	..	..	..	..	..	..	..	..
2300 Self-employed or non-employed	..	..	..	..	..	..	..	..	..	..
2310 On a payroll basis	..	..	..	..	..	..	..	..	..	..
2320 On an income tax basis	..	..	..	..	..	..	..	..	..	..
2400 Unallocable between 2100, 2200 and 2300	..	..	6 349	8 199	13 875	15 865	16 449	17 978	19 249	21 033
2410 On a payroll basis	..	..	..	..	..	..	..	..	..	..
2420 On an income tax basis	..	..	..	..	..	..	..	..	..	..
3000 Taxes on payroll and workforce	**0**	**0**	**0**	**0**	**0**	**0**	**0**	**0**	**0**	**0**
4000 Taxes on property	**965**	**4 262**	**12 617**	**9 939**	**16 896**	**18 009**	**19 411**	**21 149**	**23 583**	**24 793**
4100 Recurrent taxes on immovable property	67	639	1 788	2 600	5 595	6 138	7 271	7 101	8 523	8 478
4110 Households	67	639	1 788	2 600	5 595	6 138	7 271	7 101	8 523	8 478
Municipal property tax	0	639	1 788	2 600	5 595	6 138	7 271	7 101	8 523	8 478
Other property taxes	67	0	0	0	0	0	0	0	0	0
4120 Others	0	0	0	0	0	0	0	0	0	0
4200 Recurrent taxes on net wealth	0	0	0	0	0	0	0	0	0	0
4210 Individual	..	..	..	..	..	..	..	..	..	..
4220 Corporate	..	..	..	..	..	..	..	..	..	..
4300 Estate, inheritance and gift taxes	0	0	0	0	0	0	0	0	0	0
4310 Estate and inheritance taxes	..	..	..	..	..	..	..	..	..	..
4320 Gift taxes	..	..	..	..	..	..	..	..	..	..
4400 Taxes on financial and capital transactions	898	3 623	10 829	7 339	11 301	11 870	12 140	14 048	15 060	16 315
Stamp duty	898	3 623	10 829	7 339	11 301	11 870	12 140	14 048	15 060	16 315
4500 Non-recurrent taxes	0	0	0	0	0	0	0	0	0	0
4510 On net wealth	..	..	..	..	..	..	..	..	..	..
4520 Other non-recurrent taxes	..	..	..	..	..	..	..	..	..	..
4600 Other recurrent taxes on property	0	0	0	0	0	0	0	0	0	0
5000 Taxes on goods and services	**2 824**	**43 907**	**101 639**	**149 544**	**195 233**	**212 319**	**240 795**	**268 569**	**316 601**	**340 651**
5100 Taxes on production, sale, transfer, etc	2 760	43 107	100 317	147 500	192 381	209 302	237 456	265 064	311 911	335 189
5110 General taxes	297	22 356	65 030	84 409	109 819	121 073	138 501	149 111	171 584	187 576
5111 Value added taxes	293	22 356	63 948	82 407	107 660	118 756	135 827	146 030	168 112	183 646
General consumption tax	293	22 356	63 948	82 407	107 660	118 756	135 827	146 030	168 112	183 646
5112 Sales tax	4	0	0	0	0	0	0	0	0	0
Sales tax on used cars	4	..	..	..	..	..	..	..	..	..
5113 Other	0	0	1 082	2 002	2 159	2 318	2 674	3 081	3 472	3 930
Environmental levy	..	..	1 082	2 002	2 159	2 318	2 674	3 081	3 472	3 930
5120 Taxes on specific goods and services	2 463	20 752	35 287	63 091	82 562	88 228	98 955	115 953	140 327	147 613
5121 Excises	1 158	9 751	13 289	38 112	37 827	41 347	49 202	59 327	75 152	75 169
Special consumption tax	1 115	9 751	13 289	38 112	37 827	41 347	49 202	59 327	75 112	75 103
Quarry tax	0	0	0	0	0	0	0	0	39	66
Other excises	44	0	0	0	0	0	0	0	0	0
5122 Profits of fiscal monopolies	0	0	0	0	0	0	0	0	0	0
5123 Customs and import duties	782	8 498	18 640	19 959	25 938	26 289	28 771	34 033	37 737	41 243
5124 Taxes on exports	0	0	0	0	0	0	0	0	0	0
5125 Taxes on investment goods	0	0	0	0	0	0	0	0	0	0

Table 5.17. **Jamaica** *(cont.)*

Details of tax revenue / Ingresos tributarios detallados

Million JMD

	1990	2000	2007	2010	2013	2014	2015	2016	2017	2018
5126 Taxes on specific services	523	2 503	3 359	5 020	18 798	20 592	20 982	22 593	27 438	31 202
Travel tax	86	1 999	2 144	3 512	8 531	9 344	9 979	12 726	18 659	20 114
Telephone call tax	86	0	0	0	6 405	6 687	6 157	4 810	3 543	3 247
Betting, gaming and lottery	50	504	1 215	1 508	2 226	2 661	2 797	2 802	2 639	5 205
Accommodation tax	87	0	0	0	1 636	1 901	2 050	2 254	2 598	2 636
Bank and trust	204	0	0	0	0	0	0	0	0	0
Entertainment tax	11	0	0	0	0	0	0	0	0	0
5127 Other taxes on internat. trade and transactions	0	0	0	0	0	0	0	0	0	0
5128 Other taxes	0	0	0	0	0	0	0	0	0	0
5130 Unallocable between 5110 and 5120	0	0	0	0	0	0	0	0	0	0
5200 Taxes on use of goods and perform activities	64	800	1 322	2 045	2 852	3 017	3 339	3 505	4 690	5 463
5210 Recurrent taxes	64	800	1 322	2 045	2 852	3 017	3 339	3 505	4 690	5 463
5211 Paid by households: motor vehicles	47	751	1 012	1 775	2 493	2 666	2 901	3 032	3 768	4 334
5212 Paid by others: motor vehicles	0	0	0	0	0	0	0	0	0	0
5213 Paid in respect of other goods	17	49	310	270	359	351	438	473	922	1 129
5220 Non-recurrent taxes	0	0	0	0	0	0	0	0	0	0
5300 Unallocable between 5100 and 5200	0	0	0	0	0	0	0	0	0	0
6000 Other taxes	**16**	**266**	**907**	**748**	**1 091**	**909**	**994**	**1 245**	**1 868**	**2 410**
6100 Paid solely by business	0	0	0	0	0	0	0	0	0	0
6200 Other	16	266	907	748	1 091	909	994	1 245	1 868	2 410
Contractors levy	16	266	907	748	1 091	909	994	1 245	1 868	2 410

Note: Year ending 31st December, except for 1990-2003 which refer to fiscal year ending 31st March due to data availability.
The data are on a cash basis.
Heading 2000: The figures include contributions to National Insurance Scheme (NIS).
Heading 4400: Stamp duties have been recorded under heading 4400 in this edition. They were previously recorded under heading 6200.
Heading 5121: Quarry tax has been added as tax revenue in this edition.

Source: Ministry of Finance and the Public Service; Tax Administration Jamaica.

StatLink https://doi.org/10.1787/888934114742

Table 5.18. **Mexico / México**

Details of tax revenue / Ingresos tributarios detallados

Million MXN

	1990	2000	2007	2010	2013	2014	2015	2016	2017	2018
Total tax revenue	**102 005**	**767 216**	**1 382 103**	**1 716 243**	**2 165 501**	**2 394 279**	**2 953 480**	**3 343 314**	**3 527 123**	**3 582 463**
1000 Taxes on income, profits and capital gains	**34 673**	**276 548**	**554 099**	**683 604**	**957 213**	**979 251**	**1 230 555**	**1 427 114**	**1 571 954**	**1 671 513**
1100 Of individuals	..	..	238 938	313 473	425 621	514 208	609 384	681 784	754 109	804 236
Tax on income of individuals	..	..	238 938	313 473	425 621	514 208	609 384	681 784	754 109	804 236
1110 On income and profits	..	..	..	..	..	..	..	..	..	..
1120 On capital gains	..	..	..	..	..	..	..	..	..	..
1200 Corporate	..	..	217 790	246 745	392 199	441 317	592 443	700 925	769 193	809 834
Tax on income of corporations	..	..	217 790	246 745	392 199	441 317	592 443	700 925	769 193	809 834
1210 On profits	..	..	..	..	..	..	..	..	..	..
1220 On capital gains	..	..	..	..	..	..	..	..	..	..
1300 Unallocable between 1100 and 1200	34 673	276 548	97 370	123 386	139 393	23 726	28 728	44 405	48 652	57 443
Tax on income of other individuals and corporations	..	244 841	54 785	66 937	89 028	31 076	36 268	44 225	46 004	50 878
Tax on asset	..	13 913	15 670	-624	-1 325	-735	-502	-918	-1 069	-396
Credit on salary	..	17 794	23 177	9 708	1 274	2 423	993	1 144	1 036	1 172
Oil yields tax	..	0	3 738	2 296	3 210	4 669	0	0	0	0
IETU	..	0	0	45 069	47 205	-13 707	-11 777	-4 039	-1 648	319
Imposed by Activity Exploration and extraction of hydrocarbon	..	0	0	0	0	0	3 746	3 994	4 330	5 470
2000 Social security contributions	**17 165**	**138 223**	**236 727**	**277 459**	**351 993**	**378 373**	**409 249**	**434 998**	**467 710**	**509 087**
2100 Employees	..	..	..	..	..	..	..	..	..	..
2110 On a payroll basis	..	..	..	..	..	..	..	..	..	..
2120 On an income tax basis	..	..	..	..	..	..	..	..	..	..
2200 Employers	..	..	..	..	..	..	..	..	..	..
2210 On a payroll basis	..	..	..	..	..	..	..	..	..	..
2220 On an income tax basis	..	..	..	..	..	..	..	..	..	..
2300 Self-employed or non-employed	..	..	..	..	..	..	..	..	..	..
2310 On a payroll basis	..	..	..	..	..	..	..	..	..	..
2320 On an income tax basis	..	..	..	..	..	..	..	..	..	..
2400 Unallocable between 2100, 2200 and 2300	17 165	138 223	236 727	277 459	351 993	378 373	409 249	434 998	467 710	509 087
2410 On a payroll basis	..	138 223	236 727	277 459	351 993	378 373	409 249	434 998	467 710	509 087
2420 On an income tax basis	..	0	0	0	0	0	0	0	0	0
3000 Taxes on payroll and workforce	**1 797**	**11 217**	**28 071**	**36 911**	**53 042**	**64 713**	**70 221**	**76 762**	**84 099**	**0**
Substitute tax on salary	..	0	0	0	0	0	0	0	0	..
Payroll tax	..	11 101	20 277	27 813	41 184	64 581	69 866	76 304	0	..
Tax on remuneration to the personal work	..	65	7 578	8 841	11 645	0	152	225	0	..
Tax on professions and fees	..	36	68	71	50	51	106	99	0	..
Tax on operations by contract	..	15	148	186	163	81	96	134	0	..
4000 Taxes on property	**1 914**	**13 964**	**33 161**	**38 955**	**46 238**	**54 978**	**57 673**	**63 273**	**67 836**	**0**
4100 Recurrent taxes on immovable property	1 036	9 948	19 425	25 724	31 338	37 751	37 961	40 357	44 680	0
4110 Households	0	0	0	0	0	0	0	0	0	0
4120 Others	1 036	9 948	19 425	25 724	31 338	37 751	37 961	40 357	44 680	0
Property tax	..	9 948	19 425	25 724	31 338	37 751	37 961	40 357	44 680	0
4200 Recurrent taxes on net wealth	0	0	0	0	0	0	0	0	0	0
4210 Individual	..	..	..	..	..	..	..	..	..	0
4220 Corporate	..	..	..	..	..	..	..	..	..	0
4300 Estate, inheritance and gift taxes	8	0	0	0	0	0	0	0	0	0
4310 Estate and inheritance taxes	8	..	..	..	..	..	..	..	..	0
4320 Gift taxes	0	..	..	..	..	..	..	..	..	0
4400 Taxes on financial and capital transactions	870	4 017	13 736	13 231	14 900	17 227	19 712	22 917	23 156	0
Alienation of immovable property	..	1 763	1 076	1 122	1 271	1 308	1 595	1 723	1 623	0
Transfer of ownership of real estate	..	2 236	8 147	5 027	4 518	5 008	6 671	9 593	7 016	0
Purchasing property	..	18	4 513	7 082	9 110	10 911	11 447	11 600	14 516	0
4500 Non-recurrent taxes	0	0	0	0	0	0	0	0	0	0
4510 On net wealth	..	..	..	..	..	..	..	..	..	0
4520 Other non-recurrent taxes	..	..	..	..	..	..	..	..	..	0
4600 Other recurrent taxes on property	0	0	0	0	0	0	0	0	0	0
5000 Taxes on goods and services	**44 837**	**319 612**	**513 140**	**651 915**	**715 811**	**880 153**	**1 141 170**	**1 295 653**	**1 283 049**	**1 355 600**
5100 Taxes on production, sale, transfer, etc	44 171	310 325	491 928	630 123	696 150	859 302	1 120 610	1 274 738	1 262 770	1 354 887
5110 General taxes	26 635	189 606	409 013	504 509	556 794	667 085	707 213	791 700	816 048	922 238
5111 Value added taxes	26 635	189 606	409 013	504 509	556 794	667 085	707 213	791 700	816 048	922 238
5112 Sales tax	0	0	0	0	0	0	0	0	0	0
5113 Other	0	0	0	0	0	0	0	0	0	0
5120 Taxes on specific goods and services	17 519	120 720	82 915	125 614	139 356	192 217	413 397	483 038	446 722	432 649
5121 Excises	10 072	86 163	47 008	86 098	104 111	160 754	361 538	420 448	378 537	358 577
Special tax on production and services	..	81 544	41 532	81 427	97 860	154 327	354 294	411 390	367 834	347 435
Tax on new automobiles	..	4 619	5 476	4 671	6 252	6 427	7 244	9 058	10 703	11 142
Tax on luxury goods and services	..	0	0	0	0	0	0	0	0	0
5122 Profits of fiscal monopolies	0	0	0	0	0	0	0	0	0	0

Table 5.18. **Mexico / México** *(cont.)*

Details of tax revenue / Ingresos tributarios detallados

Million MXN

	1990	2000	2007	2010	2013	2014	2015	2016	2017	2018
5123 Customs and import duties	6 998	33 285	33 344	26 602	32 324	36 841	45 366	51 889	53 793	67 232
Step customs officer	..	423	1 156	2 071	3 065	2 913	1 270	1 336	1 463	1 690
Import taxes	..	32 861	32 188	24 531	29 260	33 928	44 096	50 553	52 330	65 543
5124 Taxes on exports	75	4	3	0	1	1	1	0	0	0
Tax on exports	..	4	3	0	1	1	1	0	0	0
5125 Taxes on investment goods	0	0	0	0	0	0	0	0	0	0
5126 Taxes on specific services	132	1 042	2 146	10 958	-967	-7 417	1 763	5 630	7 778	-629
IDE	..	0	0	8 022	-5 988	-12 322	-3 323	-1 262	-739	-629
Tax on lodging	..	504	1 059	1 384	1 890	2 067	2 561	3 009	3 598	0
Public entertainment tax	..	240	365	462	566	543	689	858	839	0
Tax on lotteries, raffles and gambling	..	267	705	923	1 213	1 218	1 416	1 828	2 717	0
Tax on commercials	..	4	17	166	203	216	210	906	1 082	0
Various indirect taxes	..	28	0	1	1 149	861	209	291	282	0
5127 Other taxes on internat. trade and transactions	0	0	0	0	0	0	0	0	0	0
5128 Other taxes	242	226	414	1 956	3 886	2 040	4 730	5 070	6 613	7 468
Mining fees	..	226	414	1 956	3 886	2 040	4 730	5 070	6 613	7 468
5130 Unallocable between 5110 and 5120	17	0	0	0	0	0	0	0	0	0
5200 Taxes on use of goods and perform activities	666	9 287	21 212	21 793	19 661	20 851	20 560	20 915	20 279	713
5210 Recurrent taxes	666	9 287	21 212	21 793	19 661	20 851	20 560	20 915	20 279	713
5211 Paid by households: motor vehicles	567	8 878	20 692	21 319	19 174	20 370	19 880	20 192	19 530	0
Tax on motor vehicules	..	8 878	20 692	21 319	19 174	20 370	19 880	20 192	19 530	0
5212 Paid by others: motor vehicles	0	301	275	281	357	367	439	503	554	640
Tax on federal auto transport	..	301	275	281	357	367	439	503	554	640
5213 Paid in respect of other goods	99	108	246	193	130	114	240	220	194	73
Sport fishing	..	40	98	59	50	65	62	68	71	73
Sport hunting	..	3	0	0	0	0	0	0	0	0
Tax on commercial activities	..	63	147	50	26	33	64	46	28	0
Trade in books and magazines	..	0	0	0	3	1	1	1	0	0
Tax on industrial activities	..	2	0	82	49	13	93	78	77	0
Mining	..	0	0	1	1	2	21	28	18	0
5220 Non-recurrent taxes	0	0	0	0	0	0	0	0	0	0
5300 Unallocable between 5100 and 5200	0	0	0	0	0	0	0	0	0	0
6000 Other taxes	**1 619**	**7 651**	**16 905**	**27 398**	**41 204**	**36 810**	**44 612**	**45 514**	**52 475**	**46 264**
6100 Paid solely by business	0	0	0	0	0	0	0	0	0	0
6200 Other	1 619	7 651	16 905	27 398	41 204	36 810	44 612	45 514	52 475	46 264
Accessories	..	5 504	12 403	22 206	25 301	23 717	23 211	28 480	32 153	45 864
Unallocable between 1000 and 5000 caused in exercices fiscal previous liquidation slopes or of payment	..	374	222	30	1 618	504	4 168	329	281	400
Additional state and local taxes	..	1 773	4 280	5 162	14 285	12 590	17 232	16 705	20 042	0

Note: Year ending 31st December.

The data are on a cash basis.

The 2018 data for tax revenues at the state and local levels of government are not available. They comprise revenues in categories 3000, 4000, 5000 and 6000.

Heading 1000: In ECLAC data, income taxes are presented net of credit on salary figures.

Heading 2000: In ECLAC data, social security contributions are presented net of transfers from the federal government for the payment of IMSS (Mexican Social Security Institute) pensions.

Some amounts of social security contributions are treated as non-tax revenue to align with the reporting to other international organisations.

Source: Ministry of Finance, Economic Department.

StatLink https://doi.org/10.1787/888934114761

Table 5.19. **Nicaragua**

Details of tax revenue / Ingresos tributarios detallados

Million NIO

	1990	2000	2007	2010	2013	2014	2015	2016	2017	2018
Total tax revenue	..	**9 300**	**25 811**	**36 162**	**57 654**	**67 119**	**77 567**	**88 482**	**98 803**	**95 166**
1000 Taxes on income, profits and capital gains	..	**1 144**	**5 746**	**8 351**	**14 832**	**18 033**	**21 313**	**24 910**	**28 557**	**29 258**
1100 Of individuals	..	..	..	..	..	..	..	..	..	..
1110 On income and profits	..	..	..	..	..	..	..	..	..	..
1120 On capital gains	..	..	..	..	..	..	..	..	..	..
1200 Corporate	..	..	..	..	..	..	..	..	..	..
1210 On profits	..	..	..	..	..	..	..	..	..	..
1220 On capital gains	..	..	..	..	..	..	..	..	..	..
1300 Unallocable between 1100 and 1200	..	1 144	5 746	8 351	14 832	18 033	21 313	24 910	28 557	29 258
2000 Social security contributions	..	**1 678**	**4 921**	**8 090**	**12 805**	**15 161**	**18 194**	**21 296**	**23 868**	**24 624**
2100 Employees	..	..	..	..	..	..	..	..	..	..
2110 On a payroll basis	..	..	..	..	..	..	..	..	..	..
2120 On an income tax basis	..	..	..	..	..	..	..	..	..	..
2200 Employers	..	..	..	..	..	..	..	..	..	..
2210 On a payroll basis	..	..	..	..	..	..	..	..	..	..
2220 On an income tax basis	..	..	..	..	..	..	..	..	..	..
2300 Self-employed or non-employed	..	..	..	..	..	..	..	..	..	..
2310 On a payroll basis	..	..	..	..	..	..	..	..	..	..
2320 On an income tax basis	..	..	..	..	..	..	..	..	..	..
2400 Unallocable between 2100, 2200 and 2300	..	1 678	4 921	8 090	12 805	15 161	18 194	21 296	23 868	24 624
2410 On a payroll basis	..	1 678	4 921	8 090	12 805	15 161	18 194	21 296	23 868	24 624
2420 On an income tax basis	..	0	0	0	0	0	0	0	0	0
3000 Taxes on payroll and workforce	..	**0**	**0**	**0**	**0**	**0**	**0**	**0**	**0**	**0**
4000 Taxes on property	..	**11**	**338**	**423**	**654**	**714**	**771**	**834**	**896**	**961**
4100 Recurrent taxes on immovable property	..	0	318	403	577	627	682	744	808	881
4110 Households	..	..	..	..	..	..	..	..	..	..
4120 Others	..	..	..	..	..	..	..	..	..	..
4200 Recurrent taxes on net wealth	..	0	0	0	0	0	0	0	0	0
4210 Individual	..	..	..	..	..	..	..	..	..	..
4220 Corporate	..	..	..	..	..	..	..	..	..	..
4300 Estate, inheritance and gift taxes	..	0	0	0	0	0	0	0	0	0
4310 Estate and inheritance taxes	..	..	..	..	..	..	..	..	..	..
4320 Gift taxes	..	..	..	..	..	..	..	..	..	..
4400 Taxes on financial and capital transactions	..	11	20	20	77	87	90	90	88	80
Stamp duties	..	11	20	20	77	87	90	90	88	80
4500 Non-recurrent taxes	..	0	0	0	0	0	0	0	0	0
4510 On net wealth	..	..	..	..	..	..	..	..	..	..
4520 Other non-recurrent taxes	..	..	..	..	..	..	..	..	..	..
4600 Other recurrent taxes on property	..	0	0	0	0	0	0	0	0	0
5000 Taxes on goods and services	..	**5 584**	**14 522**	**18 951**	**28 937**	**32 597**	**36 599**	**40 697**	**44 563**	**39 524**
5100 Taxes on production, sale, transfer, etc	..	5 584	14 283	18 608	28 367	31 923	35 798	39 855	43 619	38 489
5110 General taxes	..	2 931	9 155	11 932	19 332	22 265	23 787	26 273	29 201	25 500
5111 Value added taxes	..	2 931	8 025	10 353	16 736	19 385	20 714	22 822	25 551	21 905
5112 Sales tax	..	0	0	0	0	0	0	0	0	0
5113 Other	..	0	1 129	1 579	2 596	2 880	3 073	3 452	3 650	3 595
5120 Taxes on specific goods and services	..	2 653	5 128	6 676	9 035	9 659	12 011	13 581	14 419	12 990
5121 Excises	..	2 034	4 099	5 541	7 254	7 755	9 773	10 950	11 764	10 931
Alcoholic beverages	..	84	144	198	253	230	264	305	355	353
Beer	..	203	480	645	1 047	1 184	1 370	1 476	1 649	1 663
Cigarettes	..	70	158	45	174	0	0	0	0	0
Soft drinks	..	123	146	248	389	423	501	525	545	523
Petroleum products	..	1 359	2 108	2 699	3 418	3 938	4 396	5 021	5 534	5 395
Gaming machines	..	0	0	0	0	0	0	0	0	90
Excises on imports	..	196	1 025	1 559	1 924	1 902	3 105	3 505	3 541	2 763
Other excises	..	-1	37	148	49	78	136	117	140	145
5122 Profits of fiscal monopolies	..	0	0	0	0	0	0	0	0	0
5123 Customs and import duties	..	619	1 030	1 135	1 782	1 904	2 238	2 631	2 654	2 058
Custom duties	..	452	1 004	1 094	1 717	1 828	2 155	2 509	2 623	2 058
Temporary protection duty	..	96	0	0	0	0	0	0	0	0
On products originating in Colombia or Honduras	..	72	26	41	64	76	83	123	31	0
5124 Taxes on exports	..	0	0	0	0	0	0	0	0	0
5125 Taxes on investment goods	..	0	0	0	0	0	0	0	0	0
5126 Taxes on specific services	..	0	0	0	0	0	0	0	0	0
5127 Other taxes on internat. trade and transactions	..	0	0	0	0	0	0	0	0	0
5128 Other taxes	..	0	0	0	0	0	0	0	0	0
5130 Unallocable between 5110 and 5120	..	0	0	0	0	0	0	0	0	0
5200 Taxes on use of goods and perform activities	..	0	239	343	569	674	801	842	943	1 035
5210 Recurrent taxes	..	..	18	20	31	41	60	59	59	59

Table 5.19. **Nicaragua** *(cont.)*

Details of tax revenue / Ingresos tributarios detallados

Million NIO

	1990	2000	2007	2010	2013	2014	2015	2016	2017	2018
5211 Paid by households: motor vehicles	..	..	18	20	31	41	60	59	59	59
5212 Paid by others: motor vehicles	..	..	0	0	0	0	0	0	0	0
5213 Paid in respect of other goods	..	..	0	0	0	0	0	0	0	0
5220 Non-recurrent taxes	..	..	221	323	539	633	741	783	884	976
5300 Unallocable between 5100 and 5200	..	0	0	0	0	0	0	0	0	0
6000 Other taxes	**..**	**0**	**284**	**347**	**426**	**614**	**690**	**745**	**919**	**798**
6100 Paid solely by business	..	..	0	0	0	0	0	0	0	0
6200 Other	..	..	284	347	426	614	690	745	919	798

Note: Year ending 31st December.

The data are on a cash basis.

Revenue data before 2018 as well as local government tax revenues and social security contributions in 2018 are obtained from Inter-American Centre of Tax Administrations (CIAT). Comparable statistics for 1990 cannot be shown due to the devaluation of the Nicaraguan cordoba. Local government tax revenues have been added between 1991 and 2003 in this edition based on aggregate data from CIAT.

Heading 4400: Stamp duties have been recorded under heading 4400 in this edition. They were previously recorded under heading 6200.

Heading 5121: Special tax on gaming machines has been added under heading 5121 in this edition.

Source: Ministerio de Hacienda y Crédito Público (Ministry of Finance and Public Credit); Centro Interamericano de Administraciones Tributarias (Inter-American Centre of Tax Administrations).

StatLink https://doi.org/10.1787/888934114780

Table 5.20. **Panama / Panamá**

Details of tax revenue / Ingresos tributarios detallados

Million PAB

	1990	2000	2007	2010	2013	2014	2015	2016	2017	2018
Total tax revenue	**895**	**1 942**	**3 298**	**4 815**	**7 650**	**7 740**	**8 090**	**8 958**	**9 272**	**9 489**
1000 Taxes on income, profits and capital gains	**217**	**485**	**940**	**1 317**	**2 200**	**1 998**	**2 066**	**2 400**	**2 451**	**2 672**
1100 Of individuals	140	295	393	440	679	722	799	870	1 088	1 193
1110 On income and profits	140	295	393	440	679	722	799	870	1 088	1 193
Payroll	115	222	303	353	568	602	689	733	931	1 049
Personal income tax	14	20	28	35	52	58	45	54	68	54
Panama Canal Authority withholding	10	53	62	52	59	62	65	83	89	90
1120 On capital gains	..	..	..	..	..	..	..	..	..	..
1200 Corporate	66	159	382	603	970	896	851	1 036	943	955
1210 On profits	66	159	382	603	970	896	851	1 036	943	955
Colón Free Zone	5	3	12	20	39	43	36	36	41	53
Corporate income tax	61	155	370	584	931	853	815	1 000	902	901
1220 On capital gains	..	..	..	..	..	..	..	..	..	..
1300 Unallocable between 1100 and 1200	11	31	164	273	550	380	416	494	420	524
Dividends and complimentary tax	11	31	89	166	251	243	265	282	253	307
Capital gains	0	0	75	107	299	137	151	212	167	217
2000 Social security contributions	**271**	**742**	**1 104**	**1 637**	**2 677**	**2 794**	**3 049**	**3 380**	**3 560**	**3 654**
2100 Employees	..	..	..	..	..	..	..	..	..	..
2110 On a payroll basis	..	..	..	..	..	..	..	..	..	..
2120 On an income tax basis	..	..	..	..	..	..	..	..	..	..
2200 Employers	..	..	..	..	..	..	..	..	..	..
2210 On a payroll basis	..	..	..	..	..	..	..	..	..	..
2220 On an income tax basis	..	..	..	..	..	..	..	..	..	..
2300 Self-employed or non-employed	..	..	..	..	..	..	..	..	..	..
2310 On a payroll basis	..	..	..	..	..	..	..	..	..	..
2320 On an income tax basis	..	..	..	..	..	..	..	..	..	..
2400 Unallocable between 2100, 2200 and 2300	271	742	1 104	1 637	2 677	2 794	3 049	3 380	3 560	3 654
2410 On a payroll basis	..	..	..	..	..	..	..	..	..	..
2420 On an income tax basis	..	..	..	..	..	..	..	..	..	..
3000 Taxes on payroll and workforce	**0**	**36**	**40**	**59**	**82**	**134**	**111**	**111**	**127**	**130**
Education insurance	..	36	40	59	82	134	111	111	127	130
4000 Taxes on property	**32**	**43**	**119**	**138**	**230**	**220**	**199**	**209**	**251**	**244**
4100 Recurrent taxes on immovable property	28	34	74	108	181	176	151	168	207	209
4110 Households	28	34	74	108	181	176	151	168	207	209
4120 Others	0	0	0	0	0	0	0	0	0	0
4200 Recurrent taxes on net wealth	0	0	0	0	0	0	0	0	0	0
4210 Individual	..	..	..	..	..	..	..	..	..	..
4220 Corporate	..	..	..	..	..	..	..	..	..	..
4300 Estate, inheritance and gift taxes	0	0	0	0	0	0	0	0	0	0
4310 Estate and inheritance taxes	..	..	..	..	..	..	..	..	..	..
4320 Gift taxes	..	..	..	..	..	..	..	..	..	..
4400 Taxes on financial and capital transactions	3	9	45	30	49	45	48	41	44	36
4500 Non-recurrent taxes	0	0	0	0	0	0	0	0	0	0
4510 On net wealth	..	..	..	..	..	..	..	..	..	..
4520 Other non-recurrent taxes	..	..	..	..	..	..	..	..	..	..
4600 Other recurrent taxes on property	0	0	0	0	0	0	0	0	0	0
5000 Taxes on goods and services	**349**	**608**	**1 057**	**1 623**	**2 416**	**2 553**	**2 627**	**2 823**	**2 849**	**2 754**
5100 Taxes on production, sale, transfer, etc	332	546	961	1 473	2 193	2 319	2 376	2 555	2 570	2 474
5110 General taxes	80	69	205	766	1 269	1 351	1 357	1 510	1 529	1 477
5111 Value added taxes	80	69	205	766	1 269	1 351	1 357	1 510	1 529	1 477
ITBMS on sales	31	69	205	399	740	794	798	974	983	957
ITBMS on imports	49	0	0	367	529	558	559	536	546	519
5112 Sales tax	0	0	0	0	0	0	0	0	0	0
5113 Other	0	0	0	0	0	0	0	0	0	0
5120 Taxes on specific goods and services	251	477	756	707	924	967	1 019	1 045	1 041	997
5121 Excises	0	141	140	239	397	452	496	519	480	449
Petroleum products	..	109	90	97	117	133	157	214	190	168
Beer	..	18	25	31	36	42	48	49	49	53
Cigarette	..	0	0	0	27	24	32	23	21	24
Wine and liquor	..	12	11	11	16	23	15	10	6	18
Soft drinks	..	2	4	6	7	7	7	6	7	11
Automobiles	..	0	0	0	142	176	182	172	182	149
Other excises	..	0	11	95	53	48	53	46	25	27
5122 Profits of fiscal monopolies	0	0	0	0	0	0	0	0	0	0
5123 Customs and import duties	125	298	574	390	409	381	391	355	358	338
5124 Taxes on exports	13	0	0	0	0	0	0	0	0	0
5125 Taxes on investment goods	0	0	0	0	0	0	0	0	0	0

Table 5.20. **Panama / Panamá** *(cont.)*

Details of tax revenue / Ingresos tributarios detallados

Million PAB

	1990	2000	2007	2010	2013	2014	2015	2016	2017	2018
5126 Taxes on specific services	1	37	41	78	118	134	133	171	203	211
Insurance premiums	0	17	24	47	61	63	46	52	86	90
Cable and telecommunications	0	16	8	17	34	45	39	41	40	42
Gambling	0	0	1	1	2	2	23	53	52	53
Banks, financial institutions and exchange houses	0	2	9	12	22	24	24	25	25	26
Commercial activities and services	1	3	0	0	0	0	0	0	0	0
5127 Other taxes on internat. trade and transactions	0	0	0	0	0	0	0	0	0	0
5128 Other taxes	0	0	0	0	0	0	0	0	0	0
5130 Unallocable between 5110 and 5120	0	0	0	0	0	0	0	0	0	0
5200 Taxes on use of goods and perform activities	15	62	97	151	222	234	251	268	279	280
Other indirect taxes	0	0	0	36	55	52	59	65	69	66
5210 Recurrent taxes	12	58	83	115	168	182	192	204	210	214
5211 Paid by households: motor vehicles	0	7	10	0	0	0	0	0	0	0
5212 Paid by others: motor vehicles	0	5	5	0	0	0	0	0	0	0
5213 Paid in respect of other goods	12	46	68	115	168	182	192	204	210	214
Commercial licences	12	19	35	75	108	116	120	123	121	124
Permission to conduct commercial and service activities	0	25	31	38	57	62	69	77	84	86
Permission to conduct industrial activities	0	2	2	2	3	3	3	4	4	4
Others	0	0	0	0	0	0	0	0	0	0
5220 Non-recurrent taxes	4	4	13	0	0	0	0	0	0	0
Building and construction	0	4	13	..	..	..	..	..	..	..
Ship registration	4	0	0	..	..	..	..	..	..	..
5300 Unallocable between 5100 and 5200	2	0	0	0	0	0	0	0	0	0
6000 Other taxes	**26**	**27**	**38**	**41**	**46**	**41**	**37**	**35**	**34**	**34**
6100 Paid solely by business	0	0	0	0	0	0	0	0	0	0
6200 Other	26	27	38	41	46	41	37	35	34	34
Stamp duties	17	27	38	41	46	41	37	35	34	34
Others	9	0	0	0	0	0	0	0	0	0

Note: Year ending 31st December.

The data are on a cash basis.

Central government tax revenues between 2000 and 2014 have been updated with latest data from Contraloría General de la República, while data after 2014 have been obtained from Ministerio de Economía y Finanzas in this edition. Tax revenue data are exclusive of documentos fiscales which are considered as wastable tax credits by OECD guidelines. Municipal tax revenues are estimated in 2018.

Heading 3000: In ECLAC data, education insurance is classified as "Other taxes" (6000).

Heading 5121: Excise tax for cigarette is classified as individual country specific tax under heading 5121 in this edition. It was previously in the category of other excises. Excise tax for various products is no longer listed as country specific item and instead grouped within other excises in this edition.

Heading 5126: Tax on commercial activities and services and tax on banks, financial institutions and exchange houses are classified under heading 5126 in this edition. They were previously under heading 5127. In CIAT and ECLAC data, tax on banks, financial institutions and exchange houses is classified as a property tax (4000).

Heading 5200: Other indirect taxes are classified under heading 5200 in this edition. They were previously under heading 6200.

Heading 5213: Tax on commercial licences for business operations is classified under heading 5213 in this edition. It was previously under heading 4600.

Heading 6200: Tax on legal services is disaggregated in this edition into stamp duties which remain under heading 6200 and tax on telephone calls and cables which is merged with tax on cable and telecommunications under heading 5126. Stamp duties before 2000 include tax on telephone calls and cables which cannot be distinguished due to data availability.

Source: Contraloría General de la República de Panamá (Comptroller General of the Republic of Panama); Ministerio de Economía y Finanzas de Panamá (Ministry of Economy and Finance of Panama).

StatLink https://doi.org/10.1787/888934114799

Table 5.21. **Paraguay**

Details of tax revenue / Ingresos tributarios detallados

Million PYG

	1990	2000	2007	2010	2013	2014	2015	2016	2017	2018
Total tax revenue	**579 139**	**3 587 451**	**9 667 630**	**15 637 623**	**20 926 388**	**25 778 248**	**25 852 479**	**27 462 757**	**30 728 947**	**32 357 937**
1000 Taxes on income, profits and capital gains	**73 726**	**470 388**	**1 228 684**	**2 096 498**	**3 100 223**	**4 672 269**	**3 922 384**	**4 429 169**	**5 086 803**	**5 265 609**
1100 Of individuals	..	15 042	11 966	31 263	85 188	361 079	409 238	396 573	526 704	626 525
1110 On income and profits	..	15 042	11 966	31 263	85 188	361 079	409 238	396 573	526 704	626 525
IRAGRO-IMAGRO	..	15 042	11 200	30 113	71 813	277 157	283 401	256 019	326 555	360 003
Personal income tax	..	0	766	1 150	13 375	83 921	125 837	140 554	200 150	266 523
1120 On capital gains	..	..	..	..	..	..	..	..	..	..
1200 Corporate	..	455 346	1 216 718	2 065 235	3 015 035	4 311 190	3 513 146	4 032 596	4 560 099	4 639 084
1210 On profits	..	455 346	1 216 718	2 065 235	3 015 035	4 311 190	3 513 146	4 032 596	4 560 099	4 639 084
Income tax on small businesses	..	0	4 620	9 380	7 831	9 063	14 563	18 567	22 848	25 540
Single tax	..	4 238	8 411	715	32	72	5	3	2	1
Single tax on maquiladoras companies	..	0	1 401	3 310	4 669	9 783	10 892	12 087	20 194	27 070
IRACIS	..	451 108	1 202 286	2 051 830	3 002 503	4 292 272	3 487 686	4 001 939	4 517 056	4 586 475
1220 On capital gains	..	..	..	..	..	..	..	..	..	..
1300 Unallocable between 1100 and 1200	73 726	0	0	0	0	0	0	0	0	0
Others	73 726	..	..	..	..	..	..	..	..	..
2000 Social security contributions	**0**	**919 533**	**2 265 097**	**3 552 640**	**5 543 977**	**6 705 101**	**7 044 316**	**7 048 846**	**8 052 403**	**8 209 087**
2100 Employees	..	..	..	..	..	..	..	..	..	..
2110 On a payroll basis	..	..	..	..	..	..	..	..	..	..
2120 On an income tax basis	..	..	..	..	..	..	..	..	..	..
2200 Employers	..	..	..	..	..	..	..	..	..	..
2210 On a payroll basis	..	..	..	..	..	..	..	..	..	..
2220 On an income tax basis	..	..	..	..	..	..	..	..	..	..
2300 Self-employed or non-employed	..	..	..	..	..	..	..	..	..	..
2310 On a payroll basis	..	..	..	..	..	..	..	..	..	..
2320 On an income tax basis	..	..	..	..	..	..	..	..	..	..
2400 Unallocable between 2100, 2200 and 2300	..	919 533	2 265 097	3 552 640	5 543 977	6 705 101	7 044 316	7 048 846	8 052 403	8 209 087
2410 On a payroll basis	..	919 533	2 265 097	3 552 640	5 543 977	6 705 101	7 044 316	7 048 846	8 052 403	8 209 087
2420 On an income tax basis	..	0	0	0	0	0	0	0	0	0
3000 Taxes on payroll and workforce	**0**	**0**	**0**	**0**	**0**	**0**	**0**	**0**	**0**	**0**
4000 Taxes on property	**17 162**	**71 777**	**270 574**	**264 354**	**350 348**	**390 208**	**413 066**	**548 611**	**539 060**	**586 379**
4100 Recurrent taxes on immovable property	17 162	0	196 504	258 423	0	0	405 806	540 423	529 986	576 632
4110 Households	17 162	..	196 504	258 423	..	..	405 806	540 423	529 986	576 632
Real estate tax	17 162	..	190 924	249 697	..	..	390 772	514 404	501 873	546 045
Tax on vacant lots	0	..	2 046	2 925	..	..	4 818	10 284	13 600	14 797
Large estate and land tax	0	..	3 533	5 801	..	..	10 216	15 736	14 513	15 790
4120 Others	0	..	0	0	..	..	0	0	0	0
4200 Recurrent taxes on net wealth	0	0	0	0	0	0	0	0	0	0
4210 Individual	..	..	..	..	..	..	..	..	..	..
4220 Corporate	..	..	..	..	..	..	..	..	..	..
4300 Estate, inheritance and gift taxes	0	0	0	0	0	0	0	0	0	0
4310 Estate and inheritance taxes	..	..	..	..	..	..	..	..	..	..
4320 Gift taxes	..	..	..	..	..	..	..	..	..	..
4400 Taxes on financial and capital transactions	0	71 777	74 054	4 189	179	106	7 195	6 918	7 609	8 153
Real estate transfer tax	..	0	0	0	0	0	0	0	0	0
Municipal Seal and Stamp Paper Tax	..	0	2 923	3 857	0	0	6 912	6 515	7 464	8 121
Registration and stamp duties	..	71 777	71 130	332	179	106	282	403	144	31
4500 Non-recurrent taxes	0	0	0	0	0	0	0	0	0	0
4510 On net wealth	..	..	..	..	..	..	..	..	..	..
4520 Other non-recurrent taxes	..	..	..	..	..	..	..	..	..	..
4600 Other recurrent taxes on property	0	0	16	1 742	0	0	66	1 269	1 466	1 595
5000 Taxes on goods and services	**438 444**	**2 080 878**	**5 818 667**	**9 473 318**	**11 808 562**	**13 933 097**	**14 299 029**	**15 245 422**	**16 837 338**	**18 086 188**
5100 Taxes on production, sale, transfer, etc	438 444	2 080 878	5 684 037	9 244 989	11 524 590	13 596 422	13 858 293	14 743 302	16 354 222	17 560 560
5110 General taxes	0	1 150 496	3 496 787	5 991 694	7 843 002	9 363 648	9 768 800	10 482 238	11 221 710	11 851 394
5111 Value added taxes	0	1 150 496	3 496 787	5 991 694	7 843 002	9 363 648	9 768 800	10 482 238	11 221 710	11 851 394
5112 Sales tax	..	0	0	0	0	0	0	0	0	0
5113 Other	..	0	0	0	0	0	0	0	0	0
5120 Taxes on specific goods and services	438 444	930 382	2 187 250	3 253 295	3 681 588	4 232 774	4 089 493	4 261 064	5 132 512	5 709 165
5121 Excises	300 219	456 561	1 335 412	1 710 531	2 048 143	2 455 139	2 404 222	2 589 108	2 890 013	3 158 850
Fuels	41 087	316 694	1 000 894	1 126 143	1 427 769	1 787 112	1 775 479	1 830 782	2 032 235	2 300 601
Other excises	259 132	136 194	309 463	537 887	620 374	655 783	616 342	745 189	843 123	841 900
Animal health and quality service	0	3 673	24 923	46 501	0	12 244	12 401	13 137	14 656	16 350
Livestock trade	0	0	132	0	0	0	0	0	0	0
5122 Profits of fiscal monopolies	0	0	0	0	0	0	0	0	0	0
5123 Customs and import duties	138 225	473 821	838 494	1 524 252	1 633 378	1 776 724	1 659 535	1 642 818	2 206 934	2 512 883
5124 Taxes on exports	0	0	0	0	0	0	0	0	0	0
5125 Taxes on investment goods	0	0	0	0	0	0	0	0	0	0

Table 5.21. **Paraguay** *(cont.)*

Details of tax revenue / Ingresos tributarios detallados

Million PYG

	1990	2000	2007	2010	2013	2014	2015	2016	2017	2018
5126 Taxes on specific services	0	0	13 344	18 513	67	911	25 736	29 138	35 564	37 432
Advertising	..	..	3 613	5 249	29	0	7 428	8 424	9 489	10 325
Public transport	..	..	4 173	4 363	1	0	4 297	4 316	4 080	4 439
Gambling	..	..	162	16	0	911	4 654	3 683	7 131	6 497
Advertising and gambling	..	..	5 361	8 884	37	0	9 357	12 715	14 821	16 125
Other taxes on specific services	..	..	35	0	0	0	0	0	43	47
5127 Other taxes on internat. trade and transactions	0	0	0	0	0	0	0	0	0	0
5128 Other taxes	0	0	0	0	0	0	0	0	0	0
5130 Unallocable between 5110 and 5120	0	0	0	0	0	0	0	0	0	0
5200 Taxes on use of goods and perform activities	0	0	133 322	228 092	283 972	336 675	417 897	474 711	452 082	491 864
5210 Recurrent taxes	..	..	113 441	195 367	283 754	336 618	351 559	409 230	391 270	425 707
5211 Paid by households: motor vehicles	..	..	0	0	..	..	0	0	0	0
5212 Paid by others: motor vehicles	..	..	28 343	52 365	..	..	94 393	106 200	109 084	118 685
Motor vehicle licences	..	..	28 343	52 365	..	..	94 393	106 200	109 084	118 685
5213 Paid in respect of other goods	..	..	85 098	143 002	..	..	257 166	303 030	282 186	307 022
Licencing fees	..	..	75 323	126 965	..	..	229 686	274 468	250 528	272 578
slaughter tax	..	..	3 363	4 271	..	..	5 074	5 584	5 395	5 870
Tax to the owners of animals	..	..	6 412	11 766	..	..	22 406	22 978	26 263	28 574
5220 Non-recurrent taxes	..	..	19 881	32 725	351	57	66 338	65 482	60 812	66 157
Tax on construction	..	..	16 168	31 696	123	0	65 403	64 284	60 092	65 381
Luxury automobile tax	..	..	2 750	91	218	57	54	152	7	0
Trademarks registration	..	..	962	938	10	0	881	1 045	713	776
5300 Unallocable between 5100 and 5200	0	0	1 309	237	0	0	22 838	27 409	31 034	33 765
6000 Other taxes	**49 807**	**44 875**	**84 608**	**250 812**	**123 278**	**77 573**	**173 684**	**190 709**	**213 344**	**210 672**
6100 Paid solely by business	0	0	0	0	0	0	0	0	0	0
6200 Other	49 807	44 875	84 608	250 812	123 278	77 573	173 684	190 709	213 344	210 672
Taxes replaced	0	0	0	0	0	0	0	0	0	0
Other	49 807	44 875	84 608	250 812	123 278	77 573	173 684	190 709	213 344	210 672

Note: Year ending 31st December.

The data are on a cash basis.

The figures for years up to and including 2004, as well as for 2013 and 2014, exclude local government tax revenues as the data are not available. This affects data in categories 4000, 5000 and 6000.

Heading 1110: The proportion of data included in this category has been estimated from 1999 to 2014 based on the disaggregation provided in 2015.

Heading 1210: The proportion of data included in this category has been estimated from 1999 to 2014 based on the disaggregation provided in 2015.

Heading 2000: Data on social security contributions collected by decentralised institutions are not available for 2011 to 2014, with the exception of the contributions made to the Instituto de Previsión Social (Social Security Institute).

Heading 4110 : The land fractionation tax has been classified under heading 4100 in this edition. This tax was classified under heading 4400 in the previous edition.

Heading 4400 : The municipal seal and stamp paper tax and the registration and stamp duties have been classified under heading 4400 in this edition. These taxes were classified under heading 6200 in the previous edition.

Heading 5126 : Taxes on credit operations in "other taxes on specific services" have been classified under heading 5126 in this edition. These taxes were classified under heading 4400 in the previous edition.

Heading 5213 : The slaughter tax and the tax on the owners of animals have been classified under heading 5213 in this edition. These taxes were classified under heading 5126 and heading 4600 respectively in the previous edition.

Heading 5220 : The tax on construction,the luxury automobile tax and the trademaks registration have been classified under heading 5220 in this edition. These taxes were classified under heading 5213 and heading 6200 in the previous edition.

Source: Subsecretaría de Estado de Tributación, Ministerio de Hacienda del Paraguay (Tax Undersecretary, Ministry of Finance of Paraguay).

StatLink https://doi.org/10.1787/888934114818

Table 5.22. **Peru / Perú**

Details of tax revenue / Ingresos tributarios detallados

Million PEN

	1990	2000	2007	2010	2013	2014	2015	2016	2017	2018
Total tax revenue	**637**	**26 761**	**59 176**	**74 746**	**102 988**	**110 061**	**106 095**	**105 952**	**106 367**	**121 746**
1000 Taxes on income, profits and capital gains	**37**	**5 078**	**24 139**	**27 317**	**39 357**	**43 577**	**37 772**	**40 360**	**39 846**	**43 979**
1100 Of individuals	3	2 117	4 645	6 518	10 570	11 423	11 137	11 760	13 008	13 598
First category	..	167	217	160	310	374	443	504	532	580
Second category	..	7	611	869	1 275	1 214	1 287	1 536	1 581	1 772
Fourth category	..	234	408	521	744	834	783	871	894	960
Fifth category	..	1 641	3 241	4 735	7 820	8 473	8 044	8 248	8 444	9 162
Tax debt payments	..	68	168	233	421	529	581	601	1 558	1 125
1110 On income and profits	..	..	..	..	..	..	..	..	..	..
1120 On capital gains	..	..	..	..	..	..	..	..	..	..
1200 Corporate	32	2 526	18 724	19 561	26 207	26 593	24 266	24 786	24 604	28 830
1210 On profits	32	2 526	18 724	19 561	26 207	26 593	24 266	24 786	24 604	28 830
Third category	..	2 023	13 258	14 652	19 633	18 536	16 817	16 496	15 499	17 268
Income tax on mining	..	0	0	0	337	372	208	236	638	770
Income tax special regime	..	47	60	118	246	275	310	335	323	344
Other incomes corporate	..	18	95	148	187	193	167	215	233	251
Tax debt payments	..	438	3 829	2 856	3 029	3 703	3 066	3 204	3 327	5 244
Temporary tax on net assets	..	0	1 483	1 788	2 776	3 513	3 697	4 300	4 585	4 953
1220 On capital gains	..	..	..	..	..	..	..	..	..	..
1300 Unallocable between 1100 and 1200	1	436	770	1 239	2 579	5 561	2 369	3 814	2 233	1 550
Income tax on non-residents	1	487	961	1 511	2 848	6 027	3 248	5 205	3 462	3 560
Income tax refunds	0	-51	-191	-272	-269	-466	-879	-1 391	-1 228	-2 009
2000 Social security contributions	**50**	**3 175**	**5 233**	**7 929**	**11 259**	**11 847**	**12 680**	**13 186**	**13 676**	**14 872**
2100 Employees	..	566	1 005	2 468	3 211	3 211	3 508	3 646	3 796	4 216
2110 On a payroll basis	..	566	978	1 700	2 854	3 100	3 371	3 550	3 662	3 940
2120 On an income tax basis	..	0	26	767	357	112	137	97	134	275
Solidarity contribution for pension plan	..	..	26	767	357	112	137	97	134	275
2200 Employers	..	2 515	4 221	5 454	8 044	8 631	9 170	9 536	9 878	10 653
2210 On a payroll basis	..	2 432	4 039	5 216	7 827	8 413	8 926	9 282	9 591	10 299
2220 On an income tax basis	..	83	182	238	217	218	244	255	287	354
2300 Self-employed or non-employed	..	95	8	7	4	4	2	3	2	4
2310 On a payroll basis	..	0	0	0	0	0	0	0	0	0
2320 On an income tax basis	..	95	8	7	4	4	2	3	2	4
2400 Unallocable between 2100, 2200 and 2300	50	0	0	0	0	0	0	0	0	0
2410 On a payroll basis	50	..	..	..	..	..	..	..	..	..
2420 On an income tax basis	0	..	..	..	..	..	..	..	..	..
3000 Taxes on payroll and workforce	**0**	**1 176**	**-40**	**1**	**0**	**-82**	**4**	**1**	**-2**	**1**
Extraordinary solidarity tax (IES)	..	1 151	9	3	1	3	5	1	0	1
IES refunds	..	-2	-48	-2	-1	-86	-1	0	-2	0
National Housing Fund (FONAVI)	..	27	0	0	0	0	0	0	0	0
4000 Taxes on property	**87**	**323**	**1 931**	**2 231**	**2 131**	**2 154**	**2 429**	**2 637**	**2 573**	**2 680**
4100 Recurrent taxes on immovable property	0	298	554	727	1 127	1 230	1 463	1 629	1 718	1 748
4110 Households	..	..	..	..	..	..	..	..	..	..
4120 Others	..	..	..	..	..	..	..	..	..	..
4200 Recurrent taxes on net wealth	49	0	0	0	0	0	0	0	0	0
4210 Individual	..	..	..	..	..	..	..	..	..	..
4220 Corporate	..	..	..	..	..	..	..	..	..	..
4300 Estate, inheritance and gift taxes	0	0	0	0	0	0	0	0	0	0
4310 Estate and inheritance taxes	..	..	..	..	..	..	..	..	..	..
4320 Gift taxes	..	..	..	..	..	..	..	..	..	..
4400 Taxes on financial and capital transactions	38	25	1 377	1 504	1 005	925	966	1 008	855	932
Financial transactions tax	0	0	1 031	944	134	153	161	168	175	200
Real estate transfer tax	0	25	347	560	870	772	805	840	680	732
Tax Law Decree 519	38	0	0	0	0	0	0	0	0	0
4500 Non-recurrent taxes	0	0	0	0	0	0	0	0	0	0
4510 On net wealth	..	..	..	..	..	..	..	..	..	..
4520 Other non-recurrent taxes	..	..	..	..	..	..	..	..	..	..
4600 Other recurrent taxes on property	0	0	0	0	0	0	0	0	0	0
5000 Taxes on goods and services	**454**	**16 263**	**27 142**	**36 353**	**46 264**	**49 933**	**51 102**	**48 247**	**50 061**	**58 551**
5100 Taxes on production, sale, transfer, etc	454	16 239	27 075	36 199	46 030	49 668	50 820	47 943	49 774	58 257
5110 General taxes	109	9 646	20 151	29 094	37 953	41 779	42 612	39 462	41 036	49 038
5111 Value added taxes	109	9 646	20 151	29 094	37 953	41 779	42 612	39 462	41 036	49 038
VAT (internal)	69	6 992	13 586	19 629	27 164	28 732	30 410	31 040	32 114	35 125
VAT (imports)	41	4 961	11 673	15 908	20 655	21 620	21 259	21 652	22 529	25 541
VAT refunds	0	-2 307	-5 107	-6 442	-9 867	-8 573	-9 056	-13 231	-13 606	-11 628
5112 Sales tax	0	0	0	0	0	0	0	0	0	0
5113 Other	0	0	0	0	0	0	0	0	0	0
5120 Taxes on specific goods and services	345	6 593	6 924	7 105	8 077	7 889	8 208	8 482	8 737	9 219

Table 5.22. **Peru / Perú** *(cont.)*

Details of tax revenue / Ingresos tributarios detallados

Million PEN

	1990	2000	2007	2010	2013	2014	2015	2016	2017	2018
5121 Excises	232	3 518	4 445	4 875	5 787	5 488	5 796	6 175	6 588	7 011
Fuels	151	2 145	2 419	2 410	2 502	2 041	2 211	2 423	2 604	2 565
Gasoline sales tax	3	97	174	210	335	380	332	312	363	437
Other excises	78	1 304	1 872	2 258	2 978	3 094	3 284	3 479	3 711	4 295
Excise tax refunds	0	-28	-20	-4	-28	-27	-31	-39	-91	-286
5122 Profits of fiscal monopolies	0	0	0	0	0	0	0	0	0	0
5123 Customs and import duties	64	2 960	2 198	1 803	1 706	1 790	1 775	1 606	1 448	1 455
5124 Taxes on exports	2	0	0	0	0	0	0	0	0	0
5125 Taxes on investment goods	0	0	0	0	0	0	0	0	0	0
5126 Taxes on specific services	0	115	281	427	585	612	637	701	702	754
Casinos and slot machines	..	81	109	187	269	279	279	298	297	318
Tourism tax	..	0	87	105	118	127	144	173	174	193
Municipal taxes on services	..	34	85	135	198	206	214	230	230	243
5127 Other taxes on internat. trade and transactions	48	0	0	0	0	0	0	0	0	0
5128 Other taxes	0	0	0	0	0	0	0	0	0	0
5130 Unallocable between 5110 and 5120	0	0	0	0	0	0	0	0	0	0
5200 Taxes on use of goods and perform activities	0	25	67	154	233	264	282	303	288	294
5210 Recurrent taxes	..	25	67	154	233	264	282	303	288	294
5211 Paid by households: motor vehicles	..	..	..	..	..	..	..	..	..	..
5212 Paid by others: motor vehicles	..	..	..	..	..	..	..	..	..	..
5213 Paid in respect of other goods	..	..	..	..	..	..	..	..	..	..
5220 Non-recurrent taxes	..	0	0	0	0	0	0	0	0	0
5300 Unallocable between 5100 and 5200	0	0	0	0	0	0	0	0	0	0
6000 Other taxes	**9**	**745**	**770**	**914**	**3 976**	**2 633**	**2 108**	**1 522**	**213**	**1 662**
6100 Paid solely by business	0	84	82	108	147	158	179	185	140	133
Single simplified regime	..	84	82	108	147	158	179	185	140	133
University Development Fund	..	0	0	0	0	0	0	0	0	0
6200 Other	9	662	688	806	3 830	2 475	1 929	1 337	73	1 529
Tax debt payments	9	542	510	714	893	814	922	1 068	1 109	1 320
Other taxes	0	133	253	280	3 159	2 060	1 790	1 114	219	1 225
Other tax refunds	0	-14	-74	-188	-222	-399	-783	-845	-1 255	-1 016

Note: Year ending 31st December.

The data are on a cash basis.

The figures for years up to 2000 exclude local government tax revenues as the data are not available.

Heading 2000: All contributions pertaining to pensions are only made by employees and contributions to healthcare are made by employers. The exceptions are special regimes which apply to self-employed and are levied on an income basis.

Heading 5123: Import tax refunds are classified under 6200 because they cannot be distinguished from other tax refunds.

Source: Superintendencia Nacional de Aduanas y de Administración Tributaria (National Superintendence of Customs and Tax Administration - SUNAT); Banco de la Nación (Bank of the Nation); Ministerio de Economía y Finanzas (Ministry of Economy and Finance).

StatLink https://doi.org/10.1787/888934114837

Table 5.23. **Saint Lucia / Santa Lucía**

Details of tax revenue / Ingresos tributarios detallados

Million XCD

	1990	2000	2007	2010	2013	2014	2015	2016	2017	2018
Total tax revenue	..	**432**	**687**	**736**	**819**	**872**	**934**	**977**	**985**	**1 042**
1000 Taxes on income, profits and capital gains	..	**137**	**196**	**224**	**220**	**224**	**242**	**259**	**253**	**269**
1100 Of individuals	..	49	71	83	98	101	105	106	105	113
1110 On income and profits	..	49	71	83	98	101	105	106	105	113
1120 On capital gains	..	..	..	..	..	..	..	..	..	..
1200 Corporate	..	63	92	95	55	71	78	99	94	94
1210 On profits	..	63	92	95	55	71	78	99	94	94
1220 On capital gains of corporates	..	..	..	..	..	..	..	..	..	..
1300 Unallocable between 1100 and 1200	..	26	33	46	67	53	58	53	54	61
Withholdings	..	7	5	14	26	27	25	24	24	29
Arrears	..	25	35	42	49	33	44	39	40	43
Tax Refunds	..	-6	-8	-10	-8	-7	-10	-10	-10	-10
2000 Social security contributions	..	..	..	..	..	..	..	..	..	..
2100 Employees	..	..	..	..	..	..	..	..	..	..
2110 On a payroll basis	..	..	..	..	..	..	..	..	..	..
2120 On an income tax basis	..	..	..	..	..	..	..	..	..	..
2200 Employers	..	..	..	..	..	..	..	..	..	..
2210 On a payroll basis	..	..	..	..	..	..	..	..	..	..
2220 On an income tax basis	..	..	..	..	..	..	..	..	..	..
2300 Self-employed or non-employed	..	..	..	..	..	..	..	..	..	..
2310 On a payroll basis	..	..	..	..	..	..	..	..	..	..
2320 On an income tax basis	..	..	..	..	..	..	..	..	..	..
2400 Unallocable between 2100, 2200 and 2300	..	..	..	..	..	..	..	..	..	..
2410 On a payroll basis	..	..	..	..	..	..	..	..	..	..
2420 On an income tax basis	..	..	..	..	..	..	..	..	..	..
3000 Taxes on payroll and workforce	..	**0**	**0**	**0**	**0**	**0**	**0**	**0**	**0**	**0**
4000 Taxes on property	..	**11**	**37**	**19**	**22**	**24**	**23**	**26**	**26**	**26**
4100 Recurrent taxes on immovable property	..	0	0	0	0	0	0	0	0	0
4110 Households	..	..	..	..	..	..	..	..	..	..
4120 Others	..	..	..	..	..	..	..	..	..	..
4200 Recurrent taxes on net wealth	..	0	0	0	0	0	0	0	0	0
4210 Individual	..	..	..	..	..	..	..	..	..	..
4220 Corporate	..	..	..	..	..	..	..	..	..	..
4300 Estate, inheritance and gift taxes	..	0	0	0	0	0	0	0	0	0
4310 Estate and inheritance taxes	..	..	..	..	..	..	..	..	..	..
4320 Gift taxes	..	..	..	..	..	..	..	..	..	..
4400 Taxes on financial and capital transactions	..	9	32	16	14	14	12	14	13	17
4500 Other non-reccurrent taxes on property	..	2	5	3	8	9	11	12	12	9
4510 On net wealth	..	..	..	..	..	..	..	..	..	..
4520 Other non-recurrent taxes	..	..	..	..	..	..	..	..	..	..
4600 Other recurrent taxes on property	..	0	0	0	0	0	0	0	0	0
5000 Taxes on goods and services	..	**284**	**455**	**492**	**577**	**624**	**669**	**693**	**707**	**748**
5100 Taxes on production, sale, transfer, etc	..	277	429	467	549	602	641	662	680	720
5110 General taxes on goods and services	..	101	122	119	300	334	347	335	309	331
5111 Value added taxes	..	0	0	0	299	334	346	335	309	331
VAT (domestic)	..	..	..	..	157	183	184	177	170	181
VAT (imports)	..	..	..	..	142	151	163	159	139	149
5112 Sales tax	..	101	122	119	1	0	0	0	0	0
Consumption tax (domestic)	..	11	10	6	0	0	0	..	..	..
Consumption tax (Imports)	..	90	112	114	1	0	0	..	..	..
5113 Other	..	0	0	0	0	0	0	0	0	0
5120 Taxes on specific goods and services	..	176	307	347	249	268	294	327	372	390
5121 Excises	..	34	49	85	65	78	92	112	131	133
Excise tax (domestic)	..	28	3	14	4	4	4	4	4	4
Excise tax (imports)	..	0	43	68	57	67	74	87	106	109
Fuel Surcharge	..	3	4	4	4	8	15	21	21	20
Surcharge on international calls	..	4	0	0	0	0	0	0	0	0
5122 Profits of fiscal monopolies	..	0	0	0	0	0	0	0	0	0
5123 Customs and import duties	..	108	193	186	156	163	178	189	201	205
Import Duty	..	64	107	101	95	101	106	114	121	123
Thruput Charge	..	1	3	6	1	2	3	4	5	4
Service Charge (imports) and security charges	..	33	65	63	60	60	69	71	75	78
Environmental Levy	..	9	18	16	0	0	0	0	0	0
5124 Taxes on exports	..	0	0	0	0	0	0	0	0	0
5125 Taxes on investment goods	..	0	0	0	0	0	0	0	0	0
5126 Taxes on specific services	..	34	65	76	29	27	24	26	40	51
Hotel occupancy tax	..	23	34	34	2	3	1	0	0	0
Insurance premium tax	..	4	7	7	9	8	8	8	9	8

Table 5.23. **Saint Lucia / Santa Lucía** *(cont.)*

Details of tax revenue / Ingresos tributarios detallados

Million XCD

	1990	2000	2007	2010	2013	2014	2015	2016	2017	2018
Cellular tax	..	0	12	18	0	0	0	0	0	0
Passenger facility fee	..	0	3	5	5	4	4	3	4	3
Travel tax	..	3	3	4	3	4	4	4	5	5
Airport tax	..	5	6	9	10	8	7	11	22	35
5127 Other taxes on internat. trade and transactions	..	0	0	0	0	0	0	0	0	0
5128 Other taxes	..	0	0	0	0	0	0	0	0	0
5130 Unallocable between 5110 and 5120	..	0	0	0	0	0	0	0	0	0
5200 Taxes on use of goods and to perform activities	..	7	25	26	28	22	29	31	27	28
5210 Recurrent taxes	..	7	25	26	28	22	29	31	27	28
5211 Paid by households: motor vehicles	..	0	0	0	0	0	0	0	0	0
5212 Paid by others: motor vehicles	..	0	0	0	0	0	0	0	0	0
5213 Paid in respect of other goods	..	7	25	26	28	22	29	31	27	28
5220 Non-recurrent taxes	..	0	0	0	0	0	0	0	0	0
5300 Unallocable between 5100 and 5200	..	0	0	0	0	0	0	0	0	0
6000 Other taxes	**..**	**0**	**0**	**0**	**0**	**0**	**0**	**0**	**0**	**0**
6100 Paid solely by business	..	..	..	..	..	..	..	..	..	..
6200 Other	..	..	..	..	..	..	..	..	..	..

Note: Year ending 31st March. For example, the data for 2018 represent April 2018 to March 2019.
The data are on a cash basis.
Heading 2000: Social security contributions data are not available.
The figures for the sub-categories under the heading 4000, 5120 and 5200 are not available.
Source: The Central Statistical Office of Saint Lucia.

StatLink https://doi.org/10.1787/888934114856

Table 5.24. **Trinidad and Tobago / Trinidad y Tobago**

Details of tax revenue / Ingresos tributarios detallados

Million TTD

	1990	2000	2007	2010	2013	2014	2015	2016	2017	2018
Total tax revenue	**4 923**	**10 953**	**37 099**	**39 720**	**47 946**	**50 911**	**46 559**	**33 984**	**31 164**	**36 813**
1000 Taxes on income, profits and capital gains	**2 595**	**6 224**	**26 853**	**27 213**	**33 139**	**36 371**	**29 628**	**17 057**	**16 133**	**19 411**
1100 Of individuals	669	2 325	3 426	4 674	6 458	6 859	7 752	7 458	6 570	6 840
1110 On income and profits	669	2 325	3 426	4 674	6 458	6 859	7 752	7 458	6 570	6 840
Health surcharge	92	149	170	185	218	210	264	226	218	184
Insurance surrender tax	6	7	16	22	33	29	42	46	48	57
Individuals (Ch. 75:01)	571	2 169	3 239	4 467	6 207	6 620	7 445	7 187	6 303	6 599
1120 On capital gains	..	..	..	..	..	..	..	..	..	..
1200 Corporate	1 856	3 704	22 252	21 659	25 796	28 570	20 810	8 608	8 736	11 713
1210 On profits	1 856	3 704	22 252	21 659	25 796	28 570	20 810	8 608	8 736	11 713
Oil companies	1 439	2 441	16 206	13 834	14 772	16 970	10 513	1 036	1 116	2 093
Other companies	383	1 041	4 797	6 630	9 675	10 151	9 481	7 003	6 919	8 858
Business levy	0	65	138	206	187	210	215	438	603	608
National recovery impost	34	0	0	0	0	0	0	0	0	0
Unemployment Fund	0	157	1 111	989	1 163	1 240	601	131	99	153
1220 On capital gains	..	..	..	..	..	..	..	..	..	..
1300 Unallocable between 1100 and 1200	70	195	1 175	881	885	942	1 067	990	827	858
2000 Social security contributions	**183**	**702**	**1 502**	**2 645**	**3 304**	**3 624**	**4 261**	**4 252**	**4 608**	**4 670**
2100 Employees	..	..	..	..	..	..	..	..	..	..
2110 On a payroll basis	..	..	..	..	..	..	..	..	..	..
2120 On an income tax basis	..	..	..	..	..	..	..	..	..	..
2200 Employers	..	..	..	..	..	..	..	..	..	..
2210 On a payroll basis	..	..	..	..	..	..	..	..	..	..
2220 On an income tax basis	..	..	..	..	..	..	..	..	..	..
2300 Self-employed or non-employed	..	..	..	..	..	..	..	..	..	..
2310 On a payroll basis	..	..	..	..	..	..	..	..	..	..
2320 On an income tax basis	..	..	..	..	..	..	..	..	..	..
2400 Unallocable between 2100, 2200 and 2300	183	702	1 502	2 645	3 304	3 624	4 261	4 252	4 608	4 670
2410 On a payroll basis	..	..	..	..	..	..	..	..	..	..
2420 On an income tax basis	..	..	..	..	..	..	..	..	..	..
3000 Taxes on payroll and workforce	**0**	**0**	**0**	**0**	**0**	**0**	**0**	**0**	**0**	**0**
4000 Taxes on property	**90**	**175**	**385**	**194**	**250**	**289**	**406**	**332**	**322**	**362**
4100 Recurrent taxes on immovable property	39	64	84	22	4	3	3	3	3	4
4110 Households	..	..	..	..	..	..	..	..	..	..
4120 Others	..	..	..	..	..	..	..	..	..	..
4200 Recurrent taxes on net wealth	0	0	0	0	0	0	0	0	0	0
4210 Individual	..	..	..	..	..	..	..	..	..	..
4220 Corporate	..	..	..	..	..	..	..	..	..	..
4300 Estate, inheritance and gift taxes	1	0	0	0	0	0	0	0	0	0
4310 Estate and inheritance taxes	1	..	..	..	..	..	..	..	..	..
4320 Gift taxes	0	..	..	..	..	..	..	..	..	..
4400 Taxes on financial and capital transactions	49	111	301	172	246	285	403	329	319	359
Stamp duties	49	111	301	172	246	285	403	329	319	359
4500 Non-recurrent taxes	0	0	0	0	0	0	0	0	0	0
4510 On net wealth	..	..	..	..	..	..	..	..	..	..
4520 Other non-recurrent taxes	..	..	..	..	..	..	..	..	..	..
4600 Other recurrent taxes on property	0	0	0	0	0	0	0	0	0	0
5000 Taxes on goods and services	**2 055**	**3 852**	**8 358**	**9 667**	**11 253**	**10 627**	**12 264**	**12 344**	**10 101**	**12 370**
5100 Taxes on production, sale, transfer, etc	1 973	3 603	8 010	9 282	10 690	10 047	11 678	11 765	9 675	12 026
5110 General taxes	980	1 890	5 105	6 358	7 027	6 126	7 569	7 617	5 876	8 087
5111 Value added taxes	927	1 890	4 829	6 032	6 657	5 745	7 223	7 005	5 050	7 245
5112 Sales tax	54	0	0	0	0	0	0	0	1	0
5113 Other	0	0	276	325	370	381	346	612	825	842
Green Fund	..	..	276	325	370	381	346	612	803	813
Tax on online purchases	..	..	0	0	0	0	0	0	22	29
5120 Taxes on specific goods and services	993	1 713	2 904	2 924	3 663	3 921	4 108	4 148	3 798	3 939
5121 Excises	481	801	614	708	707	680	703	735	739	793
Alcohol products	..	..	..	156	153	157	154	168	150	183
Beer	..	..	..	202	196	172	189	181	202	202
Petroleum products	..	..	..	105	103	94	88	132	102	98
Cigarette products	..	..	..	243	238	235	243	226	253	269
Malt beverages	..	..	..	2	17	23	29	28	33	41
5122 Profits of fiscal monopolies	0	0	0	0	0	0	0	0	0	0
5123 Customs and import duties	260	748	2 004	1 905	2 588	2 861	3 014	3 016	2 684	2 732
5124 Taxes on exports	0	0	0	0	0	0	0	0	0	0
5125 Taxes on investment goods	0	0	0	0	0	0	0	0	0	0

Table 5.24. **Trinidad and Tobago / Trinidad y Tobago** *(cont.)*

Details of tax revenue / Ingresos tributarios detallados

Million TTD

	1990	2000	2007	2010	2013	2014	2015	2016	2017	2018
5126 Taxes on specific services	49	163	284	311	369	380	391	397	375	414
Insurance premium tax	0	56	130	167	194	197	191	181	163	170
Transaction tax on financial services	0	23	42	53	64	75	75	87	93	97
Hotel room tax	0	23	48	46	50	56	64	54	52	52
Betting and entertainment taxes	4	17	0	12	13	0	0	0	0	0
Other taxes on goods and services	45	44	63	33	47	52	61	75	67	95
5127 Other taxes on internat. trade and transactions	202	0	2	1	0	0	0	0	1	0
5128 Other taxes	0	0	0	0	0	0	0	0	0	0
5130 Unallocable between 5110 and 5120	0	0	0	0	0	0	0	0	0	0
5200 Taxes on use of goods and perform activities	81	249	348	386	562	580	586	580	426	344
5210 Recurrent taxes	81	249	348	386	562	580	586	580	426	344
Motor vehicle taxes and duties	76	239	338	375	552	569	575	569	415	334
5211 Paid by households: motor vehicles	..	..	..	..	..	..	..	..	..	..
5212 Paid by others: motor vehicles	..	..	..	..	..	..	..	..	..	..
5213 Paid in respect of other goods	5	10	10	10	11	11	11	11	11	11
Liquor and miscellaneous business licence fees	5	10	10	10	11	11	11	11	11	11
5220 Non-recurrent taxes	0	0	0	0	0	0	0	0	0	0
5300 Unallocable between 5100 and 5200	0	0	0	0	0	0	0	0	0	0
6000 Other taxes	**0**	**0**	**0**	**0**	**0**	**0**	**0**	**0**	**0**	**0**
6100 Paid solely by business	..	..	..	..	..	..	..	..	..	..
6200 Other	..	..	..	..	..	..	..	..	..	..

Note: Fiscal year ending on 30th September. For example, the data for 2018 represent October 2017 to September 2018.

The data are on a cash basis.

The figures exclude local government tax revenues as the data are not available.

Heading 2000: Social security contributions follow financial year from July to June, instead of October to September. For example, social security contributions in 2018 are between 1st July 2017 and 30th June 2018. The figures include total contribution income of National Insurance Board minus refunds. A small amount of voluntary contributions have been identified and removed from the figures since 2013.

Heading 4400: Stamp duties are classified under heading 4400 in this edition. They were previously under heading 6200.

Heading 5121: Revenues from alcohol and tobacco taxes are merged with excise taxes for alcohol products and cigarettes in this edition.

Heading 5126: Other taxes on goods and services include mainly club gaming tax and are classified under heading 5126 in this edition. They were previously under heading 5213.

Source: Ministry of Finance; The National Insurance Board.

StatLink https://doi.org/10.1787/888934114875

Table 5.25. **Uruguay**

Details of tax revenue / Ingresos tributarios detallados

Million UYU

	1990	2000	2007	2010	2013	2014	2015	2016	2017	2018
Total tax revenue	**2 399**	**64 183**	**141 132**	**212 907**	**324 538**	**365 043**	**397 734**	**441 071**	**494 580**	**534 208**
1000 Taxes on income, profits and capital gains	**114**	**8 698**	**20 540**	**42 583**	**68 257**	**73 120**	**84 141**	**101 584**	**125 295**	**140 537**
1100 Of individuals	0	3 597	8 362	19 148	33 378	40 334	45 451	51 679	68 948	78 571
Personal income tax (IRP)	..	3 597	3 519	0	0	0	0	0	0	0
1110 On income and profits	..	..	4 262	16 790	29 100	35 367	39 613	44 817	60 570	69 083
IRPF second category	..	..	4 262	14 643	26 048	31 365	34 881	39 883	54 327	61 077
Social security assistance	..	..	0	2 651	4 285	5 518	6 576	7 480	9 448	11 091
Personal income tax refunds	..	..	0	-504	-1 233	-1 517	-1 844	-2 545	-3 204	-3 085
1120 On capital gains	..	..	581	2 358	4 278	4 967	5 838	6 862	8 377	9 488
IRPF first category	..	..	581	2 358	4 278	4 967	5 838	6 862	8 377	9 488
1200 Corporate	114	5 102	11 829	21 772	32 200	29 549	34 814	45 382	51 169	56 326
1210 On profits	114	5 102	11 829	21 772	32 200	29 549	34 814	45 382	51 169	56 326
Income tax for economic activities (IRAE)	0	0	709	21 280	31 812	29 152	34 375	45 308	50 929	56 130
Industry and commerce income tax (IRIC)	97	5 096	11 055	491	387	396	439	72	239	197
Agricultural income tax (IRA)	10	3	65	2	1	0	0	1	0	0
Tax on agricultural activities (IMAGRO)	7	3	0	0	0	0	0	0	0	0
1220 On capital gains	..	..	..	..	..	..	..	..	..	..
1300 Unallocable between 1100 and 1200	0	0	349	1 662	2 679	3 237	3 875	4 523	5 179	5 639
Non-resident income tax (IRNR)	..	..	349	1 662	2 679	3 237	3 875	4 523	5 179	5 639
2000 Social security contributions	**717**	**17 679**	**28 485**	**49 742**	**86 012**	**100 993**	**108 742**	**118 451**	**131 224**	**139 241**
2100 Employees	..	..	..	..	..	..	..	..	..	..
2110 On a payroll basis	..	..	..	..	..	..	..	..	..	..
2120 On an income tax basis	..	..	..	..	..	..	..	..	..	..
2200 Employers	..	..	..	..	..	..	..	..	..	..
2210 On a payroll basis	..	..	..	..	..	..	..	..	..	..
2220 On an income tax basis	..	..	..	..	..	..	..	..	..	..
2300 Self-employed or non-employed	..	..	..	..	..	..	..	..	..	..
2310 On a payroll basis	..	..	..	..	..	..	..	..	..	..
2320 On an income tax basis	..	..	..	..	..	..	..	..	..	..
2400 Unallocable between 2100, 2200 and 2300	717	17 679	28 485	49 742	86 012	100 993	108 742	118 451	131 224	139 241
2410 On a payroll basis	717	17 679	28 485	49 742	86 012	100 993	108 742	118 451	131 224	139 241
2420 On an income tax basis	0	0	0	0	0	0	0	0	0	0
3000 Taxes on payroll and workforce	**0**	**0**	**0**	**0**	**0**	**0**	**0**	**0**	**0**	**0**
4000 Taxes on property	**213**	**5 508**	**13 243**	**18 965**	**25 759**	**29 226**	**32 422**	**36 441**	**38 460**	**40 508**
4100 Recurrent taxes on immovable property	87	3 248	5 686	8 140	11 572	13 016	14 884	16 812	18 180	19 648
Primary education tax	0	378	691	1 064	1 441	1 612	2 386	2 474	2 781	2 961
Farm property tax	0	155	0	189	627	921	886	852	764	728
Property tax surcharge	0	0	0	0	214	541	503	511	543	476
Primary education tax refunds	0	0	0	0	0	0	0	0	0	-3
Other property taxes	87	2 715	4 995	6 887	9 290	9 942	11 109	12 975	14 092	15 485
4110 Households	..	..	..	..	..	..	..	..	..	..
4120 Others	..	..	..	..	..	..	..	..	..	..
4200 Recurrent taxes on net wealth	94	1 769	5 392	8 760	11 700	13 714	14 776	16 652	17 057	17 473
4210 Individual	64	108	340	382	491	629	606	684	711	760
4220 Corporate	30	1 661	5 052	8 378	11 208	13 085	14 170	15 968	16 346	16 713
Corporate wealth tax	28	1 507	4 805	8 165	11 198	13 079	14 167	15 967	16 345	16 713
Tax on financial investment companies (ISAFI)	1	154	247	213	11	6	3	1	1	1
4300 Estate, inheritance and gift taxes	0	0	0	0	0	0	0	0	0	0
4310 Estate and inheritance taxes	..	..	..	..	..	..	..	..	..	..
4320 Gift taxes	..	..	..	..	..	..	..	..	..	..
4400 Taxes on financial and capital transactions	31	476	1 831	1 740	2 007	1 994	2 241	2 439	2 662	2 819
Property transfer tax (ITP)	11	372	1 405	1 347	1 516	1 442	1 601	1 724	1 927	1 984
Tax on transfer of rights over athletes	0	0	50	3	0	0	0	0	0	0
Auction tax	20	104	376	390	491	553	639	714	735	835
4500 Non-recurrent taxes	0	0	0	0	0	0	0	0	0	0
4510 On net wealth	..	..	..	..	..	..	..	..	..	..
4520 Other non-recurrent taxes	..	..	..	..	..	..	..	..	..	..
4600 Other recurrent taxes on property	1	15	335	326	480	502	522	538	560	567
Corporation control tax (ICOSA)	1	15	236	325	480	502	522	538	560	567
Financial system control tax (ICOSIFI)	0	0	99	0	0	0	0	0	0	0
5000 Taxes on goods and services	**1 358**	**32 139**	**77 673**	**100 282**	**142 683**	**159 646**	**170 279**	**182 082**	**196 669**	**210 711**
5100 Taxes on production, sale, transfer, etc	1 301	29 562	74 369	96 494	137 330	153 184	162 739	172 823	186 355	199 329
5110 General taxes	660	18 009	50 943	69 951	98 758	108 918	114 627	123 262	129 663	137 400
5111 Value added taxes	660	17 995	49 064	69 921	98 758	108 918	114 627	123 262	129 663	137 400
5112 Sales tax	1	14	1 879	30	0	0	0	0	0	0
Social security financing tax (COFIS)	0	0	1 859	30	..	..	..	..	..	..
Other sales taxes	1	14	20	0	..	..	..	..	..	..
5113 Other	0	0	0	0	0	0	0	0	0	0

Table 5.25. **Uruguay** *(cont.)*

Details of tax revenue / Ingresos tributarios detallados

Million UYU

	1990	2000	2007	2010	2013	2014	2015	2016	2017	2018
5120 Taxes on specific goods and services	641	11 553	23 426	26 543	38 572	44 266	48 111	49 561	56 692	61 928
5121 Excises	393	7 896	13 409	17 300	24 554	27 770	31 197	32 528	37 779	39 214
Fuels	203	4 067	5 694	6 551	10 269	11 816	14 096	15 222	17 129	18 662
Tobacco products	80	1 741	3 085	4 236	4 755	4 913	5 778	6 144	6 995	7 518
Motor vehicles	20	656	1 333	2 289	3 388	3 924	4 017	3 960	4 313	3 789
Non-alcoholic beverages	19	464	804	1 172	1 718	1 926	2 131	2 330	2 547	2 687
Agricultural products	4	299	1 396	1 349	1 870	2 144	2 223	2 227	2 369	2 636
Beer	8	205	372	602	1 024	1 035	1 102	1 109	1 357	1 526
Advances of import excises	0	27	-250	-136	18	398	312	-62	1 372	704
Greases and lubricants	5	119	306	390	489	519	525	559	623	652
Alcoholic beverages	22	212	415	562	811	883	789	774	766	617
Other excises	32	106	254	283	212	213	224	265	309	423
5122 Profits of fiscal monopolies	0	0	0	0	0	0	0	0	0	0
5123 Customs and import duties	214	1 967	7 077	8 478	13 020	15 167	15 440	15 384	17 198	20 878
5124 Taxes on exports	1	32	274	325	422	520	582	658	664	770
5125 Taxes on investment goods	0	0	0	0	0	0	0	0	0	0
5126 Taxes on specific services	34	1 392	2 145	440	576	809	892	991	1 052	1 067
Bank asset tax (IMABA)	31	1 092	686	2	0	1	0	0	0	0
Income tax for insurance companies	3	76	336	366	470	691	763	845	902	916
Other services taxes	0	224	1 123	72	106	117	129	146	150	152
5127 Other taxes on internat. trade and transactions	0	265	520	0	0	0	0	0	0	0
5128 Other taxes	0	0	0	0	0	0	0	0	0	0
5130 Unallocable between 5110 and 5120	0	0	0	0	0	0	0	0	0	0
5200 Taxes on use of goods and perform activities	57	2 576	3 303	3 788	5 353	6 463	7 540	9 259	10 313	11 382
5210 Recurrent taxes	57	2 576	3 303	3 788	5 353	6 463	7 540	9 259	10 313	11 382
5211 Paid by households: motor vehicles	0	0	0	0	0	0	0	0	0	0
5212 Paid by others: motor vehicles	57	2 576	3 303	3 788	5 353	6 463	7 540	9 259	10 313	11 382
5213 Paid in respect of other goods	0	0	0	0	0	0	0	0	0	0
5220 Non-recurrent taxes	0	0	0	0	0	0	0	0	0	0
5300 Unallocable between 5100 and 5200	0	0	0	0	0	0	0	0	0	0
6000 Other taxes	**-3**	**159**	**1 191**	**1 335**	**1 827**	**2 057**	**2 151**	**2 513**	**2 933**	**3 212**
6100 Paid solely by business	-10	-145	626	586	686	741	796	850	925	980
Small business tax (minimum VAT)	0	296	563	586	686	741	796	850	925	980
Credit card tax	0	0	63	0	0	0	0	0	0	0
Other tax refunds	-10	-440	0	0	0	0	0	0	0	0
6200 Other	7	303	565	748	1 141	1 316	1 355	1 663	2 008	2 232

Note: Year ending 31st December.

The data are on a cash basis.

Heading 1100: Personal income tax (IRP) has been revised based on data from Ministry of Economy and Finance in this edition.

Heading 2000: Figures for 1990-98 are estimated by the General Tax Directorate (DGI). Since 1999 the figures include income from Social Security Bank (BPS) published by the Ministry of Economy and Finance.

Heading 4100: Primary education tax refunds have been added in this edition.

Heading 5111: Diesel VAT refunds have been added in this edition.

Heading 5112: Social security financing tax (COFIS) has been added in this edition. The tax on the sale of goods by public auctions recorded under other sales taxes is classified in category 4000 in ECLAC data.

Heading 5121: Advances of import excises and excise tax on greases and lubricants have been added in this edition. Tax on the sale of agricultural goods (IMEBA) has been placed under heading 5121 in this edition, combined with the additional taxes on sale of agricultural goods (MEVIR and INIA). It was previously under heading 1210.

Heading 5126: Bank asset tax (IMABA) has been placed under heading 5126 in this edition. It was previously under heading 4600.

Heading 6100: Small business tax (minimum VAT) has been placed under heading 6100 in this edition. It was previously under heading 1210.

Source: Dirección General Impositiva (General Tax Directorate); Ministerio de Economía y Finanzas (Ministry of Economy and Finance).

StatLink https://doi.org/10.1787/888934114894

Table 5.26. **Venezuela**

Details of tax revenue / Ingresos tributarios detallados

VES

	1990	2000	2007	2010	2013	2014	2015	2016	2017	2018
Total tax revenue	**4 115**	**108 486**	**838 614**	**1 200 840**	**3 239 431**	**..**	**..**	**..**	**..**	**..**
1000 Taxes on income, profits and capital gains	**3 444**	**46 856**	**375 642**	**368 365**	**936 941**	**1 878 840**	**2 847 864**	**..**	**..**	**..**
1100 Of individuals	..	..	..	..	..	..	..	..	..	..
1110 On income and profits	..	..	..	..	..	..	..	..	..	..
1120 On capital gains	..	..	..	..	..	..	..	..	..	..
1200 Corporate	3 148	33 683	199 585	86 998	252 703	676 007	473 879	..	..	..
1210 On profits	3 148	33 683	199 585	86 998	252 703	676 007	473 879	..	..	..
Oil	3 148	33 683	199 585	86 998	252 703	676 007	473 879	..	..	..
1220 On capital gains	..	..	..	..	..	..	..	..	..	..
1300 Unallocable between 1100 and 1200	297	13 173	176 057	281 367	684 238	1 202 834	2 373 986	7 331 699	31 378 510	..
2000 Social security contributions	**202**	**5 905**	**42 176**	**96 896**	**214 220**	**..**	**..**	**..**	**..**	**..**
2100 Employees	..	..	..	..	..	..	..	..	..	..
2110 On a payroll basis	..	..	..	..	..	..	..	..	..	..
2120 On an income tax basis	..	..	..	..	..	..	..	..	..	..
2200 Employers	..	..	..	..	..	..	..	..	..	..
2210 On a payroll basis	..	..	..	..	..	..	..	..	..	..
2220 On an income tax basis	..	..	..	..	..	..	..	..	..	..
2300 Self-employed or non-employed	..	..	..	..	..	..	..	..	..	..
2310 On a payroll basis	..	..	..	..	..	..	..	..	..	..
2320 On an income tax basis	..	..	..	..	..	..	..	..	..	..
2400 Unallocable between 2100, 2200 and 2300	202	5 905	42 176	96 896	214 220	..	..	..	..	..
2410 On a payroll basis	..	..	..	..	..	..	..	..	..	..
2420 On an income tax basis	..	..	..	..	..	..	..	..	..	..
3000 Taxes on payroll and workforce	**0**	**0**	**0**	**0**	**0**	**0**	**0**	**0**	**0**	**..**
4000 Taxes on property	**11**	**3 999**	**27 147**	**2 217**	**5 298**	**10 463**	**29 459**	**90 877**	**24 353 035**	**..**
4100 Recurrent taxes on immovable property	0	0	0	0	0	0	0	0	0	..
4110 Households	..	..	..	..	..	..	..	..	..	..
4120 Others	..	..	..	..	..	..	..	..	..	..
4200 Recurrent taxes on net wealth	0	0	0	0	0	0	0	0	0	..
4210 Individual	..	..	..	..	..	..	..	..	..	..
4220 Corporate	..	..	..	..	..	..	..	..	..	..
4300 Estate, inheritance and gift taxes	11	191	1 050	2 217	5 298	10 463	29 459	90 877	361 298	..
4310 Estate and inheritance taxes	11	191	1 050	2 217	5 298	10 463	29 459	90 877	361 298	..
4320 Gift taxes	0	0	0	0	0	0	0	0	0	..
4400 Taxes on financial and capital transactions	0	3 808	26 097	0	0	0	0	0	23 991 737	..
Bank debits	..	2 918	26 097	..	..	..	..	..	0	..
Registration of immovable property rights	..	890	0	..	..	..	..	..	0	..
Tax on Large Financial Transactions (IGTF)	..	0	0	..	..	..	..	..	23 991 737	..
4500 Non-recurrent taxes	0	0	0	0	0	0	0	0	0	..
4510 On net wealth	..	..	..	..	..	..	..	..	..	..
4520 Other non-recurrent taxes	..	..	..	..	..	..	..	..	..	..
4600 Other recurrent taxes on property	0	0	0	0	0	0	0	0	0	..
5000 Taxes on goods and services	**457**	**51 726**	**393 649**	**733 363**	**2 038 941**	**3 462 719**	**9 128 199**	**25 580 149**	**148 669 517**	**..**
5100 Taxes on production, sale, transfer, etc	457	51 726	393 649	733 363	2 038 941	3 462 719	9 128 199	25 580 149	148 669 517	..
5110 General taxes	0	32 716	278 954	561 005	1 647 371	2 721 869	7 027 427	19 070 779	112 990 174	..
5111 Value added taxes	..	32 716	278 954	561 005	1 647 371	2 721 869	7 027 427	19 070 779	112 990 174	..
5112 Sales tax	..	0	0	0	0	0	0	0	0	..
5113 Other	..	0	0	0	0	0	0	0	0	..
5120 Taxes on specific goods and services	457	19 011	114 695	172 357	391 570	740 850	2 100 772	6 509 370	35 679 343	..
5121 Excises	157	7 742	29 778	88 722	163 715	305 249	1 165 755	4 399 252	29 679 186	..
Oil	57	4 679	7 039	12 798	0	0	0	0	0	..
Alcoholic beverages	58	852	9 081	21 915	59 745	108 885	444 982	1 568 778	14 113 397	..
Tobacco	42	2 201	13 641	54 009	103 969	196 364	720 772	2 830 474	15 565 789	..
Matches	0	9	17	0	0	0	0	0	0	..
5122 Profits of fiscal monopolies	0	0	0	0	0	0	0	0	0	..
5123 Customs and import duties	300	9 716	82 713	81 333	226 557	433 979	932 598	2 103 519	5 986 482	..
5124 Taxes on exports	0	0	0	0	0	0	0	0	0	..
5125 Taxes on investment goods	0	0	0	0	0	0	0	0	0	..
5126 Taxes on specific services	0	1 552	2 204	2 302	1 298	1 621	2 419	6 600	13 675	..
Telecommunications	0	1 505	1 658	0	0	0	0	0	0	..
Casinos, bingo and slot machines	0	47	546	2 302	1 298	1 621	2 419	6 600	13 675	..
5127 Other taxes on internat. trade and transactions	0	0	0	0	0	0	0	0	0	..
5128 Other taxes	0	0	0	0	0	0	0	0	0	..
5130 Unallocable between 5110 and 5120	0	0	0	0	0	0	0	0	0	..
5200 Taxes on use of goods and perform activities	0	0	0	0	0	0	0	0	0	..
5210 Recurrent taxes	..	..	..	..	..	..	..	..	..	..
5211 Paid by households: motor vehicles	..	..	..	..	..	..	..	..	..	..
5212 Paid by others: motor vehicles	..	..	..	..	..	..	..	..	..	..

Table 5.26. **Venezuela** *(cont.)*

Details of tax revenue / Ingresos tributarios detallados

VES

	1990	2000	2007	2010	2013	2014	2015	2016	2017	2018
5213 Paid in respect of other goods	..	..	..	..	..	..	..	..	..	..
5220 Non-recurrent taxes	..	..	..	..	..	..	..	..	..	..
5300 Unallocable between 5100 and 5200	0	0	0	0	0	0	0	0	0	..
6000 Other taxes	**0**	**0**	**0**	**0**	**44 031**	**80 237**	**158 333**	**263 062**	**1 225 170**	**..**
6100 Paid solely by business	..	..	..	..	0	0	0	0	0	..
6200 Other	..	..	..	..	44 031	80 237	158 333	263 062	1 225 170	..

Note: Year ending 31st December.

The data are on a cash basis.

Tax revenue data are revised in this edition based on Bolívar Soberano introduced in August 2018. Data are not available for 2018.

The figures exclude state and local government tax revenues as the data are not available.

The figures since 2015 should be interpreted with caution as they have been affected by the high rate of inflation over this period.

The total tax revenue data are not available since 2014 due to missing data for social security contributions since 2014 and oil revenues since 2016 (classified in heading 1210 taxes on corporate profits).

Source: Servicio Nacional Integrado de Administración Aduanera (National Integrated Service of Customs); Ministerio de Finanzas (Ministry of Finance).

StatLink https://doi.org/10.1787/888934114913

Chapter 6

Tax revenues by sub-sectors of general government

Capítulo 6

Ingresos tributarios por sub-sectores de gobierno general

Chapter 6 / Capítulo 6

Tax revenues by sub-sectors of general government

Revenues of both the Latin American and the OECD countries have been attributed to the different levels of government according to the revised guidelines set out in to the final version of the 2008 System of National Accounts (SNA). Under this, revenues are generally attributed to the level of government that exercises the authority to impose the tax or has the final discretion to set and vary the tax rate.

Ingresos tributarios por sub-sectores de gobierno general

Los ingresos de los países latinoamericanos y de los países de la OCDE se han atribuido a los diferentes niveles de gobierno de acuerdo con lo recogido en la versión final 2008 del Sistema de Cuentas Nacionales (SCN), según el cual, los ingresos se atribuyen por lo general al nivel de gobierno que ejerce la facultad de aplicar el impuesto o que puede a su discreción establecer y modificar la tasa del impuesto.

Table 6.1. **Argentina, tax revenues by sub-sectors of government**

Million ARS

	Federal government					State/Regional				
	1990	2000	2010	2015	2018	1990	2000	2010	2015	2018
1000 Taxes on income, profits and capital gains	**542**	**11 303**	**78 427**	**384 536**	**746 994**	**0**	**0**	**0**	**0**	**0**
1100 Of individuals	141	3 937	23 980	188 218	296 224	..	..	..	..	..
1200 Corporate	357	6 575	50 664	185 725	401 683	..	..	..	..	..
1300 Unallocable between 1100 and 1200	43	792	3 783	10 593	49 086	..	..	..	..	..
2000 Social security contributions	**0**	**0**	**0**	**0**	**0**	**0**	**0**	**0**	**0**	**0**
2100 Employees	..	..	..	..	..	..	..	..	..	..
2200 Employers	..	..	..	..	..	..	..	..	..	..
2300 Self-employed or non-employed	..	..	..	..	..	..	..	..	..	..
2400 Unallocable between 2100, 2200 and 2300	..	..	..	..	..	..	..	..	..	..
3000 Taxes on payroll and workforce	**0**	**0**	**0**	**0**	**0**	**0**	**0**	**0**	**0**	**0**
4000 Taxes on property	**616**	**1 254**	**32 674**	**117 274**	**255 531**	**549**	**2 614**	**10 864**	**48 908**	**133 542**
4100 Recurrent taxes on immovable property	0	0	0	0	0	419	1 809	5 035	21 738	58 672
4200 Recurrent taxes on net wealth	246	1 084	5 248	18 538	15 296	0	0	0	0	0
4300 Estate, inheritance and gift taxes	0	0	0	0	0	0	0	0	0	0
4400 Taxes on financial and capital transactions	330	100	27 423	98 736	240 235	130	804	5 829	27 170	74 870
4500 Non-recurrent taxes	40	70	3	0	0	0	0	0	0	0
4600 Other recurrent taxes on property	0	0	0	0	0	0	0	0	0	0
5000 Taxes on goods and services	**4 669**	**27 592**	**198 346**	**634 068**	**1 511 671**	**967**	**6 947**	**54 746**	**255 256**	**608 529**
5100 Taxes on production, sale, transfer, etc	4 671	28 174	201 402	642 899	1 546 271	791	6 114	51 148	238 221	566 740
5110 General taxes	1 594	19 009	116 386	433 076	1 104 580	791	6 114	51 148	238 221	566 740
5120 Taxes on specific goods and services	3 077	9 166	85 016	209 822	441 691	0	0	0	0	0
5130 Unallocable between 5110 and 5120	0	0	0	0	0	0	0	0	0	0
5200 Taxes on use of goods and perform activities[1]	..	..	..	..	..	177	833	3 598	17 035	41 789
5300 Unallocable between 5100 and 5200	-3	-583	-3 056	-8 831	-34 600	0	0	0	0	0
6000 Other taxes	**214**	**395**	**2 386**	**6 931**	**7 407**	**78**	**1 309**	**3 110**	**10 533**	**26 794**
6100 Paid solely by business	0	354	2 093	5 624	16 052	0	0	0	0	0
6200 Other[2]	214	41	294	1 306	-8 646	78	1 309	3 110	10 533	26 794
Total tax revenue	**6 040**	**40 544**	**311 834**	**1 142 808**	**2 521 603**	**1 594**	**10 870**	**68 720**	**314 697**	**768 864**

Million ARS

	Local government[3]					Social Security Funds				
	1990	2000	2010	2015	2018	1990	2000	2010	2015	2018
1000 Taxes on income, profits and capital gains	..	..	..	..	..	**0**	**0**	**0**	**0**	**0**
1100 Of individuals	..	..	..	..	..	..	..	..	..	..
1200 Corporate	..	..	..	..	..	..	..	..	..	..
1300 Unallocable between 1100 and 1200	..	..	..	..	..	..	..	..	..	..
2000 Social security contributions	..	..	..	..	..	**2 583**	**9 670**	**102 460**	**415 410**	**913 427**
2100 Employees	..	..	..	..	..	..	2 486	37 990	163 590	361 756
2200 Employers	..	..	..	..	..	..	6 069	54 713	235 610	514 144
2300 Self-employed or non-employed	..	..	..	..	..	98	1 115	9 757	16 210	37 527
2400 Unallocable between 2100, 2200 and 2300	..	..	..	..	..	2 485	0	0	0	0
3000 Taxes on payroll and workforce	..	..	..	..	..	**0**	**0**	**0**	**0**	**0**
4000 Taxes on property	..	..	..	..	..	**0**	**0**	**0**	**0**	**0**
4100 Recurrent taxes on immovable property	..	..	..	..	..	..	..	..	..	..
4200 Recurrent taxes on net wealth	..	..	..	..	..	..	..	..	..	..
4300 Estate, inheritance and gift taxes	..	..	..	..	..	..	..	..	..	..
4400 Taxes on financial and capital transactions	..	..	..	..	..	..	..	..	..	..
4500 Non-recurrent taxes	..	..	..	..	..	..	..	..	..	..
4600 Other recurrent taxes on property	..	..	..	..	..	..	..	..	..	..
5000 Taxes on goods and services	..	..	..	..	..	**0**	**0**	**0**	**0**	**0**
5100 Taxes on production, sale, transfer, etc	..	..	..	..	..	..	..	..	..	..
5110 General taxes	..	..	..	..	..	..	..	..	..	..
5120 Taxes on specific goods and services	..	..	..	..	..	..	..	..	..	..
5130 Unallocable between 5110 and 5120	..	..	..	..	..	..	..	..	..	..
5200 Taxes on use of goods and perform activities[1]	..	..	..	..	..	..	..	..	..	..
5300 Unallocable between 5100 and 5200	..	..	..	..	..	..	..	..	..	..
6000 Other taxes	..	..	..	..	..	**0**	**0**	**0**	**0**	**0**
6100 Paid solely by business	..	..	..	..	..	..	..	..	..	..
6200 Other[2]	..	..	..	..	..	..	..	..	..	..
Total tax revenue	..	..	..	..	..	**2 583**	**9 670**	**102 460**	**415 410**	**913 427**

1. In ECLAC data, tax on ownership of motor vehicles is classified in category 4000.
2. The tax debt payments in 2016 include revenue following the implementation of a new voluntary disclosure regime in July 2016 (Law 27260).
3. The figures exclude local government tax revenues as the data are not available.

StatLink https://doi.org/10.1787/888934114932

Table 6.2. **Bahamas, tax revenues by sub-sectors of government**

Million BSD

	Federal government[1]					State/Regional				
	1990	2000	2010	2015	2018	1990	2000	2010	2015	2018
1000 Taxes on income, profits and capital gains	**0**	**0**	**0**	**0**	**0**	..	..	..	..	..
1100 Of individuals	0	0	0	0	0	..	..	..	..	..
1200 Corporate	0	0	0	0	0	..	..	..	..	..
1300 Unallocable between 1100 and 1200	0	0	0	0	0	..	..	..	..	..
2000 Social security contributions	**0**	**0**	**0**	**0**	**0**	..	..	..	..	..
2100 Employees	..	..	..	..	..	..	..	..	..	..
2200 Employers	..	..	..	..	..	..	..	..	..	..
2300 Self-employed or non-employed	..	..	..	..	..	..	..	..	..	..
2400 Unallocable between 2100, 2200 and 2300	..	..	..	..	..	..	..	..	..	..
3000 Taxes on payroll and workforce	**0**	**0**	**0**	**0**	**0**	..	..	..	..	..
4000 Taxes on property	**56**	**208**	**269**	**298**	**237**	..	..	..	..	..
4100 Recurrent taxes on immovable property	19	32	92	107	124	..	..	..	..	..
4200 Recurrent taxes on net wealth	0	0	0	0	0	..	..	..	..	..
4300 Estate, inheritance and gift taxes	0	0	0	0	0	..	..	..	..	..
4400 Taxes on financial and capital transactions	37	176	177	191	114	..	..	..	..	..
4500 Non-recurrent taxes	0	0	0	0	0	..	..	..	..	..
4600 Other recurrent taxes on property	0	0	0	0	0	..	..	..	..	..
5000 Taxes on goods and services	**386**	**620**	**780**	**1 203**	**1 593**	..	..	..	..	..
5100 Taxes on production, sale, transfer, etc	354	552	657	993	1 405	..	..	..	..	..
5110 General taxes	0	0	0	219	680	..	..	..	..	..
5120 Taxes on specific goods and services	354	552	657	775	725	..	..	..	..	..
5130 Unallocable between 5110 and 5120	0	0	0	0	0	..	..	..	..	..
5200 Taxes on use of goods and perform activities	32	69	123	209	189	..	..	..	..	..
5300 Unallocable between 5100 and 5200	0	0	0	0	0	..	..	..	..	..
6000 Other taxes	**-4**	**21**	**60**	**0**	**0**	..	..	..	..	..
6100 Paid solely by business	0	0	0	0	0	..	..	..	..	..
6200 Other	-4	21	60	0	0	..	..	..	..	..
Total tax revenue	**438**	**849**	**1 109**	**1 500**	**1 831**	..	..	..	..	..

Million BSD

	Local government[2]					Social Security Funds[3]				
	1990	2000	2010	2015	2018	1990	2000	2010	2015	2018
1000 Taxes on income, profits and capital gains	..	..	..	..	..	**0**	**0**	**0**	**0**	**0**
1100 Of individuals	..	..	..	..	..	..	..	..	..	..
1200 Corporate	..	..	..	..	..	..	..	..	..	..
1300 Unallocable between 1100 and 1200	..	..	..	..	..	..	..	..	..	..
2000 Social security contributions	..	..	..	..	..	**66**	**115**	**167**	**260**	**320**
2100 Employees	..	..	..	..	..	..	..	60	98	..
2200 Employers	..	..	..	..	..	..	..	104	157	..
2300 Self-employed or non-employed	..	..	..	..	..	..	..	3	6	..
2400 Unallocable between 2100, 2200 and 2300	..	..	..	..	..	66	115	0	-1	320
3000 Taxes on payroll and workforce	..	..	..	..	..	**0**	**0**	**0**	**0**	**0**
4000 Taxes on property	..	..	..	..	..	**0**	**0**	**0**	**0**	**0**
4100 Recurrent taxes on immovable property	..	..	..	..	..	..	..	..	..	..
4200 Recurrent taxes on net wealth	..	..	..	..	..	..	..	..	..	..
4300 Estate, inheritance and gift taxes	..	..	..	..	..	..	..	..	..	..
4400 Taxes on financial and capital transactions	..	..	..	..	..	..	..	..	..	..
4500 Non-recurrent taxes	..	..	..	..	..	..	..	..	..	..
4600 Other recurrent taxes on property	..	..	..	..	..	..	..	..	..	..
5000 Taxes on goods and services	..	..	..	..	..	**0**	**0**	**0**	**0**	**0**
5100 Taxes on production, sale, transfer, etc	..	..	..	..	..	..	..	..	..	..
5110 General taxes	..	..	..	..	..	..	..	..	..	..
5120 Taxes on specific goods and services	..	..	..	..	..	..	..	..	..	..
5130 Unallocable between 5110 and 5120	..	..	..	..	..	..	..	..	..	..
5200 Taxes on use of goods and perform activities	..	..	..	..	..	..	..	..	..	..
5300 Unallocable between 5100 and 5200	..	..	..	..	..	..	..	..	..	..
6000 Other taxes	..	..	..	..	..	**0**	**0**	**0**	**0**	**0**
6100 Paid solely by business	..	..	..	..	..	..	..	..	..	..
6200 Other	..	..	..	..	..	..	..	..	..	..
Total tax revenue	..	..	..	..	..	**66**	**115**	**167**	**260**	**320**

1. The data for 2018 are preliminary as published by the Central Bank of The Bahamas.
2. Local government tax revenues are not available.
3. The data for social security contributions are estimated for 2017 and 2018.

StatLink https://doi.org/10.1787/888934114951

Table 6.3. **Barbados, tax revenues by sub-sectors of government**

Million BBD

	Federal government[1]					State/Regional				
	1990	2000	2010	2015	2018	1990	2000	2010	2015	2018
1000 Taxes on income, profits and capital gains	**250**	**599**	**766**	**714**	**921**	..	..	..	..	..
1100 Of individuals	140	293	395	433	482	..	..	..	..	..
1200 Corporate	95	269	294	215	355	..	..	..	..	..
1300 Unallocable between 1100 and 1200	15	37	76	66	83	..	..	..	..	..
2000 Social security contributions	**0**	**0**	**0**	**0**	**0**	..	..	..	..	..
2100 Employees	..	..	..	..	..	..	..	..	..	..
2200 Employers	..	..	..	..	..	..	..	..	..	..
2300 Self-employed or non-employed	..	..	..	..	..	..	..	..	..	..
2400 Unallocable between 2100, 2200 and 2300	..	..	..	..	..	..	..	..	..	..
3000 Taxes on payroll and workforce	**0**	**0**	**0**	**0**	**0**	..	..	..	..	..
4000 Taxes on property	**147**	**108**	**130**	**143**	**172**	..	..	..	..	..
4100 Recurrent taxes on immovable property	46	95	118	133	161	..	..	..	..	..
4200 Recurrent taxes on net wealth	0	0	0	0	0	..	..	..	..	..
4300 Estate, inheritance and gift taxes	0	0	0	0	0	..	..	..	..	..
4400 Taxes on financial and capital transactions	101	13	12	10	11	..	..	..	..	..
4500 Non-recurrent taxes	0	0	0	0	0	..	..	..	..	..
4600 Other recurrent taxes on property	0	0	0	0	0	..	..	..	..	..
5000 Taxes on goods and services	**495**	**889**	**1 276**	**1 410**	**1 719**	..	..	..	..	..
5100 Taxes on production, sale, transfer, etc	424	788	1 105	1 291	1 520	..	..	..	..	..
5110 General taxes	197	492	768	861	990	..	..	..	..	..
5120 Taxes on specific goods and services	227	296	337	430	530	..	..	..	..	..
5130 Unallocable between 5110 and 5120	0	0	0	0	0	..	..	..	..	..
5200 Taxes on use of goods and perform activities	71	101	171	119	199	..	..	..	..	..
5300 Unallocable between 5100 and 5200	0	0	0	0	0	..	..	..	..	..
6000 Other taxes	**0**	**0**	**0**	**0**	**0**	..	..	..	..	..
6100 Paid solely by business	..	..	..	..	..	..	..	..	..	..
6200 Other	..	..	..	..	..	..	..	..	..	..
Total tax revenue	**892**	**1 596**	**2 171**	**2 266**	**2 812**	..	..	..	..	..

Million BBD

	Local government[2]					Social Security Funds[3]				
	1990	2000	2010	2015	2018	1990	2000	2010	2015	2018
1000 Taxes on income, profits and capital gains	..	..	..	..	..	**0**	**0**	**0**	**0**	**0**
1100 Of individuals	..	..	..	..	..	..	..	..	..	..
1200 Corporate	..	..	..	..	..	..	..	..	..	..
1300 Unallocable between 1100 and 1200	..	..	..	..	..	..	..	..	..	..
2000 Social security contributions	..	..	..	..	..	**134**	**295**	**565**	**546**	**572**
2100 Employees	..	..	..	..	..	..	..	..	..	..
2200 Employers	..	..	..	..	..	..	..	..	..	..
2300 Self-employed or non-employed	..	..	..	..	..	..	..	..	..	..
2400 Unallocable between 2100, 2200 and 2300	..	..	..	..	..	134	295	565	546	572
3000 Taxes on payroll and workforce	..	..	..	..	..	**0**	**0**	**0**	**0**	**0**
4000 Taxes on property	..	..	..	..	..	**0**	**0**	**0**	**0**	**0**
4100 Recurrent taxes on immovable property	..	..	..	..	..	..	..	..	..	..
4200 Recurrent taxes on net wealth	..	..	..	..	..	..	..	..	..	..
4300 Estate, inheritance and gift taxes	..	..	..	..	..	..	..	..	..	..
4400 Taxes on financial and capital transactions	..	..	..	..	..	..	..	..	..	..
4500 Non-recurrent taxes	..	..	..	..	..	..	..	..	..	..
4600 Other recurrent taxes on property	..	..	..	..	..	..	..	..	..	..
5000 Taxes on goods and services	..	..	..	..	..	**0**	**0**	**0**	**0**	**0**
5100 Taxes on production, sale, transfer, etc	..	..	..	..	..	..	..	..	..	..
5110 General taxes	..	..	..	..	..	..	..	..	..	..
5120 Taxes on specific goods and services	..	..	..	..	..	..	..	..	..	..
5130 Unallocable between 5110 and 5120	..	..	..	..	..	..	..	..	..	..
5200 Taxes on use of goods and perform activities	..	..	..	..	..	..	..	..	..	..
5300 Unallocable between 5100 and 5200	..	..	..	..	..	..	..	..	..	..
6000 Other taxes	..	..	..	..	..	**0**	**0**	**0**	**0**	**0**
6100 Paid solely by business	..	..	..	..	..	..	..	..	..	..
6200 Other	..	..	..	..	..	..	..	..	..	..
Total tax revenue	..	..	..	..	..	**134**	**295**	**565**	**546**	**572**

1. Tax revenues are revised with latest data from the Central Bank of Barbados.
2. Local government tax revenues are not available.
3. The data for social security contributions are government projections for 2015-18.

StatLink https://doi.org/10.1787/888934114970

Table 6.4. **Belize, tax revenues by sub-sectors of government**

Million BZD

	Federal government[1]					State/Regional				
	1990	2000	2010	2015	2018	1990	2000	2010	2015	2018
1000 Taxes on income, profits and capital gains	**37**	**76**	**248**	**254**	**287**	..	..	..	..	..
1100 Of individuals	21	19	52	82	98	..	..	..	..	..
1200 Corporate	12	51	189	159	178	..	..	..	..	..
1300 Unallocable between 1100 and 1200	4	6	7	13	11	..	..	..	..	..
2000 Social security contributions	**0**	**0**	**0**	**0**	**0**	..	..	..	..	..
2100 Employees	..	..	..	..	..	..	..	..	..	..
2200 Employers	..	..	..	..	..	..	..	..	..	..
2300 Self-employed or non-employed	..	..	..	..	..	..	..	..	..	..
2400 Unallocable between 2100, 2200 and 2300	..	..	..	..	..	..	..	..	..	..
3000 Taxes on payroll and workforce	**0**	**0**	**0**	**0**	**0**	..	..	..	..	..
4000 Taxes on property	**33**	**11**	**16**	**29**	**40**	..	..	..	..	..
4100 Recurrent taxes on immovable property	0	0	0	0	0	..	..	..	..	..
4200 Recurrent taxes on net wealth	0	0	0	0	0	..	..	..	..	..
4300 Estate, inheritance and gift taxes	0	0	0	0	0	..	..	..	..	..
4400 Taxes on financial and capital transactions	33	11	16	29	40	..	..	..	..	..
4500 Non-recurrent taxes	0	0	0	0	0	..	..	..	..	..
4600 Other recurrent taxes on property	0	0	0	0	0	..	..	..	..	..
5000 Taxes on goods and services	**97**	**211**	**409**	**580**	**721**	..	..	..	..	..
5100 Taxes on production, sale, transfer, etc	94	207	400	571	708	..	..	..	..	..
5110 General taxes	0	82	199	275	320	..	..	..	..	..
5120 Taxes on specific goods and services	94	125	200	296	388	..	..	..	..	..
5130 Unallocable between 5110 and 5120	0	0	0	0	0	..	..	..	..	..
5200 Taxes on use of goods and perform activities	3	4	9	9	13	..	..	..	..	..
5300 Unallocable between 5100 and 5200	0	0	0	0	0	..	..	..	..	..
6000 Other taxes	**0**	**0**	**0**	**0**	**0**	..	..	..	..	..
6100 Paid solely by business	..	..	..	..	..	..	..	..	..	..
6200 Other	..	..	..	..	..	..	..	..	..	..
Total tax revenue	**167**	**298**	**673**	**864**	**1 049**	..	..	..	..	..

Million BZD

	Local government[1]					Social Security Funds				
	1990	2000	2010	2015	2018	1990	2000	2010	2015	2018
1000 Taxes on income, profits and capital gains	**0**	**0**	**0**	**0**	**0**	**0**	**0**	**0**	**0**	**0**
1100 Of individuals	..	..	..	..	..	..	..	..	..	..
1200 Corporate	..	..	..	..	..	..	..	..	..	..
1300 Unallocable between 1100 and 1200	..	..	..	..	..	..	..	..	..	..
2000 Social security contributions	**0**	**0**	**0**	**0**	**0**	**10**	**18**	**60**	**77**	**87**
2100 Employees	..	..	..	..	..	..	..	..	..	..
2200 Employers	..	..	..	..	..	..	..	..	..	..
2300 Self-employed or non-employed	..	..	..	..	..	..	..	..	..	..
2400 Unallocable between 2100, 2200 and 2300	..	..	..	..	..	10	18	60	77	87
3000 Taxes on payroll and workforce	**0**	**0**	**0**	**0**	**0**	**0**	**0**	**0**	**0**	**0**
4000 Taxes on property	**1**	**2**	**7**	**5**	**6**	**0**	**0**	**0**	**0**	**0**
4100 Recurrent taxes on immovable property	1	2	7	5	6	..	..	..	..	..
4200 Recurrent taxes on net wealth	0	0	0	0	0	..	..	..	..	..
4300 Estate, inheritance and gift taxes	0	0	0	0	0	..	..	..	..	..
4400 Taxes on financial and capital transactions	0	0	0	0	0	..	..	..	..	..
4500 Non-recurrent taxes	0	0	0	0	0	..	..	..	..	..
4600 Other recurrent taxes on property	0	0	0	0	0	..	..	..	..	..
5000 Taxes on goods and services	**0**	**0**	**0**	**0**	**0**	**0**	**0**	**0**	**0**	**0**
5100 Taxes on production, sale, transfer, etc	..	..	..	..	..	..	..	..	..	..
5110 General taxes	..	..	..	..	..	..	..	..	..	..
5120 Taxes on specific goods and services	..	..	..	..	..	..	..	..	..	..
5130 Unallocable between 5110 and 5120	..	..	..	..	..	..	..	..	..	..
5200 Taxes on use of goods and perform activities	..	..	..	..	..	..	..	..	..	..
5300 Unallocable between 5100 and 5200	..	..	..	..	..	..	..	..	..	..
6000 Other taxes	**0**	**0**	**0**	**0**	**0**	**0**	**0**	**0**	**0**	**0**
6100 Paid solely by business	..	..	..	..	..	..	..	..	..	..
6200 Other	..	..	..	..	..	..	..	..	..	..
Total tax revenue	**1**	**2**	**7**	**5**	**6**	**10**	**18**	**60**	**77**	**87**

1. The data for 2018 are revised estimates as presented by the Belize Approved Estimates of Revenue and Expenditure.

StatLink https://doi.org/10.1787/888934114989

Table 6.5. **Bolivia, tax revenues by sub-sectors of government**

Million BOB

	Federal government[1]					State/Regional				
	1990	2000	2010	2015	2018	1990	2000	2010	2015	2018
1000 Taxes on income, profits and capital gains	**68**	**1 209**	**6 294**	**12 809**	**10 591**	..	..	..	..	..
1100 Of individuals	68	214	263	508	525	..	..	..	..	..
1200 Corporate	0	995	6 031	12 302	10 066	..	..	..	..	..
1300 Unallocable between 1100 and 1200	0	0	0	0	0	..	..	..	..	..
2000 Social security contributions	**0**	**0**	**0**	**0**	**0**	..	..	..	..	..
2100 Employees	..	..	..	..	..	..	..	..	..	..
2200 Employers	..	..	..	..	..	..	..	..	..	..
2300 Self-employed or non-employed	..	..	..	..	..	..	..	..	..	..
2400 Unallocable between 2100, 2200 and 2300	..	..	..	..	..	..	..	..	..	..
3000 Taxes on payroll and workforce	**0**	**0**	**0**	**0**	**0**	..	..	..	..	..
4000 Taxes on property	**1**	**3**	**367**	**424**	**543**	..	..	..	..	..
4100 Recurrent taxes on immovable property	0	0	0	0	0	..	..	..	..	..
4200 Recurrent taxes on net wealth	0	0	0	0	0	..	..	..	..	..
4300 Estate, inheritance and gift taxes	1	3	20	36	0	..	..	..	..	..
4400 Taxes on financial and capital transactions	0	0	347	388	543	..	..	..	..	..
4500 Non-recurrent taxes	0	0	0	0	0	..	..	..	..	..
4600 Other recurrent taxes on property	0	0	0	0	0	..	..	..	..	..
5000 Taxes on goods and services	**907**	**6 697**	**17 791**	**34 759**	**35 215**	..	..	..	..	..
5100 Taxes on production, sale, transfer, etc	907	6 697	17 791	34 759	35 215	..	..	..	..	..
5110 General taxes	584	3 955	12 541	25 247	25 615	..	..	..	..	..
5120 Taxes on specific goods and services	324	2 742	5 250	9 511	9 600	..	..	..	..	..
5130 Unallocable between 5110 and 5120	0	0	0	0	0	..	..	..	..	..
5200 Taxes on use of goods and perform activities	0	0	0	0	0	..	..	..	..	..
5300 Unallocable between 5100 and 5200	0	0	0	0	0	..	..	..	..	..
6000 Other taxes	**30**	**42**	**451**	**2 452**	**2 858**	..	..	..	..	..
6100 Paid solely by business	4	6	12	25	33	..	..	..	..	..
6200 Other	25	36	439	2 427	2 825	..	..	..	..	..
Total tax revenue	**1 005**	**7 952**	**24 903**	**50 444**	**49 208**	..	..	..	..	..

Million BOB

	Local government[2]					Social Security Funds[3]				
	1990	2000	2010	2015	2018	1990	2000	2010	2015	2018
1000 Taxes on income, profits and capital gains	..	**0**	**0**	**0**	**0**	..	**0**	**0**	**0**	**0**
1100 Of individuals	..	..	..	..	..	..	..	..	..	..
1200 Corporate	..	..	..	..	..	..	..	..	..	..
1300 Unallocable between 1100 and 1200	..	..	..	..	..	..	..	..	..	..
2000 Social security contributions	..	**0**	**0**	**0**	**0**	..	**1 977**	**5 265**	**14 235**	**16 930**
2100 Employees	..	..	..	..	..	..	..	..	..	..
2200 Employers	..	..	..	..	..	..	..	..	..	..
2300 Self-employed or non-employed	..	..	..	..	..	..	..	..	..	..
2400 Unallocable between 2100, 2200 and 2300	..	..	..	..	..	..	1 977	5 265	14 235	16 930
3000 Taxes on payroll and workforce	..	**0**	**0**	**0**	**0**	..	**0**	**0**	**0**	**0**
4000 Taxes on property	..	**0**	**0**	**0**	**0**	..	**0**	**0**	**0**	**0**
4100 Recurrent taxes on immovable property	..	..	..	..	..	..	..	..	..	..
4200 Recurrent taxes on net wealth	..	..	..	..	..	..	..	..	..	..
4300 Estate, inheritance and gift taxes	..	..	..	..	..	..	..	..	..	..
4400 Taxes on financial and capital transactions	..	..	..	..	..	..	..	..	..	..
4500 Non-recurrent taxes	..	..	..	..	..	..	..	..	..	..
4600 Other recurrent taxes on property	..	..	..	..	..	..	..	..	..	..
5000 Taxes on goods and services	..	**0**	**0**	**0**	**0**	..	**0**	**0**	**0**	**0**
5100 Taxes on production, sale, transfer, etc	..	..	..	..	..	..	..	..	..	..
5110 General taxes	..	..	..	..	..	..	..	..	..	..
5120 Taxes on specific goods and services	..	..	..	..	..	..	..	..	..	..
5130 Unallocable between 5110 and 5120	..	..	..	..	..	..	..	..	..	..
5200 Taxes on use of goods and perform activities	..	..	..	..	..	..	..	..	..	..
5300 Unallocable between 5100 and 5200	..	..	..	..	..	..	..	..	..	..
6000 Other taxes	..	**575**	**1 381**	**2 585**	**4 496**	..	**0**	**0**	**0**	**0**
6100 Paid solely by business	..	0	0	0	0	..	..	..	..	..
6200 Other	..	575	1 381	2 585	4 496	..	..	..	..	..
Total tax revenue	..	**575**	**1 381**	**2 585**	**4 496**	..	**1 977**	**5 265**	**14 235**	**16 930**

1. The figures have been revised with latest data from Ministerio de Economía y Finanzas Públicas de Bolivia and Unidad de Análisis de Políticas Sociales y Económicas in this edition.
2. The figures exclude local government tax revenues for the period 1990-1993 as the data are not available. The data for 2018 are estimated.
3. The data for social security contributions include contributions to Bolivia's pension system and healthcare related funds in this edition. For healthcare related funds, the contributions for 2018 are estimated.

StatLink https://doi.org/10.1787/888934115008

Table 6.6. **Brazil, tax revenues by sub-sectors of government**

Million BRL

	Federal government					State/Regional				
	1990	2000	2010	2015	2018	1990	2000	2010	2015	2018
1000 Taxes on income, profits and capital gains	**1**	**68 667**	**258 738**	**400 993**	**489 863**	**0**	**0**	**0**	**0**	**0**
1100 Of individuals	0	3 406	87 828	148 739	193 089	..	..	..	..	..
1200 Corporate	0	25 430	128 255	164 057	194 814	..	..	..	..	..
1300 Unallocable between 1100 and 1200	0	39 831	42 656	88 196	101 961	..	..	..	..	..
2000 Social security contributions	**0**	**0**	**0**	**0**	**0**	**0**	**0**	**0**	**0**	**0**
2100 Employees	..	..	..	..	..	..	..	..	..	..
2200 Employers	..	..	..	..	..	..	..	..	..	..
2300 Self-employed or non-employed	..	..	..	..	..	..	..	..	..	..
2400 Unallocable between 2100, 2200 and 2300	..	..	..	..	..	..	..	..	..	..
3000 Taxes on payroll and workforce	**0**	**5 437**	**20 974**	**37 192**	**41 800**	**0**	**0**	**0**	**0**	**0**
4000 Taxes on property	**0**	**17 726**	**27 038**	**35 786**	**38 034**	**0**	**329**	**2 518**	**6 461**	**8 162**
4100 Recurrent taxes on immovable property	0	234	485	1 105	1 419	0	0	0	0	0
4200 Recurrent taxes on net wealth	0	0	0	0	0	0	0	0	0	0
4300 Estate, inheritance and gift taxes	0	0	0	0	0	0	329	2 518	6 461	8 162
4400 Taxes on financial and capital transactions	0	17 492	26 553	34 681	36 615	0	0	0	0	0
4500 Non-recurrent taxes	0	0	0	0	0	0	0	0	0	0
4600 Other recurrent taxes on property	0	0	0	0	0	0	0	0	0	0
5000 Taxes on goods and services	**1**	**75 502**	**254 095**	**352 985**	**416 251**	**1**	**87 573**	**289 483**	**432 647**	**522 018**
5100 Taxes on production, sale, transfer, etc	1	75 502	251 265	348 743	413 939	1	82 279	268 117	396 428	480 524
5110 General taxes[1]	0	48 358	181 532	252 466	308 237	1	82 279	268 117	396 428	480 524
5120 Taxes on specific goods and services	0	27 144	69 732	96 278	105 703	0	0	0	0	0
5130 Unallocable between 5110 and 5120	0	0	0	0	0	0	0	0	0	0
5200 Taxes on use of goods and perform activities	0	0	2 830	4 242	2 312	0	5 294	21 367	36 219	41 495
5300 Unallocable between 5100 and 5200	0	0	0	0	0	0	0	0	0	0
6000 Other taxes[2]	**0**	**1 064**	**3 330**	**4 229**	**4 971**	**0**	**322**	**17 038**	**28 983**	**37 098**
6100 Paid solely by business	0	0	0	0	0	0	0	0	0	0
6200 Other	0	1 064	3 330	4 229	4 971	0	322	17 038	28 983	37 098
Total tax revenue	**1**	**168 396**	**564 175**	**831 185**	**990 919**	**1**	**88 224**	**309 040**	**468 091**	**567 279**

Million BRL

	Local government					Social Security Funds				
	1990	2000	2010	2015	2018	1990	2000	2010	2015	2018
1000 Taxes on income, profits and capital gains	**0**	**0**	**0**	**0**	**0**	**0**	**0**	**0**	**0**	**0**
1100 Of individuals	..	..	..	..	..	..	..	..	..	..
1200 Corporate	..	..	..	..	..	..	..	..	..	..
1300 Unallocable between 1100 and 1200	..	..	..	..	..	..	..	..	..	..
2000 Social security contributions	**0**	**0**	**0**	**0**	**0**	**1**	**83 469**	**315 789**	**501 944**	**579 228**
2100 Employees	..	..	..	..	..	..	..	..	..	..
2200 Employers	..	..	..	..	..	0	18 709	64 271	118 323	124 428
2300 Self-employed or non-employed	..	..	..	..	..	..	..	..	..	..
2400 Unallocable between 2100, 2200 and 2300	..	..	..	..	..	1	64 760	251 519	383 622	454 800
3000 Taxes on payroll and workforce	**0**	**0**	**0**	**0**	**0**	**0**	**0**	**0**	**0**	**0**
4000 Taxes on property	**0**	**5 469**	**23 285**	**41 426**	**57 411**	**0**	**0**	**0**	**0**	**0**
4100 Recurrent taxes on immovable property	0	4 519	17 444	31 521	45 970	..	..	..	..	..
4200 Recurrent taxes on net wealth	0	0	0	0	0	..	..	..	..	..
4300 Estate, inheritance and gift taxes	0	0	0	0	0	..	..	..	..	..
4400 Taxes on financial and capital transactions	0	950	5 840	9 904	11 442	..	..	..	..	..
4500 Non-recurrent taxes	0	0	0	0	0	..	..	..	..	..
4600 Other recurrent taxes on property	0	0	0	0	0	..	..	..	..	..
5000 Taxes on goods and services	**0**	**6 106**	**32 756**	**54 455**	**65 916**	**0**	**0**	**0**	**0**	**0**
5100 Taxes on production, sale, transfer, etc	0	6 106	32 756	54 455	65 916	..	..	..	..	..
5110 General taxes[1]	0	6 106	32 756	54 455	65 916	..	..	..	..	..
5120 Taxes on specific goods and services	0	0	0	0	0	..	..	..	..	..
5130 Unallocable between 5110 and 5120	0	0	0	0	0	..	..	..	..	..
5200 Taxes on use of goods and perform activities	0	0	0	0	0	..	..	..	..	..
5300 Unallocable between 5100 and 5200	0	0	0	0	0	..	..	..	..	..
6000 Other taxes[2]	**0**	**377**	**8 573**	**14 627**	**18 012**	**0**	**0**	**0**	**0**	**0**
6100 Paid solely by business	0	0	0	0	0	..	..	..	..	..
6200 Other	0	377	8 573	14 627	18 012	..	..	..	..	..
Total tax revenue	**0**	**11 952**	**64 613**	**110 507**	**141 339**	**1**	**83 469**	**315 789**	**501 944**	**579 228**

1. The PASEP (Program of Formation of the Patrimony of the Public Servants) contributions are added to the PIS (Social Integration Program) contributions in heading 5110 for the years prior to 2000.
2. The FUNDAF (Special Fund for Development and Improvement of Auditing Activities) contributions are included in heading 6200 from 2008.

StatLink https://doi.org/10.1787/888934115027

Table 6.7. **Chile, tax revenues by sub-sectors of government**

Million CLP

	Federal government					State/Regional				
	1990	2000	2010	2015	2018	1990	2000	2010	2015	2018
1000 Taxes on income, profits and capital gains	**412 974**	**1 841 630**	**8 329 060**	**11 840 521**	**14 418 859**	..	..	..	..	..
1100 Of individuals	99 154	604 100	1 492 837	3 199 876	2 701 416	..	..	..	..	..
1200 Corporate	219 586	882 896	4 448 745	6 839 133	8 920 497	..	..	..	..	..
1300 Unallocable between 1100 and 1200	94 233	354 634	2 387 478	1 801 512	2 796 947	..	..	..	..	..
2000 Social security contributions	**66 738**	**232 728**	**371 386**	**434 658**	**473 962**	..	..	..	..	..
2100 Employees	61 200	209 907	310 558	370 744	391 050	..	..	..	..	..
2200 Employers	5 538	22 821	60 828	63 914	82 912	..	..	..	..	..
2300 Self-employed or non-employed	0	0	0	0	0	..	..	..	..	..
2400 Unallocable between 2100, 2200 and 2300	0	0	0	0	0	..	..	..	..	..
3000 Taxes on payroll and workforce	**0**	**0**	**0**	**0**	**0**	..	..	..	..	..
4000 Taxes on property	**59 682**	**255 371**	**245 044**	**379 603**	**736 328**	..	..	..	..	..
4100 Recurrent taxes on immovable property	10 331	3 578	8 805	15 249	22 957	..	..	..	..	..
4200 Recurrent taxes on net wealth	0	0	0	0	0	..	..	..	..	..
4300 Estate, inheritance and gift taxes	3 444	10 906	39 338	92 236	125 649	..	..	..	..	..
4400 Taxes on financial and capital transactions	45 907	240 886	196 901	272 118	587 721	..	..	..	..	..
4500 Non-recurrent taxes	0	0	0	0	..	..	..	..	..	..
4600 Other recurrent taxes on property	0	0	0	0	..	..	..	..	..	..
5000 Taxes on goods and services	**1 063 677**	**4 719 255**	**10 330 378**	**16 181 720**	**19 634 567**	..	..	..	..	..
5100 Taxes on production, sale, transfer, etc	1 060 304	4 684 525	10 294 165	16 129 953	19 465 361	..	..	..	..	..
5110 General taxes	664 421	3 306 350	8 399 926	13 273 958	16 211 646	..	..	..	..	..
5120 Taxes on specific goods and services[1]	395 883	1 378 175	1 894 239	2 855 995	3 253 715	..	..	..	..	..
5130 Unallocable between 5110 and 5120	0	0	0	0	..	..	..	..	..	..
5200 Taxes on use of goods and perform activities	3 374	34 730	36 213	51 767	169 206	..	..	..	..	..
5300 Unallocable between 5100 and 5200	0	0	0	0	..	..	..	..	..	..
6000 Other taxes	**-23 356**	**-112 195**	**-61 117**	**-579 308**	**-447 692**	..	..	..	..	..
6100 Paid solely by business	0	0	0	0	..	..	..	..	..	..
6200 Other	-23 356	-112 195	-61 117	-579 308	-447 692	..	..	..	..	..
Total tax revenue	**1 579 715**	**6 936 788**	**19 214 751**	**28 257 194**	**34 816 024**	..	..	..	..	..

Million CLP

	Local government					Social Security Funds				
	1990	2000	2010	2015	2018	1990	2000	2010	2015	2018
1000 Taxes on income, profits and capital gains	**0**	**0**	**0**	**0**	**0**	**0**	**0**	**0**	**0**	**0**
1100 Of individuals	0	0	0	0	0	0	0	0	0	0
1200 Corporate	0	0	0	0	0	0	0	0	0	0
1300 Unallocable between 1100 and 1200	0	0	0	0	0	0	0	0	0	0
2000 Social security contributions	**0**	**0**	**0**	**0**	**0**	**92 821**	**344 030**	**1 122 601**	**1 817 831**	**2 312 211**
2100 Employees	..	..	..	..	..	92 821	344 030	1 122 601	1 817 831	2 312 211
2200 Employers	..	..	..	..	..	0	0	0	0	0
2300 Self-employed or non-employed	..	..	..	..	..	0	0	0	0	0
2400 Unallocable between 2100, 2200 and 2300	..	..	..	..	..	0	0	0	0	0
3000 Taxes on payroll and workforce	**0**	**0**	**0**	**0**	**0**	**0**	**0**	**0**	**0**	**0**
4000 Taxes on property	**49 637**	**298 666**	**653 563**	**1 041 671**	**1 334 785**	**0**	**0**	**0**	**0**	**0**
4100 Recurrent taxes on immovable property	49 637	298 666	653 563	1 041 671	1 334 785	..	..	..	..	..
4200 Recurrent taxes on net wealth	0	0	0	0	0	..	..	..	..	..
4300 Estate, inheritance and gift taxes	0	0	0	0	..	..	..	..	..	..
4400 Taxes on financial and capital transactions	0	0	0	0	..	..	..	..	..	..
4500 Non-recurrent taxes	0	0	0	0	..	..	..	..	..	..
4600 Other recurrent taxes on property	0	0	0	0	..	..	..	..	..	..
5000 Taxes on goods and services	**55 045**	**322 514**	**854 778**	**1 415 658**	**1 834 406**	**0**	**0**	**0**	**0**	**0**
5100 Taxes on production, sale, transfer, etc	13 705	105 302	238 739	385 532	486 196	..	..	..	..	..
5110 General taxes	0	0	0	0	0	..	..	..	..	..
5120 Taxes on specific goods and services[1]	13 705	105 302	238 739	385 532	486 196	..	..	..	..	..
5130 Unallocable between 5110 and 5120	0	0	0	0	..	..	..	..	..	..
5200 Taxes on use of goods and perform activities	41 340	217 212	616 039	1 030 126	1 348 210	..	..	..	..	..
5300 Unallocable between 5100 and 5200	0	0	0	0	..	..	..	..	..	..
6000 Other taxes	**0**	**0**	**0**	**0**	**0**	**0**	**0**	**0**	**0**	**0**
6100 Paid solely by business	..	..	..	..	..	..	..	..	..	..
6200 Other	..	..	..	..	..	..	..	..	..	..
Total tax revenue	**104 682**	**621 180**	**1 508 341**	**2 457 329**	**3 169 191**	**92 821**	**344 030**	**1 122 601**	**1 817 831**	**2 312 211**

1. ECLAC classifies Oil Prices Stabilisation Fund (FEPP) revenues as non-tax revenues.

StatLink https://doi.org/10.1787/888934115046

Table 6.8. **Colombia, tax revenues by sub-sectors of government**

Million COP

	Federal government					State/Regional[1]				
	1990	2000	2010	2015	2018	1990	2000	2010	2015	2018
1000 Taxes on income, profits and capital gains	**771 694**	**7 103 525**	**26 218 852**	**52 656 876**	**64 043 928**	**0**	**0**	**0**	**0**	**0**
1100 Of individuals	47 210	1 499 345	5 192 384	9 736 861	12 215 963	..	..	..	..	..
1200 Corporate	359 758	5 119 828	20 405 209	41 070 208	48 529 320	..	..	..	..	..
1300 Unallocable between 1100 and 1200	364 726	484 352	621 258	1 849 807	3 298 645	..	..	..	..	..
2000 Social security contributions	**0**	**0**	**0**	**0**	**0**	**0**	**0**	**0**	**0**	**0**
2100 Employees	..	..	..	..	..	..	..	..	..	..
2200 Employers	..	..	..	..	..	..	..	..	..	..
2300 Self-employed or non-employed	..	..	..	..	..	..	..	..	..	..
2400 Unallocable between 2100, 2200 and 2300	..	..	..	..	..	..	..	..	..	..
3000 Taxes on payroll and workforce	**0**	**1 286 803**	**4 022 503**	**2 797 308**	**3 461 352**	**0**	**0**	**0**	**0**	**0**
4000 Taxes on property	**0**	**1 036 584**	**5 196 303**	**12 094 140**	**7 283 483**	**0**	**0**	**0**	**0**	**0**
4100 Recurrent taxes on immovable property	..	0	0	0	0	..	..	..	..	..
4200 Recurrent taxes on net wealth	..	0	1 970 530	5 352 940	467 925	..	..	..	..	..
4300 Estate, inheritance and gift taxes	..	0	0	0	0	..	..	..	..	..
4400 Taxes on financial and capital transactions	..	1 036 584	3 225 773	6 741 200	6 815 558	..	..	..	..	..
4500 Non-recurrent taxes	..	0	0	0	0	..	..	..	..	..
4600 Other recurrent taxes on property	..	0	0	0	0	..	..	..	..	..
5000 Taxes on goods and services	**1 035 934**	**11 108 594**	**35 382 852**	**51 725 461**	**63 898 347**	**263 429**	**1 481 725**	**3 406 301**	**4 986 314**	**6 812 676**
5100 Taxes on production, sale, transfer, etc	1 035 934	11 108 594	35 382 852	51 725 461	63 898 347	263 429	1 349 930	3 032 733	4 456 650	6 016 297
5110 General taxes	583 078	8 445 776	28 811 682	41 553 967	55 879 110	0	0	0	0	0
5120 Taxes on specific goods and services	452 856	2 662 818	6 571 170	10 171 494	8 019 237	263 429	1 349 930	3 032 733	4 456 650	6 016 297
5130 Unallocable between 5110 and 5120	0	0	0	0	0	0	0	0	0	0
5200 Taxes on use of goods and perform activities	0	0	0	0	0	0	131 795	373 568	529 665	796 379
5300 Unallocable between 5100 and 5200	0	0	0	0	0	0	0	0	0	0
6000 Other taxes	**78 306**	**480 784**	**483 762**	**424 000**	**541 027**	**0**	**241 471**	**1 374 970**	**2 624 769**	**2 606 397**
6100 Paid solely by business	0	0	0	0	0	..	0	0	0	0
6200 Other	78 306	480 784	483 762	424 000	541 027	..	241 471	1 374 970	2 624 769	2 606 397
Total tax revenue	**1 885 934**	**21 016 290**	**71 304 272**	**119 697 784**	**139 228 138**	**263 429**	**1 723 196**	**4 781 271**	**7 611 084**	**9 419 073**

Million COP

	Local government[1]					Social Security Funds[2]				
	1990	2000	2010	2015	2018	1990	2000	2010	2015	2018
1000 Taxes on income, profits and capital gains	**0**	**0**	**0**	**0**	**0**	**0**	**0**	**0**	**0**	**0**
1100 Of individuals	..	..	..	..	..	..	..	..	..	..
1200 Corporate	..	..	..	..	..	..	..	..	..	..
1300 Unallocable between 1100 and 1200	..	..	..	..	..	..	..	..	..	..
2000 Social security contributions	**0**	**0**	**0**	**0**	**0**	**203 596**	**4 989 000**	**11 478 085**	**13 585 138**	**18 192 049**
2100 Employees	..	..	..	..	..	..	..	..	..	..
2200 Employers	..	..	..	..	..	..	..	..	..	..
2300 Self-employed or non-employed	..	..	..	..	..	..	..	..	..	..
2400 Unallocable between 2100, 2200 and 2300	..	..	..	..	..	203 596	4 989 000	11 478 085	13 585 138	18 192 049
3000 Taxes on payroll and workforce	**0**	**0**	**0**	**0**	**0**	**0**	**0**	**0**	**0**	**0**
4000 Taxes on property	**56 160**	**991 070**	**3 338 935**	**6 061 965**	**7 981 989**	**0**	**0**	**0**	**0**	**0**
4100 Recurrent taxes on immovable property	56 160	991 070	3 338 935	6 061 965	7 981 989	..	..	..	..	..
4200 Recurrent taxes on net wealth	0	0	0	0	0	..	..	..	..	..
4300 Estate, inheritance and gift taxes	0	0	0	0	0	..	..	..	..	..
4400 Taxes on financial and capital transactions	0	0	0	0	0	..	..	..	..	..
4500 Non-recurrent taxes	0	0	0	0	0	..	..	..	..	..
4600 Other recurrent taxes on property	0	0	0	0	0	..	..	..	..	..
5000 Taxes on goods and services	**89 290**	**1 590 132**	**5 622 489**	**8 899 062**	**10 697 766**	**0**	**0**	**0**	**0**	**0**
5100 Taxes on production, sale, transfer, etc	89 290	1 590 132	5 622 489	8 400 241	10 020 693	..	..	..	..	..
5110 General taxes	89 290	1 140 090	4 522 121	7 025 204	8 436 909	..	..	..	..	..
5120 Taxes on specific goods and services	0	450 042	1 100 368	1 375 037	1 583 783	..	..	..	..	..
5130 Unallocable between 5110 and 5120	0	0	0	0	0	..	..	..	..	..
5200 Taxes on use of goods and perform activities	0	0	0	498 821	677 073	..	..	..	..	..
5300 Unallocable between 5100 and 5200	0	0	0	0	0	..	..	..	..	..
6000 Other taxes	**81 017**	**288 942**	**1 930 282**	**4 200 992**	**4 780 896**	**0**	**0**	**0**	**0**	**0**
6100 Paid solely by business	0	0	0	0	0	..	..	..	..	..
6200 Other	81 017	288 942	1 930 282	4 200 992	4 780 896	..	..	..	..	..
Total tax revenue	**226 467**	**2 870 144**	**10 891 707**	**19 162 019**	**23 460 651**	**203 596**	**4 989 000**	**11 478 085**	**13 585 138**	**18 192 049**

1. The data correspond to the reported consolidated revenues of the territorial entities (departments and municipalities).
2. All of the health contributions pertaining to FOSYGA (Solidarity and Guarantee Fund) are classified as social security contributions from 2013. Prior to 2013, only the portion of the contributions used to finance the subsidised regime was included and the part to finance the contributory regime was classified in the social security sector as "other incomes".

StatLink https://doi.org/10.1787/888934115065

Table 6.9. **Costa Rica, tax revenues by sub-sectors of government**

Million CRC

	Federal government					State/Regional				
	1990	2000	2010	2015	2018	1990	2000	2010	2015	2018
1000 Taxes on income, profits and capital gains	**11 820**	**128 805**	**748 093**	**1 247 308**	**1 699 258**	..	..	..	..	..
1100 Of individuals	..	..	202 849	386 241	483 645	..	..	..	..	..
1200 Corporate	..	..	450 312	659 951	915 284	..	..	..	..	..
1300 Unallocable between 1100 and 1200	11 820	128 805	94 932	201 116	300 330	..	..	..	..	..
2000 Social security contributions[1]	**1 345**	**18 677**	**61 193**	**63 458**	**85 407**	..	..	..	..	..
2100 Employees	..	..	..	..	..	..	..	..	..	..
2200 Employers	..	..	..	..	..	..	..	..	..	..
2300 Self-employed or non-employed	..	..	..	..	..	..	..	..	..	..
2400 Unallocable between 2100, 2200 and 2300	1 345	18 677	61 193	63 458	85 407	..	..	..	..	..
3000 Taxes on payroll and workforce	**0**	**0**	**0**	**0**	**0**	..	..	..	..	..
4000 Taxes on property	**366**	**3 007**	**18 270**	**37 334**	**40 191**	..	..	..	..	..
4100 Recurrent taxes on immovable property	0	0	3 527	4 076	4 468	..	..	..	..	..
4200 Recurrent taxes on net wealth	0	0	0	0	0	..	..	..	..	..
4300 Estate, inheritance and gift taxes	0	0	0	0	0	..	..	..	..	..
4400 Taxes on financial and capital transactions	366	3 007	14 743	33 258	35 724	..	..	..	..	..
4500 Non-recurrent taxes	0	0	0	0	0	..	..	..	..	..
4600 Other recurrent taxes on property	0	0	0	0	0	..	..	..	..	..
5000 Taxes on goods and services	**52 248**	**444 870**	**1 696 593**	**2 536 562**	**2 782 173**	..	..	..	..	..
5100 Taxes on production, sale, transfer, etc	49 867	425 630	1 598 789	2 385 807	2 605 079	..	..	..	..	..
5110 General taxes	21 326	222 775	920 298	1 368 601	1 513 677	..	..	..	..	..
5120 Taxes on specific goods and services[2]	28 541	202 856	678 491	1 017 206	1 091 402	..	..	..	..	..
5130 Unallocable between 5110 and 5120	0	0	0	0	0	..	..	..	..	..
5200 Taxes on use of goods and perform activities	2 380	19 240	97 804	150 755	177 093	..	..	..	..	..
5300 Unallocable between 5100 and 5200	0	0	0	0	0	..	..	..	..	..
6000 Other taxes[3]	**9 251**	**23 956**	**92 452**	**162 200**	**214 862**	..	..	..	..	..
6100 Paid solely by business	0	0	0	0	0	..	..	..	..	..
6200 Other	9 251	23 956	92 452	162 200	214 862	..	..	..	..	..
Total tax revenue	**75 030**	**619 314**	**2 616 600**	**4 046 862**	**4 821 890**	..	..	..	..	..

Million CRC

	Local government					Social Security Funds				
	1990	2000	2010	2015	2018	1990	2000	2010	2015	2018
1000 Taxes on income, profits and capital gains	**0**	**0**	**0**	**0**	**0**	**0**	**0**	**0**	**0**	**0**
1100 Of individuals	..	..	..	..	..	..	..	..	..	..
1200 Corporate	..	..	..	..	..	..	..	..	..	..
1300 Unallocable between 1100 and 1200	..	..	..	..	..	..	..	..	..	..
2000 Social security contributions[1]	**0**	**0**	**0**	**0**	**0**	**32 645**	**278 392**	**1 389 338**	**2 241 674**	**2 774 060**
2100 Employees	..	..	..	..	..	..	..	..	..	..
2200 Employers	..	..	..	..	..	3 447	37 313	207 206	318 652	368 865
2300 Self-employed or non-employed	..	..	..	..	..	..	..	..	..	..
2400 Unallocable between 2100, 2200 and 2300	..	..	..	..	..	29 198	241 079	1 182 132	1 923 022	2 405 196
3000 Taxes on payroll and workforce	**0**	**0**	**0**	**0**	**0**	**7 575**	**61 796**	**260 664**	**423 616**	**498 577**
4000 Taxes on property	**1 200**	**5 390**	**45 436**	**85 927**	**109 119**	**0**	**0**	**0**	**0**	**0**
4100 Recurrent taxes on immovable property	1 200	5 390	45 436	85 927	109 119	..	..	..	..	..
4200 Recurrent taxes on net wealth	0	0	0	0	0	..	..	..	..	..
4300 Estate, inheritance and gift taxes	0	0	0	0	0	..	..	..	..	..
4400 Taxes on financial and capital transactions	0	0	0	0	0	..	..	..	..	..
4500 Non-recurrent taxes	0	0	0	0	0	..	..	..	..	..
4600 Other recurrent taxes on property	0	0	0	0	0	..	..	..	..	..
5000 Taxes on goods and services	**1 262**	**11 981**	**70 321**	**125 341**	**136 299**	**0**	**0**	**0**	**0**	**0**
5100 Taxes on production, sale, transfer, etc	0	83	1 513	3 093	3 785	..	..	..	..	..
5110 General taxes	..	0	0	0	0	..	..	..	..	..
5120 Taxes on specific goods and services[2]	..	83	1 513	3 093	3 785	..	..	..	..	..
5130 Unallocable between 5110 and 5120	..	0	0	0	0	..	..	..	..	..
5200 Taxes on use of goods and perform activities	1 262	11 898	68 808	122 248	132 514	..	..	..	..	..
5300 Unallocable between 5100 and 5200	0	0	0	0	0	..	..	..	..	..
6000 Other taxes[3]	**0**	**1 242**	**8**	**155**	**46**	**0**	**0**	**0**	**0**	**0**
6100 Paid solely by business	..	0	0	0	0	..	..	..	..	..
6200 Other	..	1 242	8	155	46	..	..	..	..	..
Total tax revenue	**2 461**	**18 613**	**115 765**	**211 422**	**245 464**	**40 220**	**340 187**	**1 650 002**	**2 665 291**	**3 272 637**

1. The data include social security contributions paid by the governments for their employees as well as the contributions for special regimes (teachers and magistrates). In ECLAC data, social security contributions also include INA (National Institute of Apprenticeship), IMAS (Joint Social Aid Institute) and FODESAF (Social Development and Family Allowances Fund).
2. In ECLAC data, the tax on ownership of vehicles, aircraft and boats is classified in category 4000.
3. The tax revenue of decentralised bodies is classified under the central government. In Costa Rica this revenue is classified under a separate unit (decentralised) considered to be different to the central government.

StatLink https://doi.org/10.1787/888934115084

Table 6.10. **Cuba, tax revenues by sub-sectors of government**

Million CUP

	Federal government					State/Regional				
	1990	2000	2010	2015	2018	1990	2000	2010	2015	2018
1000 Taxes on income, profits and capital gains	..	..	**1 857**	..	..	..	..	..	..	..
1100 Of individuals	..	..	0	..	..	..	..	..	..	..
1200 Corporate	..	..	1 857	..	..	..	..	..	..	..
1300 Unallocable between 1100 and 1200	..	..	0	..	..	..	..	..	..	..
2000 Social security contributions	..	..	**0**	..	..	..	..	..	..	..
2100 Employees	..	..	..	..	..	..	..	..	..	..
2200 Employers	..	..	..	..	..	..	..	..	..	..
2300 Self-employed or non-employed	..	..	..	..	..	..	..	..	..	..
2400 Unallocable between 2100, 2200 and 2300	..	..	..	..	..	..	..	..	..	..
3000 Taxes on payroll and workforce	..	..	**289**	..	..	..	..	..	..	..
4000 Taxes on property	..	..	**0**	..	..	..	..	..	..	..
4100 Recurrent taxes on immovable property	..	..	..	..	..	..	..	..	..	..
4200 Recurrent taxes on net wealth	..	..	..	..	..	..	..	..	..	..
4300 Estate, inheritance and gift taxes	..	..	..	..	..	..	..	..	..	..
4400 Taxes on financial and capital transactions	..	..	..	..	..	..	..	..	..	..
4500 Non-recurrent taxes	..	..	..	..	..	..	..	..	..	..
4600 Other recurrent taxes on property	..	..	..	..	..	..	..	..	..	..
5000 Taxes on goods and services	..	..	**5 757**	..	..	..	..	..	..	..
5100 Taxes on production, sale, transfer, etc	..	..	5 757	..	..	..	..	..	..	..
5110 General taxes	..	..	4 924	..	..	..	..	..	..	..
5120 Taxes on specific goods and services	..	..	833	..	..	..	..	..	..	..
5130 Unallocable between 5110 and 5120	..	..	0	..	..	..	..	..	..	..
5200 Taxes on use of goods and perform activities	..	..	0	..	..	..	..	..	..	..
5300 Unallocable between 5100 and 5200	..	..	0	..	..	..	..	..	..	..
6000 Other taxes	..	..	**569**	..	..	..	..	..	..	..
6100 Paid solely by business	..	..	..	..	..	..	..	..	..	..
6200 Other	..	..	..	..	..	..	..	..	..	..
Total tax revenue	..	..	**8 472**	..	..	..	..	..	..	..

Million CUP

	Local government[1]					Social Security Funds				
	1990	2000	2010	2015	2018	1990	2000	2010	2015	2018
1000 Taxes on income, profits and capital gains	..	..	**1 746**	..	..	**0**	**0**	**0**	**0**	**0**
1100 Of individuals	..	..	554	..	..	..	..	..	..	..
1200 Corporate	..	..	1 193	..	..	..	..	..	..	..
1300 Unallocable between 1100 and 1200	..	..	0	..	..	..	..	..	..	..
2000 Social security contributions	..	..	**0**	..	..	**691**	**1 181**	**2 974**	**4 322**	**5 206**
2100 Employees	..	..	..	..	..	..	..	..	..	..
2200 Employers	..	..	..	..	..	..	..	..	..	..
2300 Self-employed or non-employed	..	..	..	..	..	..	..	..	..	..
2400 Unallocable between 2100, 2200 and 2300	..	..	..	..	..	691	1 181	2 974	4 322	5 206
3000 Taxes on payroll and workforce	..	..	**4 125**	..	..	**0**	**0**	**0**	**0**	**0**
4000 Taxes on property	..	..	**0**	..	..	**0**	**0**	**0**	**0**	**0**
4100 Recurrent taxes on immovable property	..	..	..	..	..	..	..	..	..	..
4200 Recurrent taxes on net wealth	..	..	..	..	..	..	..	..	..	..
4300 Estate, inheritance and gift taxes	..	..	..	..	..	..	..	..	..	..
4400 Taxes on financial and capital transactions	..	..	..	..	..	..	..	..	..	..
4500 Non-recurrent taxes	..	..	..	..	..	..	..	..	..	..
4600 Other recurrent taxes on property	..	..	..	..	..	..	..	..	..	..
5000 Taxes on goods and services	..	..	**6 526**	..	..	**0**	**0**	**0**	**0**	**0**
5100 Taxes on production, sale, transfer, etc	..	..	6 526	..	..	..	..	..	..	..
5110 General taxes	..	..	5 601	..	..	..	..	..	..	..
5120 Taxes on specific goods and services	..	..	925	..	..	..	..	..	..	..
5130 Unallocable between 5110 and 5120	..	..	0	..	..	..	..	..	..	..
5200 Taxes on use of goods and perform activities	..	..	0	..	..	..	..	..	..	..
5300 Unallocable between 5100 and 5200	..	..	0	..	..	..	..	..	..	..
6000 Other taxes	..	..	**106**	..	..	**0**	**0**	**0**	**0**	**0**
6100 Paid solely by business	..	..	..	..	..	..	..	..	..	..
6200 Other	..	..	..	..	..	..	..	..	..	..
Total tax revenue	..	..	**12 503**	..	..	**691**	**1 181**	**2 974**	**4 322**	**5 206**

1. The figures include local government tax revenues for 2002 to 2012. Local tax revenues are not available for other years

StatLink https://doi.org/10.1787/888934115103

Table 6.11. **Dominican Republic, tax revenues by sub-sectors of government**

Million DOP

	Federal government					State/Regional				
	1990	2000	2010	2015	2018	1990	2000	2010	2015	2018
1000 Taxes on income, profits and capital gains	**1 670**	**10 782**	**53 643**	**119 819**	**170 561**	..	..	..	..	..
1100 Of individuals	..	4 088	17 088	35 549	51 425	..	..	..	..	..
1200 Corporate	..	4 679	21 475	61 695	88 079	..	..	..	..	..
1300 Unallocable between 1100 and 1200	1 670	2 015	15 080	22 576	31 057	..	..	..	..	..
2000 Social security contributions	**0**	**0**	**0**	**0**	**0**	..	..	..	..	..
2100 Employees	..	..	..	..	..	..	..	..	..	..
2200 Employers	..	..	..	..	..	..	..	..	..	..
2300 Self-employed or non-employed	..	..	..	..	..	..	..	..	..	..
2400 Unallocable between 2100, 2200 and 2300	..	..	..	..	..	..	..	..	..	..
3000 Taxes on payroll and workforce	**0**	**0**	**0**	**0**	**0**	..	..	..	..	..
4000 Taxes on property	**74**	**689**	**13 315**	**19 044**	**25 716**	..	..	..	..	..
4100 Recurrent taxes on immovable property	9	115	555	1 755	2 527	..	..	..	..	..
4200 Recurrent taxes on net wealth	0	0	2 449	3 445	4 609	..	..	0	0	..
4300 Estate, inheritance and gift taxes	11	96	231	418	526	..	..	..	..	..
4400 Taxes on financial and capital transactions	40	377	8 658	12 067	15 675	..	..	..	..	..
4500 Non-recurrent taxes	3	32	488	591	553	..	..	..	..	..
4600 Other recurrent taxes on property	11	70	934	769	1 827	..	..	..	..	..
5000 Taxes on goods and services	**4 467**	**35 853**	**175 139**	**273 898**	**358 888**	..	..	..	..	..
5100 Taxes on production, sale, transfer, etc	4 398	35 135	168 641	263 435	344 706	..	..	..	..	..
5110 General taxes	970	9 912	81 226	147 039	194 725	..	..	..	..	..
5120 Taxes on specific goods and services[1]	3 429	25 224	87 415	116 396	149 981	..	..	..	..	..
5130 Unallocable between 5110 and 5120	0	0	0	0	0	..	..	..	..	..
5200 Taxes on use of goods and perform activities	69	718	6 498	10 463	14 182	..	..	..	..	..
5300 Unallocable between 5100 and 5200	0	0	0	0	0	..	..	..	..	..
6000 Other taxes[2]	**159**	**495**	**0**	**1**	**1**	..	..	..	..	..
6100 Paid solely by business	0	0	..	0	0	..	..	..	..	..
6200 Other	159	495	..	1	1	..	..	..	..	..
Total tax revenue	**6 371**	**47 820**	**242 097**	**412 762**	**555 166**	..	..	..	..	..

Million DOP

	Local government[3]					Social Security Funds[4]				
	1990	2000	2010	2015	2018	1990	2000	2010	2015	2018
1000 Taxes on income, profits and capital gains	..	..	..	..	..	**0**	**0**	**0**	**0**	**0**
1100 Of individuals	..	..	..	..	..	..	..	..	..	..
1200 Corporate	..	..	..	..	..	..	..	..	..	..
1300 Unallocable between 1100 and 1200	..	..	..	..	..	..	..	..	..	..
2000 Social security contributions	..	..	..	..	..	**53**	**490**	**1 845**	**1 483**	**2 514**
2100 Employees	..	..	..	..	..	..	..	1 720	1 321	..
2200 Employers	..	..	..	..	..	..	..	125	163	..
2300 Self-employed or non-employed	..	..	..	..	..	..	..	0	0	..
2400 Unallocable between 2100, 2200 and 2300	..	..	..	..	..	53	490	0	0	2 514
3000 Taxes on payroll and workforce	..	..	..	..	..	**0**	**0**	**0**	**0**	**0**
4000 Taxes on property	..	..	..	..	..	**0**	**0**	**0**	**0**	**0**
4100 Recurrent taxes on immovable property	..	..	..	..	..	..	..	..	..	..
4200 Recurrent taxes on net wealth	..	..	..	..	..	..	..	..	..	..
4300 Estate, inheritance and gift taxes	..	..	..	..	..	..	..	..	..	..
4400 Taxes on financial and capital transactions	..	..	..	..	..	..	..	..	..	..
4500 Non-recurrent taxes	..	..	..	..	..	..	..	..	..	..
4600 Other recurrent taxes on property	..	..	..	..	..	..	..	..	..	..
5000 Taxes on goods and services	..	..	..	..	..	**0**	**0**	**0**	**0**	**0**
5100 Taxes on production, sale, transfer, etc	..	..	..	..	..	..	..	..	..	..
5110 General taxes	..	..	..	..	..	..	..	..	..	..
5120 Taxes on specific goods and services[1]	..	..	..	..	..	..	..	..	..	..
5130 Unallocable between 5110 and 5120	..	..	..	..	..	..	..	..	..	..
5200 Taxes on use of goods and perform activities	..	..	..	..	..	..	..	..	..	..
5300 Unallocable between 5100 and 5200	..	..	..	..	..	..	..	..	..	..
6000 Other taxes[2]	..	..	..	..	..	**0**	**0**	**0**	**0**	**0**
6100 Paid solely by business	..	..	..	..	..	..	..	..	..	..
6200 Other	..	..	..	..	..	..	..	..	..	..
Total tax revenue	..	..	..	..	..	**53**	**490**	**1 845**	**1 483**	**2 514**

1. In ECLAC data, the tax on transfer of movable goods is classified as a property tax (4000).
2. In ECLAC data, the vehicle transfer tax is classified as a property tax (4000).
3. The figures exclude local government tax revenues as the data are not available.
4. The figures exclude social security contributions to general government managed by the private sector.

StatLink https://doi.org/10.1787/888934115122

Table 6.12. **Ecuador, tax revenues by sub-sectors of government**

Million USD

	Federal government					State/Regional				
	1990	2000	2010	2015	2018	1990	2000	2010	2015	2018
1000 Taxes on income, profits and capital gains	**138**	**267**	**2 348**	**4 705**	**5 165**	..	..	..	..	..
1100 Of individuals	..	10	80	192	193	..	..	..	..	..
1200 Corporate	..	53	405	1 575	1 894	..	..	..	..	..
1300 Unallocable between 1100 and 1200	138	204	1 783	2 938	3 078	..	..	..	..	..
2000 Social security contributions	**0**	**0**	**0**	**0**	**0**	..	..	..	..	..
2100 Employees	..	..	..	..	..	..	..	..	..	..
2200 Employers	..	..	..	..	..	..	..	..	..	..
2300 Self-employed or non-employed	..	..	..	..	..	..	..	..	..	..
2400 Unallocable between 2100, 2200 and 2300	..	..	..	..	..	..	..	..	..	..
3000 Taxes on payroll and workforce	**0**	**0**	**0**	**0**	**0**	..	..	..	..	..
4000 Taxes on property	**0**	**0**	**43**	**87**	**66**	..	..	..	..	..
4100 Recurrent taxes on immovable property	..	..	3	9	2	..	..	..	..	..
4200 Recurrent taxes on net wealth	..	..	35	49	30	..	..	..	..	..
4300 Estate, inheritance and gift taxes	..	..	5	29	27	..	..	..	..	..
4400 Taxes on financial and capital transactions	..	..	0	0	0	..	..	..	..	..
4500 Non-recurrent taxes	..	..	0	0	7	..	..	..	..	..
4600 Other recurrent taxes on property	..	..	0	0	0	..	..	..	..	..
5000 Taxes on goods and services	**668**	**1 596**	**5 969**	**10 751**	**10 858**	..	..	..	..	..
5100 Taxes on production, sale, transfer, etc	665	1 574	5 814	10 414	10 524	..	..	..	..	..
5110 General taxes	302	923	3 759	6 352	6 633	..	..	..	..	..
5120 Taxes on specific goods and services	363	651	2 054	4 062	3 891	..	..	..	..	..
5130 Unallocable between 5110 and 5120	0	0	0	0	0	..	..	..	..	..
5200 Taxes on use of goods and perform activities	3	22	156	336	334	..	..	..	..	..
5300 Unallocable between 5100 and 5200	0	0	0	0	0	..	..	..	..	..
6000 Other taxes	**0**	**0**	**4**	**10**	**21**	..	..	..	..	..
6100 Paid solely by business	..	..	0	0	0	..	..	..	..	..
6200 Other	..	..	4	10	21	..	..	..	..	..
Total tax revenue	**806**	**1 863**	**8 364**	**15 553**	**16 110**	..	..	..	..	..

Million USD

	Local government[1]					Social Security Funds[2]				
	1990	2000	2010	2015	2018	1990	2000	2010	2015	2018
1000 Taxes on income, profits and capital gains	**1**	**2**	**15**	**75**	**71**	**0**	**0**	**0**	**0**	**0**
1100 Of individuals	..	..	0	0	0	..	..	..	..	..
1200 Corporate	..	..	..	..	..	..	..	..	..	..
1300 Unallocable between 1100 and 1200	1	2	15	75	71	..	..	..	..	..
2000 Social security contributions	**0**	**0**	**0**	**0**	**0**	**243**	**228**	**2 541**	**5 057**	**5 553**
2100 Employees	..	..	..	..	..	..	..	..	..	..
2200 Employers	..	..	..	..	..	..	..	..	..	..
2300 Self-employed or non-employed	..	..	..	..	..	..	..	..	..	..
2400 Unallocable between 2100, 2200 and 2300	..	..	..	..	..	243	228	2 541	5 057	5 553
3000 Taxes on payroll and workforce	**0**	**0**	**0**	**0**	**0**	**0**	**0**	**0**	**0**	**0**
4000 Taxes on property	**16**	**17**	**116**	**216**	**288**	**0**	**0**	**0**	**0**	**0**
4100 Recurrent taxes on immovable property	13	8	66	125	172	..	..	..	..	..
4200 Recurrent taxes on net wealth	0	0	0	0	0	..	..	..	..	..
4300 Estate, inheritance and gift taxes	0	0	0	0	0	..	..	..	..	..
4400 Taxes on financial and capital transactions	0	0	0	0	1	..	..	..	..	..
4500 Non-recurrent taxes	0	0	0	0	0	..	..	..	..	..
4600 Other recurrent taxes on property	3	9	50	91	115	..	..	..	..	..
5000 Taxes on goods and services	**10**	**13**	**97**	**246**	**253**	**0**	**0**	**0**	**0**	**0**
5100 Taxes on production, sale, transfer, etc	6	6	49	89	84	..	..	..	..	..
5110 General taxes	4	5	41	79	74	..	..	..	..	..
5120 Taxes on specific goods and services	1	2	8	10	11	..	..	..	..	..
5130 Unallocable between 5110 and 5120	0	0	0	0	0	..	..	..	..	..
5200 Taxes on use of goods and perform activities	5	7	48	157	169	..	..	..	..	..
5300 Unallocable between 5100 and 5200	0	0	0	0	0	..	..	..	..	..
6000 Other taxes	**2**	**2**	**1**	**0**	**2**	**0**	**0**	**0**	**0**	**0**
6100 Paid solely by business	0	0	0	0	0	..	..	..	..	..
6200 Other	2	2	1	0	2	..	..	..	..	..
Total tax revenue	**29**	**34**	**228**	**537**	**615**	**243**	**228**	**2 541**	**5 057**	**5 553**

1. The local data have been revised since 1990 and their classifications have been improved, affecting headings 1000, 4400, 5120 and 5200. The figures in 2018 are estimated.
2. Social security contributions are collected from non-financial public sector operations published by the Central Bank of Ecuador and are on accrual basis.

StatLink https://doi.org/10.1787/888934115141

Table 6.13. **El Salvador, tax revenues by sub-sectors of government**

Million USD

	Federal government					State/Regional				
	1990	2000	2010	2015	2018	1990	2000	2010	2015	2018
1000 Taxes on income, profits and capital gains	**95**	**429**	**996**	**1 545**	**1 819**	..	..	..	..	..
1100 Of individuals	..	..	590	774	795	..	..	..	..	..
1200 Corporate	..	..	420	622	845	..	..	..	..	..
1300 Unallocable between 1100 and 1200	95	429	-14	148	180	..	..	..	..	..
2000 Social security contributions	**0**	**0**	**0**	**0**	**0**	..	..	..	..	..
2100 Employees	..	..	..	..	..	..	..	..	..	..
2200 Employers	..	..	..	..	..	..	..	..	..	..
2300 Self-employed or non-employed	..	..	..	..	..	..	..	..	..	..
2400 Unallocable between 2100, 2200 and 2300	..	..	..	..	..	..	..	..	..	..
3000 Taxes on payroll and workforce	**0**	**0**	**0**	**0**	**0**	..	..	..	..	..
4000 Taxes on property	**26**	**12**	**16**	**107**	**113**	..	..	..	..	..
4100 Recurrent taxes on immovable property	0	0	0	0	0	..	..	..	..	..
4200 Recurrent taxes on net wealth	16	0	0	0	0	..	..	..	..	..
4300 Estate, inheritance and gift taxes	0	0	0	0	0	..	..	..	..	..
4400 Taxes on financial and capital transactions	10	12	16	107	113	..	..	..	..	..
4500 Non-recurrent taxes	0	0	0	0	0	..	..	..	..	..
4600 Other recurrent taxes on property	0	0	0	0	0	..	..	..	..	..
5000 Taxes on goods and services	**259**	**903**	**1 871**	**2 266**	**2 747**	..	..	..	..	..
5100 Taxes on production, sale, transfer, etc	259	903	1 863	2 254	2 732	..	..	..	..	..
5110 General taxes	133	714	1 433	1 764	2 054	..	..	..	..	..
5120 Taxes on specific goods and services	127	189	431	490	678	..	..	..	..	..
5130 Unallocable between 5110 and 5120	0	0	0	0	0	..	..	..	..	..
5200 Taxes on use of goods and perform activities	0	0	7	12	15	..	..	..	..	..
5300 Unallocable between 5100 and 5200	0	0	0	0	0	..	..	..	..	..
6000 Other taxes	**58**	**0**	**0**	**0**	**0**	..	..	..	..	..
6100 Paid solely by business	0	0	..	..	..	..	..	..	..	..
6200 Other	58	0	..	..	..	..	..	..	..	..
Total tax revenue	**438**	**1 344**	**2 882**	**3 918**	**4 680**	..	..	..	..	..

Million USD

	Local government					Social Security Funds[1]				
	1990	2000	2010	2015	2018	1990	2000	2010	2015	2018
1000 Taxes on income, profits and capital gains	..	..	**0**	**0**	**0**	**0**	**0**	**0**	**0**	**0**
1100 Of individuals	..	..	..	..	..	..	..	..	..	..
1200 Corporate	..	..	..	..	..	..	..	..	..	..
1300 Unallocable between 1100 and 1200	..	..	..	..	..	..	..	..	..	..
2000 Social security contributions	..	..	**0**	**0**	**0**	**104**	**325**	**470**	**607**	**704**
2100 Employees	..	..	..	..	..	..	75	99	130	156
2200 Employers	..	..	..	..	..	..	176	238	314	380
2300 Self-employed or non-employed	..	..	..	..	..	..	13	33	45	54
2400 Unallocable between 2100, 2200 and 2300	..	..	..	..	..	104	62	100	119	114
3000 Taxes on payroll and workforce	..	..	**0**	**0**	**0**	**0**	**0**	**0**	**0**	**0**
4000 Taxes on property	..	..	**3**	**5**	**6**	**0**	**0**	**0**	**0**	**0**
4100 Recurrent taxes on immovable property	..	..	3	5	6	..	..	..	..	..
4200 Recurrent taxes on net wealth	..	..	0	0	0	..	..	..	..	..
4300 Estate, inheritance and gift taxes	..	..	0	0	0	..	..	..	..	..
4400 Taxes on financial and capital transactions	..	..	0	0	0	..	..	..	..	..
4500 Non-recurrent taxes	..	..	0	0	0	..	..	..	..	..
4600 Other recurrent taxes on property	..	..	0	0	0	..	..	..	..	..
5000 Taxes on goods and services	..	..	**7**	**12**	**15**	**0**	**0**	**0**	**0**	**0**
5100 Taxes on production, sale, transfer, etc	..	..	0	0	0	..	..	..	..	..
5110 General taxes	..	..	..	..	..	..	..	..	..	..
5120 Taxes on specific goods and services	..	..	..	..	..	..	..	..	..	..
5130 Unallocable between 5110 and 5120	..	..	..	..	..	..	..	..	..	..
5200 Taxes on use of goods and perform activities	..	..	7	12	15	..	..	..	..	..
5300 Unallocable between 5100 and 5200	..	..	0	0	0	..	..	..	..	..
6000 Other taxes	..	..	**63**	**86**	**93**	**0**	**0**	**0**	**0**	**0**
6100 Paid solely by business	..	..	0	0	0	..	..	..	..	..
6200 Other	..	..	63	86	93	..	..	..	..	..
Total tax revenue	..	..	**74**	**103**	**114**	**104**	**325**	**470**	**607**	**704**

1. Social security contributions are those paid to the Salvadoran Institute of Social Security (ISSS), National Public Employees Pension Institute (INPEP), Social Security Institute of the Armed Forces (IPSFA) and Salvadoran Institute of Teacher Welfare (ISBM). The figures exclude contributions to the privately managed regime and may include small amount of voluntary contributions which are undistinguishable from the public social security contribution data.

StatLink https://doi.org/10.1787/888934115160

Table 6.14. **Guatemala, tax revenues by sub-sectors of government**

Million GTQ

	Federal government					State/Regional				
	1990	2000	2010	2015	2018	1990	2000	2010	2015	2018
1000 Taxes on income, profits and capital gains	**507**	**3 041**	**9 933**	**17 534**	**20 893**	..	..	..	..	..
1100 Of individuals	25	137	1 225	1 826	2 603	..	..	..	..	..
1200 Corporate	482	2 902	6 134	11 801	13 633	..	..	..	..	..
1300 Unallocable between 1100 and 1200	0	2	2 574	3 907	4 656	..	..	..	..	..
2000 Social security contributions	**0**	**0**	**0**	**0**	**0**	..	..	..	..	..
2100 Employees	..	..	..	..	..	..	..	..	..	..
2200 Employers	..	..	..	..	..	..	..	..	..	..
2300 Self-employed or non-employed	..	..	..	..	..	..	..	..	..	..
2400 Unallocable between 2100, 2200 and 2300	..	..	..	..	..	..	..	..	..	..
3000 Taxes on payroll and workforce	**0**	**0**	**0**	**0**	**0**	..	..	..	..	..
4000 Taxes on property	**149**	**199**	**582**	**358**	**491**	..	..	..	..	..
4100 Recurrent taxes on immovable property	0	6	1	1	2	..	..	..	..	..
4200 Recurrent taxes on net wealth	0	0	0	0	0	..	..	..	..	..
4300 Estate, inheritance and gift taxes	0	0	0	0	0	..	..	..	..	..
4400 Taxes on financial and capital transactions	149	194	581	357	489	..	..	..	..	..
4500 Non-recurrent taxes	0	0	0	0	0	..	..	..	..	..
4600 Other recurrent taxes on property	0	0	0	0	0	..	..	..	..	..
5000 Taxes on goods and services	**1 477**	**10 317**	**23 255**	**31 719**	**37 253**	..	..	..	..	..
5100 Taxes on production, sale, transfer, etc	1 449	10 131	22 750	30 088	35 420	..	..	..	..	..
5110 General taxes	762	6 259	16 980	23 271	27 733	..	..	..	..	..
5120 Taxes on specific goods and services	687	3 872	5 770	6 816	7 687	..	..	..	..	..
5130 Unallocable between 5110 and 5120	0	0	0	0	0	..	..	..	..	..
5200 Taxes on use of goods and perform activities	28	186	505	1 631	1 834	..	..	..	..	..
5300 Unallocable between 5100 and 5200	0	0	0	0	0	..	..	..	..	..
6000 Other taxes	**0**	**4**	**1**	**0**	**0**	..	..	..	..	..
6100 Paid solely by business	..	0	0	0	0	..	..	..	..	..
6200 Other	..	4	1	0	0	..	..	..	..	..
Total tax revenue	**2 133**	**13 562**	**33 771**	**49 611**	**58 637**	..	..	..	..	..

Million GTQ

	Local government					Social Security Funds[1]				
	1990	2000	2010	2015	2018	1990	2000	2010	2015	2018
1000 Taxes on income, profits and capital gains	..	**0**	**0**	**0**	**0**	**0**	**0**	**0**	**0**	**0**
1100 Of individuals	..	..	..	..	..	..	..	..	..	..
1200 Corporate	..	..	..	..	..	..	..	..	..	..
1300 Unallocable between 1100 and 1200	..	..	..	..	..	..	..	..	..	..
2000 Social security contributions	..	**0**	**0**	**0**	**0**	**436**	**2 569**	**6 312**	**9 778**	**12 102**
2100 Employees	..	..	..	..	..	..	..	..	..	..
2200 Employers	..	..	..	..	..	..	..	..	..	..
2300 Self-employed or non-employed	..	..	..	..	..	..	..	..	..	..
2400 Unallocable between 2100, 2200 and 2300	..	..	..	..	..	436	2 569	6 312	9 778	12 102
3000 Taxes on payroll and workforce	..	**0**	**0**	**0**	**0**	**0**	**0**	**0**	**0**	**0**
4000 Taxes on property	..	**147**	**620**	**692**	**863**	**0**	**0**	**0**	**0**	**0**
4100 Recurrent taxes on immovable property	..	147	620	692	863	..	..	..	..	..
4200 Recurrent taxes on net wealth	..	0	0	0	0	..	..	..	..	..
4300 Estate, inheritance and gift taxes	..	0	0	0	0	..	..	..	..	..
4400 Taxes on financial and capital transactions	..	0	0	0	0	..	..	..	..	..
4500 Non-recurrent taxes	..	0	0	0	0	..	..	..	..	..
4600 Other recurrent taxes on property	..	0	0	0	0	..	..	..	..	..
5000 Taxes on goods and services	..	**0**	**0**	**0**	**0**	**0**	**0**	**0**	**0**	**0**
5100 Taxes on production, sale, transfer, etc	..	..	..	..	..	..	..	..	..	..
5110 General taxes	..	..	..	..	..	..	..	..	..	..
5120 Taxes on specific goods and services	..	..	..	..	..	..	..	..	..	..
5130 Unallocable between 5110 and 5120	..	..	..	..	..	..	..	..	..	..
5200 Taxes on use of goods and perform activities	..	..	..	..	..	..	..	..	..	..
5300 Unallocable between 5100 and 5200	..	..	..	..	..	..	..	..	..	..
6000 Other taxes	..	**0**	**0**	**0**	**0**	**0**	**0**	**0**	**0**	**0**
6100 Paid solely by business	..	..	..	..	..	..	..	..	..	..
6200 Other	..	..	..	..	..	..	..	..	..	..
Total tax revenue	..	**147**	**620**	**692**	**863**	**436**	**2 569**	**6 312**	**9 778**	**12 102**

1. Corresponds to social security contributions to the Guatemalan Social Security Institute (IGSS) and payments by public employees to the government's pension fund.

StatLink https://doi.org/10.1787/888934115179

Table 6.15. **Guyana, tax revenues by sub-sectors of government**

Million GYD

	Federal government[1]					State/Regional				
	1990	2000	2010	2015	2018	1990	2000	2010	2015	2018
1000 Taxes on income, profits and capital gains	1 752	16 179	39 561	55 011	78 713	..	..	..	..	..
1100 Of individuals	333	7 734	17 816	23 300	31 377	..	..	..	..	..
1200 Corporate	1 375	8 266	21 427	31 200	46 857	..	..	..	..	..
1300 Unallocable between 1100 and 1200	43	179	317	511	478	..	..	..	..	..
2000 Social security contributions	0	0	0	0	0	..	..	..	..	..
2100 Employees	..	..	..	..	..	..	..	..	..	..
2200 Employers	..	..	..	..	..	..	..	..	..	..
2300 Self-employed or non-employed	..	..	..	..	..	..	..	..	..	..
2400 Unallocable between 2100, 2200 and 2300	..	..	..	..	..	..	..	..	..	..
3000 Taxes on payroll and workforce	0	0	0	0	0	..	..	..	..	..
4000 Taxes on property	53	701	1 593	3 237	4 421	..	..	..	..	..
4100 Recurrent taxes on immovable property	40	681	1 562	3 201	4 377	..	..	..	..	..
4200 Recurrent taxes on net wealth	0	0	0	0	0	..	..	..	..	..
4300 Estate, inheritance and gift taxes	13	20	31	37	44	..	..	..	..	..
4400 Taxes on financial and capital transactions	0	0	0	0	0	..	..	..	..	..
4500 Non-recurrent taxes	0	0	0	0	0	..	..	..	..	..
4600 Other recurrent taxes on property	0	0	0	0	0	..	..	..	..	..
5000 Taxes on goods and services	2 200	20 798	59 360	83 924	112 891	..	..	..	..	..
5100 Taxes on production, sale, transfer, etc	2 162	20 530	58 846	83 227	111 796	..	..	..	..	..
5110 General taxes	1 399	14 861	27 044	35 374	48 181	..	..	..	..	..
5120 Taxes on specific goods and services	763	5 669	31 802	47 853	63 615	..	..	..	..	..
5130 Unallocable between 5110 and 5120	0	0	0	0	0	..	..	..	..	..
5200 Taxes on use of goods and perform activities	38	268	514	697	1 095	..	..	..	..	..
5300 Unallocable between 5100 and 5200	0	0	0	0	0	..	..	..	..	..
6000 Other taxes	1 037	204	1 233	1 038	2 488	..	..	..	..	..
6100 Paid solely by business	0	0	0	0	0	..	..	..	..	..
6200 Other	1 037	204	1 233	1 038	2 488	..	..	..	..	..
Total tax revenue	5 041	37 882	101 746	143 210	198 512	..	..	..	..	..

Million GYD

	Local government[2]					Social Security Funds[3]				
	1990	2000	2010	2015	2018	1990	2000	2010	2015	2018
1000 Taxes on income, profits and capital gains	..	..	0	0	0	0	0	0	0	0
1100 Of individuals	..	..	..	..	..	..	..	..	..	..
1200 Corporate	..	..	..	..	..	..	..	..	..	..
1300 Unallocable between 1100 and 1200	..	..	..	..	..	..	..	..	..	..
2000 Social security contributions	..	..	0	0	0	191	4 868	10 047	16 644	21 766
2100 Employees	..	..	..	..	..	..	..	..	..	..
2200 Employers	..	..	..	..	..	..	..	..	..	..
2300 Self-employed or non-employed	..	..	..	..	..	..	..	..	..	..
2400 Unallocable between 2100, 2200 and 2300	..	..	..	..	..	191	4 868	10 047	16 644	21 766
3000 Taxes on payroll and workforce	..	..	0	0	0	0	0	0	0	0
4000 Taxes on property	..	..	0	0	0	0	0	0	0	0
4100 Recurrent taxes on immovable property	..	..	..	..	..	..	..	..	..	..
4200 Recurrent taxes on net wealth	..	..	..	..	..	..	..	..	..	..
4300 Estate, inheritance and gift taxes	..	..	..	..	..	..	..	..	..	..
4400 Taxes on financial and capital transactions	..	..	..	..	..	..	..	..	..	..
4500 Non-recurrent taxes	..	..	..	..	..	..	..	..	..	..
4600 Other recurrent taxes on property	..	..	..	..	..	..	..	..	..	..
5000 Taxes on goods and services	..	..	0	0	0	0	0	0	0	0
5100 Taxes on production, sale, transfer, etc	..	..	..	..	..	..	..	..	..	..
5110 General taxes	..	..	..	..	..	..	..	..	..	..
5120 Taxes on specific goods and services	..	..	..	..	..	..	..	..	..	..
5130 Unallocable between 5110 and 5120	..	..	..	..	..	..	..	..	..	..
5200 Taxes on use of goods and perform activities	..	..	..	..	..	..	..	..	..	..
5300 Unallocable between 5100 and 5200	..	..	..	..	..	..	..	..	..	..
6000 Other taxes	..	..	113	41	178	0	0	0	0	0
6100 Paid solely by business	..	..	0	0	0	..	..	..	..	..
6200 Other	..	..	113	41	178	..	..	..	..	..
Total tax revenue	..	..	113	41	178	191	4 868	10 047	16 644	21 766

1. Central government tax revenues in 2018 come from Bank of Guyana. Data for earlier years come from Ministry of Finance.
2. Local government tax revenues come from Bank of Guyana.
3. Social security figures include contributions to National Insurance Scheme.

StatLink https://doi.org/10.1787/888934115198

Table 6.16. **Honduras, tax revenues by sub-sectors of government**

Million HNL

	Federal government					State/Regional				
	1990	2000	2010	2015	2018	1990	2000	2010	2015	2018
1000 Taxes on income, profits and capital gains	**431**	**2 907**	**13 232**	**25 003**	**36 071**	..	..	..	..	..
1100 Of individuals	157	992	4 528	8 147	11 368	..	..	..	..	..
1200 Corporate	274	1 916	8 705	16 856	24 702	..	..	..	..	..
1300 Unallocable between 1100 and 1200	0	0	0	0	0	..	..	..	..	..
2000 Social security contributions	**0**	**0**	**0**	**0**	**0**	..	..	..	..	..
2100 Employees	..	..	..	..	..	..	..	..	..	..
2200 Employers	..	..	..	..	..	..	..	..	..	..
2300 Self-employed or non-employed	..	..	..	..	..	..	..	..	..	..
2400 Unallocable between 2100, 2200 and 2300	..	..	..	..	..	..	..	..	..	..
3000 Taxes on payroll and workforce	**0**	**0**	**0**	**0**	**0**	..	..	..	..	..
4000 Taxes on property	**16**	**266**	**994**	**2 635**	**3 243**	..	..	..	..	..
4100 Recurrent taxes on immovable property	16	189	254	298	435	..	..	..	..	..
4200 Recurrent taxes on net wealth	0	78	359	334	278	..	..	..	..	..
4300 Estate, inheritance and gift taxes	0	0	0	0	0	..	..	..	..	..
4400 Taxes on financial and capital transactions	0	0	0	2 003	2 531	..	..	..	..	..
4500 Non-recurrent taxes	0	0	380	0	0	..	..	..	..	..
4600 Other recurrent taxes on property	0	0	0	0	0	..	..	..	..	..
5000 Taxes on goods and services	**1 401**	**12 436**	**28 937**	**52 217**	**66 735**	..	..	..	..	..
5100 Taxes on production, sale, transfer, etc	1 401	12 436	28 937	52 217	66 735	..	..	..	..	..
5110 General taxes	344	5 146	16 050	32 273	41 562	..	..	..	..	..
5120 Taxes on specific goods and services	1 057	7 290	12 887	19 944	25 173	..	..	..	..	..
5130 Unallocable between 5110 and 5120	0	0	0	0	0	..	..	..	..	..
5200 Taxes on use of goods and perform activities	0	0	0	0	0	..	..	..	..	..
5300 Unallocable between 5100 and 5200	0	0	0	0	0	..	..	..	..	..
6000 Other taxes	**1**	**2**	**9**	**8**	**17**	..	..	..	..	..
6100 Paid solely by business	0	0	0	0	0	..	..	..	..	..
6200 Other	1	2	9	8	17	..	..	..	..	..
Total tax revenue	**1 849**	**15 612**	**43 172**	**79 863**	**106 066**	..	..	..	..	..

Million HNL

	Local government[1]					Social Security Funds				
	1990	2000	2010	2015	2018	1990	2000	2010	2015	2018
1000 Taxes on income, profits and capital gains	**0**	**0**	**0**	**0**	**0**	**0**	**0**	**0**	**0**	**0**
1100 Of individuals	..	..	..	..	..	..	..	..	..	..
1200 Corporate	..	..	..	..	..	..	..	..	..	..
1300 Unallocable between 1100 and 1200	..	..	..	..	..	..	..	..	..	..
2000 Social security contributions	**0**	**0**	**0**	**0**	**0**	**179**	**1 727**	**8 671**	**13 524**	**19 302**
2100 Employees	..	..	..	..	..	..	..	..	..	..
2200 Employers	..	..	..	..	..	..	..	..	..	..
2300 Self-employed or non-employed	..	..	..	..	..	..	..	..	..	..
2400 Unallocable between 2100, 2200 and 2300	..	..	..	..	..	179	1 727	8 671	13 524	19 302
3000 Taxes on payroll and workforce	**0**	**0**	**0**	**0**	**0**	**0**	**0**	**0**	**0**	**0**
4000 Taxes on property	**0**	**0**	**0**	**0**	**0**	**0**	**0**	**0**	**0**	**0**
4100 Recurrent taxes on immovable property	..	..	..	..	..	..	..	..	..	..
4200 Recurrent taxes on net wealth	..	..	..	..	..	..	..	..	..	..
4300 Estate, inheritance and gift taxes	..	..	..	..	..	..	..	..	..	..
4400 Taxes on financial and capital transactions	..	..	..	..	..	..	..	..	..	..
4500 Non-recurrent taxes	..	..	..	..	..	..	..	..	..	..
4600 Other recurrent taxes on property	..	..	..	..	..	..	..	..	..	..
5000 Taxes on goods and services	**0**	**0**	**0**	**0**	**0**	**0**	**0**	**0**	**0**	**0**
5100 Taxes on production, sale, transfer, etc	..	..	..	..	..	..	..	..	..	..
5110 General taxes	..	..	..	..	..	..	..	..	..	..
5120 Taxes on specific goods and services	..	..	..	..	..	..	..	..	..	..
5130 Unallocable between 5110 and 5120	..	..	..	..	..	..	..	..	..	..
5200 Taxes on use of goods and perform activities	..	..	..	..	..	..	..	..	..	..
5300 Unallocable between 5100 and 5200	..	..	..	..	..	..	..	..	..	..
6000 Other taxes	**90**	**960**	**2 216**	**2 495**	**2 387**	**0**	**0**	**0**	**0**	**0**
6100 Paid solely by business	0	0	0	0	0	..	..	..	..	..
6200 Other	90	960	2 216	2 495	2 387	..	..	..	..	..
Total tax revenue	**90**	**960**	**2 216**	**2 495**	**2 387**	**179**	**1 727**	**8 671**	**13 524**	**19 302**

1. The figures may include non-tax revenues and central government transfers but it has not been possible to distinguish the different components of local government tax revenues.

StatLink https://doi.org/10.1787/888934115217

Table 6.17. **Jamaica, tax revenues by sub-sectors of government**

Million JMD

	Federal government[1]					State/Regional				
	1990	2000	2010	2015	2018	1990	2000	2010	2015	2018
1000 Taxes on income, profits and capital gains	**3 944**	**39 277**	**118 708**	**149 990**	**173 122**	..	..	..	..	..
1100 Of individuals	1 687	17 441	54 798	74 538	62 644	..	..	..	..	..
1200 Corporate	1 280	7 627	33 091	40 198	62 504	..	..	..	..	..
1300 Unallocable between 1100 and 1200	977	14 209	30 820	35 255	47 974	..	..	..	..	..
2000 Social security contributions	**0**	**0**	**0**	**0**	**0**	..	..	..	..	..
2100 Employees	..	..	..	..	..	..	..	..	..	..
2200 Employers	..	..	..	..	..	..	..	..	..	..
2300 Self-employed or non-employed	..	..	..	..	..	..	..	..	..	..
2400 Unallocable between 2100, 2200 and 2300	..	..	..	..	..	..	..	..	..	..
3000 Taxes on payroll and workforce	**0**	**0**	**0**	**0**	**0**	..	..	..	..	..
4000 Taxes on property	**965**	**3 623**	**7 339**	**12 140**	**16 315**	..	..	..	..	..
4100 Recurrent taxes on immovable property	67	0	0	0	0	..	..	..	..	..
4200 Recurrent taxes on net wealth	0	0	0	0	0	..	..	..	..	..
4300 Estate, inheritance and gift taxes	0	0	0	0	0	..	..	..	..	..
4400 Taxes on financial and capital transactions	898	3 623	7 339	12 140	16 315	..	..	..	..	..
4500 Non-recurrent taxes	0	0	0	0	0	..	..	..	..	..
4600 Other recurrent taxes on property	0	0	0	0	0	..	..	..	..	..
5000 Taxes on goods and services	**2 824**	**43 907**	**149 544**	**240 795**	**340 651**	..	..	..	..	..
5100 Taxes on production, sale, transfer, etc	2 760	43 107	147 500	237 456	335 189	..	..	..	..	..
5110 General taxes	297	22 356	84 409	138 501	187 576	..	..	..	..	..
5120 Taxes on specific goods and services	2 463	20 752	63 091	98 955	147 613	..	..	..	..	..
5130 Unallocable between 5110 and 5120	0	0	0	0	0	..	..	..	..	..
5200 Taxes on use of goods and perform activities	64	800	2 045	3 339	5 463	..	..	..	..	..
5300 Unallocable between 5100 and 5200	0	0	0	0	0	..	..	..	..	..
6000 Other taxes	**16**	**266**	**748**	**994**	**2 410**	..	..	..	..	..
6100 Paid solely by business	0	0	0	0	0	..	..	..	..	..
6200 Other	16	266	748	994	2 410	..	..	..	..	..
Total tax revenue	**7 748**	**87 074**	**276 340**	**403 919**	**532 498**	..	..	..	..	..

Million JMD

	Local government[1]					Social Security Funds[1]				
	1990	2000	2010	2015	2018	1990	2000	2010	2015	2018
1000 Taxes on income, profits and capital gains	..	**0**	**0**	**0**	**0**	..	..	**0**	**0**	**0**
1100 Of individuals	..	..	..	..	..	..	..	..	..	..
1200 Corporate	..	..	..	..	..	..	..	..	..	..
1300 Unallocable between 1100 and 1200	..	..	..	..	..	..	..	..	..	..
2000 Social security contributions	..	**0**	**0**	**0**	**0**	..	..	**8 199**	**16 449**	**21 033**
2100 Employees	..	..	..	..	..	..	..	..	..	..
2200 Employers	..	..	..	..	..	..	..	..	..	..
2300 Self-employed or non-employed	..	..	..	..	..	..	..	..	..	..
2400 Unallocable between 2100, 2200 and 2300	..	..	..	..	..	..	..	8 199	16 449	21 033
3000 Taxes on payroll and workforce	..	**0**	**0**	**0**	**0**	..	..	**0**	**0**	**0**
4000 Taxes on property	..	**639**	**2 600**	**7 271**	**8 478**	..	..	**0**	**0**	**0**
4100 Recurrent taxes on immovable property	..	639	2 600	7 271	8 478	..	..	..	..	..
4200 Recurrent taxes on net wealth	..	0	0	0	0	..	..	..	..	..
4300 Estate, inheritance and gift taxes	..	0	0	0	0	..	..	..	..	..
4400 Taxes on financial and capital transactions	..	0	0	0	0	..	..	..	..	..
4500 Non-recurrent taxes	..	0	0	0	0	..	..	..	..	..
4600 Other recurrent taxes on property	..	0	0	0	0	..	..	..	..	..
5000 Taxes on goods and services	..	**0**	**0**	**0**	**0**	..	..	**0**	**0**	**0**
5100 Taxes on production, sale, transfer, etc	..	..	..	..	..	..	..	..	..	..
5110 General taxes	..	..	..	..	..	..	..	..	..	..
5120 Taxes on specific goods and services	..	..	..	..	..	..	..	..	..	..
5130 Unallocable between 5110 and 5120	..	..	..	..	..	..	..	..	..	..
5200 Taxes on use of goods and perform activities	..	..	..	..	..	..	..	..	..	..
5300 Unallocable between 5100 and 5200	..	..	..	..	..	..	..	..	..	..
6000 Other taxes	..	**0**	**0**	**0**	**0**	..	..	**0**	**0**	**0**
6100 Paid solely by business	..	..	..	..	..	..	..	..	..	..
6200 Other	..	..	..	..	..	..	..	..	..	..
Total tax revenue	..	**639**	**2 600**	**7 271**	**8 478**	..	..	**8 199**	**16 449**	**21 033**

1. The figures refer to fiscal year ending 31st March for 1990-2003 and then calendar year ending 31st December.

StatLink https://doi.org/10.1787/888934115236

Table 6.18. **Mexico, tax revenues by sub-sectors of government**

Million MXN

	Federal government					State/Regional				
	1990	2000	2010	2015	2018	1990	2000	2010	2015	2018
1000 Taxes on income, profits and capital gains[1]	**34 668**	**276 548**	**683 604**	**1 230 555**	**1 671 513**	**3**	**0**	**0**	**0**	..
1100 Of individuals	..	..	313 473	609 384	804 236	..	..	..	..	..
1200 Corporate	..	..	246 745	592 443	809 834	..	..	..	..	..
1300 Unallocable between 1100 and 1200	34 668	276 548	123 386	28 728	57 443	3	..	..	..	..
2000 Social security contributions	**0**	**0**	**0**	**0**	**0**	**0**	**0**	**0**	**0**	..
2100 Employees	..	..	..	..	..	..	..	..	..	..
2200 Employers	..	..	..	..	..	..	..	..	..	..
2300 Self-employed or non-employed	..	..	..	..	..	..	..	..	..	..
2400 Unallocable between 2100, 2200 and 2300	..	..	..	..	..	..	..	..	..	..
3000 Taxes on payroll and workforce	**818**	**0**	**0**	**0**	**0**	**972**	**11 215**	**36 818**	**70 221**	**0**
4000 Taxes on property	**3**	**0**	**0**	**0**	**0**	**894**	**7 018**	**13 137**	**22 481**	**0**
4100 Recurrent taxes on immovable property	0	..	..	..	..	482	5 238	8 522	14 245	0
4200 Recurrent taxes on net wealth	0	..	..	..	..	0	0	0	0	0
4300 Estate, inheritance and gift taxes	0	..	..	..	..	7	0	0	0	0
4400 Taxes on financial and capital transactions	3	..	..	..	..	405	1 781	4 615	8 235	0
4500 Non-recurrent taxes	0	..	..	..	..	0	0	0	0	0
4600 Other recurrent taxes on property	0	..	..	..	..	0	0	0	0	0
5000 Taxes on goods and services	**44 605**	**318 065**	**645 623**	**1 116 026**	**1 355 600**	**118**	**1 346**	**5 805**	**24 355**	**0**
5100 Taxes on production, sale, transfer, etc	44 029	309 283	627 187	1 115 525	1 354 887	45	910	2 470	4 357	0
5110 General taxes	26 635	189 606	504 509	707 213	922 238	0	0	0	0	..
5120 Taxes on specific goods and services	17 394	119 677	122 678	408 312	432 649	30	910	2 470	4 357	0
5130 Unallocable between 5110 and 5120	0	0	0	0	0	15	0	0	0	0
5200 Taxes on use of goods and perform activities	576	8 782	18 436	501	713	73	436	3 335	19 998	0
5300 Unallocable between 5100 and 5200	0	0	0	0	0	0	0	0	0	0
6000 Other taxes	**1 340**	**5 878**	**22 236**	**27 379**	**46 264**	**165**	**907**	**2 546**	**6 489**	**0**
6100 Paid solely by business	0	0	0	0	0	0	0	0	0	0
6200 Other	1 340	5 878	22 236	27 379	46 264	165	907	2 546	6 489	0
Total tax revenue	**81 434**	**600 491**	**1 351 463**	**2 373 960**	**3 073 376**	**2 152**	**20 485**	**58 307**	**123 545**	**0**

Million MXN

	Local government					Social Security Funds[2]				
	1990	2000	2010	2015	2018	1990	2000	2010	2015	2018
1000 Taxes on income, profits and capital gains[1]	**2**	**0**	**0**	**0**	..	**0**	**0**	**0**	**0**	**0**
1100 Of individuals	..	..	..	..	..	..	..	..	..	..
1200 Corporate	..	..	..	..	..	..	..	..	..	..
1300 Unallocable between 1100 and 1200	2	..	..	..	..	..	..	..	..	..
2000 Social security contributions	**0**	**0**	**0**	**0**	..	**17 165**	**138 223**	**277 459**	**409 249**	**509 087**
2100 Employees	..	..	..	..	..	..	..	..	..	..
2200 Employers	..	..	..	..	..	..	..	..	..	..
2300 Self-employed or non-employed	..	..	..	..	..	..	..	..	..	..
2400 Unallocable between 2100, 2200 and 2300	..	..	..	..	..	17 165	138 223	277 459	409 249	509 087
3000 Taxes on payroll and workforce	**7**	**2**	**93**	**1**	**0**	**0**	**0**	**0**	**0**	**0**
4000 Taxes on property	**1 017**	**6 946**	**25 818**	**35 193**	**0**	**0**	**0**	**0**	**0**	**0**
4100 Recurrent taxes on immovable property	554	4 710	17 202	23 715	0	..	..	..	..	..
4200 Recurrent taxes on net wealth	0	0	0	0	0	..	..	..	..	..
4300 Estate, inheritance and gift taxes	1	0	0	0	0	..	..	..	..	..
4400 Taxes on financial and capital transactions	462	2 236	8 616	11 477	0	..	..	..	..	..
4500 Non-recurrent taxes	0	0	0	0	0	..	..	..	..	..
4600 Other recurrent taxes on property	0	0	0	0	0	..	..	..	..	..
5000 Taxes on goods and services	**114**	**202**	**487**	**789**	**0**	**0**	**0**	**0**	**0**	**0**
5100 Taxes on production, sale, transfer, etc	97	133	466	728	0	..	..	..	..	..
5110 General taxes	0	0	0	0	..	..	..	..	..	..
5120 Taxes on specific goods and services	95	133	466	728	0	..	..	..	..	..
5130 Unallocable between 5110 and 5120	2	0	0	0	0	..	..	..	..	..
5200 Taxes on use of goods and perform activities	17	69	21	61	0	..	..	..	..	..
5300 Unallocable between 5100 and 5200	0	0	0	0	0	..	..	..	..	..
6000 Other taxes	**114**	**866**	**2 616**	**10 743**	**0**	**0**	**0**	**0**	**0**	**0**
6100 Paid solely by business	0	0	0	0	0	..	..	..	..	..
6200 Other	114	866	2 616	10 743	0	..	..	..	..	..
Total tax revenue	**1 254**	**8 016**	**29 014**	**46 726**	**0**	**17 165**	**138 223**	**277 459**	**409 249**	**509 087**

Note: The 2018 data for tax revenues of the state and local levels of government are not available. They comprise revenues in categories 3000, 4000, 5000 and 6000.

1. In ECLAC data, income taxes are presented net of credit on salary figures.
2. Some amounts of social security contributions are now treated as non-tax revenue to align with reporting to other international organisations. In ECLAC data, social security contributions are presented net of transfers from the Federal government for the payment of IMSS (Mexican Social Security Institute) pensions.

StatLink https://doi.org/10.1787/888934115255

Table 6.19. **Nicaragua, tax revenues by sub-sectors of government**

Million NIO

	Federal government[1]					State/Regional				
	1990	2000	2010	2015	2018	1990	2000	2010	2015	2018
1000 Taxes on income, profits and capital gains	..	**1 144**	**8 351**	**21 313**	**29 258**	..	..	..	..	..
1100 Of individuals	..	..	..	..	..	..	..	..	..	..
1200 Corporate	..	..	..	..	..	..	..	..	..	..
1300 Unallocable between 1100 and 1200	..	1 144	8 351	21 313	29 258	..	..	..	..	..
2000 Social security contributions	..	**0**	**0**	**0**	**0**	..	..	..	..	..
2100 Employees	..	..	..	..	..	..	..	..	..	..
2200 Employers	..	..	..	..	..	..	..	..	..	..
2300 Self-employed or non-employed	..	..	..	..	..	..	..	..	..	..
2400 Unallocable between 2100, 2200 and 2300	..	..	..	..	..	..	..	..	..	..
3000 Taxes on payroll and workforce	..	**0**	**0**	**0**	**0**	..	..	..	..	..
4000 Taxes on property	..	**11**	**20**	**90**	**80**	..	..	..	..	..
4100 Recurrent taxes on immovable property	..	0	0	0	0	..	..	..	..	..
4200 Recurrent taxes on net wealth	..	0	0	0	0	..	..	..	..	..
4300 Estate, inheritance and gift taxes	..	0	0	0	0	..	..	..	..	..
4400 Taxes on financial and capital transactions	..	11	20	90	80	..	..	..	..	..
4500 Non-recurrent taxes	..	0	0	0	0	..	..	..	..	..
4600 Other recurrent taxes on property	..	0	0	0	0	..	..	..	..	..
5000 Taxes on goods and services	..	**5 584**	**17 029**	**32 725**	**34 894**	..	..	..	..	..
5100 Taxes on production, sale, transfer, etc	..	5 584	17 029	32 725	34 894	..	..	..	..	..
5110 General taxes	..	2 931	10 353	20 714	21 905	..	..	..	..	..
5120 Taxes on specific goods and services	..	2 653	6 676	12 011	12 990	..	..	..	..	..
5130 Unallocable between 5110 and 5120	..	0	0	0	0	..	..	..	..	..
5200 Taxes on use of goods and perform activities	..	0	0	0	0	..	..	..	..	..
5300 Unallocable between 5100 and 5200	..	0	0	0	0	..	..	..	..	..
6000 Other taxes	..	**0**	**0**	**0**	**0**	..	..	..	..	..
6100 Paid solely by business	..	..	..	..	..	..	..	..	..	..
6200 Other	..	..	..	..	..	..	..	..	..	..
Total tax revenue	..	**6 739**	**25 400**	**54 128**	**64 232**	..	..	..	..	..

Million NIO

	Local government[2]					Social Security Funds[2]				
	1990	2000	2010	2015	2018	1990	2000	2010	2015	2018
1000 Taxes on income, profits and capital gains	..	**0**	**0**	**0**	**0**	..	**0**	**0**	**0**	**0**
1100 Of individuals	..	..	..	..	..	..	..	..	..	..
1200 Corporate	..	..	..	..	..	..	..	..	..	..
1300 Unallocable between 1100 and 1200	..	..	..	..	..	..	..	..	..	..
2000 Social security contributions	..	**0**	**0**	**0**	**0**	..	**1 678**	**8 090**	**18 194**	**24 624**
2100 Employees	..	..	..	..	..	..	..	..	..	..
2200 Employers	..	..	..	..	..	..	..	..	..	..
2300 Self-employed or non-employed	..	..	..	..	..	..	..	..	..	..
2400 Unallocable between 2100, 2200 and 2300	..	..	..	..	..	..	1 678	8 090	18 194	24 624
3000 Taxes on payroll and workforce	..	**0**	**0**	**0**	**0**	..	**0**	**0**	**0**	**0**
4000 Taxes on property	..	**0**	**403**	**682**	**881**	..	**0**	**0**	**0**	**0**
4100 Recurrent taxes on immovable property	..	..	403	682	881	..	..	..	..	..
4200 Recurrent taxes on net wealth	..	..	0	0	0	..	..	..	..	..
4300 Estate, inheritance and gift taxes	..	..	0	0	0	..	..	..	..	..
4400 Taxes on financial and capital transactions	..	..	0	0	0	..	..	..	..	..
4500 Non-recurrent taxes	..	..	0	0	0	..	..	..	..	..
4600 Other recurrent taxes on property	..	..	0	0	0	..	..	..	..	..
5000 Taxes on goods and services	..	**0**	**1 922**	**3 874**	**4 630**	..	**0**	**0**	**0**	**0**
5100 Taxes on production, sale, transfer, etc	..	..	1 579	3 073	3 595	..	..	..	..	..
5110 General taxes	..	..	1 579	3 073	3 595	..	..	..	..	..
5120 Taxes on specific goods and services	..	..	0	0	0	..	..	..	..	..
5130 Unallocable between 5110 and 5120	..	..	0	0	0	..	..	..	..	..
5200 Taxes on use of goods and perform activities	..	..	343	801	1 035	..	..	..	..	..
5300 Unallocable between 5100 and 5200	..	..	0	0	0	..	..	..	..	..
6000 Other taxes	..	**0**	**347**	**690**	**798**	..	**0**	**0**	**0**	**0**
6100 Paid solely by business	..	..	0	0	0	..	..	..	..	..
6200 Other	..	..	347	690	798	..	..	..	..	..
Total tax revenue	..	**882**	**2 672**	**5 246**	**6 310**	..	**1 678**	**8 090**	**18 194**	**24 624**

Note: Comparable statistics for 1990 cannot be shown due to the devaluation of the Nicaraguan cordoba.

1. Central government tax revenues in 2018 come from the Ministry of Finance and Public Credit. Data for previous years come from Inter-American Centre of Tax Administrations (CIAT).
2. Local government tax revenues and social security contributions are obtained from Inter-American Centre of Tax Administrations (CIAT).

StatLink https://doi.org/10.1787/888934115274

Table 6.20. **Panama, tax revenues by sub-sectors of government**

Million PAB

	Federal government[3]					State/Regional				
	1990	2000	2010	2015	2018	1990	2000	2010	2015	2018
1000 Taxes on income, profits and capital gains	**217**	**485**	**1 317**	**2 066**	**2 672**	..	..	..	..	..
1100 Of individuals	140	295	440	799	1 193	..	..	..	..	..
1200 Corporate	66	159	603	851	955	..	..	..	..	..
1300 Unallocable between 1100 and 1200	11	31	273	416	524	..	..	..	..	..
2000 Social security contributions	**0**	**0**	**0**	**0**	**0**	..	..	..	..	..
2100 Employees	..	..	..	..	..	..	..	..	..	..
2200 Employers	..	..	..	..	..	..	..	..	..	..
2300 Self-employed or non-employed	..	..	..	..	..	..	..	..	..	..
2400 Unallocable between 2100, 2200 and 2300	..	..	..	..	..	..	..	..	..	..
3000 Taxes on payroll and workforce[1]	**0**	**36**	**59**	**111**	**130**	..	..	..	..	..
4000 Taxes on property	**32**	**43**	**138**	**199**	**244**	..	..	..	..	..
4100 Recurrent taxes on immovable property	28	34	108	151	209	..	..	..	..	..
4200 Recurrent taxes on net wealth	0	0	0	0	0	..	..	..	..	..
4300 Estate, inheritance and gift taxes	0	0	0	0	0	..	..	..	..	..
4400 Taxes on financial and capital transactions	3	9	30	48	36	..	..	..	..	..
4500 Non-recurrent taxes	0	0	0	0	0	..	..	..	..	..
4600 Other recurrent taxes on property	0	0	0	0	0	..	..	..	..	..
5000 Taxes on goods and services	**349**	**565**	**1 547**	**2 496**	**2 598**	..	..	..	..	..
5100 Taxes on production, sale, transfer, etc	332	546	1 473	2 376	2 474	..	..	..	..	..
5110 General taxes	80	69	766	1 357	1 477	..	..	..	..	..
5120 Taxes on specific goods and services[2]	251	477	707	1 019	997	..	..	..	..	..
5130 Unallocable between 5110 and 5120	0	0	0	0	0	..	..	..	..	..
5200 Taxes on use of goods and perform activities	15	19	75	120	124	..	..	..	..	..
5300 Unallocable between 5100 and 5200	2	0	0	0	0	..	..	..	..	..
6000 Other taxes	**26**	**27**	**41**	**37**	**34**	..	..	..	..	..
6100 Paid solely by business	0	0	0	0	0	..	..	..	..	..
6200 Other	26	27	41	37	34	..	..	..	..	..
Total tax revenue	**624**	**1 157**	**3 102**	**4 910**	**5 678**	..	..	..	..	..

Million PAB

	Local government[4]					Social Security Funds				
	1990	2000	2010	2015	2018	1990	2000	2010	2015	2018
1000 Taxes on income, profits and capital gains	..	**0**	**0**	**0**	**0**	**0**	**0**	**0**	**0**	**0**
1100 Of individuals	..	..	..	..	..	..	..	..	..	..
1200 Corporate	..	..	..	..	..	..	..	..	..	..
1300 Unallocable between 1100 and 1200	..	..	..	..	..	..	..	..	..	..
2000 Social security contributions	..	**0**	**0**	**0**	**0**	**271**	**742**	**1 637**	**3 049**	**3 654**
2100 Employees	..	..	..	..	..	..	..	..	..	..
2200 Employers	..	..	..	..	..	..	..	..	..	..
2300 Self-employed or non-employed	..	..	..	..	..	..	..	..	..	..
2400 Unallocable between 2100, 2200 and 2300	..	..	..	..	..	271	742	1 637	3 049	3 654
3000 Taxes on payroll and workforce[1]	..	**0**	**0**	**0**	**0**	**0**	**0**	**0**	**0**	**0**
4000 Taxes on property	..	**0**	**0**	**0**	**0**	**0**	**0**	**0**	**0**	**0**
4100 Recurrent taxes on immovable property	..	0	..	..	..	..	..	..	..	..
4200 Recurrent taxes on net wealth	..	0	..	..	..	..	..	..	..	..
4300 Estate, inheritance and gift taxes	..	0	..	..	..	..	..	..	..	..
4400 Taxes on financial and capital transactions	..	0	..	..	..	..	..	..	..	..
4500 Non-recurrent taxes	..	0	..	..	..	..	..	..	..	..
4600 Other recurrent taxes on property	..	0	..	..	..	..	..	..	..	..
5000 Taxes on goods and services	..	**43**	**76**	**131**	**156**	**0**	**0**	**0**	**0**	**0**
5100 Taxes on production, sale, transfer, etc	..	0	0	0	0	..	..	..	..	..
5110 General taxes	..	0	..	..	..	..	..	..	..	..
5120 Taxes on specific goods and services[2]	..	0	..	..	..	..	..	..	..	..
5130 Unallocable between 5110 and 5120	..	0	..	..	..	..	..	..	..	..
5200 Taxes on use of goods and perform activities	..	43	76	131	156	..	..	..	..	..
5300 Unallocable between 5100 and 5200	..	0	0	0	0	..	..	..	..	..
6000 Other taxes	..	**0**	**0**	**0**	**0**	**0**	**0**	**0**	**0**	**0**
6100 Paid solely by business	..	0	..	..	..	..	..	..	..	..
6200 Other	..	0	..	..	..	..	..	..	..	..
Total tax revenue	..	**43**	**76**	**131**	**156**	**271**	**742**	**1 637**	**3 049**	**3 654**

1. In ECLAC data, education insurance is classified as "Other taxes" (6000).
2. In CIAT and ECLAC data, the tax on banks, financial institutions and currency exchange is classified as a property tax (4000).
3. The figures exclude documentos fiscales as they are not considered as tax revenues.
4. Local government tax revenues are estimated in 2018.

StatLink https://doi.org/10.1787/888934115293

Table 6.21. **Paraguay, tax revenues by sub-sectors of government**

Million PYG

	Federal government					State/Regional				
	1990	2000	2010	2015	2018	1990	2000	2010	2015	2018
1000 Taxes on income, profits and capital gains	**73 726**	**470 388**	**2 096 498**	**3 922 384**	**5 265 609**	..	..	..	..	..
1100 Of individuals	..	15 042	31 263	409 238	626 525	..	..	..	..	..
1200 Corporate	..	455 346	2 065 235	3 513 146	4 639 084	..	..	..	..	..
1300 Unallocable between 1100 and 1200	73 726	0	0	0	0	..	..	..	..	..
2000 Social security contributions	**0**	**0**	**0**	**0**	**0**	..	..	..	..	..
2100 Employees	..	..	..	..	..	..	..	..	..	..
2200 Employers	..	..	..	..	..	..	..	..	..	..
2300 Self-employed or non-employed	..	..	..	..	..	..	..	..	..	..
2400 Unallocable between 2100, 2200 and 2300	..	..	..	..	..	..	..	..	..	..
3000 Taxes on payroll and workforce	**0**	**0**	**0**	**0**	**0**	..	..	..	..	..
4000 Taxes on property	**17 162**	**71 777**	**332**	**91**	**30**	..	..	..	..	..
4100 Recurrent taxes on immovable property	17 162	0	0	0	0	..	..	..	..	..
4200 Recurrent taxes on net wealth	0	0	0	0	0	..	..	..	..	..
4300 Estate, inheritance and gift taxes	0	0	0	0	0	..	..	..	..	..
4400 Taxes on financial and capital transactions	0	71 777	332	91	30	..	..	..	..	..
4500 Non-recurrent taxes	0	0	0	0	0	..	..	..	..	..
4600 Other recurrent taxes on property	0	0	0	0	0	..	..	..	..	..
5000 Taxes on goods and services	**438 444**	**2 080 878**	**9 226 584**	**13 837 266**	**17 529 671**	..	..	..	..	..
5100 Taxes on production, sale, transfer, etc	438 444	2 080 878	9 226 493	13 837 212	17 529 671	..	..	..	..	..
5110 General taxes	0	1 150 496	5 991 694	9 768 800	11 851 394	..	..	..	..	..
5120 Taxes on specific goods and services	438 444	930 382	3 234 799	4 068 411	5 678 277	..	..	..	..	..
5130 Unallocable between 5110 and 5120	0	0	0	0	0	..	..	..	..	..
5200 Taxes on use of goods and perform activities	0	0	91	54	0	..	..	..	..	..
5300 Unallocable between 5100 and 5200	0	0	0	0	0	..	..	..	..	..
6000 Other taxes	**49 807**	**44 875**	**109 001**	**128 632**	**162 604**	..	..	..	..	..
6100 Paid solely by business	0	0	0	0	0	..	..	..	..	..
6200 Other	49 807	44 875	109 001	128 632	162 604	..	..	..	..	..
Total tax revenue	**579 139**	**2 667 918**	**11 432 415**	**17 888 373**	**22 957 914**	..	..	..	..	..

Million PYG

	Local government[1]					Social Security Funds[2,3]				
	1990	2000	2010	2015	2018	1990	2000	2010	2015	2018
1000 Taxes on income, profits and capital gains	..	..	**0**	**0**	**0**	..	**0**	**0**	**0**	**0**
1100 Of individuals	..	..	..	..	..	..	..	..	..	..
1200 Corporate	..	..	..	..	..	..	..	..	..	..
1300 Unallocable between 1100 and 1200	..	..	..	..	..	..	..	..	..	..
2000 Social security contributions	..	..	**0**	**0**	**0**	..	**919 533**	**3 552 640**	**7 044 316**	**8 209 087**
2100 Employees	..	..	..	..	..	..	..	..	..	..
2200 Employers	..	..	..	..	..	..	..	..	..	..
2300 Self-employed or non-employed	..	..	..	..	..	..	..	..	..	..
2400 Unallocable between 2100, 2200 and 2300	..	..	..	..	..	..	919 533	3 552 640	7 044 316	8 209 087
3000 Taxes on payroll and workforce	..	..	**0**	**0**	**0**	..	**0**	**0**	**0**	**0**
4000 Taxes on property	..	..	**264 022**	**412 975**	**586 349**	..	**0**	**0**	**0**	**0**
4100 Recurrent taxes on immovable property	..	..	258 423	405 806	576 632	..	..	..	..	..
4200 Recurrent taxes on net wealth	..	..	0	0	0	..	..	..	..	..
4300 Estate, inheritance and gift taxes	..	..	0	0	0	..	..	..	..	..
4400 Taxes on financial and capital transactions	..	..	3 857	7 104	8 123	..	..	..	..	..
4500 Non-recurrent taxes	..	..	0	0	0	..	..	..	..	..
4600 Other recurrent taxes on property	..	..	1 742	66	1 595	..	..	..	..	..
5000 Taxes on goods and services	..	..	**246 734**	**461 763**	**556 517**	..	**0**	**0**	**0**	**0**
5100 Taxes on production, sale, transfer, etc	..	..	18 496	21 082	30 888	..	..	..	..	..
5110 General taxes	..	..	0	0	0	..	..	..	..	..
5120 Taxes on specific goods and services	..	..	18 496	21 082	30 888	..	..	..	..	..
5130 Unallocable between 5110 and 5120	..	..	0	0	0	..	..	..	..	..
5200 Taxes on use of goods and perform activities	..	..	228 001	417 843	491 864	..	..	..	..	..
5300 Unallocable between 5100 and 5200	..	..	237	22 838	33 765	..	..	..	..	..
6000 Other taxes	..	..	**141 811**	**45 052**	**48 069**	..	**0**	**0**	**0**	**0**
6100 Paid solely by business	..	..	0	0	0	..	..	..	..	..
6200 Other	..	..	141 811	45 052	48 069	..	..	..	..	..
Total tax revenue	..	..	**652 567**	**919 790**	**1 190 935**	..	**919 533**	**3 552 640**	**7 044 316**	**8 209 087**

1. The figures for years up to and including 2004, as well as for 2013 and 2014, exclude local government tax revenues as the data are not available. Data for 2018 are estimated using CIAT figures.
2. Data on social security contributions collected by decentralised institutions are not available from 2011, with the exception of the contributions made to the Instituto de Previsión Social (Social Security Institute).
3. The figures for years up to and including 1998 exclude decentralised institutions as the data are not available.

StatLink https://doi.org/10.1787/888934115312

Table 6.22. **Peru, tax revenues by sub-sectors of government**

Million PEN

	Federal government					State/Regional				
	1990	2000	2010	2015	2018	1990	2000	2010	2015	2018
1000 Taxes on income, profits and capital gains	**37**	**5 078**	**27 317**	**37 772**	**43 979**	..	..	..	..	..
1100 Of individuals	3	2 117	6 518	11 137	13 598	..	..	..	..	..
1200 Corporate	32	2 526	19 561	24 266	28 830	..	..	..	..	..
1300 Unallocable between 1100 and 1200	1	436	1 239	2 369	1 550	..	..	..	..	..
2000 Social security contributions	**0**	**0**	**0**	**0**	**0**	..	..	..	..	..
2100 Employees	..	..	..	..	..	..	..	..	..	..
2200 Employers	..	..	..	..	..	..	..	..	..	..
2300 Self-employed or non-employed	..	..	..	..	..	..	..	..	..	..
2400 Unallocable between 2100, 2200 and 2300	..	..	..	..	..	..	..	..	..	..
3000 Taxes on payroll and workforce	**0**	**1 176**	**1**	**4**	**1**	..	..	..	..	..
4000 Taxes on property	**87**	**0**	**944**	**161**	**200**	..	..	..	..	..
4100 Recurrent taxes on immovable property	0	0	0	0	0	..	..	..	..	..
4200 Recurrent taxes on net wealth	49	0	0	0	0	..	..	..	..	..
4300 Estate, inheritance and gift taxes	0	0	0	0	0	..	..	..	..	..
4400 Taxes on financial and capital transactions	38	0	944	161	200	..	..	..	..	..
4500 Non-recurrent taxes	0	0	0	0	0	..	..	..	..	..
4600 Other recurrent taxes on property	0	0	0	0	0	..	..	..	..	..
5000 Taxes on goods and services	**454**	**16 205**	**36 064**	**50 606**	**58 014**	..	..	..	..	..
5100 Taxes on production, sale, transfer, etc	454	16 205	36 064	50 606	58 014	..	..	..	..	..
5110 General taxes	109	9 646	29 094	42 612	49 038	..	..	..	..	..
5120 Taxes on specific goods and services	345	6 558	6 970	7 994	8 976	..	..	..	..	..
5130 Unallocable between 5110 and 5120	0	0	0	0	0	..	..	..	..	..
5200 Taxes on use of goods and perform activities	0	0	0	0	0	..	..	..	..	..
5300 Unallocable between 5100 and 5200	0	0	0	0	0	..	..	..	..	..
6000 Other taxes	**9**	**697**	**888**	**2 088**	**1 647**	..	..	..	..	..
6100 Paid solely by business	0	84	108	179	133	..	..	..	..	..
6200 Other	9	614	780	1 909	1 513	..	..	..	..	..
Total tax revenue	**587**	**23 156**	**65 215**	**90 631**	**103 841**	..	..	..	..	..

Million PEN

	Local government[1]					Social Security Funds				
	1990	2000	2010	2015	2018	1990	2000	2010	2015	2018
1000 Taxes on income, profits and capital gains	..	**0**	**0**	**0**	**0**	**0**	**0**	**0**	**0**	**0**
1100 Of individuals	..	..	..	..	..	..	..	..	..	..
1200 Corporate	..	..	..	..	..	..	..	..	..	..
1300 Unallocable between 1100 and 1200	..	..	..	..	..	..	..	..	..	..
2000 Social security contributions	..	**0**	**0**	**0**	**0**	**50**	**3 175**	**7 929**	**12 680**	**14 872**
2100 Employees	..	..	..	..	..	..	566	2 468	3 508	4 216
2200 Employers	..	..	..	..	..	..	2 515	5 454	9 170	10 653
2300 Self-employed or non-employed	..	..	..	..	..	..	95	7	2	4
2400 Unallocable between 2100, 2200 and 2300	..	..	..	..	..	50	0	0	0	0
3000 Taxes on payroll and workforce	..	**0**	**0**	**0**	**0**	**0**	**0**	**0**	**0**	**0**
4000 Taxes on property	..	**323**	**1 287**	**2 268**	**2 480**	**0**	**0**	**0**	**0**	**0**
4100 Recurrent taxes on immovable property	..	298	727	1 463	1 748	..	..	..	..	..
4200 Recurrent taxes on net wealth	..	0	0	0	0	..	..	..	..	..
4300 Estate, inheritance and gift taxes	..	0	0	0	0	..	..	..	..	..
4400 Taxes on financial and capital transactions	..	25	560	805	732	..	..	..	..	..
4500 Non-recurrent taxes	..	0	0	0	0	..	..	..	..	..
4600 Other recurrent taxes on property	..	0	0	0	0	..	..	..	..	..
5000 Taxes on goods and services	..	**59**	**290**	**496**	**537**	**0**	**0**	**0**	**0**	**0**
5100 Taxes on production, sale, transfer, etc	..	34	135	214	243	..	..	..	..	..
5110 General taxes	..	0	0	0	0	..	..	..	..	..
5120 Taxes on specific goods and services	..	34	135	214	243	..	..	..	..	..
5130 Unallocable between 5110 and 5120	..	0	0	0	0	..	..	..	..	..
5200 Taxes on use of goods and perform activities	..	25	154	282	294	..	..	..	..	..
5300 Unallocable between 5100 and 5200	..	0	0	0	0	..	..	..	..	..
6000 Other taxes	..	**48**	**26**	**19**	**15**	**0**	**0**	**0**	**0**	**0**
6100 Paid solely by business	..	0	0	0	0	..	..	..	..	..
6200 Other	..	48	26	19	15	..	..	..	..	..
Total tax revenue	..	**430**	**1 603**	**2 784**	**3 033**	**50**	**3 175**	**7 929**	**12 680**	**14 872**

1. The figures for years up to 2000 exclude local government tax revenues as the data are not available.

StatLink https://doi.org/10.1787/888934115331

Table 6.23. **Saint Lucia, tax revenues by sub-sectors of government**

Million XCD

	Federal government					State/Regional				
	1990	2000	2010	2015	2018	1990	2000	2010	2015	2018
1000 Taxes on income, profits and capital gains	..	**137**	**224**	**242**	**269**	..	..	..	..	..
1100 Of individuals	..	49	83	105	113	..	..	..	..	..
1200 Corporate	..	63	95	78	94	..	..	..	..	..
1300 Unallocable between 1100 and 1200	..	26	46	58	61	..	..	..	..	..
2000 Social security contributions	..	**0**	**0**	**0**	**0**	..	..	..	..	..
2100 Employees	..	..	..	..	..	..	..	..	..	..
2200 Employers	..	..	..	..	..	..	..	..	..	..
2300 Self-employed or non-employed	..	..	..	..	..	..	..	..	..	..
2400 Unallocable between 2100, 2200 and 2300	..	..	..	..	..	..	..	..	..	..
3000 Taxes on payroll and workforce	..	**0**	**0**	**0**	**0**	..	..	..	..	..
4000 Taxes on property	..	**11**	**19**	**23**	**26**	..	..	..	..	..
4100 Recurrent taxes on immovable property	..	0	0	0	0	..	..	..	..	..
4200 Recurrent taxes on net wealth	..	0	0	0	0	..	..	..	..	..
4300 Estate, inheritance and gift taxes	..	0	0	0	0	..	..	..	..	..
4400 Taxes on financial and capital transactions	..	9	16	12	17	..	..	..	..	..
4500 Non-recurrent taxes	..	2	3	11	9	..	..	..	..	..
4600 Other recurrent taxes on property	..	0	0	0	0	..	..	..	..	..
5000 Taxes on goods and services	..	**284**	**492**	**669**	**748**	..	..	..	..	..
5100 Taxes on production, sale, transfer, etc	..	277	467	641	720	..	..	..	..	..
5110 General taxes	..	101	119	347	331	..	..	..	..	..
5120 Taxes on specific goods and services	..	176	347	294	390	..	..	..	..	..
5130 Unallocable between 5110 and 5120	..	0	0	0	0	..	..	..	..	..
5200 Taxes on use of goods and perform activities	..	7	26	29	28	..	..	..	..	..
5300 Unallocable between 5100 and 5200	..	0	0	0	0	..	..	..	..	..
6000 Other taxes	..	**0**	**0**	**0**	**0**	..	..	..	..	..
6100 Paid solely by business	..	..	..	..	..	..	..	..	..	..
6200 Other	..	..	..	..	..	..	..	..	..	..
Total tax revenue	..	**432**	**736**	**934**	**1 042**	..	..	..	..	..

Million XCD

	Local government[1]					Social Security Funds[1]				
	1990	2000	2010	2015	2018	1990	2000	2010	2015	2018
1000 Taxes on income, profits and capital gains	..	..	..	..	..	..	..	..	..	..
1100 Of individuals	..	..	..	..	..	..	..	..	..	..
1200 Corporate	..	..	..	..	..	..	..	..	..	..
1300 Unallocable between 1100 and 1200	..	..	..	..	..	..	..	..	..	..
2000 Social security contributions	..	..	..	..	..	..	..	..	..	..
2100 Employees	..	..	..	..	..	..	..	..	..	..
2200 Employers	..	..	..	..	..	..	..	..	..	..
2300 Self-employed or non-employed	..	..	..	..	..	..	..	..	..	..
2400 Unallocable between 2100, 2200 and 2300	..	..	..	..	..	..	..	..	..	..
3000 Taxes on payroll and workforce	..	..	..	..	..	..	..	..	..	..
4000 Taxes on property	..	..	..	..	..	..	..	..	..	..
4100 Recurrent taxes on immovable property	..	..	..	..	..	..	..	..	..	..
4200 Recurrent taxes on net wealth	..	..	..	..	..	..	..	..	..	..
4300 Estate, inheritance and gift taxes	..	..	..	..	..	..	..	..	..	..
4400 Taxes on financial and capital transactions	..	..	..	..	..	..	..	..	..	..
4500 Non-recurrent taxes	..	..	..	..	..	..	..	..	..	..
4600 Other recurrent taxes on property	..	..	..	..	..	..	..	..	..	..
5000 Taxes on goods and services	..	..	..	..	..	..	..	..	..	..
5100 Taxes on production, sale, transfer, etc	..	..	..	..	..	..	..	..	..	..
5110 General taxes	..	..	..	..	..	..	..	..	..	..
5120 Taxes on specific goods and services	..	..	..	..	..	..	..	..	..	..
5130 Unallocable between 5110 and 5120	..	..	..	..	..	..	..	..	..	..
5200 Taxes on use of goods and perform activities	..	..	..	..	..	..	..	..	..	..
5300 Unallocable between 5100 and 5200	..	..	..	..	..	..	..	..	..	..
6000 Other taxes	..	..	..	..	..	..	..	..	..	..
6100 Paid solely by business	..	..	..	..	..	..	..	..	..	..
6200 Other	..	..	..	..	..	..	..	..	..	..
Total tax revenue	..	..	..	..	..	..	..	..	..	..

1. Local government tax revenues and social security contributions are not available.

StatLink https://doi.org/10.1787/888934115350

Table 6.24. **Trinidad and Tobago, tax revenues by sub-sectors of government**

Million TTD

	Federal government					State/Regional				
	1990	2000	2010	2015	2018	1990	2000	2010	2015	2018
1000 Taxes on income, profits and capital gains	**2 595**	**6 224**	**27 213**	**29 628**	**19 411**	..	..	..	..	..
1100 Of individuals	669	2 325	4 674	7 752	6 840	..	..	..	..	..
1200 Corporate	1 856	3 704	21 659	20 810	11 713	..	..	..	..	..
1300 Unallocable between 1100 and 1200	70	195	881	1 067	858	..	..	..	..	..
2000 Social security contributions	**0**	**0**	**0**	**0**	**0**	..	..	..	..	..
2100 Employees	..	..	..	..	..	..	..	..	..	..
2200 Employers	..	..	..	..	..	..	..	..	..	..
2300 Self-employed or non-employed	..	..	..	..	..	..	..	..	..	..
2400 Unallocable between 2100, 2200 and 2300	..	..	..	..	..	..	..	..	..	..
3000 Taxes on payroll and workforce	**0**	**0**	**0**	**0**	**0**	..	..	..	..	..
4000 Taxes on property	**90**	**175**	**194**	**406**	**362**	..	..	..	..	..
4100 Recurrent taxes on immovable property	39	64	22	3	4	..	..	..	..	..
4200 Recurrent taxes on net wealth	0	0	0	0	0	..	..	..	..	..
4300 Estate, inheritance and gift taxes	1	0	0	0	0	..	..	..	..	..
4400 Taxes on financial and capital transactions	49	111	172	403	359	..	..	..	..	..
4500 Non-recurrent taxes	0	0	0	0	0	..	..	..	..	..
4600 Other recurrent taxes on property	0	0	0	0	0	..	..	..	..	..
5000 Taxes on goods and services	**2 055**	**3 852**	**9 667**	**12 264**	**12 370**	..	..	..	..	..
5100 Taxes on production, sale, transfer, etc	1 973	3 603	9 282	11 678	12 026	..	..	..	..	..
5110 General taxes	980	1 890	6 358	7 569	8 087	..	..	..	..	..
5120 Taxes on specific goods and services	993	1 713	2 924	4 108	3 939	..	..	..	..	..
5130 Unallocable between 5110 and 5120	0	0	0	0	0	..	..	..	..	..
5200 Taxes on use of goods and perform activities	81	249	386	586	344	..	..	..	..	..
5300 Unallocable between 5100 and 5200	0	0	0	0	0	..	..	..	..	..
6000 Other taxes	**0**	**0**	**0**	**0**	**0**	..	..	..	..	..
6100 Paid solely by business	..	..	..	..	..	..	..	..	..	..
6200 Other	..	..	..	..	..	..	..	..	..	..
Total tax revenue	**4 740**	**10 251**	**37 074**	**42 298**	**32 144**	..	..	..	..	..

Million TTD

	Local government[1]					Social Security Funds[2]				
	1990	2000	2010	2015	2018	1990	2000	2010	2015	2018
1000 Taxes on income, profits and capital gains	..	..	..	..	..	**0**	**0**	**0**	**0**	**0**
1100 Of individuals	..	..	..	..	..	..	..	..	..	..
1200 Corporate	..	..	..	..	..	..	..	..	..	..
1300 Unallocable between 1100 and 1200	..	..	..	..	..	..	..	..	..	..
2000 Social security contributions	..	..	..	..	..	**183**	**702**	**2 645**	**4 261**	**4 670**
2100 Employees	..	..	..	..	..	..	..	..	..	..
2200 Employers	..	..	..	..	..	..	..	..	..	..
2300 Self-employed or non-employed	..	..	..	..	..	..	..	..	..	..
2400 Unallocable between 2100, 2200 and 2300	..	..	..	..	..	183	702	2 645	4 261	4 670
3000 Taxes on payroll and workforce	..	..	..	..	..	**0**	**0**	**0**	**0**	**0**
4000 Taxes on property	..	..	..	..	..	**0**	**0**	**0**	**0**	**0**
4100 Recurrent taxes on immovable property	..	..	..	..	..	..	..	..	..	..
4200 Recurrent taxes on net wealth	..	..	..	..	..	..	..	..	..	..
4300 Estate, inheritance and gift taxes	..	..	..	..	..	..	..	..	..	..
4400 Taxes on financial and capital transactions	..	..	..	..	..	..	..	..	..	..
4500 Non-recurrent taxes	..	..	..	..	..	..	..	..	..	..
4600 Other recurrent taxes on property	..	..	..	..	..	..	..	..	..	..
5000 Taxes on goods and services	..	..	..	..	..	**0**	**0**	**0**	**0**	**0**
5100 Taxes on production, sale, transfer, etc	..	..	..	..	..	..	..	..	..	..
5110 General taxes	..	..	..	..	..	..	..	..	..	..
5120 Taxes on specific goods and services	..	..	..	..	..	..	..	..	..	..
5130 Unallocable between 5110 and 5120	..	..	..	..	..	..	..	..	..	..
5200 Taxes on use of goods and perform activities	..	..	..	..	..	..	..	..	..	..
5300 Unallocable between 5100 and 5200	..	..	..	..	..	..	..	..	..	..
6000 Other taxes	..	..	..	..	..	**0**	**0**	**0**	**0**	**0**
6100 Paid solely by business	..	..	..	..	..	..	..	..	..	..
6200 Other	..	..	..	..	..	..	..	..	..	..
Total tax revenue	..	..	..	..	..	**183**	**702**	**2 645**	**4 261**	**4 670**

1. Data are not available for local government tax revenues.
2. The figures follow financial year from July to June.

StatLink https://doi.org/10.1787/888934115369

Table 6.25. **Uruguay, tax revenues by sub-sectors of government**

Million UYU

	Federal government					State/Regional				
	1990	2000	2010	2015	2018	1990	2000	2010	2015	2018
1000 Taxes on income, profits and capital gains	**114**	**8 698**	**42 583**	**84 141**	**140 537**	..	..	..	..	..
1100 Of individuals	0	3 597	19 148	45 451	78 571	..	..	..	..	..
1200 Corporate	114	5 102	21 772	34 814	56 326	..	..	..	..	..
1300 Unallocable between 1100 and 1200	0	0	1 662	3 875	5 639	..	..	..	..	..
2000 Social security contributions	**0**	**0**	**0**	**0**	**0**	..	..	..	..	..
2100 Employees	..	..	..	..	..	..	..	..	..	..
2200 Employers	..	..	..	..	..	..	..	..	..	..
2300 Self-employed or non-employed	..	..	..	..	..	..	..	..	..	..
2400 Unallocable between 2100, 2200 and 2300	..	..	..	..	..	..	..	..	..	..
3000 Taxes on payroll and workforce	**0**	**0**	**0**	**0**	**0**	..	..	..	..	..
4000 Taxes on property	**105**	**2 690**	**11 688**	**20 673**	**24 188**	..	..	..	..	..
4100 Recurrent taxes on immovable property	0	533	1 252	3 775	4 163	..	..	..	..	..
4200 Recurrent taxes on net wealth	94	1 769	8 760	14 776	17 473	..	..	..	..	..
4300 Estate, inheritance and gift taxes	0	0	0	0	0	..	..	..	..	..
4400 Taxes on financial and capital transactions	11	372	1 350	1 601	1 984	..	..	..	..	..
4500 Non-recurrent taxes	0	0	0	0	0	..	..	..	..	..
4600 Other recurrent taxes on property	1	15	326	522	567	..	..	..	..	..
5000 Taxes on goods and services	**1 301**	**29 556**	**96 432**	**162 611**	**199 177**	..	..	..	..	..
5100 Taxes on production, sale, transfer, etc	1 301	29 556	96 432	162 611	199 177	..	..	..	..	..
5110 General taxes	660	18 009	69 951	114 627	137 400	..	..	..	..	..
5120 Taxes on specific goods and services	641	11 546	26 480	47 983	61 777	..	..	..	..	..
5130 Unallocable between 5110 and 5120	0	0	0	0	0	..	..	..	..	..
5200 Taxes on use of goods and perform activities	0	0	0	0	0	..	..	..	..	..
5300 Unallocable between 5100 and 5200	0	0	0	0	0	..	..	..	..	..
6000 Other taxes	**-10**	**-145**	**586**	**796**	**980**	..	..	..	..	..
6100 Paid solely by business	-10	-145	586	796	980	..	..	..	..	..
6200 Other	0	0	0	0	0	..	..	..	..	..
Total tax revenue	**1 510**	**40 799**	**151 289**	**268 221**	**364 881**	..	..	..	..	..

Million UYU

	Local government					Social Security Funds[1]				
	1990	2000	2010	2015	2018	1990	2000	2010	2015	2018
1000 Taxes on income, profits and capital gains	**0**	**0**	**0**	**0**	**0**	**0**	**0**	**0**	**0**	**0**
1100 Of individuals	..	..	..	..	..	..	..	..	..	..
1200 Corporate	..	..	..	..	..	..	..	..	..	..
1300 Unallocable between 1100 and 1200	..	..	..	..	..	..	..	..	..	..
2000 Social security contributions	**0**	**0**	**0**	**0**	**0**	**717**	**17 679**	**49 742**	**108 742**	**139 241**
2100 Employees	..	..	..	..	..	..	..	..	..	..
2200 Employers	..	..	..	..	..	..	..	..	..	..
2300 Self-employed or non-employed	..	..	..	..	..	..	..	..	..	..
2400 Unallocable between 2100, 2200 and 2300	..	..	..	..	..	717	17 679	49 742	108 742	139 241
3000 Taxes on payroll and workforce	**0**	**0**	**0**	**0**	**0**	**0**	**0**	**0**	**0**	**0**
4000 Taxes on property	**107**	**2 819**	**7 277**	**11 749**	**16 320**	**0**	**0**	**0**	**0**	**0**
4100 Recurrent taxes on immovable property	87	2 715	6 887	11 109	15 485	..	..	..	..	..
4200 Recurrent taxes on net wealth	0	0	0	0	0	..	..	..	..	..
4300 Estate, inheritance and gift taxes	0	0	0	0	0	..	..	..	..	..
4400 Taxes on financial and capital transactions	20	104	390	639	835	..	..	..	..	..
4500 Non-recurrent taxes	0	0	0	0	0	..	..	..	..	..
4600 Other recurrent taxes on property	0	0	0	0	0	..	..	..	..	..
5000 Taxes on goods and services	**57**	**2 583**	**3 851**	**7 668**	**11 534**	**0**	**0**	**0**	**0**	**0**
5100 Taxes on production, sale, transfer, etc	0	7	63	128	152	..	..	..	..	..
5110 General taxes	0	0	0	0	0	..	..	..	..	..
5120 Taxes on specific goods and services	0	7	63	128	152	..	..	..	..	..
5130 Unallocable between 5110 and 5120	0	0	0	0	0	..	..	..	..	..
5200 Taxes on use of goods and perform activities	57	2 576	3 788	7 540	11 382	..	..	..	..	..
5300 Unallocable between 5100 and 5200	0	0	0	0	0	..	..	..	..	..
6000 Other taxes	**7**	**303**	**748**	**1 355**	**2 232**	**0**	**0**	**0**	**0**	**0**
6100 Paid solely by business	0	0	0	0	0	..	..	..	..	..
6200 Other	7	303	748	1 355	2 232	..	..	..	..	..
Total tax revenue	**171**	**5 705**	**11 876**	**20 772**	**30 086**	**717**	**17 679**	**49 742**	**108 742**	**139 241**

1. Figures for 1990-98 are estimated by the General Tax Directorate (DGI). Since 1999 the figures include income from Social Security Bank (BPS) published by the Ministry of Economy and Finance.

StatLink https://doi.org/10.1787/888934115388

Table 6.26. **Venezuela, tax revenues by sub-sectors of government**

VES

	Federal government[1,2]					State/Regional[3]				
	1990	2000	2010	2015	2018	1990	2000	2010	2015	2018
1000 Taxes on income, profits and capital gains	**3 444**	**46 856**	**368 365**	**2 847 864**	..	..	..	..	..	..
1100 Of individuals	..	..	..	..	..	..	..	..	..	..
1200 Corporate[1]	3 148	33 683	86 998	473 879	..	..	..	..	..	..
1300 Unallocable between 1100 and 1200	297	13 173	281 367	2 373 986	..	..	..	..	..	..
2000 Social security contributions	**0**	**0**	**0**	..	..	..	..	..	..	..
2100 Employees	..	..	..	..	..	..	..	..	..	..
2200 Employers	..	..	..	..	..	..	..	..	..	..
2300 Self-employed or non-employed	..	..	..	..	..	..	..	..	..	..
2400 Unallocable between 2100, 2200 and 2300	..	..	..	..	..	..	..	..	..	..
3000 Taxes on payroll and workforce	**0**	**0**	**0**	**0**	..	..	..	..	..	..
4000 Taxes on property	**11**	**3 999**	**2 217**	**29 459**	..	..	..	..	..	..
4100 Recurrent taxes on immovable property	0	0	0	0	..	..	..	..	..	..
4200 Recurrent taxes on net wealth	0	0	0	0	..	..	..	..	..	..
4300 Estate, inheritance and gift taxes	11	191	2 217	29 459	..	..	..	..	..	..
4400 Taxes on financial and capital transactions	0	3 808	0	0	..	..	..	..	..	..
4500 Non-recurrent taxes	0	0	0	0	..	..	..	..	..	..
4600 Other recurrent taxes on property	0	0	0	0	..	..	..	..	..	..
5000 Taxes on goods and services	**457**	**51 726**	**733 363**	**9 128 199**	..	..	..	..	..	..
5100 Taxes on production, sale, transfer, etc	457	51 726	733 363	9 128 199	..	..	..	..	..	..
5110 General taxes	0	32 716	561 005	7 027 427	..	..	..	..	..	..
5120 Taxes on specific goods and services	457	19 011	172 357	2 100 772	..	..	..	..	..	..
5130 Unallocable between 5110 and 5120	0	0	0	0	..	..	..	..	..	..
5200 Taxes on use of goods and perform activities	0	0	0	0	..	..	..	..	..	..
5300 Unallocable between 5100 and 5200	0	0	0	0	..	..	..	..	..	..
6000 Other taxes	**0**	**0**	**0**	**158 333**	..	..	..	..	..	..
6100 Paid solely by business	..	..	..	0	..	..	..	..	..	..
6200 Other	..	..	..	158 333	..	..	..	..	..	..
Total tax revenue	**3 913**	**102 581**	**1 103 944**	**12 163 855**	..	..	..	..	..	..

VES

	Local government[3]					Social Security Funds[2,4]				
	1990	2000	2010	2015	2018	1990	2000	2010	2015	2018
1000 Taxes on income, profits and capital gains	..	..	..	..	..	**0**	**0**	**0**	..	..
1100 Of individuals	..	..	..	..	..	..	..	..	..	..
1200 Corporate[1]	..	..	..	..	..	..	..	..	..	..
1300 Unallocable between 1100 and 1200	..	..	..	..	..	..	..	..	..	..
2000 Social security contributions	..	..	..	..	..	**202**	**5 905**	**96 896**	..	..
2100 Employees	..	..	..	..	..	..	..	..	..	..
2200 Employers	..	..	..	..	..	..	..	..	..	..
2300 Self-employed or non-employed	..	..	..	..	..	..	..	..	..	..
2400 Unallocable between 2100, 2200 and 2300	..	..	..	..	..	202	5 905	96 896	..	..
3000 Taxes on payroll and workforce	..	..	..	..	..	**0**	**0**	**0**	..	..
4000 Taxes on property	..	..	..	..	..	**0**	**0**	**0**	..	..
4100 Recurrent taxes on immovable property	..	..	..	..	..	..	..	..	..	..
4200 Recurrent taxes on net wealth	..	..	..	..	..	..	..	..	..	..
4300 Estate, inheritance and gift taxes	..	..	..	..	..	..	..	..	..	..
4400 Taxes on financial and capital transactions	..	..	..	..	..	..	..	..	..	..
4500 Non-recurrent taxes	..	..	..	..	..	..	..	..	..	..
4600 Other recurrent taxes on property	..	..	..	..	..	..	..	..	..	..
5000 Taxes on goods and services	..	..	..	..	..	**0**	**0**	**0**	..	..
5100 Taxes on production, sale, transfer, etc	..	..	..	..	..	..	..	..	..	..
5110 General taxes	..	..	..	..	..	..	..	..	..	..
5120 Taxes on specific goods and services	..	..	..	..	..	..	..	..	..	..
5130 Unallocable between 5110 and 5120	..	..	..	..	..	..	..	..	..	..
5200 Taxes on use of goods and perform activities	..	..	..	..	..	..	..	..	..	..
5300 Unallocable between 5100 and 5200	..	..	..	..	..	..	..	..	..	..
6000 Other taxes	..	..	..	..	..	**0**	**0**	**0**	..	..
6100 Paid solely by business	..	..	..	..	..	..	..	..	..	..
6200 Other	..	..	..	..	..	..	..	..	..	..
Total tax revenue	..	..	..	..	..	**202**	**5 905**	**96 896**	..	..

1. The figures for 2015-17 should be interpreted with caution as they have been affected by the high rate of inflation over this period. Data for revenues from taxes on oil profits (classified in heading 1200) are not available from 2016.
2. Tax revenue data are revised in this edition based on Bolívar Soberano introduced in August 2018. Data are not available for 2018.
3. The figures exclude state and local government tax revenues as the data are not available.
4. Data on social security contributions are not available from 2014.

StatLink https://doi.org/10.1787/888934115407

Annex A

The OECD classification of taxes and interpretative guide[1]

Table of contents

A.1. The OECD classification of taxes

1. 1000 *Taxes on income, profits and capital gains*
    - 1100 Taxes on income, profits and capital gains of individuals
        - 1110 On income and profits
        - 1120 On capital gains
    - 1200 Corporate taxes on income, profits and capital gains
        - 1210 On income and profits
        - 1220 On capital gains
    - 1300 Unallocable as between 1100 and 1200
2. 2000 *Social security contributions*
    - 2100 Employees
        - 2110 On a payroll basis
        - 2120 On an income tax basis
    - 2200 Employers
        - 2210 On a payroll basis
        - 2220 On an income tax basis
    - 2300 Self-employed or non-employed
        - 2310 On a payroll basis
        - 2320 On an income tax basis
    - 2400 Unallocable as between 2100, 2200 and 2300
        - 2410 On a payroll basis
        - 2420 On an income tax basis
3. 3000 *Taxes on payroll and workforce*
4. 4000 *Taxes on property*
    - 4100 Recurrent taxes on immovable property
        - 4110 Households
        - 4120 Other
    - 4200 Recurrent taxes on net wealth
        - 4210 Individual
        - 4220 Corporate
    - 4300 Estate, inheritance and gift taxes
        - 4310 Estate and inheritance taxes
        - 4320 Gift taxes
    - 4400 Taxes on financial and capital transactions
    - 4500 Other non-recurrent taxes on property
        - 4510 On net wealth
        - 4520 Other non-recurrent taxes
    - 4600 Other recurrent taxes on property

5. 5000 *Taxes on goods and services*

5100 Taxes on production, sale, transfer, leasing and delivery of goods and rendering of services

5110 General taxes

5111 Value added taxes

5112 Sales taxes

5113 Turnover and Other general taxes on goods and services

5120 Taxes on specific goods and services

5121 Excises

5122 Profits of fiscal monopolies

5123 Customs and import duties

5124 Taxes on exports

5125 Taxes on investment goods

5126 Taxes on specific services

5127 Other taxes on international trade and transactions

5128 Other taxes on specific goods and services

5130 Unallocable as between 5110 and 5120

5200 Taxes on use of goods, or on permission to use goods or perform activities

5210 Recurrent taxes

5211 Paid by households in respect of motor vehicles

5212 Paid by others in respect of motor vehicles

5213 Other recurrent taxes

5220 Non-recurrent taxes

5300 Unallocable as between 5100 and 5200

6. 6000 *Other taxes*

6100 Paid solely by business

6200 Paid by other than business or unidentifiable

A.2. Coverage

General criteria

1. In the OECD classification the term "taxes" is confined to compulsory unrequited payments to general government. Taxes are unrequited in the sense that benefits provided by government to taxpayers are not normally in proportion to their payments.

2. The term "tax" does not include fines, penalties and compulsory loans paid to government. Borderline cases between tax and non-tax revenues in relation to certain fees and charges are discussed in §11–14.

3. General government consists of the central administration, agencies whose operations are under its effective control, state and local governments and their administrations, certain social security schemes and autonomous governmental entities, excluding public enterprises. This definition of government follows that of the 2008 *System of National Accounts* (SNA).[2] In that publication, the general government sector and its sub-sectors are defined in Chapter 4, paragraphs 4.117 to 4.165.

4. Extra-budgetary units are part of the general government system. These are general government entities with individual budgets that are not fully covered by the main or general budget. These entities operate under the authority or control of a central, state, or local government. Extra-budgetary entities may have their own revenue sources, which may be supplemented by grants (transfers) from the general budget or from other sources. Even though their budgets may be subject to approval by the legislature, similar to that of budgetary accounts, they have discretion over the volume and composition of their spending. Such entities may be established to carry out specific government functions, such as road construction, or the nonmarket production of health or education services. Budgetary arrangements vary widely across countries, and various terms are used to describe these entities, but they are often referred to as "extra-budgetary funds" or "decentralised agencies".

5. Compulsory payments to supra-national bodies and their agencies are no longer included as taxes as from 1998, with some exceptions. However, custom duties collected by EU member states on behalf of the European Union are still identified as memorandum items and included in overall tax revenue amounts in the country tables (Chapter 4) of the country in which they are collected (see §99). In countries where the church forms part of general government church taxes are included, provided they meet the criteria set out in §1 above. As the data refer to receipts of general government, levies paid to non-government bodies, welfare agencies or social insurance schemes outside general government, trade unions or trade associations, even where such levies are compulsory, are excluded. Compulsory payments to general government earmarked for such bodies are, however, included, provided that the government is not simply acting in an agency capacity.[3] Profits from fiscal monopolies are distinguished from those of other public enterprises and are treated as taxes because they reflect the exercise of the taxing power of the state by the use of monopoly powers (see §65–67), as are profits received by the government from the purchase and sale of foreign exchange at different rates (see §74).

6. Taxes paid by governments (e.g. social security contributions and payroll taxes paid by governments in their capacity as an employer, consumption taxes on their purchases or taxes on their property) are not excluded from the data provided. However, where it is possible to identify the amounts of revenue involved,[4] they are shown in Chapter 4.2 of this Report.

7. The relationship between this classification and that of the System of National Accounts (SNA) is set out in Sections A.9 and A.11 below. Because of the differences between the two classifications, the data shown in national accounts are sometimes calculated or classified differently from the practice set out in this guide. These and other differences are mentioned where appropriate (e.g. in §30 below) but it is not possible to refer to all of them. There may also be some differences between this classification and that employed domestically by certain national administrations (e.g. see §12 below), so that OECD and national statistics data may not always be consistent: any such differences, however, are likely to be very slight in terms of amounts of revenues involved.

Social security contributions

8. Compulsory social security contributions, as defined in §39, and paid to general government, are treated here as tax revenues. Being compulsory payments to general government they clearly resemble taxes. They may, however, differ from other taxes in that the receipt of social security benefits depends, in most countries, upon appropriate contributions having been made, although the size of the benefits is not necessarily related to the amount of the contributions. Better comparability between countries is obtained by treating social security contributions as taxes, but they are listed under a separate heading so that they can be distinguished in any analysis.

9. The strict dividing line between tax revenues (compulsory unrequited payments to general government) and non-tax compulsory payments (NTCPs) (payments that are either requited or made to other institutions) is clearly defined. However, within the range of different compulsory payments to governments existing across countries, it is not always straightforward in practice to decide whether specific payments are either taxes or NTCPs. For example, compulsory pension savings that are controlled by general government and that accumulate on an individual account earning a market return or a rate that compensates for inflation would at first sight be categorised as NTCPs as opposed to taxes. However, even these payments might still be 'unrequited' and therefore classify as taxes instead of NTCPs (for example if these pension savings are not paid out when the taxpayer dies before reaching the pension age and the funds are then used to provide a minimum pension to all taxpayers that are insured). These issues result in the social security revenue figures reported for most countries being based on the premise that all types of compulsory payments to general government are judged to some extent to have a re-distributional element. It should be noted that this conclusion is based on a typically broad interpretation of the term 'unrequited' in the tax definition.

10. Social security contributions which are either voluntary or not payable to general government (see §1) are not treated as taxes, though in some countries, as indicated in the country footnotes, there are difficulties in completely eliminating voluntary contributions and certain compulsory payments to the private sector from the revenue figures. Imputed social security contributions are also not treated as taxes.

Fees, user charges and licence fees

11. Apart from vehicle licence fees, which are universally regarded as taxes, it is not easy to distinguish between those fees and user charges which are to be treated as taxes and those which are not, since, whilst a fee or charge is levied in connection with a specific service or activity, the strength of the link between the fee and the service provided may vary considerably, as may the relation between the amount of the fee and the cost of providing the service. Where the recipient of a service pays a fee clearly related to the cost of providing

the service, the levy may be regarded as requited and under the definition of §1 would not be considered as a tax. In the following cases, however, a levy could be considered as 'unrequited':

a. where the charge greatly exceeds the cost of providing the service;

b. where the payer of the levy is not the receiver of the benefit (e.g. a fee collected from slaughterhouses to finance a service which is provided to farmers);

c. where government is not providing a specific service in return for the levy which it receives even though a licence may be issued to the payer (e.g. where the government grants a hunting, fishing or shooting licence which is not accompanied by the right to use a specific area of government land);

d. where benefits are received only by those paying the levy but the benefits received by each individual are not necessarily in proportion to his payments (e.g. a milk marketing levy paid by dairy farmers and used to promote the consumption of milk).

12. In marginal cases, however, the application of the criteria set out in §1 can be particularly difficult. The solution adopted – given the desirability of international uniformity and the relatively small amounts of revenue usually involved – is to follow the predominant practice among tax administrations rather than to allow each country to adopt its own view as to whether such levies are regarded as taxes or as non-tax revenue.[5]

13. A list of the main fees and charges in question and their normal[6] treatment in this publication is as follows:

Non-tax revenues:	court fees; driving licence fees; harbour fees; passport fees; radio and television licence fees where public authorities provide the service.
Taxes within heading 5200:	permission to perform such activities as distributing films; hunting, fishing and shooting; providing entertainment or gambling facilities; selling alcohol or tobacco; permission to own dogs or to use or own motor vehicles or guns; severance taxes.

14. In practice it may not always be possible to isolate tax receipts from non-tax revenue receipts when they are recorded together. If it is estimated that the bulk of the receipts derive from non-tax revenues, the whole amount involved is treated as a non-tax revenue; otherwise, such government receipts are included and classified according to the rules provided in §32 below.

Royalties

15. The ownership of subsoil assets in the form of deposits of minerals or fossil fuels (coal, oil, or natural gas) depends upon the way in which property rights are defined by law and also on international agreements in the case of deposits below international waters. In some cases, either the ground below which the mineral deposits are located, the deposits themselves or both may belong to a local or central government unit.

16. In such cases, these general government units may grant leases to other institutional units that permit them to extract these deposits over a specified period of time in return for a payment or series of payments. These payments are often described as 'royalties' but they are essentially rent that accrues to owners of natural resources in return for putting these assets at the disposal of other units for specified periods of time. The rent may take the form of periodic payments of fixed amounts, irrespective of the rate of extraction, or, more commonly, they may be a function of the quantity, volume, or value of the asset extracted. Enterprises

engaged in exploration on government land may make payments to general government units in exchange for the right to undertake test drilling or otherwise investigate the existence and location of subsoil assets. Such payments are also recorded as rents even though no extraction may take place. These payments are therefore classified as non-tax revenues.

17. The same principles apply when other institutional units are granted leases that permit them to fell timber in natural forests on land owned by general government units. These payments are also classified as non-tax revenues.

18. These rents or royalties paid to general government should not be confused with taxes on income and profits, severance taxes, business licenses, or other taxes. If the payments are levied on the profits from the extraction activity, then they should be classified as taxes on incomes, profits and gains (1000). In addition, any severance payments that are imposed on the extraction of minerals and fossil fuels from reserves owned privately or by another government should be classified as taxes. Payments related to the gross value of production should be classified as other taxes on goods and services (5128). Payments for a license or permit to conduct extraction operations should be classified as taxes on use of goods and on permission to use goods or perform activities (5213).

Fines and penalties

19. In principle, fines and penalties charged on overdue taxes or penalties imposed for the attempted evasion of taxes should not be recorded as tax revenues. However it may not be possible to separate payments of fines or other penalties from the revenues from the taxes to which they relate. In this case the fines and penalties relating to a particular tax are recorded together with the revenues from that tax and fines and penalties paid with revenue from unidentifiable taxes are classified as other taxes in Category 6000. Fines not relating to tax offences (e.g. for parking offences), or not identifiable as relating to tax offences, are also not treated as tax revenues.

A.3. Basis of reporting

Accrual reporting

20. The data reported in this publication for recent years are predominantly recorded on an accrual basis, i.e. recorded at the time that the tax liability was created. Further information is provided in the footnotes to the country table in Chapter 4 of the Report.

21. However, data for earlier years are still predominantly recorded on a cash basis, i.e. at the time at which the payment was received by government. Thus, for example, taxes withheld by employers in one year but paid to the government in the following year and taxes due in one year but actually paid in the following year are both included in the receipts of the second year. Corrective transactions, such as refunds, repayments and drawbacks, are deducted from gross revenues of the period in which they are made.

22. Data on tax revenues are recorded without offsets for the administrative expenses connected with tax collection. Similarly, where the proceeds of tax are used to subsidise particular members of the community, the subsidy is not deducted from the yield of the tax, though the tax may be shown net of subsidies in the national records of some countries.

23. As regards fiscal monopolies (heading 5122), only the amount actually transferred to the government is included in government revenues. However, if any expenditures of fiscal monopolies are considered to be government expenditures (e.g. social expenditures undertaken by fiscal monopolies at the direction of the government) they are added back for the purpose of arriving at tax revenue figures (see §65 below).

The distinction between tax and expenditure provisions[7]

24. Because this publication is concerned only with the revenue side of government operations, no account being taken of the expenditure side, a distinction has to be made between tax and expenditure provisions. Normally there is no difficulty in making this distinction as expenditures are made outside the tax system and the tax accounts and under legislation separate from the tax legislation. In borderline cases, cash flow is used to distinguish between tax provisions and expenditure provisions. Insofar as a provision affects the flow of tax payments from the taxpayer to the government, it is regarded as a tax provision and is taken into account in the data shown in this publication. A provision which does not affect this flow is seen as an expenditure provision and is disregarded in the data recorded in this publication.

25. Tax allowances, exemptions and deductions against the tax base clearly affect the amount of tax paid to the government and are therefore considered as tax provisions. At the other extreme, those subsidies which cannot be offset against tax liability and which are clearly not connected with the assessment process, do not reduce tax revenues as recorded in this publication. Tax credits are amounts deductible from tax payable (as distinct from deductions from the tax base). Two types of tax credits are distinguished, those (referred to here as wastable tax credits) which are limited to the amount of the tax liability and therefore cannot give rise to a payment by the authorities to the taxpayer, and those (referred to as non-wastable tax credits) which are not so limited, so that the excess of the credit over the tax liability can be paid to the taxpayer.[8] A wastable tax credit, like a tax allowance, clearly affects the amount of tax paid to the government, and is therefore considered as a tax provision. The practice followed for non-wastable tax credits[9] is to distinguish between the 'tax expenditure component',[10] which is that portion of the credit that is used to reduce or eliminate a taxpayer's liability, and the 'transfer component', which is the portion that exceeds the taxpayer's liability and is paid to that taxpayer. Reported tax revenues should be reduced by the amount of the tax expenditure component but not by the amount of the transfer component. In addition, the amounts of the tax expenditure and transfer components should be reported as memorandum items in the country tables. Countries that are unable to distinguish between the tax expenditure and transfer components should indicate whether or not the tax revenues have been reduced by the total of these components, and provide any available estimates of the amounts of the two components. Further information is given in Chapter 1 of the Report, which illustrates the effect of alternative treatments of non-wastable tax credits on tax to GDP.

Calendar and fiscal years

26. National authorities whose fiscal years do not correspond to the calendar year show data, where possible, on a calendar year basis to permit maximum comparability with the data of other countries. There remain a few countries where data refer to fiscal years. For these the GDP data used in the comparative tables also correspond to the fiscal years.

A.4. General classification criteria

The main classification criteria

27. The classification of receipts among the main headings (1000, 2000, 3000, 4000, 5000 and 6000) is generally governed by the base on which the tax is levied: 1000 income, profits and capital gains; 2000 and 3000 earnings, payroll or number of employees; 4000 property; 5000 goods and services; 6000 multiple bases, other bases or unidentifiable bases. Where a

tax is calculated on more than one base, the receipts are, where possible, split among the various headings (see §32 and §81). The headings 4000 and 5000 cover not only taxes where the tax base is the property, goods or services themselves but also certain related taxes. Thus, taxes on the transfer of property are included in 4400[11] and taxes on the use of goods or on permission to perform activities in 5200. In headings 4000 and 5000 a distinction is made in certain sub-headings between recurrent and non-recurrent taxes: recurrent taxes are defined as those levied at regular intervals (usually annually) and non-recurrent taxes are levied once and for all (see also §47 to §50, §53, §54 and §79 for particular applications of this distinction).

28. Earmarking of a tax for specific purposes does not affect the classification of tax receipts. However, as explained in §39 on the classification of social security contributions, the conferment of an entitlement to social benefits is crucial to the definition of the 2000 main heading.

29. The way that a tax is levied or collected (e.g. by use of stamps) does not affect classification.

Classification of taxpayers

30. In certain sub-headings distinctions are made between different categories of taxpayers. These distinctions vary from tax to tax:

a. *Between individuals and corporations in relation to income and net wealth taxes*

The basic distinction is that corporation income taxes, as distinct from individual income taxes, are levied on the corporation as an entity, not on the individuals who own it, and without regard to the personal circumstances of these individuals. The same distinction applies to net wealth taxes on corporations and those on individuals. Taxes paid on the profits of partnerships and the income of institutions, such as life insurance or pension funds, are classified according to the same rule. They are classified as corporate taxes (1200) if they are charged on the partnership or institution as an entity without regard to the personal circumstances of the owners. Otherwise, they are treated as individual taxes (1100). Usually, there is different legislation for the corporation taxes and for the individual taxes.[12] The distinction made here between individuals and corporations does not follow the sector classification between households, enterprises, and so on of the System of National Accounts for income and outlay accounts. The SNA classification requires certain unincorporated businesses[13] to be excluded from the household sector and included with non-financial enterprises and financial institutions. The tax on the profits of these businesses, however, cannot always be separated from the tax on the other income of their owners, or can be separated only on an arbitrary basis. No attempt at this separation is made here and the whole of the individual income tax is shown together without regard to the nature of the income chargeable.

b. *Between households and others in relation to taxes on immovable property*

Here the distinction is that adopted by the SNA for the production and consumption expenditure accounts. The distinction is between households as consumers (i.e. excluding non-incorporated business) on the one hand and producers on the other hand. However, taxes on dwellings occupied by households, whether paid by owner-occupiers, tenants or landlords, are classified under households. This follows the common distinction made between taxes on domestic property versus taxes on business property. Some countries are not, however, in a position to make this distinction.

c. *Between households and others in relation to motor vehicle licences*

Here the distinction is between households as consumers on the one hand and producers on the other, as in the production and consumption expenditure accounts of the SNA.

d. *Between business and others in relation to the residual taxes (6000)*

The distinction is the same as in c) above between producers on the one hand and households as consumers on the other hand. Taxes which are included under the heading 6000 because they involve more than one tax base or because the tax base does not fall within any of the previous categories but which are identifiable as levyable only on producers and not on households are included under 'business'. The rest of the taxes which are included under the heading 6000 are shown as 'other' or non-identified.

Surcharges

31. Receipts from surcharges in respect of particular taxes are usually classified with the receipts from the relevant tax whether or not the surcharge is temporary. If, however, the surcharge has a characteristic which would render it classifiable in a different heading of the OECD list, receipts from the surcharge are classified under that heading separately from the relevant tax.

Unidentifiable tax receipts and residual sub-headings

32. A number of cases arise where taxes cannot be identified as belonging entirely to a heading or sub-heading of the OECD classification and the following practices are applied in such cases:

a. The heading is known, but it is not known how receipts should be allocated between sub-headings: receipts are classified in the appropriate residual sub-heading (1300, 2400, 4520, 4600, 5130, 5300 or 6200).

b. It is known that the bulk of receipts from a group of taxes (usually local taxes) is derived from taxes within a particular heading or sub-heading, but some of the taxes in the group whose amount cannot be precisely ascertained may be classifiable in other headings or sub-headings: receipts are shown in the heading or sub-heading under which most of the receipts fall.

c. Neither the heading nor sub-heading of a tax (usually local) can be identified: the tax is classified in 6200 unless it is known that it is a tax on business in which case it is classified in 6100.

A.5. Commentaries on items of the list

1000 — *Taxes on income, profits and capital gains*

33. This heading covers taxes levied on the net income or profits (i.e. gross income minus allowable tax reliefs) of individuals and enterprises. Also covered are taxes levied on the capital gains of individuals and enterprises, and gains from gambling.

34. Included in the heading are:

a. taxes levied predominantly on income or profits, though partially on other bases. Taxes on various bases which are not predominantly income or profits are classified according to the principles laid down in §32 and §81;

b. taxes on property, which are levied on a presumed or estimated income as part of an income tax (see also §47(a), (c) and (d));

c. compulsory payments to social security fund contributions that are levied on income but do not confer an entitlement to social benefits. When such contributions do confer an entitlement to social benefits, they are included in heading 2000 (see §39);

d. receipts from integrated scheduler income tax systems are classified as a whole in this heading, even though certain of the scheduler taxes may be based upon gross income and may not take into account the personal circumstances of the taxpayer.

35. The main subdivision of this heading is between levies on individuals (1100) and those on corporate enterprises (1200). Under each subdivision a distinction is made between taxes on income and profits (1110 and 1210), and taxes on capital gains (1120 and 1220). If certain receipts cannot be identified as appropriate to either 1100 or 1200, or if in practice this distinction cannot be made (e.g. because there are no reliable data on the recipients of payments from which withholding taxes are deducted) they are classified in 1300 as not-allocable.

Treatment of credits under imputation systems

36. Under imputation systems of corporate income tax, a company's shareholders are wholly or partly relieved of their liability to income tax on dividends paid by the company out of income or profits liable to corporate income tax. In countries with such systems,[14] part of the tax on the company's profits is available to provide relief against the shareholders' own tax liability. The relief to the shareholder takes the form of a tax credit, the amount of which may be less than, equal to, or more than the shareholder's overall tax liability. If the tax credit exceeds this tax liability the excess may be payable to the shareholder. As this type of tax credit is an integral part of the imputation system of corporate income tax, any payment to the shareholders is treated as a repayment of tax and not as expenditure (compare the treatment of other tax credits described in §25).

37. As the tax credit under imputation systems (even when exceeding tax liability) is to be regarded as a tax provision, the question arises whether it should be deducted from individual income tax receipts (1110) or corporate income tax receipts (1210). In this Report, the full amount of corporate income tax paid is shown under 1210 and no imputed tax is included under 1110. Thus, the full amount of the credit reduces the amount of 1110 whether the credit results in a reduction of personal income tax liability or whether an actual refund is made because the credit exceeds the income tax liability. (Where, however, such tax credits are deducted from corporation tax in respect of dividends paid to corporations the amounts are deducted from the receipts of 1210).

1120 and 1220 — Taxes on capital gains

38. These sub-headings comprise taxes imposed on capital gains, 1120 covering those levied on the gains of individuals and 1220 those levied on the gains of corporate enterprises, where receipts from such taxes can be separately identified. In many countries this is not the case and the receipts from such taxes are then classified with those from the income tax. Heading 1120 also includes taxes on gains from gambling.

2000 — Social security contributions

39. Classified here are all compulsory payments that confer an entitlement to receive a (contingent) future social benefit. Such payments are usually earmarked to finance social benefits and are often paid to institutions of general government that provide such benefits. However, such earmarking is not part of the definition of social security contributions and

is not required for a tax to be classified here. However, conferment of an entitlement is required for a tax to be classified under this heading. So, levies on income or payroll that are earmarked for social security funds but do not confer an entitlement to benefit are excluded from this heading and shown under personal income taxes (1100) or taxes on payroll and workforce (3000). Taxes on other bases, such as goods and services, which are earmarked for social security benefits are not shown here but are classified according to their respective bases because they generally confer no entitlement to social security benefits.

40. Contributions for the following types of social security benefits would, *inter alia*, be included: unemployment insurance benefits and supplements, accident, injury and sickness benefits, old-age, disability and survivors' pensions, family allowances, reimbursements for medical and hospital expenses or provision of hospital or medical services. Contributions may be levied on both employees and employers.

41. Contributions may be based on earnings or payroll ('on a payroll basis') or on net income after deductions and exemptions for personal circumstances ('on an income tax basis'), and the revenues from the two bases should be separately identified if possible. However, where contributions to a general social security scheme are on a payroll basis, but the contributions of particular groups (such as the self-employed) cannot be assessed on this basis and net income is used as a proxy for gross earnings, the receipts may still be classified as being on a payroll basis. In principle, this heading excludes voluntary contributions paid to social security schemes. When separately identifiable these are shown in the memorandum item on the financing of social security benefits. In practice, however, they cannot always be separately identified from compulsory contributions, in which case they are included in this heading.

42. Contributions to social insurance schemes which are not institutions of general government and to other types of insurance schemes, provident funds, pension funds, friendly societies or other saving schemes are not considered as social security contributions. Provident funds are arrangements under which the contributions of each employee and of the corresponding employer on his/her behalf are kept in a separate account earning interest and withdrawable under specific circumstances. Pension funds are separately organised schemes negotiated between employees and employers and carry provisions for different contributions and benefits, sometimes more directly tied to salary levels and length of service than under social security schemes. When contributions to these schemes are compulsory or quasi-compulsory (e.g. by virtue of agreement with professional and union organisations) they are shown in the memorandum item (refer to Chapter 4.2 of the Report).

43. Contributions by government employees and by governments in respect of their employees, to social security schemes classified within general government are included in this heading. Contributions to separate schemes for government employees, which can be regarded as replacing general social security schemes, are also regarded as taxes.[15] Where, however, a separate scheme is not seen as replacing a general scheme and has been negotiated between the government, in its role as an employer, and its employees, it is not regarded as social security and contributions to it are not regarded as taxes, even though the scheme may have been established by legislation.

44. This heading excludes 'imputed' contributions, which correspond to social benefits paid directly by employers to their employees or former employees or to their representatives (e.g. when employers are legally obliged to pay sickness benefits for a certain period).

45. Contributions are divided into those of employees (2100), employers (2200), and self-employed or non-employed (2300), and then further sub-divided according to the basis on which they are levied. Employees are defined for this purpose as all persons engaged in activities of business units, government bodies, private non-profit institutions, or other paid employment, except the proprietors and their unpaid family members in the case of unincorporated businesses. Members of the armed forces are included, irrespective of the duration and type of their service, if they contribute to social security schemes. The contributions of employers are defined as their payments on account of their employees to social security schemes. Where employees or employers are required to continue the payment of social security contributions when the employee becomes unemployed these contributions, data permitting, are shown in 2100 and 2200 respectively. Accordingly, the sub-heading 2300 is confined to contributions paid by the self-employed and by those outside of the labour force (e.g. disabled or retired individuals).

3000 — Taxes on payroll and workforce

46. These consist of taxes payable by enterprises assessed either as a proportion of the wages or salaries paid or as a fixed amount per person employed. They do not include compulsory social security contributions paid by employers or any taxes paid by employees themselves out of their wages or salaries

4000 — Taxes on property

47. This heading covers recurrent and non-recurrent taxes on the use, ownership or transfer of property. These include taxes on immovable property or net wealth, taxes on the change of ownership of property through inheritance or gift and taxes on financial and capital transactions. The following kinds of tax are excluded from this heading:

a. taxes on capital gains resulting from the sale of a property (1120 or 1220);

b. taxes on the use of goods or on permission to use goods or perform activities (5200); see §76;

c. taxes on immovable property levied on the basis of a presumed net income which take into account the personal circumstances of the taxpayer. They are classified as income taxes along with taxes on income and capital gains derived from property (1100);

d. taxes on the use of property for residence, where the tax is payable by either proprietor or tenant and the amount payable is a function of the user's personal circumstances (pay, dependants, and so on). They are classified as taxes on income (1100);

e. taxes on building in excess of permitted maximum density, taxes on the enlargement, construction or alteration of certain buildings beyond a permitted value and taxes on building construction. They are classified as taxes on permission to perform activities (5200);

f. taxes on the use of one's own property for special trading purposes like selling alcohol, tobacco, meat or for exploitation of land resources (e.g. United States severance taxes). They are classified as taxes on permission to perform activities (5200).

4100 — *Recurrent taxes on immovable property*

48. This sub-heading covers taxes levied regularly in respect of the use or ownership of immovable property.

- these taxes are levied on land and buildings;
- they can be in the form of a percentage of an assessed property value based on a national rental income, sales price, or capitalised yield; or in terms of other characteristics of real property, (for example size or location) from which a presumed rent or capital value can be derived.
- such taxes can be levied on proprietors, tenants, or both. They can also be paid by one level of government to another level of government in respect of property under the jurisdiction of the latter.
- debts are not taken into account in the assessment of these taxes, and they differ from taxes on net wealth in this respect.

49. Taxes on immovable property are further sub-divided into those paid by households (4110) and those paid by other entities (4120), according to the criteria set out in §30(*b*) above.

4200 — *Recurrent taxes on net wealth*

50. This sub-heading covers taxes levied regularly (in most cases annually) on net wealth, i.e. taxes on a wide range of movable and immovable property, net of debt. It is sub-divided into taxes paid by individuals (4210) and taxes paid by corporate enterprises (4220) according to the criteria set out in §30(*a*) above. If separate figures exist for receipts paid by institutions, the tax payments involved are added to those paid by corporations.

4300 — *Estate, inheritance and gift taxes*

51. This sub-heading is divided into taxes on estates and inheritances (4310) and taxes on gifts (4320).[16] Estate taxes are charged on the amount of the total estate whereas inheritance taxes are charged on the shares of the individual recipients; in addition the latter may take into account the relationship of the individual recipients to the deceased.

4400 — *Taxes on financial and capital transactions*

52. This sub-heading comprises, *inter alia*, taxes on the issue, transfer, purchase and sale of securities, taxes on cheques, and taxes levied on specific legal transactions such as validation of contracts and the sale of immovable property. The heading does not include:

a. taxes on the use of goods or property or permission to perform certain activities (5200);
b. fees paid to cover court charges, charges for birth, marriage or death certificates, which are normally regarded as non-tax revenues (see §11);
c. taxes on capital gains (1000);
d. recurrent taxes on immovable property (4100);
e. recurrent taxes on net wealth (4200);
f. once-and-for-all levies on property or wealth (4500).

4500 — *Other non-recurrent taxes on property*[16]

53. This sub-heading covers once-and-for-all, as distinct from recurrent, levies on property. It is divided into taxes on net wealth (4510) and other non-recurrent taxes on property (4520). Heading 4510 would include taxes levied to meet emergency expenditures, or for

redistribution purposes. Heading 4520 would cover taxes levied to take account of increases in land value due to permission given to develop or provision of additional local facilities by general government, any taxes on the revaluation of capital and once-and-for-all taxes on particular items of property.

4600 — *Other recurrent taxes on property*

54. These rarely exist in OECD member countries, but the heading would include taxes on goods such as cattle, jewellery, windows, and other external signs of wealth.

5000 — *Taxes on goods and services*

55. All taxes and duties levied on the production, extraction, sale, transfer, leasing or delivery of goods, and the rendering of services (5100), or in respect of the use of goods or permission to use goods or to perform activities (5200) are included here. The heading thus covers:

a. multi-stage cumulative taxes;

b. general sales taxes — whether levied at manufacture/production, wholesale or retail level;

c. value-added taxes;

d. excises;

e. taxes levied on the import and export of goods;

f. taxes levied in respect of the use of goods and taxes on permission to use goods, or perform certain activities;

g. taxes on the extraction, processing or production of minerals and other products.

56. Borderline cases between this heading and heading 4000 (taxes on property) and 6100 (other taxes on business) are referred to in §47, §52 and §78. Residual sub-headings (5300) and (5130) cover tax receipts which cannot be allocated between 5100 and 5200 and between 5110 and 5120, respectively; see §32.

5100 — *Taxes on the production, sale, transfer, leasing and delivery of goods and rendering of services*

57. This sub-heading consists of all taxes, levied on transactions in goods and services on the basis of their intrinsic characteristics (e.g. value, weight of tobacco, strength of alcohol, and so on) as distinct from taxes imposed on the use of goods, or permission to use goods or perform activities, which fall under 5200.

5110 — *General taxes on goods and services*

58. This sub-heading includes all taxes, other than import and export duties (5123 and 5124), levied on the production, leasing, transfer, delivery or sales of a wide range of goods and/ or the rendering of a wide range of services, irrespective of whether they are domestically produced or imported and irrespective of the stage of production or distribution at which they are levied. It thus covers value-added taxes, sales taxes and multi-stage cumulative taxes. Receipts from border adjustments in respect of such taxes when goods are imported are added to gross receipts for this category, and repayments of such taxes when goods are exported are deducted. These taxes are subdivided into 5111 value-added taxes, 5112 sales taxes, 5113 turnover and other general taxes on goods and services.

59. Borderline cases arise between this heading and taxes on specific goods (5120) when taxes are levied on a large number of goods, for example, the United Kingdom purchase tax

(repealed in 1973) and the Japanese commodity tax (repealed in 1988). In conformity with national views, the former United Kingdom purchase tax is classified as a general tax (5112) and the former Japanese commodity tax as excises (5121).

5111 — *Value-added taxes*

60. All general consumption taxes charged on value-added are classified in this sub-heading, irrespective of the method of deduction and the stages at which the taxes are levied. In practice, all OECD countries with value-added taxes normally allow immediate deduction of taxes on purchases by all but the final consumer and impose tax at all stages. In some countries the heading may include certain taxes, such as those on financial and insurance activities, either because receipts from them cannot be identified separately from those from the value-added tax, or because they are regarded as an integral part of the value-added tax, even though similar taxes in other countries might be classified elsewhere (e.g. 5126 as taxes on services or 4400 as taxes on financial and capital transactions).

5112 — *Sales taxes*

61. All general taxes levied at one stage only, whether at manufacturing or production, wholesale or retail stage are classified here.

5113 — *Turnover and other general taxes on goods and services*

62. These are multi-stage cumulative taxes and taxes where elements of consumption taxes are combined with multistage taxes. These taxes are levied each time a transaction takes place without deduction for taxes paid on inputs. Multi-stage taxes can be combined with elements of value-added or sales taxes.

5120 — *Taxes on specific goods and services*

63. Excises, profits generated and transferred from fiscal monopolies, and customs and imports duties as well as taxes on exports, foreign exchange transactions, investment goods and betting stakes and special taxes on services, which do not form part of a general tax of 5110, are included in this category.

5121 — *Excises*

64. Excises are taxes levied as a product specific unit tax on a predefined limited range of goods. Excises are usually levied at differentiated rates on nonessential or luxury goods, alcoholic beverages, tobacco, and energy. Excises may be imposed at any stage of production or distribution and are usually assessed as a specific charge per unit based on characteristics by reference to the value, weight, strength, or quantity of the product. Included are special taxes on individual products such as sugar, sugar beets, matches, and chocolates; taxes levied at varying rates on a certain range of goods; and taxes levied on tobacco goods, alcoholic drinks, motor fuels, and hydrocarbon oils. If a tax collected principally on imported goods also applies, or would apply, under the same law to comparable domestically produced goods, then the revenue from this tax is classified as arising from excises rather than from import duties. This principle applies even if there is no comparable domestic production or no possibility of such production. Taxes on the use of utilities such as water, electricity, gas, and energy are regarded as excises rather than taxes on specific services (5126). Excises exclude those taxes that are levied as general taxes on goods and services (5110); profits of fiscal monopolies (5122); customs and other import duties (5123); or taxes on exports (5124).

5122 — *Profits of fiscal monopolies*

65. This sub-heading covers that part of the profits of fiscal monopolies which is transferred to general government or which is used to finance any expenditures considered to be government expenditures (see §23). Amounts are shown when they are transferred to general government or used to make expenditures considered to be government expenditures.

66. Fiscal monopolies reflect the exercise of the taxing power of government by the use of monopoly powers. Fiscal monopolies are non-financial public enterprises exercising a monopoly in most cases over the production or distribution of tobacco, alcoholic beverages, salt, matches, playing cards and petroleum or agricultural products (i.e. on the kind of products which are likely to be, alternatively or additionally, subject to the excises of 5121), to raise the government revenues which in other countries are gathered through taxes on dealings in such commodities by private business units. The government monopoly may be at the production stage or, as in the case of government-owned and controlled liquor stores, at the distribution stage.

67. Fiscal monopolies are distinguished from public utilities such as rail transport, electricity, post offices, and other communications, which may enjoy a monopoly or quasi-monopoly position but where the primary purpose is normally to provide basic services rather than to raise revenue for government. Transfers from such other public enterprises to the government are considered as non-tax revenues. The traditional concept of fiscal monopoly is not generally extended to include state lotteries, the profits of which are usually accordingly regarded as non-tax revenues. However, they can be included as tax revenues if the prime reason for their operation is to raise revenues to finance government expenditure. Fiscal monopoly profits are distinguished from export and import monopoly profits (5127) transferred from marketing boards or other enterprises dealing with international trade.

5123 — *Customs and other import duties*

68. Taxes, stamp duties and surcharges restricted by law to imported products are included here. Also included are levies on imported agricultural products which are imposed in member countries of the European Union and amounts paid by certain of these countries under the Monetary Compensation Accounts (MCA) system.[17] Starting from 1998, customs duties collected by European Union member states on behalf of the European Union are no longer reported under this heading in the country tables (in Chapter 4 of the Report). Excluded here are taxes collected on imports as part of a general tax on goods and services, or an excise applicable to both imported and domestically produced goods.

5124 — *Taxes on exports*

69. In the 1970s, export duties were levied in Australia, Canada and Portugal as a regular measure and they have been used in Finland for counter-cyclical purposes. Some member countries of the European Union pay, as part of the MCA system, a levy on exports (see note 16 to §68). Where these amounts are identifiable, they are shown in this heading. This heading does not include repayments of general consumption taxes or excises or customs duties on exported goods, which should be deducted from the gross receipts under 5110, 5121 or 5123, as appropriate.

5125 — *Taxes on investment goods*

70. This sub-heading covers taxes on investment goods, such as machinery. These taxes may be imposed for a number of years or temporarily for counter-cyclical purposes. Taxes

on industrial inputs which are also levied on consumers [e.g. the Swedish energy tax which is classified under (5121)] are not included here.

5126 — *Taxes on specific services*

71. All taxes assessed on the payment for specific services, such as taxes on insurance premiums, banking services, gambling and betting stakes (e.g. from horse races, football pools, lottery tickets), transport, entertainment, restaurant and advertising charges, fall into this category. Taxes levied on the gross income of companies providing the service (e.g. gross insurance premiums or gambling stakes received by the company) are also classified under this heading. Tax revenues from bank levies and payments to deposit insurance and financial stability schemes are provisionally included here for the 2012 edition. The detailed classification is set out in §108.

72. Excluded from this sub-heading are:

a. taxes on services forming part of a general tax on goods and services (5110);

b. taxes on electricity, gas and energy (5121 as excises);

c. taxes on individual gains from gambling (1120 as taxes on capital gains of individuals and non-corporate enterprises) and lump-sum taxes on the transfer of private lotteries or on the permission to set up lotteries (5200);[18]

d. taxes on cheques and on the issue, transfer or redemption of securities (4400 as taxes on financial and capital transactions).

5127 — *Other taxes on international trade and transactions*

73. This sub-heading covers revenue received by the government from the purchase and sale of foreign exchange at different rates. When the government exercises monopoly powers to extract a margin between the purchase and sales price of foreign exchange, other than to cover administrative costs, the revenue derived constitutes a compulsory levy exacted in indeterminate proportions from both purchaser and seller of foreign exchange. It is the common equivalent of an import duty and export duty levied in a single exchange rate system or of a tax on the sale or purchase of foreign exchange. Like the profits of fiscal monopolies and import or export monopolies transferred to government, it represents the exercise of monopoly powers for tax purposes and is included in tax revenues.

74. The sub-heading covers also the profits of export or import monopolies, which do not however exist in OECD countries, taxes on purchase or sale of foreign exchange, and any other taxes levied specifically on international trade or transactions.

5128 — *Other taxes on specific goods and services*

75. This item includes taxes on the extraction of minerals, fossil fuels and other exhaustible resources from deposits owned privately or by another government together with any other unidentifiable receipts from taxes on specific goods and services. Taxes on the extraction of exhaustible resources are usually a fixed amount per unit of quality or weight, but can be a percentage of value. The taxes are recorded when the resources are extracted. Payments from the extraction of exhaustible resources from deposits owned by the government unit receiving the payment are classified as rent.

5200 — *Taxes on use of goods or on permission to use goods or perform activities*

76. This sub-heading covers taxes which are levied in respect of the use of goods as distinct from taxes on the goods themselves. Unlike the latter taxes – reported under 5100 –, they are

not assessed on the value of the goods but usually as fixed amounts. Taxes on permission to use goods or to perform activities are also included here, as are pollution taxes not based upon the value of particular goods. It is sometimes difficult to distinguish between compulsory user charges and licence fees which are regarded as taxes and those which are excluded as non-tax revenues. The criteria which are employed are noted in §11–12.

77. Although the sub-heading refers to the 'use' of goods, registration of ownership rather than use may be what generates liability to tax, so that the taxes of this heading may apply to the ownership of animals or goods rather than their use (e.g. race horses, dogs and motor vehicles) and may apply even to unusable goods (e.g. unusable motor vehicles or guns).

78. Borderline cases arise with:

a. taxes on the permission to perform business activities which are levied on a combined income, payroll or turnover base and, accordingly, are classified following the rules in §81;

b. taxes on the ownership or use of property of headings 4100, 4200 and 4600. The heading 4100 is confined to taxes on the ownership or tenancy of immovable property and – unlike the taxes of 5200 – they are related to the value of the property. The net wealth taxes and taxes on chattels of 4200 and 4600 respectively are confined to the ownership rather than the use of assets, apply to groups of assets rather than particular goods and again are related to the value of the assets,

5210 — *Recurrent taxes on use of goods and on permission to use goods or perform activities*

79. The principal characteristic of taxes classified here is that they are levied at regular intervals and that they are usually fixed amounts. The most important item in terms of revenue receipts is vehicle licence taxes. This sub-heading also covers taxes on permission to hunt, shoot, fish or to sell certain products and taxes on the ownership of dogs and on the performance of certain services, provided that they meet the criteria set out in §11–12. The sub-divisions of 5210 are user taxes on motor vehicles paid by households (5211) and those paid by others (5212).[19] Sub-heading 5213 covers dog licences and user charges for permission to perform activities such as selling meat or liquor when the levies are on a recurring basis. It also covers recurrent general licences for hunting, shooting and fishing where the right to carry out these activities is not granted as part of a normal commercial transaction (e.g. the granting of the licence is not accompanied by the right to use a specific area which is owned by government).

5220 — *Non-recurrent taxes on use of goods and on permission to use goods or perform activities*

80. This section covers non-recurrent taxes levied on the use of goods or on permission to use goods or perform activities and taxes levied each time goods are used. It includes taxes levied on the emission or discharge into the environment of noxious gases, liquids or other harmful substances.

- Payments for tradable emission permits issued by governments under cap and trade schemes should be recorded here at the time the emissions occur. No revenue should be recorded for permits that governments issue free of charge. The accrual basis of recording means that there can be a timing difference between the cash being received by government for the permits and the time the emission occurs. In the national accounts, this timing gives rise to a financial liability for government during the period.

- Payments made for the collection and disposal of waste or noxious substances by public authorities should be excluded as they constitute a sale of services to enterprises.

81. Other taxes falling under heading 5200 that are not levied recurrently are also included here. Thus, once-and-for-all payments for permission to sell liquor or tobacco or to set up betting shops are included provided they meet the criteria set out in §11–12.

6000 — Other taxes

82. Taxes levied on a base, or bases, other than those described under headings 1000, 3000, 4000 and 5000, or on bases of which cannot be considered to be related to any one of these headings, are included here. Where taxes are levied on a multiple base and it is possible to estimate the receipts related to each base the separate amounts are included under the appropriate headings. If separate amounts cannot be estimated and it is known that most of the receipts are derived from one base, the whole of the receipts are classified according to that base. Otherwise, they are classified here. Other revenues included here are presumptive taxes not included elsewhere in the classification system, taxes on individuals in the form of a poll tax or capitation tax, stamp taxes not related to financial and capital transactions nor falling exclusively on a single category of transaction, expenditure taxes where personal deductions or exemptions are applied and unidentifiable tax receipts. A subdivision is made between taxes levied wholly or predominantly on business (6100) and those levied on others (6200).

A.6. Conciliation with national accounts

83. This section of the tables provides a re-conciliation between the OECD calculation of total tax revenues and the total of all taxes and social contributions paid to general government as recorded in the country's National Accounts. Where the country is a member of the European Union (EU), the comparison is between the OECD calculation of total tax revenues and the sum of tax revenues and social contributions recorded in the combination of the general government and the institutions of the EU sectors of the National Accounts.

A.7. Memorandum item on the financing of social security benefits

84. In view of the varying relationship between taxation and social security contributions and the cases referred to in §39 to §45, a memorandum item collects together all payments earmarked for social security-type benefits, other than voluntary payments to the private sector. Data are presented as follows (refer Chapter 4.2 of the Report):

a. Taxes of 2000 series.

b. Taxes earmarked for social security benefits.

c. Voluntary contributions to the government.

d. Compulsory contributions to the private sector.

Guidance on the breakdown of (a) to (d) above is provided in §39 to §45.

A.8. Memorandum item on identifiable taxes paid by government

85. Identifiable taxes actually paid by government are presented in a memorandum item classified by the main headings of the OECD classification of taxes. In the vast majority of countries, only social security contributions and payroll taxes paid by government can be identified. These are, however, usually the most important taxes paid by governments (refer to Chapter 4.2 of the Report).

A.9. Relation of OECD classification of taxes to national accounting systems

86. A system of national accounts (SNA) seeks to provide a coherent framework for recording and presenting the main flows relating respectively to production, consumption, accumulation and external transactions of a given economic area, usually a country or a major region within a country. Government revenues are an important part of the transactions recorded in SNA. The final version of the 2008 SNA was jointly published by five international organisations: the United Nations, the International Monetary Fund, the European Union, the Organisation for Economic Co-operation and Development, and the World Bank in August 2009. The *System* is a comprehensive, consistent and flexible set of macroeconomic accounts. It is designed for use in countries with market economies, whatever their stage of economic development, and also in countries in transition to market economies. The important parts of the SNA's conceptual framework and its definitions of the various sectors of the economy have been reflected in the OECD's classification of taxes.

87. There are, however, some differences between the OECD classification of taxes and SNA concepts that are listed below. They arise because the aim of the former is to provide the maximum disaggregation of statistical data on what are generally regarded as taxes by tax administrations.

a. OECD includes compulsory social security contributions paid to general government in total tax revenues. Imputed and voluntary contributions plus those paid to private funds are not treated as taxes (§8 and §10 above);

b. there are different points of view on whether or not some levies and fees are classified as taxes (§11 and §12 above);

c. OECD excludes imputed taxes or subsidies resulting from the operation of official multiple exchange rates or from the central bank paying a rate of interest on required reserves that is different from other market rates;

d. there are differences in the treatment of non-wastable tax credits

88. As noted in §1 and §2, headings 1000 to 6000 of the OECD list of taxes cover all unrequited payments to general government, other than compulsory loans and fines. Such unrequited payments including fines, but excluding compulsory loans can be obtained from adding together the following figures in the 2008 SNA

- value-added type taxes (D.211);
- taxes and duties on imports, excluding VAT (D.212);
- export taxes (D.213);
- taxes on products, excluding VAT, import and export taxes (D.214);
- other taxes on production (D.29);
- taxes on income (D.51);
- other current taxes (D.59);
- social contributions (D.61), excluding voluntary contributions;
- capital taxes (D.91).

A.10. The OECD classification of taxes and the International Monetary Fund (GFS) system

89. The coverage and valuation of tax revenues in the GFS system and the 2008 SNA are very similar. Therefore, the differences between the OECD classification and that of the 2008 SNA (see §87 above) also apply to the GFS. In addition the International Monetary Fund subdivides the OECD 5000 heading into section IV (Domestic Taxes on Goods and Services) and section V (Taxes on International Trade and Transactions). This reflects the fact that while the latter usually yield insignificant amounts of revenue in OECD countries, this is not the case in many non-OECD countries.

A.11. Comparison of the OECD classification of taxes with other international classifications

90. The table below describes an item by item comparison of the OECD classification of taxes and the classifications used in the following:

- *i)* System of National Accounts (2008 SNA);
- *ii)* European System of Accounts (2010 ESA);
- *iii)* IMF *Government Finance Statistics Manual* (GFSM2014).

91. These comparisons represent those that would be expected to apply in the majority of cases. However in practice some flexibility should be used in their application. This is because in particular cases, countries can adopt varying approaches to the classification of revenues in National Accounts.

OECD Classification	2008 SNA	2010 ESA	GFSM2014
1000 Taxes on income, profits and capital gains			
1100 Individuals			
1110 Income and profits	D51-8.61a	D51A	1111
1120 Capital gains	D51-8.61c, d	D51C, D	1111
1200 Corporations			
1210 Income and profits	D51-8.61b	D51B	1112
1220 Capital gains	D51-8.61c	D51C	1112
1300 Unallocable as between 1100 and 1200			1113
2000 Social security contributions			
2100 Employees	D613-8.85	D613	1211
2200 Employers	D611-8.83	D611	1212
2300 Self-employed, non-employed	D613-8.85	D613	1213
2400 Unallocable as between 2100, 2200 and 2300			1214
3000 Taxes on payroll and workforce	D29-7.97a	D29C	112
4000 Taxes on property			
4100 Recurrent taxes on immovable property			
4110 Households	D59-8.63a	D59A	1131
4120 Other	D29-7.97b	D29A	1131
4200 Recurrent net wealth taxes			
4210 Individual	D59-8.63b	D59A	1132
4220 Corporations	D59-8.63b	D59A	1132
4300 Estate, inheritance and gift taxes			
4310 Estate and inheritance taxes	D91-10.207b	D91A	1133
4320 Gift taxes	D91-10.207b	D91A	1133
4400 Taxes on financial and capital transactions	D59-7.96d; D29-7.97e	D214B, C	114114; 1161
4500 Other non-recurrent taxes on property	D91-10.207a	D91B	1135
4600 Other recurrent taxes on property	D59-8.63c	D59A	1136
5000 Taxes on goods and services			

OECD Classification	2008 SNA	2010 ESA	GFSM2014
5100 Taxes on production, sale and transfer of goods and services			
5110 General taxes on goods and services			
5111 Value-added taxes	D211-7.89	D211; D29G	11411
5112 Sales taxes	D2122-7.94a; D214-7.96a	D21224; D214I	11412
5113 Other general taxes on goods and services	D214-7.96a	D214I	11413
5120 Taxes on specific goods and services			
5121 Excises	D2122-7.94b; D214-7.96b	D21223; D214A, B, D	1142
5122 Profits of fiscal monopolies	D214-7.96e	D214J	1143
5123 Customs and other import duties	D2121-7.93	D2121; D21221, 2	1151
5124 On exports	D213-7.95a	D214K	1152-4
5125 On investment goods			
5126 On specific services	D2122-7.94c; D214-7.96c	D21225; D214E, F, G, H; D29F	1144; 1156
5127 Other taxes on international trade and transactions	D2122-7.94d D29-7.95b D29-7.97g D59-8.64d	D21226; D29D; D59E	1153; 1155-6
5128 Other taxes on specific goods and services			1146
5130 Unallocable between 5110 and 5120			
5200 Taxes on use of goods and on permission to use goods or perform activities			
5210 Recurrent taxes on use of goods and on permission to use goods or perform activities			
5211 Motor vehicle taxes households	D59-8.64c	D59D	11451
5212 Motor vehicles taxes others	D29-7.97d	D214D; D29B	11451
5213 Other recurrent taxes on use of goods and on permission to use goods or perform activities	D29-7.97c, d, f D59-8.64c	D29B, E, F; D59D	11452
5220 Non-recurrent taxes on permission to use goods or perform activities			11452
5300 Unallocable as between 5100 and 5200			
6000 Other taxes			
6100 Payable solely by business			1161
6200 Payable by other than business, or unidentifiable	D59-8.64a, b	D59B, C	1162

A.12. Attribution of tax revenues by sub-sectors of general government

92. The OECD classification requires a breakdown of tax revenues by sub-sectors of government. The definition of each sub-sector and the criteria to be used to attribute tax revenues between these sub-sectors are set out below. They follow the guidance of the 2008 SNA and GFSM 2014.

Sub-sectors of general government to be identified

a) Central government

93. The central government sub-sector includes all governmental departments, offices, establishments and other bodies which are agencies or instruments of the central authority whose competence extends over the whole territory, with the exception of the administration of social security funds. Central government therefore has the authority to impose taxes on all resident and non-resident units engaged in economic activities within the country.

b) State, provincial or regional government

94. This sub-sector consists of intermediate units of government exercising a competence at a level below that of central government. It includes all such units operating independently of central government in a part of a country's territory encompassing a number of smaller

localities, with the exception of the administration of social security funds. In unitary countries, regional governments may be considered to have a separate existence where they have substantial autonomy to raise a significant proportion of their revenues from sources within their control and their officers are independent of external administrative control in the actual operation of the unit's activities.

95. At present, federal countries comprise the majority of cases where revenues attributed to intermediate units of government are identified separately. Spain is the only unitary country in this position. In the remaining unitary countries, regional revenues are included with those of local governments.

c) Local government

96. This sub-sector includes all other units of government exercising an independent competence in part of the territory of a country, with the exception of the administration of social security funds. It encompasses various urban and/or rural jurisdictions (e.g. local authorities, municipalities, cities, boroughs, districts).

d) Social security funds

97. Social security funds form a separate sub-sector of general government. The social security sub-sector is defined in the 2008 SNA by the following extracts from paragraphs 4.124 to 4.126 and 4.147:

> *"Social security schemes are social insurance schemes covering the community as a whole or large section of the community that are imposed and controlled by government units. The schemes cover a wide variety of programmes, providing benefits in cash or in kind for old age, invalidity or death, survivors, sickness and maternity, work injury, unemployment, family allowance, health care, etc. There is not necessarily a direct link between the amount of the contribution paid by an individual and the benefits he or she may receive." (Paragraph 4.124).*
>
> *"When social security schemes are separately organised from the other activities of government units and hold their assets and liabilities separately from the latter and engage in financial transactions on their own account they qualify as institutional units that are described as social security funds." (Paragraph 4.125).*
>
> *"The amounts raised, and paid out, in social security contributions and benefits may be deliberately varied in order to achieve objectives of government policy that have no direct connection with the concept of social security as a scheme to provide social benefits to members of the community. They may be raised or lowered in order to influence the level of aggregate demand in the economy, for example. Nevertheless, so long as they remain separately constituted funds, they must be treated as separate institutional units in the SNA. (Paragraph 4.126).*
>
> *"The social security funds sub-sector (of general government) consists of the social security funds operating at all levels of government. Such funds are social insurance schemes covering the community as a whole or large section of the community that are imposed by government units." (Paragraph 4.147).*

98. This definition of social security funds is followed in the OECD classification with the two following exceptions which are excluded

- Schemes imposed by government and operated by bodies outside the general government sector, as defined in §3 of this manual; and
- Schemes to which all contributions are voluntary.

Supra-national authorities

99. This sub-sector covers the revenue-raising operations of supra-national authorities within a country. In practice, the only relevant supra-national authority in the OECD area is that of the institutions of the European Union (EU). As from 1998, supra-national authorities are no longer included in the *Revenue Statistics*, to achieve consistency with the SNA definition of general government which excludes them. For example, income taxes and social security contributions collected by European Institutions and paid by European civil servants who are resident of EU member countries should not be included. However the specific levies paid by the member states of the EU continue to be included in total tax revenues and they are shown under this heading.

Criteria to be used for the attribution of tax revenues

100. When a government collects taxes and pays them over in whole or in part to other governments, it is necessary to determine whether the revenues should be considered to be those of the collecting government which it distributes to others as grants, or those of the beneficiary governments which the collecting government receives and passes on only as their agent. The criteria to be used in the attribution of revenues are set out in §101 to §104 which replicate paragraphs 3.70 to 3.73 from the 2008 SNA.

101. In general, a tax is attributed to the government unit that

   a. exercises the authority to impose the tax (either as a principal or through the delegated authority of the principal),

   b. has final discretion to set and vary the rate of the tax

102. Where an amount is collected by one government for and on behalf of another government, and the latter government has the authority to impose the tax, and set and vary its rate, then the former is acting as an agent for the latter and the tax is reassigned. Any amount retained by the collecting government as a collection charge should be treated as a payment for a service. Any other amount retained by the collecting government, such as under a tax-sharing arrangement, should be treated as a current grant. If the collecting government was delegated the authority to set and vary the rate, then the amount collected should be treated as tax revenue of this government.

103. Where different governments jointly and equally set the rate of a tax and jointly and equally decide on the distribution of the proceeds, with no individual government having ultimate overriding authority, then the tax revenues are attributed to each government according to its respective share of the proceeds. If an arrangement allows one government unit to exercise ultimate overriding authority, then all of the tax revenue is attributed to that unit.

104. There may also be the circumstance where a tax is imposed under the constitutional or other authority of one government, but other governments individually set the tax rate in their jurisdictions. The proceeds of the tax generated in each respective government's jurisdiction are attributed as tax revenues of that government.

Levies paid by member states of the European Union

105. The levies paid by the member states of the EU take the form specific levies which include

   a. custom duties and levies on agricultural goods (5123),

   b. gross monetary compensation accounts (5123 if relating to imports and 5124 if relating to exports); and

   c. Steel, coal, sugar and milk levies (5128).

106. The custom duties collected by member states on behalf of the EU are recorded

- on a gross of collection fee basis;
- using figures adjusted so that duties are shown on a 'final destination' as opposed to a 'country of first entry' basis where such adjustments can be made. These adjustments concern in particular duties collected at important (sea) ports. Although the EU duties are collected by the authorities of the country of first entry, when possible these duties should be excluded from the revenue of the collecting country and be included in the revenue of the country of final destination.

107. This is the specific EU levy that most clearly conforms to the attribution criterion described in §99 above. Consequently as from 1998, these amounts are footnoted as a memorandum item to the EU member state country tables (in Chapter 4) and no longer shown under heading 5123. However the figures are included in the total tax revenue figures on the top line for all the relevant years shown in the tables.

A.13. Provisional classification of revenues from bank levies and payments to deposit insurance and financial stability schemes

108. The OECD have adopted the following interim approach to reporting revenue from bank levies plus deposit insurance and stability fees for the 2012 and subsequent editions of *OECD Revenue Statistics*. It is recommended that the amounts should be recorded under category 5126.

- Compulsory payments of stability fees, bank levies and deposit insurance should generally be treated as tax revenues where the payments are made to General Government and allocated to the governments' consolidated or general funds so that the Government is free to make immediate use of the money for the purposes that it chooses. This principle would apply regardless of whether the Government is promising to make payments to guarantee the banks' customer deposits in some future contingency.
- If the compulsory payments are made to general government and placed in funds that are earmarked to be entirely channelled back to the sector of the economy that comprises the companies that are subject to the payment, they would still generally be treated as tax revenues on the grounds that the funds would be available for the government and would reduce its budget deficit, the fee is unrequited for an individual entity and the amounts raised could be unrelated to any eventual pay out to depositors or expenditure on wider support for the financial sector.
- Payments to made to the smaller long-standing schemes for insuring 'retail' deposits, where the payment levels are consistent with the costs of insurance should be classified as fee for service.
- Any payments which involve governments realising the assets of a failed institution or receiving a priority claim on its assets in liquidation in order to fund payments of compensation to customers for their lost deposits would be treated as a fee for a service as opposed to tax revenues.
- Compulsory payments that are made to funds operated outside the government sector and non-state institutions backed by the deposit takers and all payments to voluntary schemes should not be treated as tax revenues.

Notes

1. References in this OECD Interpretative Guide to Sections or Parts of "this Report" refer to OECD (2019), *Revenue Statistics 2019*, OECD Publishing, Paris.
2. All references to SNA are to the 2008 edition.
3. See section A.12 of this guide for a discussion of the concept of agency capacity.
4. It is usually possible to identify amounts of social security contributions and payroll taxes, but not other taxes paid by government.
5. If, however, a levy which is considered as non-tax revenue by most countries is regarded as a tax — or raises substantial revenue — in one or more countries, the amounts collected are footnoted at the end of the relevant country tables, even though the amounts are not included in total tax revenues.
6. Names, however, can frequently be misleading. For example, though a passport fee would normally be considered a non-tax revenue, if a supplementary levy on passports (as is the case in Portugal) were imposed in order to raise substantial amounts of revenue relative to the cost of providing the passport, the levy would be regarded as a tax under 5200.
7. A more detailed explanation of this distinction can be found in the special feature, 'Current issues in reporting tax revenues', in the 2001 edition of the *Revenue Statistics*.
8. Sometimes the terms 'non-refundable' and 'refundable' are used, but it may be considered illogical to talk of 'refundable' when nothing has been paid.
9. A different treatment, however, is accorded to non-wastable tax credits under imputation systems of corporate income tax (§36–38).
10. This is not strictly a true tax expenditure in the formal sense. Such tax expenditures require identification of a benchmark tax system for each country or, preferably, a common international benchmark. In practice it has not been possible to reach agreement on a common international benchmark.
11. Unless based on the profit made on a sale, in which case they would be classified as capital gains taxes under 1120 or 1220.
12. In some countries the same legislation applies to both individual and corporate enterprises for particular taxes on income. However, the receipts from such taxes are usually allocable between individuals and enterprises and can therefore be shown in the appropriate sub-heading.
13. For example, "...sufficiently self-contained and independent that they behave in the same way as corporations....... (including) keeping a complete set of accounts" (2008 SNA, section 4.44).
14. In Canada — a country also referred to as having an imputation system — the (wastable) tax credit for the shareholder is in respect of domestic corporation tax deemed to have been paid whether or not a corporation tax liability has arisen. As there is no integral connection between the corporation tax liability and the credit given against income tax under such systems, these credits for dividends are treated, along with other tax credits, on the lines described in §25.
15. This may also apply where a scheme for government employees existed prior to the introduction of a general social security scheme.
16. In the 2008 SNA these are regarded as capital transfers and not as taxes (see section A.8).
17. This is the system by which the European Union adjusts for differences between the exchange rates used to determine prices under the Common Market Agricultural Policy and actual exchange rates. Payments under the system may relate to imports or exports and where these amounts are separately identifiable they are shown under the appropriate heading (5123 or 5124). In this Report, these amounts are shown gross (i.e. without deducting any subsidies paid out under the MCA system).
18. Transfers of profits of State lotteries are regarded as non-tax revenues (see also §67).
19. See §30(c) as regards this distinction.

ANEXO A

Guía de interpretación de la OCDE[1]

Índice

A.1. Clasificación de impuestos de la OCDE

1. 1000 *Impuestos sobre la renta, las utilidades y las ganancias de capital*

    1100 Impuestos sobre la renta, utilidades y ganancias de capital de personas físicas

        1110 Renta y utilidades

        1120 Ganancias de capital

    1200 Impuesto sobre la renta, utilidades y ganancias de capital de sociedades.

        1210 Renta y utilidades

        1220 Ganancias de capital

    1300 No clasificables entre 1100 y 1200

2. 2000 *Contribuciones a la seguridad social*

    2100 Empleados

        2110 Sobre la base de la nómina

        2120 Sobre la base del impuesto sobre la renta

    2200 Empleadores

        2210 Sobre la base de la nómina

        2220 Sobre la base del impuesto sobre la renta

    2300 Trabajadores por cuenta propia o no empleados

        2310 Sobre la base de la nómina

        2320 Sobre la base del impuesto sobre la renta

    2400 No clasificables entre 2100, 2200 y 2300

        2410 Sobre la base de la nómina

        2420 Sobre la base del impuesto sobre la renta

3. 3000 *Impuestos sobre la nómina y la fuerza de trabajo*

4. 4000 *Impuestos sobre la propiedad*

    4100 Impuestos recurrentes sobre la propiedad inmueble

        4110 Hogares

        4120 Otros

    4200 Impuestos recurrentes sobre la riqueza neta

        4210 Personas físicas

        4220 Sociedades

    4300 Impuestos sobre sucesiones, herencias y donaciones

        4310 Impuestos sobre sucesiones y herencias

        4320 Impuestos sobre donaciones

    4400 Impuestos sobre transacciones financieras y de capital

    4500 Otros impuestos no recurrentes sobre la propiedad

        4510 Otros impuestos sobre la riqueza neta

        4520 Otros impuestos no recurrentes

    4600 Otros impuestos recurrentes sobre la propiedad

5. 5000 *Impuestos sobre los bienes y servicios*

5100 Impuestos sobre la producción, venta, transferencia , arrendamiento y entrega de bienes y prestación de servicios

5110 Impuestos generales

5111 Impuestos sobre el valor agregado

5112 Impuestos sobre las ventas

5113 Otros impuestos generales sobre ingresos brutos y sobre bienes y servicios

5120 Impuestos sobre bienes y servicios específicos

5121 Impuestos selectivos

5122 Utilidades de los monopolios fiscales

5123 Derechos de aduanas y otros derechos de importación

5124 Impuestos sobre las exportaciones

5125 Impuestos sobre los bienes de inversión

5126 Impuestos sobre servicios específicos

5127 Otros impuestos sobre el comercio y las transacciones internacionales

5128 Otros impuestos sobre bienes y servicios específicos

5130 No clasificables entre 5110 y 5120

5200 Impuestos sobre el uso de bienes y sobre el permiso para usar bienes y realizar actividades

5210 Impuestos recurrentes

5211 Pagados por los hogares sobre vehículos automotores.

5212 Pagados por otros sobre vehículos automotores

5213 Otros impuestos recurrentes

5220 Impuestos no recurrentes

5300 No clasificables entre 5100 y 5200

6. 6000 *Otros impuestos*

6100 Pagados únicamente por empresas

6200 Pagados por otros distintos de las empresas o no identificables

A.2. Cobertura

Criterios generales

1. En la clasificación de la OCDE, el término "impuestos" se circunscribe exclusivamente a los pagos sin contraprestación efectuados al gobierno general. Los impuestos carecen de contraprestación en el sentido en que, normalmente, las prestaciones proporcionadas por el gobierno a los contribuyentes no guardan relación directa con los pagos realizados por estos.

2. El término "impuestos" no incluye las multas, sanciones pecuniarias, ni préstamos obligatorios pagados al gobierno. La delimitación entre ingresos tributarios y no tributarios en relación con ciertas tasas y cargos se abordan en los § 11–14.

3. El gobierno general comprende la Administración central y los organismos que se hallan bajo su control efectivo, los gobiernos estatales y locales y sus respectivas administraciones, y ciertos regímenes de seguridad social y entidades gubernamentales autónomas, excluidas las empresas públicas. Esta definición del gobierno proviene del *Sistema de Cuentas Nacionales* (SCN) 2008;[2] en esa publicación, el sector del gobierno general y sus subsectores se hallan definidos en el capítulo 4, párrafos 4.117 a 4.165 de la versión en inglés.

4. Las unidades extrapresupuestarias son parte del sistema de gobierno general. Estas son entidades del gobierno general con presupuestos individuales que no están completamente cubiertos por el presupuesto principal o general. Estas entidades operan bajo la autoridad o el control de un gobierno central, estatal o local. Las entidades extrapresupuestarias pueden tener sus propias fuentes de ingresos, que pueden complementarse con subvenciones (transferencias) del presupuesto general o de otras fuentes. A pesar de que sus presupuestos pueden estar sujetos a la aprobación de la legislatura, similar a la de las cuentas presupuestarias, tienen discreción sobre el volumen y la composición de sus gastos. Dichas entidades pueden establecerse para llevar a cabo funciones gubernamentales específicas, como la construcción de carreteras o la producción de servicios de salud o educación pública. Los arreglos presupuestarios varían ampliamente entre países, y se utilizan diversos términos para describir estas entidades, pero a menudo se los denomina "fondos extrapresupuestarios" o "agencias descentralizadas".

5. Los pagos obligatorios a autoridades supranacionales y a los organismos vinculados a ellas no se incluyen como impuestos desde 1998, con contadas excepciones; sin embargo, los derechos de aduana recaudados por los estados miembros de la Unión Europea en nombre de esta siguen registrándose como partidas informativas y se incluyen en los cuadros de países (Capítulo 4 de la publicación *Revenue Statistics* de la OCDE), concretamente en la recaudación tributaria total del país en el que se cobran (véase el § 99). Por otra parte, en los países en los que la Iglesia forma parte del gobierno general, se computan los impuestos eclesiásticos, siempre que reúnan los criterios establecidos en el § 1. Además, habida cuenta de que los datos hacen referencia a las entradas que recibe el gobierno general, quedan excluidos los gravámenes abonados a órganos no gubernamentales, organismos de bienestar o regímenes de seguro social externos al gobierno general, y sindicatos u organizaciones profesionales, aun cuando dichos gravámenes sean obligatorios; sin embargo, los pagos obligatorios al gobierno general asignados a esos entes sí están incluidos aquí siempre que el gobierno no actúe como mero agente de estos.[3] Las utilidades de los monopolios fiscales se diferencian de las de otras empresas públicas, y se tratan como impuestos porque reflejan el ejercicio del poder tributario del Estado mediante el uso de prerrogativas monopolísticas (véanse los §§ 65–67), al igual que las utilidades percibidas por el gobierno por la compra y la venta de divisas a diferentes tipos de cambio (véase el § 74).

6. Los impuestos pagados por el gobierno (p. ej., contribuciones a la seguridad social e impuestos sobre la nómina pagados por el gobierno en su calidad de empleador, impuestos sobre el consumo en sus compras o impuestos sobre sus propiedades) no se han excluido de los datos presentados. Sin embargo, cuando ha sido posible identificar las cantidades de ingreso implicadas,[4] se han mostrado en el Capítulo 4.2 de la publicación Estadísticas Tributarias en países de la OCDE.

7. La relación entre esta clasificación y la del Sistema de Cuentas Nacionales (SCN) se aclara en los apartados A.9 y A.11 *infra.*; dado que estas dos clasificaciones no coinciden en todos sus aspectos, en ocasiones, los datos presentados en las cuentas nacionales se calculan o clasifican de forma diferente a lo establecido en la presente guía y, aunque esas y otras diferencias se han mencionado en determinados casos (p. ej., en el § 30 *infra.*), no ha sido posible hacer referencia a todas ellas. Por otra parte, pueden darse asimismo ciertas disparidades entre la presente clasificación y la empleada internamente por algunas administraciones nacionales (véase el § 12), por lo que quizá las estadísticas de la OCDE y las nacionales no siempre concuerden; sin embargo, es más que probable que esas diferencias sean mínimas en lo que a la cuantía de ingresos se refiere.

Contribuciones a la seguridad social

8. Las contribuciones obligatorias a la seguridad social, tal y como se definen en el § 39, abonadas al gobierno general, se tratan aquí como ingresos tributarios, ya que, al tratarse de pagos preceptivos al gobierno general, se asemejan claramente a los impuestos. No obstante, pueden diferir de otros impuestos por el hecho de que la recepción de prestaciones de la seguridad social depende, en numerosos países, de que se hayan aportado las debidas contribuciones, aunque la magnitud de dichas prestaciones no tiene por qué estar supeditada obligatoriamente al importe de las contribuciones. Al tratar las contribuciones sociales como impuestos, se obtiene un mayor grado de comparabilidad entre países, aunque se han consignado en una categoría separada para poder distinguirlas en cualquier análisis.

9. La estricta distinción entre los ingresos tributarios (pagos obligatorios sin contraprestaciones directas a los gobiernos generales) y los pagos obligatorios no tributarios (NTCPs por sus siglas en inglés) (pagos que con derechos a contraprestaciones o que se realizan a otras instituciones) está claramente definida. Sin embargo, dentro del rango de diferentes pagos obligatorios realizados a los gobiernos en todos los países, no siempre es sencillo en la práctica decidir si los pagos específicos son impuestos o NTCPs. Por ejemplo, los ahorros de pensión obligatorios que son controlados por el gobierno general y que se acumulan en una cuenta individual obteniendo una rentabilidad del mercado o una tasa que compensa la inflación se clasificarían a primera vista como NTCPs en lugar de impuestos. Sin embargo, incluso estos pagos podrían no dar origen a "reembolsos" y clasificarse como impuestos en lugar de NTCPs (por ejemplo, si estos ahorros no se pagan cuando el contribuyente muere antes de alcanzar la edad de jubilación y los fondos se utilizan para proporcionar una pensión mínima a todos los contribuyentes que están asegurados). Estos problemas hacen que las cifras de ingresos de la seguridad social reportadas para la mayoría de los países se basen en la premisa de que todos los tipos de pagos obligatorios a las administraciones públicas se consideran en cierta medida como elementos de redistribución. Cabe señalar que esta conclusión se basa en una interpretación generalmente amplia del término "no correspondido" en la definición del impuesto.

10. Por el contrario, las contribuciones a la seguridad social voluntarias o no pagaderas al gobierno general (véase el § 1) no se tratan como impuestos, aunque en ciertos países, tal

y como se indica debidamente en cada caso en las notas que figuran al pie de los cuadros, plantea dificultades el eliminar tanto las contribuciones voluntarias como algunos pagos obligatorios al sector privado de las cifras de recaudación tributaria. Las contribuciones a la seguridad social imputadas tampoco son considerados impuestos.

Tasas, cargos a usuarios y licencias

11. Aparte de las tasas por licencia de vehículos, universalmente consideradas como impuestos, no resulta fácil distinguir entre las tasas y cargos a usuarios que deben tratarse como impuestos y las que no, ya que, aunque toda tasa o cargo se impone en conexión con un servicio o una actividad específicos, la intensidad del vínculo entre el derecho cobrado y el servicio prestado puede variar considerablemente, al igual que puede hacerlo la relación entre la cuantía de la tasa y el costo que supone proporcionar el servicio en cuestión. En todo caso, cuando el beneficiario del servicio pague una tasa claramente relacionada con el costo que supone prestar un servicio, puede inferirse que el gravamen tiene contraprestación y, de acuerdo con la definición reseñada en el § 1, no se considerará como impuesto. En sentido contrario, puede estimarse que el gravamen "carece de contraprestación" cuando:

a. el cargo exceda con creces el costo que supone prestar el servicio;

b. el pagador o sujeto pasivo del gravamen no sea el beneficiario del servicio (p. ej., tasas recaudadas de los mataderos para financiar un servicio proporcionado a los titulares de explotaciones agropecuarias);

c. el gobierno no proporcione un servicio específico a cambio del pago del gravamen, aun y cuando se emita un permiso en beneficio del sujeto pasivo (p. ej., cuando el gobierno concede licencias de caza, pesca o tiro que no otorgan el derecho a usar una zona específica propiedad del gobierno);

d. los servicios beneficien únicamente a los pagadores del gravamen, pero las utilidades recibidas por cada persona no guarden necesariamente proporción con sus pagos (p. ej., el gravamen sobre la comercialización de la leche que recae en los criadores de ganado lechero y que se utiliza para fomentar el consumo de la leche).

12. Pese a las anteriores consideraciones, en ciertos casos excepcionales la aplicación de los criterios plasmados en el § 1 puede resultar particularmente compleja. La solución adoptada – dada la conveniencia de uniformidad internacional y las cantidades de ingreso relativamente bajas implicadas por lo general– ha consistido en seguir la práctica dominante en la mayoría de las administraciones, en lugar de permitir que cada país aplique su propia visión sobre si estos gravámenes deben considerarse como ingresos tributarios o no tributarios.[5]

13. Seguidamente, se ofrece una lista de las principales tasas y cargos en cuestión, y su tratamiento normal[6] en esta publicación:

Ingresos no tributarios:	tasas procesales, permisos de conducir, tasas portuarias, tasas por expedición de pasaportes, licencias de radio y televisión cuando las autoridades públicas proporcionan el servicio de difusión.
Impuestos de la partida 5200:	permiso para realizar actividades tales como distribución cinematográfica; caza, pesca o tiro; suministro de instalaciones para actividades recreativas o de ocio o juegos de azar; venta de bebidas alcohólicas o tabaco; posesión de animales domésticos o uso de vehículos automotores; derechos sobre la extracción.

14. En la práctica, puede que no siempre resulte posible aislar las entradas tributarias de las no tributarias cuando estas se registran conjuntamente. En ese caso, si se considera que la mayoría de las entradas proviene de ingresos no tributarios, se tratará el importe total como tal; de lo contrario, esas entradas del gobierno se incluirán y clasificarán según las normas recogidas en el § 32.

Regalías

15. La propiedad de los activos del subsuelo en forma de depósitos de minerales o combustibles fósiles (carbón, petróleo o gas natural) depende de la forma en que los derechos de propiedad están definidos por la ley y también de los acuerdos internacionales en el caso de depósitos bajo aguas internacionales. En algunos casos, ya sea en el terreno por debajo del cual se encuentran los depósitos minerales, los depósitos en sí o ambos pueden pertenecer a una unidad del gobierno local o central.

16. En tales casos, estas unidades del gobierno general pueden otorgar arrendamientos a otras unidades institucionales que les permitan extraer estos depósitos durante un período de tiempo específico a cambio de un pago o una serie de pagos. Estos pagos a menudo se describen como "regalías", pero son esencialmente rentas que se acumulan a los propietarios de los recursos naturales a cambio de poner estos activos a disposición de otros agentes durante períodos de tiempo específicos. El alquiler puede tomar la forma de pagos periódicos de cantidades fijas, independientemente de la tasa de extracción, o, más comúnmente, pueden ser una función de la cantidad, el volumen o el valor del activo extraído. Las empresas dedicadas a la exploración en tierras del gobierno pueden hacer pagos a las unidades del gobierno general a cambio del derecho a realizar perforaciones de prueba o investigar de otro modo la existencia y ubicación de los activos del subsuelo. Dichos pagos también se registran como rentas aunque no se realice ninguna extracción. Por lo tanto, estos pagos se clasifican como ingresos no tributarios.

17. Los mismos principios se aplican cuando a otras unidades institucionales se les conceden arrendamientos que les permiten talar madera en bosques naturales en tierras que son propiedad de unidades del gobierno general. Estos pagos también se clasifican como ingresos no tributarios.

18. Estas rentas o regalías pagadas al gobierno general no deben confundirse con los impuestos sobre los ingresos y las ganancias, los impuestos sobre la extracción de recursos naturales, las licencias comerciales u otros impuestos. Si los pagos se aplican a las ganancias de la actividad de extracción, entonces deben clasificarse como impuestos sobre ingresos, utilidades y ganancias (1000). Además, cualquier pago que se imponga a la extracción de minerales y combustibles fósiles de las reservas de propiedad privada o de otro gobierno se debe clasificar como impuestos. Los pagos relacionados con el valor bruto de la producción deben clasificarse como otros impuestos sobre bienes y servicios (5128). Los pagos de una licencia o permiso para realizar operaciones de extracción se deben clasificar como impuestos sobre el uso de bienes y sobre el permiso para usar bienes o realizar actividades (5213).

Multas y sanciones pecuniarias

19. En principio, las multas y sanciones pecuniarias impuestas por el pago tardío de los impuestos o por el intento de evasión de los impuestos no deben registrarse como ingresos tributarios. Sin embargo, en ocasiones no es posible distinguir y separar los pagos por multas y penalidades de la recaudación del impuesto a los que estos están relacionados. En este caso, las multas y sanciones pecuniarias vinculadas a un determinado impuesto se registran

con los ingresos de ese impuesto. Las multas y penalidades pagadas sobre la recaudación de impuestos no identificados se clasifican como otros impuestos en la partida 6000. Las multas que no están relacionadas con delitos tributarios (por ejemplo, las infracciones por estacionamiento indebido), o que no puedan ser identificadas como ofensas tributarias, no serán tratadas como ingresos tributarios.

A.3. Principios de registro

Criterio de devengo

20. Los datos recogidos en esta publicación relativos a los últimos años se han registrado predominantemente según el criterio de devengo, esto es, se han computado en el momento en que nace la obligación. Se ofrece más información al respecto en las notas que figuran al pie de los cuadros de países en el Capítulo 4 del informe.

21. Sin embargo, los datos relativos a años anteriores han seguido registrándose principalmente según el criterio de caja, es decir, en el momento en que el gobierno recibió el pago. Por lo tanto, por ejemplo, los impuestos descontados por los empleadores en un año pero pagados al gobierno al año siguiente y los impuestos debidos un año pero liquidados el año después constan ambos en las entradas del segundo año. Las transacciones correctoras, tales como devoluciones, reembolsos y reintegros, se deducen de los ingresos brutos del periodo en que se realizan.

22. Los datos sobre ingresos tributarios se registran sin deducción de los gastos administrativos propios de la recaudación impositiva. De igual modo, cuando los recursos generados por un impuesto se emplean para subvencionar a miembros particulares de la comunidad, el subsidio no se descuenta del producto impositivo, aunque puede que el impuesto aparezca sin los subsidios en los registros nacionales de algunos países.

23. En lo que a los monopolios fiscales se refiere (5122), únicamente se incluye en los ingresos del gobierno el importe realmente transferido a este. Sin embargo, si cualquier gasto de los monopolios fiscales se considera gasto del gobierno (p. ej., gastos sociales emprendidos por los monopolios fiscales en beneficio del gobierno), se añadirán posteriormente con el fin de llegar a cifras de ingreso tributario (véase el § 65 *infra*.).

Distinción entre disposiciones tributarias y disposiciones relativas al gasto[7]

24. Dado que la presente publicación aborda únicamente la actividad del gobierno desde el punto de vista del ingreso, sin tener en cuenta los aspectos relacionados con el gasto, resulta preciso realizar una distinción entre las disposiciones que rigen estos dos elementos. Por lo general, no existe dificultad alguna en diferenciar ambos aspectos, ya que los gastos operan en un ámbito externo al sistema tributario y sus cuentas, y se rigen por una legislación separada de la impositiva. En los casos de difícil delimitación, se emplea el flujo de caja para distinguir entre disposiciones tributarias y disposiciones relativas al gasto. En la medida en que una disposición incida en el flujo de pagos tributarios del contribuyente al gobierno, se entenderá que reviste un carácter tributario y se tendrá en cuenta en los datos recogidos en esta publicación. Cualquier disposición que no afecte a ese flujo se reputará como relativa al gasto y no se tendrá en consideración en la información plasmada en la publicación.

25. Las desgravaciones, exenciones y deducciones tributarias sobre la base imponible afectan claramente a la cantidad transferida al gobierno y, por ende, se consideran disposiciones de naturaleza tributaria. En el extremo opuesto, los subsidios o exoneraciones que no compensen la obligación tributaria y que estén claramente desvinculados del proceso de evaluación, no

reducen los ingresos tributarios consignados en esta publicación. De particular interés en este ámbito resultan los créditos fiscales, que son cantidades deducibles del impuesto liquidable (lo que los diferencia de las deducciones sobre la base imponible). Cabe distinguir dos tipos de créditos fiscales: los créditos fiscales no exigibles (a veces denominados desaprovechables), limitados al importe de la obligación tributaria y que, por ende, no pueden generar un pago de las autoridades al contribuyente; y los créditos fiscales exigibles (o no desaprovechables), que no están sometidos a dicho límite, de forma que toda cantidad que exceda la obligación tributaria puede abonarse al contribuyente.[8] Al igual que las desgravaciones, un crédito fiscal no exigible afecta claramente a la cantidad transferida al gobierno y, por ende, se considerará como tributario. La práctica seguida para los créditos fiscales exigibles[9] consiste en distinguir entre "el componente de gasto tributario"[10] que es la porción del crédito empleada en reducir o eliminar la obligación del contribuyente" y el "componente de transferencia", constituido por la parte que excede la obligación del contribuyente y que se paga a este. Al registrar los ingresos tributarios deberá restarse la parte equivalente al componente de gasto tributario, pero no la correspondiente al componente de transferencia. Además, las cantidades de ambos componentes deberán figurar como partidas informativas en los cuadros de países. Los países que no puedan diferenciar entre estos dos componentes deberán indicar si se ha restado de los ingresos tributarios el total de ellos y presentar las evaluaciones disponibles del valor que ambos representan. Para mayor información, consúltese el Capítulo 1 de la publicación *Revenue Statistics* de la OCDE, que examina el efecto de los diversos tratamientos de los créditos fiscales exigibles en la relación impuestos sobre PIB.

Calendario y ejercicio fiscal

26. Las autoridades nacionales cuyos ejercicios fiscales no coinciden con el año calendario deben presentar los datos, siempre que sea posible, sobre la base del año calendario, a fin de permitir el mayor grado posible de comparación con la información de otros países. Subsisten algunos países en los que los datos hacen referencia a los ejercicios fiscales; para ellos, los datos relativos al PIB utilizados en los cuadros comparativos corresponden igualmente a los ejercicios fiscales.

A.4. Criterios generales de clasificación

Principales criterios de clasificación

27. El desglose de las entradas fiscales en las diversas categorías (1000, 2000, 3000, 4000, 5000 y 6000) se rige en general por la base sobre la cual recae el impuesto: 1000, renta, utilidades y ganancias de capital; 2000 y 3000, remuneraciones, nómina o número de empleados (fuerza de trabajo); 4000, propiedad; 5000, bienes y servicios; 6000, bases múltiples, otras bases o bases no identificables. Cuando un impuesto se calcula sobre más de una base, las entradas que genera se distribuyen, en la medida de lo posible, entre las diversas categorías (véanse los §§ 32 y 81). Las categorías 4000 y 5000 no sólo cubren aquellos impuestos en los que la base tributaria está constituida por la propiedad, los bienes o los servicios en sí mismos, sino también ciertos impuestos afines; y así, por ejemplo, los impuestos sobre transmisiones patrimoniales se incluyen en la partida 4400,[11] y los impuestos sobre el uso de bienes y sobre el permiso para realizar actividades, en la 5200. En las categorías 4000 y 5000, se distingue en ocasiones entre impuestos recurrentes y no recurrentes: son impuestos recurrentes los que se recaudan a intervalos regulares (por lo general, anualmente), y no recurrentes, los que se imponen una sola vez (véanse los § 47-§50, §53–§54 y §79 para profundizar en las aplicaciones particulares de esta distinción).

28. La asignación de un impuesto a fines específicos no afecta a la clasificación de las entradas fiscales que genera. Sin embargo, tal y como se explica en el § 39 en relación con la clasificación de las contribuciones a la seguridad social, el hecho de que estas confieran un derecho a recibir prestaciones sociales es decisivo para la definición de la categoría 2000.

29. La forma en que se establece o recauda un impuesto (p.ej., mediante el uso de timbres) no afecta a su clasificación.

Clasificación de los contribuyentes

30. En ocasiones, se distingue entre diversas clases de contribuyentes. Esas distinciones dependen de cada impuesto.

a. *Entre personas físicas y sociedades en relación con los impuestos sobre la renta y sobre la riqueza neta*

La distinción básica aquí es que los impuestos sobre la renta de sociedades (impuesto de sociedades), a diferencia de los impuestos sobre la renta de personas físicas, gravan a la sociedad como entidad y no a sus propietarios, independientemente de las circunstancias personales de estos; la misma distinción se aplica a los impuestos sobre la riqueza neta de sociedades y de personas físicas. Los impuestos liquidados sobre las utilidades de las asociaciones y sobre la renta de las instituciones, tales como seguros de vida o fondos de pensiones, se clasifican siguiendo la misma regla, y así, se considerarán impuestos sobre las sociedades (1200) si se cargan a la asociación o institución como persona jurídica sin tener en cuenta las circunstancias personales de sus propietarios, o impuestos sobre personas físicas en el caso contrario (1100). Por lo general, los impuestos aplicados a las sociedades y a las personas físicas se rigen por legislaciones diferentes.[12] La distinción realizada aquí entre personas físicas y sociedades no sigue la categorización por sectores entre hogares, empresas, etcétera, del Sistema de Cuentas Nacionales para las cuentas de ingresos y desembolsos. La clasificación del SCN requiere que ciertas empresas no constituidas en sociedad[13] se excluyan del sector de los hogares y vengan a sumarse a las empresas no financieras y las instituciones financieras. Sin embargo, el impuesto sobre las utilidades de esos negocios no siempre puede separarse del impuesto sobre la renta de sus propietarios o, como mucho, puede deslindarse sólo arbitrariamente. Por ello, no se ha intentado reproducir aquí esa separación, y la totalidad del impuesto sobre la renta de personas físicas se ha recogido en un solo bloque, independientemente de la naturaleza del ingreso imponible.

b. *Entre hogares y otros en relación con los impuestos sobre la propiedad inmueble*

Esta distinción es la misma que la adoptada por el SCN para las cuentas de gasto del consumo final de los hogares y de producción. Se trata pues de diferenciar a los hogares como consumidores (esto es, excluidas las empresas no constituidas en sociedad), por una parte, y a los productores, por otra. Los impuestos sobre las viviendas ocupadas por los hogares, tanto a cargo de los propietarios-ocupantes como de los arrendatarios o de los arrendadores, se incluyen en los hogares, lo que coincide con la diferenciación que suele hacerse comúnmente entre los impuestos sobre la propiedad doméstica y los impuestos sobre la propiedad empresarial. No obstante, algunos países no se hallan en situación de operar esta distinción.

c. *Entre hogares y otros en relación con las licencias de vehículos automotores*

Se distingue aquí entre los hogares como consumidores, por una parte, y los productores, por otra, al igual que en las cuentas de gasto del consumo final de los hogares y de producción del SCN.

d. Entre empresas y otros en relación con los impuestos residuales (6000)

La distinción es la misma que en c), esta vez, entre los productores, por una parte, y los hogares como consumidores, por otra. Los impuestos recogidos en la categoría 6000 bien porque gravan más de una base tributaria, o bien porque su base no entra dentro del ámbito de ninguna de las categorías anteriores pero es identificable como imponible sobre los productores, y no sobre los hogares, se incluyen en 'empresas'. El resto de los impuestos de la categoría 6000 se imputan a 'otros' o no identificables.

Recargos

31. Las entradas procedentes de recargos relacionados con impuestos particulares se clasifican por lo general en base al impuesto correspondiente, ya sea el recargo temporal o no. Pero si el recargo posee una característica que lo califica para ser clasificada en una categoría diferente de la lista de la OCDE, las entradas generadas por el recargo se recogen en dicha categoría, separadas de las del correspondiente impuesto.

Entradas tributarias no identificables y partidas residuales

32. En un cierto número de casos, no logra determinarse que los impuestos pertenezcan enteramente a una categoría o partida de la clasificación de la OCDE y, en esos casos, se aplican las siguientes pautas:

a. Se conoce la categoría, pero no la forma de distribuir las entradas entre las diversas subdivisiones: las entradas se clasifican en la correspondiente partida o subpartida residual (1300, 2400, 4520, 4600, 5130, 5300 o 6200).

b. Se sabe que la mayor parte de las entradas procedentes de un grupo de impuestos (normalmente, impuestos locales) proviene de impuestos de una categoría o una partida particulares, pero algunos de los impuestos del grupo cuya cuantía no puede determinarse con exactitud pueden clasificarse en otras categorías o partidas: las entradas se consignan en la categoría o partida a la que pertenezca la mayoría de ellas.

c. No puede identificarse ni la categoría ni la partida correspondiente al impuesto (normalmente, local): el impuesto se incorpora a la partida 6200, a menos que se conozca que se trata de un impuesto sobre las empresas, en cuyo caso se incluye en la partida 6100.

A.5. Comentarios sobre ítems de la lista

1000 – *Impuestos sobre la renta, las utilidades y las ganancias de capital*

33. Esta categoría cubre los impuestos aplicados a la renta o a las utilidades netas (esto es, la renta bruta menos las deducciones permitidas) de personas físicas y sociedades, así como los impuestos a los que se someten las ganancias de capital de esos mismos sujetos pasivos, y las ganancias obtenidas en juegos de azar.

34. Se incluyen en esta categoría:

a. los impuestos que gravan predominantemente la renta o las utilidades, aunque recaigan parcialmente sobre otras bases; los impuestos aplicados a varias bases que no sean mayoritariamente la renta o las utilidades se clasifican de acuerdo con los principios establecidos en los §§ 32 y 81;

b. los impuestos sobre la propiedad aplicados a un ingreso presunto o estimado como parte de un impuesto sobre la renta (véase el § 47(*a*), (*c*) y (*d*));

c. los pagos obligatorios al fondo de contribuciones de la seguridad social impuestos sobre la renta que no confieran un derecho a prestaciones sociales; si esas contribuciones otorgan derecho a prestaciones sociales, se incluyen en la categoría 2000 (véase el § 39);

d. el producto de los sistemas integrados de impuestos sobre la renta de régimen cedular se clasifican como un todo en esta categoría, aunque algunos de los impuestos cedulares puedan basarse en la renta bruta y no tener en cuenta las circunstancias personales del contribuyente.

35. La principal división de esta categoría se efectúa entre los gravámenes a personas físicas (1100) y aquellos a sociedades (1200). A su vez, en cada partida, se separa entre impuestos sobre la renta y las utilidades (1110 y 1210) e impuestos sobre las ganancias de capital (1120 y 1220). Si algunas entradas no pueden atribuirse pertinentemente a la partida 1100 o a la 1200, o si no puede realizarse esta distinción en la práctica (p. ej., por falta de datos fiables sobre los receptores de los pagos de los que se deducen los impuestos con retención en la fuente), las entradas se incorporan a la partida 1300 como "no clasificables".

Tratamiento de los créditos fiscales en los sistemas de imputación

36. En los sistemas de imputación del impuesto de sociedades, los accionistas están exentos, total o parcialmente, de responder en concepto del impuesto sobre la renta por los dividendos abonados por la compañía a partir de la renta o de las utilidades sometidas al impuesto de sociedades. En los países con este sistema,[14] una parte del impuesto sobre las utilidades de la sociedad está disponible para exonerar a los accionistas de su propia obligación tributaria. La exoneración del accionista reviste la forma de un crédito fiscal, cuyo importe puede ser inferior, igual o superior al pasivo tributario total del accionista. Si el crédito fiscal excede al pasivo tributario, puede que ese exceso sea pagadero al accionista. Dado que este tipo de crédito fiscal es parte integrante del sistema de imputación del impuesto sobre la renta de sociedades, cualquier pago a los accionistas se trata como devolución tributaria, y no como gasto (compárese con el tratamiento de otros créditos fiscales descrito en el § 25).

37. Puesto que en los sistemas de imputación el crédito fiscal (incluso cuando excede la obligación tributaria) debe considerarse como disposición tributaria, se plantea la cuestión de determinar si deberá deducirse de las entradas en concepto de impuesto sobre la renta de personas físicas (1110) o de las entradas atribuibles al impuesto sobre la renta de sociedades (1210). En este informe, la cantidad total pagada a título del impuesto sobre la renta de sociedades se recoge en la subpartida 1210, y el impuesto no imputado en la subpartida 1110. Por lo tanto, la cuantía total del crédito se resta de esta última subpartida, tanto si el crédito da lugar a una reducción de la obligación tributaria por renta personal, como si se realiza un reembolso porque el crédito fiscal excede el pasivo tributario por este concepto. (No obstante, si los créditos fiscales se deducen del impuesto de sociedades por dividendos repartidos a otras sociedades, las correspondientes cantidades se descuentan de las entradas registradas en la subpartida 1210.)

1120 y 1220 – Impuestos sobre las ganancias de capital

38. Como su nombre indica, estas subpartidas engloban los impuestos sobre las ganancias de capital, ya de personas físicas (1120), ya de sociedades (1220), siempre que las entradas procedentes de estos impuestos puedan identificarse por separado. Ese no es el caso en numerosos países, y las entradas de estos impuestos se clasifican junto con las del impuesto

sobre la renta. La subpartida 1120 contiene asimismo los impuestos sobre las ganancias obtenidas en juegos de azar.

2000 – Contribuciones a la seguridad social

39. Entran en esta categoría todos los pagos obligatorios que confieran un derecho a recibir una prestación social futura (contingente). Esos pagos suelen estar asignados al financiamiento de prestaciones sociales y, a menudo, se pagan a las instituciones del gobierno general que proporcionan dichas prestaciones. Sin embargo, esa asignación no forma parte de la definición de las contribuciones a la seguridad social y no es necesaria para que un impuesto sea clasificado en esta categoría, pero, para que un impuesto se incluya aquí, sí será preciso que confiera un derecho. Y así, los gravámenes sobre la renta o la nómina asignados a los fondos de seguridad social pero que no confieran el derecho a recibir prestaciones sociales quedan excluidos de la presente categoría y se registran bien entre los impuestos sobre la renta de personas físicas (1100), bien junto con los impuestos sobre la nómina y la fuerza de trabajo (3000). Los impuestos aplicados sobre otras bases, como los bienes y servicios, no se consignarán aquí aunque estén asignados a prestaciones de la seguridad social, sino que se catalogarán según sus respectivas bases, ya que por lo general no otorgarán derecho alguno a prestaciones sociales.

40. Entre otras, se incluirán aquí las contribuciones a los siguientes tipos de prestaciones de la seguridad social: prestaciones y suplementos por seguro de desempleo; prestaciones por accidente, lesión o enfermedad; pensiones por jubilación, invalidez y supervivencia; ayudas familiares; reembolsos de gastos médicos u hospitalarios o prestación de servicios médicos u hospitalarios. Las contribuciones pueden recaudarse tanto de los empleados como de los empleadores.

41. Las contribuciones pueden tener como base bien las remuneraciones o la nómina ('sobre la base de la nómina'), bien la renta neta tras deducciones y exenciones por circunstancias personales ('sobre la base del impuesto sobre la renta'), y el producto de ambas bases deberá identificarse separadamente en la medida de lo posible. Cuando las contribuciones al régimen general de la seguridad social se basen en la nómina, pero las de grupos particulares (tales como los trabajadores por cuenta propia) no puedan evaluarse en función de esta base y se emplee en ese caso la renta neta como una aproximación de las remuneraciones brutas, las entradas seguirán clasificándose sobre la base de la nómina. En principio, esta categoría excluye las contribuciones voluntarias aportadas a los regímenes de seguridad social, que, cuando sea posible identificarlas de forma separada, se recogerán en la partida informativa sobre el financiamiento de las prestaciones sociales; sin embargo, en la práctica, estas aportaciones no siempre pueden desvincularse de las contribuciones obligatorias, en cuyo caso se incluirán igualmente en esta categoría.

42. Las contribuciones a los regímenes de seguro social no vinculados a instituciones del gobierno general, así como las aportaciones a otros tipos de sistemas de seguro, tales como planes de previsión o planes de pensiones, mutualidades u otros planes de ahorro, no se consideran contribuciones a la seguridad social. Los planes de previsión son acuerdos por los que las contribuciones de cada empleado y la parte correspondiente del empleador en nombre de aquél se conservan en una cuenta separada que genera interés, de la que pueden retirarse en circunstancias específicas. Por su parte, los planes de pensiones son regímenes organizados separadamente, negociados entres empleados y empleadores, que conllevan disposiciones sobre diversas contribuciones y prestaciones, a veces más directamente vinculadas a los niveles salariales y a la duración del servicio que en otros esquemas sociales.

Cuando las contribuciones a esos regímenes son obligatorias o cuasiobligatorias (p. ej., en virtud de un acuerdo con sindicatos u organizaciones profesionales), se hacen constar en la partida informativa (véase el Capítulo 4.2 de este Reporte).

43. Las contribuciones de los empleados del gobierno y de este con respecto a sus empleados a los regímenes de seguridad social incluidos en el gobierno general se clasifican en esta categoría. También se consideran impuestos las contribuciones de los empleados del gobierno a regímenes diferentes que puedan reputarse sustitutivos de los regímenes generales de seguridad social.[15] Por el contrario, cuando un régimen diferente no pueda considerarse sustitutivo de uno general y haya sido negociado entre el gobierno, en su papel de empleador, y sus empleados, no se estimará como régimen de seguridad social y, por lo tanto, las contribuciones a él no se tendrán como impuestos, aunque el régimen haya sido instaurado por la legislación.

44. Esta categoría excluye las contribuciones 'imputadas', que corresponden a las prestaciones sociales pagadas directamente por los empleadores a sus empleados, antiguos empleados o personas a cargo de estos (p. ej., cuando los empleadores están legalmente obligados a correr con las prestaciones por enfermedad durante cierto tiempo).

45. Las contribuciones se dividen en tres partidas principales – empleados (2100), empleadores (2200) y trabajadores por cuenta propia o no empleados (2300) – y se subdividen posteriormente en función de la base que gravan. A efectos de la presente publicación, se entiende por empleados todas las personas contratadas en actividades de unidades empresariales, órganos gubernamentales, instituciones privadas sin ánimo de lucro u otro tipo de empleo remunerado, con excepción de los dueños de empresas no constituidas en sociedad y de los miembros no remunerados de sus familias. También se consideran empleados los miembros de las Fuerzas Armadas, independientemente de la duración y del tipo de su servicio, siempre que coticen a regímenes de la seguridad social. Por su parte, las contribuciones de los empleadores se definen como las aportaciones que estos realizan por cuenta de sus empleados a los sistemas de seguridad social. Si los empleados o los empleadores tienen la obligación de continuar cotizando a la seguridad social en el caso de desempleo de un empleado, esas contribuciones se muestran en las partidas 2100 y 2200, respectivamente, siempre que los datos lo permitan. En consecuencia, la partida 2300 queda reservada a las contribuciones abonadas por los trabajadores por cuenta propia y por quienes no se hallan incluidos en la población activa (p. ej., incapacitados o jubilados).

3000 – Impuestos sobre la nómina y la fuerza de trabajo

46. Consiste en los impuestos pagados por las firmas o empresas, ya sea como una proporción de los salarios o la nómina, ya como una cantidad fija por persona empleada. No incluyen pagos a la seguridad social obligatorios pagados por empleadores u otros impuestos pagados por los empleados mismos de sus salarios o remuneraciones.

4000 – Impuestos sobre la propiedad

47. Esta categoría engloba los impuestos, recurrentes y no recurrentes, sobre el uso, la titularidad o la transmisión de la propiedad, lo que incluye impuestos sobre la propiedad inmueble y la riqueza neta, sobre el cambio de titularidad en la propiedad por herencia o donación, y sobre transacciones financieras y de capital. Quedan excluidas de esta categoría los siguientes tipos de impuestos:

a. los impuestos sobre las ganancias de capital procedentes de la venta de propiedad (1120 o 1220);

b. los impuestos sobre el uso de bienes y sobre el permiso para usar bienes o realizar actividades (5200): véase el § 76;

c. los impuestos sobre los bienes inmuebles gravados sobre la base de un ingreso neto presunto que tiene en cuenta las circunstancias personales del contribuyente: se clasifican como impuestos sobre la renta junto con los impuestos sobre la renta y sobre las ganancias de capital derivadas de la propiedad (1100);

d. los impuestos sobre el uso de la propiedad con fines residenciales, tanto si debe responder del impuesto el propietario como el arrendatario, siempre que la cantidad debida tenga en cuenta las circunstancias personales del usuario (ingresos, personas a cargo, etcétera): se integran en los impuestos sobre la renta (1100);

e. los impuestos sobre los edificios con una densidad máxima superior a la permitida; sobre la ampliación, construcción o modificación de ciertos edificios más allá de un valor umbral; y sobre la construcción de edificios: todos ellos se integran en los impuestos sobre el permiso para realizar actividades (5200);

f. los impuestos sobre el uso de la propiedad propia para fines comerciales especiales, tales como la venta de bebidas alcohólicas, tabaco o carne, o para la explotación de tierras (p. ej., impuestos sobre la extracción en Estados Unidos): se integran en los impuestos sobre el permiso para realizar actividades (5200).

4100 – Impuestos recurrentes sobre la propiedad inmueble

48. Esta partida comprende los impuestos con que se grava de forma regular el uso o la titularidad de bienes inmuebles.

- Estos impuestos gravan las tierras y los edificios.
- Pueden consistir en un porcentaje del valor tasado de una propiedad, basado a su vez en un ingreso por alquiler hipotético, en el precio de venta, en un rendimiento capitalizado o en otras características de la propiedad inmueble (por ejemplo, el tamaño o la ubicación) de las que quepa inferir un alquiler o un valor de capital hipotéticos.
- Estos impuestos pueden aplicarse a los propietarios, a los arrendatarios o a ambos. También pueden pagarse de un nivel de gobierno a otro en relación con los bienes bajo jurisdicción de este último.
- Para la evaluación de estos impuestos, no se tienen en cuenta las deudas y, en ese sentido, difieren de los impuestos sobre la riqueza neta.

49. Los impuestos recurrentes sobre la propiedad inmueble se subdividen a su vez en los pagados por los hogares (4110) y los abonados por otros sujetos pasivos (4120), de acuerdo con los criterios establecidos en el § 30(*b*) *supra*.

4200 – Impuestos recurrentes sobre la riqueza neta

50. Esta partida abarca los impuestos con que se grava periódicamente (por lo general, anualmente) la riqueza neta, esto es, los impuestos sobre un amplio abanico de bienes muebles e inmuebles, descontadas sus deudas. Esta partida se subdivide a su vez en los impuestos pagados por las personas físicas (4210) y los abonados por las sociedades (4220), de acuerdo con los criterios establecidos en el § 30(*a*) *supra*. Si existen cifras separadas para las entradas correspondientes a pagos realizados por instituciones, se añaden a la subpartida de las sociedades.

4300 – *Impuestos sobre sucesiones, herencias y donaciones*

51. Esta partida se divide entre impuestos sobre sucesiones o herencias (4310) e impuestos sobre donaciones (4320).[16] Los impuestos sobre sucesiones gravan el valor total de la sucesión o del caudal hereditario, mientras los impuestos sobre herencias se aplican a las cuotas recibidas por los causahabientes individualmente considerados o en función de la relación de estos con el difunto.

4400 – *Impuestos sobre transacciones financieras y de capital*

52. Esta partida incluye, entre otros, los impuestos sobre la emisión, transmisión, compra y venta de valores, sobre los cheques, y sobre transacciones legales específicas, tales como la validación de contratos o la venta de bienes inmuebles. La partida no incluye:

a. los impuestos sobre el uso de bienes y sobre el permiso para realizar ciertas actividades (5200);
b. las tasas abonadas en concepto de costos procesales o expedición de actas de nacimiento, matrimonio o defunción, que suelen considerarse como ingresos no tributarios (véase el § 11);
c. los impuestos sobre ganancias de capital (1000);
d. los impuestos recurrentes sobre la propiedad inmueble (4100);
e. los impuestos recurrentes sobre la riqueza neta (4200);
f. otros impuestos no recurrentes sobre la propiedad o la riqueza (4500).

4500 – *Otros impuestos no recurrentes sobre la propiedad*[16]

53. Esta partida cubre los gravámenes sobre la propiedad que, a diferencia de los impuestos recurrentes, se recaudan una sola vez. Se divide en impuestos no recurrentes sobre la riqueza neta (4510) y otros impuestos no recurrentes sobre la propiedad (4520). La subpartida 4510 contiene los impuestos que se recaudan a fin de hacer frente a gastos excepcionales o de redistribuir la riqueza. Por su parte, la subpartida 4520 comprende los impuestos que gravan los incrementos de valor de la tierra, debido, por ejemplo, a permisos para su desarrollo concedidos por el gobierno general o a la provisión por parte de este de instalaciones locales adicionales; cualesquiera impuestos sobre la reevaluación del capital; y aquellos impuestos gravados una sola vez sobre determinados tipos de propiedad.

4600 – *Otros impuestos recurrentes sobre la propiedad*

54. Aunque este tipo de impuestos rara vez se dan en los países miembros de la OCDE, esta partida incluye los impuestos sobre bienes tales como ganado bovino, joyas, ventanas y otros signos externos de riqueza.

5000 – *Impuestos sobre los bienes y servicios*

55. Se incluyen en esta categoría todos los impuestos y derechos sobre la producción, extracción, venta, transmisión, arrendamiento y entrega de bienes, así como sobre la prestación de servicios (5100), y también los impuestos aplicados al uso de bienes y al permiso para usar bienes o realizar actividades (5200). Por lo tanto, esta categoría comprende:

a. los impuestos acumulativos de etapas múltiples;
b. los impuestos generales sobre las ventas aplicados, ya sea en la fabricación/producción, ya sea en la venta al por mayor o al por menor;
c. los impuestos sobre el valor agregado;

d. los impuestos selectivos;
e. los impuestos sobre las importaciones y exportaciones de bienes;
f. los impuestos sobre el uso de bienes y sobre el permiso para usar bienes o realizar ciertas actividades;
g. los impuestos sobre la extracción, el procesamiento o la producción de minerales y otros productos.

56. Los casos de difícil delimitación entre esta categoría y la categoría 4000 (impuestos sobre la propiedad) o la partida 6100 (otros impuestos pagados únicamente por empresas) se tratan en los § 47, §52 y §78. La partida 5300 y la subpartida 5130, ambas residuales, incluyen, respectivamente, las entradas tributarias que no hayan podido clasificarse entre las partidas 5100 y 5200 o entre las subpartidas 5110 y 5120, respectivamente, veáse §32.

5100 – Impuestos sobre la producción, venta, transmisión, arrendamiento y entrega de bienes, y la prestación de servicios

57. Esta partida comprende todos los impuestos aplicados a transacciones de bienes y servicios por las características intrínsecas de estos (p. ej., valor, peso del tabaco, graduación de las bebidas alcohólicas, etcétera) a diferencia de los impuestos determinados por el uso de bienes o por el permiso para usar bienes o realizar actividades, que entran dentro del ámbito de la partida 5200.

5110 – Impuestos generales

58. En esta subpartida, se incluyen todos los impuestos, aparte de los derechos de importación y exportación (5123 y 5124, respectivamente), que gravan la producción, el arrendamiento, la transmisión, la entrega o la venta de un amplio abanico de bienes o la prestación de una gran variedad de servicios, independientemente de que sean de producción nacional o importados, o de la etapa de producción o de distribución en la que recaigan. Por ende, comprende los impuestos sobre el valor agregado, los impuestos sobre las ventas y los impuestos acumulativos de etapas múltiples. A las entradas brutas generadas, se añaden las entradas por ajustes fronterizos en concepto de esos impuestos cuando se importan bienes, y se restan las devoluciones de dichos impuestos cuando se exportan bienes. Esta subpartida se divide a su vez en los epígrafes 5111, impuestos sobre el valor agregado; 5112, impuestos sobre las ventas; y 5113, otros impuestos generales sobre los ingresos brutos y sobre bienes y servicios.

59. Suelen plantearse dificultades de delimitación entre esta subpartida y la dedicada a los impuestos sobre bienes y servicios específicos (5120) cuando los impuestos se aplican a un gran número de bienes, como, por ejemplo, en el caso del impuesto sobre las compras del Reino Unido (abolido en 1973) o el impuesto sobre mercancías de Japón (abolido en 1988). De acuerdo con las respectivas perspectivas nacionales, el antiguo impuesto sobre las compras británico se ha clasificado como impuesto general (5112), mientras el desaparecido impuesto sobre mercancías japonés se ha incluido entre los impuestos selectivos (5121).

5111 – Impuestos sobre el valor agregado

60. Todos los impuestos generales al consumo cargados sobre el valor agregado entran dentro de este epígrafe, independientemente del método de deducción y de las etapas en las que recaiga el impuesto. En la práctica, todos los países de la OCDE con este tipo de impuestos permiten que todos los intermediarios, excepto el consumidor final, se deduzcan inmediatamente los impuestos sobre las compras e imponen tributación en todas las etapas.

Para algunos países, puede que se incluyan en este epígrafe otros impuestos, tales como los aplicados sobre actividades financieras y de seguros, o bien porque las entradas que generan no pueden identificarse separadamente de las procedentes del impuesto sobre el valor agregado, o bien porque se considera que forman parte de este último, aunque esos mismos impuestos puedan clasificarse diferentemente en terceros países (p. ej., como impuestos sobre servicios específicos (5126) o impuestos sobre transacciones financieras y de capital (4400).

5112 – *Impuestos sobre las ventas*

61. Se clasifican aquí todos los impuestos generales aplicados a una sola etapa, ya sea en la fabricación/producción, o en la venta al por mayor o al por menor.

5113 – *Otros impuestos generales sobre los ingresos brutos y sobre bienes y servicios*

62. Estos son impuestos acumulativos de etapas múltiplese impuestos en los que el impuesto al consumo se combina con otros impuestos multifásicos. Estos impuestos se aplican cada vez que se realiza una transacción sin deducción del valor de los impuestos pagados sobre los insumos. Los impuestos multifásicos pueden combinarse con elementos de los impuestos sobre el valor agregado o sobre las ventas.

5120 – *Impuestos sobre bienes y servicios específicos*

63. Se incluyen en esta subpartida los impuestos selectivos, las utilidades generadas y transferidas por los monopolios fiscales, y los derechos de aduana y otros derechos de importación, así como los impuestos sobre las exportaciones, las transacciones de divisas, los bienes de inversión y las apuestas, y los impuestos especiales sobre los servicios que no formen parte de uno de los impuestos generales de la subpartida 5110.

5121 – *Impuestos selectivos*

64. Los impuestos selectivos gravan la unidad de un producto específico de una gama predefinida y limitada de bienes. Los impuestos generalmente se aplican a tasas diferenciadas sobre bienes no esenciales o de lujo, bebidas alcohólicas, tabaco y la energía. Los selectivos pueden imponerse en cualquier etapa de la producción o distribución y generalmente se aplican como un cargo específico por unidad en función de las características del bien con referencia al valor, peso, intensidad o cantidad del producto. Se incluyen impuestos especiales sobre productos como el azúcar, la remolacha azucarera, fósforos y chocolates; e impuestos que gravan a tasas variables una cierta gama de bienes; e impuestos aplicados a los productos de tabaco, bebidas alcohólicas, combustibles para motores e hidrocarburos. Si un impuesto recaudado principalmente sobre bienes importados también se aplica, o se aplicaría, bajo la misma ley a bienes comparables de producción nacional, entonces los ingresos de este impuesto se clasifican como impuestos selectivos más que de derechos de importación. Este principio se aplica incluso si no hay producción nacional comparable o no hay posibilidad de tal producción. Los impuestos sobre el uso de servicios como agua, electricidad, gas y energía se consideran como impuestos selectivos más que impuestos sobre servicios específicos (5126). Los selectivos no incluyen los gravámenes que se aplican como impuestos generales sobre bienes y servicios (5110); beneficios de los monopolios fiscales (5122); derechos de aduana y otros derechos de importación (5123); o impuestos a las exportaciones (5124).

5122 – *Utilidades de los monopolios fiscales*

65. Este epígrafe comprende la parte de las utilidades de los monopolios fiscales transferida al gobierno general o usada para financiar gastos considerados como gastos del gobierno (véase el § 23). Las cantidades implicadas se registran cuando se transfieren al gobierno general o cuando se usan para gastos considerados como gastos del gobierno.

66. Los monopolios fiscales reflejan el ejercicio del poder tributario del gobierno mediante el uso de prerrogativas monopolísticas. Se trata de empresas públicas no financieras que ejercen un monopolio, en la mayoría de los casos sobre la producción o la distribución de tabaco, bebidas alcohólicas, sal, fósforos, cartas de juego, productos derivados del petróleo y productos agrícolas (es decir, sobre el tipo de productos susceptibles de estar sometidos, alternativa o adicionalmente, a los impuestos selectivos del epígrafe 5121), con el fin de recaudar ingresos para el gobierno que en otros países se obtienen gravando las operaciones que sobre dichos bienes efectúan las unidades empresariales privadas. El monopolio del gobierno puede intervenir en la etapa de producción o, en el caso de los establecimientos de licores propiedad del gobierno o bajo control de éste, en la etapa de distribución.

67. Cabe distinguir los monopolios fiscales de los servicios públicos, tales como el transporte ferroviario, la electricidad, los servicios de correos y otras comunicaciones, que pueden gozar también de una posición monopolística o cuasi-monopolística, pero cuyo fin primero suele ser la prestación de servicios básicos y no la obtención de ingresos para el gobierno; las transferencias de esas otras empresas públicas al gobierno se consideran ingresos no tributarios. Generalmente, el concepto tradicional de monopolio fiscal no abarca a las loterías estatales, cuyas utilidades usualmente se consideran, en consecuencia, ingresos no tributarios. No obstante, se pueden considerar como ingresos tributarios si su función principal es la de recaudar para financiar gasto gubernamental. Las utilidades de los monopolios fiscales se han separado de las de los monopolios de importación y exportación (5127) transferidas de juntas de comercialización u otras empresas dedicadas al comercio internacional.

5123 – *Derechos de aduana y otros derechos de importación*

68. Se incluyen aquí los impuestos, derechos de timbre y sobrecargas limitados por ley a los productos importados, así como los gravámenes sobre los productos agrícolas importados impuestos en los países miembros de la Unión Europea y las cantidades satisfechas por algunos de esos países a tenor del sistema de montantes compensatorios monetarios (MCM).[17] Desde 1998, los derechos de aduana recaudados por los Estados miembros de la Unión Europea en nombre de ésta ya no se registran en este epígrafe en los cuadros de países (Capítulo 4 de la publicación *Revenue Statistics* de la OCDE). Quedan excluidos aquí los impuestos recaudados de las importaciones como parte de un impuesto general sobre los bienes y servicios, así como los impuestos selectivos aplicables tanto a bienes importados como a bienes de producción nacional.

5124 – *Impuestos sobre las exportaciones*

69. En los años 1970, los derechos de exportación se aplicaban en Australia, Canadá y Portugal como una medida de carácter regular, y en Finlandia se han utilizado con fines contracíclicos. Algunos países miembros de la Unión Europea pagan un gravamen sobre las exportaciones, en el marco del sistema MCM (véase la nota a pie de página §16 en el § 68). Cuando las cantidades recaudadas son identificables, se integran en este epígrafe, que no incluye, sin embargo, las devoluciones de impuestos generales al consumo, de impuestos selectivos o de derechos de aduana sobre los bienes exportados, que se deducirán de las entradas brutas de 5110, 5121 o 5123, según corresponda.

5125 – Impuestos sobre los bienes de inversión

70. Este epígrafe cubre los impuestos sobre los bienes de inversión, tales como la maquinaria. Estos impuestos pueden cargarse por un cierto número de años o temporalmente con fines contracíclicos. No se incluyen aquí aquellos impuestos sobre los insumos industriales que recaen también en los consumidores (p. ej., el impuesto sobre la energía en Suecia, que se clasifica en 5121).

5126 – Impuestos sobre servicios específicos

71. Todos los impuestos sobre el pago por servicios específicos, tales como los impuestos sobre las primas de seguro, los servicios bancarios, los juegos de azar y las apuestas (p. ej., carreras de caballos, quinielas de fútbol, lotería), el transporte, las actividades recreativas o de ocio, los restaurantes y la publicidad, entran dentro de este epígrafe. También se clasifican aquí los impuestos sobre el ingreso bruto de las empresas que prestan el servicio (p. ej., primas de seguro o apuestas brutas recibidas por una empresa). Los ingresos tributarios procedentes de gravámenes bancarios y pagos a sistemas de seguro de depósitos y de estabilidad financiera se han incluido provisionalmente en este epígrafe para la edición de 2012. La clasificación detallada figura en § 108.

72. Se excluyen de este epígrafe:

a. los impuestos sobre servicios que formen parte de un impuesto general sobre los bienes y servicios (5110);

b. los impuestos sobre la electricidad, el gas y la energía (5121, impuestos selectivos);

c. los impuestos sobre las ganancias de personas físicas en los juegos de azar (1120, impuestos sobre las ganancias de capital de las personas físicas o de las empresas no constituidas en sociedad) y los impuestos fijos sobre la transferencia de loterías privadas o sobre el permiso para crear loterías (5200);[18]

d. los impuestos sobre los cheques y sobre la emisión, transmisión o compra y venta de valores (4400, impuestos sobre transacciones financieras y de capital).

5127 – Otros impuestos sobre el comercio y las transacciones internacionales

73. Este epígrafe abarca los ingresos percibidos por el gobierno por la compra y la venta de divisas a diferentes tipos de cambio. Cuando el gobierno ejerce poderes monopolísticos para obtener un margen entre los precios de compra y de venta de divisas superior al que sería necesario para cubrir los costos administrativos, el ingreso generado constituye un gravamen obligatorio impuesto en proporciones indeterminadas tanto sobre el comprador como sobre el vendedor de divisas. Es un equivalente común de los derechos de importación y exportación cargados en un sistema con tipo de cambio único o de un impuesto sobre la compraventa de divisas. Al igual que las utilidades de los monopolios fiscales o de los monopolios de importación y exportación transferidas al gobierno, representa el ejercicio de las prerrogativas monopolísticas con fines fiscales y, por lo tanto, se incluye en los ingresos tributarios.

74. El epígrafe engloba asimismo las utilidades de los monopolios de importación y exportación, que, sin embargo, son inexistentes en los países de la OCDE; los impuestos sobre la compraventa de divisas; y cualesquiera otros impuestos que recaigan sobre el comercio o las transacciones internacionales.

5128 – Otros impuestos sobre bienes y servicios específicos

75. Este epígrafe incluye los impuestos sobre la extracción de minerales, combustibles fósiles y otros recursos agotables de yacimientos de propieddad privada o de otro nivel de

gobierno, así como cualesquiera otras entradas no identificables procedentes de impuestos sobre bienes y servicios específicos. Los impuestos sobre la extracción de recursos agotables suelen traducirse en un importe fijo por cantidad o peso, pero también pueden adoptar un valor porcentual. Los impuestos se registran en el momento de extracción de los recursos. Los pagos por extracción de recursos agotables de yacimientos propiedad de la unidad de gobierno que recibe el pago se clasifican como alquiler.

5200 – Impuestos sobre el uso de bienes y sobre el permiso para usar bienes o realizar actividades

76. Esta partida incluye los impuestos aplicados al uso de bienes a diferencia de los impuestos sobre los propios bienes. Al contrario que los impuestos de este último tipo (registrados en la partida 5100), los impuestos considerados aquí no se basan en el valor de los bienes, sino que suelen revestir la forma de importes fijos. Los impuestos sobre el permiso para usar bienes o realizar actividades entran asimismo en esta partida, como, por ejemplo, los impuestos sobre la contaminación que no se basan en el valor de bienes particulares. En ocasiones, resulta complejo distinguir entre cargos obligatorios a los usuarios y tasas de licencia que se consideran como impuestos y aquellos que quedan excluidos por reputarse como ingresos no tributarios; los criterios de deslinde empleados se explican en los § 11 y §12.

77. Aunque el título de esta partida menciona el "uso" de bienes, es posible que sea el registro de la propiedad, y no el uso, lo que dé lugar a la obligación tributaria, y que los impuestos contenidos aquí se apliquen más al hecho de ser titular de ciertos animales o bienes (p. ej., caballos de carreras, perros y vehículos automotores) que al uso que se hace de ellos, o que recaigan incluso en bienes inutilizables (p. ej., vehículos automotores o armas inservibles).

78. Se plantean casos de difícil delimitación con respecto a:

a. los impuestos sobre el permiso para realizar actividades empresariales que parten de una base combinada de renta, nómina o volumen de ventas, que se clasifican de acuerdo con las normas del § 81;

b. los impuestos sobre la propiedad o el uso de la propiedad de las partidas 4100, 4200 y 4600; la partida 4100 se dedica exclusivamente a los impuestos sobre la titularidad o la posesión de bienes inmuebles y, a diferencia de los impuestos de la partida 5200, recaen siempre sobre el valor de la propiedad; los impuestos sobre la riqueza neta (4200) y otros impuestos recurrentes sobre la propiedad (4600) se circunscriben al hecho de ser titular de propiedades, y no al uso de activos; se aplican a grupos de activos, y no a bienes particulares; y están en todo caso relacionados con el valor de los activos en cuestión.

5210 – Impuestos recurrentes sobre el uso de bienes y sobre el permiso para usar bienes o realizar actividades

79. La principal característica de los impuestos consignados aquí es que se recaudan a intervalos regulares y se cobran por lo general según una cantidad fija. En términos de ingresos, el elemento más importante está constituido por los impuestos por licencia de vehículos, aunque también integran esta subpartida los impuestos sobre los permisos de caza, pesca o tiro o sobre la venta de ciertos productos, así como los impuestos sobre la propiedad de animales domésticos y sobre la prestación de ciertos servicios siempre que estos reúnan los criterios establecidos en los § 11 y §12. Los epígrafes en que se divide la partida 5210 son: los impuestos sobre vehículos automotores pagados por los hogares (5211)

y los satisfechos por otros sujetos pasivos (5212);[19] por su parte, el epígrafe 5213 abarca las licencias a propietarios de animales domésticos y los cargos a usuarios por el permiso de realizar actividades, tales como la venta de carne o de bebidas alcohólica cuando los gravámenes se imponen de forma recurrente, así como las licencias generales periódicas de caza, pesca y tiro cuando el derecho a emprender esas actividades no se otorga como parte de una transacción comercial normal (p. ej., la concesión de la licencia no implica el derecho a usar una zona específica propiedad del gobierno).

5220 – Impuestos no recurrentes sobre el uso de bienes y sobre el permiso para usar bienes o realizar actividades

80. Se incluyen aquí los impuestos no recurrentes aplicados sobre el uso de bienes y sobre el permiso para utilizar bienes o realizar actividades, así como los impuestos aplicados cada vez que se utilizan los bienes.

- Entran en esta subpartida los impuestos sobre la emisión o liberación en el medio ambiente de gases y líquidos nocivos y otras sustancias peligrosas. Los pagos por permisos negociables de emisión expedidos por los gobiernos en el marco de programas de límites máximos y comercio de emisiones deberán registrarse aquí en la fecha en que se produzcan las emisiones. No se computarán ingresos por los permisos que los gobiernos expidan a título gratuito. El registro según el criterio de devengo implica que habrá una diferencia temporal entre el momento en que el gobierno reciba el pago por los permisos y el momento en que se produzca la emisión. En las cuentas nacionales, esta diferencia genera un pasivo para el gobierno durante ese periodo.
- Se excluirán los pagos efectuados por la recogida y eliminación de desechos o sustancias nocivas por parte de los poderes públicos, ya que constituyen una venta de servicios a las empresas.

81. También se incluyen aquí otros impuestos que entren dentro del ámbito de aplicación de la partida 5200 y que no se recauden recurrentemente. Por lo tanto, quedarán comprendidos los pagos únicos por permisos para la venta de alcohol o tabaco o para la creación de centros de apuestas, siempre que cumplan los criterios de los § 11–12.

6000 – Otros impuestos

82. Esta categoría recoge los impuestos que reposan en una o varias bases diferentes de las descritas en las categorías 1000, 3000, 4000 y 5000, o en bases que no puedan considerarse relacionadas a ninguna de estas categorías, se incluyen aquí. Los impuestos de base múltiple, y si es posible estimar las entradas relacionadas con cada base las cantidades desglosadas se repartirán en las correspondientes categorías de acuerdo a su base. Si no pueden calcularse los valores por separado y se sabe que la mayoría de las entradas proceden de una base determinada, el total de estas se atribuirán de acuerdo con dicha base. En caso contrario, las entradas se clasificarán aquí. Otros ingresos incluidos aquí son los impuestos presuntos no incluidos en el sistema de clasificación, los impuestos a las personas en forma de impuesto de capitación, impuestos de sellos no relacionados con las transacciones financieras y de capital que no pertenecen exclusivamente a una sola categoría de transacción, impuestos a los gastos donde se aplican deducciones o exenciones personales y recibos de impuestos no identificables. Esta categoría se subdivide entre los impuestos pagados completa o principalmente por las empresas (6100) y los abonados por otros sujetos pasivos (6200).

A.6. Conciliación con las cuentas nacionales

83. Esta sección de los cuadros reconcilia el cálculo de la recaudación tributaria total realizado por la OCDE y el total de todos los impuestos y contribuciones sociales pagados al gobierno general tal y como figuran en el registro de las cuentas nacionales de cada país. Cuando el país es miembro de la Unión Europea (UE), la comparación se establece entre el cálculo de la recaudación tributaria total realizado por la OCDE y la suma de los ingresos tributarios y contribuciones sociales registrado en la combinación del gobierno general y de las instituciones de los sectores de la UE de las cuentas nacionales.

A.7. Partida informativa sobre el financiamiento de las prestaciones sociales

84. A la vista de la variedad de relaciones entre la tributación y las contribuciones a la seguridad social y de los casos mencionados en los § 39 al §45, se ha previsto una partida informativa que recopile todos los pagos asignados a las prestaciones tipo de la seguridad social, aparte de los pagos voluntarios al sector privado. Los datos se presentan de la forma siguiente (véase el Capítulo 4.2 de este Reporte):

a. Impuestos de la categoría 2000.

b. Impuestos asignados a las prestaciones de la seguridad social.

c. Contribuciones voluntarias al gobierno.

d. Contribuciones obligatorias al sector privado.

Los § 39 al §45 ofrecen las debidas orientaciones para efectuar el desglose entre las rúbricas (*a*) a (*d*).

A.8. Partida informativa sobre impuestos identificables pagados por el gobierno

85. Los impuestos identificables realmente pagados por el gobierno se presentan en una partida informativa, desglosados según las principales categorías de la clasificación de impuestos de la OCDE. En la vasta mayoría de los países, sólo pueden identificarse las contribuciones a la seguridad social y los impuestos sobre la nómina satisfechos por el gobierno, que, sin embargo, suelen ser los gravámenes más importantes liquidados por los gobiernos (véase el Capítulo 4.2 de este Reporte).

A.9. Relación de la clasificación de impuestos de la OCDE con el Sistema de Cuentas Nacionales

86. El Sistema de Cuentas Nacionales (SCN) pretende proporcionar un marco coherente para registrar y presentar los principales flujos relacionados con la producción, el consumo, la acumulación y las transacciones con el exterior de una determinada zona económica, por lo general, un país o una región destacada de un país, y, en este sentido, los ingresos del gobierno constituyen una importante parte de las transacciones registradas en todo sistema de cuentas nacionales. En agosto de 2009, la versión final del SCN 2008 se publicó conjuntamente por cinco organizaciones internacionales: la Organización de las Naciones Unidas, el Fondo Monetario Internacional, la Unión Europea, la Organización para la Cooperación y el Desarrollo Económicos, y el Banco Mundial. La publicación está diseñada para ser empleada en países con economías de mercado, sea cual sea su estadio de desarrollo económico, así como en países en transición hacia economías de mercado. Las principales partes del marco conceptual y las definiciones de los diversos sectores económicos del SCN se han plasmado en la clasificación de impuestos de la OCDE.

87. Sin embargo, existen ciertas diferencias, reseñadas seguidamente, entre la clasificación de impuestos de la OCDE y los conceptos del SCN, debidas a que la finalidad de la clasificación de la OCDE consiste en lograr la máxima desagregación posible de los datos estadísticos en relación con lo que, por lo general, las Administraciones tributarias consideran como impuestos. Y así:

a. la OCDE incluye las contribuciones a la seguridad social obligatorias, pagadas al gobierno general en la recaudación tributaria total. No se consideran como impuestos las contribuciones imputadas y voluntarias, además de aquellas pagadas a fondos privados (véanse los § 8 y §10 *supra.*);
b. los puntos de vista sobre la calificación de algunos gravámenes y tasas como impuestos son diferentes (§ 11y §12 *supra.*);
c. la OCDE excluye los impuestos imputados o los subsidios procedentes de la aplicación de múltiples tipos de cambio oficiales, o del pago de una tasa diferente a otras del mercado sobre reservas requeridas que pueda hacer el banco central;
d. los créditos fiscales exigibles se tratan de forma diferente.

88. Tal y como se ha apuntado en los § 1 y §2, las categorías 1000 a 6000 de la lista de impuestos de la OCDE cubren todos los pagos sin contraprestación al gobierno general, aparte de las multas y los préstamos obligatorios. Esos pagos sin contraprestación, incluidas las multas pero excluidos los préstamos obligatorios, pueden obtenerse añadiendo los siguientes valores del SCN 2008:

- impuestos sobre el valor agregado (D211);
- impuestos y derechos sobre las importaciones, IVA no incluido (D212);
- impuestos sobre las exportaciones (D213);
- impuestos sobre los productos, IVA e impuestos sobre las importaciones y exportaciones no incluidos (D214);
- otros impuestos sobre la producción (D29);
- impuestos sobre la renta (D51);
- otros impuestos corrientes (D59);
- contribuciones sociales (D61), excluidas las contribuciones voluntarias;
- impuestos sobre el capital (D91).

A10. Relación de la clasificación de impuestos de la OCDE con el sistema de estadísticas de finanzas públicas del Fondo Monetario Internacional

89. La cobertura y la valoración de los ingresos tributarios en el sistema de estadísticas de finanzas públicas (EFP) y en el SCN 2008 son muy similares. Por lo tanto, a excepción del tratamiento dado a los créditos fiscales exigibles, las diferencias entre la clasificación de la OCDE y la del SCN 2008 (véase el § 87 *supra.*) son de aplicación igualmente al sistema de EFP. Además, el Fondo Monetario Internacional (FMI) escinde la categoría única 5000 de la OCDE en dos categorías distintas dedicadas a los impuestos nacionales sobre bienes y servicios (114) y a los impuestos sobre el comercio y las transacciones internacionales (115). Esto refleja el hecho de que, mientras estos últimos impuestos suelen generar insignificantes cantidades de ingresos en la zona de la OCDE, ese no es el caso en la mayoría de los países no pertenecientes a la Organización.

A.11. Comparación de la clasificación de impuestos de la OCDE con otras clasificaciones internacionales

90. El cuadro siguiente recoge una comparación ítem por ítem entre la clasificación de impuestos de la OCDE y las clasificaciones empleadas en:

i) el Sistema de Cuentas Nacionales (SCN 2008);

ii) el Sistema Europeo de Cuentas (SEC 1995);

iii) el *Manual de estadísticas de finanzas públicas* del FMI (MEFP 2001).

91. Estas comparaciones representan equivalencias que podrán aplicarse en la mayoría de los casos. Con todo, deberán emplearse con cierta flexibilidad, ya que, en casos particulares, los países pueden adoptar enfoques diferentes para la clasificación de los ingresos en las cuentas nacionales.

Clasificación de la OCDE	SNA 2008	ESA 2010	GFSM2014
1000 Impuestos sobre los ingresos, utilidades y ganancias de capital			
1100 Personas			
1110 Ingresos y utilidades	D51-8.61a	D51A	1111
1120 Ganancias de capital	D51-8.61c, d	D51C, D	1111
1200 Corporaciones			
1210 Ingresos y ganancias	D51-8.61b	D51B	1112
1220 Ganancias de capital	D51-8.61c	D51C	1112
1300 No clasificables entre 1100 y 1200			1113
2000 Contribuciones a la seguridad social			
2100 Empleados	D613-8.85	D613	1211
2200 Empleadores	D611-8.83	D611	1212
2300 Auto-empleados y no empleados	D613-8.85	D613	1213
2400 No asignables entre 2100, 2200 y 2300			1214
3000 Impuestos sobre la nómina y fuerza de trabajo	D29-7.97a	D29C	112
4000 Impuesos sobre la propiedad			
4100 Impuestos recurrentes sobre la propiedad inmueble			
4110 Hogares	D59-8.63a	D59A	1131
4120 Other	D29-7.97b	D29A	1131
4200 Impuestos recurrentes sobre la riqueza neta			
4210 Hogares	D59-8.63b	D59A	1132
4220 Corporaciones	D59-8.63b	D59A	1132
4300 Impuestos sobre sucesiones, herencias y donaciones			
4310 Impuestos sobre sucesiones y herencias	D91-10.207b	D91A	1133
4320 Impuestos sobre donaciones	D91-10.207b	D91A	1133
4400 Impuestos sobre transacciones financieras y de capital	D59-7.96d; D29-7.97e	D214B, C	114114; 1161
4500 Otros impuestos no recurrentes sobre la propiedad	D91-10.207a	D91B	1135
4600 Otros impuestos recurrentes sobre la propiedad	D59-8.63c	D59A	1136
5000 Impuestos sobre los bienes y servicios			
5100 Impuestos sobre la producción, venta y transmisión de bienes y prestación de servicios			
5110 Impuestos generales sobre bienes y servicios			
5111 Impuestos sobre el valor agregado	D211-7.89	D211; D29G	11411
5112 Impuestos sobre las ventas	D2122-7.94a; D214-7.96a	D21224; D214I	11412
5113 Otros impuestos generales sobre los ingresos brutos y sobre bienes y servicios	D214-7.96a	D214I	11413
5120 Impuestos sobre bienes y servicios específicos			
5121 Impuestos selectivos	D2122-7.94b; D214-7.96b	D21223; D214A, B, D	1142
5122 Utilidades de los monopolios fiscales	D214-7.96e	D214J	1143
5123 Derechos de aduanas y otros derechos de importación	D2121-7.93	D2121; D21221, 2	1151

Clasificación de la OCDE	SNA 2008	ESA 2010	GFSM2014
5124 Sobre las exportaciones	D213-7.95a	D214K	1152-4
5125 Sobre los bienes de inversión			
5126 Sobre servicios específicos	D2122-7.94c; D214-7.96c	D21225; D214E, F, G, H; D29F	1144; 1156
5127 Otros impuestos sobre el comercio y las transacciones internacionales	D2122-7.94d D29-7.95b D29-7.97g D59-8.64d	D21226; D29D; D59E	1153; 1155-6
5128 Otros impuestos sobre bienes y servicios específicos			1146
5130 No clasificables entre 5110 y 5120			
5200 Impuestos sobre el uso de bienes y sobre el permiso para usar bienes y realizar actividades			
5210 Impuestos recurrentes			
5211 Sobre vehículos automotores: hogares	D59-8.64c	D59D	11451
5212 Sobre vehículos automotores: otros	D29-7.97d	D214D; D29B	11451
5213 Otros impuestos recurrentes en el uso de bienes y en el permiso para el uso de bienes y la realización de actividades	D29-7.97c, d, f D59-8.64c	D29B, E, F; D59D	11452
5220 Impuestos no recurrentes sobre el permiso para el uso de bienes o la realización de actividades			11452
5300 No clasificables entre 5100 y 5200			
6000 Otros impuestos			
6100 Pagados únicamente por empresas			1161
6200 Pagados por otros distintos de las empresas o no identificables	D59-8.64a, b	D59B, C	1162

A.12. Atribución de ingresos tributarios por subsectores del gobierno general

92. La clasificación de la OCDE requiere un desglose de los ingresos tributarios por subsectores del gobierno general. Seguidamente, se establecen la definición de cada subsector y los criterios que deben emplearse para atribuir los ingresos tributarios entre ellos, que siguen las orientaciones del SCN 2008 y del MEFP 2014.

Identificación de los subsectores del gobierno general

a) Gobierno central

93. El subsector del gobierno central incluye todos los departamentos, oficinas y establecimientos del gobierno, así como otros órganos que constituyen organismos o instrumentos de la autoridad central, cuya competencia se extiende a todo el territorio, con excepción de la administración de los fondos de seguridad social. En consecuencia, el gobierno central tiene la facultad de someter a tributación a todas las unidades residentes y no residentes que emprendan actividades económicas en el país.

b) Gobierno estatal, provincial o regional

94. Este subsector está compuesto por unidades intermedias del gobierno que ejercen su competencia a un nivel inferior al del gobierno central. Incluye a todas las unidades que operan independientemente del gobierno central en una parte del territorio de un país que engloba numerosas pequeñas localidades, con la excepción de la administración de los fondos de seguridad social. En los países unitarios, puede considerarse que los gobiernos regionales tienen una existencia separada, en la que cuentan con la suficiente autonomía como para recaudar sus ingresos de fuentes bajo su control, y sus funcionarios son independientes del control administrativo externo en el ejercicio de las actividades de la unidad.

95. En la actualidad, los países federales representan la mayoría de los casos en los que los ingresos atribuidos a unidades intermedias del gobierno se identifican de forma separada. España es el único país unitario en ese caso; en el resto de los países unitarios, los ingresos regionales se computan junto con los de los gobiernos locales.

c) Gobierno local

96. Este subsector incluye todas las demás unidades del gobierno que ejercen una competencia independiente en parte del territorio de un país, con excepción de la administración de los fondos de seguridad social. Engloba varios entes urbanos o rurales (p. ej., autoridades locales, municipios, ciudades, delegaciones, distritos).

d) Fondos de seguridad social

97. Los fondos de seguridad social forman un subsector separado del gobierno general. El SCN 2008 define el subsector de la seguridad social según lo expuesto en sus párrafos 4.124 a 4.126 y 4.147, citados seguidamente:

> *"Los regímenes de seguridad social son sistemas de seguros sociales que cubren a la comunidad en su conjunto o a amplios sectores de la misma, y que son impuestos y controlados por unidades del gobierno. Los sistemas abarcan una gran variedad de programas, y ofrecen prestaciones en dinero o en especie por vejez, invalidez o muerte, supervivencia, enfermedad y maternidad, accidentes de trabajo, desempleo, ayudas familiares, asistencia sanitaria, etc. No existe necesariamente una relación directa entre la cuantía de la contribución pagada por un individuo y las prestaciones que este pueda recibir." (Párrafo 4.124)*
>
> *"Cuando los sistemas de seguridad social se organizan por separado de las demás actividades de las unidades del gobierno, mantienen sus activos y pasivos separados de estas últimas, y realizan operaciones financieras por cuenta propia, se califican de unidades institucionales, que reciben el nombre de fondos de seguridad social." (Párrafo 4.125)*
>
> *"Las cantidades recaudadas y pagadas por contribuciones y prestaciones de la seguridad social pueden modificarse deliberadamente con el fin de alcanzar determinados objetivos de la política del gobierno que no tengan relación directa con el concepto de la seguridad social como sistema destinado a ofrecer prestaciones sociales a los miembros de la comunidad. Pueden aumentarse o disminuirse, por ejemplo, con el fin de influir en el nivel de la demanda agregada de la economía. No obstante, mientras se mantengan como fondos constituidos por separado, han de ser tratados, en el SCN, como unidades institucionales diferentes." (Párrafo 4.126)*
>
> *"El subsector de los fondos de seguridad social [del gobierno general] está conformado por los fondos de seguridad social que operan en todos los niveles del gobierno. Dichos fondos son sistemas de seguros sociales que cubren a la comunidad en su conjunto o a amplios sectores de la misma, y que son impuestos por unidades del gobierno." (Párrafo 4.147)*

98. La clasificación de la OCDE sigue esta definición de los fondos de seguridad social con las dos siguientes excepciones, por las se excluyen:

- los sistemas impuestos por el gobierno pero administrados por órganos externos al sector del gobierno general, tal y como se ha definido en el § 3 de este manual, y
- los sistemas en los que todas las contribuciones son voluntarias.

Autoridades supranacionales

99. Este subsector engloba las operaciones de recaudación fiscal de autoridades supranacionales dentro de un país. En la práctica, la única autoridad supranacional que cabe tener en cuenta en la zona de la OCDE es la que conforman las instituciones de la Unión Europea (UE). Desde 1998, las autoridades supranacionales no se incluyen en *Revenue Statistics*, a fin de ser coherentes con la definición que el SCN da del gobierno general, que las excluye. Por ejemplo, los impuestos sobre la renta y las contribuciones a la seguridad social recaudados por instituciones europeas y pagados a empleados públicos europeos que residen en países miembros de la OCDE no deberían incluirse. Pese a todo, ciertos gravámenes específicos pagados por los Estados miembros de la UE siguen incorporándose a la recaudación tributaria total y, en ese caso, se muestran bajo esta denominación.

Criterios de atribución de los ingresos tributarios

100. Cuando un gobierno recauda impuestos y los transfiere, en todo o en parte, a otros gobiernos, es necesario determinar si esos ingresos se imputarán al gobierno recaudador que los distribuye a otros en forma de donaciones, o si se atribuirán a los gobiernos beneficiarios para los que el gobierno recaudador actúa como mero agente, recibiendo el producto de los impuestos y transfiriéndolos posteriormente. Los criterios de atribución de los ingresos se establecen en los § 101–§104 siguientes, y siguen lo dispuesto en los puntos 3.70 a 3.73 del SCN 2008.

101. Por regla general, un impuesto se atribuye a la unidad de gobierno que:

a. ejerce la facultad de aplicar el impuesto (como entidad principal o a través de la autoridad delegada por la entidad principal), y

b. puede a su discreción establecer y modificar la tasa del impuesto.

102. Cuando un gobierno recauda impuestos para y en nombre de otro, y este último tiene la facultad de aplicar el impuesto y establecer y modificar su tasa impositiva, entonces el gobierno recaudador actúa como agente de este, y el impuesto se reasigna. Cualquier cantidad retenida por el gobierno recaudador como cargo por la recaudación deberá tratarse como pago por un servicio. Cualquier otra cantidad retenida por el gobierno recaudador, por ejemplo, en el marco de un arreglo de coparticipación de impuestos, deberá tratarse como una donación corriente. Si se delegó al gobierno recaudador la autoridad para establecer y modificar la tasa impositiva entonces las cantidades recaudadas deberán tratarse como ingresos tributarios de este gobierno.

103. Cuando diferentes gobiernos establecen conjuntamente y por igual la tasa de un impuesto y el uso de los recursos, sin que ninguno de ellos tengan la autoridad final y exclusiva, entonces los ingresos tributarios se atribuyen a cada gobierno según la proporción de recursos que le corresponda; si el acuerdo permite a una unidad del gobierno ejercer el control final y exclusivo, entonces todos los ingresos tributarios se atribuirán a dicha unidad.

104. También puede ocurrir que un gobierno tenga la autoridad constitucional o de otra índole de aplicar un impuesto, pero que otros gobiernos establezcan individualmente la tasa de ese impuesto en sus jurisdicciones; los recursos generados por el impuesto en cuestión en la jurisdicción de cada gobierno se atribuirán como ingresos tributarios a los respectivos gobiernos.

Gravámenes satisfechos por los Estados miembros de la Unión Europea

105. Los gravámenes satisfechos por los Estados miembros de la Unión Europea (UE) revisten la forma de:

a. derechos de aduana y gravámenes sobre los bienes agrícolas (5123),
b. cuentas de compensación monetaria brutas (5123 en relación con las importaciones y 5124 en relación con las exportaciones), y
c. gravámenes sobre el acero, el carbón, el azúcar y la leche (5128).

106. Los derechos de aduana recaudados por los Estados miembros de la UE en nombre de esta se registran de la siguiente forma:

- sobre la base de un coeficiente de recaudación bruta;
- ajustando los resultados, siempre que sea posible, de forma que esos derechos se muestren en relación con una base de "destino final", por oposición a la base de "país de primera entrada"; estos ajustes atañen particularmente a los derechos colectados en importantes puertos (marítimos); aunque los derechos de la UE se perciben por las autoridades del país de primera entrada, siempre que sea posible cabrá excluir esos derechos del ingreso del país recaudador e incluirlos en el ingreso del país de destino final.

107. Este es el gravamen específico de la UE que más claramente se ciñe al criterio de atribución consignado en el § 99. En consecuencia, desde 1998, las cantidades en relación con este gravamen se registran como partida informativa en los cuadros de países de los Estados miembros de la UE (en el Capítulo 4 de la publicación *Revenue Statistics* de la OCDE) y no se integran ya en la partida 5123. Sin embargo, se incluyen en las cifras de recaudación tributaria total de la línea superior para los años correspondientes mostrados en los cuadros.

A.13. Clasificación provisional de los ingresos tributarios procedentes de gravámenes bancarios y pagos a sistemas de seguro de depósitos y de estabilidad financiera

108. La OCDE ha adoptado el siguiente enfoque provisional para el registro de los ingresos procedentes de gravámenes bancarios, así como de seguro de depósitos y tasas de estabilidad para la edición 2012 y las posteriores publicaciones de *Revenue Statistics* de la OCDE. Se recomienda que los importes sean registrados bajo la subpartida 5126.

- Los pagos obligatorios de tasas de estabilidad, gravámenes bancarios y primas de seguro de depósitos se tratarán por lo general como ingresos tributarios cuando se abonen al gobierno general y se asignen a los fondos consolidados o generales de este, de forma que el gobierno pueda utilizar libre e inmediatamente el dinero para los fines que elija. Este principio se aplicará independientemente de que el gobierno prometa revertir esos pagos para garantizar los depósitos de los clientes de los bancos en caso de necesidad futura.
- Si los pagos obligatorios se abonan al gobierno general y se destinan a fondos afectados exclusivamente a volver al sector de la economía que engloba a las sociedades sujetas a dichos pagos, éstos seguirán considerándose ingresos tributarios dado que los fondos estarán disponibles para el gobierno y podrán reducir su déficit presupuestario, que la tasa no conlleva contraprestación para una entidad individual y que las cantidades recaudadas no tienen relación con cualquier pago posterior a los depositantes o cualquier gasto realizado como medio de respaldo más amplio al sector financiero.

- Se clasificarán como tasa por servicio los pagos que deban aportarse a sistemas permanentes más reducidos para garantizar los depósitos de "particulares" cuando los niveles de pago concuerden con el coste del seguro.
- También se clasificarán como tasa por servicio, y no como ingreso tributario, los pagos que impliquen que el gobierno ejecute los activos de una institución en quiebra o tenga un derecho prioritario sobre la liquidación de activos de esta con objeto de financiar los pagos de compensación a los clientes por la pérdida de sus depósitos.
- No se tratarán como ingresos tributarios los pagos obligatorios destinados a fondos externos al sector de gobierno y a instituciones no estatales respaldadas por los tomadores de depósitos, ni los pagos hechos a sistemas voluntarios.

Notas

1. Las referencias a la publicación *Revenue Statistics* de la OCDE en esta Guía Interpretativa, aluden a OECD (2019), *Revenue Statistics 2019*, OECD Publishing, Paris.
2. Todas las referencias al SCN deberán entenderse hechas a la edición de 2008.
3. Véase el apartado K de la presente guía para el análisis del concepto de agente.
4. Por lo general, es posible identificar la cuantía de las contribuciones a la seguridad social y de los impuestos sobre la nómina, pero no otros impuestos asumidos por el gobierno.
5. Sin embargo, si un gravamen considerado como ingreso no tributario en la mayoría de los países se califica de tributario –o permite recaudar sustanciales ingresos– en uno o más países, las entradas en concepto de dicho gravamen se indican en las notas que figuran al pie de los cuadros de países, pero no se incluyen en la recaudación tributaria total.
6. Obsérvese, no obstante, que los nombres pueden dar lugar a confusión. Por ejemplo, aunque una tasa sobre los pasaportes se trataría normalmente como ingreso no tributario, si se impone un gravamen suplementario sobre los pasaportes (como en el caso de Portugal) con el fin de conseguir un ingreso sustancialmente mayor que el costo que supone proporcionar el pasaporte, dicho gravamen deberá considerarse como un impuesto sobre el uso de bienes (5200).
7. Para una explicación más detallada de esta distinción, consúltese el estudio especial sobre cuestiones de actualidad en relación con el registro de los ingresos tributarios *Current issues in reporting tax revenues*, en la edición 2001 de *Revenue Statistics*.
8. En ocasiones, se emplean asimismo los términos "no reembolsable" y "reembolsable", pero puede parecer ilógico hablar de "reembolsable" cuando no se ha pagado nada.
9. Con la excepción del diferente tratamiento dado a los créditos fiscales exigibles en los sistemas de imputación del impuesto sobre sociedades (§§ 36–38).
10. No se trata aquí de verdaderos gastos tributarios en sentido formal, ya que tales gastos requieren que se identifique un sistema tributario de referencia para cada país o, mejor si cabe, una referencia internacional común y, en la práctica, no se ha logrado acuerdo sobre esta última.
11. A menos que se basen en la plusvalía obtenida con la venta, en cuyo caso se clasificarían como impuestos sobre las ganancias de capital, en las subpartidas 1120 o 1220.
12. Con todo, algunos países aplican la misma legislación a ambos en impuestos particulares sobre la renta, aunque las entradas procedentes de dichos impuestos suelen ser fácilmente atribuibles a uno u otro caso y pueden, por lo tanto, consignarse en la debida partida.
13. Por ejemplo, "[...] que son suficientemente autónomas e independientes y se comportan como si fueran sociedades [...] (incluido en el hecho de llevar) conjuntos completos de cuentas" (SCN 2008, 4.44).
14. En Canadá, país en el que se considera que rige un sistema de imputación, el crédito fiscal (no exigible) para el accionista nace en relación con el impuesto nacional sobre sociedades que se reputa haber pagado, tanto si ha surgido una obligación tributaria para la sociedad como si no. Habida cuenta de que no existe una conexión íntegra entre la obligación tributaria de la sociedad y el crédito concedido en relación con el impuesto sobre la renta en esos sistemas, los créditos por dividendos se tratan, junto con otros créditos fiscales, según lo descrito en el § 25.

15. Esto puede darse, por ejemplo, cuando ya existía un régimen para los empleados del gobierno previo a la introducción de un régimen general de seguridad social.
16. En el SCN 2008, se consideran transferencias de capital y no impuestos (véase la sección A.8.).
17. Mediante este sistema, la Unión Europea ajusta las diferencias entre los tipos de cambio empleados para determinar los precios de la política agrícola común (PAC) y los tipos de cambio reales. Los pagos realizados en este sistema pueden estar relacionados con importaciones o exportaciones y, cuando ha sido posible identificar por separado las respectivas cantidades, se han mostrado en el correspondiente epígrafe (5123 o 5124). En el presente informe, esas cantidades se han consignado en valores brutos (esto es, sin deducir ningún subsidio otorgado en el marco del sistema MCM).
18. Las transferencias de las utilidades de las loterías del Estado se consideran ingresos no tributarios (véase el § 67).
19. Véase el § 30(c) en relación con esta distinción.

www.ingramcontent.com/pod-product-compliance
Ingram Content Group UK Ltd.
Pitfield, Milton Keynes, MK11 3LW, UK
UKHW051457290926
15471UKWH00008B/1257